NEUROIMMUNOMODULATION: INTERVENTIONS IN AGING AND CANCER

FIRST STROMBOLI CONFERENCE ON AGING AND CANCER

ANNALS OF THE NEW YORK ACADEMY OF SCIENCES

Volume 521

NEUROIMMUNOMODULATION: INTERVENTIONS IN AGING AND CANCER
FIRST STROMBOLI CONFERENCE ON AGING AND CANCER

Edited by
Walter Pierpaoli and Novera Herbert Spector

The New York Academy of Sciences
New York, New York
1988

Cover (paper edition): Snail and turtle emblem of the conference by Paolo Carosone (see the Preface).

Library of Congress Cataloging-in-Publication Data

Stromboli Conference on Aging and Cancer (1st : 1987)
Neuroimmunomodulation : interventions in aging and cancer / First Stromboli Conference on Aging and Cancer ; edited by Walter Pierpaoli and Novera Herbert Spector.

p. cm. — (Annals of the New York Academy of Sciences ; v. 521)
Papers presented at the NATO Advanced Research Workshop held by the Institute for Integrative Biomedical Research, the International Working Group on Neuroimmunomodulation, and the Italian National Research Centers on Aging in Stromboli, Sicily, June 7-11, 1987.
Bibliography: p.
Includes index.
ISBN 0-89766-431-0. ISBN 0-89766-432-9 (pbk.)
1. Aging—Physiological aspects—Congresses. 2. Cancer—Immunological aspects—Congresses. 3. Cancer—Endocrine aspects— Congresses. 4. Neuroimmunology—Congresses. I. Pierpaoli, Walter. II. Spector, Novera Herbert. III. Title. IV. Series.
QP86.S76 1987
612'.67—dc19

PCP
Printed in the United States of America
ISBN 0-89766-431-0 (cloth)
ISBN 0-89766-432-9 (paper)

ANNALS OF THE NEW YORK ACADEMY OF SCIENCES

Volume 521
March 29, 1988

NEUROIMMUNOMODULATION: INTERVENTIONS IN AGING AND CANCER
FIRST STROMBOLI CONFERENCE ON AGING AND CANCER[a]

Editors
WALTER PIERPAOLI AND NOVERA HERBERT SPECTOR

Conference Coordinator
IONE AUSTON

CONTENTS

[a]The papers in this volume were presented at the NATO Advanced Research Workshop (NATO-ARW 397/86) entitled Neuroimmunomodulation: Interventions in Aging and Cancer, First Stromboli Conference on Aging and Cancer, held by the Institute for Integrative Biomedical Research, the International Working Group on Neuroimmunomodulation, and the Italian National Research Centers on Aging (INRCA) in Stromboli, Sicily, June 7-11, 1987.

Concluding Remarks

Financial assistance was received from:

- FIDIA, ABANO TERME, ITALY
- ITALIAN NATIONAL RESEARCH CENTERS ON AGING
- NEW YORK ACADEMY OF SCIENCES
- NORTH ATLANTIC TREATY ORGANIZATION
- SIGMA-TAU, ROME, ITALY
- SWISS CANCER LEAGUE, BERN, SWITZERLAND

Welcoming Remarks

WALTER PIERPAOLI

Institute for Integrative Biomedical Research
Lohwisstrasse 50
CH-8123 Ebmatingen, Switzerland

My dear friends, we are meeting in an unusual and haunting place—near the active volcano of Stromboli—a place that fascinates through the immanent presence of primeval Nature dwelling under the constant surveillance of this benevolent but sometimes explosive volcano.

Let us together and in full intellectual and spiritual freedom enjoy the all-pervasive sense of solitude and isolation of being on this small island. The mysterious Bronze Age inhabitants of Stromboli here buried testify to the ancient fascination of *strongylos,* the Greek snail. What the Greeks called the spiral of the amnion, these early peoples called our volcano. The enormous fertility of the soil is constantly regenerated by new, fresh volcanic dust, which contains a lot of zinc among the other rare elements that play an important, but still largely unknown role in homeostasis. A *gerontology* center would certainly be appropriate on Stromboli.

Let us invoke Epictetus, who invites us to reflect on the complexity of Nature. "It is impossible," he says, "for anyone to begin to learn what he believes he already knows."

The emblem of this Conference—a turtle—was developed by the artist Paolo Carosone. It represents a symbiosis or conjugation of development and evolution, and of research through introspection, analysis, and technology. This emblem of the long-lived turtle with a man-made mechanism represents a search for life and for the cause of aging. It is a reference point for meditation upon our presence on this planet and its significance. Prolongation of life or postponement of aging and death can be achieved only by investigating the diseases of aging. Can cancer be avoided by an equilibrated and joyful life? How far is distress avoidable? There are only personal answers to these general questions.

For support of this meeting thanks are due to the North Atlantic Treaty Organization. We thank, too, Dr. Fabris of the Italian National Research Centers on Aging, which aims at understanding the causes of aging and rendering our senescence, if not evitable, at least more acceptable. Our gratitude is also addressed to the Swiss Cancer League of Bern, Switzerland, to FIDIA, Inc. of Abano Terme, and SIGMA-TAU, Inc. of Pomezia, Italy for their financial support.

We are particularly indebted to Ione Auston for her masterly low-key and high-class help in the preparation and delivery of the manuscripts and in the coordination of the book. The New York Academy of Sciences is to be thanked both for its generous financial contribution and for the rapidity, the efficiency, and the quality of its editorial work. We thank Dr. Cook Kimball especially for seeing this book through the press.

We warmly thank Dr. Giuseppe Naro and Dr. Umberto Pidalà and the Ente Provinciale del Turismo, Messina, Italy, for the unforgettable performance of the

Canterini Peloritani, and the Russo family of the Sirenetta Park Hotel, Stromboli, for the very high standard of their hospitality and their exquisite personal touch.

Finally, we are grateful to Anna Fabris and the staff of Up-Service, Ancona, Italy, for their help in the complex and problematic organizational work required to hold a small conference on a small volcano in the Mediterranean, a conference that, it is hoped, will generate a great yield of human and scientific achievement.

Let us use what we have learned to help achieve a long-lived, healthy body. It can be done if we do not underestimate another great truth of Epictetus: "Always doubt what you believe." We should emerge somehow younger from this Stromboli adventure. We can grow younger if we accept the idea that aging is, as I strongly believe (*pace* Epictetus), at least partly an avoidable malaise. Thus, my dear friends, cheer up and grow younger!

In closing I would like to dedicate the following sentence composed by myself to the anthropologist and humanist Ashley Montagu, who has inspired my work on aging:

They killed me when I was a child. They told me I would reach adulthood and become a man. When I was forty, I became conscious that I had been deceived, and slowly retraced my steps to regain my stolen childhood.

Psychosocial Stress, Aging and Cancer

HANS-JOACHIM F. BALTRUSCH, JOCHEN SEIDEL,
WALTER STANGEL, AND MILLARD E. WALTZ

*Division of Immunohematology and Transfusion Medicine
(Bloodbank)
Department of Internal Medicine and Dermatology
Hannover Medical School
Hannover, Federal Republic of Germany[a]*

Some Demographic Background Data

During the past two decades in most European countries a marked increase in the total population, but also in the population over 65 years of age, has been observed. In West Germany with a population of over 60 million inhabitants, 12 million are over 60 years old, of which 62 percent (7.5 million) are women. In 1977, life expectancy in this country for men was 68.7 and for women, 72.5 years. There are more than twice the number of single women between 60 and 70 than men. Every sixth man over 60 is widowed, whereas more than half of the women beyond age 60 are widowed or divorced.

Even though the European population has increased generally, the proportion of elderly persons, those 65 years or older, has increased considerably faster. In Sweden, at present 16.8 percent of the total population is beyond age 65 in contrast to 11.4 percent in the United States. It is estimated that in Sweden during the next 15 years this group will increase by 33 percent in contrast to an estimated increase of 3.4 to 4.5 percent of the total population.[1] These data are of great social, medical and economic importance, as the risk of poor health increases with advancing age.

Pathologic Changes During Age

From a biologic point of view aging is characterized by disturbed homeostatic functions, decrease of the psychophysiologic capacity for adaptation, as well as by changes in molecular biologic functions. It is characterized by changed enzymatic reactions in environmental situations, increase of DNA repair with advancing age, and disturbances in RNA synthesis and in the loading of transfer RNA. The state of

[a] Correspondence address: Blutbank 8350, Hannover Medical School, Konstanty-Gutschow-Strasse 8, D-3000 Hannover, Federal Republic of Germany.

1

the neuroendocrine system is of decisive importance for the aging process. The incidence of diseases and their duration increase with age. Clinical observations have shown that 25 percent of persons between age 60 and 75, and only 16 percent of persons aged 75 were free from illnesses.[2] It is also known that aged people suffer from a variety of physical disturbances, often of long duration (multimorbidity).

Older people also appear to be a marked risk group for psychic illness because of their increased exposure to psychosocial, physical and economic strains.[3] Depression is a prominent condition in elderly people. It is estimated that between 25 to 30 percent of persons beyond age 65 suffer from psychic conditions. On the other hand, gerontologic research has demonstrated that there is no general decrease in psychologic functions in aged people.[4] Chronologic age was found to be of minor importance in regard to learning ability.

Incidence of "Psychosomatic" Illnesses During Aging

It has been noted that classic psychosomatic diseases, like bronchial asthma, hypertension and ulcerative colitis, which usually manifest in the younger or middle age groups can prevail without change in the higher and also in the high age groups, and that these often are followed by increasing tissue changes and other diseases.[5] But psychosomatic illness, manifested at previous life phases may also reappear after a latency period, sometimes between 20 to 30 years, during adverse life situations in later life or during crises typical of aging. Furthermore, the first manifestation of typical psychosomatic diseases has been observed in persons beyond age 55.

Aging and Immunity

It is well known that aging is associated with alterations of the immune system. The higher incidence of malignancies, the increased susceptibility to infections, as well as the occurrence of antibodies and monoclonal antibodies in senescent persons of both sexes are undisputed facts. The study of immunocompetence in young and old people yields quite regularly an increase in the coefficient of variation of the parameters under investigation the older the subjects become. Thymic involution accompanied by a fall in serum thymic hormones can be detected in all aging individuals. After 60 years of age there are virtually no thymic hormones detectable.[6] A rise of immature T-cells in peripheral blood as a consequence of decreased thymic maturation can also be found. In healthy old subjects (age 65-84) percentage and absolute numbers of OKT-8 positive cells are significantly lower, yielding an augmented T4/T8 ratio.[7] T-cell proliferation responses to plant mitogens and antigens are all depressed in the elderly. Expression of Tac-antigen, as well as high- and low-affinity receptors for Il-2 are reduced.[8–10] This may be attributed to the observation that these cells are more readily inhibited by prostaglandin E_2 which is produced by macrophages.[11,12] In line with these findings are observations reporting decreased reactivity in the mixed lymphocyte culture,[13] decreased cytotoxic T-cells responses to allogenic tumor cells[14] and a decline in delayed-type hypersensitivity to recall antigens,[15] as well as impaired *in-vitro* proliferation to antigens to which sensitization has previously occurred.[16] Some of these aspects of T-cell functions may be relieved by treatment with thymopentin which shows an improvement in cutaneous delayed-type hypersensitivity reaction to recall antigens and enhanced production of Il-2 after PHA-stimulation of T-lymphocytes *in vitro.*[17]

As far as the B-cell compartment is concerned, quite regularly an increase in IgG- and IgA-class immunoglobulins can be observed, while the IgM level seems to be reduced along with all naturally occurring immunoglobulins.[18] After challenge with pneumococcal vaccine, furthermore, a poor IgM-class response has been noted in persons from 71 to 95 years of age.[19] *In-vitro* functions of B-lymphocytes as assessed by plaque-forming cell capability have been seen to be impaired in senescent persons.[20] A defect in B- and T-cell cooperation with increased suppressor activity residing in surface Ig-negative cell populations has also been suspected to be the cause for the reduced humoral response in aging.[21] There is also an age-related increase in monoclonal gammopathies: in a study of 111 patients, aged 62 to 95 years, monoclonal gammopathy was found in 11 (10 percent) instances.[22] Although there is practically no augmented autoimmune disease frequency associated with aging,[23] there is a higher rate of autoantibodies in the serum directed against mitochondria, thyreoglobulin, lymphocytes, nucleic acid, and smooth muscles, as well as possibly also against idiotypes[7] which may play a crucial role in immunoregulation.

An impairment of granulocyte functions could not be corroborated, employing strict study admission criteria especially designed for immunogerontologic investigations.[24,25] As far as the functions of monocytes and macrophages are concerned, there have been no shortcomings identified in senescent persons.[14,26] The possible increase in generation of prostaglandin E_2 by macrophages in aging and its possible immunomodulatory efficiency has been already mentioned.[12,13]

Butenko[27] in this connection stresses that changes that occur in the immune system with age are not a consequence of loss or decrease in certain cells or substances; rather, they appear to be disturbances of the regulation of cell differentiation and of cooperative interaction between various types of cells during active suppression of the immune response. They are dependent on systemic influences, including age-related dynamics of thymic function, and reflect the expression of the organism's ontogenetic programme. Primary disturbances of the immune system can cause a number of secondary aging phenomena, such as the age-associated spectrum of pathology, including infections, cancer, amyloidosis and degenerative processes of internal organs.

Aging and Cancer

According to Doll,[28] a rapid increase in cancer incidence with age is characteristic for a number of cancer sites (lungs, prostate, breast, large bowel, chronic lymphatic leukemia, polycythaemia vera and multiple myeloma). However, this is not universal and cancer cannot be regarded as a direct result of aging. Animal experiments carried out in order to discover whether susceptibility to cancer induction varies with age yield different and conflicting results, and also human data are difficult to interpret. Following the Hiroshima atomic bomb explosion, the incidence of leukemia has been equal at all ages, whereas the incidence of other cancer sites appears to have increased with age. Doll concludes that the susceptibility of a tissue to cancer induction depends in part on the extent of its past exposure to other factors.

Contrary to these findings, Oeser[29] maintains that on account of the statistical evaluation of the age-specific incidence rates of malignant tumors, there is an age-specific risk for cancer, and that the relatively constant cancer risk may lead to the assumption of an endogeneous cancer proneness in which carcinogenic agents, as well as stress play only a role of promoting factors. The increase in total cancer mortality in age appears to be a consequence of heightened life expectancy, as more human beings today are reaching the critical age for neoplasia. This is contrasted by a recent German investigation in 301 persons with a documented age of over 100 years.[30] Absolute survival after the 100th birthday was 30 ± 1 months. Main causes of death were protracted cardiovascular diseases; malignancies were rare in this sample—only 2 persons (one percent) suffered from cancer. The authors point to German death statistics, according to which the incidence of malignant disease decreases from 35.4 percent in the age group of 55 to 10.9 percent in persons who succumb beyond the age of 85.[31]

Psychosocial Stresses of Aging

Aging cannot be viewed as a static period of time, but as a process within a frame of a psychodynamically oriented life cycle concept.[4,5] This concept is characterized by coping with different life strains, the experience of becoming older, and its final acceptance, including dying and death. Three phases of aging may be distinguished: the first is initiated at about 50 years of age and includes the transition from termination of biologic (fathering and bringing up of children) and social tasks (becoming adult, getting married, having a family with children growing up, finding and working at a job) until retirement from the working process at age 60-65. This includes also the experience of getting older and the finding of new values in partnership or marriage when children leave home.

The second phase dates from the beginning of retirement and includes the seeking and finding of new life goals and orientations for the remainder of life.

The third phase begins at about 75 years of age and lasts until high age and death. This period is characterized by a certain loss of independence and autonomy and an increasing dependency on environment. During all these phases the individual is subjected to numerous physical, psychological, social and economic changes.

The coping resources of the individual are of utmost importance for the adequate adjustment to different strains and threats. People who have a sense of meaningfulness and commitment to self, a vigorous attitude towards life, and self-confidence are less likely to develop disease in the wake of stressful life events or role strains. At the cognitive and emotional levels, they cope more effectively with life's vicissitudes. The same is true of individuals with sufficient social coping resources or social support available. The psychologically hardy person is often socially competent and, therefore, possesses an adequate social support network. Social bonds to significant others which provide socio-emotional supports and which are not associated with substantial interpersonal friction and conflict appear conducive to successful adaptation to stress and long-term health enhancement.[32] This also holds true for aging people. In this connection some adverse life situations and their importance for the vulnerability of senescent persons shall be briefly discussed. Losses and separations are known to be important health hazards, in particular during childhood and aging.[3,33,34] There are two categories of bereavement, actual losses and separations, such as death and/or separations from highly cathected relationships (loss of spouse, children, close family members and friends, and, under certain conditions also unemployment or retirement), as well as impending losses and separations (life-threatening illness or hospitalization of prominent relations, children leaving home, and, under certain conditions, also change of residency). It is well known that conjugal bereavement is a predisposing factor for depressive conditions and that the mortality rates after conjugal bereavement in every age group are higher than for married people.[36–38] Widowerhood and widowhood are associated with higher mortality rates, but the excess risk is much greater for men than for women.[37] Marriage acts as a stress buffer and protects people, in particular men, from a number of health consequences which begin to affect them when this marital protection becomes endangered or has been removed. This buffer seems to be less likely to be compensated in men by other and new social networks, because men's networks are smaller.

Bereavement was shown to be a factor in the onset of malignancy in 45 male and female cancer patients with different sites and in the age between 58 and 74 years (mean age 63.7 years). In this ongoing study we found the occurrence of actual losses in 14 (31.1 percent) and of impending losses in 18 (40 percent) patients. Furthermore 16 patients (35.5 percent) had childhood losses or longstanding separations from a parental figure.[39] This seems to confirm our previous findings that cancer patients of both sexes have a significantly higher amount of parental losses and separations during early childhood and youth.[35] It is further known that temporarily decreased lymphoblast transmission can be observed in healthy subjects for eight weeks, respectively 5-7 weeks post bereavement.[40,41]

Marital quality appears also to be an important factor for psychic and physical well-being. A recent investigation has compared 38 married with 38 separated/divorced women. Among the married subjects, poorer marital quality was associated with greater depression and a poorer response on three qualitative immune assays, lymphocytic proliferation in response to two mitogens and antibody titers to EBV VCA. Women who had been separated one year or less had significantly poorer immune function than their married controls, including lower percentages of NK and helper cells, poorer blastogenic responsiveness and higher antibody titers to EBV VCA. Within the separated/divorced group shorter separation times and greater attachment to the (ex)husband were associated with poorer immune function and greater depression. These data are in line with epidemiological findings linking marital discord with increased morbidity and mortality.[42] In our group of 45 unselected elderly cancer patients, 17 (37.7 percent) reported severe marital discord and disruption preceding the onset of their neoplasms. Interesting also in this connection is, that in elderly polycythaemia vera patients with conditions like loss and isolation and also marital discord, shorter intervals between erypheresis treatments became necessary in order to keep erythrocyte count within balanced ranges. We also observed an increase of tumor cell mass as assessed by an increase in serum myeloma protein level in patients with plasmocytoma in periods of impending loss and marital discord.[39]

Strong social support systems are associated with decreased morbidity and mortality; they have been hypothesized to mitigate the harmful effects of stressful stimuli on the individual. A recent investigation showed that subjects who feel the least helped by their social networks tend to have larger, but more superficial networks. They generally do not feel as helped by all these relationships, but the greatest contribution to their feelings of not being helped arises from the lack of success in their help-seeking efforts with a significant close relationship—the inner core of their network. They report more major events in their current, recent and distant past, confirming Bowlby's statement that there is a strong causal relationship between an individual's attachment experience with his parents and his later capacity to form affectional bonds.[43]

The effect of social support on stress-related changes in cholesterol level, uric acid level and immune function in an elderly sample was studied by Thomas et al.[44] These authors found among 256 healthy adults (61-89 years), that individuals with good social support systems had lower serum cholesterol and uric acid levels and higher indices of immune function. However, significant differences between men and women could be found in regard to physiological functions, which is ascribed to the fact that women have a greater sensitivity to close relationships and that they are more versatile in their choice of relationships.

A further strain, especially to old people is understimulation. In a controlled study, Arnetz et al.[45,46] examined the psychoendocrine and metabolic effects of social isolation and understimulation. The authors found that social activation led to an increase of testosterone, dehydroepiandrosterone and estradiol levels, while hemoglobin A_{1c} decreased significantly in the stimulated group. It is concluded that social isolation and understimulation may be associated with a wide range of psychophysiologic effects in elderly people. Kiecolt-Glaser and co-workers[47] assessed the enhancement of immunocompetence by relaxation and social contact in geriatric residents of independent-living facilities. Subjects were randomly assigned to one of three protocols: (1) relaxation training, (2) social contact, and (3) no contact. Subjects in the relaxation and social-contact groups were seen individually three times a week for a month. At the end of the intervention, the relaxation group showed a significant increase in NK-activity and significant decreases in antibody titers to herpes simplex virus and self-related distress, while the other two groups showed no significant changes. There was also a general increase in the T-lymphocyte response to phytohemagglutinin stimulation at the end of the intervention period, with a greater change at lower mitogen concentrations. These data suggest also that immunocompetence may be enhanced by psychosocial interventions in elderly populations.

In summary, aging is characterized by changes in the autonomous nervous system and in regulation mechanisms of the internal organs, and by a number of immunologic changes. However, we also have to face the fact that in aging these processes are influenced by emotional stress and by inadequate coping of the individual. As major strains, actual and impending losses and separations, lack of social support, marital discord and disruption, as well as social isolation and understimulation have been outlined. In respect to aging and cancer, a number of irreversible changes in neuroendocrine, neurotransmitter and immune function may be found as a consequence of chronic psychosocial stress exposure, low self-esteem and dissatisfaction with life and other psychological markers of long-term environmental conditions. On the other hand, aging persons appear to be more vulnerable to environmental demands and strains. Impaired adaptive and homeostatic mechanisms lead to an increased risk for disease and to earlier death, when aging people are subjected to unfavorable environmental conditions. Most recent studies, however, give some hints that in aged people psychological intervention may also lead to an enhancement of homeostatic and immunological functions.

Psychosocial Stress and Cancer

Dilman[48] has suggested that long-term adverse environmental demands can lead to pathological alterations in neuroendocrine and metabolic function; these processes are possibly similar to those leading to essential hypertension and arteriosclerosis and its concomitant disease states in the cerebro- and cardiovascular systems. Dilman and Ostroumova[49] have coined the term hyperadaptosis to refer to the organism's inability to regain homeostasis after an extended exposure to stress and the maintenance of a state of continuing chronic physiological stress; this state is seen as associated with reduced antitumor defense in the immune system. Early psychological and physiological 'sensitization' due to traumatic childhood experiences, as well as longstanding stress exposure during life-span, may lead to a permanent decrease in immunocompetence as a part of the aging process.

According to Balitsky,[50-52] extreme stress exposure, has a pervasive effect on the organism. He speculates that an overload of stress causes disorders at all body levels, spreading over the hypothalamic link, the hypothalamic-hypophysis-adrenal system, and the adreno-reactive structure, leading to the damage of the neurohormonal regulatory mechanisms, and, finally, the regulation of immunological reactivity.[51] Metastasis of a tumor correlates rather strictly with the intensity of stress reactions. An accumulation of different stress factors, as the psychological make up of the individual and his or her coping ability, the tumor process itself, surgery and chemotherapy, as well as 'pain stress' of the individual are important factors in this complex process; the metastatic process appears to be considerably enhanced as the tumor process decreases natural resistance in reducing stress and preventing stress damage.[52]

Although clinical biobehavioral research on stress and carcinogenesis is beset with considerable methodological difficulties,[53] some generalizations and themes emerge from a number of studies.[54] One consistently appearing theme in most studies is that cancer patients have difficulties in expressing emotions, or even feeling them. From prospective, longitudinal and retrospective studies there is today enough convergent evidence to discern a constellation of factors that predispose certain individuals to develop cancer or to progress through its stages more quickly. There is also evidence from prospective and retrospective investigations that there is little substance to the argument that knowing one has cancer (or has knowledge without conscious awareness) results in psychological and physiological reactions that compromise the validity of retrospective findings. Personality traits or longstanding characteristics of persons who develop cancer or who have a less favorable outcome include niceness, pleasantness, industriousness, perfectionism, exaggerated sociability, conventionality and a more rigid control of defensiveness. Underlying attitudes or tendencies of blockage or interpersonal repression, of helplessness/hopelessness, and of giving up rather than fighting are characteristics of persons with a more rapid course of cancer.[54,55] The existence and number of past or recent life events appears to be of lesser importance than how these were cognitively, emotionally, or behaviorally dealt with. Recent investigations show further that NK-activity may be a marker of psychopathology and coping ability.[56,57]

Type C and Psychosocial Factors Linked to Coping with Stress and Cancer Proneness

For several decades research in biobehavioral oncology has been focused on stress as a dispositional factor associated with the development and outcome of malignant neoplasia. New insights in the transduction of environmental influences by the brain and hormonal transmitters to the immune and other body systems have recently increased the salience of this approach in biobehavioral medicine.

Behavioral medicine in the area of cardiovascular disease has been quite successful due to the use of a Type A, or coronary-prone pattern concept in large-scale epidemiological studies in many countries. As an important moderating factor in the stress-disease process, this Type A behavior pattern probably influences the cognitive processing of environmental stressors and the individual's emotional reaction to them. The psychological components underlying this particular behavior pattern are not yet completely understood, but hostility is seen as an important component, as well as a need for control. Type A's respond to stress with physiological hyperreactivity. In a longitudinal study of coronary patients, the Type A pattern was also found to be associated with a psychological hyperresponsiveness at the cognitive and affective levels, particularly in respect to elevated anxiety levels.[58] More recently, cancer researchers have similarly attempted to conceptualize and operationalize a Type C or cancer-prone behavior pattern.[59–63] The majority of these investigators have noted a suppression of negative emotions, and/or an inability to express emotions, in particular anger.[64] Other marked traits are the avoidance of conflicts, and so-called "harmonizing behavior," exaggerated social desirability and social conformity, compliance, unassertiveness and patience (TABLE 1).

TABLE 1. Cancer-Prone Behavior (Type C)[a]

1. Behavioral features
   Overcooperative
   Appeasing
   Unassertive
   Patient
   Avoidance of conflicts, "harmonizing behavior"
   Unexpressive of negative emotions, in particular anger
   Compliant with external authorities
   Defensive response to stress, high on both self-reported social desirability and anxiety

2. Possible psychobiologic concomitants
   Decrease in biogenic amine concentrations in the hypothalamus, deficiency in homeostatic regulation, and a metabolic shift to enhanced utilization of FFA as fuel. As a consequence, cellular and macrophage functions are lowered, promotion of division of malignant cells and also inhibition of the activity of the DNA repair system (Dilman[48,49]).
   Association between IgA level and the tendency to suppress anger in female breast cancer patients (Pettingale et al.[68]).
   Increased electrodermal activity during experimental stress associated in breast cancer patients with higher scores on social desirability, suggesting a relationship between social compliance/conformity and increased autonomic arousal (Watson et al.[59]).
   Changes in endogeneous opiod systems (Zagon & McLaughlin[69]).
   Changes in NK-activity (Levy et al.,[56] Locke[55]) and impairment of DNA repair in human lymphocytes (Kiecolt-Glaser et al.[66,67]).

[a] Type C is a prognostic indicator in patients with malignant melanoma, significantly associated with thicker and more invasive tumors (Temoshok et al.[65]); breast cancer patients score higher than healthy controls on measures of social desirability, emotional suppression and state anxiety (Greer et al.[59]).

Temoshok[61] stresses that as a result of genetic predisposition and/or family interaction patterns, a child learns to cope with the inevitable challenges, stressors, and traumatic events of early life in a certain manner. A given coping style is successful to the extent that it reliably ensures psychological, biological and environmental homeostasis, even under stressful conditions. The Type C coping style is characterized as abrogating one's own needs in favor of others, suppressing of negative emotions, and being overly-cooperative, unassertive, appeasing and accepting. This coping style appears to be effective, as long as environmental and psychological homeostasis is maintained and sufficient self-esteem from the reflected acceptance and social rewards by the environment is gained. However, chronically blocked expression of needs and affects have negative biologic and psychologic consequences. It is thought that this pattern, which is concealed behind a facade of pleasantness and happiness may not cause problems immediately in ideally nurturing environments. In the course of time, however, the accumulated life strains take a toll on the individual who has become numb to biologic needs and demands. In this situation, the Type C coping style interacts with stresses and creates increased stress, which, in turn, is handled by the reinforcement of the Type C pattern. It is speculated that at this point the stage is set for the promotion of the disease.

According to Temoshok,[61] the Type C coping style is a fragile accommodation to the world; homeostasis with the environment may be achieved only partly and at a high cost, while biologic homeostasis appears to be severely strained. In an earlier, more comprehensive multidimensional theory of emotion, Temoshok[65] proposed that an internalizing versus externalizing mode of adapting was associated with the development of physical rather than psychological problems under stress. The Type C individual eventually develops a coping style that is dependent upon the suppression of conscious recognition of feelings and biological needs, whereas cardiovascular disorders (Type A pattern) arise from stressful situations that are chronically accommodated at the mental level of "motivation" which has as biological substrate the autonomous nervous and endocrine system. It is speculated that cancer arises from stressful conditions that are chronically accommodated at a lower level of organization which has as its biologic substrate immunomodulatory neuropeptides. A number of biologic sequelae of this behavior pattern, such as impairment of DNA repair,[66,67] changes in stress hormones,[68] and of neuropeptides[69] have been elucidated or are under active investigation. It hardly needs to be pointed out in this connection that further clinical and laboratory work is warranted in order to clarify the role of stress, coping style and its biological concomitants in neoplastic disease.

Cancer in the Aged, Own Studies

It has been argued that one problem with clinical studies lies in their failure to take full account of the medical risk factors with which psychological variables may be confounded. Of special interest is the foremost among risk factors: age.[70] It has been speculated that psychologic factors may be of greater importance in the etiology of cancer among younger persons than among persons who are at risk by virtue of their advanced age.[53]

At our Department we are presently pursuing this problem. An investigation has been started of patients with polycythaemia vera and multiple myeloma with advancing age. As the study is still ongoing, only limited data are available from patients with polycythaemia vera, and some of these will be presented here. Thirty-five polycythaemia vera (PV) patients were thus far studied. All patients were outpatients and were randomly selected. Eighteen were men with a mean age of 60.6 years, while 17 were women with a mean age of 60.8 years. The patients were studied by a structured interview technique regarding their curriculum vitae, a biographic questionnaire, a defense scale, the Courtauld Emotional Control Scale (CECS) and the Thomas Family Attitude Questionnaire (FAQ). The interviews with the patients revealed that in 33/

35 patients the clinical onset of PV occurred in a setting of severe and unresolved psychosocial stress, including: losses of close object relationships by death, divorce and separation; severe life-threatening illness of a partner or spouse; severe marital discord, as well as severe, unresolved dissensions with other family members living in the patients' household; and also real or impending vocational losses, ensued by feelings of hopelessness and giving up (TABLE 2).

The basic underlying conflict appeared to be a deeply rooted disturbance in their ability to relate to other people, in particular the marital partner. Most patients also complained of having insufficient outlets for their problems and worries, and were also often reluctant to share their problems with others.

Comparison of the biographic questionnaire with age-matched healthy controls yielded significant differences ($p = \leq 0.5$) in male and female PV patients. PV patients were more externally controlled and showed considerably higher suppression of anger and hostility, as well as attitudes of resignation and giving up. There was also a more rigid compliance with external authorities and a minor incidence of neurotic traits in childhood and youth, which may be indicative of early denial and suppression.

Immune status was measured in 15 patients. Decrease of natural killer cell activity (8 patients), impaired mitogenic stimulation (5 patients) and decreased lymphoblast transformation (7 patients) were psychologically associated with high suppression of anger and rigid defensiveness (score of 12 or higher on the 16-points defense scale). Two patients were unobtrusive.

With the exception of two patients, both male and female PV patients fulfilled the criteria for Type C behavior. The most outstanding trait was their inability to express negative emotions, in particular anger.[71-73]

Handling of Negative Emotions in Elderly Cancer Patients

In an additional study we studied suppression of anger, anxiety, and depressive mood in two groups of male and female patients with malignant tumors of different sites. One was a younger group in the age range of 40 to 59 years, and the other was an older group of 60 years and above. The male subgroups consisted of 48 patients, and the older group differed significantly in respect to scale scores on repression of

TABLE 2. Adverse Life Situations up to Three Years prior to Onset of Polycythaemia Vera (N = 35)

Death of spouse with ensuing change in patients' behavior	5
Divorce or separation from spouse or partner	5
Severe, life-threatening illness of close family member with ensuing change of behavior	6
Longstanding unresolved emotional conflicts with close family members other than spouse with ensuing change of behavior	3
Chronic marital discord in married or remarried patients	12
Death of other close family members with ensuing change in patients' behavior	5
Separation from other close family members with ensuing change in patients' behavior	3
Longstanding vocational conflicts with ensuing change in behavior	9
Life situation unclear or unobstrusive	2

TABLE 3. Courtauld Emotional Control Scale (Suppression of Anger, Anxiety and Depressive Mood in Two Age Groups of Cancer Patients; Different Sites (N = 87)

	Group I (40–59 yrs)	Group II (over 60 yrs)	t	p
Male patients (N = 48), no.	28	20		
Age variation, years	41–58	60–80		
Mean age	48.1	67.0		
Anger scale (7–28), range	11–22	14–28		
Mean score	16.9	18.5		n.s.
Anxiety scale (7–28), range	11–28	11–28		
Mean score	20.1	20.8		n.s.
Depressive mood scale (7–28), range	11–27	16–27		
Mean score	18.6 ± 5.2	21.7 ± 3.5	2.5759	<0.02
Total score (21–84), range	39–72	48–74		
Mean score	55.7 ± 12.3	61.7 ± 8.5	2.0675	<0.05
Female patients (N = 39), no.	23	16		
Age variation, years	40–59	60–74		
Mean age, years	50.2	67.8		
Anger scale (7–28), range	7–26	12–28		
Mean score	15.6 ± 6.3	20.3 ± 5.9	2.5759	<0.02
Anxiety scale (7–28), range	11–28	10–28		
Mean score	17.1 ± 5.8	20.9 ± 5.8	2.0729	<0.05
Depressive mood scale (21–84), range	11–26	12–28		
Mean score	17.1 ± 6.1	21.7 ± 5.3	2.5369	<0.02
Total score (21–84), range	35–76	28–76		
Mean score	50.0 ± 16.3	62.7 ± 14.4	2.7285	<0.01

depressive mood and of total suppression. The female subgroup consisted of 39 patients, and on the three subscales, as well as the total suppression score of the CECS the older patients have statistically significantly higher scores. These findings suggest that cancer patients belonging to older age groups use suppression more than younger subjects (TABLE 3).

Conclusions

The clinical, experimental and epidemiological findings reported here suggest the following. (a) Aging is accompanied by changes in the immunological and other biological systems in the body, but these processes appear to be influenced by the psychosocial context of aging. The latter concept refers to environmental demands and the way the individual reacts to these at the cognitive, emotional, and physiological level. (b) It is quite noticeable that some individuals age in good health with an intact immune system, whereas others develop disorders connected to senescence of the immune system. Cancer in the elderly has rarely been dealt with from a biobehavioral point of view: according to our own investigations, it does not appear to be an inevitable part of the aging process, but on the other hand it does appear to be a result of psychological coping with chronic demands during the life-span. (c) Although it is known that aged people are more vulnerable to adverse psychological and physiological stress factors, our studies point to the fact that, just as in other age groups, cancer among the aged becomes manifest under conditions of environmental demands or strains with which the person is unable to cope effectively. (d) The pathology of psychosocial stress appears to lie in a pattern of coping which is defined as the Type C pattern: this particular coping pattern seems to be as much related to psycho-emotional as to physiological responses. (e) Psychological intervention can be aimed at various levels: the alteration of environmental conditions that lead to stress, the enhancement of intrapsychic modes of reacting to those demands, and, finally, the physiological level.

REFERENCES

1. ARNETZ, B. B. 1985. Interaction of biomedical and psychosocial factors in research of aging. Annu. Rev. Gerontol. Geriatrics 5: 56-94.
2. SCHETTLER, G. 1974. Innere Aspekte des Leistungsabfalls. In Aktivitätsprobleme des Alternden. K. Fellinger, Ed. Editiones Roche. Basel.
3. RADEBOLD, H. 1979. Geriatrie. In Die Psychologie des 20. Jahrhunderts. P. Hahn, Ed. Vol. 9: 786-803. Kindler. Munich.
4. LEHR, U. 1977. Psychologie des Alterns. Quelle & Meyer. Heidelberg.
5. RADEBOLD, H. 1979. Psychosomatische Aspekte des Alterns und des Alters. In Lehrbuch der psychosomatischen Medizin. Th. Üxküll, Ed. 728-744. Urban & Schwarzenberg. Munich.
6. EFFROS, R. B. 1984. Aging and immunity. In Stress, Immunity and Aging. E. L. Cooper, Ed. 277-290. Marcel Dekker. New York, NY.
7. SCHWAB, R., L. STAIANO-COICO & M. E. WEKSLER. 1983. Immunological studies of aging. IX. Quantitative differences in T-lymphocyte subsets in young and old individuals. Diagn. Immunol. 1: 195-198.
8. LEWIS, V. M., J. J. TWOMEY, G. BEALMEAR & R. A. GOOD. 1978. Age, thymic involution and circulation of thymic hormone activity. J. Clin. Endocrinol. Metab. 47: 145-149.
9. SCHWAB, R., P. B. HAUSMAN, E. RINNOY-KAN & M. E. WEKSLER. 1985. Immunological studies of aging. X. Impaired T-lymphocytes and normal monocyte response form elderly humans to the mitogenic antibodies OKT 3 und Leu 4. Immunology 55: 677-684.
10. STAIANO-COICO, L., Z. DARZYNKIEWICZ, M. R. MELAMED & M. E. WEKSLER. 1984. Immunological studies of aging. XI. Impaired proliferation of T-lymphocytes detected in elderly humans by flow cytometry. J. Immunol. 132: 1788-1792.
11. NEGORO, S., H. HARA, S. MIYATA, O. SAIKI, T. TANAKA, K. YOSHIZAKI, T. IGARASHI & S. KISHIMOTO. 1986. Mechanism of age related decline in antigen-specific T-cell proliferative response: Il-2 receptor expression and recombinant Il-2 induced proliferative response of purified Tax-positive cells. Mech. Aging Dev. 36: 223-241.
12. ANTONACI, S., E. JIRILLO, E. SERLENGA & L. BONOMO. 1985. Monocyte chemotactic responsiveness triggered by lymphocyte derived factor in aged donors. Definitive report. Lymphokine Res. 4: 359-365.
13. GOODWIN, J. S. & R. P. MESSMER. 1979. Sensitivity of lymphocytes to prostaglandin E_2 increases in subjects over age 70. J. Clin. Invest. 64: 434-437.
14. WEKSLER, M. E. & T. H. TUTTEROTH. 1974. Impaired lymphocyte function in aged humans. J. Clin. Invest. 53: 99-103.
15. ROBERTS-THOMSON, I. C., S. WITTINGHAM, U. YOUNGCHAIYUD & I. R. MACKAY. 1974. Ageing, immune response and mortality. Lancet 2: 368-370.
16. MILLER, A. E. 1980. Selective decline in cellular immune response to varicella zoster in the elderly. Neurology 30: 582-585.
17. MERONI, P. L., W. BARCELLINI, D. FRASCA, C. SGUOTTI, M. D. BORGHI, G. DEBARTOLO, G. DORIA & C. ZANUSSI. 1987. In vivo immunopotentiating activity of thymopentin in aging humans—increase of IL-2 production. Clin. Immunol. Immunopathol. 42: 151-159.

18. RAJCZY, K., P. VARGHA & E. BEREGI. 1986. Relationship between immunoglobulin levels and specific antibody titers in the elderly. Z. Gerontol. **19:** 158-161.

19. RUBEN, F. L. & M. UHRING. 1985. Specific immunoglobulin-class antibody responses in the elderly before and after 14-valent pneumococcal vaccine. J. Infect. Dis. **151:** 845-849.

20. TAURIS, P., P. ANDERSEN & S. E. CHRISTIANSEN. 1985. Plaqueforming cell capability in the senescent. Immunol. Lett. **9:** 3-8.

21. KIM, Y. T., G. W. SISKIND & M. E. WEKSLER. 1985. Plaque-forming cell response of human blood lymphocytes. III. Cellular basis of the reduced immune response in the elderly. Isr. J. Med. Sci. **21:** 317-322.

22. CRAWFORD, J., M. K. EYE & H. J. COHEN. 1987. Evaluation of monoclonal gammopathies in the "well" elderly. Am. J. Med. **82:** 39-45.

23. GOIDL, E. A., M. MICHELIS, G. W. SISKIND & M. E. WEKSLER. 1981. Effect of age on the induction of autoantibodies. Clin. Exp. Immunol. **44:** 24-29.

24. CORBERAND, J. X., P. F. LAHARRAGUE & G. FILOLLA. 1986. Neutrophils of healthy aged humans are normal. Mech. Ageing Dev. **36:** 57-63.

25. HORAN, M. A., R. S. GULATI & R. A. FOX. 1985. Assessment of neutrophil function in the elderly using coated polyacrylamide gel (immunobeads) and nitroblue tetrazolium (NBT) reduction as a combined test. Mech. Ageing Dev. **29:** 29-33.

26. MUNAN, L. & A. KELLY. 1979. Age-dependent changes in blood monocyte populations in man. Clin. Exp. Immunol. **35:** 161-165.

27. BUTENKO, G. M. 1986. Ageing of the immune system and disease. *In* Age-related Factors in Carcinogenesis. IARC Sci. Publ. no. **58:** 71-83.

28. DOLL, R. 1962. Susceptibility to carcinogenesis at different ages. Geront. Clin. **4:** 211-221.

29. OESER, H. 1979. Krebs: Schicksal oder Verschulden? Thieme. Stuttgart.

30. SCHRAMM, A., H. FRANKE, B. SIMS & I. HAUBITZ. 1983. Gesundheitszustand, Lebenserwartung und Todesursache von Hundertjährigen. Versicherungsmedizin **35:** 50-53.

31. MIKAT, B. 1975. Zur Häufigkeit alter Menschen in der Bundesrepublik Deutschland und in West-Berlin. *In* Altern und Langlebigkeit. V. Böhlau, Ed. Schattauer. Stuttgart.

32. BALTRUSCH, H. J. F. & M. E. WALTZ. 1987. Stress and cancer: a sociobiological approach to aging, neuroimmunomodulation and host-tumor relationships. *In* Human Stress: Current Advances in Research, Vol. 2. J. H. Humphrey, Ed. AMS Press, New York, NY. In press.

33. BALTRUSCH, H. J. F. & M. E. WALTZ. 1985. Cancer from a biobehavioural and social epidemiological perspective. Soc. Sci. Med. 789-794.

34. BALTRUSCH, H. J. F., I. SCHEDEL, W. STANGEL & M. E. WALTZ. 1985. Biobehavioral perspective on the environment-immunologic interface. *In* Neuroimmunomodulation. Proceedings of the First International Workshop on Neuroimmunomodulation. N. H. Spector, Ed. 278-282. IWGN. Bethesda, MD.

35. BALTRUSCH, H. J. F., W. STANGEL & M. E. WALTZ. 1985. Early losses and family climate of cancer patients: possible relations to NIM. *In* Neuroimmunomodulation. Proceedings of the First International Workshop on Neuroimmunomodulation. N. H. Spector, Ed. 283-290. IWGN. Bethesda, MD.

36. BALTRUSCH, H. J. F. & M. E. WALTZ. 1986. Early family attitudes and the stress process: a life-span and personological model of host-tumor relationships. *In* Cancer, Stress and Death. 2nd ed. S. B. Day, Ed. 261-283. Plenum Medical Books. New York, NY.

37. BOWLING, A. 1987. Mortality after bereavement: a review of the literature on survival periods and factors affecting survival. Soc. Sci. Med. **24:** 117-124.

38. JACOBS, S. & A. OSTFELD. 1977. An epidemiological review of the mortality of bereavement. Psychosom. Med. **39:** 344-357.

39. BALTRUSCH, H. J. F. 1987. Unpublished data.

40. BARTROP, R. W., L. LAZARUS, E. LOCKHURST, L. G. KILOH & R. PENNY. 1977. Depressed lymphocyte function after bereavement. Lancet **1:** 834-836.

41. SCHLEIFER, S. J., S. E. KELLER, M. CAMERINO, J. C. THORNTON & M. STEIN. 1983. Suppression of lymphocyte stimulation following bereavement. JAMA **250:** 374-377.

42. KIECOLT-GLASER, J. K., L. D. FISHER, P. OGROCKI, J. C. STOUT, C. E. SPEICHER & R. GLASER. 1987. Marital quality, marital disruption, and immune function. Psychosom. Med. **49:** 13-34.

43. McFARLANE, A. H., G. R. NORMAN, D. L. STREINER & R. G. ROY. 1984. Characteristics and correlates of effective and ineffective social supports. J. Psychosom. Res. **28:** 501-510.
44. THOMAS, P. D., J. M. GOODWIN & J. S. GOODWIN. 1985. Effect of social support on stress-related changes in cholesterol level, uric acid level, and immune function in an elderly sample. Am. J. Psychiat. **142:** 735-737.
45. ARNETZ, B. 1983. Psychophysiological Effects of Social Understimulation in Old Age. Laboratory for Clinical Stress Research, Karolinska Institute, and National Institute for Psychosocial Factors and Health. Stockholm.
46. ARNETZ, B. B., T. THEORELL, L. LEVY, A. KALLNER & P. ENEROTH. 1983. An experimental study of social isolation of elderly people: psychoendocrine and metabolic effects. Psychosom. Med. **45:** 391-406.
47. KIECOLT-GLASER, J. K., R. GLASER, D. WILLINGER, J. STOUT, G. MESSICK, D. RICKER, S. C. ROMISHER, W. BRINER, G. BONNELL & R. DONNERBERG. 1985. Psychosocial enhancement of immunocompetence in a geriatric population. Health Psychol. **4:** 25-41.
48. DILMAN, V. M. 1978. Ageing, metabolic immunodepression and carcinogenesis. Mech. Ageing Dev. **8:** 153-173.
49. DILMAN, V. M. and M. N. OSTROMOUVA. 1984. Hypothalamic, metabolic and immune mechanisms of the influence of stress on the tumor process. *In* Impact of Psychoendocrine Systems in Cancer and Immunity. B. H. Fox and B. H. Newberry, Eds. 58-85. D. J. Hogrefe. Lewiston.
50. BALITSKY, K. P. 1983. Nervnaya Sistema i protivoopucholevaye zaslcite. Kiev. Naukova Dumka.
51. BALITSKY, K. P. & V. B. VINNITSKY. 1981. The central nervous system and cancer. *In* Stress and Cancer. K. Bammer & B. H. Newberry, Eds. 1-42. C. J. Hogrefe. Toronto.
52. BALITSKY, K. P. & Y. P. SHMALKO. 1987. Stress i metastasivanye elocestvennije opuchole. Naukova Dumka. Kiev.
53. FOX, B. H. 1978. Premorbid psychological factors as related to cancer incidence. J. Behav. Med. **1:** 45-133.
54. TEMOSHOK, L. & B. W. HELLER. 1984. On comparing apples, oranges and fruit salad: a methodological overview of medical outcome studies in psychosocial oncology. *In* Psychosocial Stress and Cancer. C. L. Cooper, Ed. 231-260. Wiley & Sons. Chichester.
55. LOCKE, S. E., L. KRAUS, J. LESERMAN, M. W. HURST, S. HEISSEL & M. WILLIAMS. 1984. Life change stress, psychiatric symptoms, and natural killer cell activity. Psychosom. Med. **46:** 441-453.
56. LEVY, S. M., R. B. HERBERMAN, A. M. MALUISH, B. SCHLIEN & M. LIPPMAN. 1985. Prognostic risk assessment in primary breast cancer by behavioral and immunological parameters. Health Psychol. **4:** 99-113.
57. CROSSARTH-MATICEK, G., J. SIEGRIST & H. VETTER. 1982. Interpersonal repression as a predictor of cancer. Soc. Sci. Med. **16:** 493-498.
58. WALTZ, M. E. 1987. Krankheit und Lebensqualität. *In* Leben mit dem Herzinfarkt. B. Badura, G. Kaufhold, H. Lehmann, H. Pfaff, T. Schott & M. Waltz, Eds. 87-125. Springer. Berlin.
59. GREER, S. & M. WATSON. 1985. Towards a psychobiological model of cancer: psychological considerations. Soc. Sci. Med. **20:** 773-777.
60. TEMOSHOK, L. 1987. Personality, coping style, emotion, and cancer: toward an integrative model. Cancer Surv. In press.
61. TEMOSHOK, L. 1983. Emotion, adaptation and disease. *In* Emotions in Health and Illness. Theoretical Research Foundations. L. Temoshok, C. Van Dyke & L. A. Zegans, Eds. 207-234. Grune & Stratton. New York, NY.
62. BALTRUSCH, H. J. F. & M. E. WALTZ. 1986. Psychosocial stress, identity and disease: the Type C pattern. Presented at the 14th International Cancer Congress, Budapest. Abstract no. 2085.
63. BALTRUSCH, H. J. F., G. A. RIGATOS & M. E. WALTZ. 1987. Repression of negative affects in cancer and other 'organic' diseases. Presented at the 11th Congress of the Italian Psychosomatic Society, Messina, 28th-30th May.
64. COX, T. & C. MACKAY. 1982. Psychosocial factors and psychophysiological mechanisms in the aetiology and development of cancers. Soc. Sci. Med. **16:** 381-396.

65. TEMOSHOK. L. 1985. Biopsychosocial studies on cutaneous malignant melanoma: psychosocial factors associated with prognostic indicators, progression, psychophysiology and tumor-host response. Soc. Sci. Med. **20:** 833-840.
66. KIECOLT-GLASER, J. K., R. E. STEPHENS, P. D. LIPETZ, C. SPEICHER & R. GLASER. 1985. Distress and DNA repair in human lymphocytes. J. Behav. Med. **8:** 311-320.
67. GLASER, R., B. E. THORNS, K. L. TARR, J. K. GLASER & S. M. D'AMBROSIO. 1985. Effects of stress on methyltransferase synthesis: an important DNA repair enzyme. Health Psychol. **4:** 403-412.
68. PETTINGALE, K. W. 1985. Towards a psychobiological model of cancer: biological considerations. Soc. Sci. Med. **20:** 779-788.
69. HEIJNEN, C. & R. E. BALLIEUX, 1987. The influence of opioid peptides on the immune system. Advances **3:** 114-121.
70. BLANEY, P. H. 1985. Psychological considerations in cancer. *In* Behavioral Medicine: The Biopsychosocial Approach. N. Schneidermann & J. T. Tapp, Eds. 533-563. Erlbaum. Hillsdale, NJ.
71. BALTRUSCH, H. J. F. & W. STANGEL. 1982. Psychosomatische Faktoren und Polycythaemia vera. *In* Haematologie im Alter. J. Böhnel, R. Heinz & A. Stacher, Eds. 80-81. Urban & Schwarzenberg. Vienna.
72. BALTRUSCH, H. J. F. & W. STANGEL. 1981. Psychosomatic aspects of polycythaemia vera. *In* Psychosomatic Factors in Chronic Illness. K. Achte & A. Pakaslahti, Eds. Psychiat. Fenn. Suppl., 133-142.
73. BALTRUSCH, H. J. F., J. SEIDEL, W. STANGEL & M. E. WALTZ. 1987. The biobehavioral setting of polycythaemia vera. In preparation.

Epidemiologic Aspects of Stress, Aging, Cancer and the Immune System

BERNARD H. FOX

Boston University School of Medicine
85 East Newton Street
Boston, Massachusetts

INTRODUCTION

The relationship among cancer, the immune system, stress, and aging can be addressed in a number of ways. Here the choice will be how stress and the immune system may interact with or even, in part, be responsible for the incidence of cancer associated with aging. It will first be necessary to set forth some data relating aging and cancer, to establish the epidemiologic baseline of events in general. Then, several relevant facts and some hypotheses regarding phenotypic biologic events will be presented. Next, the behavioral and biologic aspects of stress (and some associated reactions and personal characteristics) will be discussed. Finally, but also throughout the discussion, the possible interrelations among the four topics will be given, and tentative conclusions drawn.

EPIDEMIOLOGY OF CANCER

The causes of cancer can be characterized along a continuum from remote to immediate. The remote and intermediate causes are generally broad-gauge, characterized in social rather than individual terms.[1] They include factors like geographic-climatic, economic, sociocultural, and political. While these may affect cancer incidence and mortality independently, their influence on stress as it relates to cancer and aging is difficult to assess. Cancer rates overall, but especially rates for single sites, can vary enormously between countries, and even between locations within a country.[2] For some tumor sites (*e.g.,* cervix, lung, stomach, oro- and nasopharynx) we are fairly sure of the *major* environmental reasons for these differences. For other sites (*e.g.,* the leukemias, brain and nervous system) we are pretty much in the dark. For example, there is no peak of incidence of acute lymphocytic leukemia at 4 years of age of blacks in the U.S.A., as there is in whites. The ratio of peak rates in the groups is about 3:1.

16

Following a decline from the peak, the two rates approach each other at about age 13.[3] In view of such extreme variation it has been assumed (based on carefully defined sampling conditions) that most cancers—some 80%—are avoidable; further, that those countries or areas showing the lowest rates describe the tumor incidence level that would be achievable if proper steps were taken to avoid tumors.[4] FIGURE 1 shows examples of such variation among countries.

This is an interesting assumption because it involves exceptions, specified within the defined sampling conditions, that have genetic origins. For example, skin cancers were not considered because pigmentation is so potent a discriminator of susceptibility. But if omission of that genetic attribute is justified, might there not be other genetic uniformities in various world areas that could yield large differences in susceptibility? All that would be needed would be a cultural isolate that began with an extreme level of susceptibility, either high or low. Such an event is not likely to happen often, since we have had considerable population mixing in the last 10,000 years. Nevertheless, the point is not trivial. For example, it has been estimated that several cancers, especially breast cancer, are found in excess (rate ratios 1.6 in men, 2.0 in women) among adult blood relatives of patients with ataxia-telangiectasia (AT), an autosomal recessive disease reflecting chromosomal instability and probably DNA repair deficiency. Heterozygotes with the AT gene are variously estimated to make up 0.68 to 7.7 percent of the U.S. white population.[5] A similar disease (in that victims are cancer prone) is Bloom's syndrome. In this disease a so-called "founder effect" is evident. Ashkenazi Jews earlier living in a small area near the Ukraine-Poland border were an originating gene pool.[6] The number of cancer events discovered to be related to genetic features keeps growing. For example, patients having extra copies of the oncogene HER-2/neu in breast tumor cells have a poorer prognosis than other patients, and the same is true for the oncogene N-myc in children with neuroblastoma.[7]

A point of particular importance in regard to the problem of isolating the contribution of stress to cancer, if it exists, is the variation in the curves of cancer incidence (and mortality) among various cancer sites. They can appear in essentially four types:

a. Peaking early in life. Some peak in early childhood, like Wilms' tumor, and fall to zero by age 20. Others peak in early adulthood. For example, in testicular tumors, the peak is 25–35 years of age; thereafter the rate falls, but rises again after age 65. This pattern is found in U.S. whites, but the peak in early adulthood is practically nonexistent in blacks, whose rate in early adulthood is a fourth that of whites. The pattern in blacks also appears in Africa.[3]

b. Rising throughout life from initial appearance. Examples are stomach, starting around age 35, and prostate, starting around age 50.

c. Rising to a peak in late maturity and falling at about age 80. Examples are uterine body and lung, beginning about age 40.

d. Rising to a maximum in adulthood and remaining at that peak or rising rapidly to a near maximum and very slowly thereafter throughout life, e.g., cervix. Variations of these are known; e.g., breast rises to menopause, flattens for a few years (a break known as Clemmesen's hook) and rises with increasing slope thereafter.[8]

These variations are important because one must ask, if stress or personality acts to increase or decrease cancer risk, when must its effects manifest themselves? How long an exposure to such influences must the body or the affected organ endure before risk is increased because of their presence? At what point can we say that such effects are no longer zero or negligible? For example, in retinoblastoma the tumor is known to arise very early in life, as is the case with medulloblastoma. For such childhood tumors, would stress find a place as a contributing or potentiating feature?

These genetic variations are not inconsistent with the notion that some oncogenes might be excess baggage and might not appear in certain people.

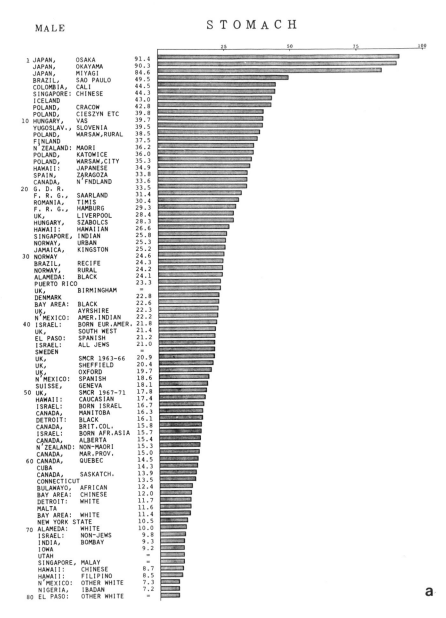

FIGURE 1. Age-adjusted incidence rates (cases/100,000 per year) among 80 world groups, variously late 1960s to early 1970s: (**a**) stomach cancer in males and (**b**) breast cancer in females. (Data from Waterhouse *et al.*[4a] Figure from Segi;[4b] reprinted by permission from the Segi Institute of Cancer Epidemiology.)

BREAST

FEMALE

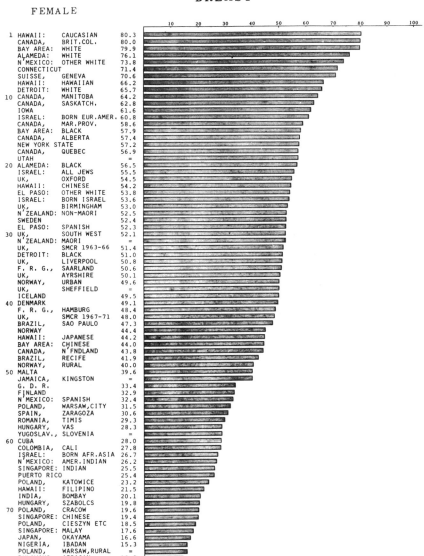

1 HAWAII:	CAUCASIAN	80.3
CANADA,	BRIT.COL.	80.0
BAY AREA:	WHITE	79.9
ALAMEDA:	WHITE	76.1
N'MEXICO:	OTHER WHITE	73.8
CONNECTICUT		71.4
SUISSE,	GENEVA	70.6
HAWAII:	HAWAIIAN	66.2
DETROIT:	WHITE	65.7
10 CANADA,	MANITOBA	64.2
CANADA,	SASKATCH.	62.8
IOWA		61.6
ISRAEL:	BORN EUR.AMER.	60.8
CANADA,	MAR.PROV.	58.6
BAY AREA:	BLACK	57.9
CANADA,	ALBERTA	57.4
NEW YORK STATE		57.2
CANADA,	QUEBEC	56.9
UTAH		=
20 ALAMEDA:	BLACK	56.5
ISRAEL:	ALL JEWS	55.5
UK,	OXFORD	54.5
HAWAII:	CHINESE	54.2
EL PASO:	OTHER WHITE	53.8
ISRAEL:	BORN ISRAEL	53.6
UK,	BIRMINGHAM	53.0
N'ZEALAND:	NON-MAORI	52.5
SWEDEN		52.4
EL PASO:	SPANISH	52.3
30 UK,	SOUTH WEST	52.1
N'ZEALAND:	MAORI	=
UK,	SMCR 1963-66	51.4
DETROIT:	BLACK	51.0
UK,	LIVERPOOL	50.8
F. R. G.,	SAARLAND	50.6
UK,	AYRSHIRE	50.1
NORWAY,	URBAN	49.6
UK,	SHEFFIELD	=
ICELAND		49.5
40 DENMARK		49.1
F. R. G.,	HAMBURG	48.4
UK,	SMCR 1967-71	48.0
BRAZIL,	SAO PAULO	47.3
NORWAY		44.4
HAWAII:	JAPANESE	44.2
BAY AREA:	CHINESE	44.0
CANADA,	N'FNDLAND	43.8
BRAZIL,	RECIFE	41.9
NORWAY,	RURAL	40.0
50 MALTA		39.6
JAMAICA,	KINGSTON	=
G. D. R.		33.4
FINLAND		32.9
N'MEXICO:	SPANISH	32.4
POLAND,	WARSAW,CITY	31.5
SPAIN,	ZARAGOZA	30.6
ROMANIA,	TIMIS	29.3
HUNGARY,	VAS	28.3
YUGOSLAV.,	SLOVENIA	=
60 CUBA		28.0
COLOMBIA,	CALI	27.8
ISRAEL:	BORN AFR.ASIA	26.7
N'MEXICO:	AMER.INDIAN	26.2
SINGAPORE:	INDIAN	25.5
PUERTO RICO		25.4
POLAND,	KATOWICE	23.2
HAWAII:	FILIPINO	21.5
INDIA,	BOMBAY	20.1
HUNGARY,	SZABOLCS	19.8
70 POLAND,	CRACOW	19.6
SINGAPORE:	CHINESE	19.4
POLAND,	CIESZYN ETC	18.5
SINGAPORE:	MALAY	17.6
JAPAN,	OKAYAMA	16.6
NIGERIA,	IBADAN	15.3
POLAND,	WARSAW,RURAL	=
BULAWAYO,	AFRICAN	13.8
JAPAN,	MIYAGI	13.0
JAPAN,	OSAKA	12.1
80 ISRAEL;	NON-JEWS	11.0

b

THE INITIATION OF CANCER

Statistical incidence of cancer is defined by discovery of its presence. This happens after about 30 doublings of a growing tumor, and usually longer. Thus, "causes of cancer incidence" are a combination of the causes of transformation and the influences on the growth of tumors until diagnosis. Therefore, one must distinguish clearly the initiation of cancer from its progress. The first event, transformation, is connected to the immune system only in limited ways. If a virus invades a cell, it can produce a precursor to cancer; that is, a transformed cell that may be mortal, as in some dysplasias that can regress to normal tissue—*e.g.,* mild cervical dysplasia. (We assume that cervical cancer and the dysplasias usually preceding it are virally induced.) In that case the immune system (IS) may be one agent that causes regression of the abnormality, either through antigenic stimulation or through the agency of cells like NK cells. Similar reasoning applies to chemically or radiologically induced transformations. Further, immortal but nonmalignant transformations like benign tumors may be subject to regression by IS attack, thus reducing the probability that they may mutate to malignant tumors. However, when an immortal transformation to malignancy does occur, the action of the IS is addressed to prognosis, that is, probability of continued growth and dissemination of the malignancy. Aside from the conditions where the IS may or may not prevent malignant transformation, various other events affecting malignant transformation are generally not associated with the IS. They include, among other things, DNA repair, chromosomal instability (CI), enzymes transforming substances to carcinogens or carcinogens to harmless substances, radiation effects, and last, but of considerable theoretical importance in the theory relating stress and coping to cancer, viral invasion with long-term residence in transformed but quiescent cells.

We know little enough about the effects associated with carcinogen-transforming enzymes in a biologic sense, let alone the possible effect of psychological stimuli.

However, in respect to DNA repair and chromosomal instability, we have some evidence. It is suspected that sister chromatid exchange (crossover of chromosomal segments) (SCE) reflects DNA repair status, and may itself be a kind of DNA repair mechanism, since it is observed to diminish with aging, and its induction occurs in increased amount following stimuli known to damage DNA. With small amounts of such agents (cyclophosphamide, mitomycin C, doxorubicin), young and old mice showed equal levels of SCE induction; with a larger mutagenic dose the older mice displayed less SCE increase than the younger.[9]

The role of DNA repair is fairly clear from an overall viewpoint. If there were none, most advanced organisms would not reach reproductive years. Some invertebrates do not show tumors. They might remove them by losing and replacing tissue, as in lost limbs. Or they may not engender tumors because there is very little cellular turnover, and that may be a major source of transformation. (Is this why there are no pure nerve tissue cancers in higher organisms? Man's central nervous system (CNS) tumors are distributed as follows: gliomas, about 45%; meningiomas, 15%; acoustic nerve, 2–3%; pituitary adenomas, 7%; neurilemmomas, 7%; metastases to CNS, 6%; angiomas, sarcomas, etc., the remainder.) Some authors, *e.g.,* Good and Finstad,[10] have proposed that DNA repair evolved to handle neoplasia. Its development presumably arose from wide differentiation of cell types and from their duplication, which makes errors more likely. However, since the amount of DNA in vertebrate and invertebrate cells does not differ much, the number of redundant genes is supposedly fewer in higher organisms, tending to increase the probability of mutations becoming manifest.[11] It has been suggested that there are nonfunctional genes. If so, it occurs to me that their presence might be explained by a simple stochastic argument. If there is a constant probability of DNA disturbances (cosmic rays, bodily radioactive materials from food, chemical carcinogens, etc.), their distribution among a large number of genes lessens the chance of any particular gene (including active ones) being damaged.

What is, now, the relevance of DNA repair and SCE to stress and cancer? If repair and SCE offer protection against cancer, and if stress and coping ability affect their level of activity, stress and coping ability may affect initiation of cancer. There have been studies showing just such effects. Seredenin et al.[12] reported that, using two stressors on mice, open field test with flashes and movement restraint, chromosomal aberrations (CA) increased markedly in both cases compared with controls. When the mice were pretreated with a tranquilizer the CA did not differ from those of controls. Fischman et al.[13] found results consistent with those findings. They exposed rats to warm and cold swims, white noise, intermittent inescapable footshock, continuous footshock, and no stress. All of the stressors increased SCE's, although to different degrees. Also, two hours after stress termination, unscheduled DNA synthesis was measured in leukocytes. Stressed rats showed twice the level of unstressed. In that test for dose-response changes, 3 shock frequencies were compared with no shock. SCE's and CA were found to be graded according to the shock frequencies. Rats exposed to no shock but placed in the cages used to shock test animals showed intermediate elevations in the two measures. Finally, Kiecolt-Glaser et al.[14] found that the lymphocytes of nonpsychotic depressives before medication (whom they called "distressed") showed reduced DNA repair capability after radiation of their leucocytes.

The meaning of these results is not entirely clear, since the DNA repair results, both involving unscheduled DNA synthesis, were in opposite directions. My hypothesis is that depressed individuals are likely to show increased output of glucocorticoids with resultant poor synthesis, and that the rats were exposed for short periods of time to stimuli that initially provoke catecholamine products, with resultant improved synthesis. This hypothesis is directly testable. Another hypothesis, proposed by Fischman et al.,[13] is that the DNA itself was altered by the stress, yielding both the SCE results and DNA results that they found.

In any case, the potential effect on DNA transformation and chromosomal aberrations is clear. Mattern and Cerutti,[15] cited by Hayflick,[16] reported that DNA repair capability declines with the number of cell population doublings (translatable as aging).

Thus, the combination of stress and aging, under conditions not yet specifiable (per the above conflict) can theoretically have an effect on the initial transformation to a malignant cell.

THE PROGRESSION OF CANCER

Once a cell has been transformed to a malignant one, all phenomena thereafter associated with reproduction or cloning of itself belong in the realm of progression of a tumor, not initiation. This leads to uncertainties in particular matters pertaining to etiology, as will be explained below. But first, it should be noted that some aspects of tumor development are both progression and initiation: namely, mutation of cancer cells to produce new cells as originators of a clone. This phenomenon bears very strongly on the present topic in two ways. First, as a tumor grows, with increasing size the number of dividing cells grows. If there is a constant probability of mutation, the number of mutations grows as the population of dividing cells grows. Since the population to begin with is malignant there will appear a cluster of clones of mutated cells, each with an original parent that was the first transformed cell of its own clone. The various clones are, it has been shown, differentially sensitive to individual chemotherapeutic agents. Thus, some of the clones will die when single-agent treatment begins, but others will not. The latter regrow and the newly regrown tumor is not responsive to that agent. For that reason, chemotherapeutic cocktails are more successful than unit agents.[17] If the patient is lucky, he or she will not have developed mutations, and if further lucky, the agent chosen will kill the tumor cells; or the mutations that do occur may be sensitive to the agents used.

The second way that mutation is relevant to the progression of tumors is the degree to which the mutations produce antigens detectable to the host's immune system. If detectable, they may be attacked provided the host's immune system has not been weakened by existing tumor cells. But the greater the number of mutations the greater the chance that at least one of them will not cause an immune reaction and, therefore, will proliferate unhindered.

Stress and coping enter the picture during growth of the tumor. These are two different aspects of a person's or animal's reaction to threatening of disequilibrating stimuli, and they may be partially dependent. If the stimuli are emotionally disturbing, there may as a result be depression of immune reactivity, either through stimulation of glucocorticoids or through release of opioids that can render parts of the immune system less active or efficient;[18] or, under some conditions, more efficient.[19,20] These data refer to animals, but similar results have been shown in humans. A recent study showed that women who had undergone major life events had lower NK cell activity than those who had not. Among them, the severity of depressive symptoms was correlated with impairment.[21] Of course, it does not necessarily follow that either cancer incidence or prognosis is affected by such events. In fact, the whole issue of which, if any, psychosocial factors bear on survival in cancer patients is rather uncertain. It has been discussed in some detail by Levy and Fox.[22] Their conclusion was that in some patients, under some conditions, stress, coping style, or personality is associated with (but does not necessarily cause) changes in survival. See TABLE 1.

In addition, a number of variables have been examined to see whether cancer patients can be distinguished from noncancer patients. The conclusions from these studies are in some doubt because it has been shown that when the patient is in a dysphoric mood, stressful events are more often recalled than nonstressful.[23]

GENERAL THEORETICAL CONSIDERATIONS

One point to note in regard to the above relationships is that those changes associated with decreased IS efficiency, especially cell-mediated reactions, can theoretically arise either from stable states such as personality structure or from intermittent states such as stress responses or from their combination. Any of the stable personality characteristics listed in TABLE 1 may belong to the first group. A number of repeated stressful situations have been described in various places; *e.g.*, an unhappy, but indissoluble marriage,[24] a distressing job situation (*e.g.*, social work among the poor, teaching in U.S.A. ghetto schools, transoceanic flight personnel, air traffic control personnel; prison; concentration camps). It has been judged that personality may be a two-way street. Life distress may induce personality traits such as denial or a helpless-hopeless attitude, or not. Or personality may govern, in part, the response to the stressor; for example, regarding the stressor as a challenge, one of the components of Kobasa's hardiness concept.[25] In any case, it is the way the organism copes with the stressor, plus the severity of the stressor, that govern the total product of the stress

TABLE 1. Psychosocial Factors That Have Been Associated with Cancer Surival and Incidence

A number of psychosocial variables have been associated with shorter (s) or longer (l) survival time or time to relapse in human cancer patients—[mixed (m), melanoma (mel), breast (b)] (only the first author is listed):

Stavraky[40]	hostility without loss of emotional control	l	m
Schonfield[41]	social introversion	s	b
Jensen[42]	suppression or repression of emotion	s	mel
Temoshok[43]	Type C personality (accepting, tries to please, does not express emotion, pleasant facade)	s	mel
Greer[44]	helpless-hopeless attitude	s	b
	stoic acceptance	s	b
	denial	l	b
	fighting spirit (I can beat this disease)	l	b
Derogatis[45]	bad patient—noncompliant, complaining, aggressive	l	b
Viitamäki[46]	aggressiveness	s	m
Rogentine[47]	needed little life adjustment to melanoma surgery	s	mel
Visintainer[48]	problem-solving attitude toward disease	l	mel
Ikemi[49]	strong system of belief (partly religion)	l	m
Reynolds[50]	social isolation (in men)	s	m

For comparison, the following have yielded a positive relationship (pr) or no relationship (nr) to later incidence of cancer or mortality from cancer; all but two are for mixed sites:

Ragland[26]	Type A personality (in men for lung cancer)	nr
Ragland[26]	Type A personality (in men for nonlung cancer)	pr
Kaplan[51]	depressed attitude but not clinically ill	nr
Shekelle[52]	depressed attitude but not clinically ill (men)	pr
Thomas[53]	little closeness to parents while growing up (men)	pr
Hagnell[54]	warm-hearted, extroverted (women)	pr
Keehn[55]	discharged from Army for psychoneurosis (men)	nr
Keehn[56]	having been prisoners of war (men)	nr
Kaplan[57]	poor well-being (in both sexes but especially for hormonal tumors in women)	pr
Reynolds[50]	social isolation	pr
Kerr[58]	hospitalized depression	pr
Evans[59]	hospitalized depression	nr
Morrison[60]	somatic symptoms	nr
Wagner[61]	psychotropic drugs in mental patients (breast)	nr

induction. If a malignant transformation takes place, and early in the development of the tumor—before it gets too large to be dealt with by the IS—there is a stressful situation that reduces IS competence, the tumor may indeed grow large enough not to be affected, or it may, before being destroyed by the IS if the latter recovers competence, yield enough mutant cells with small antigenic stimulus value so that they can escape immune surveillance.

At this point the statistical nature of the risk of stress can be brought in. In one situation, that of Type A men being at greater risk of cancer mortality than Type B,[26] the following theory was proposed to explain that finding.[27] Type A persons seem continually to try to achieve more. They seem to seek out challenges to overcome, are impatient, driving, sometimes hostile. Because successive challenges always involve unsolved problems at first, during those times before success, they are frustrated and do not have control of the situation. This produces the typical hormonal response of increased ACTH and cortisol output, usually tending to reduce IS competence, especially cell-mediated response competence, which seems the most important IS element in combatting tumors, together with NK cells. Thus it is proposed that Type A persons suffer a series of frustrations and IS depressions, larger in number than Type B's, and hence increase the probability that among all the transformations, one will yield a tumor that would not be destroyed by the IS.

I will hypothesize that failure to cope, which goes along with certain personalities, and a helpless, giving-up attitude, both already having been observed in some studies, will go along with decreased survival in cancer patients, and also go along with increase in probability of cancer, following reasoning similar to that given for the Type A personality. That is, there will be an increased number of cases where reduced IS efficiency due to poor coping may occur together with a transformed cancer clone. But I will further hypothesize that such susceptibility will be very broad. It is known that a number of viral diseases involve inactive resident viruses that are repressed and quiescent after initial invasion. These can be derepressed and released into the bloodstream to activate a disease once again; e.g., herpesvirus I, herpesvirus II, EBV, and possibly cytomegalovirus and leukemia. In animals such derepression has been known for some time and a number of such viruses can be released to activity with greater or lesser ease, based on *genetic* characteristics whose allelic location is known. A table of 22 such alleles and the associated mouse strains in which the allelic expression has been recorded is given by Upton,[28] citing Tooze.[29] If such a viral genome is associated with an oncogene, its release, due perhaps to a carcinogen such as a chemical or X-rays, yields a tumorous cell. Another possibility is that the viral genome is maintained in the repressed state by the IS, and if that influence is reduced, as by stress, the possibility of transformation exists. Since we live in a sea of ionizing radiation, *e.g.,* radioactivity in foods, housing minerals, etc., derepression is to be expected. Viral transformation is more frequent *in vitro* among cells from patients with more CA than those with less.[30] Further, it is known that CA increase with age.[31] These facts are consistent with the accelerating increases in cancer incidence with age.

Current theory on the development of cancer says that there are at least two events involved.[32] This theory, generally accepted, is consistent with the fact that for any site with positively accelerating incidence, the rate of increase of incidence can be described as a power function. For example, the incidence of colon cancer rises as the 5th or 6th power of age; that of lung cancer as the 4th power; and that of prostate cancer, amazingly, as the 11th power of age.[33] The effect on the incidence curve as the power becomes greater is to reduce the slope in early years and to increase its rate of rise after it starts to show a perceptible turn upward on the graph, making the curve turn upward more sharply. Biologic events are likely to be the prepotent influencers in this picture, but to the degree that psychosocial phenomena can affect them, to that degree such phenomena can also affect incidence. Besides the accumulation of carcinogenic cell alterations, other influences include decline in IS competence, activation of oncogenic viruses, hormonal changes, and DNA repair capability.

One interesting finding is that in almost all animals the female outlives the male. Aside from the possible influence of hormones (*e.g.,* premenopausal ovariectomized women are at lower risk of breast cancer than intact women), one theory has proposed that the reason for this is that females have two copies of immunoregulatory genes residing on the X-chromosome, whereas males have only one.[34] If this is the case females ought to be less affected by equivalent stress, and if stress affects cancer incidence, they should experience lower cancer and other viral disease incidence. Females should also, for similar cancers, experience longer survival, all other things being equal. Women do indeed, have lower incidence of many tumors.[35]

It may be possible to relate stress changes as one ages and cancer risk changes as one ages. It is known that with aging, CNS function declines, although with different speeds and in different degrees for various functions. Generally, lower cell count, slowing of nerve conduction velocity, fragmentation of reticulation, Nissl substance reduction, chromatin loss, and increase in lipofucsin have been observed in nerve cells.[36] Together with these phenomena, functional loss has also been reported, for example, for vibrotactile, cutaneous, pain, and corneal sensitivity.[37] Of particular interest is the finding that although reports of pain showed a small, though real, reduction in sensitivity, there was a substantial rise in pain tolerance. This was established by a signal detection procedure involving the relative operating characteristic (ROC). ROC procedures permit the separation and separate identification of first, threshold variation unaffected by frame of reference and second, frame of reference itself, reflecting attitudinal bias or response set.[38] One can hypothesize that increased pain tolerance is a general phenomenon, rendering any noxious stimulus more tolerable, and calling forth less autonomic reactivity (e.g., ACTH and opioid release). One would then predict, all other things being equal, a lesser effect of life events on cancer induction. Such a hypothesis is almost impossible to test, because of the considerable variability in a number of relevant factors. For example, the number of stressful events is said to decrease with age, since the older person is more settled; but depending on financial circumstances, old age may yield more pressing stressors, especially ones producing increased states of reduced IS function: loneliness, rejection, loss of mate, and sexual problems, all of which tend toward a depressive reaction. In spite of its initial attractiveness to me, overall the hypothesis, on more detailed consideration, does not seem to be useful, partly because it is not easily testable, and partly because it is almost certain to involve severely confounding variables.

A more productive approach would be based on stochastic principles. What events yielding stressful reaction occur frequently? Among what groups? What stressors produce feelings of lost control, or are, as cumulative events, stimuli to a feeling of helplessness and hopelessness? What personal attributes produce such feelings in some people but not in others? Among those with such feelings, one would predict poorer disease outcome and more frequent disease—especially cancer—incidence. The literature on personality and cancer tends, in a mild degree, to support the first prediction, that on survival,[22] but the second, on incidence, is much more doubtful.[39]

CONCLUSION

In summary, biological phenomena suggest that stress can increase cancer susceptibility with age, but that it must ride on top of the biological etiologic agents for cancer whose effects are much more potent. Further, the probability is that stress affects survival, or progress of cancer, more than it does initiation, although new information on virus-induced cancer suggests that stress may increase the probability of viral derepression, and hence cancer risk. This possibility has been addressed in the research literature only by implication. It would be valuable if such a hypothesis were tested directly.

REFERENCES

1. FOX, B. H. 1984. Remote life-style causes of cancer. Cancer Detection Prev. **7:** 21-29.
2. FOX, B. H. 1982. Endogenous psychosocial factors in cross-national cancer incidence. *In* Social Psychology and Behavioral Medicine. J. R. Eiser, Ed. 101-141. John Wiley. London.
3. MILLER, R. W. 1977. Ethnic differences in cancer occurrence: genetic and environmental influences with particular reference to neuroblastoma. *In* Genetics of Human Cancer. J. J. Mulvihill, R. W. Miller & J. F. Fraumeni, Jr., Eds. 1-14. Raven Press. New York, N.Y.
4. DOLL, R. AND R. PETO. 1981. The causes of cancer: quantitative estimates of avoidable risks of cancer in the United States today. J. Natl. Cancer Inst. **66:** 1191-1308.
4a. WATERHOUSE, J., C. MUIR, P. CORREA & J. POWELL. 1976. Cancer on Five Continents. Vol. 3. International Agency for Research on Cancer. Lyon.
4b. SEGI, M. 1977. Graphic Presentation of Cancer Incidence by Site and by Area. 12, 24. Segi Institute of Cancer Epidemiology. Nagoya, Japan.
5. SWIFT, M., P. J. REITNAUER, D. MORRELL & C. L. CHASE. 1987. Breast and other cancers in families with ataxia telangiectasia. N. Engl. J. Med. **316:** 1289-1294.
6. HECHT, F. & B. K. McCAW. 1977. Chromosome instability syndromes. *In* Genetics of Human Cancer. J. J. Mulvihill, R. W. Miller & J. F. Fraumeni, Jr., Eds. 105-123. Raven Press. New York, N.Y.
7. 1987. Breast cancer: *neu* clue. Sci. Am. **256** (3): 71,74.
8. 1981. Surveillance, Epidemiology, and End Results: Incidence and Mortality Data, 1973-1977. Natl. Cancer Inst. Monog. 57. National Cancer Institute. Bethesda, MD.
9. NAKANISHI, Y., D. KRAM & E. L. SCHNEIDER. 1979. Aging and sister chromatid exchange. IV. Reduced frequencies of mutagen-induced sister chromatid exchanges in vivo in mouse bone marrow cells with aging. Cytogenet. Cell Genet. **24:** 61-67.
10. GOOD, R. A. & J. FINSTAD. 1969. Essential relationship between the lymphoid system, immunity, and malignancy. Natl. Cancer Inst. Monog. **31:** 41-58.
11. DAWE, C. J. 1973. Comparative neoplasia. *In* Cancer Medicine. J. F. Holland and E. Frei, Eds. 209-256. Lea and Febiger. Philadelphia, P.A.
12. SEREDENIN, S. B., A. D. DURNEV & A. A. VEDERNIKOV. 1980. Bull. Exp. Biol. Med. (translated from the Russian) **89:** 972-973.
13. FISCHMAN, H. K. & D. D. KELLY. 1987. Sister chromatid exchanges induced by behavioral stress. Ann. N. Y. Acad. Sci. **496:** 426-435.
14. KIECOLT-GLASER, J. K., R. E. STEPHENS, P. D. LIPETZ, C. E. SPEICHER & R. GLASER. 1985. Distress and DNA repair in human lymphocytes. J. Behav. Med. **8:** 311-320.
15. MATTERN, M. R. & P. A. CERUTTI. 1975. Age dependent excision repair of damaged thymidine from gamma-irradiated DNA by isolated nuclei from fibroblasts. Nature **254:** 450-452.
16. HAYFLICK, L. 1977. The cellular basis of biological aging. *In* The Handbooks of Aging. J. E. Birren, Ed. in Chief. Vol. 1. Handbook of the Biology of Aging. C. E. Finch and L. Hayflick. Eds. 159-186. Van Nostrand Reinhold. New York, N.Y.
17. BLUM, R. H., E. FREI, III & J. F. HOLLAND. 1982. Principles of dose, schedule, and combination chemotherapy. *In* Cancer Medicine (2nd Edition). J. F. Holland & E. Frei, III, Eds. 730-751. Lea and Febiger. Philadelphia, PA.
18. RILEY, V. 1981. Psychoneuroendocrine influences on immunocompetence and neoplasia. Science **212:** 1100-1109.
19. MONJAN. A. A. & M. I. COLLECTOR. 1977. Stress-induced modulation of the immune response. Science **196:** 307-308.

20. KEAST, D. 1981. Immunosurveillance and cancer. *In* Stress and Cancer. K. Bammer & B. H. Newberry, Eds. 71-97. Hogrefe, Inc. Toronto.
21. IRWIN, M., M. D. DANIELS, E. T. BLOOM, T. SMITH & H. WEINER. 1987. Life events, depressive symptoms and immune function. Am. J. Psychiat. **144:** 437-441.
22. LEVY, S. & B. H. FOX. Psychological risk factors and mechanisms in cancer prognosis. CA: A Cancer Journal for Clinicians. In press.
23. BOWER, G. H. 1981. Mood and memory. Am. Psychologist **36:** 129-148.
24. FOX, B. H. 1978. Premorbid psychological factors as related to cancer incidence. J. Behav. Med. **1:** 45-133.
25. KOBASA, S. C., S. R. MADDI & M. C. PUCCETTI. 1982. Personality and exercise as buffers in the stress-illness relationship. J. Behav. Med. **5:** 391-404.
26. RAGLAND, D. R., R. J. BRAND & B. H. FOX. 1987. Type A behavior and mortality in the Western Collaborative Group Study. (Abstract). Psychosom. Med. **49:** 209.
27. FOX, B. H., D. R. RAGLAND, R. J. BRAND & R. H. ROSENMAN. 1987. Type A behavior and cancer mortality. Ann. N. Y. Acad. Sci. **496:** 620-627.
28. UPTON, A. C. 1977. Pathobiology. *In* The Handbooks of Aging. J. E. Birren, Ed. in Chief. Vol. 1. Handbook of the Biology of Aging. C. E. Finch & L. Hayflick, Eds. 513-535. Van Nostrand Reinhold. New York, N.Y.
29. TOOZE, J., ED. 1973. The Molecular Biology of Tumor Viruses. Cold Spring Harbor Laboratory. Cold Spring Harbor, N.Y.
30. MILLER, R. W. & G. TODARO. 1969. Viral transformation of cells from persons at high risk of cancer. Lancet **1:** 81-82.
31. JARVIK, L. F., FU-SUN YEN & E. MORALISHVILI. 1974. Chromosome examination in aging institutionalized women. J. Gerontol. **29:** 269-276.
32. KNUDSON, A. G., JR. 1973. Mutation and human cancer. Adv. Cancer Res. **17:** 317-352.
33. DOLL, R. 1971. The age distribution of cancer: implications for models of carcinogenesis. J. R. Stat. Soc. 134 (Part 2): 133-166.
34. PURTILO, D. T. & J. L. SULLIVAN. 1979. Immunological bases for superior survival in females. Am. J. Dis. Child. **133:** 1251-1253.
35. PURTILO, D. T. 1977. Opportunistic non-Hodgkins lymphoma in X-linked recessive immunodeficiency and lymphoproliferative syndromes. Semin. Oncol. **4:** 335-343.
36. BRODY, H. & N. VIJAYASHANKAR. 1977. Anatomical changes in the nervous system. *In* The Handbooks of Aging. J. E. Birren, Ed. in Chief. Vol. 1. Handbook of the Biology of Aging. C. E. Finch & L. Hayflick. Eds. 241-261. Van Nostrand Reinhold. New York, N.Y.
37. KENSHALO, D. R. 1977. Age changes in touch, vibration, temperature, kinesthesis and pain sensitivity. *In* The Handbooks of Aging, J. E. Birren, Ed. in Chief. Vol. 2. Handbook of the Psychology of Aging. J. E. Birren & K. W. Schaie, Eds. 562-579. Van Nostrand Reinhold. New York, N.Y.
38. GREEN, D. M. & J. A. SWETS. 1966. Signal Detection Theory and Psychophysics. Robert E. Krieger. Huntington, N.Y.
39. FOX, B. H. 1983. Current theory of psychogenic effects on cancer incidence and prognosis. J. Psychosoc. Oncol. **1:** 17-31.
40. STAVRAKY, K. M. 1968. Psychological factors in the outcome of human cancer. J. Psychosom. Res. **12:** 251-259.
41. SCHONFIELD, J. 1981. Psychologic factors in the recovery from and recurrence of early breast cancer. *In* Living and Dying with Cancer. P. Ahmed, Ed. 121-130. Elsevier. New York, NY.
42. JENSEN, M. R. 1984. Psychobiological Factors in the Prognosis and Treatment of Neoplastic Disorders. Doctoral Dissertation. Yale University. New Haven, CT.
43. TEMOSHOK, L., B. W. HELLER, R. W. SAGEBIEL, M. S. BLOIS, D. M. SWEET, R. J. DICLEMENTE & M. C. GOLD. 1985. The relationship of psychosocial factors to prognostic indicators in cutaneous malignant melanoma. J. Psychosom. Res. **29:** 139-153.
44. GREER. S., T. MORRIS & K. W. PETTINGALE. 1979. Psychological response to breast cancer: effect on outcome. Lancet **2:** 785-787.
45. DEROGATIS, L. R., M. D. ABELOFF & N. MELISARATOS. 1979. Psychological coping mechanisms and survival time in metastatic breast cancer. J. Am. Med. Assoc. **242:** 1504-1508.

46. VIITAMÄKI, R. O. 1970. Part II. Psychological determinants of cancer. *In* Cancer and Psyche. Monograph #1. 45-153. Psychiatric Clinic, Helsinki University Central Hospital. Helsinki.

47. ROGENTINE, G. N., D. P. VAN KAMMEN, B. H. FOX. J. P. DOCHERTY, J. E. ROSENBLATT, S. C. BOYD & W. E. BUNNEY. 1979. Psychological factors in the prognosis of malignant melanoma: a prospective study. Psychosom. Med. **41:** 647-655.

48. VISINTAINER, M. A. & R. N. CASEY. 1984. Adjustment and outcome in melanoma patients. Presented at the Annual Meeting of the American Psychological Association, Toronto.

49. IKEMI, Y., S. NAKAGAWA, J. NAKAGAWA & M. SUGITA. 1975. Psychosomatic consideration on cancer patients who have made a narrow escape from death. Dynamic Psychiatry **8:** 77-93.

50. REYNOLDS, P. & G. A. KAPLAN. 1986. Social connections and cancer: a prospective study of Alameda County residents. Presented at the Annual Meeting of the Society of Behavioral Medicine, San Francisco.

51. KAPLAN, G. A. & P. REYNOLDS. Depression and cancer mortality and morbidity: prospective evidence from the Alameda County study. J. Behav. Med. In press.

52. SHEKELLE, R. B., W. J. RAYNOR, A. M. OSTFELD, D. C. GARRON, L. A. BIELIAUSKAS, S. C. LIU & O. PAUL. 1981. Psychological depression and 17-year risk of death from cancer. Psychosom. Med. **43:** 117-125.

53. THOMAS, C. B., K. R. DUSZYNSKI & J. W. SHAFFER. 1979. Family attitudes reported in youth as potential predictors of cancer. Psychosom. Med. **41:** 287-302.

54. HAGNELL, O. 1966. The premorbid personality of persons who develop cancer in a total population investigated in 1947 and 1957. Ann. N. Y. Acad. Sci. **125:** 846-855.

55. KEEHN, R. J., I. D. GOLDBERG & G. W. BEEBE. 1974. Twenty-four year follow-up of army veterans with disability separations for psychoneurosis in 1944. Psychosom. Med. **36:** 27-46.

56. KEEHN, R. J. 1980. Follow-up studies of World War II and Korean conflict prisoners. III. Mortality to January 1, 1976. Am. J. Epidemiol. **111:** 194-211.

57. KAPLAN, G. A., P. REYNOLDS & R. D. COHEN. 1987. Psychological Well-being and Cancer Risk: Prospective Evidence from the Alameda County Study. Human Population Laboratory. California Dept. of Health Services. Berkeley, CA.

58. KERR, T. A., A. SCHAPIRA & M. ROTH. 1969. The relationship between premature death and affective disorders. Br. J. Psychiatry **115:** 1277-1282.

59. EVANS, N. J. R., J. A. BALDWIN & D. GATH. 1974. The incidence of cancer among inpatients with affective disorders. Br. J. Psychiatry **124:** 518-525.

60. MORRISON, F. R. 1981. Psychosocial factors in the etiology of cancer. Dissertation Abstracts International **42:** 155-156B.

61. WAGNER, S. & N. MANTEL. 1978. Breast cancer at a psychiatric hospital before and after the introduction of neuroleptic agents. Cancer Res. **38:** 2703-2708.

Augmentation of Natural Immunity and Regulation of Tumor Growth by Conditioning[a]

VITHAL K. GHANTA,[b,c,d,e] TAKAJI MIURA,[g]
NANCY S. HIRAMOTO,[c] AND RAYMOND
N. HIRAMOTO [b,c,d,e,f]

[b]Departments of Biology and [c]Microbiology
[d]Neurosciences Program
[e]Comprehensive Cancer Center
[f]Veterans Administration Medical Research
University of Alabama at Birmingham
Birmingham, Alabama 35294

and

[g]Third Department of Internal Medicine
School of Medicine
Gunma University
Maebashi, Gunma 372, Japan

INTRODUCTION

The immune system is a regulatory system involved in recognition of self from nonself. The action of this system is carried out by partially autoregulatory cellular mechanisms (suppressor/helper, idiotype-anti-idiotype, regulatory lymphokines, etc.). An increasing body of evidence suggests that the central nervous system (CNS) and peripheral nervous system and endocrine systems also regulate the host defense system. It has been demonstrated that antibody responses can be modulated by discrete CNS lesions,[1-4] by stimulation of specific sites in the CNS,[5-7] and by classical Pavlovian conditioning.[8,9]

Our studies showed that BALB/c mice injected with MOPC 104E cells and subsequently treated with cisplatinum could spontaneously regulate tumor growth *in vivo* for > 200 days.[10] Evidence that host immune resistance could develop was suggested.[11] We were able to demonstrate augmentation of natural killer cell (NK) activity in mice conditioned with camphor smell as the conditioning stimulus (CS) and poly I:C as the unconditioning stimulus (US). Mice were conditioned with the association of camphor and poly I:C to augment NK activity and were subsequently injected i.v. with myeloma cells. The conditioned mice were able to resist myeloma growth when

[a]This work was supported by grants CA37570 and CA42337 from the National Institutes of Health, and by Veterans Administration medical research funds.

29

they were repeatedly exposed to the CS only.[12] This study reports the possible natural and immune host response to myeloma that might be involved in the *in-vivo* regulation of tumor growth of MOPC 104E.

METHODS

Mice

Six-week-old female BALB/c mice were purchased from Simonsen Laboratories, Gilroy, CA. The mice were maintained on standard laboratory chow (Wayne Feed Co., Chicago, IL) and water *ad libitum*.

Myeloma cells

The MOPC 104E (*in-vivo*) line is maintained as an ascites tumor by serial passage in BALB/c mice. For the *in-vitro* studies, an *in-vitro* tumor line designated MOPC 104E-KI81 was used. The *in-vitro* line has been maintained in continuous culture for more than one year in RPMI 1640 medium containing 10% heat-inactivated fetal calf serum (FCS), 100 U/ml penicillin and 100 μg/ml streptomycin (Gibco, Grand Island, NY).

Murine Model

The MOPC 104E plasmacytoma is a transplantable tumor which produces a monoclonal IgM. This monoclonal IgM has the unique characteristic of reacting with bacterial Dextran B-1355 (a generous gift from Dr. M. E. Slodki, Northern Regional Research Laboratory, United States Department of Agriculture, Peoria, IL). Sheep red blood cells (SRBC) conjugated with Dextran B-1355 can be used in the presence of MOPC 104E IgM and complement, thus permitting precise quantification of total-body idiotype IgM.[10] Dextran B-1355 coated SRBC were used in the radial hemolysis in gel assay for the quantitation of MOPC 104E IgM. Sera from tumor-bearing mice were transferred into the wells of an agarose plate of SRBC coated with Dextran B-1355 and were allowed to diffuse at 5°C for 22 hr, followed by lysis with complement at 37°C. The area of lysis of unknown samples was compared with that of standard samples to obtain the amount of MOPC 104E IgM. MOPC 104E tumor cells per mouse were calculated from the total circulating MOPC 104E IgM measured for individual animals.[13]

Conditioning Paradigm

Solid camphor was dissolved in mineral oil and dispensed into bottles with caps. The animals were exposed to camphor smell for 1 hr in their own cages. The cages were placed in an enclosed area. One bottle of heated camphor was placed on the cage metal top for each large cage and the tops of the bottles were removed. The assembly was covered with another cage and the doors of the enclosed area were closed. The exposure was started at 8 a.m. Polyinosinic:polycytidylic acid, poly I:C, (P. L. Biochemicals, Milwaukee, WI) was dissolved in 0.85% NaCl solution. One-tenth ml (20 μg/mouse) of poly I:C was given i.p. to each mouse immediately following exposure to the camphor vapor. Ten camphor and poly I:C conditioning trials were given for the conditioned groups. Twenty-four hr after the last conditioning trial, 1×10^4 MOPC 104E cells were given in 0.1 ml i.v. Forty-eight hr after the tumor inoculation the animals were re-exposed to the CS (camphor smell) and this was continued every 72 hr thereafter. Mice were bled from the tail vein (~ 80 μl of blood) every 4 or 5 days to monitor for the tumor-specific anti-dextran IgM, starting from day 10 post tumor inoculation.

Thymectomy

Adult thymectomy (ATx) was performed when the mice were 6 weeks old. The mice were anesthetized with pentobarbital, and the thymus was removed by vacuum extraction through a surgical incision. The incision was closed with autoclips. Thymectomized mice were given MOPC 104E 10 days postthymectomy. At the time of death, mice were autopsied for the successful removal of the thymus. Six ATx mice and 6 control mice were used in this study.

Spleen Cell Preparation

Spleen cell suspensions were prepared from the spleens of 8-16-week-old normal, female BALB/c mice (H-2^d, Simonsen Laboratories, Gilroy, CA) or from female BALB/c mice injected i.p. with 1×10^7 mitomycin C (50 μg/ml) treated MOPC 104E-KI81 cells seven days before. A pool of cells from more than 5 spleens was used in individual experiments. Single cell suspension of spleen was prepared by gentle teasing with forceps in RPMI 1640 medium. After gravity sedimentation to remove fragments and debris, the cells were washed and treated with Tris-NH$_4$Cl buffer to lyse red blood cells. The cell suspension was washed three times with RPMI 1640 medium and was resuspended in the culture medium. To remove plastic adherent cells, spleen cell suspensions were cultured in 35 mm plastic Petri dishes for 1 hr at 37°C in a humidified CO$_2$ incubator.

Nonadherent spleen cells (NSC) were collected by gentle aspiration of the culture medium. To collect plastic adherent cells, one ml of spleen cell suspensions (1×10^7/ml) were cultured in a 24-well plate (Costar, Cambridge, MA) for 2-3 hr at 37°C in a humidified CO$_2$ incubator, and plastic nonadherent cells were removed by gentle aspiration and several washings with prewarmed (37°C) RPMI 1640 medium. The number of spleen cells was adjusted for the assays before the culture, but the number of plastic adherent cells was not adjusted, since the 24 hr viability of plastic adherent cells collected by using Versene buffer (1:5000 dilution, Gibco, Grand Island, NY) or by rubber policemen was not good (< 5% viability).

The percentages of macrophages in plastic adherent cell preparation was determined by morphological and functional criteria. Enumeration of adherent cells by morphological criteria was done by Wright stain and by functional criteria by determining the percentage of cells that ingest latex beads (Sigma Chemical Co., St. Louis, MO) according to the method of Rosenstreich, et al.[14] More than 95% of plastic adherent cells were macrophages by both methods.

Generation of Effector Cells

For stimulating NSC *in vitro,* 2×10^7 freshly harvested NSC from normal or *in-vivo* primed mice were cultured with 8×10^5 MOPC 104E-KI81 tumor cells treated with 50 μg/ml mitomycin-C for 30 min. Cultures were incubated in Corning 25 cm^2 culture flasks (Corning, Cambridge, NY) containing 10 ml culture medium with 5×10^{-5} M 2-mercaptoethanol in an upright position. Following five days of culture in a humidified CO_2 incubator, the cells were washed and used as effector cells. The effector cells were used to study their effect on the function of MOPC 104E-KI81 cells at a low effector-target (E:T) ratio of 5:1. The low E:T ratio was used specifically to circumvent the cytotoxicity which is produced by CTL at high E:T ratios. To determine that cytotoxicity was minimal, a 4-hr ^{51}Cr-release assay was used with modifications to measure cytotoxic activity. The percentage of specific ^{51}Cr released in the presence of effector cells at effector (E) to target (T) cell ratio of 100:1 was usually 30 to 70%. However, the percentage of specific ^{51}Cr released at E:T ratio of 10:1 was usually < 5%. The stimulated lymphocytes from BALB/c mice (H-2^d) were cytotoxic against MOPC 104E-KI81 cells, and to a lesser degree, cytotoxic against DBA/2(H-2^d) P815 mastocytoma cells, which is maintained by serial i.p. passage in syngeneic DBA/2 mice. BALB/c spleen cells sensitized against DBA/2 P815 were cytotoxic against P815, but not MOPC 104E-KI81.

Coculture of Lymphocytes with MOPC 104E-KI81 Cells

In the short-term 24-hr culture experiments, 1×10^5 viable tumor cells were cultured with or without 5×10^5 effector lymphocytes in 1 ml medium. The low 5:1 E:T ratio produces negligible cytotoxicity. Tumor cells were also plated directly into wells to which plastic adherent cells were attached.

In the long-term 7-day culture experiments, the method of colony formation in 0.8% methylcellulose (a semi-liquid culture system) was used as described earlier.[15] Viable tumor cells (1×10^3) were cultured in 1 ml of 0.8% methylcellulose with 20% FBS in RPMI 1640 medium in the presence or absence of 1×10^4 effector lymphocytes (E:T ratio 10:1). This mixture was plated into the wells of a 24-well cluster plate. To examine the effects of plastic adherent cells on tumor cells, 1×10^3 viable tumor cells in 1 ml of 0.8% methylcellulose with 20% FBS and RPMI 1640 medium was directly plated into > 3 wells to which adherent cells were attached. Both 24-hr and 7-day cultures were incubated at 37°C in a humidified CO_2 incubator. At the end of the culture period, viable tumor cells cultured for 24 hr were counted with trypan blue. For the long-term culture experiments, the number of colonies formed in 7-day cultures in methylcellulose (colonies consisting of > 20 cells) were scored with a Nikon inverted microscope at $100\times$ magnification. Cells from both 24-hr and 7-day cultures were harvested and washed twice with RPMI 1640 medium. Tumor cells are 3-5 times larger than lymphocytes and are easily distinguishable from lymphocytes. To detect antibody-secreting tumor cells, a modified method of the localized hemolytic plaque (PFC) assay of Jerne *et al.* was used.[16] Fifty μl (1×10^4) viable tumor cell suspension was mixed with 25 μl of 14% sheep erythrocytes coated with dextran and 100 μl 0.5% agarose in RPMI 1640 medium. The mixture was plated in a 33-mm Petri dish and was incubated for 3-4 hr at 37°C, followed by the addition of 1 ml of a 1:10 dilution of guinea pig complement, and was incubated for an additional 30 min at 37°C. The plaques were counted with a Nikon microscope at $100\times$ magnification. PFC assays were done in triplicate with appropriate controls.

RESULTS

Effect of Conditioning with Camphor Odor and Poly I:C on Growth of MOPC 104E in Vivo

In this repeat study 2 groups with 10 mice/group were used. The conditioned group (CND) was paired with camphor and poly I:C, 10 times and subsequent to tumor inoculation, treated with CS every 72 hr. The conditioned zero (CNDo) group was also conditioned but not re-exposed to the camphor odor after tumor implantation.

The results show a statistically significant delay in growth of MOPC 104E in the CND group when compared with the CNDo group, as measured by IgM production by the tumor cells (FIGURE 1). The survival data (FIGURE 2) supports the observations of tumor IgM values. The CND group re-exposed to camphor vapor every 72 hr showed better survival characteristics and indicated that the tumor was growing at a slower rate than in the CNDo group. It was evident that the conditioned animals were regulating tumor growth. Camphor odor itself had no therapeutic value for the animals with MOPC 104E myeloma.[12] It would be of great interest to determine by what mechanisms the host might regulate MOPC 104E growth *in vivo*.

Effect of Immune Suppression on Innate Resistance to MOPC 104E

Our studies show that BALB/c mice injected with MOPC 104E and subsequently treated with cisplatinum[10] or irradiation[11] have the capacity to regress and resist tumor growth *in vivo*. These results indicate that there are cells in the body of the BALB/c mouse that can resist and/or regulate MOPC 104E growth *in vivo*.

Studies were therefore carried out to see if the host possesses innate resistance to tumor growth. In the first experiment, animals were treated with 200 mg/kg cyclophosphamide 24 hr before i.v. injection of MOPC 104E cells to immunosuppress or deplete innate resistance. IgM produced by the tumor cells were measured every 4 or 5 days. On day 19, the number of tumor cells in the cyclophosphamide-treated group was 11 times greater than in the untreated normal control group. The rate of growth, *i.e.,* the doubling time, of the tumor was 1.47 days and 2.59 days in the immunosuppressed vs control, respectively. In the second experiment, adult thymectomy (ATx) was used as a means of immunosuppression. At 16 days the ATx group had 3.4 times more tumor cells than its corresponding controls.

In the third study, mice with 19-day-old tumors were treated with prednisolone. Prednisolone was given at a dose of 12 mg/kg for 7 consecutive days starting from day 19 post tumor transplantation; a slight facilitation of growth was observed. The fact that less difference was seen between the prednisolone-treated vs the untreated control group may be due to the late start in treatment. There were 1.6 times more tumor cells in the prednisolone-treated mice by day 25 (TABLE 1).

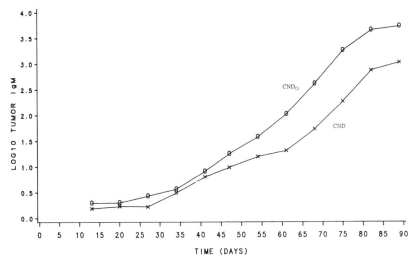

FIGURE 1. Changes in tumor IgM levels in conditioned (X) and conditioned-zero (O) mice. Both groups of mice were exposed to camphor smell (CS) and given poly I:C injection (US) every 72 hr for 10 association trials before injection with 1×10^4 MOPC 104E tumor cells i.v. The conditioned group was then re-exposed to CS every 72 hr. The CNDo group was left untreated.

These studies show normal mice possess or can develop measurable resistance against the growing MOPC 104E *in vivo.* Systemic treatment with cyclophosphamide which removes all resistance showed the greatest enhancement of growth. ATx, which removes a further source of T-cell, enhanced tumor growth to some extent but only partial resistance was obtained when compared with cyclophosphamide-treated mice. When prednisolone treatment was started in animals with relatively large tumors, growth facilitation occurred but was of much lower magnitude.

These results suggest that 1) normal spleen cells and macrophages provide resistance to tumor growth or 2) MOPC 104E tumor during its course of growth *in vivo* sensitizes the host and generates activated effector spleen cells and macrophages which can provide resistance against tumor growth *in vivo.*

TABLE 1. Growth of MOPC 104E in Immunosuppressed Mice

Treatment Groups	No. of Tumor Cells $\times\ 10^6$/Mouse	Increase over Control
Cyclophosphamide	730 ± 176[a,b]	11.1
Untreated control	66 ± 16	
ATx	1800 ± 530[c]	3.4
Nonthymectomized control	530 ± 90	
Prednisone	4100 ± 160[d,e]	1.6
Untreated control	2540 ± 930	

[a] Calculated from the IgM measurement taken 19 days after tumor implantation.
[b] Average/group ± S.E.
[c] Number of tumor cells/mouse at 16 days after tumor implantation.
[d] Number of tumor cells/mouse at 25 days after tumor implantation.
[e] Prednisolone, 12 mg/kg/day for 7 days was administered 19 days after tumor implantation.

To investigate this possibility *in-vitro* coculture studies were carried out with MOPC 104E-KI81. The ability to inhibit the growth of MOPC 104E-KI81 by normal non-adherent spleen cells (NSC) and plastic adherent cells (macrophages) and sensitized NSC and plastic adherent cells were compared *in vitro*. Two culture systems were used, a short-term 24-hr assay and a long-term 7-day coculture assay. In both culture systems the effect of spleen cells on the secretion of IgM by PFC assay and the growth of the plasmacytoma by cell counts were measured. In these studies low effector-to-target-cell ratios (E:T) which did not produce cytotoxicity to MOPC 104E-KI81 cells were used.

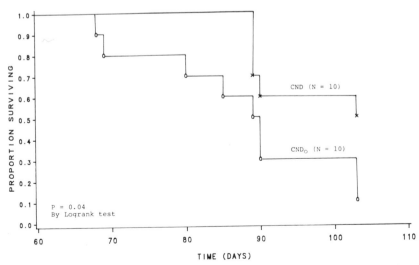

FIGURE 2. Survival curve of CND (X) and CND (O) groups. Both groups were conditioned and subsequently treated as described in FIGURE 1. Animals were observed daily for survival.

MOPC 104E Growth Pattern in Vitro

MOPC 104E-KI81 cells (1×10^5 cells/ml) were cultured and the viable cell number was determined at various intervals (FIGURE 3). The tumor cells grew slowly during the first 24 hr. By 96 hr of culture, the cell number had reached a plateau level at a cell density of $1.2 \pm 0.2 \times 10^6$ cells/ml. There was an increase in the proportion of cells in S phase (68%) and a decline in cells in G_1 phase (16%) by 36 hr. Before reaching the plateau level (72 hr), the proportion of cells in S phase declined and the proportion of cells in G_1 increased. At the plateau level (96 hr), about half of the cells were in G_1 phase (51%) (data not shown). (For uniformity the term G_1 will be used in the text, although analysis by flow cytometry was unable to distinguish G_1 from cells in the G_0 state.)

Effects of NSC or Plastic Adherent Spleen Cells on MOPC 104E-KI81

Nonadherent spleen cells (NSC) or plastic adherent cells from *in-vitro*-sensitized or from *in-vivo*-primed mice were cocultured with MOPC 104E-KI81 cells for 24 hr or 7 days. Their effect on MOPC 104E cell viability, colony-forming capacity and IgM-producing ability (PFC) were examined (TABLES 2 and 3).

The effect of different preparations of effector cells cocultured with MOPC 104E is shown (TABLE 2). NSC sensitized *in vitro* (A), normal NSC (B), and *in-vivo*-primed NSC (C), all enhanced growth of MOPC 104E (column 4, compare with F). These cell preparations inhibited MOPC 104E PFC (columns 5 and 6). Plastic adherent cells from normal spleen (D) or from spleen cells of mice primed with MOPC 104E (E) also enhanced growth, but the plastic adherent cells from nonprimed normal

FIGURE 3. Growth curve of *in-vitro* cultured MOPC 104E-KI81 cells. MOPC 104E-KI81 cells (1×10^5/ml) were cultured for 96 hr. Cell number was established at 24, 36, 48, 72 and 96 hr after culture. Values are mean ± S.D. of at least 3 samples.

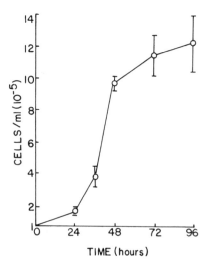

TABLE 2. Effect of Spleen Cells on MOPC 104E-KI81 Function after 24 Hr of Coculture[a]

Cell Preparation	Effector Cells from	E:T Ratio	Viable Tumor Cells ($\times 10^5$/Well)	PFC/10^4 MOPC 104E Cells	% Inhibition of PFC
A	Normal NSC sensitized *in vitro*	5:1	2.4 ± 0.3[b]	162 ± 35[b,c]	85
B	Normal NSC	5:1	2.5 ± 0.3	329 ± 146[c]	70
C	*In-vivo-* primed NSC	5:1	2.6 ± 0.2	102 ± 17[c]	91
D	Adherent cells from 10^7 normal spleen cells		2.4 ± 0.2	694 ± 31[d]	37
E	Adherent cells from 10^7 *in-vivo-* primed spleen cells		2.2 ± 0.2	148 ± 18[c]	87
F	None (MOPC 104E alone)		1.3 ± 0.1	1097 ± 170	

[a] BALB/c spleen cells were sensitized *in vitro* against mitomycin-C-treated MOPC 104E cells for 5 days. These sensitized cells were cocultured with 1×10^5 viable MOPC 104E cells (T) to examine the effect on the growth and function of MOPC 104E cells (cell preparations A-C). Freshly collected adherent cells from normal or *in-vivo*-primed mice (mice were injected with 1×10^7 mitomycin-C-treated MOPC 104E 7 days before) were used as effector cells (cell preparations D and E).
[b] Mean $\pm$ S.D. of triplicate samples.
[c] $p < 0.01$, compared with cell preparation F.
[d] $0.02 > p < 0.05$, compared with cell preparation F.

spleen reduced PFC by only 37%. The growth stimulatory effect produced by NSC or plastic adherent cells on MOPC 104E was significant. The number of viable tumor cells recovered from 24-hr cocultures was nearly twice that of the control group (F) (TABLE 2).

In the second series of experiments, we examined the effects of nonadherent and plastic adherent cells on colony-forming units and IgM secretion at 7 days following coculture in methylcellulose (TABLE 3). MOPC 104E cells recovered from methylcellulose were in the plateau phase and a large proportion ($\sim 50\%$) of cells were in the G_1 state. These cells behaved like late tumor cells in that a smaller fraction of cells were in cell cycle and the number of cells secreting and expressing IgM were high.[15] MOPC 104E cells cultured alone showed the number of PFC/10^4 cells in 7-day methylcellulose culture was 2100 PFC vs 1097 PFC in 24-hr cultures (TABLE 3, L, and TABLE 2, F). In contrast to the 24-hr culture where MOPC 104E cells were in proliferation (TABLE 2, A, B, C), little or no inhibition of PFC was observed with normal NSC or *in-vitro*- or *in-vivo*-sensitized NSC in the methylcellulose cultures (TABLE 3, G-I). The number of CFU were not affected, when compared with the control under the same conditions.

Plastic adherent cells from normal spleen cells or *in-vivo*-primed mice showed an inhibitory effect on PFC of 68 and 98 percent respectively. While plastic adherent cells from nonprimed normal mice (preparation J) had no effect on CFU, plastic adherent cells from spleens of mice primed *in vivo* with MOPC 104E (K) reduced significantly the number of CFU/well.

TABLE 3. Effect of Spleen Cells on MOPC 104E-KI81 Function following 7 Days of Coculture[a]

Cell Preparation	Effector Cells from	E:T Ratio	Colonies/Well	PFC/10⁴ MOPC 104E Cells	% Inhibition of PFC
G	Normal NSC sensitized *in vitro*	10:1	289 ± 23^b	$1696 \pm 359^{b,c}$	19
H	Normal NSC	10:1	274 ± 40	3078 ± 83^c	0
I	*In-vivo*- primed NSC	10:1	219 ± 21	2855 ± 397^c	0
J	Adherent cells from 1×10^7 normal spleen cells		240 ± 16	667 ± 231^d	68
K	Adherent cells from 1×10^7 *in-vivo*-primed spleen cells		183 ± 8^e	33 ± 58^f	98
L	None (MOPC 104E cells alone)		270 ± 36	2100 ± 849	

[a] BALB/c spleen cells were sensitized *in vitro* against mitomycin-C-treated MOPC 104E. These sensitized cells (effector cells) were cocultured with 1×10^3 viable MOPC 104E cells (T) to examine the effect on the colony-forming capacity in methylcellulose and on the function of MOPC 104E cells (cell preparations G-I). Freshly collected adherent cells from normal or *in-vivo*-primed mice (mice were injected with 1×10^7 mitomycin-C-treated MOPC 104E 7 days before) were used as effector cells (cell preparations J and K).
[b] Mean $\pm$ S.D. of triplicate samples.
[c] Not significant, when compared with cell preparation L.
[d] $0.02 > p < 0.05$, compared with cell preparation L.
[e] $0.01 > p < 0.02$, compared with cell preparation L.
[f] $0.01 > p < 0.02$, compared with cell preparation L.

DISCUSSION

We have successfully conditioned the enhancement of the NK cell response with either camphor[12] or saccharin-LiCl[17] as the CS. Moreover, we have conditioned mice to resist the growth of MOPC 104E *in vivo*.[12] This study was carried out to corroborate the previous observations made on conditioned resistance induced by camphor odor and extend these observations to the possible cellular mechanisms involved in host resistance to MOPC 104E. Conditioning of resistance was achieved by associating exposure to camphor odor for 1 hr, followed by poly I:C injection within 5 min in 10 learning trials prior to injection with myeloma cells i.v. Subsequent to tumor injection, the CND group was re-exposed to camphor odor every 3 days, whereas the CNDo group was untreated. Survival and IgM data indicate that significant resistance was detected in the CND group re-exposed to camphor odor only. At the termination of the experiment one animal remained free of disease in the CND group while there were no survivors in the CNDo group. In our previous experiment mice were exposed to camphor odor for 4 hr rather than 1 hr. In that series 2 animals remained free of disease in the CND group whereas none survived in the control groups.[12] These results indicate that while only small numbers of animals were cured the effect of the resistance imparted by conditioning is quite powerful. If we can establish the optimal trials for learning, and subsequent scheduling of the CS, with perhaps "reinforcement trials" during the period of tumor growth, we may be able to improve our cure rates in the CND group.

The mechanisms by which resistance is imparted to CND mice would be essential to further our understanding of the model. Our studies show that BALB/c mice have an innate capacity to resist the MOPC 104E. Systemic immunosuppression of the mice with a high dose of cyclophosphamide prior to implantation of the tumor leads to enhanced growth of MOPC 104E over untreated controls. Similarly, removal of the thymus prior to tumor inoculation also leads to some loss in tumor resistance. Animals with growing neoplasm when immunosuppressed with prednisolone (12 mg/kg $\times$ 7) starting from day 19 after tumor implantation also showed some suppression. These results are consistent with previous reports[18-20] that suppression of the host effector function could negate the effects of chemotherapy and cause rapid growth of MOPC 104E in the host. Because ATx lowers resistance to MOPC 104E growth *in vivo,* it is possible that the T-cell may be an important cell in the effector function. However, since T-cells also play an important role in activating macrophages the loss of T-cells might affect the macrophage effector function; therefore, effector functions by macrophages and T-cells are interrelated. The mechanisms of immunosuppression by glucocorticoid operates through T-cell proliferation. Glucocorticoid suppresses leukocyte-activating factor production and exerts its effects on the macrophage and the T-cell subsets that are involved in the production of TCGF (IL-2). The inhibition of IL-2 production leads to prevention of IL-2-mediated T-cell proliferation and lympholysis.[21]

In the course of our conditioning we injected poly I:C which can stimulate the production of interferon (IFN). Both the nonspecific cytotoxic macrophages and NK cells are stimulated by IFN[22,23] and show natural cell-mediated cytotoxicity (NCMC). The cytotoxicity is defined as, and measured by, the lysis of tumor cells *in vitro* by lymphocytes from normal donors with no history of prior sensitization to tumor cells.[24,25] It is significant for our study that: 1) interferon stimulates both macrophages and NK cells for NCMC; 2) IFN levels and cytotoxic response have been shown to be modulated by restraint and other stressors;[26-28] 3) NK cells, but not pre-NK cells, have been shown to be suppressed by hydrocortisone and cortisone-acetate which are synthetic corticosteroids;[22,29] and finally, that nonspecific cytotoxicity by macrophages is inhibited by both corticosteroids and restraint stress.[28] In early studies on natural cytotoxicity, NK cell levels were depressed for one week after shipping. Moving animals from building to building, resulted in similar depressed levels.[30,31] This is relevant to our studies because of work done by Vernon Riley on the stress effects of shipping, which includes elevated corticosterone levels in mice and thymic involution:[32] the classical responses observed due to exposure to a stressor. A recent publication demonstrated suppression of NK activity after exposure to cold swim stress.[33] These data suggest a modulatory effect of psychoneuroendocrine influences on macrophage function and NK activity and support our primary thesis of CNS modulation of immunity.

We have investigated at the cellular level those cells which we believe are activated to myeloma cells *in vivo*. Both short-term 24-hr culture and long-term 7-day cultures of NSC and adherent cells (macrophage) with MOPC 104E cells were investigated. The effect of both normal and sensitized NSC and macrophages on the viability, MOPC 104E growth, colony-forming capacity and secretion of IgM by the tumor cells were studied. Both sensitized and unsensitized NSC enhanced the growth of MOPC 104E but inhibited PFC (ability to produce IgM) in the short-term culture. Spleen macrophages from normal or sensitized animals also enhanced MOPC 104E growth, but adherent cells from normal spleen reduced PFC by only 37% whereas the macrophages from sensitized spleen reduced PFC by 87% (TABLE 2).

In the second series of experiments, we examined the effects of NSC and macrophages on myeloma stem cell growth by measuring colony-forming units. NSC from normal or sensitized spleen did not enhance or suppress CFU and had no inhibitory effect on PFC, in contrast to the 24-hr cultures. Macrophages from normal spleen had no effect on CFU but suppressed PFC by 68%. Macrophages from sensitized spleen reduced the proliferation of MOPC 104E stem cells significantly (32%) and also reduced the ability of the tumor to secrete IgM (98%) (TABLE 3).

The identified number of cell types exhibiting cytostatic and cytolytic antitumor effects has steadily increased to include: cytotoxic T-lymphocytes (CTL), K (killer) cells participating in antibody-dependent cell mediated cytotoxicity (ADCC), nonspecific cytotoxic macrophages, and natural killer (NK) cells. In our studies a low E:T ratio which did not produce cytoxicity to MOPC 104E cells was used, the purpose being to probe for those effector cells that can affect the myeloma tumor even at very low effector cell numbers. These results point to sensitized macrophages as the possible cells involved in retarding tumor growth by reducing stem cell proliferation *in vivo*. Sensitized NSC used at low E:T ratio, *i.e.*, under conditions where cytotoxicity was not produced, had little effect on the tumor stem cell proliferation or IgM secretion by the MOPC 104E.

While association of camphor odor and poly I:C had led to the conditioning of the NK cell response and demonstrable resistance to MOPC 104E growth *in vivo*, the actual cells involved in the tumor resistance is unknown. In our studies we have attempted to test for effector cells which might show functional activity against MOPC 104E tumor at the lowest E:T ratios. Effector function was found in the sensitized, activated macrophage fraction. Although not proved, it is therefore likely that the conditioned resistance to MOPC 104E tumor imparted to BALB/c mice by association of camphor odor and poly I:C injection might be due to the activation of tumor cytostatic macrophages.

SUMMARY

We have reported the effect of classical (Pavlovian) conditioning of natural immunity on survival of tumor-bearing mice. In the first study, we have observed that mice conditioned, transplanted with tumor, and re-exposed to conditioned stimulus (camphor odor) had an increase in median survival (day 43, as compared to days 34, 38, and 37 of various control groups). Two of these conditioned mice lived more than 120 days and showed early tumor growth, but were free of disease at day 97. We report the observations of a repeat study. Two groups of conditioned mice were used for these studies. One group was re-exposed to the conditioning stimulus following transplantation with tumor (CND) and the second group was not re-exposed to odor of camphor (CNDo). Statistically significant delay in growth of MOPC 104E in the CND group was observed when compared with the CNDo group. The survival data supports the observations of tumor IgM values. In an independent study, we investigated the possible mechanisms of MOPC 104E regulation *in vitro*. Plastic adherent spleen cells (macrophage cells) from mice primed *in vivo* with MOPC 104E tumor cells suppressed tumor IgM production by MOPC cells by 98% and also reduced colony formation by MOPC cells. The possible mechanism(s) of regulation of tumor growth in conditioned mice might be mediated by plastic adherent activated macrophages.

REFERENCES

1. STEIN, M., R. C. SCHIAVI & M. S. CAMERINO. 1976. Influence of brain and behavior on immune system. Science **191**: 435-440.
2. MAURIS, N., R. SCHIAVI, M. CAMERINO & M. STEIN. 1970. Effect of hypothalamic lesions on immune processes in the guinea pig. Am. J. Physiol. **219**: 1205-1209.
3. KORNEVA, E. A. & L. M. KHAI. 1964. Effect of destruction of hypothalamic areas on immunogenesis. Fed. Proc. Trans. Suppl. **23**: 88-92.
4. BROOKS, W. H., R. J. CROSS, T. L. ROSZMAN & W. R. MARKESBERY. 1982. Neuroimmunomodulation: neural anatomical basis for impairment and facilitation. Ann. Neurol. **12**: 56-61.
5. SPECTOR, N. H. 1983. Anatomic and physiologic connections between the central nervous and immune systems: neuroimmunomodulation. *In* Immunoregulation. N. Fabris, E. Graci, J. Hadden & N. A. Mitchison, Eds. Plenum Press. New York, NY.
6. SPECTOR, N. H. 1980. The central state of the hypothalamus in health and disease: old and new concepts. *In* Physiology of the Hypothalamus: Handbook of the Hypothalamus. P. Morgane & J. Panksepp, Eds. Vol. 2, Ch. 6. Marcel Dekker. New York, NY.
7. ROSZMAN, T. L., R. J. CROSS, W. H. BROOKS & W. R. MARKESBERY. 1983. *In* Experimental and Clinical Interventions in Aging. R. F. Walker & R. L. Cooper, Eds.: 163. Marcel Dekker. New York, NY.
8. LUK'YANENKO, V. I. 1961. The problem of conditioned reflex regulation of immunobiologic reactions. Usp. Sovrem. Biol. **51**(2): 170-187.
9. ADER, R. 1981. A historical account of conditioned immunobiologic responses. *In* Psychoneuroimmunology. R. Ader, Ed.: 321-349. Plenum Press. New York, NY.
10. GHANTA, V. K., R. N. HIRAMOTO, D. W. DAVIS & N. S. HIRAMOTO. 1980. Maintenance of MOPC 104E in plateau phase. Cancer Res. **40**: 2372-2376.
11. GHANTA, V. K., P. J. COX, N. S. HIRAMOTO, W. B. MILLS, H. J. COHEN & R. N. HIRAMOTO. 1985. Host regulation of MOPC 104E plasmacytoma after reduction of tumor burden by total body irradiation. Cancer Invest. **3**: 217-223.
12. GHANTA, V. K., R. N. HIRAMOTO, B. SOLVASON & N. H. SPECTOR. 1987. Influence of conditioned natural immunity on tumor growth. Ann. N.Y. Acad. Sci. **496**: 637-646.
13. GHANTA, V. K. & R. N. HIRAMOTO. 1974. Quantitation of total body tumor cells (MOPC 104E). I. Subcutaneous tumor model. J. Natl. Cancer Inst. **52**: 1199-1201.
14. ROSENSTREICH, D. L., J. T. BLAKE & A. S. ROSENTHAL. 1971. The peritoneal exudate lymphocyte. I. Differences in antigen responsiveness between peritoneal exudate and lymph node lymphocytes from immunized guinea pig. J. Exp. Med. **134**: 1170-1186.

15. MIURA, T., R. N. HIRAMOTO & V. K. GHANTA. 1983. MOPC 104E plasmacytoma functional heterogeneity and maturational potential in culture. Cancer Res. **43:** 953-958.
16. JERNE, N. K. & A. A. NORDIN. 1963. Plaque formation in agar by a single antibody producing cell. Science **140:** 405.
17. HIRAMOTO, R. N., N. S. HIRAMOTO, H. B. SOLVASON & V. K. GHANTA. 1987. Regulation of natural immunity (NK activity by conditioning). Ann. N.Y. Acad. Sci. **496:** 545-552.
18. LUBET, R. A. & D. E. CARLSON. 1977. Tumor immunity directed against MOPC 104E effects and various therapeutic regimens. Cancer Immunol. Immunother. **2:** 267-270.
19. LUBET, R. A. & D. E. CARLSON. 1978. Immunity against MOPC 104E plasmacytoma: effects of tumor size and time post-therapy on *in vivo* immunity. J. Natl. Cancer Inst. **60:** 1107-1111.
20. LUBET, R. A. & D. E. CARLSON. 1978. Therapy of the murine plasmacytoma MOPC 104E: role of the immune response. J. Natl. Cancer Inst. **61:** 897-903.
21. SMITH, K. A. 1980. T-cell growth factor. Immunol. Rev. **51:** 337-357.
22. OEHLER, J. R. & R. B. HERBERMAN. 1978. Natural cell-mediated cytotoxicty in rats. III. Effects of immunopharmacologic treatments on natural reactivity and on reactivity augmented by polyinosinic:polycytidylic acid. Int. J. Cancer **21:** 221-229.
23. SCHULTZ, R. M. 1981. Factors limiting tumoricidal function of interferon-induced effector systems. Cancer Immunol. Immunother. **10:** 61-66.
24. HERBERMAN, R. B., ED. 1982. NK Cell and Other Natural Effector Cells. Academic Press. New York, NY.
25. KISSLING, R. & O. HALLER. 1978. Natural killer cells in the mouse: an alternative immune surveillance mechanism? Contemp. Top. Immunobiol. **8:** 171-201.
26. DE CLERCQ, E. & T. C. MERIGAN. 1970. Current concepts of interferon and interferon induction. Annu. Rev. Med. **21:** 17-46.
27. JENSEN, M. M. 1968. Transitory impairment of interferon production in serotonin treated mice. Proc. Soc. Exp. Biol. Med. **128:** 174-178.
28. SCHULTZ, R., M. CHIRIGOS, J. STOYCHKOV & N. PAVLIDIS. 1979. Factors affecting macrophage cytotoxic activity with particular emphasis on corticosteroids and acute stress. J. Reticuloendo. Soc. **26:** 83-92.
29. HOCHMAN, P. S. & G. CUDKOWICZ. 1979. Suppression of natural cytotoxicity by spleen cells of hydrocortisone treated mice. J. Immunol. **123:** 968-976.
30. KIESSLING, R. & H. WIGZELL. 1979. An analysis of the murine NK cell as to structure, function, and biological relevance. Immunol. Rev. **44:** 165-208.
31. HERBERMAN, R. B. & H. T. HOLDEN. 1978. Natural cell-mediated immunity. Adv. Cancer Res. **27:** 305-377.
32. RILEY, V., M. A. FITZMAURICE & D. H. SPACKMAN. 1981. Psychoneuroimmunologic factors in neoplasia: studies in animals. *In* Psychoneuroimmunology. R. Ader, Ed.: 31-102. Academic Press. New York, NY.
33. AARSTAD, H. J., G. GAUDERNACK & R. SELJELID. 1983. Stress causes reduced natural killer activity in mice. Scand. J. Immunol. **18:** 461-464.

Psychoimmunologic and Endorphin Function in the Aged[a]

GEORGE F. SOLOMON, MARIA A. FIATARONE,
DONNA BENTON, JOHN E. MORLEY, EDA BLOOM,
AND TAKASHI MAKINODAN

*Geriatric Research, Education and
Clinical Centers
Sepulveda and West Los Angeles Veterans
Administration Medical Centers
and
Departments of Psychiatry and Medicine
University of California, Los Angeles
Los Angeles, California 90024*

IMMUNE FUNCTION IN THE ELDERLY

In humans and all mammalian species which have been studied so far, the immune system undergoes significant changes with advancing age.[1-4] Immunosenescence may be defined as those alterations in immune function which occur to some degree in all older individuals, and which are distinguishable from immunodeficiency secondary to underlying disease, malnutrition, toxic exposure, or genetic disorder. The increased incidence of malignancy, infectious disease, autoimmune disorders, monoclonal gammopathies, and amyloidosis with age is felt to be linked with this decline of immunocompetence.[5-9] In addition, the immunologic theory of aging[10] proposes genetically programmed changes in immune cells as the determinant of maximum lifespan. Support for this theory may be found in the fact that intervention which increases the lifespan of rodents (dietary restriction, hypothermia) also causes profound changes in immune function.[11-13] Conversely, in humans, derangements of immunity such as high autoantibody titers,[14] low suppressor cell activity,[15] and impaired cutaneous hypersensitivity[16] have been correlated with increased mortality.

Immunosenecence is characterized by its high prevalence, interindividual variability, and complexity. The immune system is not uniformly affected by the aging process. For example, total numbers of white blood cells, lymphocytes, and granulocytes, as well as phagocytic function of neutrophils and the complement system do not change appreciably with age.[17-19] The most significant decrements occur in cellular immunity, in such functions as delayed type hypersensitivity,[20] resistance to tumor cells,[21] viruses and protozoans,[6,8] primary allograft rejection, and graft versus host

[a]This study was supported by funds from the Veterans Administration and from the Joan B. Kroc Foundation, through the auspices of the University of California, Los Angeles Program in Psychoneuroimmunology and Norman Cousins.

disease.[22] The frequency of individuals with autoantibodies,[23] circulating immune complexes, and monoclonal gammopathies[9] increases with age. This dysregulation of immune homeostasis, leading to *vulnerability and failure under stress,* may be attributed to changes in the immune cells themselves and their secretory products, as well as in the cellular milieu in which they function. The most important of these processes appears to be reduced cellular efficiency, since total numbers of immune cells are little altered with age.[24] A brief review of the most important age-related changes is presented below.

Stem cells in mice have a reduced ability to repair injury,[25] capacity for clonal expansion,[26] and ability to migrate to the thymus with age.[27] Macrophages from old mice secrete inadequate amounts of interleukin-1 (IL-1),[28] leading to decreased stimulation of T helper cells and thereby contributing to diminished interleukin-2 (IL-2) production.[29] Abnormal augmentation by splenic T cells in mice appears to contribute to this decline in IL-1 production by macrophages.[30] Increased production of prostaglandin E by macrophages from old animals may also inhibit the proliferative responses of T lymphocytes.[31,32]

B cells appear to function relatively well in old age in both human and animal models. They proliferate normally in response to antigenic challenge; however, their differentiation into mature plasma cells capable of secreting appropriate levels of high affinity antibody is slightly diminished.[33] This decline may be related to changes in the B cells themselves (such as decreased density of surface immunoglobulin[34]), or secondary to T cell dysfunction. In man, decreased primary antibody response to immunization is commonly seen; whereas secondary responses to antigens produce normal titers of antibody.[35-38] A decline in autotolerance, signaled by increased autoantibody production by B cells, is another common finding in older individuals and is also felt to be related to altered B and T cell interactions.[11,22]

T cells are indisputably the component of the immune system most sensitive to the aging process. The onset of decline in T cell function can be demonstrated as early as puberty, at which time thymic involution begins.[39] Thymic hormones, which are required for both T and B cell maturation, begin to decline in the third decade of life; and by age 50, the thymus retains less than 15% of its original mass attained in early adolescence.[40] Although total T cell numbers are not dramatically altered, functionally mature T cells are decreased in number with age.[41] Shifts in T cell subpopulations,[42] changes in surface receptors (*e.g.,* IL-2 and glucocorticoid receptors[43]), impaired adenylate cyclase activity,[44] increased sensitivity to prostaglandin inhibition,[45] prolonged cell cycle duration,[46] and decreased calcium uptake required for proliferation[47] also occur with advancing age. Although helper T cell numbers may be normal or reduced with age, function is usually found to be diminished secondary to both impaired IL-2 production and responsiveness.[48,49] The defect limiting IL-2 production is a diminished number of lyphokine-producing T cells, but there may be an alteration in IL-2 receptor expression in aged humans and experimental animals.[50] In combination, these changes in the T cell population lead to decreased mitogenesis in response to plant lectins, such as phytohemagglutinin (PHA) and concanavalin A (ConA), mixed lymphocyte reactions, or cytotoxic T cell assays *in vitro.*[51,52] Suppressor T cells have been reported to increase,[53] decrease,[54] or not change with age.[55] The emergence of autoimmune disorders with age points to either decreased suppressor cell function or resistance of other lymphoid cells to suppressive influences.[56] (The onset and course of autoimmune disorders are also related to psychosocial factors, particularly failure of psychological defenses[57]).

Natural killer cells are a heterogeneous subpopulation of lymphocytes contained within the null cell population and comprise approximately 5-15% of peripheral blood lymphocytes.[58] They are capable of target cell lysis without prior sensitization or major histocompatability complex restriction. In mice, they have been found to play a major role in suppression of local and metastatic tumor growth, lysis of viral-infected cells, and to contribute to the longevity of long-lived strains.[59] The data in humans are controversial, as natural killer (NK) cell activity has been reported to be maintained, increased, or decreased in the elderly.[60–75] A summary of the major reports in the literature is found in TABLE 1. These studies differ greatly in population size and characteristics; but it appears that in healthy populations where an adequate sample size is obtained, NK activity is preserved or increased with age in the absence of disease. Because NK cells are felt to represent a primary line of defense against viral infection and malignant clones of cells, modulation of NK activity is being actively investigated as a potentially valuable approach to the prevention and/or therapy for cancer.

OPIOID PEPTIDES AND THE IMMUNE SYSTEM

Endogenous opioids (endorphins) have been implicated as mediators of a number of responses to stressful stimuli.[76] In view of the close connections between the central nervous system and the immune system and the marked responses of the immune system to stressful stimuli, it is not surprising that the endogenous opioids should play a role in the modulation of the immune system.[77]

In-vivo studies in animals have shown that stressors that produce prolonged endogenous opioid release lead to suppression of splenic natural killer (NK) cell activity.[78] This suppression appears to be secondary to tolerance developing to the acute effects of endogenous opioids on NK cell activity.

Endogenous opioids have also been shown to be involved in modulation of tumor growth.[79–81] The effects of endogenous opioids on tumor growth are not only secondary to the effects they have on the immune system, but also are due to direct effects on opioid receptors present on some tumors and indirectly secondary to the ability of opioids to release growth hormone and prolactin.

In 1979, Wybran *et al.*[82] showed that there are methionine-enkephalin receptors on T cell lymphocytes. Opioids have been shown to increase NK cell activity, alpha-interferon and interleukin-2 production, enhance chemotaxis, release histamine from mast cells, modulate PHA-stimulated lymphocyte proliferation, increase superoxide production and bind to terminal complexes of complement (see REFERENCES 81,83,84 for a review).

The effects of endogenous opioids on NK cells have been particularly well studied. Peripheral blood lumphocyte natural killer (NK) cell activity is a spontaneous cytotoxic function that is involved in mediating host defense to viral and other infections and in natural resistance to malignant cells. Results from three laboratories have shown that beta-endorphin and methionine enkephalin enhance NK activity.[85–87] The dose-response curve has an inverted-U shape. Kay *et al.*[88] have demonstrated that the des-tyrosine endorphins are more potent than beta-endorphin in enhancing NK activity. The ability of endorphins to stimulate NK activity appears to reside in the (6-9) amino acid fragment, *i.e.,* the alpha-helical nonopioid portion of beta-endorphin. The nonopioid endorphin fragment effects are reversed by naloxone, suggesting that the opioid receptor site is of the double-lock variety with the (6-9) portion acting as

TABLE 1. Natural Killer Cell Activity with Aging

Authors	Population	Methods	Results
Increased activity with age			
Onsrud, 1981[60]	15 residents of Salvation Army Home (76-93); 15 SAH workers (20-39)	20 hr Cr^{51} release assay against K562 cells	Increased NK activity in peripheral blood and T lymphocytes. No change in NK activity per unit of blood in old subjects. Increased lymphocytes with + Fc receptors in old.
Batory et al., 1981[61]	44 old (70-98) 69 young (20-45)	4 hr Cr^{51} release assay	Increased NK activity; increased granular lymphocytes; increased lymphocytes with + Fc receptors in old.
Fernandes and Gupta, 1981[62]	50 independently living without significant illness or recent hospitalization (mean 71.2); 43 (mean 32.3)	4 hr Cr^{51} release assay	Increased non-T cell NK activity in males only; no change in T cell NK activity in old subjects.
Abo et al., 1982[63]	112 healthy subjects from 0-88 years; 54 males, 58 females	6 hr Cr^{51} release assay; HNK-1 immunofluorescence	Increased NK activity; increased HNK-1 expression with age. Increased HNK-1 expression in males.
Thompson et al., 1984[64]	17 old (100-103) 25 young (less than 57 years)	Leu 11b and Leu 7 immunofluorescence	Increased percentage of Leu 11b and Leu 7 cells in old.
Tilden et al., 1986[65]	105 healthy subjects (0-79, 12 between 60-79)	4 hr Cr^{51} release assay	Increased NK activity, Leu 7, Leu 11, large granular lymphocytes with age. NK activity correlated with granular lymphocytes and Leu 11 cells.

Lighart et al., 1986[66]	33 aged 75-84 and 35 aged 25-34; all fulfilling strict SENIEUR protocol for immunological studies.	CD-16 monoclonal antibody staining	Increase in CD-16 positive cells in the old subjects. (NK activity not measured.)

Decreased activity with age

Rabinowich et al., 1985[67]	9 old (patients hospitalized for elective surgery 66-89). 10 young (22-51). None with organic disease.	4 hr Cr^{51} release assay; IL-2 stimulation of NK activity.	Decreased NK activity; decreased IL-2 stimulation of NK activity in old. Decreased PHA responsiveness and IL-2 production in old. Correlation between NK activity and IL-2 production and PHA responsiveness.
Mysliwska et al., 1985[68]	20 old (mean 76); 20 young (mean 25). Old in nursing home without acute or chronic illness; no medications.	4 hr Cr^{51} release assay with murine L 1210 target cells (DBA/2 mice)	Decreased NK activity in old, not accounted for by female predominance in sample.
Rytel et al., 1986[69]	16 old (mean 79) 21 young (mean 28)	K562 target cells	Decreased NK activity in old. Interferon stimulation of NK activity in old less than in young subjects.
Mariani et al., 1986[70]	Not specified	K562 and P815-IgG cell lines. Immunofluorescent antibody staining for CD-4, CD-5, CD-8, CD-16.	CD-5/CD-8 and CD-5/CD-16 clones were less cytotoxic in old subjects than in young subjects.

No change in activity with age

Sato et al., 1979[71]	7 old (65-75) 8 young (25-35) 11 newborn	16 hr Cr^{51} release assay against RSb and Rsa (human transformed cell lines). Interferon stimulated cytotoxicity.	Cytotoxic activity nonsignificantly lower in old compared to young, increased over levels in neonates. Interferon stimulated cytotoxicity of all groups.

TABLE 1. *Continued*

Authors	Population	Methods	Results
Nagel et al., 1981[72]	200 adults aged 20-95 from BLSA. Healthy.	4 hr Cr^{51} release assay	No change in NK activity with age; no change after 20-month follow-up period in subset. Some increase in levels in 80 to 95-year-old group.
Marcano et al., 1982[73]	11 old (80-114) in nursing home	4 hr Cr^{51} release assay. Antibody dependent cell cytotoxicity; cell-mediated lympholysis; mixed lymphocyte culture.	No change in NK activity in old; decreased T lymphocyte function: ADDC, CML, MLC, in old.
Murasko et al., 1986[74]	260 old (70-106) living in geriatric community; 39 young (23-35)	4 hr Cr^{51} release assay	No difference young vs. old. Those over 90 compared to those 70-84 showed decline.
Tsukayama et al., 1986[75]	13 old (mean 79.5), malnourished, functionally impaired nursing home residents; 9 young (mean 33.7), healthy.	4 hr Cr^{51} release assay	No change in NK activity with age.

the key to allow access to the opioid receptor.[89] A similar double-lock opioid receptor conformation has been proposed for the dynorphin molecule.[90,91]

Of particular interest is the finding that both interferon-[87] and interleukin-2-[89] stimulated NK activity are reversed by naloxone. Radioactively-labeled interleukin-2 is displaced from PHA-stimulated lymphocytes by beta-endorphin and naloxone (Kay, Allen and Morley: submitted for publication). Others have also shown that naloxone decreases the expression of the IL-2 receptor as measured by the monoclonal antibody, anti-TAC. These findings demonstrate that the TAC protein is only one component of the high-affinity receptor for interleukin-2.[92] They suggest, therefore, that the opioids may modulate immune function through their effects on the TAC protein component of the high-affinity IL-2 receptor.

OPIOID PEPTIDES AND AGING

Several studies have provided evidence that the endogenous opioid (endorphin) systems are altered with aging.[93] Concentrations of beta-endorphin and other endogenous opioids have been reported to be lower in the hypothalamus and other central nervous system areas of older rats compared to younger rats.[94-96] In addition, a decrease in opioid receptor binding has been reported in the central nervous system of older animals.[97] The physiological correlate to these reduced biochemical parameters with aging is that older animals have a marked decrease in sensitivity to morphine analgesia.[98,99] Opioid feeding systems also appear to be markedly attenuated with advancing age.[100] In addition, tolerance to opiates occurs more commonly in younger compared to older animals.[101] Taken together, these studies suggest that there is a reduction in the activity of the endorphin system with advancing age. It was for this reason that we felt it would be useful to study the effects of beta-endorphin on natural killer cell activity from young and old individuals.

NATURAL KILLER CELLS, BETA-ENDORPHIN AND AGING

We examined age-related differences in basal natural killer (NK) cell activity and *in-vitro* stimulation with beta-endorphin (BE) and interleukin-2 (IL-2) in 45 free-living elderly volunteers (mean age 73, range 65-89) and 29 young volunteers (mean age 29, range 22-39). Most subjects were studied twice, four months apart. There were significantly higher NK values in the elderly subjects (16.4 ± 1.7 lytic units/ 10^6 cells vs. 10.8 ± 1.0, p < 0.05). The percentage of Leu-11a and Leu-19 lymphocytes, which have been correlated with NK activity, was quantified. Leu-11a cells were significantly higher in the elderly (17 ± 2% vs. 13 ± 1%, p < 0.05), as were Leu-19 cells (23 ± 2% vs. 16 ± 2%, p < 0.05). Stimulation with BE (10^{-7} or 10^{-8} M) produced a statistically significant increase in NK activity (outside the 95% confidence interval) in 21% of the young and 43% of the old on at least one of the two test days. The concordance rate for stimulation on these two days was 71% in the young and 58% in the elderly, suggesting an increased variability in lymphocyte responsiveness in the older group. Stimulation with IL-2 (10 units/ml) occurred in 57% of both the young and the old groups.

In summary, healthy elderly subjects demonstrate enhanced NK activity both at baseline and after stimulation with beta-endorphin, as compared to a younger population. Analysis of the Leu-11a and Leu-19 lymphocytes subgroups indicates that this enhanced activity may reflect an increase in the proportion of cells with NK activity in the healthy elderly. We suggest that this difference between healthy young and old subjects may represent a cohort effect of increased immune surveillance in those surviving to old age.

NATURAL KILLER CELLS, BETA-ENDORPHIN AND EXERCISE

We also have studied an *in-vivo* model of acute physical stress-exercise, which is known to cause elevations of beta-endorphin in humans.[102–104] Two previous studies have found NK activity to be enhanced after exercise in young subjects.[105–106] Our preliminary results in nine women aged 24-75 indicate that NK activity is significantly stimulated by an acute bout of maximal exercise (6.3 $\pm$ .8 lytic units/10^6 cells before exercise vs. 14.1 $\pm$ 1.8 lytic units post exercise, p <0.01) in both young and old subjects (FIG. 1). In addition, the ability to stimulate NK cells with beta-endorphin

FIGURE 1. The effect of exercise on NK cell activity.

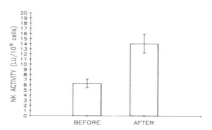

in vitro is markedly suppressed post-exercise (15 $\pm$ 4% vs. 1 $\pm$ 4%, p <0.05), suggesting that an exercise-induced rise in beta-endorphin may have maximally stimulated these cells and prevented further *in-vitro* augmentation of their activity. These data are compatible with a role for beta-endorphin in the stimulation of NK cells that occurs during exercise.

PSYCHOLOGICAL FACTORS AND NATURAL KILLER CELL STIMULATION IN HEALTHY YOUNG AND OLD SUBJECTS

Clinical depression of a significant degree[107] and bereavement[108] have been associated with immunosuppression. Bereavement, dysphoria and depression are more common among the elderly.[109] Healthy elderly persons with good social support systems tend to show stronger indices of immune function, particularly mitogen response of lymphocytes.[110] Natural killer cell activity can be enhanced in an elderly population by a relaxation inducing intervention.[111] Dilman relates the process of aging to a complex variety of centrally "programmed," hypothalamically mediated metabolic and immunologic changes in which psychological depression may be an involved variable, in both cause and effect roles.[112]

Physically healthy relatives of patients with rheumatoid arthritis who showed the rheumatoid arthritis-predisposing autoantibody, rheumatoid factor (an IgM anti-IgG), in their sera were more emotionally healthy than their physically healthy relatives without rheumatoid factor.[113] Thus, emotional health may protect against autoimmune disease. The above data support an hypothesis that physically healthy elderly persons are likely to be emotionally healthy as well.

We hypothesize that a cohort of healthy elderly persons will have low levels of dysphoric affect (*e.g.*, depression, helplessness, anxiety) and adaptive coping and personality trait patterns. The same trends might be expected in a younger population of healthy persons but would be less critical to health because of the greater vulnerability of the aging immune system to failure under stress. We correlated state and trait psychological variables with measures of immune function, particularly numbers of natural killer (NK) cells and their function under baseline conditions and under stimulation by beta-endorphin and IL-2, in cohorts of elderly and young persons.

Methods Forty-eight persons ages 65-89 (mean 73), who currently were and for the past five years had been in good physical health and who currently showed no significant cognitive impairments, were compared with 28 healthy persons ages 21-40 (mean 29) on psychological and immunological variables. All subjects were recruited from the clientele or staffs of two senior centers and staffs of two Veterans Administration hospitals.

At baseline (the only data herein reported) the following psychological variables were measured:

1. Anxiety as assessed by the Taylor Manifest Anxiety Scale (short form).[114]
2. Hopelessness as assessed by the Beck Hopelessness Scale.[115]
3. Social desirability (an index of socially acceptable attitudes and beliefs) as assessed by the Marlow Browne Scale.[116]
4. Overall "hardiness" as assessed by the Kobasa Hardiness Scale.[117] (Hardiness, which can be divided into components of commitment, control, and challenge, appears to serve as a buffer against the effects of stressful life events in producing illness[111].)

At baseline, the following immunologic studies were performed:

1. Baseline (NK) cell activity.
2. Maximum observed stimulation of NK cells by beta-endorphin.
3. IL-2 stimulation of NK cells (above the 95% confidence level).
4. Percentage of lymphocytes bearing Leu-11a and Leu-19 markers, both of which are correlated with NK cell activity. (Those psychological or immunologic tests performed on fewer than 20 subjects are not included in this initial report.)

RESULTS

Data were analyzed using the SAS program. There was a trend toward significance between IL-2 stimulation of NK cell activity and "hardiness" ($p < 0.10$, $n = 32$) when all subjects (young and old) were combined. Looking at the young subjects, maximum beta-endorphin stimulation of NK cells was significantly *negatively* correlated with the Taylor Manifest Anxiety Scale ($p < 0.003$, $n = 26$). Maximum beta-endorphin stimulation was significantly correlated ($p < 0.01$) with the Hardiness Scale in the elderly group ($n = 42$). There was a definite trend toward correlation of hardiness with IL-2 stimulation in the elderly ($n = 19$, $p < 0.10$). (Unfortunately, a considerable number of "hardy" elderly subjects were evaluated prior to inclusion of IL-2 stimulation studies in the research protocol.)

The elderly group showed significantly higher mean hopelessness (6.0 vs 4.3, $p < 0.02$) and social desirability scores (12.3 vs 9.9, $p < 0.03$) than the young group.

INTERPRETATION

A trend toward psychoimmunologic correlation between "hardiness"—a measure of commitment, control, and challenge that is known to correlate with health—and stimulability of NK cells was found especially in old subjects. That stimulation by beta-endorphin and IL-2 were correlated with these adaptive traits may be related to the contribution these peptides make to immune failure in the aged. Healthy old persons are similar to healthy young persons in regard to hardiness, a stress "buffer", but have more dysphoria and are more conventional. However, hardiness appears more strongly related to immune function in the elderly.

Continued psychoimmunologic studies of large numbers of old and young subjects with longitudinal follow-ups every four months will likely reveal more relationships between psychological and immunological status and health.

CONCLUSION

Our preliminary data support the concept that NK activity is enhanced in the elderly. The elderly also demonstrate an enhanced stimulation of NK activity by beta-endorphin. It is suggested that beta-endorphin, which is released from the pituitary in concert with ACTH in response to stress, provides a potential link among stress, altered immunity, and diseases related to dysregulation of the immune system. Support for this hypothesis comes from our finding that beta-endorphin plays a role in the stimulation of NK activity associated with exercise. "Hardiness," a constellation of personality traits and coping patterns reflecting commitment, control, and challenge that has previously been found to be related to health, correlates with beta-endorphin stimulation and tends also to correlate with IL-2 stimulation of NK cell activity. Since IL-2 may be important for augmentation of NK activity *in vivo*, augmented activity would mediate stronger surveillance against malignant and infectious diseases. The correlation found between emotional "hardiness", beta-endorphin and IL-2 stimulation of NK cells suggest a mechanism by which emotional hardiness influences maintenance of physical health, especially in the elderly.

Future studies will be needed to determine whether both superior psychological and immunological functions are necessary to maintain health in old age.

ACKNOWLEDGMENTS

The authors express appreciation to Denise Reeves and Shelley McClelland for technical assistance and to S. Mary Jackson, University of Southern California, for statistical consultation. The authors also would like to thank Jo Ann Phillips for preparation of the manuscript.

REFERENCES

1. BILDER, G. E. 1975. Studies on immune competence in the rat: changes with age, sex, and strain. J. Gerontol. **30:** 641-646.
2. JAROSLOW, N., K. M. SUHRBIER & T. E. FRITZ. 1974. Decline and restoration of antibody forming capacity in aging beagle dogs. J. Immunol. **112:** 1467-1476.
3. MATHIES, M., L. LIPPS, G. S. SMITH & R. L. WALFORD. 1973. Age-related decline in response to phytohemagglutinin and pokeweed mitogen by spleen cells from hamster and a long-lived mouse strain. J. Gerontol. **28:** 425-430.
4. NOMAGUCCI, T. A., Y. OKUMA-SAKURAI & I. KIMURA. 1976. Changes in immunological potential between juvenile and presenile rabbits. Mech. Ageing Dev. **5:** 409-417.
5. MAKINODAN, T., S. J. JAMES, T. INAMIZU & M-P. CHANG. 1984. Immunologic basis for susceptibility to infection in the aged. Gerontology **30:** 279-289.
6. GARDNER, I. D. & J. S. REMINGTON. 1978. Aging and immune response. I. Antibody formation and chronic infection in toxoplasma gondii-infected mice. J. Immunol. **120:** 939-943.
7. GRUYS, E. 1979. A comparative approach to secondary amyloidosis: minireview. Dev. Comp. Immunol. **3:** 23-36.
8. PAZMINO, N. H. & J. M. YUHAS. 1973. Senescent loss of resistance to murine sarcoma virus (Moloney) in the mouse. Cancer Res. **33:** 2668-2672.
9. AXELSSON, U., R. BACHMAN & J. HALLEN. 1966. Frequency of pathological proteins (M components) on 6,995 sera from an adult population. Acta Med. Scand. **179:** 235-247.
10. WALFORD, R. L. 1969. The Immunologic Theory of Aging. Williams and Wilkins. Baltimore, MD.
11. FERNANDES, G., E. J. YUNIS, D. G. JOSE & R. A. GOOD. 1973. Dietary influence on antinuclear antibodies and cell-mediated immunity in NZB mice. Int. Arch. Allergy Appl. Immunol. **44:** 770-782.
12. WEINDRUCH, R., S. R. S. GOTTESMAN & R. L. WALFORD. 1982. Modification of age-related immune decline in mice dietarily restricted from or after midadulthood. Proc. Natl. Acad. Sci. USA **79:** 898-902.
13. LIU, R. K. & R. L. WALFORD. 1975. Mid-life temperature transfer effects on life span of annual fish. J. Gerontol. **30:** 129-131.
14. MACKAY, I. R., S. F. WHITTINGHAM & J. D. MATHEWS. 1977. The immunoepidemiology of aging. *In* Immunology and Aging. T. Makinodan & E. Yunis, Eds. 35-49. Plenum Medical Book Co. New York, NY.
15. WECKSLER, M. E. & P. B. HAUSMAN. 1982. Effects of aging in the immune response. *In* Basic and Clinical Immunology. D. P. Stites, J. B. Stobo & H. H. Fedenberg, Eds. 306-313. Lange Medical Publications. Los Altos, CA.
16. ROBERTS-THOMSON, I. C., U. YOUNGCHAIZUD, S. WITTINGHAM & I. R. MAKAY. 1974. Aging, immune response, and mortality. Lancet **2:** 368-370.
17. CORBERAND, J. X., P. F. LAHARRAGUE & G. FILLOLA. 1986. Neutrophils of healthy aged humans are normal. Mech. Ageing Dev. **36:** 57-63.
18. SPARROW, D., J. E. SILBERT & J. W. ROWE. 1980. The influence of age on peripheral lymphocyte count in men: a cross-sectional and longitudinal study. J. Gerontol. **35:** 163-166.

19. NAGAKI, K., S. HIRAMATSU, S. INAI & A. SASAKI. 1980. The effect of aging on complement activity (CH50) and complement protein levels. J. Clin. Lab. Immunol. 3: 45-50.
20. DWORSKY, R., A. PAGANINI-HILL, M. ARTHUR & J. PARKER. 1983. Immune responses of healthy humans 83-104 years of age. J. Natl. Cancer Inst. 71: 265-268.
21. LIPSCHITZ, D. A., S. GOLKDSTEIN, R. REIS, M. E. WEKSLER, R. BRESSLER & B. A. WEILAN. 1985. Cancer in the elderly: basic science and clinical aspects. Ann. Intern. Med. 102: 218-228.
22. BLOOM, E. T., W. J. PETERSON, M. TAKASUGI & T. MAKINODAN. 1985. Immunity and ageing. In Principles and Practice of Geriatric Medicine. M. S. J. Pathy, Ed., 57-65. John Wiley and Sons, Ltd. Chichester, England.
23. CAMMARATA, R. J., G. P. RODNAN & R. H. FENNEL. 1967. Serum antigamma globulin and antinuclear factors in the aged. JAMA 199: 456-458.
24. DYBKAER, R., M. LAURITZEN & R. KRAKAUER. 1981. Relative reference values for clinical, chemical and haematological quantities for healthy elderly people. Acta Med. Scand. 209: 1-9.
25. CHEN, M. G. 1971. Age-related changes in hematopoietic stem cell populations of a long-lived hybrid mouse. J. Cell Physiol. 78: 225-232.
26. ALBRIGHT, J. & T. MAKINODAN. 1976. Decline in the growth potential of spleen colonizing bone marrow stem cells of long-lived aging mice. J. Exp. Med. 144: 1204-1213.
27. TYAN, M. L. 1977. Age-related decrease in mouse T cell progenitors. J. Immunol. 118: 846-851.
28. INAMIZU, T., M-P. CHANG & T. MAKINODAN. 1983. Decline in interleukin (IL)-1 production with age. Gerontologist 23: 249.
29. CHANG, M-P., T. MAKINODAN, W. J. PETERSON & B. L. STREHLER. 1982. Role of T cells and adherent cells in age-related decline in murine interleukin-2 production. J. Imunol. 129: 2426-2430.
30. INAMIZU, T., M-P. CHANG & T. MAKINODAN. 1985. Influence of age on the production and regulation of interleukin-1 in mice. Immunology 55: 447-455.
31. ROSENSTEIN, M. M. & H. R. STRAUSSER. 1980. Macrophage-induced T cell mitogen suppression with age. J. Reticuloendoth. Soc. 27: 159-166.
32. LICASTRO, F. & R. L. WALFORD. 1986. Effects exerted by prostaglandins and indomethacin on the immune response during aging. Gerontology 32: 1-9.
33. GOIDL, E. A., J. B. INNES & M. E. WEKSLER. 1976. Immunological studies on aging. II. Loss of IgG and high avidity plaque-forming cells and increased suppressor cell activity in aging mice. J. Exp. Med. 144: 1037-1048.
34. WODA, B. A. & J. D. FELDMAN. 1979. Density of surface immunoglobulins and capping on rat B lymphocytes. I. Changes with aging. J. Exp. Med. 149: 416-423.
35. HOWELLS, C. H. L., C. T. VESSELINOVA-JENKINS, A. D. EVANS & J. JAMES. 1975. Influenza vaccination and mortality from bronchopneumonia in the elderly. Lancet 1: 381-383.
36. RUBEN, F. L., J. NAGEL & P. FIREMAN. 1973. Antitoxin responses in the elderly to tetanus-diptheria (Td) immunization. Am. J. Epidemiol. 103: 145-149.
37. LANDESMAN, S. H. & G. SCHIFFMAN. 1981. Assessment of the antibody response to pneumococcal vaccine in high-risk populations. Rev. Infect. Dis. 3(Suppl): 184-197.
38. MAKINODAN, T. & W. J. PETERSON. 1962. Relative antibody-forming capacity of spleen cells as a function of age. Proc. Natl. Acad. Sci. USA 48: 234-238.
39. BOYD, E. 1932. The weight of the thymus gland in health and disease. Am. J. Clin. Dis. Child. 43: 1162-1214.
40. WEKSLER, M. E. 1981. The senescence of the immune system. Hosp. Pract. 16: 53-64.
41. O'LEARY, J. J., D. P. JACKOLA, H. M. HALLGREN, M. ABBASNEZHAD & W. G. YASMINEH. 1983. Evidence for a less differentiated subpopulation of lymphocytes in people of advanced age. Mech. Ageing Dev. 21: 109-120.
42. NAGEL, J. E., F. J. CHREST & W. H. ADLER. 1981. Enumeration of T lymphocyte subsets by monoclonal antibodies in young and aged humans. J. Immunol. 127: 2086-2088.
43. GILLIS, S., R. KOZAK, M. DURANTE & M. E. WEKSLER. 1981. Immunological studies

of aging. Decreased production of and response to T cell growth factor by lymphocytes from aged humans. J. Clin. Invest. **67:** 937-942.

44. ABRASS, I. B. & P. J. SCARPACE. 1982. Catalytic unit of adenylate cyclase: reduced activity in aged human lymphocytes. J. Clin. Endocrinol. Metab. **55:** 1026-1028.

45. DORIA, G., C. MANCINI & L. ADORINI. 1982. Immunoregulation in senescence: increased inducibility of antigen-specific suppressor T cells and loss of cell sensitivity to immunosuppression in aging mice. Proc. Natl. Acad. Sci. USA **79:** 3803-3807.

46. TICE, R. R., E. L. SCHNEIDER, D. KRAM & P. THORNE. 1979. Cytokinetic analysis of the impaired proliferative response of peripheral lymphocytes from aged humans to phytohemagglutinin. J. Exp. Med. **150:** 1029-1041.

47. KENNES, B., C. HUBERT, D. BROHEE & P. NEVE. 1981. Early biochemical events associated with lymphocyte activation in aging. Immunology **42:** 119-126.

48. THOMAN, M. L. & W. O. WEIGLE. 1981. Lymphokines and aging: interleukin-2 production and activity in aged animals. J. Immunol. **127:** 2102-2106.

49. ERSHLER, W. B., A. L. MOORE, K. ROESSNER & G. E. RANGES. 1985. Interleukin-2 and aging: decrease interleukin-2 production in healthy older people does not correlate with reduced helper cell numbers of antibody response to influenza vaccine and is not corrected *in vitro* by thymosin alpha-1. Immunopharmacology **10:** 11-17.

50. THOMAN, M. L. 1985. The role of Interleukin-2 in the aged-related impairment of immune function. J. Am. Geriatr. Soc. **33:** 781-787.

51. MOODY, C. E., J. B. INNES, L. STAIANO-COICO, G. S. INCEFY, H. T. THALER & M. E. WEKSLER. 1981. Lymphocyte transformation induced by autologous cells. XI. The effect of age on the autologous mixed lymphocyte reaction. Immunology **44:** 431-438.

52. TOLLEFSBOL, T. O. & H. J. COHEN. 1986. Expression of intracellular biochemical defects of lymphocytes in aging: proposal of a general aging mechanism which is not cell-specific. Exp. Gerontol. **21:** 129-148.

53. GUPTA, S. & R. A. GOOD. 1979. Subpopulations of human T lymphocytes. X. Alterations in T, B, third population cells, and T cells with receptors for immunoglubulin M (T mu) or G (T gamma) in aging humans. J. Immunol. **122:** 1214-1219.

54. HALLGREN, H. M. & E. YUNIS. 1977. Suppressor lymphocytes in young and aged humans. J. Immunol. **118:** 2004-2008.

55. BARRETT, D. J., S. STENMARK, D. W. WARA & A. J. AMMANN. 1980. Immunoregulation in aged humans. Clin. Immunol. Immunopathol. **17:** 203-211.

56. ANTEL, J. P. & B. G. W. ARNASON. 1979. Suppressor cell function in man: evidence for altered sensitivity of responder cells with age. Clin. Immunol. Immunopathol. **13:** 119-124.

57. SOLOMON, G. F. 1981. Emotional and personality factors in the onset and couse of autoimmune disease, particularly rheumatoid arthritis. *In* Psychoneuroimmunology. R. A. Ader, Ed. 259-278. Academic Press. New York, NY.

58. HERBERMAN, R. B., J. Y. DJEU, H. D. KAY, J. R. ORTALDO, C. RICCARDI, G. D. BONNARD, H. T. HOLDEN, H. FAGNANI, A. SANTONI & P. PUCCETTI. 1979. Natural killer cells: characteristics and regulation of activity. Immunol. Rev. **44:** 43-70.

59. LOTZOVA, E. & K. B. MCCREDIE. 1973. Natural killer cells in mice and man and their possible biological significance. Cancer Immunol. Immunother. **4:** 215-221.

60. ONSRUD, M. 1981. Age-dependent changes in some human lymphocyte subpopulations. Changes in natural killer cell activity. Acta Pathol. Microbiol. Scand., Sect. C **89:** 55-62.

61. BATORY, G., M. BENCZUR, M. VARGA, T. GARAM, C. ONODY & G. G. PETIANYI. 1981. Increased killer cell activity in aged humans. Immunobiology **158:** 393-402.

62. FERNANDES, G. & S. GUPTA. 1981. Natural killing and antibody-dependent cytotoxicity by lymphocyte subpopulations in young and aging humans. J. Clin. Immunol. **1:** 141-148.

63. ABO, T., M. D. COOPER & C. M. BALCH. 1982. Postnatal expansion of the natural killer and killer cell population in humans identified by the monoclonal HNK-1 antibody. J. Exp. Med. **155:** 321-326.

64. THOMPSON, J. S., D. R. WEKSTEIN, J. L. RHOADES, C. KIRKPATRIC, S. A. BROWN, T. ROSZMAN, R. STRAUS & N. TIETZ. 1984. The immune status of healthy centenarians. J. Am. Geriatr. Soc. **32:** 274-281.

65. TILDEN, A. B., C. E. GROSSI, K. ITOH, G. A. CLOUD, P. A. DOUGHERTY & C. M. BALCH. 1986. Subpopulation analysis of human granular lymphocytes: associations with age, gender and cytotoxic activity. Natl. Immunol. Cell Growth Regul. 5: 90-99.

66. LIGHART, G. J., P. C. VAN VLOKHOVEN, H. R. E. SCHUIT & W. HIGMANS. 1986. The expanded null cell compartment in ageing: increase in the number of natural killer cells and changes in T-cell and NK-cell subsets in human blood. Immunology 59: 353-357.

67. RABINOWICH, H., Y. GOSES, T. RESHEF & A. KLAJMAN. 1985. Interleukin-2 production and activity in aged humans. Mech. Ageing Dev. 32: 213-226.

68. MYSLIWSKA, J., A. MYSLIWSKI & J. WITKOWSKI. 1985. Age dependent decline of natural killer and antibody-dependent cell-mediated cytotoxicity activity of human lymphocytes is connected with decrease of their acid phosphatase activity. Mech. Ageing Dev. 31: 1-11.

69. RYTEL, M. W., N. KERMANI, K. S. LARRATT & P. A. TURNER. 1986. Immune interferon response and natural killer cell activity in the elderly and young adults. (Abstract) J. Am. Geriatr. Soc. 34: 685-686.

70. MARIANI, E., M. VITALE, P. RODA, A. DEGRASSI, A. R. MARIANI & A. FACCHINI. 1987. T and NK clones in old individuals. (Abstract) Fed. Proc. 46: 1090.

71. SATO, T., A. FUSE & T. KUWATA. 1979. Enhancement by interferon of natural cytotoxic activities of lymphocytes from human cord blood and peripheral blood of aged persons. Cell. Immunol. 45: 458-463.

72. NAGEL, J. E., G. D. COLLINS & W. H. ADLER. 1981. Spontaneous or natural killer cytotoxicity of K562 erythroleukemic cells in normal patients. Cancer Res. 41: 2284-2288.

73. MARCANO, N. B., A. RIVAS, E. F. FIGARELLA, I. BLANCA, G. K. PENCHASZADEH, M. PEREZ-ROJAS & N. E. BLANCO. 1982. Cell-mediated effector mechanisms in aging humans. Arch. Allergy Appl. Immunol. 69: 7-11.

74. MURASKO, D. M., B. J. NELSON, R. SILVER, D. MATOUR & D. KAYE. 1986. Immunologic response in an elderly population with a mean age of 85. Am. J. Med. 81: 612-618.

75. TSUKAYAMA, D., R. BREITENBUCHER, S. STEINBERG, T. ALLEN, R. NELSON, G. GEKKER, W. KEANE & P. PETERSON. 1986. Polymorphonuclear leukocyte, T-lymphocyte, and natural killer cell activities in elderly nursing home residents. Eur. J. Clin. Microbiol. 5: 468-471.

76. MORLEY, J. E. 1983. Neuroendocrine effects of endogenous opioid peptides in human subjects: a review. Psychoneuroendocrinology 8: 361-379.

77. SOLOMON, G. F. 1987. Psychoneuroimmunology: interactions between central nervous system and immune system. J. Neurosci. Res. In press.

78. SHAVIT, Y., J. W. LEWIS, G. W. TERMAN, R. P. GALE & J. C. LEIBESKIND. 1984. Opioid peptides mediate the suppressive effect of stress on natural killer cell cytotoxicity. Science 223: 188-190.

79. AYLESWORTH, C. F., C. A. HODSON & J. MEITES. 1979. Opiate antagonists can inhibit mammary tumor growth in rats. Proc. Soc. Exp. Biol. Med. 161: 18-20.

80. ZAGON, I. S. & P. J. MCLAUGHLIN. 1983. Opioid antagonists inhibit the growth of metastatic murine neuroblastoma. Cancer Lett. 21: 89-94.

81. MORLEY, J. E., N. KAY, J. ALLEN, T. MOON & C. J. BILLINGTON. 1985. Endorphins, immune function and cancer. Psychopharmacol. Bull. 21: 485-488.

82. WYBRAN, J., T. APPELBOOM, J. P. FARALY & A. GOVAERTS. 1979. Suggestive evidence for morphine and methionine-enkephalin-like receptors on normal blood T lymphocytes. J. Immunol. 123: 1068-1070.

83. SOLOMON, G. F., N. KAY & J. E. MORLEY. 1986. Endorphins: a link between personality, stress, emotions, immunity and disease? In Enkephalins and Endorphins: Stress and the Immune System. N. P. Plotnikoff, R. E. Faith, A. J. Mungo & R. A. Good, Eds. 129-144. Plenum Press. New York, NY.

84. TESCHEMACHER, H. & L. SCHWEIGERER. 1985. Opioid peptides: do they have immunological significance? Trends. Pharmacol. Sci. 6: 368-370.

85. FAITH, R. E., H. J. LIANG, A. J. MURGO & N. P. PLOTNIKOFF. 1984. Neuroimmunomodulation with enkephalins: enhancement of natural killer (NK) cell activity in vitro. Clin. Immunol. Immunopathol. 31: 412-418.

86. MATTHEWS, P. M., C. J. FOELICH, W. L. SIBBITT & A. D. BANKHURST. 1983. Enhancement of natural cytotoxicity by beta-endorphins. J. Immunol. **130:** 1658-1662.

87. KAY, N., J. ALLEN & J. E. MORLEY. 1984. Endorphins stimulate normal human peripheral blood lymphocyte natural killer cell activity. Life Sci. **35:** 53-59.

88. KAY, N., J. E. MORLEY & J. M. VANREE. 1987. Enhancement of human lymphocyte natural killing function by non-opioid fragments of beta-endorphin. Life Sci. **40:** 1083-1087.

89. MORLEY, J. E. & N. KAY. 1986. Neuropeptides as modulators of immune function. Psychopharmacol. Bull. **22:** 1089-1092.

90. CHAVKIN, C. & A. GOLDSTEIN. 1981. Dynorphin-specific receptor for the opioid peptide, dynorphin: structure-activity relationships. Proc. Natl. Acad. Sci. USA **78:** 6543-6547.

91. MORLEY, J. E. & A. S. LEVINE. 1983. Involvement of dynorphin and the kappa opioid receptor in feeding. Peptides **4:** 797-800.

92. TSUDO, M., R. W. KOZAK, C. K. GOLDMAN & T. A. WALDMANN. 1986. Demonstration of a non-TAC peptide that binds interleukin-2: a potential participant in a multichain interleukin-2 receptor complex. Proc. Natl. Acad. Sci. USA **83:** 9694-9698.

93. MORLEY, J. E. 1986. Neuropeptides, behavior and aging. J. Am. Geriatr. Soc. **34:** 52-62.

94. DUPONT, A., P. SAVARD & Y. MESAND. 1981. Age-related changes in central nervous system enkephalins and substance P. Life Sci. **29:** 2317-2323.

95. GAMBERT, S. R. 1981. Interaction of age and thyroid hormone status on beta-endorphin content in rat corpus striatum and hypothalamus. Neuroendocrinology **32:** 114-119.

96. BARDEN, N., A. DUPONT & F. LABRIE. 1981. Age-dependent changes in the beta-endorphin content of discrete rat brain nuclei. Brain Res. **9:** 209-215.

97. MESSING, R. B., B. J. VASQUEZ & B. SAMANIEGO. 1981. Alterations in dihydromorphine binding in cerebral hemispheres of aged male rats. J. Neurochem. **36:** 784.

98. SPRATTO, G. R. & R. E. DONO. 1978. Effect of age on acute morphine response in the rat. Res. Commun. Chem. Pathol. Pharamacol. **19:** 23-28.

99. WEBSTER, G. W., L. SHUSTER & B. E. ELEFTHERIUS. 1976. Morphine analgesia in mice of different ages. Exp. Aging Res. **2:** 221-223.

100. GOSNELL, B. A., A. S. LEVINE & J. E. MORLEY. 1983. The effects of aging on opioid modulation of feeding in rats. Life Sci. **32:** 2793-2799.

101. NICAK, A. & A. KOHUT. 1978. Development of tolerance to morphine and pethidine in rats is dependant on age. Act. Nerv. Super. (Praha) **20:** 231-235.

102. FRAIOLI, F., C. MORETTI, D. PAOLUCCI, E. ALICICCO, F. CRESCENZI & G. FORTUNIO. 1980. Physical exercise stimulates marked concomitant release of beta-endorphin and adrenocorticotropic hormone (ACTH) in peripheral blood in man. Experientia **36:** 987-989.

103. CARR, D. B., B. A. BULLEN, G. S. SKRINER, M. A. ARNOLD, M. ROSENBLATT, I. Z. BETTINS, J. B. MARTIN & J. N. MCARTHUR. 1981. Physical conditioning facilitates the exercise induced secretion of beta-endorphin and beta-lipotropin in women. N. Engl. J. Med. **305:** 560-563.

104. COLT, E. W. D., S. L. WARDLAW & A. G. FRANTZ. 1981. The effect of running on plasma beta-endorphin. Life Sci. **28:** 1637-1640.

105. TARGAN, S., L. BRITVAN & F. DOREY. 1981. Activation of human NKCC by moderate exercise: increased frequency of NK cells with enhanced capability of effector-target lytic interactions. Clin. Exp. Immunol. **45:** 352-360.

106. BRAHMI, Z., J. E. THOMAS, M. PARK & I. R. G. DOWDESWELL. 1985. The effect of acute exercise on natural killer cell activity of trained and sedentary human subjects. J. Clin. Immunol. **5:** 321-328.

107. SCHLEIFER, S. J., S. E. KELLER, S. G. SAMUEL, L. D. KENNETH & M. STEIN. 1985. Depression and immunity lymphocyte function in ambulatory depressed patients, hospitalized schizophrenic patients, and patients hospitalized for heriorrhaphy. Arch. Gen. Psychiatry **42:** 129-133.

108. BARTROP, R. W., L. LAZARUS, E. OUCKHURST, L. G. KILOH & R. PENNY. 1977. Depressed lymphocyte function after bereavement. Lancet **1:** 834-836.

109. BLAZER, D. & C. D. WILLIAMS. 1980. Epidemiology of dysphoria and depression in an elderly population. Am. J. Psychiatry **137:** 439-444.

110. THOMAS, P. D., J. M. GOODWIN & J. S. GOODWIN. 1985. Effect of social support on stress-related changes in cholesterol level, uric acid level, and immune function in an elderly sample. Am. J. Psychiatry **142:** 735-737.
111. KIECOLT-GLASER, J. K., R. GLASER, D. WILLIGER, J. STOUT, G. MESSICK, S. SHEPPARD, D. RICKER, S. C. ROMISHER, W. BRINER, G. BONNELL & R. DONNERBERG. 1985. Psychosocial enhancement of immunocompetence in a geriatric population. Health Psychol. **4:** 25-41.
112. DILMAN, V. M. 1981. The Law of Deviation of Homeostasis and Diseases of Aging. John Wright PSG. Boston, MA.
113. SOLOMON, G. F. & R. H. MOOS. 1964. The relationship of personality to the presence of rheumatoid factor in asymptomatic relatives of patients with rheumatoid arthritis. Psychosom. Med. **27:** 350-360.
114. TAYLOR, J., 1955. A personality scale of manifest anxiety. J. Abnorm. Soc. Psychol. **48:** 285-290.
115. BECK, A. T., C. H. WARD, M. MENDELSON, J. E. MOCK & J. ERBAUGH. 1961. An inventory for measuring depression. Arch. Gen. Psychiatry **4:** 561-571.
116. CROWNE, D. P., & D. MARLOW. 1960. A new scale of social desirability independent of psychopathology. J. Cons. Psychol. **24:** 349.
117. KOBASA, S. C. 1979. Stressful life events, personality and health: an inquiry into hardiness. J. Pers. Soc. Psychol. **37:** 1-11.

The Effects of Cortisone on Acetylcholinesterase (AChE) in the Neonatal and Aged Thymus[a]

KAREN BULLOCH AND ROBERT LUCITO

*Neuroimmune Physiology Laboratory
The Helicon Foundation
4622 Santa Fe Street
San Diego, California 92109*

INTRODUCTION

AChE-positive nerve fibers and terminals from the vagus nerve are first observed during the eleventh embryonic day penetrating the parenchyma of the primordial thymus while the gland still maintains its cervical locale. As the gland descends into the thoracic cavity, these nerves divide, elaborate, and form a dense network defining the boundaries between the future thymic cortex and medulla. During this migratory phase of thymic development, other AChE-positive fibers derived from the phrenic and recurrent laryngeal nerves penetrate the gland and are distributed to the subcapsular and outer cortical regions.[1,2] The development and distribution of acetylcholinesterase (AChE)-positive nerves within the normal thymus, and within embryonic thymic tissue transplanted under the kidney capsule of syngeneic nude mice,[3] precedes the differentiation of thymic structure and function. This finding suggests that AChE may play an important role in the maturation of the gland within the context of neural transmission, or as an independent inducer of developmental events, or both.

This hypothesis is further supported by pharmacological research showing that potent cholinesterase inhibitors can both cause developmental abnormalities[4] and modulate T-cell-dependent immune responses.[5] Although it is not known how the enzyme operates in these cases, the experimental evidence makes it clear that AChE is a critical component of thymic development and function.

In addition to its role in neural transmission, AChE has been noted within neural crest cells during discrete phases of their migration and within certain organ tissues as they undergo organogenesis.[6] It is also present in hematopoietic-derived tissues such as erythrocytes[7,8] and in some types of peripheral T-lymphocytes.[9]

The thymus gland functions optimally in its production of mature T-cells within a discrete time period of the vertebrate's life. Although the exact time of optimal immune-related thymic functions can differ somewhat among the vertebrates, it occurs for most species from late embryonic development throughout the prepubescent period.

[a]This work was supported by Grant N00014-85K-0528 from the Office of Naval Research and by a grant from the Joan B. Kroc Foundation of Psychoneuroimmunology.

With the onset of puberty the thymus shrinks and the number of thymocytes that are processed within the gland drops markedly. This drop in T-cell production parallels the gradual decrease of immune competency in vertebrates.

In addition to the natural aging phenomenon, stress and an increase in adrenal corticosteroids can also initiate a temporary depletion of thymocytes in the thymic parenchyma. Injected corticosteroids such as cortisone have a profound affect on immature thymocytes in the thymic cortex, and within the thymic medulla they increase the number of mature thymocytes, which are cortisone-resistant and bear muscarinic acetylcholine receptors on their cell surfaces.[10]

In an earlier anatomical study, Muller and Muntener[11] observed that cortisone injections caused a dramatic increase in AChE activity within the cortex of the thymus. A peak activity was observed at 10 hours after the injection of the hormone. However, no biochemistry was carried out to determine which molecular species of the enzyme was involved.

At the molecular level, AChE (EC 3.1.1.7) is a glycoprotein enzyme best known for its ability to terminate cholinergic neural transmission by hydrolysing acetylcholine into choline and acetate.[12] More recently, AChE glycoprotein has also been shown to function within other neurotransmitter systems as a possible peptidase.[13]

The distribution of molecular forms of acetylcholinesterase (AChE) has been extensively studied in the rat and mouse thymus. The data now indicate that the mouse thymus displays predominantly one globular low-molecular-weight 3-4S species of AChE (14-16) whereas two species (4S and 10S) are evident in the rat thymus.[15] Three to seven forms of AChE, ranging from a low-molecular-weight 3-4.5S monomeric form to a 16-19S tetrameric form, have been identified in different tissues of various species of vertebrates by using zone sedimentation in sucrose gradients or gel filtration chromatography.[17,18] The monomeric form is believed to be a secreted, globular molecule, whereas the higher-molecular-weight forms of the enzyme are asymmetrical molecules in which globular catalytic subunits are associated with a rod-shaped collagen tail piece.

In light of the fact that this cholinergic enzyme has been identified within the nerves that innervate the thymus and that cortisone has a profound effect on both the increase in thymic AChE activity and the production of muscarinic acetylcholine receptor-bearing mature thymocytes, it seems important to further our understanding of this cortisone-AChE phenomenon. In the current work, we have characterized anatomically and biochemically the effects of cortisone on the AChE activity within the thymus as a function of age in order to gain a better understanding of the possible role of this cholinergic enzyme in the production and/or education of the muscarinic acetylcholine receptor-bearing mature thymocytes.

Experimental Methods

Animals

A total of fifty neonatal through year-old male and female BALB/C mice (Teconic farms) were used in this study. The adult mice were housed 4-5 mice per cage and maintained on a diurnal lighting schedule with free access to food and water.

Injection Protocol

Adult mice were inoculated interperitoneally with 1 milligram cortisone acetate or with saline, whereas neonatal mice received 0.25 mg of the steroid. The animals were sacrified at six, ten, eighteen and twenty-four hours post-inoculation. Immediately after sacrifice, the thymuses were removed from each animal and prepared for histochemical or biochemical analysis.

The acetylcholinesterase (AChE) histochemical method of Koelle[19] as modified by Bulloch and Pomerantz[2] was used to identify AChE-positive structures anatomically. Mice were lethally anesthetized with phenobarbitol and were perfused transcardially, first with a cold solution of 5% dextrose in phosphate buffer (pH 7.4) and then with a cold solution of 4% paraformaldehyde in phosphate buffer (pH 7.4). The thymus was removed and put in the same fixative which, after 2 additional hours, was replaced with a 10% sucrose buffer solution for 12 hours. Sections, 28 microns thick, were cut on a cryostat and mounted on gelatin-coated slides which when dry were washed 3 times with sodium acetate buffer (pH 5.5) and then incubated in a medium containing 50 mM acetate buffer (pH 5.5), 2 mM copper sulfate, 10 mM glycin (Sigma; molecular weight, 75), 4 mM acetylcholine iodide as the substrate, and 0.8 mM tetraisopropyl pyrophosphoramine (iso-OMPA) to inhibit nonspecific esterase activity. Control slides were incubated in the above buffer minus either the substrate or the nonspecific esterase inhibitor. The specific acetylcholinesteasse inhibitor BW284c51 (Sigma) was used as the positive control. Following incubation, the slides were rinsed with deionized water and developed in 2.5% sodium sulfide (pH 6.8-7.0) using a 0.1% silver nitrate solution to intensify the sulfur reaction product. The slides were washed again with deionized water, dehydrated and coverslipped with Permount. The tissues were inspected and photographed with a Nikon photomicroscope.

Preparation of Thymus Homogenate

Tissue was prepared as described elsewhere.[16] In brief, mice were quickly sacrificed by decapitation, and the thymus tissue was removed, cleaned of external connective tissue, washed, and minced at 4°C into small pieces, which were then homogenized in a Teflon-glass Potter homogenizer using a total of 10 volumes of 100 mM phosphate buffer, pH 7.0 (0.15 M NaCl, 0.5% Triton X-100 and 0.25 mM EDTA). Although the initial thymus tissue preparations of the nondrug-treated mice produced a gelatinous homogenate, persistence with homogenization eventually yielded a uniform product. (A reduction in the salt concentration of the buffer according to the methods of Skau[15] results in a more easily homogenated tissue preparation.) The homogenate was centrifuged for 30 minutes at 14,500 rev/min in a Sorvall RC2-B superspeed centrifuge outfitted with an SS-34 rotor at 4°C. The supernatant was then removed and subjected to the various assay systems described below.

Sucrose Gradient Purification

Linear sucrose gradients (4.8 ml., 5-20%) were prepared using a Buchler gradient maker in 100 mM phosphate buffer, pH 7.0 containing 0.15 M NaCl, 0.5% Triton

X-100 and 0.25 mM EDTA. Two hundred μl of thymus homogenate were layered onto the gradient. The following enzymes were included as sedimentation coefficient standards: B-galactosidase (16S) and catalase (11.2S). The gradients were centrifuged at 4°C for 4.25 hours at 65,000 rev/min. Aliquots of the fractions were assayed for AChE and for the marker proteins. AChE was assayed according to the above method; B-galactosidase was assayed as described by Sigma Chemical Corp., St. Louis, MO, using o-Nitrophenyl-B-d-Galactopyranoside as substrate, and the catalase was identified by its absorbance at 404 nm. A graph of the DPM-versus-fraction was plotted from the data of the AChE assay to show peaks of activity of the enzyme. The sedimentation coefficients of these peaks were then determined by comparing the AChE-containing fraction numbers to the fraction numbers of the calibrating markers.

AChE Assay

To control for nonspecific cholinesterase activity, extracts of thymus tissue were routinely preincubated at room temperature (RT) with iso-OMPA (Sigma) before being subjected to the assay for true cholinesterase activity.

AChE activity was evaluated by placing in duplicate 25 μl of each fraction of the thymus extract directly into scintillation vials containing 4.76×10^{-4} M [3-H] acetylcholine iodide (NET-113 from New England Nuclear, Boston, MA). The assay was terminated after 20 minutes by placing 2 ml of a stopping solution (glycine/HCL buffer, pH 2.5) directly into the vials. Five ml of an extractive scintillation cocktail (17.2 g PPO; 1.1 g dimethyl-POPOP; 400 ml isoamyl alcohol plus toluene to bring the volume up to 4 liters) was then added to each scintillation vial. The samples were counted directly in a Packard Tri-Carb 460 CD scintillation counter.

RESULTS

Our histochemical analysis in this and in other studies[2] clearly shows that most of the AChE within the thymus is nerve-related. The AChE activity in the cortex of the postnatal thymus (neonate to two weeks of age) is quite intense, making it difficult to visualize the dense plexus of nerve fibers at the cortico-medullary boundaries. However, the large nerves that course along the blood vessels and penetrate deep into the gland are easily viewed, and branches can be seen entering the area of intense AChE activity. A subcapsular nerve plexus is also observed. These nerves radiate into the cortex. This pattern of AChE-thymic innervation is observed throughout the life of the mouse (FIGURE 1) and is also seen to develop in embryonic normal thymic tissue transplanted under the kidney capsule of syngeneic nude mice (FIGURE 2). The cortisone-treated thymuses of the neonate-2-week-old mice are very much reduced in size, and the activity appeared somewhat denser than in the nontreated mouse thymus.

By the third postnatal week, AChE activity of the nondrug-treated thymus is confined to the nerves at the cortico-medullary boundary and in the subcapsular plexus. The intense diffuse staining pattern of the younger ages is greatly reduced. However, cortisone-treated mice show a dramatic increase in staining within the cortex of the thymus (FIGURES 3 and 4). The thymus revealed a marked increase in the distribution of AChE activity within the nerves and nerve terminals of the cortico-medullary boundary at six hours postinjection that spread into the cortex over the next six hours. An increase in activity in the subcapsular region was also noted with similar spreading into the cortex over the same time period. In both areas new nerve-associated structures were observed that were not visualized in the nonsteroid-injected thymus. In addition it was apparent that the cortical epithelial cells demonstrated a marked increase in cholinergic activity that peaked during the 12th postnatal hour postinjection. The long delicate fibers demonstrated strong activity and aggregation of thymocytes was observed along their full extension. AChE activity persisted in the thymus through the 24-hour time period. By 18 hours the thymus cortex was saturated with AChE-positive nerves and related structures and only with 14-μm sections could the nature of the distribution be clearly established. Small thymocytes within the shrunken cortex also appeared to contain AChE activity.

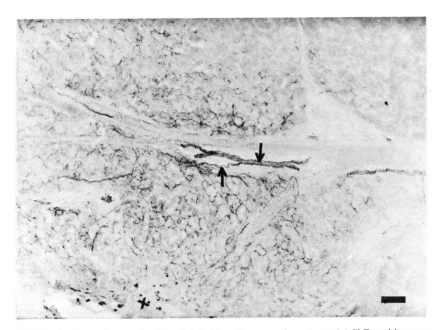

FIGURE 1. Photomicrograph of the distribution of a noncortisone-treated AChE-positive nerve accompanying a thymic medullary blood vessel and penetrating into the adjacent parenchyma of the cortico-medullary boundary of a six-week-old mouse thymus. Marker bar = 10 μm. *Arrows* designate nerve trunk and branching fibers.

During the following five weeks, AChE activity in the normal mouse thymus gradually became less prevalent in regions surrounding the nerve plexuses (FIGURE 1), and there was a general inconsistency throughout the gland in the intensity of the stain. The drug-treated eight-week-old thymuses also displayed an inconsistent staining pattern in response to cortisone treatment. Vast regions of the cortex showed little or no staining. This was particularly evident in sections of the cortex that interface with

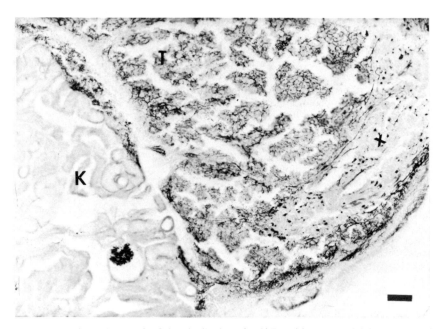

FIGURE 2. Photomicrograph of the distribution of AChE-positive nerves (X) in a C57B1/6 normal thymic tissue (T) transplanted under the kidney (K) capsule of a syngeneic nude mouse six weeks postoperatively.

the cortex of the other lobe. No pattern could be assigned to one lobe versus the other, as the pattern was seen throughout both lobes (FIGURE 5).

By the time the mouse was eight months old and older, the AChE activity was evident only within, and surrounding, the nerve plexuses. The mouse thymus was no longer capable of responding to cortisone and serial sections of the nondrug-treated and drug-treated thymus yielded virtually no differences in the distribution of the AChE staining pattern (FIGURE 6).

BIOCHEMICAL ANALYSIS

Our initial biochemical analysis of the overall AChE activity in the different ages was carried out at ten and twenty-four hours. AChE activity in the neonatal mouse thymus is so intense that no changes in AChE activity can be noted in either the drug-treated or control thymus at ten hours. However, the twenty-four-hour time point does demonstrate a greater depletion in overall AChE activity than the ten-hour point.

The overall activity in both the normal and drug-treated mice peaks (per thymus) during the third to sixth week then gradually drops off as the mouse ages. The ten-hour time point constantly yields the greatest activity up to the eighth month. At this point, cortisone no longer has an effect on the enhancement of AChE activity over controls.

Our analysis of the sucrose gradients of normal and drug treated mice thymuses revealed that the predominant activity is almost entirely that of the 4S species at all ages (FIGURE 7). In the neonatal to two-week-old thymus, small peaks do appear within the 6S and 10S range but are so insignificant that we cannot say with confidence that they reflect real forms of the enzyme.

Biochemical analysis of sucrose gradients of the three-week-old normal and drug-treated thymuses reveal a large 4S peak of activity. Small peaks are again evident in the 6-8S and 10S range. However, with the injection of cortisone, a significant increase is observed in all of the peaks. The maximum activity is reached during the 10-12th hour after cortisone injection. (FIGURE 8) and drops below the controls by the twenty-fourth hour. This finding parallels both the overall biochemical analysis and the histochemical analysis.

The appearance of the other peaks became more evident as the animal grew older, and in a few of the older mice (6 months), the peaks were of equal value. By the time the mouse was 9 months old, the AChE activity in the thymus no longer responded to cortisone. The 4S peak remained the predominant species with few exceptions; however, the other peaks were clearly visible.

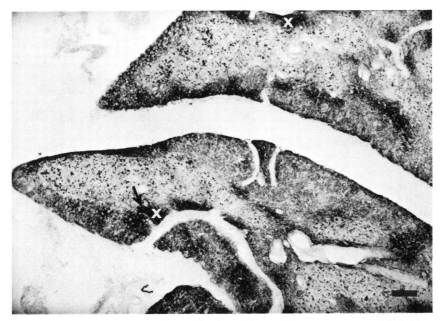

FIGURES 3. FIGURES 3-6 are photomicrographs of a series of mice thymuses all processed at the same time and cut at the same thickness. The differences noted in these photomicrographs correlate well with the differences noted in a biochemical analysis of AChE activity of three similar-age thymuses, again all processed at the same time. FIGURE 3 shows the dense AChE-positive staining of a three-week-old thymus ten hours after the injection of cortisone. Note that the entire cortex is darkened by the AChE activity and the increase in AChE-positive cells within the cortex (X). Marker bar = 500 μm. The *arrow* designates visible nerve fibers.

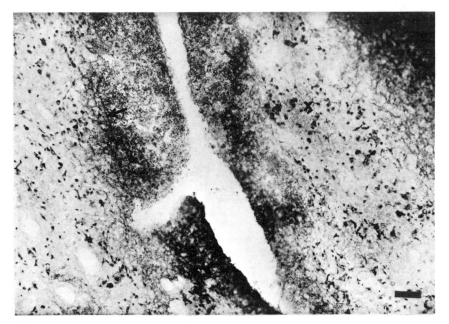

FIGURE 4. A high-power photomicrograph of the strong AChE activity in the two adjacent thymic lobes of a three-week-old mouse thymus. Marker bar = 100 μm. *Arrows* designate areas where AChE-positive nerves are visible and surrounded by a dense staining pattern. (X) designates the area within the medulla rich in AChE-positive cells after cortisone treatment.

DISCUSSION

In a previous publication[16] a complete biochemical analysis of the thymic enzyme in the normal mouse was carried out. There, we designated the 4S fraction as 3S but use of better marker proteins in the present study showed that this peak falls more in the 4S range. By comparing the sedimentation coefficient of the 4S thymic enzyme to those of the marker proteins, an approximate molecular weight of 80,000 could be assigned to this slowly sedimenting thymic AChE. The previous study also revealed that the AChE of the thymus was completely inhibited by the specific acetycholinesterase inhibitor BW284c51 but was unaffected by the nonspecific esterase inhibitor iso-OMPA.[14] Those experiments further revealed that the specific inhibitor of AChE, BW284c51, blocked the activity of the thymic enzyme by more than 95% at a concentration of 1×10^{-5} M, whereas iso-OMPA, an inhibitor of pseudo-cholinesterase, at a concentration of 1×10^{-4} M inhibited only 5% of the enzyme's activity. The thymuses of cortisone-treated mice showed the same pattern in their response to the drug, thereby indicating that the cholinesterase present in the thymuses of normal and drug-treated mice is almost entirely the true AChE. The kinetics (Km and Vmax) and sensitivity to inhibitors of the thymic AChE are similar to those found for this enzyme in other mammalian species.[18] These data are also compatible with reports that true AChE accounts for most of the cholinesterase activity in the thymus of the rat, rabbit, and pig.[19]

In this study we did determine AChE activity per milligram of protein but chose not to express our data in these terms. We reasoned that to do so might result in an artifactual interpretation of the data, since most of the changes in thymic size after cortisone injections are caused by the destruction of thymocytes, not of the AChE-producing nerves and resident cells.

Although there is predominantly a 4S form of the enzyme within the thymus, two other forms (a 10S and a 16S) of the enzyme appear during development. All of these forms are associated with nerves or nerve-related structures.[17,18] Our histochemistry has now demonstrated that the highest activity of this enzyme is in fact localized to nerves and their immediate surroundings.

Skau[15] recently reported that the rat thymus has two molecular forms of AChE, a 10S and a 4S form, whereas in the mouse, he found only one. Our previous report on the mouse thymus indicated only one form of the enzyme. However, in the present study, the use of cortisone shows an exacerbation of the enzyme. After analyzing many mouse thymuses we can clearly detect in the normal state a small activity that represents 10S and 16S peaks. Even in Skau's data on the mouse there is a small peak of activity at 10S. However, it is not surprising that he felt, as we did previously, that this activity was insignificant.

All forms of AChE are enhanced by cortisone injections during specific phases of the animal's life. However, we do not know if cortisone affects the enzyme directly

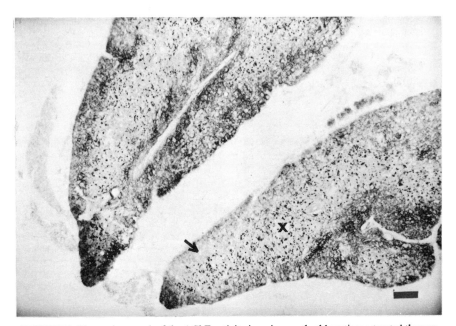

FIGURE 5. Photomicrograph of the AChE activity in a six-month-old cortisone-treated thymus. Marker bar = 500 μm. The *arrow* designates the distinctive lack of AChE activity in some regions of the cortex. Also note the generalized loss of AChE activity throughout the cortex compared to the three-week-old thymus. As with the younger thymus, there is an increase of AChE-positive cells within the medulla of the gland (X).

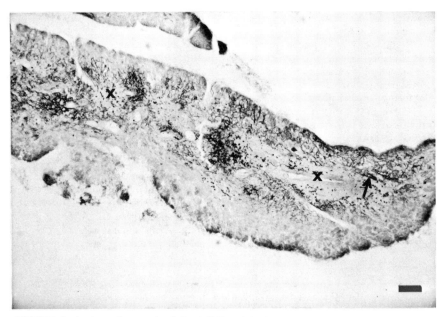

FIGURE 6. A photomicrograph of the AChE activity in a year-old thymus ten hours after cortisone injection. Note the overall lack of the dense AChE-staining pattern. Marker bar = 500 μm. Nerve fibers (*arrow*) are visible within the cortico-medullary boundaries and within some areas of what remains of the cortical areas. Note inconsistent pattern of AChE staining pattern around medullary blood vessels. Note also that AChE-positive cells are not as dense as in the younger mice (X).

and/or activates cholinergic nerves within the thymus, or instead if cholinergic and/or enzymatic mechanisms are activated in response to the effect of cortisone on some other target. However, we do know that cortisone and other hormones under either experimental conditions or conditions of stress exert an effect on the thymus that results in the production of mature T-cells and the killing of masses of immature thymocytes. We now also know that AChE is involved in this process and that its role in the thymus is tied into the neuroendocrine system. A deeper understanding of this age-dependent induction of nerve-related AChE activity by cortisone may offer new insight into how the neuroendocrine system interacts with the thymus in both normal and aberrant development.

SUMMARY

    Acetylcholinesterase (AChE) histochemistry and biochemistry was used to characterize the distribution and species of this enzyme within the developing thymus gland of the mouse. The results indicate that AChE-positive nerves and related structures are involved in a steroid-induced mechanism for regulating thymocyte populations. Low doses of cortisone injected into mice produce an activation of quiescent cholinergic nerves and the appearance of several new molecular forms of AChE within areas of the thymus where thymocyte death is prevalent. The action of cortisone on AChE is age dependent. In neonates, AChE activity is extremely high in the cortex of the gland, and cortisone causes little or no increase in AChE activity. In mice three to six weeks old, cortisone exerts its most profound effect on the AChE activity within the thymus. In mice eight months old and older, the AChE activity of the normal thymus is restricted to nerves and nerve-related structures at the cortical-medullary boundaries, with little or no activity observed in the cortex. Injections of cortisone in these mice does not cause an increase in AChE activity in the cortex and only slightly enhances activity within the cortico-medullary boundaries.

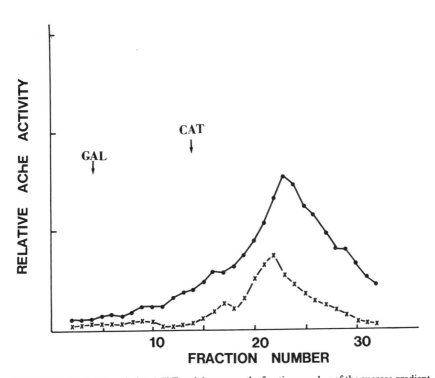

FIGURE 7. Plot of the relative AChE activity versus the fraction number of the sucrose gradient 10 (●) and 24 (x) hours after i.p. injections of cortisone or diluent (control) into six-week-old mice. Note the marked increase of AChE activity and the enhancement of two previously undetected forms of the enzyme. GAL = Beta galactosidase; CAT = Catalase.

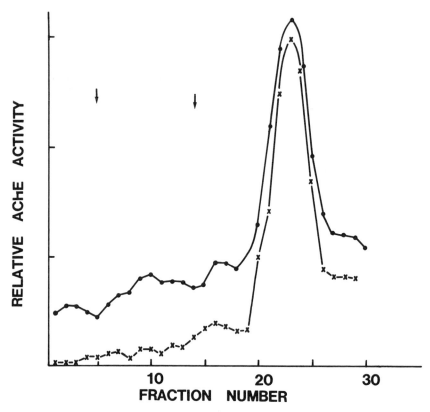

FIGURE 8. Plot of the relative AChE activity versus the fraction number of the sucrose gradient of a two-week-old normal thymus (x) and a year-old thymus (●). Note the slight 10S peak of both the two-week-old and year-old mouse thymus. *Arrows* designate GAL and CAT respectively (see FIG. 7).

ACKNOWLEDGMENTS

A debt of gratitude is owed to Theodore Melnechuk for his editorial and professional advice and to Dr. Tricia Radojcic and Leslie Tollefson for their help in the preparation of this manuscript.

REFERENCES

1. BULLOCH, K. 1985. *In* Neural Modulation of Immunity. R. Guillemin *et al.,* Eds. Raven Press. New York, NY.
2. BULLOCH, K. & W. POMERANTZ. 1984. J. Comp. Neurol. **228:** 56-68.

3. BULLOCH, K. 1987. J. Neurosci. Res. **18:** 16-27.
4. LANDAUER, A. & N. SALAM. 1974. J. Neurosci. Res. **1:** 51-66.
5. MIERZEJENSKI, J. 1970. Exp. Med. Microbiol. **12(3):** 269-275.
6. SKAER, R. 1973. J. Cell Sci. **12:** 911-923.
7. ROGISTER, G. *et al.* 1955. Acta Anat. **25:** 361-371.
8. HERTZ, F. & E. KAPLAN. 1973 Pediatr. Res. **7:** 204.
9. SZELENYI, J. G. *et al. 1982. Br. J. Haematol.* **50:** 241-248.
10. MASLINSKI, W. *et al.* 1983. Biochim. Biophys. Acta **758:** 93-97.
11. MULLER, E. & M. MUNTENER. 1979. Histochemistry **60:** 169-180.
12. DALE, H. H. 1914. J. Pharmacol. Exp. Ther. **6:** 147-190.
13. LOCKRIDGE, O. 1982. J. Neurochem. **39:** 106-110.
14. SKAU, K. A. & W. S. BRIMYOIN. 1979. Soc. Neurosci. Abst. **5:** 416.
15. ISRAEL, D. & K. A. SKAU. 1986. Thymus **8:** 193-199.
16. BULLOCH, K. & S. BASSONE. 1987. Ann. N. Y. Acad. Sci. In press.
17. ROTONDO, R. & D. M. FAMBROUGH. 1979. J. Biol. Chem. **254(11):** 4790-4799.
18. MASSOULIE, J. & S. BON. 1982. Annu. Rev. Neurosci. **5:** 57-106.
19. KOELLE, G. B. 1954. J. Comp. Neurol. **193:** 435-465.

Neuroendocrine-Thymus Interactions: Perspectives for Intervention in Aging[a]

N. FABRIS,[b] E. MOCCHEGIANI, M. MUZZIOLI,
AND M. PROVINCIALI

[b]Chair of Immunology
Medical Faculty
University of Pavia
Italian National Research Centers on Aging (INRCA)
Via Birarelli, 8
60121 Ancona, Italy

INTRODUCTION

It is generally accepted that the immune system, although regulated to a large extent by intrinsic cellular and humoral events, is sensitive to signals generated out of the immune network, namely, in the nervous and endocrine systems. This assumption is supported by two lines of experimental evidence: first, that spontaneous or induced alterations in the neuroendocrine system may cause functional modifications of immune reactivity[1] and, second, that present on the membrane of lymphoid cells are receptor sites for many low molecular weight and protein hormones.[2] On the other hand, the neuroendocrine system seems to act not only as a modulator of the immune network, but also as a target for signals generated within the immune system. Examples of such interactions are the alterations that can be induced in the neuroendocrine balance either by removal of relevant lymphoid organs, such as the thymus,[3] or by the functioning of the immune system itself, such as reactions to immunogenic or tolerogenic doses of antigen.[4,5]

Although these interactions are not fully defined, it is already possible to distinguish two levels of neuroendocrine-immune interrelationship.[6] The first level may be based on the interactions between the neurendocrine system and the thymus (FIGURE 1A), as organ deputed to induce proliferation and differentiation of stem cells into mature T-lymphocytes. Such interactions should take into account the fact that the thymus is synthetizing and secreting various hormone-like peptides with differentiation prop-

[a]This work was supported by the National Research Council (CNR) through "Progetto finalizzato Medicina Preventiva e Riabilitativa," Sottoprogetto "Meccanismi di invecchiamento" to N.F. (No. 85.00555.56, 86.01765.56) and by Health Ministery Targeted Program on "Geriatric Pharmacology" through the Italian National Research Centers on Aging (INRCA).

erties on the T-cell lineage,[7] and which are also found in the blood circulation, where they can be measured by bioassay or radioimmunoassay. The second level of interaction would be at the periphery (FIGURE 1B) between neuroendocrine signals and the humoral products which are secreted by immune cells during specific reactions to various antigens.[8]

The rationale for distinguishing these two levels is based on the evidence that either the humoral mediators, at least on the immune site, responsible for such neuroendocrine-immune interactions, or the targets of their action are different. The first level of interaction may be involved, in fact, in maturative steps of both immune and neuroendocrine systems as well as in the maintenance of their efficiency throughout life,[9] independent of the rate of antigenic stimulation. The second level may serve as extrinsic regulation of the immune reaction itself as well as a neurohormone-mediated defense against antigenic noxae.[10]

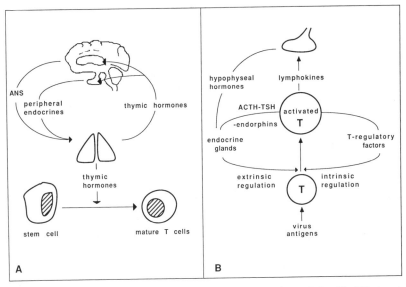

FIGURE 1. Schematic representation of neuroendocrine-immune interrelationship (**A**) at central level, mediated by thymic factors, and (**B**) at peripheral level, mediated by lymphocyte products released under antigenic stimulation.

The thymus plays a key role in the context[11] of these neuroendocrine-immune interactions. It is directly involved in the first level of interactions and indirectly relevant for the second level, since it produces the mature T-cells which are responsible for the peripheral immune-neuroendocrine network.

The key role played by the thymus is even more evident during aging,[11] since a progressive decline of its function and particularly of its endocrine activity is a common finding in animals and man. The data collected until now clearly show that, on the one hand, such an age-related thymic deterioration is not an irreversible process: different neuroendocrinological manipulation may restore thymic function to the young level, even when performed in old age.[12-15] On the other hand, age-related thymic failure is associated with, and in some instances it seems to be cause of, some age-associated alterations of the neuroendocrine balance.[6,11,16]

In the present paper we would like to summarize the experimental evidences supporting the existence of neuroendocrine-thymus interactions and their impact on the aging processes.

THE COMBINED PITUITARY-IMMUNODEFICIENCY STATE ASSOCIATED WITH CONGENITAL HYPOPITUITARISM OR POSTTHYMECTOMY WASTING SYNDROME

One of the first evidences of the existence of thymus-neuroendocrine interactions was based on the discovery that, on the one hand, congenital mutation affecting the pituitary (dwarf mice) caused concomittant alterations in the thymus and in the thymus-dependent system,[17,18] and, on the other hand, that removal of the thymus in neonatal age was followed by a wasting syndrome, one of its feature being a pituitary disfunction.[3]

Both of these experimental models served also to point out that thymus-neuroendocrine interactions might play a relevant role either at developmental stages[9] or during aging.[1,11]

The Dwarf Model

Congenital hypopituitarism, which occurs, as a recessive autosomal character, in Snell (genetic symbol, dw) dwarf mice, is characterized by nearly absent production of growth hormone and diminished synthesis of thyroid-stimulating hormone, adrenocorticotropic hormone, and prolactin. Pituitary dwarf mice show a normal development of the lymphoid system during the first 2 weeks of life, whereas in the following periods they suffer from a progressive involution of the immune system. Such an immunodeficiency affects primarily the thymus-dependent system, as indicated by the prolonged allogeneic skin-graft survival, the depressed capability of spleen cells to induce graft-vs-host reactions, or to react to T mitogens, and the reduced humoral antibody response to thymus-dependent antigens, while the synthesis of immunoglobulins is within normal range.[17]

The relevance of the pituitary-thymus interaction for the immunodeficiency state of the dwarf mouse is supported by the findings that the thymus underdevelopment and the immunologic deficiencies may be completely corrected by treating dwarf mice daily for 30 days with growth hormone and thyroxine, provided, however, that the thymus is not previously removed.[18]

The Wasting Syndrome Model

The idea that the thymus may act, particularly during early stages of life, on the physiologic development of nonimmunologic functions, originated from the observation that postthymectomy wasting disease, in addition to the obvious immunological disturbances, is characterized by pathological signs, which can hardly be linked to the direct effect of immune deficiency itself. Mice thymectomized at birth, show, in fact, a progressive impairment of body growth with reduced length of ears and tail, microsplancnia, microsomia, thinness of the skin and lack of subcutaneous fat, osseal alterations, particularly evident in the vertebrae with consequent hunched posture, and hypotrophy of various tissues including submaxillary gland, hair follicles and bone marrow.

At pituitary level it was demonstrated that thymectomized mice show a progressive degranulation of pituitary acidophilic growth-hormone-producing cells,[4] whereas other cell lineages in the hypophysis are left unmodified (FIGURE 2).

These data suggested that the thymus might, directly or indirectly, modulate the rate of synthesis and/or secretion of pituitary hormones relevant for its own efficiency, in the feedback fashion other endocrine glands do, and prompted a number of studies aimed to define the physiological extent and the mechanism of action of such a thymus-hypophysis axis, and more in general of the neuroendocrine-immune network.

Implications for Aging

The relevance of the dwarf and of the wasting syndrome model for the study of the impact of neuroendocrine-thymus interactions in the aging processes originated from findings showing that in both kinds of animals a number of signs which normally are considered as reflecting the physiological aging process appear much earlier than in normal mice.

In dwarf mice, death, which occurs at three-five months of age is preceded by the appearance of distinct signs of accelerated aging, such as greying and loss of hairs, general weakness, occasionally catarats (FIGURE 3), and precocious alterations of various age-related parameters such as cell turnover in different tissues, outgrowth potential of spleen or kidney fragments *in vitro,* and the mitotic index of cell colonies outgrown from explants.[19]

The precocious alterations observed in dwarf mice could be completely prevented by daily treatment with growth hormone and thyroxine for 30 days in the postweaning period of life, provided the thymus remains intact.[19] These data have suggested to us that a) dwarf mice suffer from an early-aging syndrome; b) such an early aging is due to a deficient thymus functioning; c) certain developmental hormones can prevent early aging through their action on the lymphoid tissue and primarily on the thymus.

With regard to thymectomized mice a relevant piece of information has been given by the observation that one of the best "aging parameters" in rodents, such as the progressive reduction of responsiveness of submanibular glands to beta-adrenoceptor stimulation[16] occurs much earlier in thymectomized mice than in normal littermates. Furthermore, tetraploid cells in the liver, which are also a feature of aging, appear much earlier in thymectomized mice.[20] A syngenic neonatal thymus transplant is able to completely recover both these defects.[16]

All these findings, though quite fragmentary have strongly supported the idea that the thymus might play, likely through its integration in the hormonal homeostatic mechanisms, a relevant role in basic aging processes, well beyond its responsibility for the age-associated immune deterioration.[12]

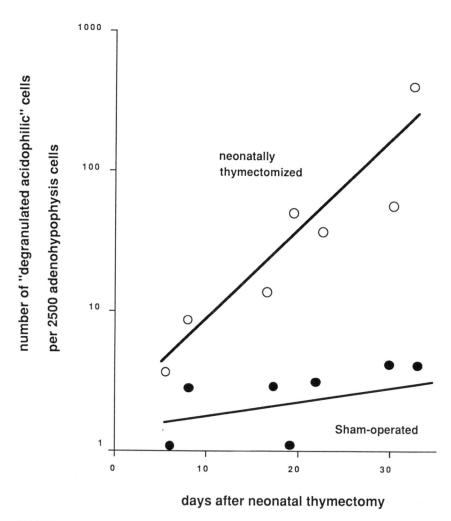

FIGURE 2. Number of "degranulated" acidophilic cells in the adenohypophysis of neonatally thymectomized mice and sham-operated littermates at various times after operation (redrawn from REFERENCE 3).

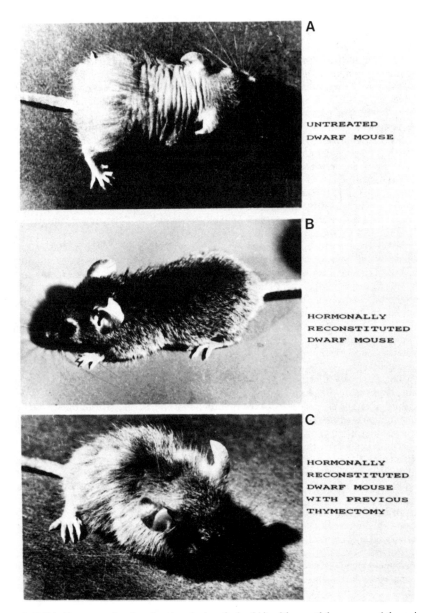

FIGURE 3. Recovery of early aging signs in dwarf mice (**A**), with growth hormone and thyroxine therapy (**B**), provided the thymus is not previously removed (**C**) (partially redrawn from REFERENCE 19).

INFLUENCE OF THE NEUROENDOCRINE NETWORK ON
THYMUS FUNCTION

In order to prove that the neuroendocrine system may influence the efficiency of the thymus, a number of experimental designs have been drawn following the original observation in dwarf mice. The majority of them have been based on the removal of endocrine glands and on the observation of the consequent functional modifications of the thymus, as measured by its size or by its histological picture or, indirectly, by the peripheral efficiency of the thymus-dependent lymphoid system.

Such an approach has been quite fruitful. It has in fact demonstrated that thymus growth is negatively influenced by removal of hypophysis or of thyroid or by chemical blockade of endocrine pancreas, whereas enlargement of the thymus was reported after removal of sexual and adrenal glands (for review see REFERENCES 1 and 11). These studies have furthermore pointed out that the efficiency of the thymus-dependent branch, as measured by different functional parameters, such as mitogen responsiveness, skin graft rejection time and antibody response to T-dependent antigens was also modified by those endocrinological manipulations.[12–22]

While the relevance of such findings for the understanding of the modulatory role played by the neuroendocrine system on different immune functions is beyond doubt, they were unable, however, to discriminate between influences directly exerted on the thymus from actions exerted on the mature T-cell, and even within the thymus, between influences exerted on thymocytes from those directed to the endocrine activity of thymic epithelial cells, deputed to synthetize and secrete thymic factors.

Such a limitation was mainly linked to the existence on the membrane of both thymocytes and mature T-cells of receptors for different hormones and neurotransmitters,[2–21] and therefore, to the likelihood of a direct "in-vivo" hormonal effect on these cells.

The discovery that some thymic factors are secreted into the blood stream and that the measure of the circulating level of at least one of them, the facteur thymique serique (FTS),[22] more recently called thymulin in its zinc-bound form,[23] strictly reflects the functional activity of the thymus, has offered a new technical approach to evaluate neuroendocrine thymus interaction both in animal and in man.

Thus it has been demonstrated (FIGURE 4) that congenital hypopituitarism, experimental diabetes and thyroidectomy all cause a rapid reduction of plasma level of thymulin, whereas removal of the gonads or of the adrenals does not induce any significant modification. Reconstitution experiments by means of specific substitutive hormonal therapy have demonstrated that the circulating level of thymulin returns to normal levels a few days after the beginning of the hormonal treatment.[13] The short period of time required in order to detect hormonal influences on thymic endocrine activity clearly supports the modulatory nature of the hormonal influence.

Furthermore, the fact that the modifications of thymulin levels precede other hormone-dependent alterations of the thymus, such as size and cellularity, which occur weeks later, suggests that the modulation of thymulin production is one of the earliest events induced by endocrinological manipulation, and makes it likely that the other effects are to a certain extent a consequence of it.

Also in humans, many disendocrinopathies (FIGURE 5) are associated with alterations of circulating thymulin. Thus hypopituitarism[24] due to congenital defect, type 1 diabetes and hypothyroidism[26] following surgical thyroidectomy, are associated with consistent reduction of thymulin level; by contrast, hyperthyroidism, due to diffuse nodular goitre, is associated with high levels of thymulin, particularly evident in old individuals. since at this age the physiological level of thymulin is usually quite low.[25]

In addition, it was recently observed that premature infants, who are characterized by low triiodothyronine (T3) serum level due to peripheral alteration in the T4 to T3 conversion rate (with normal T4 values) also show low thymulin plasma levels, thus suggesting that T3 rather than T4 is responsible for the modulation of the synthesis and/or release of thymulin from the thymus.[26]

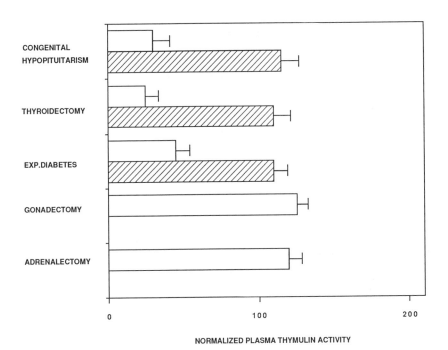

NORMALIZED PLASMA THYMULIN ACTIVITY

FIGURE 4. Reduced plasma thymulin concentrations in different experimental endocrine unbalances (*open columns*) when compared to normal values (age-matched controls = 100) and recovery of physological levels (*dashed columns*) by means of appropriate hormonal therapy.

While these observations definitely confirm that the thymus is under the physiological influence of various signals coming from the neuroendocrine network, the extent of such interactions and the hormone/neurotransmitters involved remain to be established.

These data would not exclude, furthermore, that hormones and neurotransmitters may also act on mature T-cells, as demonstrated by a good body of experimental and clinical evidence, summarized in recent reviews.[21]

INFLUENCE ON THE THYMUS ON THE NEUROENDOCRINE NETWORK

Following the original observation of the pituitary involvement in the postthymectomy wasting disease,[3] studies were undertaken to verify the neuroendocrine alterations caused by the absence and/or removal of the thymus. Part of the work was performed with the use of nude mice (nu/nu), which are characterized by congenital absence of the thymus (for review see REFERENCE 11).

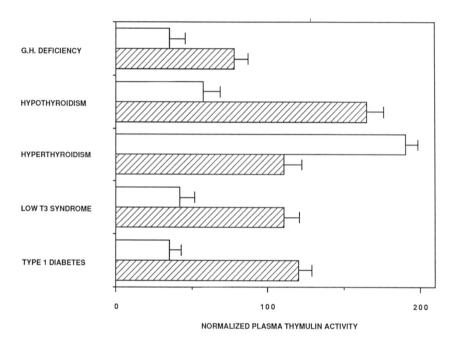

FIGURE 5. Modifications of plasma thymulin concentrations in different human disendocrinopathies (*open columns*) when compared to normal values (age-matched controls = 100) and recovery of physiological levels (*dashed columns*) by means of appropriate therapy.

At hypophyseal level, progressive degranulation of growth hormone and prolactin-producing cells was also observed in thymusless nude mice. Determination of blood levels of pituitary hormones demonstrated a reduction of plasma level of prolactin and an increased level of luteotropic hormone (LH) in thymectomized mice. In neonatally thymectomized rats transitory decrements of ACTH levels and increased blood concentrations of LH were observed.

Transitory signs of thyroid stimulation have been observed in thymectomized guinea pigs and ascribed to pituitary involvement.[32] In nude mice features of hypotrophy of the gland with reduced plasma levels of T3 and T4 have been reported.[27] Unpublished data from our laboratory recently confirmed that even adult thymectomy causes reduction of plasma levels of both T3 and T4 and that a syngeneic neonatal transplant completely recovers such a defect.

Both neonatally thymectomized and nude mice have been reported to show an abnormal histological picture of adrenals accompanied by a transient increase of plasma levels of corticosterone. According to other authors, neonatal thymectomy in rats, on the contrary, induces reduction of corticosterone plasma levels, which, in the presence of the concomitant low levels of ACTH, would suggest an action of the thymus on the adrenals via the hypophysis.

Gonadal function in thymus-deprived animals has been deeply investigated, since it was demonstrated that neonatal thymectomy in hamster had quite different effects according to sex (males undergo wasting diseases, females do not). In mice, thymectomy causes sterility in females, but not in males.[31,35] Further investigations in both thymectomized and athymic nude mice have shown that both thymus-deprived conditions are characterized by a delayed vaginal opening time, with deeper sexual underdevelopment in nude mice than in thymectomized animals.

With regard to the endocrine pancreas very little is presently known. Preliminary experiments in nude mice have shown that while there are no differences in the basal levels of plasma insulin between nude and normal littermates, the insulin-dependent esokinase pattern in the liver is strongly altered in nude animals.

Finally, some physiological reaction induced by the stimulation of beta-adrenergic receptors, such as the increased rate of DNA synthesis in submandibular glands or the increment of total water intake shortly after the injection of isoproterenol, are found greatly reduced in both thymectomized and nude mice, and are restored to normal values by a syngeneic neonatal thymus transplant.[28] Recent data from our laboratory have furthermore demonstrated that the beta-adrenoceptor density in different tissues (submandibular glands, brain) is reduced in thymusless mice, and it can be recovered by syngenic thymus transplant.[28]

With regard to the mechanism of action of the thymus on the neuroendocrine network, both thymic humoral factors or the cellular product of the thymus, *i.e.*, the mature T-lymphocytes, might be involved. The first ones because of their hormone-like nature, the second ones because in given circumstances they may produce lymphokines capable of influencing some pituitary functions[8] or even pituitary-hormone-like substances, such as ACTH, TSH and gamma-endorphins.[10]

The relevance of these products of mature T-cells in the context of the above reported experimental designs can be questioned; firstly, because such products are secreted upon stimulation with specific antigens and therefore might exert only a temporarily limited effect; secondly, because thymus-neuroendocrine interactions are working also in germ-free conditions, where even the background antigenic stimulation is supposed to be nearly absent.

Furthermore, at least with respect to some altered neuroendocrine pattern in thymus-deprived animals, such as IPR response and reduced T3 and T4 plasma levels, no recovery has been achieved when mature lymphocytes have been used instead of neonatal thymus grafts.

A possible role played by thymic factors may, on the contrary, be supported by the following considerations: a) they do not require, in order to act, any specific antigenic stimulation; b) some neuroendocrine abnormalities, such as the degranulation of growth-hormone-producing cells in the pituitary of thymus-deprived mice, can be prevented by injection of thymic extracts;[29] and c) evidence was recently gathered of a direct effect of some thymosins on pituitary cells.[30]

RELEVANCE OF THYMUS-NEUROENDOCRINE INTERACTIONS FOR AGING

With advancing age both the thymic function and the neuroendocrine balance are found altered.

The thymus attains its maximum size at puberty, after which it starts to progressively involute and to be replaced by fat. This process is nearly complete in man by the 5th to 6th decade: the cortical areas are depleted of lymphoid cells and epithelial cells show cystic changes and reduction of intracellular granules.

Measurement of circulating level of thymic factors has demonstrated that in both animal and man, the plasma level of thymulin declines progressively from birth to old age and is virtually undetectable over 60 years of age in man. According to a recent more precise determination of thymulin, which takes into account the interference due to the marginal zinc deficiency present with advancing age,[31] the decline of thymulin levels is less pronounced than that previously reported, and even in very old age a residual significant production of thymulin is observable. The age-associated decline of thymic endocrine activity seems to be one of the major causes for the peripheral immune deterioration observed in old age.[32]

With regard to the neuroendocrine system, a number of age-associated alterations have been documented: reduced activity of hypothalamic neuro-secretory cells; increased hypothalamic threshold level to negative feedback mechanisms; abnormalities in nearly all endocrine glands and in particular in the pituitary-adrenal axis and in thyroid hormone secretion; and reduced peripheral sensitivity to the stimulation of hormones and neurotransmitters.[33]

Since it has been demonstrated that modifications induced by experimental manipulation of the thymus alter the neuroendocrine system and vice-versa, it may also be expected that the physiological decline with advancing age either of the thymus or of the neuroendocrine system may be in part responsible for the alterations observed in the other partner.

With these premises, studies have been undertaken to verify whether experimental functional restoration of some neuroendocrine patterns in old age might recover thymic functional activity and vice-versa.

Thymus Rejuvenation in Old Age by Hormonal Treatment

In mice with advancing age there occurs a progressive alteration of thyroid hormone turnover: both T3 and T4 serum levels decline with age.[12] If old mice are treated with L-thyroxine, their thymus regains the capacity to produce thymulin,[12,13] and such a recovery is followed by a reappearance of a young-like histological picture of the organ, though the size remains somewhat reduced when compared to young thymuses (FIGURE 6). Such a thymic rejuvenation is further supported by the findings that when the thymus from an old thyroxine-treated mouse is transplanted into a young

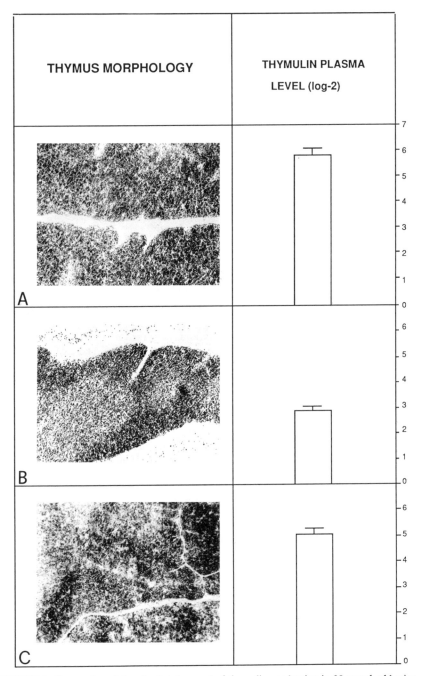

FIGURE 6. Restoration of thymic structure and of thymulin production in 20-month-old mice by 15-day treatment with L-thyroxine. (**A**) Young mouse, (**B**) old mouse, (**C**) old thyroxine-treated mouse.

thymectomized recipient, its capacity to restore thymulin activity in the host is comparable to that of a "young" thymus, whereas thymuses from old untreated mice are much less effective.[13]

The recovery of thymulin secretion in old mice is not a sterile event, since it induces an increased functionality of the peripheral immune system as assessed by the reconstitution of the number of T-lymphocytes and of their responsiveness to mitogen stimulation, which are abnormally low in old mice.[12] The capacity of thyroid hormones to restore thymic function in old age is further supported by the clinical observation that hypertyroidism in old humans is associated with thymic enlargement[34] and with high circulating plasma levels of thymulin comparable to those recorded in young normal individuals.[25]

The major deduction from these findings, i.e., that the age-related thymic involution is not an irreversible process, and that functional recovery can be achieved even in old age, gained further support from recent observations that thymus regrowth can be induced in old age by other endocrine manipulation such as implantation of a growth hormone secreting tumor cell line,[14] or by castration.[15]

Recovery of Age-related Neuroendocrine Unbalance by Neonatal Thymus Grafting

The rationale of this approach is based on the fact that a neonatal thymus, when transplanted into an old organism, maintains its vitality, as measured by thymulin production, at least for 30-50 postgrafting days; afterward, a rapid involution takes place, this phenomenon likely being due to the "old" microenvironment.[13] On this basis, whether such a neonatal thymus graft into old individuals might be able to recover some age-related alterations in the neuroendocrine network has been investigated.

In mice, with advancing age, there occur modifications of the plasma level of some hormones, such as an increased insulin and a decreased T3 level and reduction of the adaptive reaction to beta-adrenergic stimuli,[16] the latter likely being due to a decreased beta-adrenoceptors density on the membrane of different cell lineages.[28] As shown in FIG. 7, all these alterations are fully recovered in old animals by neonatal thymus grafts.[16, 28] Furthermore, a neonatal thymus graft is able to correct also the increased poliploidity present in liver cells as a consequence of aging.[20]

It is of interest to note that the majority of the neuroendocrine alterations taken into consideration in these studies are strictly age-dependent, i.e., they display a linear progression starting early in life. Their interconnection with the thymus, which shows a quite similar age-dependent progression of its deterioration, does not seem, therefore, to be casual, and this consideration adds further support to the idea that the thymic factors are to play the major role in these contexts,[11] rather than the humoral products of T-activated cells, which do not show a similar linear progressive deterioration with age.

CONCLUSIONS AND PERSPECTIVES

The data merging from authors and other research groups stress the following points:

1. The neuroendocrine system influences immune functions and primarily thymus efficiency by modulating its hormonal activity.
2. The thymus interacts with other endocrine glands and may influence body homeostatic mechanisms.
3. Thymus-neuroendocrine interactions work during the entire life of the organism.
4. Neuroendocrine manipulations are able in old age to rejuvenate the thymus, fully recovering its endocrine activity.

Future work should aim to elucidate the intimate mechanisms and to clarify the humoral mediators of these neuroendocrine-thymus interactions.

FUNCTIONAL PARAMETERS

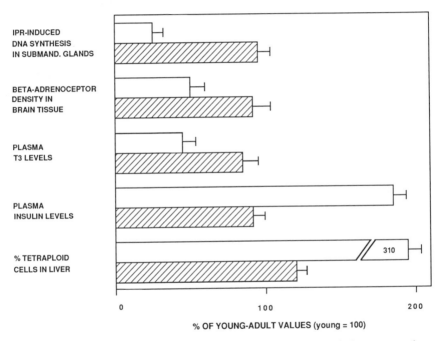

FIGURE 7. Aging associated modifications of different nonimmunological parameters (*open columns*) when compared with the values recorded in young mice (= 100) and their recovery by a neonatal thymus graft performed in old age (*dashed columns*).

ACKNOWLEDGMENTS

We thank Mrs. N. Gasparini, Mr. M. Marcellini and Miss. R. Stecconi for their excellent technical assistance.

REFERENCES

1. FABRIS, N. 1981. Body homeostatic mechanism and aging of the immune system. *In* Immunology and Aging. M. M. B. Kay & I. Makinodan, Eds. 61-78. CRC Press. Boca Raton, FL.
2. FABRIS, N. 1987. Hormones and natural immunity. D. Nelson Ed. Academic Press. New York, NY. In press.
3. PIERPAOLI, W., N. FABRIS & E. SORKIN. 1970. Developmental hormones and immunological maturation. *In* Hormones and the Immune Response. G. E. W. Wolstenholme & J. Knight, Eds. Ciba Study Group No. 36. 126-143. Churchill. London.
4. BESEDOVSKY, H. O., E. SORKIN, M. KELIER & J. MULLER. 1975. Changes in blood hormone levels during the immune response. Proc. Soc. Exp. Biol. Med. 150: 466-502.
5. PIERPAOLI, W., H. G. KOPP & E. BIANCHI. 1976. Interdependence of thymic and neuroendocrine functions in ontogeny. Clin. Exp. Immunol. 24: 501-506.
6. FABRIS, N. 1986. Pathways of neuroendocrine-immune interactions and their impact with aging processes. *In* Immunoregulation in Aging. A. Facchini, J. J. Haaijman & G. Labò, Eds. 117-130. Eurage. Rijswijk, The Netherlands.
7. ZATZ, M. M. & A. L. GOLDSTEIN. 1985. Thymosins, lymphokines, and the immunology of ageing. Gerontology 31: 263-272.
8. DUMONDE, D. 1987. The therapeutic potential of lymphokines in neoplastic disease. This volume.
9. FABRIS, N. 1981. Ontogenetic and phylogenetic aspects of neurendocrine-immune network. Dev. Comp. Immunol. 5: 46-53.
10. BLALOCK, J. E. 1984. The immune system as a sensory organ. J. Immunol. 132: 1067-1070.
11. FABRIS, N. & L. PIANTANELLI. 1982. Thymus-neuroendocrine interactions during development and aging. *In* Hormones and Aging. R. C. Adelman & G. S. Roth, Eds. 167-181. CRC Press. Boca Raton, FL.
12. FABRIS, N., M. MUZZIOLI & E. MOCCHEGIANI. 1982. Recovery of age-dependent immunological deterioration in Balb/c mice by short-term treatment with L-thyroxine. Mech. Ageing Dev. 18: 327-343.
13. FABRIS, N. & E. MOCCHEGIANI. 1985. Endocrine control of thymic serum factor in young-adult and old mice. Cell. Immunol. 91: 325-335.
14. KELLEY, K. W., S. BRIEF, H. J. WESTLY, J. NOVAKOFSKI, P. J. BECHTEL, J. SIMON & E. B. WALKER. 1986. GH3 pituitary adenoma cells can reverse thymic aging in rats. Proc. Natl. Acad. Sci. USA 83: 5663-5667.
15. GREENSTEIN, B. D., F. T. FITZPATRICK, M. D. KENDALL & M. J. WHEELER. 1987. Regeneration of the thymus in old male rats treated with a stable analogue of LHRH. J. Endocrinol. 112: 345-350.
16. PIANTANELLI, L., A. BASSO, M. MUZZIOLI & N. FABRIS. 1978. Thymus-dependent reversibility of physiological and isoproterenol evoked age-related parameters in athymic (nude) and old normal mice. Mech. Ageing Dev. 7: 171-182.
17. FABRIS, N., W. PIERPAOLI & E. SORKIN. 1971. Hormones and the immunological capacity. III. The immunodeficiency diseases of the hypopituitary Snell-Bagg dwarf mouse. Clin. Exp. Immunol. 9: 209-225.
18. FABRIS, N., W. PIERPAOLI & E. SORKIN. 1971. Hormones and the immunological capacity. IV. Restorative effects of developmental hormones or of lymphocytes on the immunodeficiency syndrome of the dwarf mouse. Clin. Exp. Immunol. 9: 227-240.
19. FABRIS, N., W. PIERPAOLI & E. SORKIN. 1972. Lymphocytes, hormones and ageing, Nature 240: 557-559.
20. PIERI, C., C. GIULI, M. DEL MORO & L. PIANTANELLI. 1980. Electron microscopic morphometric analysis of mouse liver. II. Effect of aging and thymus transplantation in old animals. Mech. Aging Dev. 13: 275-280.
21. ONG, M. L., D. G. MALKIN & A. MALKIN. 1986. Alteration of lymphocytes reactivities by thyroid hormones. Int. J. Immunopharmacol. 8: 755-762.
22. BACH, J. F., M. DARDENNE, J. M. PLEAU & A. M. BACH. 1975. Isolation, biochemical characteristic and biological activity of a circulating thymic hormone in the mouse and in the human. Ann. N. Y. Acad. Sci. 249: 186-191.

23. DARDENNE, M., J. M. PLEAU, B. NABAMA, P. LEFANCIER, M. DENIEN, J. CHOAY & J. F. BACH. 1982. Contribution of zinc and other metals to the biological activity of the serum thymic factors. Proc. Natl. Acad. Sci. USA **79**: 5370-5374.

24. FABRIS, N., E. MOCCHEGIANI, M. MUZZIOLI & R. IMBERTI. 1983. Thymus-neuroendocrine network. *In* Immunoregulation. N. Fabris, E. Garaci, J. Hadden & N. A. Mitchison, Eds. Plenum Press. 341-362. New York, NY.

25. FABRIS, N., E. MOCCHEGIANI, S. MARIOTTI, F. PACINI & A. PINCHERA. 1986. Thyroid function modulates thymus endocrine activity. J. Clin. Endocrinol. Metab. **62**: 474-478.

26. FABRIS, N., E. MOCCHEGIANI, S. MARIOTTI, F. PACINI & A. PINCHERA. 1987. Thymulin deficiency and low T-3 syndrome in infants with low-birth-weight syndromes. J. Clin. Endocrinol. Metab. **65**: 247-252.

27. PIERPAOLI, W. & E. SORKIN. 1972. Alteration of adrenal cortex and thyroid in mice with congenital absence of the thymus. Nature New Biol. **238**: 282-286.

28. PIANTANELLI, L., S. GENTILE, P. FATTORETTI & C. VITICCHI. 1985. Thymic regulation of brain cortex beta-adrenoceptors during development and aging. Arch. Gerontol. Geriatr. **4**: 179-185.

29. DESCHAUX, P., B. MASSENGO & R. FONTANGES. 1979. Endocrine interaction of the thymus with the hypophysis, adrenals and testes: effect of two thymic extracts. Thymus **1**: 95-100.

30. GROSSMAN, C. J. 1985. Interactions between the gonadal steroids and the immune system. Science 227-230.

31. FABRIS, N., E. MOCCHEGIANI, L. AMADIO, M. ZANOTTI, F. LICASTRO & C. FRANCESCHI. 1984. Thymic hormone deficiency in normal ageing and Down's syndrome: Is there a primary failure of the thymus? Lancet **1**: 983-986.

32. HIROKAWA, K., J. W. ALBRIGHT & T. MAKINODAN. 1976. Restoration of impaired immune function in aging animals. I. Effect of syngeneic thymus and bone marrow grafts. Clin. Immunol. Immunopathol. **5**: 371-376.

33. MEITES, J., R. GOYA & S. TAKAHASHI. 1987. Why the neuroendocrine system is important in aging processes. Exp. Gerontol. **22**: 1-15.

34. SIMPSON, J. C., E. S. GRAY, W. MICHIE & J. S. BECK. 1975. The influence of preoperative drug treatment on the extent of hyperplasia of the thymus in primary thyrotoxicosis. Clin. Exp. Immunol. **22**: 249-253.

A Pituitary-Thymus Connection during Aging[a]

KEITH W. KELLEY,[b] DONNA R. DAVILA,[b] SUSAN
BRIEF,[b] JOSEPH SIMON,[c] AND SEAN ARKINS [b]

[b] Laboratory of Immunophysiology
Department of Animal Sciences
and
[c] Department of Veterinary Pathobiology
University of Illinois
162 Animal Sciences Laboratory
1207 West Gregory Drive
Urbana, Illinois 61801

INTRINSIC DEFECTS IN LYMPHOID CELLS

Defects in T-cell responses of aged individuals may arise from either intrinsic or extrinsic causes. Historically, immunologists have considered that most of the deficiencies in cellular immune responses of aged individuals are due to intrinsic defects in lymphoid cells. However, the concept that changes in the immune system of aging individuals can be neatly compartmentalized into defects that are intrinsic or extrinsic to the T cell should be re-evaluated. We believe that the emerging concept of the immune system's integration with the neuroendocrine system provides support for extrinsic causes being more important than previously recognized. However, before discussing the role of the endocrine environment in immunosenescence, it is pertinent to briefly review the mechanism of activation of T cells.

A number of theories have been proposed through the years to explain defects in T-cell responses of aged individuals, such as a finite life span of progenitor T cells in the bone marrow, age-related defects in chromosomal integrity or fidelity of transcription. It was once postulated that stem cells were defective in aged subjects, but it is now known that progenitor T cells of old animals possess the capability to develop into functional T cells with a complete antigen receptor repertoire.[1-3] It is clear, however, that there are reductions in the number of precursor helper cells and cytolytic cells,[4] and that this deficiency contributes to the reduction in clonal expansion of T cells from aged subjects.

Since age-associated defects in T-cell responses may involve defects in signal transmission across the plasma membrane, a brief review of some aspects of cellular

[a]This research was supported by grants to Keith W. Kelley from the National Institutes of Health (AG06246-01), the United States Department of Agriculture (86-CRCR-1-2003) and the Moorman Manufacturing Company.

88

activation and its alteration with age is appropriate. The co-recognition of antigen and autologous MHC-encoded proteins by T cells is considered to be mediated by a single T-cell receptor/T3 complex (TCR). Activation of T cells requires the interaction of antigen with antigen-presenting cells and resting T cells in conjunction with the production of at least two cytokines, IL-1 and IL-2. These specific and nonspecific signals act together to produce a rapid expansion of antigen-reactive T cells, culminating in the development of cells with specialized effector functions. T cells can be activated *in vitro* by ligands (*e.g.,* monoclonal antibodies directed against the TCR), plant lectins such as phytohemagglutinin (PHA) and concanavalin A (Con A) or, indirectly, by a combination of phorbol esters and calcium ionophores.

The use of phorbol esters and calcium ionophores has allowed the development of an activation model which postulates that interaction of ligands or lectin with membrane receptors triggers two synergistically acting signal pathways in which the activation of protein kinase C (PKC) and the mobilization of intracellular calcium function as important intermediates.[5] The use of monoclonal antibodies directed against the TCR and of mutant cell lines lacking the TCR complex have shown that a functional TCR complex is essential for both ligand and lectin activation of T cells.[6] Perturbation of the TCR complex thus appears to activate a phosphodiesterase (PDE) which catalyzes the hydrolysis of the membrane phospholipid, phosphatidylinositol 4,5-biphosphate (PIP_2) to inositol triphosphate (IP_3), which functions in mobilizing calcium release from a nonmitochondrial pool, and to 1,2-diacylglycerol, which activates PKC. The increased metabolic and proliferative activity of stimulated lymphocytes is a direct result of PKC activation and calcium mobilization, which has a net effect of enhancing G_0-to-G_1 transition, augmenting expression of IL-2 receptors, augmenting IL-2 production and, ultimately, enhancing the progression from the G_1 to the S phase.

A number of authors have addressed the issue of signal reception and transduction in T cells of aged animals. Miller[7] found that a combination of a calcium ionophore and the PKC activator (PMA) could stimulate proliferation of T cells from aged mice to a degree characteristic of the responses of T cells from young mice that were not treated with these agents, suggesting that an inability to elevate PKC activity and/or calcium after lectin stimulation contributes to the age-associated decline in T-cell activation signals. In support of this finding, Joncourt *et al.*[8] found that intracytoplasmic calcium elevations in old mice were reduced and delayed relative to their younger counterparts, and Kennes *et al.*[9] demonstrated that T cells of aged individuals showed an increased sensitivity to agents that reduced the effective gradient of calcium across the plasma membrane. The reported decreases in synthesis of IL-2 and IL-2 receptors[10] and the resulting decrease in T-cell activation might also arise from defects in nuclear activation,[11] although this explanation is not consistent with the data of Miller.[7]

An intriguing possibility that has not, to our knowledge, been investigated is that the level of transcription of the TCR or of other signal-generating mechanisms across the plasma membrane declines with age. Such an explanation would be consistent with the overall decline in protein synthesis with age[12] and with the observation made by Schwab *et al.*[13] that the proliferative response to monoclonal antibodies directed against the TCR complex was a more sensitive discriminator of donor age than was the response to lectins.

These data would argue that age-related defects in chromosomal integrity of T lymphocytes do not contribute to their inability to proliferate. Based on the findings of Miller[7] and others, we suggest that the primary defect in T cells of aged animals lies between antigen recognition at the cell membrane and activation of PKC activity and elevation of intracellular cytoplasmic free calcium. It is possible that growth hormone and/or prolactin act at this level to partially reverse these intracellular defects. The following sections address the role of the endocrine environment in thymic involution of aged animals. The role is much larger than has been previously appreciated.

THE THYMUS GLAND, T LYMPHOCYTES AND AGING

The thymus gland functions to attract bone-marrow derived pre-thymic stem cells to the gland, to process these progenitor T cells into T lymphocytes through rearrangement of T-cell receptor genes for antigen, and to secrete thymic hormones. The thymus is also involved in the clonal elimination of T cells that react with self-antigens of the major histocompatibility complex. Thymic atrophy during aging is associated with a decline in a number of T-cell responses in peripheral lymphoid tissues. These include proliferative responses to T-cell lectins, antibody synthesis to T-dependent antigens and cytolytic T-cell activity. A number of arguments support the idea that thymic atrophy is involved in, and may be responsible for, the decline in T-cell functions of aged animals:

- Thymic involution, which begins around puberty, preceeds the decline in T-cell functions that occur with age.[14,15]
- The ability of the thymus gland to repopulate T-dependent areas of lymph nodes and to generate mature T cells declines with age.[16,17]
- Syngeneic thymus grafts reconstitute a number of T-dependent immune functions in aged mice.[3,18,19]
- As the thymus involutes during aging, there is an elevated number of peripheral immature T cells in humans.[20]
- Plasma levels of thymulin,[21,22] thymosin-α_1 and the number of thymic medullary cells have been reported to decline with age,[15] although some reports have not shown a change in blood levels of thymic hormones of aged subjects.[23,24]
- Replacement of hormones that are normally secreted by the thymus gland can augment a number of T-dependent immune functions in aged animals (reviewed in REFERENCES 25–26).
- Supplementation with the T-cell-derived hormone, IL-2, reconstitutes a number of immune responses of aged animals both *in vitro* and *in vivo*.[27]

Studies such as these have led to the general concept that thymic atrophy causes the subsequent decline in T-cell responses of aged animals. However, this hypothesis has been difficult to test until recently, since there has not been an experimental model for regenerating autologous thymus glands in aged animals.

THE ENDOCRINE ENVIRONMENT, THYMUS GLAND AND AGING

The pioneering research conducted by Fabris, Pierpaoli and Sorkin in the early 70's with dwarf Snell-Bagg mice offered some of the first evidence that pituitary hormones, particularly growth hormone, thyroid stimulating hormone (acting via thyroxine) and prolactin, can cause growth of the thymus gland, augment T-dependent immune responses[28-30] and extend life span.[31] These efforts not only demonstrated that pituitary hormones could affect the thymus gland, but they also showed that the thymus gland affects a number of hormones from the pituitary gland.[32-34] Denckla[35] and Regelson[36] also summarized many studies which implicated the pituitary gland as a major regulator in a number of physiological changes that occur during aging. Excellent reviews of the early work on pituitary hormones, immune responses and aging, have been written by Fabris.[37,38]

It is now clear that a number of pituitary hormones affect lymphoid cells, and these effects have recently been summarized by Berczi.[39] It also appears that cells of the immune system actually synthesize and secrete classic pituitary hormones, and it has been postulated that the immune system serves a sensory function to recognize infectious agents and communicate this information to the central nervous system by secreting protein hormones.[40,41] For example, we have shown that virus-infected spleen cells express mRNA encoding a large prohormone (proopiomelanocortin) for a number of smaller peptide hormones (REFERENCE 42; reviewed in REFERENCE 43). Activated lymphoid cells also express mRNA for both growth hormone and prolactin,[44] and new results suggest that at least the prolactin mRNA is translated and secreted in a biologically-active moiety.[45] Thymic hormones augment the release of prolactin from transformed pituitary cells,[46] which supports the concept of an active and functional thymic-pituitary axis. Therefore, it is important to understand whether neuroendocrine-immune-system circuits are altered during the aging process, and whether any of these changes are related to the decline in T-cell responses that occurs during senescence.

ENDOCRINE RECONSTITUTION OF THYMIC GROWTH OF AGED ANIMALS

Until recently, it was generally considered impossible to reverse the thymic atrophy that normally occurs during aging. However, recent evidence that is summarized below clearly indicates that thymic aging is a reversible process:

- We have employed an experimental model using cells that secrete pituitary hormones to show that it is possible to reconstitute histologically-normal thymus glands in aged rats.[47,48] Reappearance of thymus glands in aged rats was accompanied by restored proliferative responses of peripheral T cells to lectins and synthesis of IL-2.
- Castration of aged males results in substantial growth of the thymus gland,[49,50] and thymic growth in these castrates can be prevented by administration of

exogenous testosterone.[51] These studies were based on gross thymic morphology, and no functional responses of T cells from these aged castrates have yet been reported.

- Hypophysectomy and supplementation with a hormone cocktail restored thymic growth in middle-aged mice.[52] Thymic growth was associated with augmented proliferative responses of spleen cells to PHA and delayed-type hypersensitivity responses, although there was no change in the capability of mice to synthesize antibodies to a T-dependent antigen.

- An early report demonstrated that thyroxine injections augmented antibody synthesis and thymulin secretion in aged mice,[53] and these findings with thymulin have been confirmed in aged mice[21] and humans.[22] These data support the hypothesis that the decline in thymulin secretion by thymic epithelial cells during aging may be caused by age-associated endocrine imbalances in thyroid hormones.

These combined results clearly show that thymic involution which occurs during aging is a reversible process, and they suggest that changes in the endocrine system that occur during aging may, in fact, lead to atrophy of the thymus gland. These data are important because they offer compelling evidence which argues against the concept that age-associated thymic involution is due to a programmed destruction of thymic precursor cells. It now remains to be determined whether restoration of thymus glands in old rats is the cause of, or, is simply associated with, augmented lectin-induced proliferative responses of spleen cells and enhanced IL-2 synthesis.

SPECIFIC EFFECTS OF GH₃ PITUITARY CELLS IN AGED RATS

In our original report, growth hormone- and prolactin-secreting GH₃ pituitary cells were implanted into 16- and 22-month-old female Wistar-Furth rats.[47] These rats were sacrificed two months later. Although only thymic remnants could be found in control rats, the 18-month-old rats implanted with GH₃ cells had thymus glands that were morphologically and histologically indistinguishable from thymus glands of young rats. Thymic growth also occurred in the 24-month-old rats as evidenced by the appearance of many more cortical thymocytes and fewer fat vacuoles, but the small size of thymic lobules and lack of completely formed trabeculae suggested that thymic restoration was not complete.

We also asked whether T-cell responses of aged rats implanted with GH₃ cells were improved. Results are shown in TABLE 1. There was a 5-fold reduction in T-lymphocyte proliferation by 18 months of age, and negligible PHA-induced proliferation was detected at 24 months of age. However, following implantation of GH₃ cells into 18-month-old rats, T-cell proliferation returned to those levels seen in 3-month-old animals. In very old animals, T-cell responses were significantly augmented to the level of normal 18-month-old rats, but remained below those of the 3-month-old controls. We speculated that this finding was related to the lack of totally restored thymus glands in these very old rats. Similar results were observed when IL-2 synthesis was measured in supernatants of Con A-stimulated spleen cells from 24-month-old animals. Conditioned supernatants derived from aged rats contained very low concentrations of IL-2, but supernatants from GH₃-implanted rats contained significantly more IL-2.

We next asked whether similar results could be obtained by injecting purified growth hormone into aged rats.[54] Aged Fischer 344 female rats (26 months) were injected twice daily with 750 μg of pituitary-derived ovine growth hormone for five weeks. Although morphologic characteristics of the thymus were not altered in these rats, proliferative responses of spleen cells to both Con A and PHA (FIGURE 1) were augmented more than twofold ($p < 0.05$) compared to aged-matched controls injected with saline. Natural killer cell activity was also consistently elevated in aged rats injected with growth hormone, although IL-2 synthesis was unaffected. Furthermore, we found in another experiment[54] that mice transgenic for the rat metallothionein-growth hormone gene have greater numbers of thymic epithelial cells and Hassall's corpuscles and enhanced proliferative responses to sub-optimal doses of lectins than littermate mice that do not carry the exogenous growth hormone gene. These combined data support the postulate that exogenous hormones can augment some T-cell responses, and that the improved T-cell responses observed in GH_3-implanted aged rats were probably caused by growth hormone and/or prolactin that were secreted by the GH_3 cells.

TABLE 1. Role of GH_3 Cells in Stimulating Thymic Growth and T-cell Responses in Aged Rats[40, a]

Rat Age	Thymus Size	PHA-induced Proliferation	IL-2 Production
3 mos	.07%	12,700 cpm	16.0 units
18 mos	not detectable	2,500	not done
18 mos + GH_3	0.05%[b]	13,900[b]	not done
24 mos	not detectable	300	0.4
24 mos + GH_3	0.05%[b]	1,900[c]	6.9[c]

[a] Statistical comparisons made within age groups.
[b] $p < 0.01$.
[c] $p < 0.05$.

Interestingly, distinct improvements in thymic histology were not observed in aged Fischer 344 rats injected with ovine growth hormone. While it remains possible that functional activities of thymus glands in aged rats injected with growth hormone were different from control rats, it is also possible that growth hormone might directly affect lymphoid cells independently of the presence of the thymus gland. To examine this possibility, we implanted GH_3 cells into Rowett nude rats to determine whether hormones secreted by these cells could induce the appearance of functional T cells.[54] Nude rats could not produce antibodies to a T-dependent antigen, proliferate in response to T-cell lectins or synthesize high amounts of IL-2, and GH_3 cells did not affect any of these responses. We interpret these results to indicate that GH_3 cells cannot directly induce maturation of progenitor T cells into functional T cells.

Since nude rodents do not possess mature, functional T cells, it remains possible that pituitary hormones directly affect activities of mature T cells. For instance, both growth hormone and prolactin display a number of immunopotentiating activities (reviewed in REFERENCE 55). Exogenous growth hormone partially reverses thymic atrophy in dwarf, immunodeficient Weimaraner puppies[56] and augments plasma concentrations of the thymic hormone thymulin in normal aged dogs.[57] Snow *et al.*[58] also demonstrated that growth hormone augmented the activity of cytotoxic T cells grown *in vitro,* and Spangelo *et al.*[59] recently found that prolactin augmented lectin-induced proliferative responses of rat splenocytes *in vitro.* We have confirmed these latter results using a serum-free system, in which approximately a 40% elevation in proliferation of spleen cells was observed in response to both PHA and Con A at 10^{-8} ng/ml of either rat growth hormone or rat prolactin (Roza *et al.,* unpublished). These direct effects on proliferative capacity may be mediated through surface receptors for both growth hormone and prolactin on lymphoid cells (reviewed in REFERENCE 55), although the identification of these receptors on lymphoid cells has been somewhat inconsistent. Perhaps the number of hormone receptors on lymphoid cells can be explained by their activation status, similar to the manner in which Con A-stimulated lymphocytes express more glucocorticoid and β-adrenergic receptors than nonstimulated cells.[60]

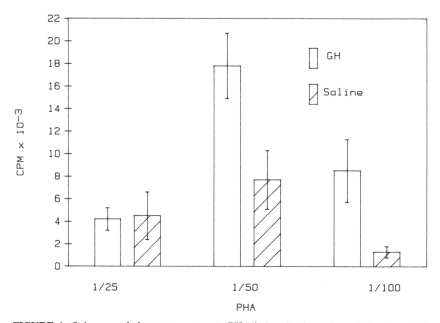

FIGURE 1. Ovine growth hormone augments PHA-induced splenocyte proliferation of 26-month-old rats.[46]

CONCLUSION

Until recently, it was generally considered impossible to reverse the thymic atrophy that normally occurs during aging. One of the central issues in research on aging and immune responses revolves around learning why the thymus gland involutes with advancing age and whether this atrophy is indeed the cause of suppressed T-cell-mediated immune events. In the past, this problem could only be approached by transplanting thymus glands from aged animals into nude or thymectomized, irradiated and bone-marrow-reconstituted syngeneic young recipients and determining the functional status of newly-developed peripheral T cells. Recently, four different systems have been described that permit the regeneration of thymus glands in aged rodents, and all of these systems share the common property of causing perturbations in the endocrine environment. It would appear, therefore, that factors extrinsic to lymphoid cells play a more important role in the decline in T-cell-mediated immunity than has previously been recognized.

SUMMARY

Thymic involution is a normal consequence of aging. It has often been speculated that if this age-associated atrophy of the thymus gland could be prevented, the natural decline that occurs in a number of T-cell-mediated immune responses could be reversed. It has recently become clear that thymic involution can indeed be reversed by altering the hormonal environment of aged animals. These data support the concept of an active and functional pituitary-thymus axis. Since thymic reconstitution can result in restoration of some T-cell responses, it would appear that intrinsic defects which exist in T cells of aged animals can be at least partially reversed. This suggests that the aged environment plays a greater role in the decline of T-cell functions than has been previously recognized. Furthermore, phorbol esters and calcium ionophores can restore suppressed proliferative responses of T cells from aged rodents, so we speculate that intrinsic defects in T cells of aged subjects lie between the recognition system for antigen/lectin and intracellular transmission of this signal.

REFERENCES

1. CHANG, M. & R. M. GORCZYNSKI. 1984. Peripheral (somatic) expansion of the murine cytotoxic T lymphocyte repertoire. I. Analysis of diversity in recognition repertoire of alloreactive T cells derived from the thymus and spleen of adult or aged DBA/2J mice. J. Immunol. **133:** 2375-2380.
2. GORCZYNSKI, R. M. & M. CHANG. 1984. Peripheral (somatic) expansion of the murine cytotoxic T lymphocyte repertoire. II. Comparison of diversity in recognition repertoire of alloreactive T cells in spleen and thymus of young or aged DBA/2J mice transplanted with bone marrow cells from young or aged donors. J. Immunol. **133:** 2381-2389.
3. ASTLE, C. M. & D. E. HARRISON. 1984. Effects of marrow donor and recipient age on immune responses. J. Immunol. **132:** 673-677.
4. MILLER, R. A. & D. E. HARRISON. 1987. Clonal analysis of age-associated changes in T-cell reactivity. *In* Aging and the Immune Response: Cellular and Humoral Aspects. E. A. Goidl, Ed. 1-26. Marcel Dekker, Inc. New York, NY.
5. DROGE, W. 1986. Protein kinase C in T-cell regulation. Immunol. Today **7:** 340-343.
6. WEISS, A., J. IMBODEN, K. HARDY, B. MANGER, C. TERHORST & J. STOBO. 1986. The role of the T3/antigen receptor complex in T cell activation. Annu. Rev. Immunol. **4:** 593-619.
7. MILLER, R. A. 1986. Immunodeficiency of aging: restorative effects of phorbol ester combined with calcium ionophore. J. Immunol. **137:** 805-808.

8. JONCOURT, F., F. BETTENS, F. KRISTENSEN & A. L. DE WECK. 1981. Age-related changes of mitogen responsiveness in different lymphoid organs from outbred NMRI mice. Immunobiology **158:** 439-449.
9. KENNES, B., CL. HUBERT, D. BROHEE & P. NEVE. 1981. Early biochemical events associated with lymphocyte activation ageing. 1. Evidence that Ca^2-dependent processes induced by PHA are impaired. Immunology **43:** 119-126.
10. THOMAN, M. L. & W. O. WEIGLE. 1987. Age-associated changes in the synthesis and function of cytokines. *In* Aging and the Immune Response: Cellular and Humoral Aspects. E. A. Goidl, Ed. 199-223. Marcel Dekker, Inc. New York, NY.
11. GUTOWSKI, J. K., J. B. INNES, M. E. WEKSLER & S. COHEN. 1986. Impaired nuclear responsiveness to cytoplasmic signals in lymphocytes from elderly humans with depressed proliferative responses. J. Clin. Invest. **78:** 40-43.
12. CHEUNG, H. T., J. SHIN TWU & A. RICHARDSON. 1984. Mechanism of the age related decline in lymphocyte proliferation: role of IL-2 production and protein synthesis. Exp. Geront. **18:** 451-460.
13. SCHWAB, R., P. B. HAUSMAN, E. RINNOOY-KAN & M. E. WEKSLER. 1985. Immunological studies of aging: X. Impaired T lymphocytes and normal monocyte response from elderly humans to the mitogenic antibodies OKT3 and Leu4. Immunology **55:** 677-684.
14. HIROKAWA, K. 1977. The thymus and aging. *In* Immunology and Aging. T. Makinodan & E. Yunis, Eds. 51-72. Plenum Press. New York, NY.
15. MAKINODAN, T., M. CHANG, D. C. NORMAN & S. LI. 1987. Vulnerability of the T-cell lineage to aging. *In* Aging and the Immune Response: Cellular and Humoral Aspects. E. A. Goidl. Ed. 27-43. Marcell Dekker, Inc. New York, NY.
16. HIROKAWA, K. & T. MAKINODAN. 1975. Thymic involution: effect on T cell differentiation. J. Immunol. **114:** 1659-1664.
17. HIROKAWA, K., K. SATO & T. MAKINODAN. 1982. Influence of age of thymic grafts on the differentiation of T cells in nude mice. Clin. Immunol. Immunopathol. **24:** 251-262.
18. HIROKAWA, K., J. W. ALBRIGHT & T. MAKINODAN. 1976. Restoration of impaired immune function in aging animals. I. Effect of syngeneic thymus and bone marrow grafts. Clin. Immunol. Immunopathol. **5:** 371-376.
19. HIROKAWA, K., K. SATO & T. MAKINODAN. 1982. Restoration of impaired immune functions in aging animals. V. Long-term immunopotentiating effects of combined young bone marrow and new-born thymus grafts. Clin. Immunol. Immunopathol. **22:** 297-304.
20. HALLGREN, H. M., D. R. JACKOLA & J. J. O'LEARY. 1983. Unusual pattern of surface marker expression on peripheral lymphocytes from aged humans suggestive of a population of less differentiated cells. J. Immunol. **131:** 191-194.
21. FABRIS, N. & E. MOCCHEGIANI. 1985. Endocrine control of thymic serum factor production in young-adult and old mice. Cell. Immunol. **91:** 325-335.
22. FABRIS, N., E. MOCCHEGIANI, S. MARIOTTI, F. PACINI & A. PINCHERA. 1986. Thyroid function modulates thymic endocrine activity. J. Clin. Endocrinol. Metab. **62:** 474-478.
23. ERSHLER, W. B., A. L. MOORE, M. P. HACKER, J. T. NINOMIYA, P. B. NAYLOR & A. L. GOLDSTEIN. 1984. Specific antibody synthesis *in vitro.* II. Age-associated thymosin enhancement of antitetanus antibody synthesis. Immunopharmacology **8:** 69-77.
24. FABRIS, N., E. MOCCHEGIANI, L. AMADIO, M. ZANNOTTI, F. LICASTRO & C. FRANCESCHI. 1984. Thymic hormone deficiency in normal ageing and Down's syndrome: Is there a primary failure of the thymus? Lancet **1:** 983-986.
25. DORIA, G., L. ADORINI & D. FRASCA. 1987. Immunoregulation of antibody responses in aging mice. *In* Aging and the Immune Response: Cellular and Humoral Aspects. E. A. Goidl, Ed. 143-176. Marcel Dekker, Inc. New York, N.Y.
26. HIRAMOTO, R. N., V. K. GHANTA & S. SOONG. 1987. Effect of thymic hormones on immunity and life span. *In* Aging and the Immune Response: Cellular and Humoral Aspects. E. A. Goidl, Ed. 177-198. Marcell Dekker, Inc. New York, NY.
27. THOMAN, M. L. & W. O. WEIGLE. 1987. Age-associated changes in the synthesis and function of cytokines. *In* Aging and the Immune Response: Cellular and Humoral Aspects. E. A. Goidl, Ed. 199-223. Marcel Dekker, Inc. New York, NY.
28. PIERPAOLI, W., C. BARONI, N. FABRIS & E. SORKIN. 1969. Hormones and immunological capacity. II. Reconstitution of antibody production in hormonally deficient mice by somatotrophic hormone, thyrotropic hormone and thyroxin. Immunology **16:** 217-230.

29. FABRIS, N., W. PIERPAOLI & E. SORKIN. 1971. Hormones and the immunological capacity. III. The immunodeficiency diseases of the hypopituitary Snell-Bagg dwarf mouse. Clin. Exp. Immunol. **9:** 209-225.
30. FABRIS, N., W. PIERPAOLI & E. SORKIN. 1971. Hormones and the immunological capacity. IV. Restorative effects of developmental hormones or of lymphocytes on the immunodeficiency syndrome of the dwarf mouse. Clin. Exp. Immunol. **9:** 227-240.
31. FABRIS, N., W. PIERPAOLI & E. SORKIN. 1972. Lymphocytes, hormones and ageing. Nature **240:** 557-559.
32. PIERPAOLI, W. & E. SORKIN. 1967. Relationship between thymus and hypophysis. Nature **215:** 834-837.
33. PIERPAOLI, W., H. G. KOPP & E. BIANCHI. 1976. Interdependence of thymic and neuroendocrine functions in ontogeny. Clin. Exp. Immunol. **24:** 501-506.
34. PIANTANELLI, L., A. BASSO, M. MUZZIOLI & N. FABRIS. 1978. Thymus-dependent reversibility of physiological and isoproterenol evoked age-related parameters in athymic (nude) and old normal mice. Mech. Ageing Dev. **7:** 171-182.
35. DENCKLA, W. D. 1978. Interactions between age and the neuroendocrine and immune systems. Fed. Proc. **37:** 1263-1267.
36. REGELSON, W. 1983. The evidence for pituitary and thyroid control of aging: Is age reversal a myth or reality?! The search for a "death hormone." *In* Intervention in the Aging Process, Part B: Basic Research and Preclinical Screening. 3-52. Alan R. Liss, Inc. New York, NY.
37. FABRIS, N. 1977. Hormones and aging. *In* Immunology and Aging. T. Makinodan & E. Yunis, Eds. 73-89. Plenum Press. New York, NY.
38. FABRIS, N. 1981. Body homeostatic mechanisms and aging of the immune system. *In* Handbook of Immunology and Aging. M. B. Kay & T. Makinodan, Eds. 61-78. CRC Press, Inc. Boca Raton, FL.
39. BERCZI, I. 1986. Immunoregulation by pituitary hormones. *In* Pituitary Function and Immunity. I. Berczi, Ed. 227-240. CRC Press, Inc. Boca Raton, FL.
40. BLALOCK, J. E. 1984. Relationships between neuroendocrine hormones and lymphokines. Lymphokines **9:** 1-13.
41. BLALOCK, J. E. 1984. The immune system as a sensory organ. J. Immunol. **132:** 1067-1070.
42. WESTLY, H. J., A. J. KLEISS, K. W. KELLEY, P. K. Y. WONG & P. H. YUEN. 1986. Newcastle disease virus-infected splenocytes express the proopiomelanocortin gene. J. Exp. Med. **163:** 1589-1594.
43. WESTLY, H. J., A. J. KLEISS, K. W. KELLEY, P. K. Y. WONG & P. H. YUEN. 1987. The postulated lymphoid-adrenal axis: a molecular approach. *In* Neuroimmunomodulation. B. D. Jankovic, B. M. Markovic & N. H. Spector, Eds. 98-103. The New York Academy of Sciences. New York, NY.
44. HIESTAND, P. C., P. MEKLER, R. NORDMANN, A. GRIEDER & C. PERMMONGKOL. 1986. Prolactin as a modulator of lymphocyte resonsiveness provides a possible mechanism of action for cyclosporine. Proc. Natl. Acad. Sci. USA **83:** 2599-2603.
45. MONTGOMERY, D. W., C. F. ZUKOSKI, G. N. SHAH, A. R. BUCKLEY, T. PACHOLCZYK & D. H. RUSSELL. 1987. Concanavalin A-stimulated murine splenocytes produce a factor with prolactin-like bioactivity and immunoreactivity. Biochem. Biophys. Res. Commun. **145:** 692-698.
46. SPANGELO, B. L., N. R. HALL, A. J. DUNN & A. L. GOLDSTEIN. 1987. Thymosin fraction 5 stimulates the release of prolactin from cultured GH_3 cells. Life Sci. **40:** 283-288.
47. KELLEY, K. W., S. BRIEF, H. J. WESTLY, J. NOVAKOFSKI, P. J. BECHTEL, J. SIMON & E. R. WALKER. 1986. GH_3 pituitary adenoma cells can reverse thymic aging in rats. Proc. Natl. Acad. Sci. USA **83:** 5663-5667.
48. KELLEY, K. W., S. BRIEF, H. J. WESTLY, J. NOVAKOFSKI, P. J. BECHTEL, J. SIMON & E. R. WALKER. 1987. Hormonal regulation of the age-associated decline in immune function. *In* Neuroimmunomodulation. B. D. Jankovic, B. M. Markovic & N. H. Spector, Eds. 91-97. The New York Academy of Sciences. New York, NY.
49. GREENSTEIN, B. D., F. T. A. FITZPATRICK, M. D. KENDALL & M. J. WHEELER. 1987. Regeneration of the thymus in old male rats treated with a stable analogue of LHRH. J. Endocrinol. **112:** 345-350.

50. FITZPATRICK, F. T. A. & B. D. GREENSTEIN. 1987. Effects of various steroids on the thymus, spleen, ventral prostate and seminal vesicles in old orchidectomized rats. J. Endocrinol. **113:** 51-55.
51. GREENSTEIN, B. D., F. T. A. FITZPATRICK, I. M. ADCOCK, M. D. KENDALL & M. J. WHEELER. 1986. Reappearance of the thymus in old rats after orchidectomy: inhibition of regeneration by testosterone. J. Endocrinol. **110:** 417-422.
52. HARRISON, D. E., J. R. ARCHER & C. M. ASTLE. 1982. The effect of hypophysectomy on thymic aging in mice. J. Immunol. **129:** 2673-2677.
53. FABRIS, N., M. MUZZIOLI & E. MOCCHEGIANI. 1982. Recovery of age-dependent immunological deterioration in Balb/C mice by short-term treatment with L-thyroxine. Mech. Ageing Dev. **18:** 327-338.
54. DAVILA, D. R., S. BRIEF, J. SIMON, R. E. HAMMER, R. L. BRINSTER & K. W. KELLEY. 1987. Role of growth hormone in regulating T-dependent immune events in aged, nude, and transgenic rodents. J. Neurosci. Res. **18:** 108-116.
55. BERCZI, I. & E. NAGY. 1987. The effect of prolactin and growth hormone on hemolymphopoietic tissue and immune function. *In* Hormones and Immunity. I. Berczi and K. Kovacs, Eds. 145-171. MTP Press. Norwell, MA.
56. ROTH, J. A., M. L. KAEBERLE, R. L. GRIER, J. G. HOPPER, H. E. SPIEGEL & H. A. MCALLISTER. 1984. Improvement in clinical condition and thymus morphologic features associated with growth hormone treatment of immunodeficient dwarf dogs. Am. J. Vet. Res. **45:** 1151-1155.
57. GOFF, B. L., J. A. ROTH, L. H. ARP & G. S. INCEFY. 1987. Growth hormone treatment stimulates thymulin production in aged dogs. Clin. Exp. Immunol. **68:** 580-587.
58. SNOW, E. C., T. L. FELDBUSH & J. A. OAKS. 1981. The effect of growth hormone and insulin upon MLC responses and the generation of cytotoxic lymphocytes. J. Immunol. **126:** 161-164.
59. SPANGELO, B. L., N. R. S. HALL, P. C. ROSS & A. L. GOLDSTEIN. 1987. Stimulation of *in vivo* antibody production and concanavalin-A-induced mouse spleen cell mitogenesis by prolactin. Immunopharmacology. **14:** 11-20.
60. WESTLY, H. J. & K. W. KELLEY. 1987. Down-regulation of glucocorticoid and β-adrenergic receptors on lectin-stimulated splenocytes. Proc. Soc. Exp. Biol. Med. **185:** 211-218.

Cancer and Aging: From the Kinetics of Biological Parameters to the Kinetics of Cancer Incidence and Mortality[a]

LUCIO PIANTANELLI

Center of Biochemistry
Gerontological Research Department
Italian National Research Centers on Aging (INRCA)
Via Birarelli 8
I-60100 Ancona, Italy

INTRODUCTION

Epidemiological data very likely represent the strongest fact supporting the existence of a strict link between cancer and aging. Over one half of all cancer cases in the United States can be found in the elderly population.[1] In spite of the relevance of the problem, there were numerous pitfalls in epidemiological investigation until a few years ago.[1,2] An apparent decrease of cancer incidence in later middle life has been revealed to be a misconception based on lack of sufficient appreciation for changing population size. When this demographic aspect is taken into account, age-specific total cancer incidence continues to rise until old age.

The problems, however, are not yet completely solved. Some authors faced a new important fact which apparently gives rise to new conflicting hypotheses. They postulate a levelling off of the increase of age-specific cancer incidence and mortality at very advanced ages, let's say over about 75-80 for humans, as shown in FIGURE 1. Due to the methods used in collecting data, including autopsy, this pattern cannot be attributed to inaccuracy of observations, performed in both the USA and Sweden.[1,3] From these findings a problem arises, because such a pattern does not seem to be in agreement with biological data, which for the most part suggest strict relationships between cancer and aging processes throughout the whole lifespan, though contradictory results are also present.[4] In addition to the fact that passage of time may allow more chance for expression of carcinogenic stimuli, aging processes lead to changes that may enhance the development of cancer. Findings on DNA repair, antioxidants, and food restrictions give strong support to the idea of a strict link between the two processes.[1] Since it seems correct to state that an aging-associated process should

[a]This paper, written under the auspices of EURAGE, was partly supported by the Ministry of Health, Italian National Research Centers on Aging (INRCA), Progetto finalizzato "Nutrizione e Invecchiamento."

99

increase progressively with aging,[1,5] the slowing-down kinetics of cancer incidence and mortality observed at very advanced ages leads to speculation about the development of some unknown mechanism capable of increasing the resistance to cancer induction in very old subjects.[6]

In this paper it will be shown that the contrast between biological and epidemiological data is only apparent. Although the existence of some alterations which can counteract cancer development cannot be excluded, a more detailed analysis of data,

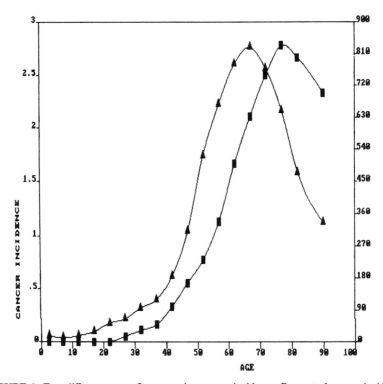

FIGURE 1. Two different ways of representing cancer incidence. Percentual cancer incidence versus age (▲) may lead to the misconception that cancer is a matter of later middle age. When, however, data are expressed as age-specific cancer incidence/100.000 population (■) an increasing trend is observed up to old age. Nevertheless, at very advanced ages this type of representation also shows a slowing down or even a decrease, depending upon the type of tumor considered. Data reported here are drawn from Crawford and Cohen[1] and deal with total cancer incidence.

which also takes into account the statistical distribution of biological parameters in a population, can explain epidemiological and experimental findings on aging and cancer without any contradiction. In this way, a progressively increasing rate of susceptibility to cancer of individual subjects leads to a biphasic pattern of age-specific cancer incidence observed in the whole population. The problem is quite similar to that one occurring in gerontology when attempting to interpret mortality kinetics on the basis of aging processes. In the gerontological field, in 1942 Simms[7] indicated the importance of considering the statistical distribution of the biological parameters in order to understand correctly the relationships between aging processes and mortality kinetics. But only recently was the problem extensively analyzed by Economos[8] who emphasized the necessity of considering the statistical aspects in addition to the biological ones in building models of mortality kinetics. Such kinetics are not fitted by Gompertzian-like models at very advanced ages,[9] where a late slowing down of the rate of mortality has been demonstrated in a great variety of species.[8]

Even more recently, a mathematical model has been developed, linking biological and statistical aspects of aging parameters, and capable of fitting the empirical kinetics of mortality also at very advanced ages.[10] An analogous approach can be followed in relating the kinetics of biological parameters indicative of susceptibility to cancer on the one hand and the kinetics of cancer incidence or mortality on the other. From such an analysis it will be shown that, even at very advanced ages, epidemiological data do not necessarily clash with biological ones in relating cancer and aging on the basis of present knowledge. In the following paragraphs only cancer incidence will be considered, for the sake of simplicity, but similar reasoning and calculations can be performed in treating data on cancer mortality.

BASIC CONCEPTS USED IN BUILDING THE MATHEMATICAL MODEL

The biological and mathematical bases of the model of mortality kinetics used in the present paper have been previously described,[10] and only the very essential points will be given here. Since, however, an improvement of the structure of the model is in progress, some of the relevant modifications already performed will also be described briefly. The model is based on some hypotheses about the function vitality and its statistical distribution in the population under study. The concept of vitality, extensively used by authors who faced such a problem, is usually defined as an index of integrated physiological functions which allow the individual to survive.[8] Mean vitality $\bar{v}(t)$ of the whole population is hypothesized to decrease at an accelerating pace with advancing age, while its statistical distribution is assumed to be normal with a standard deviation $S(t)$ increasing at an accelerating pace. These hypotheses stand on the assumption that the less vitality an individual has, that is, the less efficient he is, the more rapid his further decrease of vitality will be. Moreover, the vitality among the subjects is considered to be spreading out more rapidly when vitality decreases more rapidly and vice versa. Equations 1 and 2 describe this in mathematical terms:

$$\bar{v}(t) = \frac{K_1}{a_2} - \frac{K_3}{a_2} \exp(a_2 t) \qquad (1)$$

$$S(t) = \frac{K_2}{a_2} + \frac{K_3}{a_2} \exp(a_2 t) \qquad (2)$$

A threshold for vitality is put at $v(t) = 0$, that is, individuals are considered alive when their value of vitality $v(t)$ is positive and dead when their $v(t)$ value equals zero. Two points deserve attention in Equation 1. Firstly, the type of kinetics postulated for an individual's vitality is also assumed to be approximately valid for the mean vitality of the overall population. It has to be noted that with advancing age the initial cohort reduces in number as more and more individuals die. This selection leads to the second point. In order to simplify the mathematical structure, $\bar{v}(t)$ is defined as the mean vitality of all subjects both dead and alive. Since, therefore, negative values also contribute to $\bar{v}(t)$, this function does not represent the mean vitality of survivors and cannot be estimated experimentally. Nevertheless, it represents a fundamental step in setting the model and from it the mean vitality of survivors $\bar{v}_s(t)$ can easily be calculated, when necessary.

The kinetics of the biological and statistical aspects of mortality data are simply linked together assuming that for any t, $v(t)$ is normally distributed around its mean $\bar{v}(t)$, as expressed by Equation 3.

$$Z_1(v,t) = \frac{No}{\sqrt{2\pi}\, S(t)} \exp\left(-\frac{(v(t) - \bar{v}(t))^2}{2(S(t))^2}\right) \tag{3}$$

In Equation 3 $\bar{v}(t)$ and $S(t)$ will assume values given by Equation 1 and Equation 2, respectively. Z_1 is the density function of the distribution of $v(t)$ and No is the initial number of individuals of the cohort. Since both $\bar{v}(t)$ and $S(t)$ are functions of age t, Z_1 changes according to vitality v and age t. In order to take into account the experimental findings claiming for finite values of vitality, its distribution has to be truncated at a certain level. This can be accomplished by substracting a function $Z_2(v,t)$ from $Z_1(v,t)$. $Z_2(v,t)$ has the same standard deviation of $Z_1(v,t)$ but a higher mean vitality. The function $Z = Z_1 - Z_2$ will be considered with its actual values when positive, and will be equalled to zero when negative. This procedure reduces the area under the curve Z with respect to that of the original Z_1. This fact can be taken into account by multiplying Z by a corrective factor Fc.

$$Fc = No/\int_0^{v_x(0)} Z(v,t = 0)\, dv \tag{4}$$

where $v_x(0)$ is representative of the higher value of $v(t)$ at the age $t = 0$. The resulting density function describing vitality of living subjects will be:

$$
\begin{array}{ll}
Fc(Z_1 - Z_2) & \text{for } 0 \le v(t) \le v_x(t) \\
Z(v,t) = 0 & \text{for } v(t) < 0 \\
0 & \text{for } v(t) > v_x(t)
\end{array}
\tag{5}
$$

An example of the distribution can be observed in FIGURE 2. The integration of Equation 5 for every t gives the function survivorship $l(t)$:

$$1(t) = \int_0^{v_x(t)} Z(v,t) \, dv \qquad (6)$$

The estimation of the parameters k_i, a_2 entering the function can be performed by nonlinear regression analysis. The model used here has been made to fit mortality data from about sexual maturation to death. An improvement of the model capable also of fitting mortality data at early ages is in progress. In what follows, however, early mortality is not taken into account as it is not relevant to the problem discussed in the present paper.

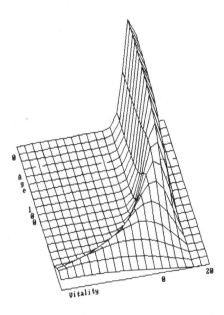

FIGURE 2. Density function of the distribution of a population according to their vitality v and age t. The vitality value $v = 0$ is a threshold for individuals when alive. At any age, distribution of living individuals is given by the surface to the right of vitality value $v = 0$. Data from Witten.[11]

ACCELERATING DECREASE OF INDIVIDUAL VITALITY LEADS TO A SLOWING OF THE INCREASE OF THE MORTALITY RATE AT VERY ADVANCED AGES

An application of the model described above has been made using the same experimental data[11] from which FIGURE 2 was drawn, in order to make comparison easier. An example of the goodness of fitting of function survivorship $1(t)$, as given by Equation 6, is shown in FIGURE 3. The effect of considering statistical distribution of biological parameters in modelling mortality kinetics, however, can better be understood by expressing data as rate of mortality Rm versus age, also shown in FIGURE 3. The slowing down tail of the curve at later ages is the part of the curve that the Gompertzian model cannot fit, as Gompertz's law just assumes for Rm an exponential increase throughout the whole lifespan.

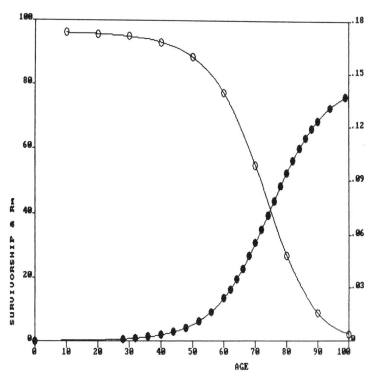

FIGURE 3. An example of the application of the mathematical model to an empirical survivorship curve (0). Data are also expressed as mortality rate Rm (●) in order to show the slowing down at very advanced ages. The mathematical fitting is represented by *solid lines*. Empirical data are drawn from the same source[11] used in FIGURE 2.

It is worth noting that the observed levelling off is obtained though a continuously accelerating decrease for individual vitality has been assumed. FIGURE 4 shows an example of the kinetics of $\bar{v}(t)$, which can be representative of the type of individual vitality kinetics. As mentioned above, the mean vitality $v_s(t)$ of survivors can also easily be estimated given a type of kinetics also shown in FIGURE 4. It can be observed that $\bar{v}_s(t)$ shows a much slower decrease than $\bar{v}(t)$, due to the progressive selection of subjects with higher physiological functions. Comparison of the kinetics of FIGURE 3 and FIGURE 4 gives an idea of the dramatic effect induced on mortality behavior by taking into account the statistical distribution of biological parameters within the population.

APPLICATION OF THE MODEL TO DATA ON CANCER INCIDENCE

Results shown in the previous paragraph allow us to explain, at least in a qualitative way, the slowing down of cancer incidence observed at very advanced ages. It can be due to the progressive positive selection of the population with advancing age. The mathematical model, however, may also be applied directly to empirical data restricted to that part of the population suffering from cancer. In this case the general concept of vitality can be considered as restricted to that of resistance to cancer or, equivalently, inversely correlated to cancer proneness. In this application individual vitality decrease has been assumed to follow the same kinetics hypothesized for the general model. All the other characteristics are assumed to be similar to those considered for general mortality.

An example of fitting is shown in FIGURE 5, where data are presented in a survivorship-like way, the most suitable for entering the mathematical model. The meaning, however, of each point is the number of subjects which do not yet evidentiate any tumors calculated within the group from the general population that will suffer from cancer. The same figure also reports data expressed as rate of cancer incidence versus age within the same population. The fact that incidence rate also shows a slowing down pattern at very advanced ages leads to two considerations at least. First, it confirms the importance of considering statistical distribution of biological param-

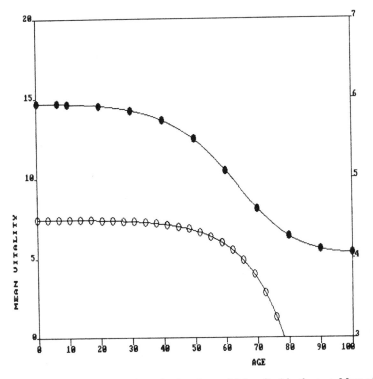

FIGURE 4. Vitality kinetics as estimated using the model described in the text. Mean vitality (O) calculated from the whole population, that is, including all subjects at any age regardless of whether they are dead or alive, gives a rough representation of the type of kinetics assumed for single individuals. Mean vitality of survivors (●), which can be compared to experimental findings, shows a late slowing down, due to the progressive selection of individuals with high levels of physiological functions.

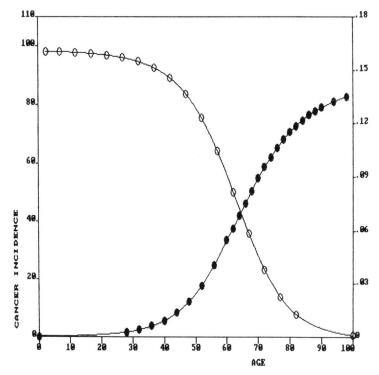

FIGURE 5. Data on total cancer incidence given in FIGURE 1 are expressed in a survivorship-like (O) way in order to enter the model. In this case, however, each value represents the number of subjects that will evidentiate but have not yet evidentiated cancer. Data are also expressed as rate of cancer incidence within the group of cancer patients versus age (●), showing a late slowing down indicative of a selective process within the group.

eters in order to get a correct pattern of cancer incidence or mortality. Moreover, it claims for a significant selective process just within the group of subjects suffering from cancer, in addition to the selection of highly efficient individuals in the whole population. Consequently, the late decrease in age-specific cancer incidence of the type shown in FIGURE 1 may result from both the above-mentioned selective processes. In FIGURE 6 an attempt to describe the pattern of FIGURE 1 from the combined selective effects is shown. As expected, the pattern elicited by the theoretical approach evidentiates a more pronounced effect of selective action exerted at advanced ages. Although given in arbitrary units, a kinetic very similar to that of age-specific cancer incidence shown in FIGURE 1, can easily evidentiated.

On the basis of the data reported here, it seems reasonable to state that epidemiological data do not necessarily clash with biological findings. It has been shown that an accelerating rate of individual cancer proneness is compatible with an accelerating pace of cancer induction throughout most of the lifespan, followed by a slowing down in the very final part at very advanced ages.

DISCUSSION

Many experimental data suggest a strict link between cancer and aging. Relevant processes found altered during aging are also altered in cancer. Changed adaptive responsiveness, altered DNA repair capacity, increased chromosomal aberrations induced by mitogens, and increased karyotypic abnormalities are common characteristics shared by both aged and cancer-bearing organisms. Manipulations capable of causing modulatory effects on aging also influence cancer susceptibility. So dietary intervention such as undernourishment increases the lifespan of different species, and decreases their susceptibility to cancer. Antioxidant treatment reduces the aging rate and neoplasia, also suggesting some common mechanism as regards the basic deleterious steps of the two processes, which could be mediated by free radical insults.[1]

Epidemiological data also contribute to the view of a strong relationship between cancer and aging. Although a detailed analysis of data from different types of cancer in humans and in experimental animals reveals a complex picture which cannot be generalized in a simplistic way,[4,6] a general increasing trend can be elicited in cancer

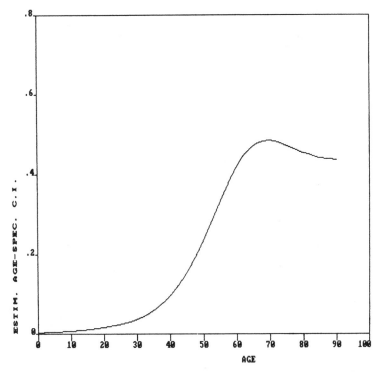

FIGURE 6. The selective action within the group of cancer patients and the general one within the whole population are combined. The estimated pattern, given in arbitrary units, shows a late decreasing pace more pronounced than that of FIGURE 5 and is very similar to the age-specific cancer incidence found for the USA population given in FIGURE 1.

incidence and mortality with advancing age. In the light of the data presented here, the slow down or even the decrease observed at very advanced ages in cancer incidence, is not in contrast to the hypothesis of a strict link between cancer and aging throughout the whole lifespan.[1] For the sake of simplicity, there seems to be no need for hypothesizing unknown mechanisms developing at extreme stages of life capable of enhancing resistance to cancer.[6] Taking into account the statistical distribution of biological parameters among the individuals of a population, the accelerating pace of individual susceptibility to cancer suggested by the link between cancer and aging, can be reconciled with a levelling off of cancer incidence and mortality. As with advancing age subjects are progressively selected for positive characteristics, we may have a population of individuals with high physiological capacities able to better counteract internal and external insults, among which damages favoring cancer induction can be included.[6]

A reasoning like that reported above leads to the suggestion that differences in susceptibility should be preferentially searched for in different genetic backgrounds and/or in the exposure to different environments. This view is in agreement with the "oncogene" model for cancer, which takes into account both genetic and environmental aspects of cancer initiation and promotion. Since various proto-oncogenes and oncogenes encode proteins involved in the regulation of important physiological functions,[12] one can tentatively speculate that altered regulatory mechanisms in aging[13] may facilitate the functional and/or temporal derangement of the mechanisms involved in carcinogenesis. In such a context, particularly intriguing could be the study of those alterations which can be reversed by some manipulations such as the neuro-immunoendocrinological ones.[14,15] Although it cannot be excluded that some alterations may contribute to limit the progression and even initiation of some cancer,[4,6] the late slow down in population cancer incidence could mainly be considered a matter of statistical distribution of biological functions among the subjects.

SUMMARY

Epidemiologic and biological data strongly support the existence of a strict link between cancer and aging. In spite of the relevance of the problem, there were numerous pitfalls in epidemiologic investigation until a few years ago. An apparent decrease of cancer incidence in old age was revealed to be a misconception based on lack of sufficient appreciation for changing population size. But not all problems are solved by using age-specific cancer incidence, as recently stressed by some authors. At very advanced ages a slowing of the rate of increase of age-specific cancer incidence is clearly demonstrated. These findings apparently clash with the majority of biological data and suggest that some mechanism may develop at advanced ages capable of decreasing cancer susceptibility. In this paper, it will be shown that just a slowing-down kinetics is predicted for cancer incidence by using a mathematical model of mortality kinetics recently proposed in the gerontologic field. The slowing of the increasing rate or even a decreasing trend of cancer incidence of an aging population is compatible with a continuously accelerating pace of loss of physiological capacity of the single subjects, as with advancing age there is a selection of individuals with better physiological functions.

ACKNOWLEDGMENTS

We thank A. Antognini for his assistance in data processing and Monica Glebocki and Paola Bolognini, respectively, for kindly reading and preparing the manuscript.

REFERENCES

1. CRAWFORD, J. & H. J. COHEN. 1984. Aging and neoplasia. *In* Annual Review of Gerontology and Geriatrics. C. Eisdorfer, Ed. Vol. 4: 3-32. Springer Publishing Company. New York, NY.
2. OOTA, K. 1980. Indian J. Cancer **17**: 139-147.
3. LUNDBERG, S. & T. BERGE. 1970. Scand. J. Urol. Nephrol. **4**: 93-104.
4. EBBESEN, P. 1984. Mech. Ageing Dev. **25**: 269-283.
5. PONTEN, J. 1977. Abnormal cell growth and aging. *In* Handbook of the Biology of Aging. C. E. Finch & L. Hayflick, Eds. 536-548. Van Nostrand Reinhold Co. New York, NY.
6. MACIEIRA-COELHO, A. 1976. Exp. Gerontol. **21**: 483-495.
7. SIMMS, H. S. 1942. J. Gen. Physiol. **28**: 169-178.
8. ECONOMOS, A. C. 1982. Arch. Gerontol. Geriatr. **1**: 3-27.
9. GOMPERTZ, B. 1825. On the nature of the function expressive of the law of human mortality, and on a new mode of determining the value of life contingencies. Philos. Trans. R. Soc. London, Ser. A 115, 513. Abstract. *In* Abstr. Philos. Trans. R. Soc. London. 252-253.
10. PIANTANELLI, L. 1986. Arch. Gerontol. Geriatr. **5**: 107-118.
11. WITTEN, M. 1986. Mech. Ageing Dev. **33**: 177-190.
12. BISHOP, J. M. 1987. Science **235**: 305-311.
13. PIANTANELLI, L., C. VITICCHI, P. FATTORETTI & A. BASSO. 1986. Arch. Gerontol. Geriatr. **5**: 325-333.
14. PIANTANELLI, L. & N. FABRIS. 1978. Hypopituitary dwarf and athymic nude mice and study of the relationship among thymus, hormones, and aging. *In* Genetic Effects on Aging. D. Harrison & D. Bergsma, Eds. Birth Defects Series. Vol. 14: 315-333. Alan R. Liss, Inc. New York, NY.
15. FABRIS, N. & L. PIANTANELLI. 1982. Thymus neuroendocrine interactions during development and aging. *In* Hormones and Aging. R. C. Adelman & G. S. Roth, Eds. Vol. 1: 167-174. CRC Press. Palm Beach, FL.

Altered Striatal Dopaminergic and Cholinergic Reciprocal Inhibitory Control and Motor Behavioral Decrements in Senescence

J. A. JOSEPH [a] AND G. S. ROTH [b]

[a] *The Armed Forces Radiobiology Research Institute*
Bethesda, Maryland 20814
and
[b] *Gerontology Research Center*
Francis Scott Key Medical Center
Baltimore, Maryland 21044

INTRODUCTION

It is generally accepted that declines in motor performance are a normal consequence of aging. These declines can occur not only because of diseases of one or more of several major physiological systems (*e.g.*, musculoskeletal, endocrine, or cardiovascular), but they can also be the result of primary, superimposed, region-specific, age-related alterations in central neuronal activity. The point in the life span at which these psychomotor difficulties become salient depends upon the particular endeavor in which the person is engaged. Numerous systematic evaluations (*e.g.* REFERENCES 1-8) have indicated that motor performance deficits vary directly with the level of difficulty of the task, with the most demanding task exhibiting the greatest debilitating effects of age. Experiments that have examined the components of these motor declines have utilized tasks that vary the degree to which conventional sensory modalities, such as vision or hearing, are involved. Generally they have indicated that consistent age-related declines are observed in tests which require the person to exhibit balance, strength, coordination and/or sensory-motor integration, such as those which assess the ability to carry out tiring work or to adequately respond on tests of complex reaction time. Complex reaction time is essentially the time needed to both recognize that a signal has occurred and to initiate a previously prepared response. Welford[4] believes that since these reaction times are greater than reflex times (which do not show consistent age-related changes), the deficits may reflect age-related alterations in central processing of afferent and efferent information.

Additional experiments[5-10] have provided evidence indicating that decrements in the ability to maintain balance and control posture lead to increases in the incidence of falls in the elderly. It appears that the decrease in balance control follows a neuronal hierarchy. As they become less stable, the elderly become more dependent upon somatosensory inputs and less dependent on central processing for postural adjust-ments. This may lead them to decrease walking speed and stride length, and restrain their walking in an effort to obtain maximum stability and security. The deficits observed in both sets of these experiments suggest that age-related differences in central information processing may be just as much involved in these decrements in motor behavior as those concerned with peripheral variables such as muscle weakness. In everyday terms, motor behavioral aberrations in the elderly can be translated into losses of independence, since they appear as components of everyday tasks such as driving an automobile or taking an afternoon walk in the park.

The problem becomes one of understanding the basic central processing areas involved in the mediation of motor behavior and examining how neuronal functioning in these areas might change with age. With this understanding, methods might be developed which can: (a) retard these age-related changes or (b) enhance performance in individuals where the changes have already occurred. Since the development of this understanding requires the use of relevant animal models, it is important that possible parallel, age-related changes in motor function be examined in other species besides the human. Fortunately for this line of research there is great deal of evidence to indicate that several species show some strikingly similar age-related declines in motor function to those seen in the human. Both rats and mice, for example, show decrements in performance on several tasks requiring coordinated control of motor and reflexive responses such as suspension time on a horizontal wire[2] or inclined wire mesh screen,[95-97] as well as the length of time that is taken by the animal to traverse a wooden rod or plank.[97]

These studies have not only demonstrated the occurrence of these declines in motor function but have also indicated that alterations in one particular "central processing system" play an important role in these declines. This is the nigrostriatal system. The purposes of the present review are to elaborate upon age-related changes that take place within this system, to show how these changes may lead to a "cascade" of effects which can ultimately effect motor performance, and to demonstrate how ma-nipulations designed to modulate nigrostriatal functioning can have a profound effect upon motor performance.

"CENTRAL PROCESSING" AND THE RELATIONSHIP TO NIGROSTRIATAL DOPAMINERGIC AND CHOLINERGIC FUNCTION

It has been known for a long time that interference with striatal function by any one of several methods can retard motor performance in young animals. Many of these procedures have involved the use of pharmacologic or surgical interventions which alter striatal dopamine (DA) activity. These techniques have included blockade of DA synthesis (alpha methyl p tyrosine[11]), induction of decreases in DA levels (reserpine[12-14]), antagonism of DA receptors with injection of neuroleptics (e.g., chlorpromazine[15]), and chemical (6-hydroxydopamine, 6-OHDA[16,17])ablation of ni-grostriatal fiber bundles. The results from these studies and many others have been to associate the neostriatal dopamine system with motor functions such as muscle tone, postural maintenance, and movement initiation.

More recent studies have expanded our understanding of the role of the neostriatum and have postulated that the striatal dopamine system is important for programming complex behavior patterns associated with feeding,[18] behavioral arousal,[19] and sensory processing.[20] It (the striatal dopamine system) also appears to be important in ordering and sequencing behaviors that are not directed by exteroceptive stimuli.[21,22] For instance, Cools and his associates have shown in two experiments that haloperidol treatment will reduce motor behavior that is directed by internal cues rather then those governed by external stimuli. In the first, cats were trained to walk on a specifically designed treadmill in which they were able to collect food pellets by switching motor patterns with or without looking at the treadmill or a window above the food box. Haloperidol treatment resulted in an increased number of occurrences where the animals were able to utilize the window and treadmill cues to adjust their gait.[21] In the second study,[23] rats were placed in a tank where they had to swim without escape. Their behaviors were divided into those that were exteroceptively directed and those which were nonstimulus directed. Behaviors of the first type included those such as scanning or swimming against or trying to cling to the tank wall, while behaviors of the second category included those such as treading water or swimming in circles. Intrastriatal administration of low doses of (250 ng) haloperidol decreased behaviors of the second type and increased exteroceptive behaviors, while intrastriatal apomorphine (250-300 ng) administration had the opposite effect. Additionally, the haloperidol-treated animals had trouble switching their behavior to that necessary for climbing when an escape rope was introduced into the task. Neither of these agents had any gross effects on motor behavior at these dose levels. Findings from such studies as these suggest that the striatum is an important structure for programming complex motor behavior and for integrating sensory and motor stimuli.

The importance of the nigrostriatum system and motor behavior is also seen when clinical data from persons suffering from diseases of the extrapyramidal motor system such as Parkinson's disease[24] is examined. In this disease there is reduced dopaminergic receptor binding in the putamen,[25,26,61] lowered dopamine levels in the basal ganglia,[27] and cell loss in the substantia nigra.[27] These persons display resting tremor, disturbances of walking gait, and rigidity. These same kinds of motor behavioral aberrations are exhibited by persons who have intravenously self-administered a meperidine analog contaminated with N-methyl-4-phenyl-1,2,3,6-tetrahydropyridine (MPTP),[28] a neurotoxin which selectively destroys DA cells in the substantia nigra.[29,30] In both Parkinson's disease and MPTP poisoning, some alleviation of symptoms can be achieved by enhancing striatal DA levels with L-Dopa.

Some of the symptoms of Parkinson's disease (e.g., tremor) can also be alleviated by inhibiting cholinergic (ACh) activity with muscarinic antagonists such as atropine.[31] Other studies have indicated that administration of centrally active ACh agents can induce Parkinsonian-like tremors, dyskinesias, catalepsy and related motor behavioral disturbances (e.g., REFERENCES 32, 33) suggesting that the striatal ACh system may be inhibitory upon the DA system. The exact nature of this inhibition remains to be specified, but recent evidence indicates that it may involve inhibition of DA-stimulated adenylate cyclase activity[34] or DA autoreceptor function (see below).

The idea that there is a close association between DA and ACh in the striatum stems not only from pharmacological but also from morphological evidence. The nigrostriatum is a very heterogeneous structure which contains a wide range of neurotransmitters which are located on striatal afferent, intrinsic, or efferent neurons.[35] Dopaminergic afferents project onto cholinergic interneurons[35] and depending upon the striatal area under consideration, cholinergic interneurons can either be inhibited[36-38] or excited[39-41] by DA neurons. In the rostral portion of the striatum DA was found to stimulate the function of the cholinergic fibers,[37] while in others, such as the medioventral striatum, DA was found to suppress the activity of the cholinergic interneurons.[42,43] Thus, these findings indicate that depending upon the particular portion of the striatum examined, reciprocal inhibitory control (RIC) may exist between DA and ACh.

Proper striatal functioning may depend upon the precise interplay between these two systems. Any age- or disease-related changes in their relationship could subsequently involve a myriad of other neurotransmitters and neuromodulators and be translated ultimately into motor behavioral deficits. Numerous previous experiments have indicated that in the senescent organism, there are a variety of changes which occur in the function of both of these nigrostriatal neurotransmitters. Morphologically, McGeer and McGeer[44] have reported in the human that of 400,000 nigral DA cells present at birth less than 200,000 survive to age 75. If their regression line is extrapolated, the projected number of cells surviving at age 100 would be 140,000. These numbers may be compared to the 60,000 to 120,000 range reported for Parkinson patients.[45] These changes appear to occur in concert with other alterations in nigrostriatal morphology such as axonal dilations in the nigrostriatal pathways, accumulations of lipofuscin granules, and markedly reduced DA histofluorescence in the pars compacta of the substantia nigra.[46] Pharmacologically, in the striatum, many of the indices of DA functioning appear to be much more species specific. For example, while age-related declines in striatal DA levels are seen with some regularity in the aged human,[47] DA loss is more intrastriatally regionally selective (selective decreases in the caudal striatum[48] or not observed[49] in the aged rodent). Moreover, several experiments have indicated that there are no age-related differences in either K+-evoked ^{3}H DA release or reuptake[50] from rat striatal tissue slices. Endogenous DA release from superfused striatal tissue slices also appears unaffected by aging.[50] Similar findings have also been reported by Rose et al.[51] These investigators used in-vivo electrochemical analyses of striatal DA release from one group of 6 mo., three groups of 24 mo., and one group of 29 mo. old Fischer rats. The results were variable in this study with two groups of the 24 mo. old animals showing no differences in K+-evoked release of striatal DA from that exhibited by 6 mo. animals. However, the third 24 mo. group and 29 mo. group did show significantly lower K+-evoked release of DA when compared to the 6 mo. group. It is unclear why these within age-group differences exist, since the experimental conditions were the same in all the groups. The authors suggest that they may have been slight differences in the rostro-caudal placement of the electrodes in these animals, and since there are regional intrastriatal age-related alterations in several indices of synaptic function (see below), some of the electrodes could have been placed into areas of the striatum which are relatively unaffected by aging. It appears that the data collected using the slice superfusion systems are much less susceptible to these regional variations, since slices are aliquoted from homogenous pools of tissue (see below).

If other aspects of striatal synaptic functioning are considered, variations become even more salient. This is seen in two important DA synthetic enzymes, tyrosine hydroxylase (TH) and dopa decarboxylase (DDC), which show no consistent changes as a function of age. Tyrosine hydroxylase activity in the human shows either no decrease in activity[52] or primary deceases before 20 years of age.[27] At least part of this discrepancy can be accounted for by such factors as post mortem delay and specification of the various age groups. For example, the lack of TH decline in aging men reported by Grote et al.[53] may result from the fact that comparisons were made to a 30-40 year old "young" group. If the major declines occur prior to this age then no differences will be seen between this age group and groups comprised of older aged individuals.

In the rodent, the findings range from those which report significant decreases in

TH activity from 10 months of age (rat[27]), to those which have shown no consistent, significant age-related declines with senescence (mouse; [54,55] rat[56]). In one very elegant study carried out by Strong and his colleagues[56] striata obtained from male rats of three different ages were divided into as many as eight different mediodorsal sections and TH activity was found to be declined in the old group in only one (the caudal) of the regions. All other regions examined showed no consistent age-related declines.

Findings with respect to DDC range from those which show a 66% decline in human[57] to 0% decline in rat[58] and mouse.[54] Since brain DDC occurs in four- to fivefold greater concentrations than brain TH and TH is rate limiting in DA synthesis, alterations in DDC may be less important than other indicators of striatal synaptic functioning which may be changing with age.

One such index that has been studied with respect to striatal aging that appears to be of primary importance in the motor behavioral changes that have been observed involves assessment of the striatal dopamine receptors. These receptors were originally divided into two classes (D_1 and D_2[59]), and subsequent findings indicate that each receptor subtype shows a different pattern of change with age. It appears that while the D_2 receptor shows remarkably consistent age-related declines in concentration (B max), the changes occurring in B max of D_1 are much more variable. In an initial assessment of D_2 receptor loss with age our first report indicated a 35% decline in haloperidol binding with no loss of binding affinity (Kd) in the aged rat.[60] This observation has been repeated numerous times under a variety of experimental conditions in several species, including human,[61] rat,[62] mouse,[63] and rabbit.[64] The actual percentage of decline as a function of age depends upon the assay conditions and the particular dopamine-sensitive ligand that is utilized. Findings from studies using ³H-spiroperidol, for example, which is also selective for the D_2 receptor subtype, indicate consistent decreases in D_2 receptor concentrations of about 36-66% which occur over the life-span of the animal.[60,62]

If age-related changes in B max or Kd of the striatal D_1 receptor (cyclase-linked[59]) are assessed, the results from at least one laboratory show parallel losses between D_1 receptor concentration (but not affinity) (assessed with ³H-piflutixol) and DA-stimulated adenylate cyclase activity that are greatest between 3 and 12 months of age in the rat.[65] However, results from other laboratories using Sprague-Dawley rats[66] or C57BL6 mice[66] indicate no change in striatal D_1 receptor levels throughout the life-span. Examination of post mortem human material indicates an actual increase in D_1 receptors with age.[67] These findings suggest that there are increases in striatal D_1/D_2 receptor ratio in senescence, a finding which has been confirmed in humans[67] and rats.[65]

Since the original division of striatal DA receptors into D_1 and D_2 subtypes,[59] they have been further subdivided into categories based upon the interaction of the receptors with a guanine nucleotide binding regulatory protein (N).[68] The coupling of receptor and N is dissociated by GTP resulting in a low-affinity agonist binding configuration. If agonist binding assays are conducted using agonists such as ³H-N-propylnorapomorphine (³H-PNA), which binds specifically to the high-affinity component of the D_2[69] in the presence of GTP there will be fewer sites in the high affinity and agonist displacement curves will be shifted to the right.[70] Using this technique, Severson and his associates[71] have determined that while there were no age differences in the ability of guanine nucleotides to decrease ³H-PNA binding as a function of age, there were fewer ³H-PNA binding sites in striatal membranes from aged mice. Further determinations indicated the percent of D_2 receptors in the high-affinity state was significantly less in the 12 and 24 mo. groups than in the 3 mo. group.[71] Thus, there appear to be shifts in the proportion of high- to low-affinity striatal D_2 sites as a function of aging which occur in concert with the decrease of D_2 sites.[71] Similarly, assessments of D_1 receptor changes with age using ^{3}H-2-amino-6,7 dihydroxy 1,2,3,4 tetrahydronapthalene (^{3}H-ADTN) which, under certain assay conditions, binds to the high-affinity form of this receptor,[70] have indicated that the age-related loss in density of this form of the receptor may be greater than 50%.[64]

It would appear, then, that there are some significant changes in striatal DA receptors in aging including alterations in striatal DA receptor number, in the ratio of high- to low-affinity agonist binding, and in the D_1/D_2 ratio. There also are some indications that the biosynthetic rates of both D_1[72] and D_2 receptor[72,73] subtypes show declines in animals beginning at about 12 months of age.[73]

Just as was seen with respect to striatal DA function and aging, the findings with respect to ACh tend to vary when synaptic functions concerned with synthesis, content and catabolism are examined. ACh is synthesized from choline (taken up from pre-synaptic terminals) and acetyl coenzyme A (synthesized in the mitochondria). The reaction is catalyzed by choline acetyltransferase (ChAT). Both choline and ChAT have been used as indices for ACh function in the striatum, and the results have generally been equivocal. For example, significant decreases have been reported in ChAT activity in the rodent[48,74,75,79] striatum by some investigators. Others have reported no change.[76,77,78] One reason for these disparate findings seems to be that, just as was seen for striatal DA, there appears to be regional specificity for the distribution of ChAT within the striatum. It is highest in the rostral relative to the caudal neostriatum, and age-related decreases occur primarily in the caudal regions. Therefore, differences in the precise area of the striatum utilized for dissection by these various studies could account for the variability of these effects.[48]

Since ACh is activated by acetylcholinesterase (AChE), it has also been used to study ACh function in aging with results that are even more contradictory than those for ChAT or choline. Various studies have indicated that declines in AChE range from 0% to 36% in the rodent[77] and less than 20% in the human.[80]

Direct measurement of striatal ACh levels in aging has not been possible until very recently, but here again the results have not been very clear. However, if cholinergic receptor binding is considered, there is better general agreement that there are decreases in the number of binding sites in the striatum as a function of age in the rodent. Using the ligand, ^{3}H (-) [^{3}H]-quinuclidinyl benzilate (^{3}H-QNB), these studies have generally indicated changes in concentration of about 25-29% in the rodent.[77,56] The distribution of these receptors within the striatum was similar to that seen for the D_2 receptors, being highest in the rostral region and lowest in the caudal portion of the striatum. ACh receptors were lost, as a function of age, primarily from medial and caudal portions of the striatum.[56]

Besides these age-related, intraregional losses in ^{3}H-QNB binding, there is some evidence from an extrastriatal brain area (hippocampus) that there are conformational changes in the muscarinic ACh receptors that remain. In hippocampal tissue from young rats oxotremorine inhibits ^{3}H-QNB binding in accordance with mass action (i.e., Hill coefficients approach one[81]). However, beginning with middle age, the binding curves for oxotremorine inhibition of ^{3}H-QNB binding deviate significantly from a simple binding isotherm and produce Hill coefficients less than one. Such results suggest that there is much more muscarinic receptor heterogeneity in the older animals, with a greater number of receptors being in desensitized conformational/orientational states.[82] Muscarinic ACh receptors in these desensitized states would be decoupled from their respective effectors and would be less able to support synaptic responses. For example, recent electrophysiological[82] evidence indicates that the responsiveness of hippocampal ACh neurons to the iontophoretic application of muscarinic agonists such as oxotremorine is blunted in aged animals. Other studies have indicated that scopolamine-induced locomotor activity was reduced.[83] Thus, in the case of the muscarinic ACh receptors it may not be just the lowered receptor number in the aged animal that is involved in motor behavioral deficits but also the responsivity of the remaining receptors.

ALTERED STRIATAL CHOLINERGIC-DOPAMINERGIC INTERACTIONS IN SENESCENCE

In the previous section, we attempted to outline briefly the changes in indices of synaptic function that occur in striatal dopamine and acetylcholine as a function of age. For the purposes of clarity, these changes were presented separately for each system; but, as alluded to above, there is evidence to suggest that there is a great deal of interactive modulation that takes place between these systems. Recent studies have shown that striatal DA-stimulated adenylate cyclase activity is inhibited by muscarinic agonists such as oxotremorine,[34] and that DA agonists such as apomorphine can inhibit the release of ACh from the striatum.[84] However, extensions of these experiments carried out in our laboratory have indicated that both of these parameters may be altered in senescence. When oxotremorine and carbachol were used to inhibit DA-stimulated adenylate cyclase activity from striatal broken cell preparations in young, middle-aged and old animals, these agents were only shown to be effective in young and middle-aged animals (e.g., 100 μM oxo inhibited DA-stimulated adenylate cyclase in both groups by 30%) but not in old (0%).

Additional assessments carried out to examine DA modulation of ^{3}H-ACh release from striatal slices from mature, middle-aged, and senescent rats indicated that apomorphine inhibited K+-evoked release from mature and middle-aged animals (35% in each) but not in old (0%).

These findings, when considered in light of those discussed above indicate, that as receptors from both of these transmitter systems are lost with age, alterations in one may profoundly affect the functioning of the other. RIC (reciprocal inhibitory control) that is normally exerted between these two systems is significantly diminished. This seems to be true even if there is not necessarily an age-related decline in some portions of the two systems. To elaborate, findings were discussed above that indicated that there were no age-related differences in K+-evoked DA release from superfused striatal tissue slices. This release is under the control of a group of striatal D_2 receptors[85] known as autoreceptors.[86] If these autoreceptors are inhibited or enhanced K+-evoked release of DA will be respectively enhanced or inhibited.[87,88] Normally, this control is mediated through striatal presynaptic cholinergic heteroreceptors[89] presumably located on the same terminals as the autoreceptors.[90] This control may be exerted on the autoreceptor as a result of TH modulation of DA synthesis.[91]

Age-related changes in this control were investigated in a recent set of experiments in which striatal tissue slices obtained from mature (6 mo.), middle-aged (12 and 18 mo.), and senescent (24 mo.) Wistar rats superfused initially with a modified Krebs-Ringer basal (containing, among other components, 2.5 mM KCl) release medium and later with a "Hi KCl" (Krebs-Ringer solution containing 30 mM KCl) medium. To this Hi CKl medium was added one of four concentrations (0 μM, 100 μM, 500 μM, and 1 mM) of one of four muscarinic agonists (i.e., oxotremorine, carbachol, pilocarpine and bethanecol). DA release was assessed in 5 minute fractions taken during depolarization with Hi KCl using high performance liquid chromatography coupled to electrochemical detection. Just as we reported previously,[50] no age-related differences were seen in the striatal tissue obtained from the various groups of animals in K+-evoked release of DA without muscarinic enhancement (e.g., mean DA release for all experiments, 6 mo. = 40.51 + 7.20 p moles DA/mg protein, 24 mo. 46.06 + p moles). In the presence of the muscarinic agonists, however, there were selective, significant decreases in enhancement of KCl-induced release of DA as a function of age. These deficits were dependent upon the particular agonist that was used to enhance the release. Peak enhancement of DA release was higher in striata from 6 and 12 mo. groups than those from 18 and 24 mo. groups when oxotremorine or pilocarpine was applied to the tissue (e.g., oxotremorine peak enhancement between 0 and 1 mM concentrations 6 mo. 269 + 17%, 12 mo. 208 + 20%, 18 mo. 176 + 15%, and 24 mo. 0 + 5%). When either bethanecol or carbachol was used to enhance K+-evoked DA release, age-related decrements appeared as early as 12 mo. (e.g., carbachol peak enhancement 6 mo. 191 + 22%, 12-24 mo. 0-20 + 19%).

We believe that these deficits in ACh control of DA autoreceptor function lie primarily with the muscarinic cholinergic portion of this interaction for two reasons. (a) Neither the addition of haloperidol (which directly inhibits DA autoreceptors) nor the addition of nicotine to striatal slices from young and old animals revealed any age-related differences in the enhancement of K+-evoked release of DA. (b) The muscarinic agonists employed here were separated previously into two classes based on their ability to stimulate phosphoinositide turnover. Class A agonists, such as carbachol, maximally stimulate phosphoinositide and inositol lipids from hippocampus and cortex, while Class B agonists such as oxotremorine and pilocarpine only poorly stimulate this turnover. It is believed that Class A agonists such as carbachol can alter the microenvironment of the muscarinic receptor allowing a change in the conformation/orientation of the receptor to a desensitized, decoupled (from the effector) state.[92] As indicated in the previous section more receptors appear to be in such decoupled states in old animals; so, if a Class A agonist is applied with desensitizes an even greater number of them deficits should be seen earlier in the life span. Age effects should be seen later in the life span if Class B agonists are employed, since these agents do not further desensitize the receptors. The pattern of effects among the various muscarinic agonists employed here reflects these A-B differences.

ALTERATIONS IN STRIATAL DA-RECEPTOR DENSITY AND IMPROVEMENTS IN MOTOR PERFORMANCE

It is surprising from the data concerning the alterations in nigrostriatal DA receptors presented in the previous sections that their biosynthetic mechanisms, although reduced in senescence, continue to retain these capabilities. If these biosynthetic mechanisms are accessed, striatal functioning might be enhanced and motor performance deficits subsequently reduced. In one of the early observations[60] we found that although there were age differences in amphetamine-induced rotational behavior in rats unilaterally lesioned in the substantia nigra, no differences were seen with respect to apomorphine-induced rotation. It had been shown previously that after lesioning, the denervated striatal DA receptors proliferate,[93] and agonists, such as apomorphine, would have a greater effect on the "up-regulated" dopamine receptors in the lesioned striatum, resulting in increased contralateral (to the lesion) turning. Since no age-related differences in contralateral turning were seen, these findings suggested that increases in striatal DA receptor density could still occur in the striata from the old animals and that these striata had retained their "plastic" capabilities. Subsequent biochemical analyses indicated that both ^{3}H-spiroperidol binding and DA-stimulated adenylate cyclase activity were higher in the lesioned striata than in the nonlesioned striata irrespective of age or sex.[94]

In an effort to further explore the generality of the "up-regulation effect" to other types of motor tasks (e.g., inclined screen performance, wire suspension,[95,96] etc.) behavior was examined in young, middle-aged, and old mice by inducing striatal DA receptor up-regulation via chronic haloperidol administration and withdrawal.[97] The results indicated that haloperidol-treated animals of all age groups showed better performance than those that were given chronic vehicle treatment.

These findings were replicated in a later experiment[98] in which chronic prolactin (which had been shown previously to up-regulate striatal DA receptors) was administered to senescent animals. These animals improved on tests such as the inclined screen and rod walking tasks beginning 4-6 days after the pumps were implanted, and behavior declined within 2 weeks after the pumps were withdrawn. The induction of the behavioral improvements coincided with the increases in ^{3}H-spiroperidol binding.[99] Tests in other groups of animals chronically treated with prolactin showed enhanced rotational behavior to intrastriatally administered DA.[100]

Although there were some previous reports in which prolactin was administered directly,[101] indirectly stimulated via domperidone,[102] or stimulated through the implantation of prolactin secreting pituitary tumors,[103] which have not shown increases in striatal ^{3}H-spiperone binding, these studies only examined prolactin effects in young animals. We have shown that the prolactin effect is even greater in old animals (37% increase in ^{3}H-spiperone binding) than in young (15-20%[99]). It could be that some of these changes were missed in studies where old animals were not examined. It is also possible that if there is an overstimulation of prolactin production, such as might be expected following the implantation of a prolactin secreting tumor, the effect is reversed. At the dose of prolactin which we employed, increased blood levels of prolactin were undetectable.

In addition to inducing increases in receptor density to enhance motor performance, we have employed one rather interesting method to retard the loss of striatal DA receptors and alter the age-related progressive deterioration of these behaviors. This method involves the use of dietary restriction. It has been known for a long time that if rats receive food only on alternate days (EOD) from the time that they are weaned, life span is extended by 40% (see REFERENCE 104). Recent evidence indicates that striatal DA receptor concentrations as measured by both ^{3}H-ADTN and specific ^{3}H-spiroperidol binding are maintained at young levels well into middle age before declining and that 24 mo. old EOD animals have striatal DA receptor compliments which are equivalent to that of a 12 mon. old ad-lib fed animal.[105] When rotational behavior was examined in these 24 mo. old EOD animals, it was found to be comparable to that of young animals.[106]

Taken together, the data from all of these techniques which induce striatal DA receptor up-regulation suggest a critical role for these receptors in the mediation of motor function in senescence. Additionally, it might be postulated from these findings, and those above, that there may be a critical concentration range for striatal DA receptors. If the receptor number is lowered via age, it could lead to decreased motor performance. Conversely, increasing the concentration of DA receptors by a variety of methods results in improved motor performance on a variety of tasks.

While the effects of specific cholinergic receptor up-regulation on motor behavior remains to be determined, it appears that the "striatal DA receptor-motor behavioral link" may be stronger in old animals than it is in young. In a recent experiment,[107] both old and young animals were treated with the irreversible DA receptor antagonist N-ethoxycarbonyl-2-ethoxy-1,2-dihydroquinoline (EEDQ) and tested at various times on the inclined screen. The results indicated that although young animals had returned to pre-EEDQ levels of performance at 48 hrs. post-EEDQ, their striatal DA receptor concentrations were only at 40% of control for both the D_1 and D_2 receptor subtypes. Old animals did not reach pre-EEDQ levels of inclined screen performance even when tested at 192 hrs. post-EEDQ (45% of control) even though their striatal DA receptor concentrations were closer to pre-EEDQ levels than those in the young animals (90% and 60% of control for the D_1 and D_2 receptor subtypes, respectively). Thus, in young animals the return of pre-EEDQ levels of performance is, to some extent independent of the recovery of pre-EEDQ concentrations of striatal DA receptors, and subsequent attempts to compromise inclined performance in young animals by treating them at 48 hrs. post-EEDQ with spiroperidol (2 mg/kg) have been unsuccessful.

These findings suggest that when striatal function is compromised in young animals, they are able to utilize other control mechanisms, possibly extrastriatal, in their behavioral recovery that are unavailable to old animals. One of these areas may be the cerebellum. It has been shown in a number of studies that cerebellar function is morphologically altered and physiologically comprised in senescence. Hence, the old animal is probably less able to utilize cerebellar mediation in its post-EEDQ recovery than is the young animal and must rely more heavily on the return of pre-EEDQ levels of striatal DA functioning for its recovery. Unfortunately, because of the non-specific nature of some of these up- and down-regulation procedures used to alter striatal DA function, it is difficult, at this point, to specify which DA-receptor subtype may be most critical in the regulation of these types of motor tasks. But evidence from three sources suggests that it might be the D_2 receptor subtype. (a) There is a more progressive age-related change in the concentration of this striatal DA receptor subtype than in that of the D_1, cyclase-linked receptors. (b) Historically, there is a well-established link between D_2 receptor function and motor performance.[108] (c) In ongoing experiments from this laboratory, only D_2 receptor blockade via 2 mg/kg spiperone has been found to be effective in disrupting inclined screen performance. Doses of the D_1 antagonist SCH 23390 as high as 3 mg/kg were found to be ineffective in disrupting performance.

In this regard, however, there are some recent reports which have shown that the D_1 receptors have a role in the mediation of rotational behaviors.[109] Therefore, the exact specification of the role of each of these receptor subtypes in mediating age changes in motor function awaits further research. But it is clear that future efforts, which are directed toward the further delineation of the mechanisms involved in striatal dopaminergic-cholinergic interactions and the design of methodologies which can take advantage of the "plastic capabilities" of striatal receptors, might enable us to forestall or reduce some of the motor behavioral deficits seen in senescence.

REFERENCES

1. BARTUS, R. T. 1979. *In* Aging. Vol. 10. Sensory Systems and Communications in the Elderly. J. M. Ordy, Ed. 35-73. Raven Press. New York, NY.
2. WALLACE, J. E., E. KRAUTER & B. A. CAMPBELL. 1980. J. Gerontol. **35:** 364-370.

3. WELFORD, A. T. 1982. *In* The Aging Motor System. J. A. Mortimer, F. J. Pirozzolo & G. J. Maletta, Eds. 159-188. Praeger Publishers. New York, NY.
4. WELFORD, A. T. 1977. *In* Handbook of the Psychology of Aging. J. E. Birren & K. W. Schaie, Eds. 450-497. Van Nostrand Reinhold Co. New York, NY.
5. HASSELKUS, B. R. & G. M. SHAMBES. 1975. J. Gerontol. **30:** 661-667.
6. SHELDON, J. H. 1963. Gerontol. Clin. **5:** 129-138.
7. WOOLLACOTT, M. H., A. SHUMWAY-COOK & L. NASHNER. 1982. Ibid; 3.
8. MURRAY, M. P., R. C. KORY & B. T. CLARKSON. 1969. J. Gerontol. **24:** 169-178.
9. MCFARLAND, R. A., G. S. TUNE & A. T. WELFORD. 1964. J. Gerontol. **19:** 190-197.
10. RIFFLE, K. 1982. Geriatric Nursing. May-June: 165-169.
11. RECH, R. H., H. K. BORYS & K. E. MOORE. 1966. Exp. Ther. **153:** 412-419.
12. BLASCHKO, H. & T. L. CHRUSCIEL. 1960. J. Physiol. **151:** 272-284.
13. CARLSSON, A., A. LINDQUIST & T. MAGNUSSON. 1957. Nature **180:** 1200.
14. SMITH, C. B. & P. B. DEWS. 1962. Psychopharmacology **3:** 55-59.
15. CARP, J. S. & R. J. ANDERSON. 1979. Pharmacol. Biochem. Behav. **10:** 513-520.
16. MARSHALL, J. F. 1979. Brain Res. **17:** 311-324.
17. KOZLOWSKI, M. R. & J. F. MARSHALL. 1981. Exp. Neurol. **74:** 318-323.
18. UNGERSTEDT, U. 1971. Acta Physiol. Scand. (Suppl.) **367:** 1-48.
19. MARSHALL, J., D. LEVITAN & E. STRIKER. 1980. J. Comp. Physiol. Psychol. **90:** 536-546.
20. MARSHALL, J., N. BERRIOS & S. SAWYER. 1980. J. Comp. Physiol. Psychol. **94:** 833-846.
21. JASPERS, R., M. SCHWARZ, K. H. SONTAG & A. R. COOLS. 1984. Brain Behav. Res. **14:** 17-28.
22. COOLS, A. R. 1980. Behav. Brain Res. **1:** 361-378.
23. VRIJMOED-DE VRIES, M. C. & A. R. COOLS. 1986. Brain Res. **364:** 77-90.
24. BERNHEIMER, H. W., O. BIRKMAYER, K. HORNYKIEWICZ, K. JELLINGER & F. J. SEITELBERGER. 1973. J. Neurol. Sci. **20:** 415-455.
25. REISINE, T. D., J. Z. FIELDS & H. I. YAMAMURA. 1977. Life Sci. **21:** 335-345.
26. LEE, T., P. SEEMAN, A. RAJPUT & I. J. FARLEY. 1978. Nature **273:** 59-61.
27. MCGEER, P. L. & E. G. MCGEER. 1978. *In* Parkinson's Disease II. Aging and Neuroendocrine Relationships. C. E. Finch, D. E. Potter & A. D. Kennny, Eds. 41-57. Plenum Press. New York, NY.
28. LANGSTON, J. W., P. BALLARD, J. W. TETRUD & I. IRWIN. 1983. Science **219:** 979-980.
29. HEIKKILLA, R. E., A. HESS & R. C. DUVOISIN. 1984. Science **224:** 1451-1453.
30. HALLMAN, H., J. LANGE, L. OLSON, I. SHOMBER & G. JANSON. 1985. J. Neurochem. **44:** 117-127.
31. STERN, G. M. 1980. *In* Parkinson's Disease—Current Progress, Problems and Management. U. K. Rinne, M. Klinger & B. Stamm, Eds. 357-361. Elsevier/North Holland Biomedical Press. Amsterdam.
32. DE FEUDIS, F. 1974. Central Cholinergic Systems & Behavior. Academic Press. New York, NY.
33. COSTALL, B. & R. J. NAYLOR. 1973. Arzneim.-Forsch. **23:** 67-683.
34. OLINAS, M. C., P. ONALI, N. H. NEFF & E. COSTA. 1983. Mol. Pharmacol. **23:** 383-398.
35. GRAYBIEL, A. M. & C. W. RAGSDALE, JR. 1979. *In* Development and Chemical Specificity of Neurons, Progress In Brain Research. Vol. 51. M. Cuenod, G. W. Kruetzberg & F. E. Bloom, Eds. 239-283 Elsevier. Amsterdam.
36. BARTHOLINI, G. 1980. Trends Neurol. Sci. 138-140.
37. SCHEEL-KRUGER, J. 1985. *In* Central Cholinergic Mechanisms and Adaptive Dysfunctions. M. M. M. Singh, H. Luy & I. H. Warburton, Eds. 105-140. Plenum Press. New York, NY.
38. STOOF, J. C., R. E. THIEME, M. C. VRIJMOED-DE VRIES & A. H. MULDER. 1979. Naunyn-Schmiedeberg's Arch. Pharmacol. **309:** 119-124.
39. COOLS, A. R., G. HENDRIKS & L. KORTEN. 1975. J. Neural. Trans. **36:** 91-105.
40. HOWARD, S. G. & E. GARCIA-RILL. 1983. Brain Res. Bull. **10:** 437-440.
41. WESTERMANN, K. H. 1981. Pharmacol. Biochem. Behav. **15:** 687-690.
42. BECKSTEAD, R. M., V. B. DOMESICK & W. J. H. NAUTA. 1979. Brain Res. **175:** 191-217.
43. FALLON, J. H. & R. Y. MOOE. 1978. J. Comp. Neurol. **180:** 545-580.
44. MCGEER, P. L., E. G. MCGEER & J. S. SUZUKI. 1977. Arch. Neurol. **34:** 33-35.

45. MORTIMER, J. A. & D. D. WEBSTER. 1982. Ibid; 3.
46. MCNEILL, T. H., L. I. KOEK & J. W. HAYCOCK. 1984. Mech. Aging Dev. 24: 293-307.
47. CARLSSON, A. & B. WINBLAD. 1976. J. Neural. Trans. 38: 271-276.
48. STRONG, R., T. SAMORAJSKI & Z. GOTTESFELD. 1982. J. Neurochem. 39: 831-836.
49. PAPAVASILIOU, P. S., S. T. MILLER, L. J. THAL, L. J. NERDER, G. HOULIHAN, S. N. RAO & J. M. STEVENS. 1981. Life Sci. 28: 2947-2952.
50. THOMPSON, J. M., J. WHITAKER & J. A. JOSEPH. 1981. Brain Res. 224: 436-440.
51. ROSE, G. M., G. A. GERHARDT, G. L. CONBOY & B. J. HOFFER. 1986. Neurobiol. Aging 7: 77-83.
52. ROBINSON, D. S., R. L. SOURKES, A. NIES, L. S. HARRIS, S. SPECTOR, D. L. BARTLETT & I. S. KAYE. 1977. Arch. Gen. Psychiatry 34: 89-92.
53. GROTE, S. S., S. G. MOSES, E. ROBINS, R. W. HUDGENS & A. B. CRONINGER. 1974. J. Neurochem. 23: 791-802.
54. REIS, D. J., R. A. ROSS & T. H. JOH. 1977. Brain Res. 136: 465-474.
55. WALLER, S. B., D. K. INGRAM, M. A. REYNOLDS & E. D. LONDON. 1981. Age 4: 143.
56. STRONG, R., J. C. WAYMIRE, T. SAMORAJSKI & Z. GOTTESFELD. 1984. Neurochem. Res. 9: 1641-1652.
57. MCGEER, P. L. & E. G. MCGEER. 1976. J. Neurochem. 26: 65-76.
58. JOSEPH, J. A., C. FILBURN, L. P. TZANKOFF, J. M. THOMPSON & B. T. ENGEL. 1980. Neurobiol. Aging 1: 119-125.
59. KEBABIAN, J. W. & D. CALNE. 1979. Nature 277: 93-96.
60. JOSEPH, J. A., R. E. BERGER, B. T. ENGEL & G. S. ROTH. 1978. J. Gerontol. 33: 643-649.
61. SEVERSON, J. A., J. MARCUSSON, B. WINBLAD & C. E. FINCH. 1982. J. Neurochem. 39: 1623-1631.
62. SEVERSON, J. A. & C. E. FINCH. 1980. Fed. Proc. 39: 508.
63. SEVERSON, J. A. & C. E. FINCH. 1980. Brain Res. 192: 147-162.
64. THAL, L. J., S. G. HOROWITZ, B. DVORKIN & M. H. MAKMAN. 1980. Brain Res. 192: 185-194.
65. HENRY, J. M., C. R. FILBURN, J. A. JOSEPH & G. S. ROTH. 1986. Neurobiol. Aging 7: 357-361.
66. O'BOYLE, K. M. & J. L. WADDINGTON. 1984. Eur. J. Pharmacol. 105: 171-174.
67. MORGAN, D. G., J. O. MARCUSSON, B. WINBLAD & C. E. FINCH. 1984. Soc. Neurosci. Abstr. 10: 445.
68. CREESE, I. D. R., S. SIBLEY & E. LEFF. 1984. Fed. Proc. 43: 2779-2784.
69. HAMBLIN, M. W., S. E. LEFF & I. CREESE. 1984. Biochem. Pharmacol. 33: 877-887.
70. HAMBLIN, M. W. & I. CREESE. 1982. Life Sci. 30: 1587-1595.
71. SEVERSON, J. A. & P. K. RANDALL. 1985. J. Pharmacol. Exp. Ther. 233: 361-369.
72. HENRY, J. M. & G. S. ROTH. 1984. Life Sci. 35: 899-904.
73. LEFF, S. E., R. GARIANO & I. CREESE. 1984. Proc. Natl. Acad. Sci. USA 81: 3910-3914.
74. ENNA, S. J. & R. STRONG. 1981. In Brain Neurotransmitters and Receptors in Aging and Age-Related Disorders. S. Enna, T. Samorajski & B. Beer, Eds. 133-142. Raven Press. New York, NY.
75. MEEK, J. L., L. BERTILSSON, D. L. CHENEY, G. ZSILLA & E. COSTA. 1977. J. Gerontol. 32: 129-131.
76. CARLSSON, A., R. ADOLFSSON, S. M. AQUILONIUS. C. G. GOTTFRIES, L. ORELAND, L. SVENNERHOLM & B. WINBLAD. 1980. In Ergot Compounds and Brain Function. M. Goldstein, A. Lieberman, D. Calne & M. Thorner, Eds. 295-304. Raven Press. New York, NY.
77. MORIN, A. M. & C. G. WASTERLAIN. 1980. Neurochem. Res. 5: 301-308.
78. PERRY, E. K., R. H. PERRY, P. H. GIBSON, G. BLESSED & B. E. TOMLINSON. 1977. Neurosci. Lett. 6: 85-89.
79. MCGEER, E. G., H. C. FIBIGER, P. L. MCGEER & V. WICKSON. 1971. Exp. Gerontol. 6: 85-89.
80. MCGEER, E. G. & P. L. MCGEER. 1976. J. Neurochem. 26: 65-76.
81. BIRDSALL, N. J. M. & E. C. HULME. 1976. J. Neurochem. 27: 7-16.
82. LIPPA, A. S., C. C. LOULLIS, J. ROTROSEN, D. M. CORDASCO, D. J. CRITCHETT & J. A. JOSEPH. 1985. Neurobiol. Aging 6: 317-325.

83. PEDIGO, N. W., JR., L. D. MINOR & T. N. KRUMREI. 1984. Neurobiol. Aging 5: 227-233.
84. DE BELLEROCHE, J., J. COUTINHO-NETTO & H. F. BRADFORD. 1982. J. Neurochem. 39: 217-222.
85. FARNEBO, L. B. & B. HAMBERGER. 1971. Acta Physiol. Scand. 84: 35-44.
86. CEBEDDU, L. X. & I. S. HOFFMANN. 1982. J. Pharmacol. Exp. Ther. 223: 497-501.
87. KEHR, W., A. CARLSSON, M. LINDQVIST, T. MAGNUSSON & C. ATACK. 1972. J. Pharm. Pharmacol. 24: 744-747.
88. PARKER, E. M. & L. X. CEBEDDU. 1985. J. Pharmacol. Exp. Ther. 232: 492-500.
89. RAITERI, M., R. LEARDI & M. MARCHI. 1984. J. Pharmacol. Exp. Ther. 228: 209-214.
90. GOTHERT, M. 1985. Arzneim.-Forsch. Drug Res. 35 (II): 1909-1916.
91. SALLER, C. F. & A. I. SALAMA. 1984. J. Neurochem. 43: 675-688.
92. FISHER, S. K., P. D. KLINGER & B. W. AGRANOFF. 1983. J. Biol. Chem. 258: 7358-7353.
93. UNGERSTEDT, U. 1971. Acta Physiol. Scand. (Suppl.) 367: 69-93.
94. JOSEPH, J. A., C. R. FILBURN & G. S. ROTH. 1981. Life Sci. 29: 575-584.
95. DEAN, R. L., J. SCOZZAFAVA, J. A. GOAS, B. REGAN, B. BEER & R. T. BARTUS. 1981. Exp. Aging Res. 35: 427-451.
96. BARTUS, R. T. 1979. In Aging. Vol. 10. Sensory Systems and Communications in the Elderly. J. M. Ordy, Ed. 35-73. Raven Press. New York, NY.
97. JOSEPH, J. A., R. T. BARTUS, D. CLODY, D. MORGAN, C. FINCH, B. BEER & S. SESACK. 1983. Neurobiol. Aging 4: 313-319.
98. JOSEPH, J. A. & A. S. LIPPA. 1986. Neurobiol. Aging 7: 37-40.
99. LEVIN, P., M. HAJII, J. A. JOSEPH & G. S. ROTH. 1983. Life Sci. 32: 1743-1749.
100. JOSEPH, J. A., G. S. ROTH & A. S. LIPPA. 1986. Neurobiol. Aging 7: 31-35.
101. MORGAN, D. G., C. V. MOBBS, C. P. ANDERSON, Y. N. SINHA & C. FINCH. Eur. J. Pharmacol. In press.
102. MORGAN, D. G., Y. N. SINHA & C. E. FINCH. 1984. Neuroendocrinology 38: 407-410.
103. CRONIN, M. J., A. RECHES, R. M. MACLEOD & I. S. LOGIN. 1983. Eur. J. Pharmacol. 91: 229-234.
104. BURROWS, C. H. & G. C. KOKKONEN. 1977. In Advances in Nutrition. H. H. Draper, Ed. Vol. 1: 253-298. Plenum Press. New York, NY.
105. ROTH, G. S., D. K. INGRAM & J. A. JOSEPH. 1984. Brain Res. 300: 27-29.
106. JOSEPH, J. A., J. WHITAKER, G. S. ROTH & D. K. INGRAM. 1983. Neurobiol. Aging 4: 191-197.
107. HENRY, J. M., J. A. JOSEPH & G. S. ROTH. Brain Res. In press.
108. CREESE, I. 1982. Trends Neurosci. Res. Feb: 40-43.
109. BARONE, P., T. DAVIS, A. R. BROWN & T. N. CHASE. 1986. Eur. J. Pharmacol. 123: 109-114.

Can Opioids Regulate Hemopoietic Differentiation?

EDWARD S. GOLUB,[b,d] TERESITA DIAZ DE' PAGAN,[d]
IRIS SUN,[d] ALISON K. HALL,[c,d] FRED L. CRANE,[d]
AND GARY ISOM [e]

[d] Department of Biological Sciences
and
[e] Department of Pharmacology
Purdue University
West Lafayette, Indiana 47907

INTRODUCTION

Whole body X-irradiation results in the destruction of the blood forming system, but death can be prevented by repopulating animals with compatible bone marrow. All of the repopulated cells of the blood (erythroid, granuloid, monocytic, megakaryocytic and lymphoid) are descendants of a small number of stem cells in the repopulating bone marrow. These cells, called pluripotent hemopoietic stem cells, are in very low frequency (ca 10^{-5}) in the bone marrow. In response to external stimuli (hemorrhage, infection, stress, etc.) the system must respond by generating large numbers of functional differentiated cells. This is brought about by increased proliferation and differentiation of the stem cell and the committed progenitors. The mechanisms of this regulation are unknown and pose some of the more intellectually profound and clinically important subjects in biology.[1] Some of these problems and *in-vitro* approaches to studying hemopoietic differentiation are discussed in REFERENCES 2 and 3.

There is an abundant literature, some of it summarized in REFERENCE 1, showing that antigens are shared by cells of the nervous, hemopoietic and germ cell systems. We have shown that antiserum to mouse brain contained antibodies which react with the hemopoietic stem cell,[4] T-lymphocytes[5] and erythrocytes.[6] Others have shown reactivity to pre-T cells[7] and granulocyte precursors.[8] Granger and Lazarides have found the 70,000-dalton core polypeptide of neruofilament which was thought to be exclusively associated with neurons in chicken erythrocytes.[9] Moreover, this seems to be associated with hemopoietic development since it is present in embryonic and young

[a] Supported by National Science Foundation Grant DCB 8411716 and National Institutes of Health Grants CA-36761 and GM-K6-21839.

[b] To whom correspondence should be addressed.

[c] Present address: Department of Developmental Genetics, Case Western Reserve University Medical School, Cleveland, OH 44101.

erythrocytes but absent in adults. The reason for the presence of shared antigens between nervous, hemopoietic and germ cell systems is, of course, unknown, but we have suggested that the shared antigens could be receptors for neurohormones and that endogenous opioids could play regulatory roles in developing systems.[1]

There is a rather extensive literature on the wide distribution of peptide messenger molecules in various animals. Neurotransmitters such as catecholamines, serotonin and acetylcholine have been identified in protozoa.[10,11] Molecules similar to human chorionic gonadotrophin have been identified in extracts of bacteria.[12,13] Several classical neurohormones have been found in extraneural vertebrate tissue,[14] and gut and pituitary hormones have been found in the brain.[15] ACTH and β-endorphin have been identified in *E. coli, Neurospora* and *Tetrahymena.*[16,17] There are a few instances in which vertebrate hormones have a biological function in unicellular organisms, *e.g.,* the stimulation of adenylate cyclase in protozoa by epinephrine[18] and the alteration of feeding behavior of ameba by opioid peptides.[19] Both of these effects are blocked by traditional antagonists such as naloxone, an indication that the binding is to traditional receptors. Lymphocytes and granulocytes of the mammalian hemopoietic system bind opioids, but often the binding is not antagonized by naloxone, suggesting binding to nontraditional receptors.

Roth and his co-workers have argued that the appearance of hormones in species where they do not carry out the function known in higher vertebrates or where they are produced by apparently inappropriate cells in the host indicates that a whole new notion of hormone functions should be considered.[20,21] They have proposed that the APUD theory which explains the overlap of the endocrine and nervous systems by proposing that the endocrine system was derived from the nervous system[22,23] be replaced by a "unification theory" which postulates a common phylogenetic origin for both.[24] We have no desire to enter this interesting discussion as a partisan of either view, only to use the fact that there is a question of the appearance of apparently inappropriate molecules as a premise in the hypothesis that endogenous opioids may play a role in regulation and differentiation of the hemopoietic system.

There is growing evidence that neuropeptides react with cells of the hemopoietic system. For example, substance P binds to the chemotactic receptor on rabbit neutrophils,[25,26] and β-endorphin and met-enkaphalin cause increases in the migration index of human neutrophils and monocytes over a wide range of doses (10^{-9} to 10^{-6}).[27] Met-enkaphalamide induces degranulation of human PMN at 10^{-4} to 10^{-3} M and increases in motility at 10^{-5} to 10^{-3} M.[28] Human phagocytic cells also have opiate receptors.[29]

There is much more evidence that opioids bind to and have an effect on the cells of the immune system. Harum *et al.*[30] showed that β-endorphin binds specifically to RPMI 6258 cells, a human B-cell line. Others have shown with rosette formation that there are receptors for morphine and met-enkaphalin on normal human T-cells[31] and on peripheral blood cells of lymphoma patients.[32] The proliferative response of human cells to PHA is suppressed by β-endorphin[33] as it is in rat cells.[34] Morphine was shown to increase an anti-SRBC response *in vivo* in mice[35,36] and decrease an *in-vitro* response.[36] NK activity has been reported to be enhanced by β-endorphins.[37] The psychological effects on the immune response (reviewed in REFERENCES 38 and 39) are thought to be due to the action of the opioids.

All of this taken together suggested the possibility that the endogenous opioids may play a regulatory role in hemopoiesis and other stem cell systems.[1] The presence of opioid receptors on differentiated hemopoietic cells and functional alterations by opioids in encouraging. But if these molecules play a physiologically important role in hemopoiesis, it is likely to be at the earliest differentiated stages.

RESULTS

To test the idea that endogenous opioids can affect differentiation we decided to test their effect on hemopoietic differentiation *in vitro*. Bone marrow from 6-8 week old CBA mice were plated *in vitro* in soft agar with colony stimulating fraction (CSF) and that number of granulocyte macrophage colonies counted 10 days later.[40,41] In a typical experiment (FIGURE 1), β-endorphin, met-enkaphalin and naloxone all inhibited the generation of colonies. However, while the results in any given experiment showed this trend, the variation between experiments was too great to give us confidence to continue with this system. In retrospect, if the hypothesis is correct the variation should not have been unexpected, since mice housed under ordinary conditions are subjected to stress and probably have varying levels of endogenous opioids.

Because of the problem of variability we turned to an established cell line which can be induced to differentiate *in vitro*. HL60 is a human myelomonocytic cell line[42,43] which is induced to granulocyte differentiation by retinoic acid (RA)[44] or macrophage differentiation by TPA.[45,46] We felt that this would be a good candidate on which to test the effect of endogenous opioids.

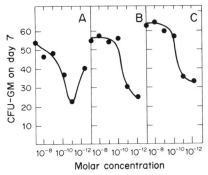

FIGURE 1. Effect of opioids on *in-vitro* colony formation. (**A**) β-endorphin; (**B**) met-enkaphalin; (**C**) naloxone.

We have recently shown that the events leading to the activation of granulocyte-specific genes in HL60 can be divided into two discrete phases[47] and have suggested a possible cascade of events leading to this gene activation.[48,49] Briefly, we showed that RA inhibits membrane electron transport, almost certainly through the inhibition of membrane diferric transferrin reductase.[50] Inhibiting the flow of electrons from NADH to diferric transferrin causes a decrease in the concentration of cellular NAD^+. The lowered NAD^+ concentration causes a decrease of GTP synthesis by down regulating the enzyme inosine monophosphate dehydrogenase (IMPD) which is exquisitely sensitive to NAD^+ concentration. We postulate that the lowered concentration of NAD^+ causes the dissociation of GTP from a hypothetical inducer molecule. For the purposes of this paper however, we will focus on the possible effect of endogenous opioids on the membrane phenomena.

We tested the ability of several opioids to induce differentiation in HL60. It can be seen (TABLE 1) that none induced the cells. When we tested the effect of these

TABLE 1. Effect on β-endorphin and Leu-enkephalin on HL60 Differentiation

Addition[a]	Percent NBT[+]
RA	94
βE 10^{-9}	<10
10^{-10}	<10
10^{-11}	<10
10^{-12}	<10
leu-enk 10^{-9}	<10
10^{-11}	<10

[a] RA = retinoic acid; βE = β-endorphin; leu-enk = leu-enkephalin.

compounds on the inhibition of electron transport (TABLE 2) we found that they did inhibit electron transport. This was very surprising to use because we have never before seen a compound which inhibited electron transport which did not induce differentiation.[48] But even more surprising was the fact that β-endorphin combined with RA *prevented* the action of RA on electron transport.

We are now in the process of determining the effect of the opioids on the ability of RA to induce differentiation. To date our very preliminary results show that β-endorphin does not appear to have a significant effect on the ability of RA to induce granulocyte differentiation. We have been able to show that HL60 has a significant number of opioid receptors (TABLE 3). This value was obtained with labeled naloxone, and we are currently determining the nature of these receptors and their affinity.

DISCUSSION AND CAUTIONARY NOTE

The data in this report show that endogenous opioids can, under certain circumstances, inhibit the differentiation of the hemopoietic system. The effect is complex, an ability to inhibit electron transport but not initiate differentiation and also to abrogate the ability of RA to inhibit electron transport. The mechanism is not obvious and further work is being done.

TABLE 2. Effect of Opioids on Electron Transport

Addition[a]	Electron Transport nmol/min/gww
Control	4.9
RA 10^{-5}	1.8
βE 10^{-9} M	0.7
RA + βE	5.1

[a] RA = retinoic acid; βE = β-endorphin.

TABLE 3. Specific Opiate Binding[a]

Cell Line	f mol/mg Protein	Est. Number Receptors
HL60	21	2,000
NG108	73	10,000
AC glioma	6	0

[a] fmole ^{3}H-naloxone bound per mg HL60 plasmamembrane protein.

It is crucial to emphasize that we do not know if endogenous opioids have any physiological role in hemopoiesis. All animals are constantly subjected to stress and probably have fluctuating levels of endogenous opioids. Can a process as essential as hemopoiesis be at the mercy of such uncertain regulatory control? While the phenomena which we report are of interest, we urge extreme caution in interpretation until much more work is done.

REFERENCES

1. GOLUB, E. S. 1982. Nature **299:** 483.
2. GOLUB, E. S. 1982. Cell **28:** 687.
3. HALL, A. K. 1983. Cell **33:** 11.
4. GOLUB, E. S. 1972. J. Exp. Med. **136:** 369.
5. GOLUB, E. S. 1971. Cell Immunol. **2:** 353.
6. GOLUB, E. S. 1973. Exp. Hematol. **1:** 105.
7. BASCH, R. S., J. L. KADISH & G. GOLDSTEIN. 1978. J. Exp. Med. **147:** 1843.
8. BERMAN, J. W. & R. S. BASCH. 1980. J. Supramoloc. Struc. Suppl. **4:** 212.
9. BRANGER, B. L. & E. LAZARIDES. 1983. Science **221:** 553.
10. JANAKIDEVI, K., V. C. DEWEY & G. W. KIDDER. 1966. J. Biochem. **241:** 2576.
11. JANAKIDEVI, K., V. C. DEWEY & G. W. KIDDER. 1966. Arch. Biochem. **113:** 758.
12. ACEVEDO, H. F., M. SLIFKIN, M. POUCHET & M. PARDO. 1978. Cancer **41:** 1217.
13. MAROU, T., H. CHEN, S. J. SEGAL & S. S. KOIDE. 1979. Proc. Natl. Acad. Sci. USA **79:** 6622.
14. HOKEFT, T., O. JOHANNSSON, J. M. LUNDBERG & M. SCHULTZBERG. 1980. Nature **284:** 515.
15. KRIEGER, D. T. & A. S. LIOTTA. 1979. Science **205:** 366.
16. LE ROITH, D., J. SHILOACH, J. ROTH & M. A. LESNIAK. 1980. Proc. Natl. Acad. Sci. USA **77:** 6184.
17. LE ROITH, D., A. S. LIOTTA, J. ROTH, J. SHILOACH, M. E. LEWIS, C. B. PERT & D. T. KRIEGER. 1982. Proc. Natl. Acad. Sci. USA **79:** 2086.
18. ROZENSWEIG, A. & S. H. KINDLER. 1972. FEBS Lett. **25:** 221.
19. JOSEFSSON, J.-O. & P. JOHANSON. 1979. Nature **282:** 78.
20. ROTH, J., D. LE ROITH, J. SHILOACH, J. L. ROSENZWEIG, M. A. LESNIAK & J. HAVRANKOVA. 1982. N. Engl. J. Med. **306:** 523.
21. ROTH, J., D. LE ROITH, J. SHILOACH & C. RUBINOVITZ. 1983. Clin. Res. **31:** 354.
22. PEARSE, A. G. E. 1968. Proc. R. Soc. London B **170:** 71.
23. PEARSE, A. G. E. & J. M. POLAK. 1972. Endocrinology, 1971. S. Taylor, Ed. 145. Heinemann. London.
24. LE ROITH, D., J. SHILOACH & J. ROTH. 1982. Peptides **3:** 211.
25. O'DORISIO, M. S., T. M. O'DORISIO, S. CATLAND & S. P. BULCERZAK. 1980. J. Lab. Clin. Med. **96:** 667.

26. MARASCO, W. A., H. J. SHOWELL & E. L. BECKER. 1981. Biochem. Biophys. Res. Commun. **99:** 1065.
27. VAN EPPS, D. E., L. SALAND, C. TAYLOR & R. C. WILLIAMS, JR. 1983. Prog. Brain Res. **59:** 361.
28. SICH, J. J. & J. D. STINNETT. 1984. Abstract, Am. Soc. Microbiol. In Press.
29. LOPKER, A. L., L. G. ABGOOD, W. HESS & F. J. LIONETTI. 1980. Biochem. Pharmacol. **29:** 1361.
30. HAZUM, E., K.-K. CHANG & P. CUATRECASAS. 1979. Science **205:** 1033.
31. WYBRAN, J., T. APPELBOOM, J.-P. FAMAEY & A. GOVAERTS. 1979. J. Immunol. **123:** 1068.
32. MILLER, G. C., A. J. MURGO & N. POLOTNIKOFF. 1983. Clin. Immunol. Immunopathol. **26:** 466.
33. MCCAIN, H. W., I. B. LAMSTER, J. M. BOZZONE & J. T. GORBIC. 1982. Life Sci. **31:** 1619.
34. GILMAN, S. C., J. M. SCHWARTZ, R. J. MILNER, F. E. BLOOM & J. D. FELDMAN. 1982. Proc. Natl. Acad. Sci. USA **79:** 4226.
35. LEFKOWITZ, S. S. & C. Y. CHIANG. 1975. Life Sci. **17:** 1763.
36. GÜNGÖR, M., E. GENC, H. SAGDUYU, L. EROGLU & H. KOYUNCOUGLE. 1980. Experientia **36:** 1309.
37. MATHEWS, P. M., C. J. FROELICH, W. L. SIBBIT, JR. & A. D. BANKHURST. 1983. J. Immunol. **130:** 1658-1662.
38. SOLOMAN, G. F. & A. A. AMKRAUT. 1981. Annu. Rev. Microbiol. **35:** 155.
39. SPECTOR, N. H. & E. A. KORNEVA. 1981. *In* Psychoneuroimmunology. 449.
40. METCALF, D. 1984. Clonal Culture of Hemopoietic Cells: Techniques and Applications. Elsevier. Amsterdam.
41. VAN DEN EUGH, G. & E. S. GOLUB. 1974. J. Exp. Med. **139:** 1621.
42. COLLINS, S. J., R. C. GALLO & R. E. GALLAGHER. 1977. Nature **270:** 347.
43. COLLINS, S. J., F. W. RUSCETTI, R. S. GALLAGHER & R. C. GALLO. 1978. Proc. Natl. Acad. Sci. USA **75:** 2458.
44. BREITMAN, T. R., S. E. SELONICK & S. J. COLLINS. 1980. Proc. Natl. Acad. Sci. USA **77:** 2936.
45. ROVERA, G. D., D. SANOLI & D. DAMSKY. 1979. Proc. Natl. Acad. Sci. USA **76:** 5158.
46. LOTEM, J. & L. SACHS. 1979. Proc. Natl. Acad. Sci. USA **76:** 5158.
47. GOLUB, E. S. & T. PAGAN. 1986. Prog. Clin. Biol. Res. **226:** 235.
48. GOLUB, E. S., T. DIAZ DE PAGAN, I. SUN & F. L. CRANE. 1987. Submitted.
49. DIAZ DE PAGAN, T. & E. S. GOLUB. 1987. Submitted.
50. SUN, I., F. L. CRANE, T. DIAZ DE PAGAN & E. S. GOLUB. 1987. Submitted.

Tetrahydrobiopterin and Biogenic Amine Metabolism in Neuropsychiatry, Immunology, and Aging

ROBERT A. LEVINE

Laboratory of Molecular Neurobiology
Lafayette Clinic and Wayne State University
951 East Lafayette Avenue
Detroit, Michigan 48207

INTRODUCTION

Tetrahydrobiopterin (BH_4) is a reduced pterin molecule that is best known for its role as the cofactor for phenylalanine hydroxylase in the liver, tyrosine hydroxylase in catecholamine neurons and adrenal medullary chromaffin cells, and tryptophan hydroxylase in serotonin neurons and the pineal gland. The role of BH_4 as the hydroxylase cofactor has been extensively studied in order to understand its involvement in the regulation of biogenic amine neurotransmitter synthesis and the potential role of altered BH_4 metabolism in human disease. There have been numerous studies indicating the important role of BH_4 in regulating the rate of hydroxylase reactions and biogenic amine synthesis (for review, see REFERENCE 1). BH_4 is also required for melatonin production in the pineal gland. There is evidence in humans that the metabolism of BH_4, catecholamines, and serotonin is altered in neuropsychiatric illness and in aging (to be discussed below).

Biopterin, the fully oxidized form of BH_4, was originally isolated from human urine by Patterson in 1956.[4] The first indication of a functional role for BH_4 in mammals was the observation by Kaufman in 1963 that BH_4 served as the cofactor for phenylalanine hydroxylase in the conversion of phenylalanine to tyrosine in the liver.[5] Reduced pterins (*i.e.,* BH_4) were later shown by Lovenberg and co-workers to be required by tryptophan hydroxylase for serotonin synthesis in brain, as well as for melatonin production in the pineal gland.[6] BH_4 was later tentatively identified[7] as the required cofactor for tyrosine hydroxylase activity in the synthesis of the catecholamines (dopamine, norepinephrine, and epinephrine). More recently, the presence of BH_4 and other pterins in cells not carrying out aromatic amino acid hydroxylation[2] indicates the possibility that pterins may have other functions in addition to BH_4 serving as the hydroxylase cofactor, although there is currently no good evidence for other physiological roles for BH_4.[3]

This paper will review the current perspective of BH_4 biosynthesis, the involvement of BH_4 metabolism in neuropsychiatric illness and aging, and what is known about the synthesis and presence of BH_4 and other pterins in the neuroendocrine and immune systems. The interaction between BH_4 and catecholamine and serotonin metabolism will be emphasized to illustrate the potential importance of altered BH_4 metabolism in diseases where alterations in catecholamine or serotonin metabolism have been recognized. Additionally, it is hoped that a discussion of pterin metabolism covering diverse fields of interest may serve as a catalyst for experts in these fields to formulate an integrated approach to the study of pterin metabolism in neuropsychiatry, immunology and aging.

TETRAHYDROBIOPTERIN BIOSYNTHESIS AND BIOGENIC AMINE METABOLISM

Our understanding of BH_4 biosynthesis has been enhanced by the opportunity to study a relatively rare disease in newborns (called atypical phenylketonuria [PKU] or BH_4-dependent hyperphenylalaninemia) in which BH_4 metabolism is impaired. In spite of information obtained by studying BH_4 deficiencies occurring at birth, aspects of BH_4 biosynthesis in mammalian systems have remained controversial, although recent advances have helped clarify some issues. FIGURE 1 depicts BH_4 biosynthesis (shown in the middle of the figure) with dopamine and serotonin metabolism in the central nervous system (CNS). It is generally accepted that guanosine triphosphate (GTP) is converted in mammals directly to dihydroneopterin triphosphate (NH_2P_3) by GTP cyclohydrolase. NH_2P_3 is transformed to 6-pyruvoyl-tetrahydropterin (6-PPH_4) by the enzyme, 6-PPH_4 synthase. It is thought that sepiapterin reductase (SR) catalyzes one and possibly both reductions of the two keto functions in the side-chain during BH_4 formation from 6-PPH_4.[8-10] Another keto reductase (for review, see REFERENCE 11) has been described that may catalyze the reduction of one keto function (at the step indicated by the question mark in FIGURE 1), however the physiological importance of this other reductase has not been determined.

After BH_4 is formed in the cell from GTP, it donates an electron in the process of aromatic amino acid hydroxylation, which yields quinoid dihydrobiopterin (q-BH_2); q-BH_2 is reduced back to BH_4 by (quinoid) dihydropteridine reductase (DHPR), which requires NADH as cofactor. The mechanism by which BH_4 is eliminated from the cell is not known, and turnover studies have been extremely difficult to perform for several reasons including that each BH_4 molecule may recycle through q-BH_2 and back to BH_4 for an undetermined number of cycles.

Before the discovery of 6-PPH_4 as an intermediate, the pathway to BH_4 was thought to proceed from NH_2P_3 to 6-pyruvoyl-dihydropterin (instead of 6-PPH_4), followed by the formation of sepiapterin (instead of the tetrahydro form of sepiapterin as is currently thought). Sepiapterin was thought to be converted to dihydrobiopterin (BH_2), which can be converted to BH_4 by dihydrofolate reductase (DHFR) *in vitro*. Though it had been proposed that DHFR was on the pathway to BH_4 since it could catalyze the conversion of BH_2 to BH_4,[12] there were initial clues that DHFR might not be involved in BH_4 synthesis *in vivo*. Young patients at the National Institutes of Health with CNS tumors receiving chronic methotrexate (DHFR inhibitor) via a CNS reservoir did not exhibit a diminution of cerebrospinal fluid (CSF) BH_4 levels (Levine, unpublished observations), nor were markers of biogenic amine metabolism affected. That DHFR was not on the de novo pathway to BH_4 was finally demonstrated in a variety of systems (for review, see REFERENCE 13). Once the bias toward DHFR and BH_2 being on the BH_4 biosynthetic pathway was convincingly eliminated,[13] several

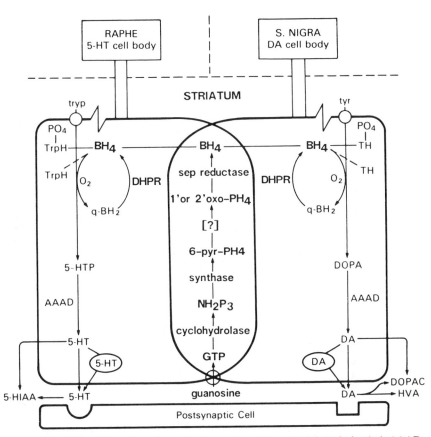

FIGURE 1. BH₄ and biogenic amine metabolism. Abbreviations (in alphabetical order): AAAD, aromatic amino acid decarboxylase; DA, dopamine; DHPR, dihydropteridine reductase; DOPA, dihydroxyphenylalanine; DOPAC, dihydroxyphenylacetic acid; 5-HT, serotonin; 5-HIAA, 5-hydroxy-indoleacetic acid; HVA, homovanillic acid, PH₄, tetrahydropterin; pyr, pyruvoyl; q-BH₂, quinoid-dihydrobiopterin; sep, sepiapterin; tryp, tryptophan; TrpH, tryptophan hydroxylase (PO₄-phosphorylated); tyr, tyrosine; TH, tyrosine hydroxylase (PO₄-phosphorylated).

groups quickly were able to discover that the tetrahydropterin ring appeared immediately after NH_2P_3 during the formation of 6-PPH_4, leading to the current view of
BH_4 biosynthesis as shown in FIGURE 1.

REGULATION OF BH₄ BIOSYNTHESIS IN HUMANS AND NONPRIMATES

In nonprimates such as the rat, GTP cyclohydrolase is thought to be the rate-
limiting enzyme in BH_4 biosynthesis, because at the present time, no identifiable
intermediates between GTP and BH_4 have been detected in tissue. However, in human
and monkey tissues and fluids, dihydroneopterin (NH_2) and neopterin can be detected
as well as BH_4 (and BH_2 to a much lesser extent). NH_2 and neopterin would appear
in the circulation only after the dephosphorylation of NH_2P_3, and NH_2P_3 and neopterin have been detected in postmortem human but not in rat liver (Levine, unpublished
observations). Since a stable pool of NH_2P_3 exists in human tissues, this indicates
that an enzyme after NH_2P_3 is rate limiting in human BH_4 biosynthesis,[14] possible
6-PPH_4 synthase or sepiapterin reductase. The selective appearance of NH_2 and
neopterin in humans as opposed to nonprimates may have great significance when
considering the involvement of BH_4 and biogenic amine metabolism in aging and
neuropsychiatric illness as will be discussed below. It may be that nonprimate models
are inappropriate under certain circumstances for examining BH_4 metabolism, and
especially its interaction with biogenic amine metabolism.

BH₄ AND ATYPICAL PKU

At first it might seem odd to discuss BH_4 deficiencies that occur at birth in a
paper focusing on aspects of adult diseases and the process of aging. However, it is
important to note that alterations in the genetic expression of BH_4 metabolism occurring at birth can lead to neurological and psychiatric impairment in the developing
children. Thus, the BH_4 system may be a focal point for genetic alterations that could
contribute to neuropsychiatric illnesses and the aging process in adults.

Atypical PKU is caused by a reduced activity of one of the BH_4 metabolic enzymes,
either GTP cyclohydrolase, 6-PPH_4 synthase, or DHPR. A deficiency in sepiapterin
reductase activity (and the other reductase) has yet to be detected in newborns, though
detection may be possible in the future given that specific antibodies recognizing
human sepiapterin reductase have been generated[15] and may aid in the recognition
of a potential sepiapterin reductase deficiency.

Cases of atypical PKU are detected at birth by PKU screening techniques, which
measure elevated circulating phenylalanine levels coupled with a BH_4 deficiency. A
deficiency of 6-PPH_4 synthase leads to high circulating neopterin and NH_2 with low
BH_4, whereas a GTP cyclohydrolase deficiency reduces all pterins. A DHPR deficiency
causes elevated neopterin and NH_2 with BH_4 being reduced and BH_2 elevated. BH_4
deficiency usually occurs in both the liver and the brain, although recently there have
been reports of a few cases where only the liver exhibits a lack of BH_4, whereas brain
BH_4 and biogenic amine metabolism appear normal.[16] If a BH_4 deficiency can be

restricted to the liver, it may be possible that a deficit of BH_4 can occur selectively in the brain, which has been referred to as a CNS-selective BH_4 deficiency.[14] A CNS-selective BH_4 deficiency at birth would not be detected by classical PKU screening techniques, since peripheral phenylalanine levels would be normal. The question remains if this possibility could explain certain cases of adult neuropsychiatric illnesses.

BH_4 therapy has been shown to be effective in some children with a CNS BH_4 deficiency.[16,17] However, not all cases are responsive to BH_4 alone. Some patients also require the neurotransmitter precursors, 5-hydroxytrypotophan (5-HTP) and L-dihydroxyphenylalanine (L-DOPA) to alleviate adverse clinical symptoms caused by deficiencies of BH_4 and biogenic amines in the CNS.[18,19] In these patients, it is possible that not enough BH_4 is able to enter the brain after peripheral administration, since it is known that BH_4 enters the brain poorly from the periphery.[20-22] Alternatively, there could be an additional problem with the expression of tyrosine and tryptophan hydroxylases (or other required factors) that would cause BH_4 therapy to be ineffective. Still other newborns are totally unresponsive to BH_4 or neurotransmitter precursor therapy and continue to exhibit CNS disturbances.[18] One possible explanation is that a severe BH_4 deficiency could cause irreversible damage to the fetus in utero.

Since genetic defects in BH_4 metabolism leading to CNS biogenic amine deficiencies occur in newborns, it is possible that the etiology of certain adult neurological and psychiatric illnesses are caused by an altered expression of BH_4 biosynthetic enzymes. It is also conceivable that part of the failings of normal aging could be related to a progressive decline in the expression of BH_4 biosynthetic capability leading to a biogenic amine deficiency with age (to be discussed below). This is plausible since many of the mechanisms for regulating tyrosine and tryptophan hydroxylase activities revolve around BH_4.

BH_4 INVOLVEMENT IN NEUROPSYCHIATRIC ILLNESS AND AGING

Age-related metabolic alterations have been reported in many systems, ranging from intracellular molecular events to organ system integration. Thus, it becomes extremely difficult to identify which of these changes can be tolerated with minimal adverse effects and which may cause the deterioration of certain bodily functions that occurs during normal aging. Compounding the problem is that dysfunctions of neuronal systems causing neuropsychiatric diseases may be interactive with aging processes, making the isolation and detection of aberrant systems difficult.

Alterations in BH_4 and biogenic amine metabolism have been observed in several neuropsychiatric disorders as well as in aging. BH_4 content in the CSF is decreased in Parkinson's disease,[23] familial dystonia,[24,25] Alzheimer's disease,[26,27] as well as certain other neurological diseases.[26] Age-related changes in pterin metabolism have also been observed.[28,29] In postmortem cortical samples from Alzheimer's-disease patients, in-vitro BH_4 biosynthesis from GTP was shown to be decreased from control.[30] Regarding biogenic amine metabolism, tyrosine hydroxylase activity in postmortem striatal samples was shown to decline with age in samples from patients dying without neurological symptoms.[31] An age-related decline in DOPA decarboxylase has also been reported.[32] One of the major biogenic amine degrading enzymes, monoamine oxidase, has been shown by several groups to increase with age (for review, see REFERENCE 33). In accordance with the above observations, it was shown that HVA and 5-HIAA varied inversely with age from birth to age 45, although the number of points at the older ages were few.[34] While this observation has been substantiated,[35] others have not reported similar decreases in metabolites at the older ages.[36,37]

A decrease of BH_4 in the CSF has been observed[28,29] with age, although the decrease may not be dramatic. BH_4 levels in CSF have been shown to be well correlated with CSF HVA levels.[23] Regarding pterin metabolism and aging, it may be important that neopterin levels rise dramatically with age, and the increase in the neopterin:biopterin ratio with age also may reflect some age-related alteration in pterin metabolism.[38] It is possible that there is a declining capacity to synthesize BH_4 with age, which may contribute to some of the observed decreases in markers of biogenic amine metabolism. It is also possible that the observed decreases in BH_4 content in brain and CSF are the result of biogenic amine neuronal loss. However, any involvement of altered biogenic amine metabolism in disease or aging may be the result of, or influenced by, defects in BH_4 metabolism.

With regard to BH_4 therapy in neuropsychiatric illness, this approach is designed to achieve a higher intracellular concentration of BH_4 in the CNS and stimulate tyrosine and/or tryptophan hydroxylase activities in biogenic amine neurons to elevate neurotransmitter synthesis (for conceptual review, see REFERENCE 1). While there have been sporadic reports of successful treatment of neuropsychiatric patients,[14] a convincing study by LeWitt and co-workers[39] demonstrated that 3 out of 10 patients with familial dystonia responded in double blind fashion to a single dose of BH_4 (10 mg/kg i.v.). Familial dystonia is sometimes characterized as a nigrostriatal dopamine deficiency condition, as some of the patients will respond positively to L-DOPA. In one of the dystonia patients responding to BH_4, dose-response studies indicated that no beneficial therapeutic response to BH_4 was observed at 2.5 mg/kg i.v.; however, a positive response occurred at 5 and 10 mg/kg i.v. CSF BH_4 content 4 hours after each dose was elevated only 50% at 2.5 mg/kg, whereas 5 and 10 mg/kg of administered BH^4 raised the CSF BH_4 level by 7- and 16-fold, respectively.[39] This limited data suggests the possibility that there is a threshold dosing level which must be surpassed in order to increase proportionately BH_4 levels in the brian after peripheral administration. This can be inferred because with no threshold, a dose of 2.5 mg/kg i.v. might have been expected to increase CSF BH_4 3 to 4 times (rather than only the observed 50%) to be proportional to CSF BH_4 levels achieved by the higher doses. If it were necessary to overcome a threshold dosage level, this would suggest that single high doses of BH_4 might be more appropriate than divided daily doses or constant infusions when treating patients. BH_4 supplementation should also be considered when attempting to treat aging-related phenomena associated with biogenic amine deficits. The full potential for using BH_4 as a therapeutic tool in neurological and psychiatric illnesses or aging may not be known until high concentrations of BH_4 or synthetic analogues in brain can be attained.

OTHER POSSIBLE PHYSIOLOGICAL ROLES FOR BH_4

BH_4 has been detected in certain neuroendocrine tissues, although no evidence has been gathered to suggest another physiological function for BH_4 or other pterins. For instance, the ratio of BH_4 content to hydroxylase enzyme activity is much higher in the pineal and whole pituitary glands,[39] and especially the anterior pituitary (Levine, unpublished data) than in most brain areas. This trend is also seen in the hypothalamus, although not to as great an extent.[40]

The apparent excessive content of hydroxylase cofactor in hypothalamus, pituitary gland, and pineal gland may indicate a role for this substance in neuroendocrine function, apart from serving as an electron donor for the hydroxylase enzymes. This observation is supported by studies which demonstrated an antigonadotropic effect by aqueous extracts of sheep pineal glands both *in vitro*[41,42] and *in vivo.*[43] The active constituent of the sheep pineal extract was identified as biopterin.[43] Thus, it is possible that the large concentration of cofactor found in neuroendocrine tissues may act to modulate hypothalamic-hypophyseal function. However, one could also speculate that the hydroxylase enzymes in these tissues are regulated by different mechanisms from the enzymes found in brain areas, whereby more cofactor would be required. It has also been suggested that pteridines have some involvement in the regulation of hydroxyindole-0-methyltransferase in the pineal gland.[44] Roles for BH_4 have also been suggested (based on *in-vitro* evidence) in ether lipid oxidation, proline hydroxylation, and mitochondrial electron transport (for review, see REFERENCE 3). Pterins are also contained in cells of the bone marrow, and pterins can be synthesized in lymphocytes and macrophages as discussed below. It remains a challenge for the future to determine whether BH_4 or other pterins have a physiological role in any of these or other systems.

PTERINS AND THE IMMUNE SYSTEM

Recently, there has been a great deal of interest generated in the possible involvement of pterin compounds in immune system function. It was first observed by Wachter and co-workers that the urinary excretion of neopterin was elevated in patients with various types of viral infections as well as certain cancers (for review, see REFERENCE 45). Increased neopterin excretion has also been detected in patients with autoimmune deficiency syndrome (AIDS)[46,47] and AIDS related complex (ARC).[47] This increase in neopterin excretion seemed to be related to diseases exhibiting hyper-immune function.

It was presumed that the elevated neopterin was derived from NH_2P_3 after dephosphorylation and oxidation in the body, although which cells were the source of the neopterin remained a mystery. It was later demonstrated that immunologically activated mononuclear cells were capable of synthesizing neopterin.[48] FIGURE 2 shows diagrammatically the proposed pterin metabolism in cells of the immune system and the cascade for how neopterin is produced from immune system activation, as advanced by Huber and co-workers[49] and Schoedon and co-workers.[50] Presentation of antigen activates T-lymphocytes (left side of FIGURE 2), causing the release of interferon-gamma (IFN-g) from stimulated lymphocytes. The lymphocytes are also stimulated to synthesize NH_2P_3 and "release" NH_2 (after dephosphorylation) and BH_4, which are detected in culture media as neopterin and biopterin.[50] This presumably occurs as a result of activation of GTP cyclohydrolase, and possibly other later enzymes in BH_4 biosynthesis, all of which are contained in lymphocytes. In contrast to lymphocytes, macrophages do not contain measurable 6-PPH_4 synthase activity. Through as yet an unknown process, IFN-g released from lymphocytes can stimulate GTP cyclohydrolase activity in macrophages and cause a large increase in the synthesis of NH_2P_3 and release of NH_2 after dephosphorylation (right side of FIGURE 2). Since

6-PPH$_4$ synthase is not contained in macrophages, they do not synthesize BH$_4$ in response to IFN-g (N.D., FIGURE 2).

Neopterin levels in blood or neopterin excretion may be a valuable marker in certain instances, and indeed has shown promise for predicting a rejection episode following certain allograft transplantations.[51] It has also been proposed that monitoring neopterin may be a sensitive marker for appraising the status of endogenous IFN-g release.[52] Whether NH$_2$ or neopterin has a primary role in immune system function

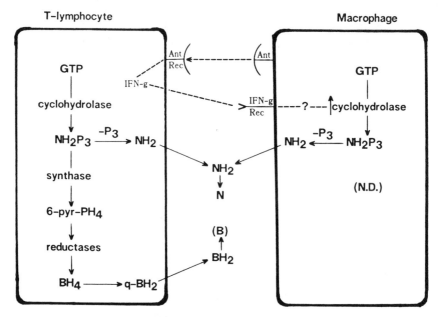

FIGURE 2. Interactions between immune cells and pterin metabolism. Presentation of antigen to T-lymphocyte increases the synthesis of NH$_2$P$_3$ and BH$_4$, as well as the release of IFN-g. IFN-g stimulates macrophages, which activates GTP cyclohydrolase and dramatically elevates NH$_2$P$_3$, leading to increased release of NH$_2$ and neopterin. 6-PPH$_4$ synthase has not been detectable in macrophages under any conditions, so macrophages do not produce BH$_4$. Abbreviations (not contained in FIGURE 1): Ant, antigen; B, biopterin; IFN-g, interferon-gamma; N, neopterin; NH$_2$, dihydroneopterin; N.D., not detectable; -P$_3$, minus triphosphate; Rec, receptor.

is unclear, although an atypical PKU patient with a GTP cyclohydrolase deficiency and low neopterin and biopterin had an apparently normally functioning immune system.[53] Since nonprimates do not have significant amounts of circulating neopterin under most conditions, this also argues against a primary role for neopterin. However, this remains an open question. The presence of pterin metabolism in the immune system remains a phenomenon searching for a function.

SUMMARY

Tetrahydrobiopterin (BH_4) is essential for biogenic amine synthesis, and alterations in its metabolism occur at birth (atypical PKU), in neuropsychiatric illnesses, and in aging. BH_4 therapy has been attempted in atypical PKU and in neuropsychiatric illness with some success and may become more viable as more is learned about BH_4 metabolism and ways are discovered to elevate brain BH_4 levels. It is intriguing to consider that a genetic defect in BH_4 biosynthesis occurring at birth might go unrecognized and contribute to altered biogenic amine metabolism that occurs in neuropsychiatric illness. Since there seems to be a sensitivity of BH_4 metabolism to genetic alterations, it is possible that altered BH_4 metabolism is involved in some of deleterious effects associated with the aging process. A link between genetic alterations in BH_4 metabolism at birth and adult neuropsychiatric illness and aging remains to be established, although this seems plausible. The presence of BH_4 and other pterins in cells of the immune system as well as the pineal gland and other neuroendocrine tissues suggests the potential for other functions of pterins. Hopefully, future research will uncover the full potential for the therapeutic use of BH_4 in a variety of diseases as well as elucidating other potential roles for pterin molecules which are present in many different systems.

REFERENCES

1. LEVINE, R. A. & M. P. GALLOWAY. 1987. The regulation of biogenic amine synthesis and role of tetrahydrobiopterin. In Unconjugated Pterins in Neurobiology: Basic and Clinical Aspects. W. Lovenberg & R. A. Levine, Eds. 119-130. Taylor and Francis. London and New York.
2. FUKUSHIMA. T. & J. C. NIXON. 1980. Anal. Biochem. **102:** 176-188.
3. MILSTIEN, S. 1987. Tetrahydrobiopterin: other physiological roles in addition to aromatic amino acid hydroxylation? In Unconjugated Pterins and Related Biogenic Amines. H.-CH. Curtius & N. Blau, Eds. Walter de Gruyter. Berlin.
4. PATTERSON, E. L., R. MITSTREY & E. L. R. STOKSTAD. 1956. J. Am. Chem. Soc. **78:** 5868-5871.
5. KAUFMAN, S. 1963. Proc. Natl. Acad. Sci. USA **50:** 1085-1093.
6. LOVENBERG, W., E. JEQUIER & A. SJOERDSMA. 1967. Science **155:** 217-219.
7. LLOYD, T. & N. WEINER. 1971. Mol. Pharmacol. **7:** 569-580.
8. MILSTIEN, S. & S. KAUFMAN. 1983. Biochem. Biophys. Res. Commun. **115:** 888-893.
9. HEINTEL, D., S. GHISLA, H.-CH. CURTIUS, A. NIEDERWIESER & R. A. LEVINE. 1984. Neurochem. Int. **6:** 141.
10. SMITH, G. K. & C. A. NICHOL. 1983. Studies on the biosynthesis of tetrahydrobiopterin in bovine adrenal medulla preparations. In Biochemical and Clinical Aspects of Pteridines. H.-Ch. Curtius, W. Pfleiderer & H. Wachter, Eds. Vol. 2: 123-131. Walter de Gruyter. Berlin and New York.
11. MILSTIEN, S. & S. KAUFMAN. 1986. The biosynthesis of tetrahydrobiopterin in rat brain. In Chemistry and Biology of Pteridines. B. A. Cooper & V. M. Whitehead, Eds. 169-181. Walter de Gruyter. Berlin and New York.
12. KAUFMAN, S. 1967. J. Biol. Chem. **242:** 3934-3943.
13. NICHOL, C. A., G. K., SMITH, J. F. REINHARD, J., E. C. BIGHAM, M. M. ABOU-DONIA, O. H. VIVEROS & D. S. DUCH. 1987. Regulation of tetrahydrobiopterin biosynthesis and cofactor replacement by tetrahydropterins. In Unconjugated Pterins in Neurobiology:

      Basic and Clinical Aspects. W. Lovenberg & R. A. Levine, Eds. 81-106. Taylor and Francis. London and New York.

14. LEVINE, R. A., D. HEINTEL, W. LEIMBACHER, A. NIEDERWIESER, H.-CH. CURTIUS & S. GHISLA. 1983. Recent advances in tetrahydrobiopterin biosynthesis and the treatment of human disease. In Biochemical and Clinical Aspects of Pteridines. H. Wachter, H.-Ch. Curtius & W. Pfleiderer, Eds. Vol. 2: 325-337. Walter de Gruyter. Berlin and New York.

15. LEVINE, R. A., G. KAPATOS, S. KAUFMAN & S. MILSTIEN. 1987. Biochem. Biophys. Res. Commun. Submitted.

16. MCINNES, R. R., S. KAUFMAN, J. J. WARSH, G. R. VAN LOON, S. MILSTIEN, G. KAPATOS, S. SOLDIN, P. WALSH, D. MACGREGOR & W. B. HANLEY. 1984. J. Clin. Invest. 73: 458.

17. NIEDERWIESER, A., H.-CH. CURTIUS, M. WANG & D. LEUPOLD. 1982. Eur. J. Pediatr. 138: 110-112.

18. ENDRES, W. 1985. In Inherited Diseases of Amino Acid Metabolism. H. Bickel and U. Wachtel, Eds. 124-132. Thieme. Stuttgart.

19. BARTHOLOME, K. & D. J. BYRD. 1975. Lancet 2: 1042-1043.

20. KAPATOS, G. & S. KAUFMAN. 1981. Science 212: 955-956.

21. LEVINE, R. A., W. LOVENBERG, A. NIEDERWIESER, W. LEIMBACHER, U. REDWICK, W. STAUDENMANN & H.-CH. CURTIUS. 1983. Penetration of reduced pterins into rat brain: effect on biogenic amine synthesis. In Chemistry and Biology of Pteridines. J. A. Blair, Ed. 176-182. Walter de Gruyter. Berlin and New York.

22. LEVINE, R. A., P. ZOPHEL, A. NIEDERWIESER & H.-CH. CURTIUS. 1987. J. Pharmacol. Exp. Ther. In press.

23. LOVENBERG, W., R. A. LEVINE, D. S. ROBINSON, M. EBERT, A. C. & D. B. CALNE. 1979. Science 204: 624-626.

24. WILLIAMS, A. C., R. ELDRIDGE, R. A. LEVINE, W. LOVENBERG & G. PAULSON. 1979. Lancet 2: 8139: 410-411.

25. LEWITT, P., L. MILLER, R. LEVINE, W. LOVENBERG, R. NEWMAN, A. PAPAVASILIOU, A. RAYES, R. ELDRIDGE & R. BURNS. 1986. Adv. Neurol. In press.

26. WILLIAMS, A. C., R. A. LEVINE, D. B. CALNE, T. N. CHASE & W. LOVENBERG. 1980. J. Neurol. Neurosurg. Psychiatry 43: 735-738.

27. KAY, A. D., S. MILSTIEN, S. KAUFMAN, H. CREASEY, J. V. HAXBY, N. R. CUTLER & S. I. RAPOPORT. 1986. Arch. Neurol. 43: 996-999.

28. WILLIAMS, A., J. BALLENGER, R. A. LEVINE, W. LOVENBERG & D. B. CALNE. 1980. Neurology 30: 1244-1246.

29. LEVINE, R. A., D. M. KUHN, A. C. WILLIAMS & W. LOVENBERG. 1981. The influence of aging on biogenic amine synthesis: the role of the hydroxylase cofactor. In Influence of Age on the Pharmacology of Psychoactive Drugs. A. Raskin, D. S. Robinson & J. Levine, Eds. 37-46. Elsevier. New York.

30. BARFORD, P. A., J. A. BLAIR, C. S. EGGAR, C. G. B. HAMON & S. B. WHITBURN. 1984. J. Neurol. Neurosurg. Psychiatry 47: 736.

31. MCGEER, P. L., E. G. MCGEER & J. S. SUZUKI. 1977. Arch. Neurol. 34: 33-35.

32. MCGEER, P. L. & E. G. MCGEER. 1976. J. Neurochem. 26: 65-76.

33. BRIDGE, T. P., S. POTKIN, C. D. WISE, B. H. PHELPS & R. J. WYATT. 1981. Monoamine oxidase and aging. In Age and the Pharmacology of Psychoactive Drugs. A. Raskin, D. S. Robinson & J. Levine, Eds. 79-89. Elsevier. New York.

34. SEIFERT, W. E., JR., J. L. FOXX & I. J. BUTLER. 1980. Ann. Neurol. 8: 38-42.

35. CARLSSON. A. 1976. Some aspects of dopamine in the basal ganglia. In The Basal Ganglia, M. D. Yahr, Ed. 181-189. Raven Press. New York.

36. BOWERS, M. B. & F. A. GERBODE. 1968. Nature 219: 1256.

37. GOTTFRIES, C. G., J. GOTTFRIES, B. JOHANSSON, et al. 1971. Neuropharmacology 10: 665-672.

38. LEWITT, P. A., R. A. LEVINE, W. LOVENBERG, N. POMARA, M. STANLEY, D. GUREVICH, P. SCHLICK & R. ROBERTS. 1986. Monoamine neurotransmitter metabolites and hydroxylase cofactor in Alzheimer-type dementia and normals. In Alzheimer's and Parkinson's Diseases: Strategies for Research and Development. A. Fisher, I. Hanin & C. Lachman, Eds. 323-327. Plenum Press. New York.

39. LeWitt, P., L. Miller, R. Levine, W. Lovenberg, R. Newman, A. Papavasilious, A. Rayes, R. Eldridge & R. Burns. 1986. Neurology **36:** 760-764.
40. Levine, R. A., D. M. Kuhn & W. Lovenberg. 1979. J. Neurochem. **32:** 1575-1578.
41. Ebels, I., A. L. Citharel & A. Moszkowska. 1975. J. Neural Trans. **36:** 281-302.
42. Moszkowska, A., A. Hus-Citharel, A. L'Heritier, W. Zurburg & Ebels. 1977. J. Neural Trans. **38:** 239-247.
43. Van der Have-Kirchberg, M. L. L., A. D. Moree, J. F. van Laar, G. J. Gerwig, C. Versluis & E. Ebeis. 1977. J. Neural Trans. **40:** 205-330.
44. Ebels, I. & G. Cremer-Bartels. 1982. Life Sci. **30:** 1369-1377.
45. Fuchs, D., et al. 1984. Eur. J. Clin. Microbiol. **3:** 70.
46. Wachter, H., H.-Ch. Curtius & W. Pfleiderer, Eds. 1985. Biochemical and Clinical Aspects of Pteridines. Walter de Gruyter. Berlin and New York.
47. Abita, J. P., et al. 1985. Lancet **1:** 51.
48. Huber, Ch., D. Fuchs, A. Hausen, et al. 1983. J. Immunol. **130:** 1047.
49. Huber, Ch., J. R. Batchelor, D. Fuchs, A. Hausen, A. Lang, D. Niederwieser, G. Reibnegger, P. Swetly, J. Troppmair & H. Wachter. 1984. J. Exp. Med. **160:** 310-316.
50. Schoedon, G. & A. Niederwieser. 1985. Metabolism of pterins in human peripheral blood mononuclear cells. In Biochemical and Clinical Aspects of Pteridines. H. Wachter. H.-Ch. Curtius & W. Pfleiderer, Eds. 368-377. Walter de Gruyter. Berlin and New York.
51. Margreiter, R., D. Fuchs, A. Hausen, C. Huber, G. Reibnegger, Spielberger & H. Wachter. 1983. Transplantation **36:** 560-653.
52. Huber, C. & J. Troppmair. 1985. Immune response-associated neopterin release: an overview. In Biochemical and Clinical Aspects of Pteridines: Cancer Immunology Metabolic Diseases. H. Wachter, H.-Ch. Curtius & W. Pfleiderer, Eds. 279-295. Walter de Gruyter. Berlin and New York.
53. Joller, P. W., N. Blau M. Atares & A. Niederwieser. 1983. Guanosine—triphosphate cyclohydrolase—deficiency: analysis of the influence on immune parameters in a girl. In Biochemical and Chemical Aspects of Pteridines: Cancer Immunology Metabolic Diseases. H. Wachter, H.-Ch. Curtius, and W. Pfleiderer, Eds. 167-176. Walter de Gruyter. Berlin and New York.

Pineal Melatonin, Its Fundamental Immunoregulatory Role in Aging and Cancer

GEORGES J. M. MAESTRONI,[a] ARIO CONTI,[a] AND
WALTER PIERPAOLI [b]

[a]Instituto Cantonale di Patologia
6604 Locarno, Switzerland
and
[b]Institute for Integrative Biomedical Research
8123 Ebmatingen, Switzerland

INTRODUCTION

A closely interwoven network of immune and neuroendocrine mechanisms protects our organism against a variety of environmental threats. Derangements of neuroendocrine functions such as those associated with or caused by failure to cope with stressful events or "distress" may lead in turn to an impairment of immunologic functions and possibly to an increased incidence of infections, autoimmune diseases and cancer.[1,3] As a matter of fact, functional connections and feedback loops between the immune and the neuroendocrine systems are being increasingly recognized.[4,6] Thus, primary defects in the neuroendocrine system or psychologic disturbances may adversely affect the immunologic machinery. The opposite is also true. In the case of aging, for example, the associated decline of both psychic and immune performance might, therefore, be triggered either by primary psycho-neuroendocrinologic or by immune alterations.

The pineal gland is a fundamental modulator of the entire neuroendocrine system. The pineal gland functions as a true "biologic clock" secreting in a circadian fashion its main neurohormone melatonin or N-acetyl-5-methoxytryptamine. Melatonin synthesis and release is regulated mainly by the light-dark cycle with a peak during the night, darkness hours.[7,8] However, other environmental variables such as temperature, humidity and, perhaps, pheromones and magnetism may influence its rhythm.[7,8] Also various physiopathologic states can affect melatonin rhythms. For example, in man alterations of melatonin production have been associated, amongst other things, with aging and cancer. In particular, low or impaired melatonin production has been described in aging[9] and various modifications of the melatonin rhythm have been found in cancer patients.[10]

We have recently found that the circadian synthesis and release of melatonin exerts an important immunomodulatory role.[4,11] Melatonin appears to be a physiologic "upregulator" of the immune system and to operate via the endogenous opioid system (EOS) on antigen-activated cells.[12,13] Here we report further on other immunologic properties of exogenous melatonin in the reversal of the immune impairment and thymus atrophy induced either by restraint stress or by pharmacologic corticosterone. Furthermore, we show that when properly administered in the course of primary immunization, melatonin can specifically and permanently enhance the "memory" immune reactivity against a specific antigen.

MELATONIN AS PHYSIOLOGIC "UP-REGULATOR" OF THE IMMUNE RESPONSE

When administered to mice in the evening, melatonin increased the primary antibody response (IgM + IgG) to T-dependent antigens. On the contrary, when administered in the morning, no effect on the immune response was apparent.[12] This circadian immunoenhancing effect was exerted by a broad range of melatonin doses (10 μg to 10 mg/kg body weight). On the basis of these findings we investigated if treatment with evening melatonin in the course of primary immunization against sheep red blood cells (SRBC) and/or vaccinia virus (VV) leads to any modification of the secondary response against the same antigen. TABLES 1 and 2 describe the results of

TABLE 1. Administration of Melatonin During Primary Immunization Enhances the Secondary Antibody Response to SRBC in Mice[a]

Group	(n)	Treatment during the Primary Immunization	Secondary Response PFC/Spleen (Ig M + Ig G)
A	(14)	Melatonin for 7 days	125413 ± 45271[b]
B	(14)	PBS for 7 days	64706 ± 32964

[a] Two groups of mice were immunized with 4×10^8 SRBC intraperitoneally (i.p.) and were injected subcutaneously (s.c.) for the following 7 days with melatonin (20 μg/kg b.w.) at 4 p.m., 2 hours before onset of darkness. Control mice were inoculated s.c. with 0.5 ml of PBS at the same hour. After this treatment the mice were left undisturbed for a further 3 weeks and then boostered i.p. with 4×10^8 SRBC. *Neither melatonin nor PBS* was inoculated during this second immunization. The secondary antibody response to SRBC was evaluated 3 days after the booster injection.
[b] $p \leq 0.01$: A vs B.

these experiments in which mice were immunized with SRBC or VV and treated by evening administration of melatonin for 6 days. The mice were then left undisturbed for 4 weeks and then boostered in order to evaluate the secondary antibody response to SRBC and the secondary T-cytotoxic response to VV, *without any further melatonin injection.* As is shown on TABLES 1 and 2, melatonin treatment during primary immunization against T-dependent antigens permanently enhanced the humoral and cellular immune reactivity against that given antigen. The mechanism of this remarkable action of melatonin is still unknown. However, it is possible that melatonin stimulates the differentiation and/or proliferation of memory cells via the EOS.

IS MELATONIN THE ANTI-STRESS HORMONE?

We have already reported that melatonin has the interesting property of reversing the depression of antibody production induced by corticosterone given to mice in the drinking water.[11] Here we report on experiments in which we investigated whether melatonin is able to counteract the effect of restraint-anxiety stress on antibody production, on thymus weight and on resistance against lethal infections with the very aggressive murine encephalomyocarditis virus (EMCV). TABLE 3 shows that evening administration of melatonin could completely buffer the depression of antibody production and thymus weight induced by the acute restraint stress in mice inoculated with SRBC (group B vs A). This effect of melatonin appeared to be dependent on

TABLE 2.[a]

Effector to Target (Ratio)	% of Specific ^{51}Cr Release $\pm$ S.D.[b]		% Variation (Melatonin vs PBS)
	PBS (n = 8)	Melatonin (n = 8)	
50 : 1	40.0 ± 4.6	52.3 ± 4.1[c]	+ 30
25 : 1	31.7 ± 6.1	44.8 ± 3.8[c]	+ 41
12 : 1	23.5 ± 4.6	32.7 ± 3.0[c]	+ 39
6 : 1	14.4 ± 3.8	23.2 ± 3.5[c]	+ 64

[a] C3H/He female mice, two months old, were injected i.v. with 1×10^6 PFU of vaccinia virus (VV) at 12 noon. In the following 6 days the mice were injected s.c. with melatonin (40 μg/kg b.w.) at 4 p.m., 2 hours before onset of darkness. Control mice were inoculated s.c. with 0.5 ml of PBS at the same hour. After this treatment the animals were kept undisturbed for 7 weeks with free access to food and water and under a 12-hour light cycle. A booster injection of 8×10^6 PFU of VV i.v. was then performed. *Neither melatonin nor PBS* was inoculated during this second immunization. After 4 days the antiviral cytotoxic T cell response was tested by the ^{51}Cr release assay. Effector spleen cells were diluted with L929 target cells at the following ratios: 50:1, 25:1, 12:1 and 6:1.
[b] % of specific ^{51}Cr release $\pm$ standard deviation (S.D.) was calculated according to the formula: $\dfrac{\text{Exp. release-Spontaneous release}}{\text{Total cpm}} \cdot 100 = \%$ spec. rel.
[c] $p < 0.01$.

antigen-activated T cells, because unprimed mice (groups G and H) or mice injected with T-independent antigens (LPS, groups E and F) did not show any melatonin effect. The anti-stress action of melatonin appeared also to be antagonized completely by the contemporary administration of the specific-opioid antagonist naltrexone. This suggested that even in stress situations, melatonin operates via the EOS (group C vs B). On the other hand, naltrexone alone had no effect either on antibody production or on thymus (group D). This showed that no direct naltrexone-sensitive opiatergic mechanisms are involved in the immunologic effect of acute stress. Most interesting, evening melatonin was able to confer resistance against lethal doses of EMCV in infected and stressed mice. TABLE 4 reports the survival of mice that were stressed

TABLE 3. Melatonin Counteracts the Effect of Restraint-Anxiety Stress on Thymus Weight and Antibody Production of Mice Injected with T-dependent Antigens[a]

Group	(n)	Stress	LPS	SRBC	Treatment	PFC/Spleen	mg Thymus Weight / g Body Weight
A	(15)	+	-	+	PBS	99903 ± 34230[b]	1.67 ± 0.57[c]
B	(15)	+	-	+	melatonin	199157 ± 62888[b]	2.35 ± 0.75[c]
C	(9)	+	-	+	melatonin + naltrexone	93391 ± 39509	1.61 ± 0.53
D	(5)	+	+	-	naltrexone	84149 ± 26795	1.60 ± 0.48
E	(10)	+	+	-	PBS	3773 ± 1187	0.76 ± 0.14
F	(10)	+	-	-	melatonin	1786 ± 392	0.76 ± 0.065
G	(18)	+	-	-	PBS	—	1.55 ± 0.46
H	(18)	+	-	+	melatonin	182035 ± 65881	1.62 ± 0.45
I	(14)	-	-	+	—	—	2.39 ± 0.63
L	(14)	-	-	-	—	—	2.67 ± 0.42

[a] Female, 2-3-months-old BALB/cJ mice kept under a 12-hour light cycle at 23 ± 1°C, with free access to food and water, were randomized in groups. Some groups were then stressed by restraining the mice in 50 ml plastic tubes with ventilation holes, for 2 hours/day for 4 days, starting from the day of antigen injection. Sheep red blood cells (SRBC) were injected i.p. (4×10^8/mouse) at 1 p.m., 1 hour after the first stress session. *Escherichia coli* lipopolysaccharide (LPS, type 055:B5, Sigma Co., St. Louis, USA) was also injected i.p. (100 μg/mouse) at 1 p.m. From the day of antigen injection, the mice were injected each evening at 4 p.m. (2 hours before onset of darkness) with melatonin (40 μg/kg body weight, s.c., Biosynth. AG, Staad, Switzerland), phosphate saline (PBS, 0.5 ml s.c.) and/or with naltrexone (1 mg/kg body weight, Sigma Co., St. Louis, USA). The number of spleen plasma cells producing direct (IgM-mediated) plaques after immunization of mice with SRBC or LPS was evaluated by the conventional hemolytic plaque-forming cells (PFC) assay in petri dishes. Anti-LPS, IgM-producing cells were detected after coating the SRBC by incubation with 2 mg/ml LPS 1 hour at 37°C. The values are expressed ± the standard deviation and the differences have been evaluated by the analysis of variance.
[b] $p < 0.01$: A vs I; B vs A, C, D.
[c] $p < 0.05$: A vs I, L; B vs A, C, D, G, H.

TABLE 4. Evening Administration of Melatonin Reverses the Impaired Immune Resistance of Mice Stressed Acutely by Physical Restraint and Inoculated with a Sublethal Dose of Encephalomyocarditis Virus (EMCV)[a]

(n)	Stress	EMCV	Treatment	% Survival ± S.D.				
				3 Days	6 Days	10 Days	30 Days
(25)	+	+	PBS only	92.3 ± 10.9	68.3 ± 9.5	7.7 ± 10.9	7.7 ± 10.9
(25)	+	+	melatonin	91.9 ± 0.45	88.1 ± 4.9	84.3 ± 10.4	84.3 ± 10.4
(25)	−	+	untreated	100.0 ± 0.0	88.2 + 4.9	88.2 ± 4.9	88.2 ± 4.9

[a] Female, 2-3-months-old BALB/cJ mice were inoculated with 0.2 ml of 2×10^8 dilutions of EMCV in saline on day 0. The mice were divided in groups and two of them were restrained two hours per day for 4 days as described (see TABLE 3). One of these groups was treated daily for 10 days with 1 μg of melatonin i.p. at 4 p.m. The remaining stressed group was treated with saline and served as control. The third group was neither stressed nor treated. Survival of 3 experiments is recorded as percentage and reported ± the standard deviation (S.D.).

by physical restraint and treated with melatonin or PBS. Other mice were inoculated with EMCV, received no melatonin and served as a nonstressed control group. It is evident that melatonin administered in the evening during 10 days after EMCV infection exerted a striking protective activity against EMCV and reversed completely the immunosuppressive influence of restraint stress (TABLE 4).

CONCLUSIONS AND PERSPECTIVES

The findings presented here, together with those previously reported,[9,11,13] point to a general immunoaugmenting effect of endogenous and/or exogenous melatonin. In particular, the present report shows that when administered in the course of primary immunization, melatonin possesses the remarkable property of permanently stimulating the immunologic reactivity against a given antigen. This attribute of melatonin holds promising obvious implications for vaccination procedures.

It seems clear that melatonin does not act directly but rather via the EOS.[12,13] Also the astonishing anti-stress properties of melatonin are, in fact, abrogated by the specific-opioid antagonist naltrexone. Furthermore, melatonin seems to exert its effect only in mice inoculated with T-dependent antigens. This indicates that antigen-activated T lymphocytes are possible targets for the melatonin-opioid action, and that final effector molecules could be products of these activated T cells. The identification of the specific opioid peptide involved in the melatonin action will allow a deeper analysis of the mechanisms involved. Experiments in this direction are in progress.

Another important aspect to be studied concerns the nature of the protection exerted by melatonin on the thymus of stressed and/or corticosterone-treated mice. We have performed preliminary studies by comparing histologic sections of thymuses from stressed and melatonin-treated mice with similar sections of thymuses from stressed and saline-treated mice. Although we did not perform any quantitative morphometric analysis, it is evident that melatonin did not protect the thymus cortex from the thymolitic action of corticosteroids, but rather produced a striking enlargement of the thymic medulla.[14] Obviously, this important point needs further investigation. The fact that exogenous, evening melatonin exerts this astonishing anti-stress effect might reflect a physiologic role of the neurohormone. Along this line, a prerequisite to any successful coping with stressful events would be an optimal synthesis and/or release of pineal melatonin. As a matter of fact, it has been suggested that failure to cope with "negative" events or distress (e.g., during aging) may depend on an exhausted EOS,[13] whose function seems also to be the coordination of the neuroendocrine response to a variety of nonspecific stressors.[3] In this regard, melatonin may have the physiologic function of restoring the EOS and thus the capacity of the organism to respond and adapt to environmental variables (e.g., temperature or antigens) and to psychosocial stress.

Many immunologic effects of stress closely resemble those associated with aging. For example, in both situations the thymus gland becomes atrophic and immune functions are impaired or imbalanced. As reported above, aging has been associated with impaired melatonin production.[9] It is thus reasonable that exogenous melatonin, i.e., the pineal neurohormone that tunes the entire neuroendocrine system according to basic environmental variables, might be able to correct the immune impairment associated with aging.

As far as neoplasia is concerned, the mechanism of the widely reported oncostatic activities of melatonin is still obscure. On the basis of our findings, the obvious suggestion would be that such activity depends on immunologic mechanisms. Experiments are now being carried out to help elucidate this important point.

All together, the present findings delineate a fundamental neuroimmunomodulatory mechanism that may open new physiologic prophylactic and immunotherapeutic interventions.

PROLONGATION OF LIFE IN MICE BY MELATONIN

The variety of the neuroendocrine mechanisms affected by melatonin, combined with our first clear findings on its immunoenhancing and anti-stress activity, guided us to the idea that the pineal gland could be considered a sort of "homeostatic headquarters," i.e., the organ in which afferent information of the most diverse nature and origin (light-darkness cycle, temperature, stress, antigens) is integrated, elaborated and finally transmitted as efferent signals able to coordinate and to modulate the neuroendocrine and immune adaptive responses of the organism to the external and/ or internal environment. On the other hand, the aging process can be synthetically and generally defined as a progressive decline and finally the loss of the capacity to cope with the environmental challenges. In addition, it is known that aging is associated with a progressive impairment of a most basic pineal function, namely the circadian production of melatonin.[9]

The duration of life of an organism is the result of a series of biologic processes in which any event is conditioned and determined by the preceding one. However, nature has provided all living creatures with rhythmic mechanisms able to reset the homeostatic capacity or, in other words, the adaptive functions of the organism. In this context, the pineal gland and in particular the circadian rhythm of melatonin synthesis seem to play a central role, both as a primary biologic clock which tunes the entire organism according to the basic light-darkness cycle, and as a pacemaker, via the rhythmic melatonin signal to the whole neuroendocrine system.[7,8]

On the basis of these considerations we thought of investigating the effect of chronic, exogenous melatonin on the life span of aging mice kept under a 12-hour light cycle at $23 \pm 1°C$ with free access to food.

Starting in November 1985, 10 male C57BL/6J inbred mice were given melatonin (10 μg/ml) in the drinking water every day. Another group of 10 mice were given tap water containing the same concentration of ethanol (0.01%) used to dissolve the neurohormone for the treated group. In order to avoid irregular drinking habits and to guarantee that the mice would ingest melatonin only during the night (darkness) hours, all the bottles with or without melatonin were always removed in the morning at 8:30 a.m. and put back in the evening at 6:00 p.m. The drinking water with or without melatonin was changed twice weekly. When the experiment started (November 1985) all the mice were 575 days (about 19 months) old and perfectly healthy.

To our surprise chronic, circadian, night administration of melatonin resulted in a progressive, striking improvement of the general state of the mice and, most important, in a remarkable prolongation of their life.

In fact, starting at 5 months from the initiation of melatonin administration, the body weight of the untreated mice still surviving started to decrease rapidly, and also astonishing differences in the fur and in the general conditions of the two groups (vigor, activity, posture) became increasingly evident. Melatonin treatment preserved completely optimal pelage conditions and the body weight was maintained at the original values (about 36 grams). Furthermore, the mean survival time $\pm$ standard deviation was 931 $\pm$ 80 days in the melatonin-treated group versus 752 $\pm$ 81 days in the untreated controls. This difference is significant with $p < 0.01$ (analysis of variance).

It would be premature to speculate on the significance of our preliminary results and the mechanism by which night, chronic administration of melatonin in aging mice prolongs their life span by approximately 20% (6 months) and, most important, greatly improves their general body conditions. Also, these preliminary findings need to be confirmed and extended in other strains of mice and other species. However, as proposed above, the melatonin-dependent circadian resetting of neuroendocrine and immune functions might account for this astonishing prolongation of the life span in melatonin-treated mice.

ACKNOWLEDGMENTS

We thank Ms. E. Hertens for skillful technical assistance.

REFERENCES

1. ADER, R., Ed. 1981. Psychoneuroimmunology. Academic Press. New York, NY.
2. GUILLEMIN, R., M. COHM & T. MELNECHUCK, Eds. 1985. Neural Modulation of Immunity. Raven Press. New York, NY.
3. PLOTNIKOFF, N. P., R. E. FAITH, A. J. MURGO & R. A. GOOD, Eds. 1986. Enkephalins and Endorphins: Stress and the Immune System. Plenum Press. New York, NY.
4. MAESTRONI, G. J. M. & W. PIERPAOLI. 1981. Pharmacologic control of the hormonally mediated immune response. *In* Psychoneuroimmunology. R. Ader, Ed. 405-425. Academic Press. New York, NY.
5. BLALOCK, J. E. & E. M. SMITH. 1985. A complete regulatory loop between the immune and the neuroendocrine systems. Fed. Proc. **44:** 108-112.
6. BESEDOVSKY, H., A. DEL REY, E. SORKIN & A. DINARELLO. 1986. Immunoregulatory feedback between interleukin-1 and glucocorticoid hormones. Science **233:** 652-654.
7. REITER, R., Ed. 1984. The Pineal Gland. Raven Press. New York, NY.
8. AXELROD, J., F. FRASCHINI & G. P. VELO, Eds. 1982. The Pineal Gland and Its Endocrine Role. Plenum Press. New York, NY.
9. IGUCHI, H., K. I. KATO & H. IBAYASHI. 1982. Age dependent reduction in serum melatonin concentrations in healthy human subjects. J. Clin. Endocrinol. Metab. **55:** 27-29.
10. BLASK, D. E. 1984. The pineal: an oncostatic gland? *In* The Pineal Gland. R. J. Reiter, Ed. 253-285. Raven Press. New York, NY.
11. MAESTRONI, G. J. M., A. CONTI & W. PIERPAOLI. 1986. Role of the pineal gland in immunity. Circadian synthesis and release of melatonin modulates the antibody response and antagonizes the immunosuppressive effect of corticosterone. J. Neuroimmunol. **13:** 19-30.
12. MAESTRONI, G. J. M., A. CONTI & W. PIERPAOLI. 1987. Role of the pineal gland in immunity. II. Melatonin enhances the antibody response via an opiatergic mechanism. Clin. Exp. Immunol. **68:** 384-391.
13. MAESTRONI, G. J. M., A. CONTI & W. PIERPAOLI. 1987. The pineal gland and the circadian, opiatergic, immunoregulatory role of melatonin. Ann. N.Y. Acad. Sci. In press.

14. MAESTRONI, G. J. M., A. CONTI & W. PIERPAOLI. 1987. Melatonin antagonizes the effect
     of acute stress via an opiatergic and T-cell dependent mechanism. In press.
15. COHEN, M. R., D. PICKAR, M. DUBOIS & R. M. COHEN. 1986. Studies of the endogenous
     opioid system in the human stress response. *In* Enkephalins and Endorphins: Stress and
     the Immune System. N. P. Plotnikoff, R. E. Faith, A. J. Murgo & R. A. Good, Eds.
     35-47. Plenum Press. New York, NY.

Modulation of Glucocorticoid Receptor from Development to Aging[a]

MOHAMMED KALIMI,[b] JOHN HUBBARD, AND SUBHENDU GUPTA

Department of Physiology
Medical College of Virginia
Virginia Commonwealth University
Richmond, Virginia 23298

INTRODUCTION

The responsiveness of target tissues to glucocorticoids is known to be altered in an age-dependent manner. Glucocorticoids are unable to induce many rat hepatic enzymes prior to a certain stage of maturation[1-3] and glucocorticoid induction of various liver enzymes decreases with increasing age.[4-7] Since glucocorticoid induction of hepatic enzymes is mediated by specific glucocorticoid receptors present in the target tissues, possible explanations for this age-dependent attenuation of enzyme induction may be (a) the absence of glucocorticoid receptors, (b) differences in the physiocochemical nature of rat liver glucocorticoid receptors, or (c) an alteration in the mechanism at a step distal to the initial binding of the hormone to the receptor, its activation and subsequent nuclear binding (presumably at the gene regulatory regions of discrete genes).

This paper will present a broad overview of the work carried out in our laboratory to investigate the developmental and age-related changes in rat liver glucocorticoid receptor binding, physiocochemical properties, and activation to explain the observed age-related changes in glucocorticoid induction of various hepatic enzymes.[8-10]

MATERIALS AND METHODS

Male Sprague-Dawley rats (CD strain from Charles River Breeding Laboratories, Wilmington, MA) were used throughout the present studies. Animals were maintained

[a]This work was supported by National Institutes of Health (NIH) Grant AM-24059 and NIH Research Career Development Award AM-00731 to M. Kalimi.

[b]Address for correspondence: Department of Physiology, Box 551, Medical College of Virginia, Richmond, VA 23298.

on a 12-h light/12-h dark cycle for up to 18-22 months. Animals having pathological abnormalities such as tumors were excluded. For developmental studies, offspring of male and female rats of Sprague-Dawley rats were used. Day of birth is designated as day 0.

The animals were adrenalectomized 2-6 days before being used and were kept on standard purina chow and 0.9% NaCl solution (saline) in addition to water ad libitum.

Steroids: 1,2,4[³H]dexamethasone (specific activities 31 Ci/mmol and 48.5 Ci/mmol) was obtained from New England Nuclear Corp. (Boston, MA). Unlabeled steroids were obtained from Sigma Chemical Co. (St. Louis, MO). Preparation of cytosol, steroid binding assays and nuclear binding assay were described previously.[8–10]

Protein was determined by the procedure of Lowry et al.[11] using bovine serum albumin as standard. DNA was estimated by the diphenylamine assay of Burton.[12]

The Scatchard[13] was employed to determine the number and affinity of specific dexamethasone binding sites. Statistical analysis was carried out employing the method of Dunnett.[14] Gel filtration and DEAE-cellulose chromatography methods were described previously.[8,9]

RESULTS

Estimation and Physicochemical Characterization of Glucocorticoid Receptors in Developing Rat Liver

Glucocorticoid receptors were present in the liver cytosol of 15-20-day-old fetal rats.[8] The receptor concentration increased steadily up to 21 days (postnatally) and remained almost constant thereafter for up to 2 months. No differences were observed in the affinity (Kd) of the receptor for the steroid (data not shown).

We observed that steroid-unoccupied glucocorticoid receptor of neonatal (3-7 days) rat liver cytosol significantly (about 60%) loses its binding ability to [³]dexamethasone within 8 h of incubation at 0°C. On the other hand, cytosol from adult animals displayed only 20% loss in binding during 8 h of incubation at 0°C. Similarly, we noted that steroid-occupied receptor complex from cytosol of neonatal (3-7 days) rats was less stable than that of adult rats. The T $\frac{1}{2}$ of dissociation of the neonatal [³H]dexamethasone-receptor complex was about 4 h, whereas the glucocorticoid receptor complex of adult rats dissociated with a T $\frac{1}{2}$ of almost 12 h (TABLE 1).

Next we examined whether known stabilizers of glucocorticoid receptors such as dithiothreitol and molybdate are able to enhance the stability of [³H]dexamethasone-receptor complexes of neonatal cytosol. Results presented in TABLE 1 suggest that addition of 5 mM dithiothreitol or 10 mM sodium molybdate to the cytosol of adult animals significantly enhanced the stability of the preformed [³H]dexamethasone-receptor complexes. However, these reagents were found to be ineffective in protecting [³H]dexamethasone-receptor complexes of neonatal rat liver cytosol (TABLE 1).

Thermally (25°C for 45 min) activated [³H]dexamethasone-receptor complexes from both neonatal and adult rat liver cytosol bound equally well to the nuclei prepared from both age groups (TABLE 2). Surprisingly, when activation was carried out at 0°C for 45 min by addition of 20 mM Ca²⁺, significantly more activation was observed in adult than in neonatal (as judged from the binding to nuclei) rat liver cytosols (TABLE 2).

Unactivated [³H]dexamethasone-receptor complexes of adult animals displayed two distinct peaks when applied on minicolumns of Sephadex G-100 and eluted with 0.3 M KCl. The first peak was eluted just after void volumes having a stokes radius of 70 A and representing about 70% of total specific bound radioactivity. The second peak eluted with a stokes radius of 55 Å and corresponded to about 30% of the total specific bound radioactivity (TABLE 3).

Unactivated [³H]dexamethasone-receptor complexes from neonatal cytosol resolved into two peaks. The first peak was eluted just after the void volume having

TABLE 1. Inactivation Rate of Steroid-occupied GR at 4°C[a]

	T ½ of Inactivation
Neonatal (3-7 days)	
Control cytosol	4 h
+ 5 mM dithiothreitol	4 h
+ 10 mM molybdate	4 h
Adult (45-60 days)	
Control cytosol	12 h
+ 5 mM dithiothreitol	14 h
+ 10 mM molybdate	20 h

[a] Cytosol prepared from neonatal and adult livers was incubated at 0°C for 2 h with 20 nM [³H]dexamethasone in the presence or absence of 1000-fold excess of unlabelled dexamethasone; chemical reagents were added as mentioned. The samples were then treated with charcoal-dextran and centrifuged. The supernatant was incubated at 0°C at various time intervals, 0.2 ml aliquots were removed and treated with charcoal-dextran, and bound radioactivity was determined as described in Materials and Methods. Results represent the mean of three determinations done in triplicates.

identical stokes radius (70 Å) as obtained for adult cytosol and consisted of about 40% of total specific bound radioactivity. Interestingly, the second peak consistently eluted with a Stokes radius of about 30 Å representing about 60% of the total specific bound radioactivity (TABLE 3).

Estimation and Physicochemical Characterization of Hepatic Glucocorticoid Receptors of Old Rats

We observed no difference in the affinity (Kd) of glucocorticoid receptor for glucocorticoids with aging. However, there was slight (20-30%) increase in receptor number with aging (data not presented).

No differences were noted in the inactivation rates between unoccupied cytosol receptors of both age groups when examined by incubating the samples at 0°C or 25°C. Interestingly, [³H]dexamethasone-bound glucocorticoid receptors of older an-

TABLE 2. Thermal and Ca^{2+}-dependent Activation of Hepatic [³H]Dexamethasone-Receptor Complex of Neonatal and Adult Rats[a]

	Nuclear Binding CPM/50 μg DNA
Neonatal (3-7 days)	
Unactivated cytosol (0°C for 2 h)	940 ± 142
Thermally activated cytosol (25°C for 45 min)	3180 ± 245
Ca^{2+}-activated cytosol (20 mM Ca^{2+}, 0°C for 45 min)	2300 ± 189
Adult (45-60 days)	
Unactivated cytosol (0°C for 2 h)	926 ± 89
Thermally activated cytosol (25°C for 45 min)	3040 ± 320
Ca^{2+}-activated cytosol (20 mM Ca^{2+}, 0°C for 45 min)	2986 ± 412

[a] Samples were incubated for 2 h at 0°C with 20 nM [³H]dexamethasone in the presence and absence of 1000-fold excess of unlabelled dexamethasone. The samples were further incubated as indicated. Following incubation, specific nuclear binding was determined as described in Materials and Methods.[9] The results are the mean ± S.E. of four determinations done in triplicate.

imals inactivated faster (about 20-30%) within 24 h at 0°C when compared with that of adult cytosols.

[³H]Dexamethasone-bound glucocorticoid receptors of older animals inactivated faster (about 20-30%) than that of adult ones when examined by incubating at 0°C for 24 h. However, no differences were noted in the activation rate between steroid-unoccupied cytosol receptors of both age groups when studied by incubating the samples at 0°C or 25°C. Interestingly, known stabilizers of glucocorticoid receptors such as molybdate, molybdate plus dithiothreitol or ATP plus dithiothreitol were found to protect the steroid-unoccupied glucocorticoid receptors of older rats more effectively than that of adult rats at both 25°C or 0°C (data not shown).

Thermal activation (25°C for 45 min) of [³H]dexamethasone-receptor complexes of both adult as well as old rat liver cytosols equally enhanced the nuclear binding of [³H]dexamethasone-receptor complexes. Surprisingly, the Ca^{2+}-dependent activation obtained at 0°C was significantly decreased in old liver cytosol when compared with adult (TABLE 4).

TABLE 3. Sephadex G-100 Gelfiltration Profile of Unactivated [³H]Dexamethasone-Receptor Complexes[a]

	Peak I 70 Å	Peak II 55 Å	Peak III 30 Å
Neonatal (3-7 days)	40%	—	60%
Adult (45-60 days)	70%	30%	—

[a] Samples were treated with [³H]dexamethasone at 0°C for 2 h—30 l of cytosol treated with charcoal-dextran were layered on a Sephadex G-100 minicolumns (0.6 × 20 cm) and were eluted with 10 mM Tris-HCl, pH 7.6, containing 0.3 M KCl. The total radioactivity in each fraction was determined as described in Materials and Methods.

We also observed no age-related changes in either Sephadex G-100 or DEAE-cellulose minicolumn elution profiles of both unactivated or thermally activated [³H]dexamethasone-receptor complexes (data not shown).

DISCUSSION

Alterations in glucocorticoid hormones responses with development and aging provide an interesting system to study how cellular components such as the glucocorticoid receptor or its gene structure change with age and how these changes may influence glucocorticoid hormone action. In the past, several investigators have characterized hepatic glucocorticoid receptors in immature and senescent rodents.[1-10] Unfortunately, little consistent information is currently available to explain the age-

TABLE 4. Thermal and Ca^{2+}-dependent Activation of Hepatic [³H]Dexamethasone-Receptor Complex of Adult and Old Rats[a]

	Nuclear Binding CPM/100 μg DNA
Adult (45-60 days)	
Unactivated cytosol (0°C for 2 h)	984 ± 186
Thermally activated cytosol (25°C for 45 min)	6500 ± 1284
Ca^{2+}-activated cytosol (20 mM Ca^{2+}, 0°C for 45 min)	4200 ± 1024
Old (24-28 months)	
Unactivated cytosol (0°C for 2 h)	1120 ± 240
Thermally activated cytosol (25°C for 45 min)	6142 ± 1486
Ca^{2+}-activated cytosol (20 mM Ca^{2+}, 0°C for 45 min)	2945 ± 1245

[a] Samples were incubated for 2 h at 0°C with 20 nM [³H]dexamethasone in the presence and absence of 1000-fold excess of unlabelled dexamethasone. The samples were further incubated as indicated. Following incubation, specific nuclear binding was determined as described in Materials and Methods.[8] The results are the mean ± S.E. of four determinations done in triplicate.

dependent changes in the glucocorticoid receptor to the observed changes in target tissue responsiveness. In order to understand this relationship, we have focused our studies for the past several years on probably maturation and age-related impairment (if any) in the initial steps in glucocorticoid hormone action, namely, (a) binding of the steroid to its receptor, (b) activation of the steroid-receptor complex, and (c) binding of the activated steroid-receptor complex to nuclei.

We have observed some interesting changes in liver glucocorticoid receptors of both immature and senescent rats. For example, both unoccupied and steroid-occupied rat hepatic glucocorticoid receptors of fetal and neonatal animals have a short half life compared to adult mature animals. A significant decrease in Ca^{2+}-dependent activation of glucocorticoid receptor was also observed in fetal and neonatal cytosols when compared to adult animals. Finally, whereas the adult rat hepatic thermally activated dexamethasone-receptor complex was largely eluted as a 55-Å species, cytosols from immature animals showed a large amount of a smaller fragment having a stokes radius of 30 Å.[9]

Liver cytosols of senescent rats displayed about a 20% increase in the inactivation rate of steroid-occupied glucocorticoid-receptor complexes. Interestingly, when stabilizing agents such as molybdate, ATP or dithiothreitol were added to the samples, there was significantly more protection obtained from dissociation of dexamethasone-receptor complexes by these reagents in senescent animals as compared to adult rats. Finally, a significant decrease in low-temperature, CA^{2+}-dependent activation was noted in glucocorticoid-receptor complexes of senescent animals as compared to adult animals.[8-10]

Recently, Belisle et al.[15] reported that a decrease in receptor activation is primarily responsible for the reduced estrogenic responsiveness in aging mice. Similarily, Chilton et al.[16] concluded that an increased dissociation rate and decreased activation rate of the estrogen receptor in immature rabbit uteri may represent a mechanism for the attunation of estrogen action before sexual maturation of rabbit uterus. Overall, the data obtained by our laboratory suggests that beside other yet unknown factors, a decrease in the rat hepatic glucocorticoid-receptor stability and impairment in the Ca^{2+}-dependent activation of glucocorticoid-receptor complexes observed in both immature and aged rats may be linked to the observed lack or delayed induction by glucocorticoids of various hepatic enzymes in the fetal and neonatal rat liver.

REFERENCES

1. SERENI, F., F. KENNY & N. KRETCHMER. 1959. J. Biol. Chem. **234:** 609-612.
2. HOLT, P. & I. OLIVER. 1968. Biochem. J. **108:** 339-341.
3. YEOH, G., T. ARBUCKLE & I. OLIVER. 1979. Biochem. J. **108:** 545-549.
4. ADELMAN, R. & G. FREEMAN. 1972. Endocrinology **90:** 1551.
5. FROLKIS, V. 1970. Exp. Gerontol. **5:** 37.
6. PATNAIK, S. & M. KANUNGO. 1974. Biochem. Biophys. Res. Commun. **56:** 845.
7. RAO, S. & M. KANUNGO. 1972. Mech. Aging Dev. **1** 61-64.
8. KALIMI, M., S. GUPTA, J. HUBBARD & K. GREENE. 1983. Endocrinology, **112:** 341-347.
9. KALIMI, M. & S. GUPTA. 1982. J. Biol. Chem. **257:** 13324-13328.
10. KALIMI, M. 1986. Mech. Aging Dev. **35:** 59-70.
11. LOWRY, O., N. ROSEBROUGH, A. FARR & R. RANDALL. 1951. J. Biol. Chem. **193:** 265-275.
12. BURTON, K. 1956. Biochemistry **62:** 315-322.
13. SCATCHARD, G. 1949. Ann. N.Y. Acad. Sci. **51:** 660-664.
14. DUNNETT, C. 1955. J. Am. Stat. Assoc. **50:** 1096-1121.
15. CHILTON, B., N. DAWNWILLIAMS, A. COBB & C. WILEAVITT. 1987. Endocrinology **120:** 750-757.
16. BELISLE, S., D. BELLABARBA, J. LEHONX, P. ROBEL & E. BAULIEU. 1986. Endocrinology **118:** 750-758.

Life and Death of Neurons: The Role of Senescent Cell Antigen

MARGUERITE M. B. KAY,[a] GEILJAN BOSMAN,[a]
MARY NOTTER,[b] AND PAUL COLEMAN [b]

[a] Departments of Medicine, Medical Biochemistry and Genetics, and
Medical Microbiology and Immunology
Texas A&M University College of Medicine
1901 South First Street
Teague Veterans Center (151)
Temple, Texas 76501
and
[b] Department of Anatomy
University of Rochester
Rochester, New York

INTRODUCTION

One of the homeostatic activities vital to the evolution of vertebrates and to the development and survival of individuals is the ability to remove cells programmed for death at the end of their useful life span. Daily maintenance of homeostasis in adults requires removal of senescent and damaged cells and tissue repair following trauma. For example, approximately 360 billion senescent red cells are removed daily in humans. An understanding of this basic homeostatic mechanism is essential to both development and aging, and to the concept of recognition and specificity which permeates disciplines in biomedicine.

METHODS

General Methods. See REFERENCES 1 and 2 for detailed methods.
Human Neuroblastoma Cell Preparation. The human neuroblastoma line IMR-32 was obtained from the American Type Culture Collection. Cells were grown in Eagles' minimal essential medium with 10% FCS, 50 μg/ml gentamicin and 2.5 μg/ml fungizone under the same environmental conditions as described above. Cells were subcultured and exposed to band 3 antiserum in suspension for flow cytometric analysis as described for mouse neuroblastoma cells.

Differentiation of IMR-32 cells was as previously described[3] and consisted of mitomycin C treatment (0.5 gmg/ml) of cells followed by 10^{-5} μ bromodeoxyuridine added six hours later. Morphological differentiation as seen by extensive neuritic branching occurred after four days.

Cell Differentiation. N_2AB-1 were grown in flasks and treated with prostaglandin E_1 (PGE_1, 10 μg/ml) and dibutyryl cyclic adenosine monophosphate (cAMP, 500 μg/ml) for a minimum of four days. After this time, 90% of the cells show bipolar neuritic extensions and are inhibited in cell growth as determined by cytometric analysis of propidium iodide (PI) stained DNA.[4]

Immunofluorescent Staining. To examine cells for the senescent cell antigen segment of band 3 protein, aliquots of N_2AB-1 were treated with 0.25 ml rabbit antiserum to human band 3 (diluted 1:2 with PBS) in suspension on ice for 30 min. Cells were rinsed two times with PBS-FCS, pelleted and resuspended in 0.25 ml of FITC conjugated goat anti-rabbit IgG (1:20). After 30 min cells were rinsed and resuspended in PBS-FCS for flow cytometric analysis. Controls included elimination of the primary antibody as well as elimination of both antibodies.

Cell viability was determined by adding 0.74 mM PI to each aliquot. PI binds to nucleic acids and can only penetrate fixed or dead cells; therefore, the percentage of red fluorescing cells per aliquot of treated cells is a measure of cell death.

Immunofluorescence staining of band 3 on N_2AB-1 cells in a monolayer was the same as that described above except cells were grown on 15-mm round, sterile coverslips, treated with drugs for differentiation and processed for staining at room temperature. Cells were examined for fluorescence with a Nikon fluorescence microscope equipped with epi-illuminescence and phase-contrast optics.

DNA Analysis. For cytometric analysis of cellular DNA, control cells and drug-treated N_2AB-1 cells were removed from the flasks and were fixed in suspension with cold 95% ethanol for 1 h on ice. After pelleting, cells were treated with 0.1 mg/ml ribonuclease (Worthington) for 30 min at 37°C. Cells were then rinsed and stained with 0.74 mM PI in PBS. Cells were excited by the 488-nm line of the sorter's argon-ion laser and fluorescence beyond 610 nm was measured on a cell-by-cell basis. A DNA cell cycle analysis program, PARA-1,[5] was employed for plotting cell cycle-DNA histograms of neuroblastoma cells.

Flow Cytometry. Multiparameter flow cytometric analysis and cell sorting of neural cells was accomplished using an EPICS V cell sorter (Coulter Electronics, Hialeah, FL). Cells were excited with an argon-ion laser (Model 2025, Spectra Physics, Mountain View, CA) tuned to 488 nm at 500 m W output power. Band 3 immunofluorescence was measured between 515 and 560 nm. PI fluorescence was collected beyond 630 nm and was used to gate on PI-negative (live) cells which excluded the dye. Light scatter pulse-width time-of-flight was measured using a homebuilt outboard module recently modified to subtract out the laser beam width. With real-time beam subtraction, the time required for a cell to cross the laser beam is directly proportional to the cell diameter. Data were acquired on an 8086-based microcomputer (MDADS, Coulter Electronics) and analyzed on a PDP11/23 minicomputer (Terak, Scottsdale, AZ) using homebuilt software packages 'ROMP' and 'ROC3D.'

Band 3 Senescent Cell Antigen Segment Surface Density. Cell surface receptor density was analyzed by flow cytometry as previously described by us for toxin receptors of N_2AB-1 cells.[6] For simultaneous analysis of band 3 senescent cell antigen segment expression and cell cycle phase, N_2AB-1 cells were first stained in suspension by immunofluorescence for band 3 protein. Cells were then fixed and treated for DNA visualization by RNase treatment and PI staining. For each cell, green fluorescence was collected from 515-560 nm and red fluorescence above 610 nm. Date were taken in listmode and reprocessed to calculate the square of the LSPW signal as a measure of cell surface area, and the ratio of green fluorescence to surface area as a measure of the mean surface protein density.

RESULTS AND DISCUSSION

Mechanism of Removal of Senescent Cells

Investigation of the mechanism by which senescent cells are removed from the body was approached by postulating that Ig in normal serum attaches to the surface of senescent human red cells until a critical level is reached, which results in removal of these cells by macrophages.[7,8] These studies demonstrated that Ig is required to initiate phagocytosis of senescent and stored cells and that IgG attaches *in situ* to senescent human RBC.[8] Old RBC separated by density centrifugation from freshly drawn blood had ~100 molecules of IgG but no IgA or IgM on their surface as determined by scanning immunoelectron microscopy.[8] Young RBC did not have immunoglobulin on their surface. Incubation of old RBC with autologous macrophages resulted in their phagocytosis regardless of whether incubations were performed in medium without serum, autologous Ig-depleted serum or whole serum.[8] Young RBC were not phagocytized under any of these conditions. Thus, it appeared that the IgG attached *in situ* to senescent human RBC and rendered them vulnerable to phagocytosis by macrophages. The presence of IgG autoantibodies indicates that a new antigen has appeared on the surface of old cells that is not present on other cells. This was the first indication that a "neo-antigen" appears on senescent cells.

These results were confirmed *in vivo* using mice which were bred and maintained in a Maximum Security Barrier devoid of viruses, mycoplasma, and pathogenic bacteria thus excluding an exogenous source for the senescent cell antigen.[9] RBC were labeled *in situ* with ^{59}Fe which labels the newly synthesized hemoglobin in young cells. Red cells were separated on Percoll gradients, 1 or 40 days after radioactive iron injection, into young and old populations, and injected into separate groups of syngeneic mice. Kinetic studies revealed that less than 90% of the ^{59}Fe-labeled young RBC were removed from the circulation within 45 days. In contrast, more than 90% of the ^{59}Fe-labeled old RBC were removed within 20 days. The difference in the rate of removal of young and old RBC was statistically significant (P ≤ 0.001). Kinetic studies on density-separated spleen cell populations revealed that the radioactivity decreased in the RBC fraction concomitantly with an increase in radioactivity in the splenic macrophage fraction. The radioactivity was found to be inside macrophages.[9] Studies performed *in vitro* with mouse splenic macrophages and autologous young and old RBC revealed that mouse macrophages phagocytized senescent but not young RBC (P ≤ 0.001). The phagocytosis of middle-aged RBC (~23%) was intermediate between that of young RBC (~5%) and old RBC (~50%). This suggested that the appearance of the senescent cell antigen, and, thus, molecular aging of membranes, was a cumulative process.

The IgG attached to senescent cells *in situ* was shown to be an autoantibody.[10] The antibodies could be dissociated from senescent cells. The dissociated antibodies specifically reattached via the antigen binding (Fab) portion of the IgG molecule to homologous old, but not young cells.[10] Fab binding was demonstrated by antigen blockade studies, scanning immunoelectron microscopy, and ^{125}I-labeled Protein A binding to the Fc region of IgG bound to senescent cells and vesicles.[10–12] Thus, the antibody to senescent cell antigen is an autoantibody and not a nonspecific or a cytophilic antibody.[10] It exhibited specific immunologic binding via the Fab region. Binding of an IgG autoantibody to senescent RBC through immunologic mechanisms indicated that antigenic determinants recognized by these IgG autoantibodies appeared on the membrane surface as RBC aged.

Senescent cell antigen was isolated from sialoglycoprotein mixtures with affinity columns prepared with IgG eluted from senescent cells.[13] Material specifically bound by the column was eluted with glycine-HCl buffer, pH 2.3. Both glycoprotein and protein stains of gels of the eluted material revealed a band migrating at a relative molecular weight of $\sim 62,000$ daltons in the component 4.5 region. These experiments suggested that the $\sim 62,000$ M_r glycopeptide carried the antigenic determinants recognized by IgG obtained from freshly isolated senescent cells. The $\sim 62,000$ M_r peptide, but not the remaining sialoglycoprotein mixture from which it was isolated, abolished the phagocytosis-inducing ability of IgG eluted from senescent RBC in the erythrophagocytosis assay.[13–15] This indicated that the 62,000 M_r peptide was the antigen which appeared on the membrane of cells as they aged.

Examination of other somatic cells for the antigen which appears on senescent RBC revealed its presence on lymphocytes, platelets, neutrophils, cultured human adult liver cells, and primary cultures of human embryonic kidney cells as determined by a phagocytosis inhibition assay.[13] The senescent cell antigen was isolated from lymphocytes[13,15] with the senescent RBC IgG affinity column. Gel electrophoresis of the material obtained from the column revealed a band migrating at a M_r of 62,000 at the same position as the antigen isolated from senescent RBC. This finding confirmed the results obtained with the phagoctytosis inhibition assay, indicating that the antigen which appeared on senescent RBC also appeared on other somatic cells.

Appearance of the $\sim 62,000$ M_r antigen on RBC initiates binding of IgG autoantibodies in situ and phagocytosis of senescent cells by macrophages.[7,8,13] The antigen is present on stored human lymphocytes, platelets, and neutrophils, and on cultured liver and kidney cells. In addition, IgG autoantibodies in normal serum have been shown to bind to senescent RBC in situ in humans,[8] mice,[9] rats,[16] cows,[17] and rabbits.[18,19] Thus, the immunological mechanism for removing senescent and damaged red cells appears to be a general physiological process for removing cells programmed for death in mammals and, possibly, other vertebrates.[7,8,13] This work demonstrates that macrophages distinguish between senescent and mature RBC on the basis of selective IgG attachment, and firmly establishes the existence of autoantibodies with intrinsic physiologic and homeostatic functions. The IgG that binds to senescent RBC in situ and stored RBC in vitro is an autoantibody, as it specifically attaches to old cells via the Fab region, thus initiating their selective destruction by macrophages. The IgG autoantibody is directed against an altered membrane protein, not a cryptic antigen.

The IgG autoantibody induces phagocytosis of senescent RBC by macrophages. As a result, senescent cells are removed from the circulation instead of lysing.[20–23] Thus, the membranes and hemoglobin of the approximately 1.93×10^{11} senescent cells that are removed daily are enzymatically degraded by macrophages rather than being released into the circulation by lysis. Lysis of RBC could be detrimental to an individual's survival. For example, individuals with elevated plasma iron levels, as are seen with overt hemolytic anemia or destruction of ferritin-containing liver cells (e.g., viral hepatitis), are extremely susceptible to even a small inoculum of invading pathogens.[24] Iron enhances the virulence of bacteria and can neutralize the microbiostatic action of serum (for review, see REFERENCE 24).

The IgG described herein is a physiologic autoantibody, as it contributes to the maintenance of homeostasis by permitting the more efficient mature cells to carry out their vital functions without hindrance from the less efficient senescent cells, or from pathological reactions which could arise as a consequence of senescent cells dying or decaying within the organism. This was the first experimental demonstration of the existence of homeostatic autoantibodies. Since these autoantibodies are part of the normal immune mechanism for removing cells, the B cell clones producing these antibodies cannot be "forbidden,"[25,26] nor need the presence of these autoantibodies be attributed to an age-related decrease in suppressor cell function.[27,28] Many other physiologic autoantibodies, such as auto-anti-idiotypic antibodies, have since been demonstrated (for a review, see REFERENCE 11).

It appears that autoantibodies function as a regulatory mechanism for initiating as well as terminating metabolic processes. This is suggested by studies of the pathophysiology of certain disease processes. For example, thyroid-stimulating immunoglobulin (TSI) is an IgG autoantibody that binds to the thyroid follicular cell's receptor or a component thereof. TSI stimulates cyclic adenosine monophosphate and endocytosis of colloid droplets, displaces thyroid stimulating hormone from membrane sites and results in excessive levels of circulating thyroid hormone.[29] The existence of an autoantibody that can initiate the activities of an endocrine gland, even though it is associated with a disease, suggests the possibility that other autoantibodies may exist which act as initiators of homeostatic processes. Less dramatic examples of immunoglobulins initiating metabolic processes are the "capping" that is observed following binding of anti-immunoglobulin reagents to lymphocyte membranes and the DNA synthesis initiated by culturing lymphocytes with anti-immunoglobulin.[30–32]

It is interesting that greater than 90% of the immunoglobulin molecules in human serum are of the IgG class. IgG has the longest half-life and the highest rate of synthesis of any immunoglobulin class.[33] A calculation of the amount of IgG in a human being reveals that each of us has approximately a quarter of a kilogram. This is rather excessive unless IgG serves physiologic functions other than opsonization of occasional bacteria. One of these physiologic functions is the removal of senescent cells. Others remain to be elucidated.

Like the neuroendocrine system, the immune system is organismal and is in contact with most organs and tissues in the body. The immune system and the brain share some antigens such as a T cell related, "theta-like" antigen. Both systems synthesize and secrete macromolecules that have far-reaching effects on other systems. The time has come to consider the possibility that autoantibodies may serve as intercellular communicators and that an overlooked function of these antibodies may be that of "messengers."

Mechanism(s) of Cellular Aging

Since mature erythrocytes cannot synthesize proteins, the senescent cell antigen was probably generated by modification of a preexisting protein of higher molecular weight.[14,15] It was postulated that the senescent cell antigen was a component of the band 4.5 region that was derived from band 3[15] based on both extraction and isolation conditions, relative molecular weight, and its characterization as a glycosylated peptide.[13]

Experiments designed to test this hypothesis revealed that the senescent cell antigen is immunologically related to band 3 and may represent a physiologically significant breakdown product of the parent molecule.[11,34] Both band 3 and senescent cell antigen abolished the phagocytosis-inducing ability of IgG eluted from senescent cells; whereas, spectrin, bands 2.1, 4.1, actin, glycophorin A, PAS staining bands 1-4, and desialylated PAS staining bands 1-4 did not. In addition, rabbit antibodies to both purified band 3 and the senescent cell antigen reacted with band 3 and its breakdown products as determined by immunoautoradiography of RBC membranes indicating that these molecules share common antigenic determinants not possessed by other red cell membrane components.[11,34,35]

Senescent cell antigen was mapped along the band 3 molecule using topographically defined fragments of band 3. Both binding of IgG eluted from senescent red blood cells ("senescent cell IgG") to defined proteolytic fragments of band 3 in immunoblots, and two-dimensional peptide mapping of senescent cell antigen, band 3, and defined proteolytic fragments of band 3 were used to localize senescent cell antigen along the band 3 molecule.[35] The data suggested that the antigenic determinants of the senescent cell antigen that are recognized by physiologic IgG autoantibodies reside on an external portion of a naturally occurring transmembrane fragment of band 3 that has lost an M_r 40,000 cytoplasmic (NH_2-terminal) segment and part of the anion transport region. A critical cell age specific cleavage of a band 3 appears to occur in the transmembrane, anion transport region of band 3.

TABLE 1. Effect of Cellular Aging and Vitamin E Deficiency on Anion Transport System of Rat Erythrocytes[a]

	K_m (mM)	V_{max} (Mol $\times 10^{-8}$ per 10^8 Cells per Min)
Cell age		
Middle-aged	0.5 ± 0.2	41.8 ± 1.9
Old	1.6 ± 0.4[b]	17.3 ± 3.8[b]
Vitamin E diet		
Normal	0.7 ± 0.1	41.2 ± 3.7
Deficient	2.0 ± 0.3[b]	16.2 ± 2.0[b]
Deficient + vitamin E	2.0 ± 0.3[b]	12.1 ± 1.7[b]

[a] Results presented as the mean ± 1 SD. There is no statistical difference between deficient, deficient + vitamin E, and old cells. K_m, concentration at half-maximal exchange, corresponding to an apparent Michaelis-Menten constant (in mM); V_{max}, maximal flux, determined at 37°C and pH 7.2. From REFERENCE 51.
[b] $P \leq 0.01$.

From these studies indicating that a cleavage of band 3 occurs in the anion transport region,[35-37] we suspected that anion transport might be altered with cellular aging. If this suspicion proved to be correct, then we would have a functional assay for aging of band 3, the major anion transport protein of the erythrocyte membrane.

Transport studies on age-separated rat and human erythrocytes indicated that anion transport decreased with age (TABLE 1). The Michaelis-Menten constant (K_M) increased and the maximal velocity (V_{max}) decreased in old red cells as compared to middle-aged red cells.

A decrease in band 3 functioning with erythrocyte age supports the data indicating the alteration of band 3 occurs during erythrocyte aging and generation of senescent cell antigen.[35-37]

Since the senescent cell antigen and band 3 share antigenic determinants, the effect of cellular age on the accumulation of band 3 breakdown products was investigated using the immunoblotting technique.[36,37] Antibodies to band 3 and the senescent cell antigen were used to determine the relative amount of band 3 breakdown products in the membranes of young, middle-aged, and old cells by immunoautoradiography using the gel overlay and immunoblotting procedures.[35,36] Results revealed binding of both antibodies to band 3 and IgG eluted from senescent cells to a polypeptide migrating at $M_r \sim 62,000$ in membranes of old but not young cells. The results indicated that band 3 breakdown products increase with cell age and that antigenic determinants recognized by the IgG eluted from senescent cells reside on a $M_r \sim 62,000$ fragment of band 3. Although band 3 comprises 25% of the erythrocyte membrane protein, circulating, naturally occurring autoantibodies to band 3 in normal human serum[11] do not bind to RBC unless they are senescent, stored, or damaged.[8,10,38]

As a mechanism for cellular aging and generation of senescent cell antigen, free radical reactions and oxidation are considered probable candidates.[39] Most free radical reactions involve the reduction of molecular oxygen, leading to the formation of highly reactive oxygen species such as superoxide anion (O_2^-), hydroxyl radical ($\cdot OH$), hydrogen peroxide (H_2O_2) and singlet oxygen ($^1O_2$). The production of these highly reactive oxygen species as metabolic intermediates appears to be an evolutionary consequence of aerobic existence because the spin state of oxygen favors univalent pathways of reduction.[40] We used vitamin E deficiency as a model for studying oxidation because studies show that, in mammals, vitamin E functions as an antioxidant, and because vitamin E deficiency simulates conditions encountered *in situ* more closely than does chemical treatment of cells *in vitro*.

As an approach to evaluating oxidation as a possible mechanism responsible for generation of senescent cell antigen, we studied red cells from vitamin E deficient rats. The importance of vitamin E as an antioxidant, providing protection against free radical-induced membrane damage, has been well documented.[41-44] Vitamin E is primarily localized in cellular membranes, and a major role of vitamin E is the termination of free radical chain reactions propagated by the polyunsaturated fatty acids of membrane phospholipids. Vitamin E deficient red cells are defective in their ability to free radical scavenge.[44,45]

In humans, vitamin E deficiency shortens red cell life span causing a compensated hemolytic anemia in patients with cystic fibrosis.[46] In newborns, vitamin E deficiency causes a hemolytic anemia that develops by 4 to 6 weeks of age.[47]

The role of free radical damage in aging has received a great deal of attention. It is interesting that there is a correlation between life span and natural antioxidant levels in a variety of species and that the level of such antioxidants appears to correlate with metabolic activity of individual species.[48] Evidence for free radical damage associated with aging is the presence of lipofusion and ceroid, so-called aging pigments which represent accumulated breakdown products of polyunsaturated fatty acids and proteins. It has been suggested that free radicals may be mediators of aging and specific pathologies such as inflammation, arthritis, adult respiratory distress syndrome and other conditions.[49,50] Free radicals have also been implicated as causative agents in mutagenesis and carcinogenesis as well as causing crosslinking of macromolecules and the formation of age pigments.[50]

Clinical studies on Vitamin E deficient rats indicated accelerated destruction of red cells and were consistent with the vitamin E deficient rats having a compensated hemolytic anemia[51] as is observed in vitamin E deficient humans. Serum haptoglobin was significantly reduced in vitamin E deficient rats.

Haptoglobin binds specifically and tightly to the protein (globin) in hemoglobin.

The hemoglobin-haptoglobin complex is cleared within minutes by the mononuclear-phagocyte system while free haptoglobin has a prolonged circulation time. The number of reticulocytes was increased in vitamin E deficient rats.

Anion transport studies were performed to evaluate band 3 function. Results of the anion transport studies on red cells from vitamin E deficient rats revealed that their anion transport was impaired as was transport in old red cells (TABLE 1).

The phagocytosis assay was performed on both age-separated and unseparated red cells from rats fed a diet containing normal amounts of vitamin E or a diet deficient in vitamin E (TABLE 2). Old red cells obtained from rats fed a diet containing normal amounts of vitamin E were phagocytized; whereas, young and middle-aged red cells were not. In contrast, young and middle-aged as well as old red cells were phagocytized when obtained from vitamin E deficient rats. There was a significant difference in phagocytosis between red cells obtained from normal rats and vitamin E deficient rats even when unfractionated red cells were used for the assay (TABLE 2).

Our studies indicate that G3PD activity is reduced in old red cells and in red cells from vitamin E deficient rats.[51] Thus, cells from vitamin E deficient rats behave like old cells in respect to G3PD activity.

TABLE 2. Phagocytosis of Unfractionated and Age-separated Erythrocytes from Vitamin E Deficient and Normal Rats[a]

Vitamin E Diet	Erythrocyte Fraction	% Phagocytosis
Normal (50 mg/kg)	young	2 ± 3
	middle-aged	1 ± 1
	old	72 ± 3
	unfractionated	13 ± 3
Deficient (0 mg/kg)	young	89 ± 1
	middle-aged	88 ± 1
	old	99 ± 0
	unfractionated	87 ± 1

[a] The phagocytosis assay was performed with U937 cells. Erythrocytes were incubated with macrophages overnight at 37°C in a humidified atmosphere containing 5% CO_2. Data are presented as the mean ± 1 SD; n = 3. Diet is expressed as mg of vitamin E per kg of diet. From REFERENCE 51.

Differences were not detected in protein or glycoprotein composition of erythrocyte membranes from control and vitamin E deficient rats. Although high molecular weight polypeptides or polymers were detected with Coomassie blue staining of 2-16% polyacrylamide gels, there were no differences in the number or amount of these polypeptides between control and experimental samples. Immunoblotting studies revealed increased breakdown products of band 3 in cells from vitamin E deficient rats.[51]

Results of the experiments on Vitamin E deficiency suggest that oxidation can cause aging of band 3. We suspect that this may be one of the mechanisms of cellular aging in situ. At this time, it appears that general cellular damage such as lysis (Kay, unpublished), and oxidation can result in the generation of senescent cell antigen. We suspect that many different cellular insults have a final common pathway that results in generation of senescent cell antigen.

Band 3 in Nonerythroid Cells

We suspected that band 3 was present in nucleated somatic cells as well as red cells because senescent cell antigen which is immunologically related to band 3[11,34] is present on lymphocytes, platelets, adult liver cells, and embryonic kidney cells.[13,14] Furthermore, antibodies prepared against the senescent cell antigen isolated from white blood cells react with erythrocyte band 3;[34] and other cells are known to transport anions.[52]

As a test of this hypothesis, primary cultures of human fibroblasts, lung cells, neutrophils, mononuclear white cells, squamous epithelial (mouth) cells, lung squamous epithelial carcinoma, rhabdomyosarcoma, mouse neuroblastoma cells, and rat hepatocytes were examined for the presence of immunoreactive forms of band 3 by immunofluorescence, immunoelectron microscopy, and immunoautoradiography.[53] Band 3 related polypeptides were demonstrated in all of these cells. Peptide mapping indicated that these polypeptides share peptide homology with erythrocyte band 3. However, band 3 polypeptides were present in nucleated cells in much smaller quantities than in red cells.[53] Rather than appearing on one of the major bands as they do in red cells, they were one of many minor bands and could be identified only with immunoautoradiography.

Antibodies to erythrocyte band 3 bind to the surface of nucleated somatic cells as determined by surface immunofluorescence and immunoelectron microscopy studies. Immunofluorescence studies indicate that the band 3-like proteins in nucleated cells are mobile because they participate in antiband 3 induced cell surface patching and capping.[53] We suggested that band 3-like proteins present in nucleated cells were the attachment site for the cytoskeletal protein network (*e.g.,* spectrin, bands 1 and 2, band 2.1, band 4.1) in the plasma membrane as band 3 is in erythrocytes based on the observation that binding of antibodies to band 3 to nucleated cells induces cell surface capping.[35] Work by other investigators showing that band 3 in rat kidney is associated with spectrin (bands 1 and 2) and band 2.1 supports our suggestion.[54]

Immunoautoradiographic analysis revealed that antibodies to band 3 react with a $M_r \sim 95,000$ polypeptide in membranes of freshly isolated white cells, polypeptides $M_r \sim 60,000$, 48,000, and 38,000 in cultured human lung cells, and polypeptides $M_r \sim 69,000$ and $\sim 60,000$ in cultured neoplastic cells. These polypeptides were present in cell membranes prepared with DFP, EDTA, and EGTA to avoid artifactual proteolysis. Therefore, these lower molecular weight immunoreactive forms of band 3 may be present in the membranes of cultured cells and neoplastic cells *in vivo*. We suspect that band 3 molecule varies structurally as an adaptation *in situ* to specific cell types and environments.[53]

Other investigators have confirmed the presence of band 3 in other cell types and tissues,[54,55] and have presented evidence indicating that band 3 in other cell types does bind to the cytoskeletal network.[54] Further, evidence indicates that large amounts of band 3 are found in the basolateral plasma membrane of the intercalated cells of renal distal tubules and collecting ducts.[54,56] These results were anticipated based on the premise that band 3 performs anion transport in non-erythroid cells just as it does in erythroid cells.[53] Thus, transport of chlorine, bicarbonate, etc. in the collecting ducts of the kidney would be mediated by the same mechanism as it is in erythrocytes.

Cox, *et al.*[56] were able to demonstrate the presence of band 3-like peptides in avian (chicken) kidney by immunofluorescence, peptide mapping, and a cDNA probe. However, they stated that they were unable to demonstrate band 3 in any other tissues in contrast to the results of other investigators in the field.[53,54] This discrepancy may be simply a matter of sensitivity or quality of biological preparations, or may be related to the quality, specificity or other characteristics of the antisera. For example, Cox *et al.* used NaDodSO$_4$ denatured band 3 obtained from polyacrylamide slab gels to produce antisera. This treatment can destroy antigenic determinants, alter antigenic characteristics, etc. Furthermore, the antibodies appeared weak based on immunoblots. Methionine-labeled rather than unlabeled polypeptides were used to characterize binding of the antisera. Thus, band 3 could be detected even with a low-affinity, low-titer antisera. Both red cells and renal proximal tubule cells have large amounts of band 3 relative to other cells (*e.g.,* 25% of membrane protein for RBC or 1×10^6 copies/cell) because anion transport represents one of their major functions. This undoubtedly facilitated detection of band 3 by Cox *et al.*[56] in these cell types.

It is interesting that the band 3 polypeptides detected in avian kidneys were slightly larger ($M_r100,000$ and $105,000$) than those detected in erythrocytes.

Band 3, Senescent Cell Antigen, Neuronal Differentiation, and Aging

A polyclonal antibody against the segment of band 3 containing senescent cell antigen was used to determine whether senescent cell antigen was altered by differentiation. In order to assess the amount of band 3 protein on living mitotic and differentiated cells, immunofluorescence was measured on a single-cell basis by flow cytometry. FIGURE 1 shows fluorescence histograms of senescent cell antigen/band

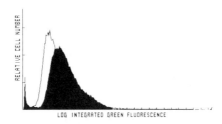

FIGURE 1. Histograms of band 3 expression (green fluorescence) on the surface of mitotic and differentiated neuroblastoma cells. Fluorescence intensity is greater for differentiated cells indicating more band 3 protein on these cells. □ Mitotic, mean = 0.6431; ■ differentiated, mean = 0.714.

3 protein on control and treated N$_2$AB-1 expressed as logarithmic curves. Differentiated N$_2$AB-1 were shown to have more senescent cell antigen/band 3 protein on the cell surface on an individual cell basis (FIGURES 1 and 2). Since these cells do not change in size following differentiation, increased surface band 3 protein must be due to a change in density of this protein. These results were confirmed using immunoelectron microscopy. Preliminary studies on anion (sulfate) transport indicated that it increased following differentiation of N$_2$AB-1.

Examination of frozen brain sections from 10 year old and 96 year old individuals revealed labeling of fibrilary structures and processes with senescent cell antigen-band 3 antibodies in sections from old but not young brains (FIGURE 3). These studies, while preliminary, suggest a fruitful area of research. They are being expanded, and extended to tissue from individuals who died with Alzheimer's disease. Complementary biochemical studies are being done in parallel with the immunohistochemistry.

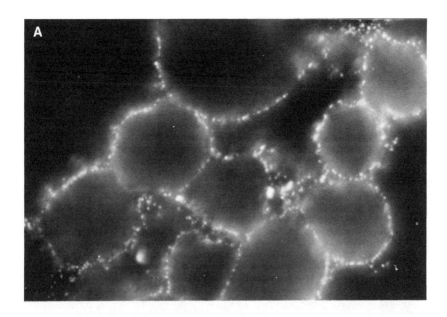

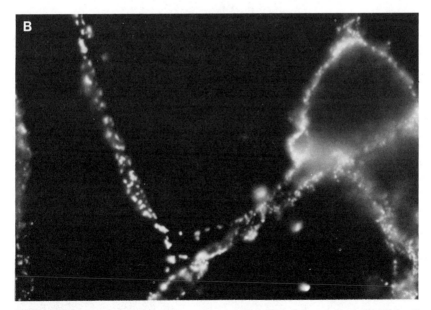

FIGURE 2. (A) and (B) Immunofluorescence staining of band 3 protein on N_2AB-1 cells differentiated by PGE_1/cAMP. Fluorescence can be seen outlining the cell body and neuritic extensions. 1200x.

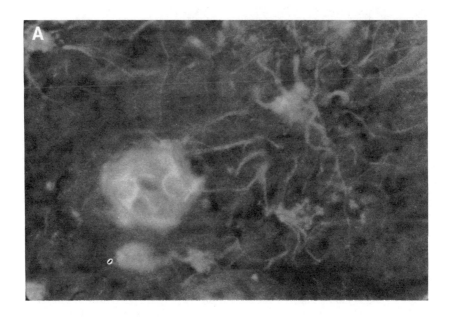

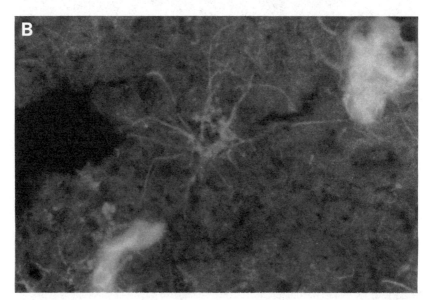

FIGURE 3. (A) and (B) Brain sections from a 96 year old stained with antibodies to senescent cell antigen-band 3 segment followed by fluoroscein isothiocycinate labeled anti-rabbit IgG.

REFERENCES

1. KAY, M. M. B. 1986. Senescent cell antigen: a red cell aging antigen. *In* Red Cell Antigens and Antibodies. G. Garratty, Ed. 35-82. American Association of Blood Banks. Arlington, Va.
2. KAY, M. M. B. 1985. Aging of cell membrane molecules leads to appearance of aging antigen and removal of senescent cells. *In* Gerontology. H. P. von Hahn, (Basel), G. Andrews (London) & M. Ermini (Basel), Eds. Vol. 31: 215-235. S. Karger, A. G. Basel.
3. GUPTA, M., M. F. D. NOTTER, S. FELTON & D. M. GASH. 1985. Differentiation characteristics of human neuroblastoma cells in the presence of growth modulators and antimitotic drugs. Dev. Brain Res. **19**: 21-29.
4. NOTTER, M. F. D. & J. F. LEARY. 1986. Tetanus toxin binding to neuroblastoma cells differentiated by antimitotic agents. Dev. Brain Res. **26**: 59-68.
5. BAGWELL, C. B., J. L. HUDSON & G. L. IRWIN. 1979. Non-parametric flow cytometric analysis. J. Histochem. Cytochem. **27**: 293-296.
6. NOTTER, M. F. D. & J. F. LEARY. 1985. Flow cytometric analysis of tetanus toxin binding to neuroblastoma cells. J. Cell. Physiol. **125**: 476-484.42.
7. KAY, M. M. B. 1974. Mechanism of removal of senescent red cells. Gerontologist **14**: 33.
8. KAY, M. M. B. 1975. Mechanism of removal of senescent cells by human macrophages *in situ.* 1975. Proc. Natl. Acad. Sci. USA **72**: 3521-3525.
9. BENNETT, G. D. & M. M. B. KAY. 1981. Homeostatic removal of senescent murine erythrocytes by splenic macrophages. Exp. Hematol. **9**: 297-307.
10. KAY, M. M. B. 1978. Role of physiologic autoantibody in the removal of senescent human red cells. J. Supramol. Struct. **9**: 555-567.
11. KAY, M. M. B., P. WONG & P. BOLTON. 1982. Antigenicity, storage & aging: physiologic autoantibodies to cell membrane and serum proteins. Mol. Cell. Biochem. **49**: 65-85.
12. LUTZ, H. U. & M. M. B. KAY. 1981. An age-specific cell antigen is present on senescent human red blood cell membranes. Mech. Ageing Dev. **15**: 65-75.
13. KAY, M. M. B. 1981. Isolation of the phagocytosis inducing IgG-binding antigen on senescent somatic cells. Nature. **289**: 491-494.
14. KAY, M. M. B. 1981. The IgG autoantibody binding determinant appearing on senescent cells resides on a 62,000 MW peptide. Acta Biol. Med. Ger. **40**: 385-391. (Presented at the Berlin/GDR: IXth International Symposium on Structure and Function of Erythroid Cells.)
15. KAY, M. M. B. 1982. Molecular aging: a termination antigen appears on senescent cells. *In* Protides of the Biological Fluids. Vol. 29: 325-38. Peeters. Oxford. (Presented in Belgium: XXIXth Annual Colloquium on Protides of the Biological Fluids).
16. GLASS, G. A., H. GERSHON & D. GERSHON. 1983. The effect of donor and cell age on several characteristics of rat erythrocytes. Exp. Hematol. **11**: 987-995.
17. BARTOSZ, G., M. SOSYNSKI & A. WASILEWSKI. 1982. Aging of the erythrocyte XVII. Binding of autologous immunoglobin. Mech. Ageing Dev. **20**: 223-232.
18. KHANSARI, N. & H. H. FUDENBERG. 1984. Phagocytosis of senescent erythrocytes by autologous monocytes: requirement of membrane-specific autologous IgG for immune elimination of aging red blood cells. Cell. Immunol. **78**: 114-121.
19. VOMEL, T. H. & D. PLATT. 1981. Phagocytic activity of the reticulohistiocyte system in rabbits after splenectomy and activation with ink. Mech. Ageing Dev. **17**: 267-273.
20. MORITA, C. R. & E. H. PERKINS. 1965. A simple quantitative method to assess the in vitro engulfing and degradative potentials of mouse peritoneal phagocytic cells. J. Reticuloendothel Soc. **2**: 406-419.
21. JENKIN, C. R. & K. KARTHIGASU. 1967. Elimination hepatique des erythrocytes agés et alterés chez le rat. Compt. Rend. Soc. Biol. **161**: 1006-1007.
22. NELSON, D. S. 1969. Macrophages in auto-immunity, the disposal of effete cells and chronic inflammation. *In* Macrophages and Immunity. Nelson, Ed. Elsevier. New York, NY.
23. SMITH, F. 1958. Erythrophagocytosis in human lymph-glands. J. Path. Bact. **78**: 383-392.
24. WEINBERG, E. D. 1974. Iron and susceptibility to infectious disease. Science **148**: 952-956.
25. BURNET, F. M. 1970. Immunological Surveillance. Pergammon Press. Oxford.
26. MOHANDAS, N. & S. B. SHOHET. 1981. The role of membrane-associated enzymes in regulation of erythrocyte shape and deformability. Clin. Hematol. **10**: 223-237.

27. FUDENBERG, H. H. 1971. Genetically determined immune deficiency as the predisposing cause of "autoimmunity" and lymphoid neoplasia. Am. J. Med. **51:** 295-298.
28. GERSHWIN, M. E. & A. D. STEINBERG. 1975. Suppression of autoimmune hemolytic anemia in New Zealand (NZB) mice by syngeneic young thymocytes. Clin. Immunol. Immunopathol. **4:** 38-45.
29. SOLOMAN, D. H. 1978. Autoimmune thyroid diseases—Graves' and Hashimoto's. Ann. Intern. Med. **88:** 379-391.
30. KAY, M. M. B. 1975. Multiple labeling technique used for kinetic studies of activated human B lymphocytes. Nature. **254:** 424-426.
31. RAFF, M. C. 1970. Two distinct populations of peripheral lymphocytes in mice distinguishable by immunofluorescence. Immunology **19:** 637-650.
32. SCRIBNER, D. J., H. L. WEINER & J. W. MOORHEAD. 1978. Anti-immunogloblin stimulation of murine lymphocytes. V. Age-related decline in Fc receptor-mediated immunoregulation. J. Immunol. **121:** 377-382.
33. EISEN, H. N. 1974. Immunology. Harper and Row. Hagerstown, MD.
34. KAY, M. M. B., S. GOODMAN, C. WHITFIELD, P. WONG, L. ZAKI & V. RUDOLOFF. 1983. The senescent cell antigen is immunologically related to band 3. Proc. Natl. Acad. Sci. USA **80:** 1631-1635.
35. KAY, M. M. B. 1984. Localization of senescent cell antigen on band 3. Proc. Natl. Acad. Sci. USA **81:** 5753-5757.
36. KAY, M. M. B. 1982. Accumulation of band 3 breakdown products is a function of cell age. Blood **60:** 21a. (Presented in Washington, DC: XXIVth Annual Meeting of the American Society of Hematology.)
37. KAY, M. M. B. 1984. Band 3, the predominant transmembrane polypeptide undergoes proteolytic degradation as cells age. Monogr. Dev. Biol. **17:** 245-253.
38. KAY, M. M. B. & J. R. GOODMAN. 1984. IgG antibodies do not bind to band 3 in intact erythrocytes; enzymatic treatment of cells is required for IgG binding. Biomed. Biochim. Acta **43:** 841-846. (Presented in Berlin/GDR: Xth International Symposium on the Structure and Function of Erythroid Cells.)
39. KAY, M. M. B., S. GOODMAN, K. SORSENSEN, et al. 1982. The senescent cell antigen is immunologically related to band 3. J. Cell Biol. **95:** 244a. (Presented in Baltimore, MD: XXIInd Annual Meeting of the American Society of Cell Biology.)
40. FRIDOVICH, I. 1975. Superoxide dismutase. Nutr. Rev. Biochem. **44:** 147-159.
41. MCCAY, P. B. & M. M. KING. 1980. In Vitamin E, a Comprehensive Treatise. L. J. Machlin, Ed. 289-317. Marcel Dekker. New York, NY.
42. MENZEL, D. B. 1980. In Vitamin E, a Comprehensive Treatise. L. J. Machlin, Ed. 473-494. Marcel Dekker. New York, NY.
43. WALTON, J. R. & L. PACKER. 1980. In Vitamin E, a Comprehensive Treatise. L. J. Machlin, Ed. 495-518. Marcel Dekker. New York, NY.
44. FARRELL, P., J. G. BIERI, J. F. FRATANTONI, R. E. WOOD & P. A. DISANT'AGREE. 1977. The occurrence and effects of human Vitamin E deficiency. J. Clin. Invest. **60:** 233-241.
45. DODGE, J. T., G. COHEN, H. J. KAYDEN & G. B. PHILLIPS. 1967. Peroxidative hemolysis of red blood cells from patients with abetalipoproteinemia. J. Clin. Invest. **46:** 357-368.
46. JAIN, S. K. & S. B. SHOHET. 1984. A novel phospholipid in irreversibly sickled cells: evidence for in vivo peroxidative membrane damage in sickle cell disease. Blood **63:** 362-367.
47. OSKI, F. A. 1983. Anemia related to mutrinal deficiencies other than Vitamin B_{12} and folic acid. In Hematology. W. J. Williams, E. Beutler, A. J. Erslev & M. A. Lictman, Eds. 532-537. McGraw-Hill. New York, NY.
48. CUTLER, R. G. 1976. Cellular aging: concepts and mechanisms. Interdiscip. Top. Gerontol. **9:** 83-133.
49. AUTOR, A. P. 1982. Pathology of Oxygen. Academic Press. New York, NY.
50. PACKER, L. 1984. Vitamin E, physical exercise and tissue damage in animals. Med. Biol. **62:** 105-109.
51. KAY, M. M. B., G. J. C. G. M. BOSMAN, S. S. SHAPIRO, A. BENDICH & P. S. BASSEL. 1986. Oxidation as a possible mechanism of cellular aging: vitamin E deficiency causes premature aging and IgG binding to erythrocytes. Proc. Natl. Acad. Sci. USA **83:** 2463-2467.

52. CHENG, S. & L. D. N. LEVY. 1980. Characterization of the anion transport system in hepatocyte plasma membranes. J. Biol. Chem. **255**: 2637-2640.
53. KAY, M. M. B., C. TRACEY, J. GOODMAN, J. C. CONE & P. S. BASSEL. 1983. Polypeptides immunologically related to band 3 are present in nucleated somatic cells. Proc. Natl. Acad. Sci. USA **80**: 6882-6886.
54. DRENCKHAHN, D., K. SCHÜLTER, D. P. ALLEN & V. BENNETT. 1985. Colocalization of band 3 with ankyrin and spectrin at the basal membrane of intercalated cells in the rat kidney. Science **230**: 1287-1289.
55. DRENCKHAHN, D., K. ZINKE, U. SCHAUER, K. C. APPELL & P. S. LOW. 1984. Identification of immunoreactive forms of human erythrocyte band 3 in nonerythroid cells. Eur. J. Cell. Biol. **34**: 144-150.
56. COX, J. V., R. T. MOON & E. LAZARIDES. 1985. Anion transporter: highly cell-type-specific expression of distinct polypeptides and transcripts in erythroid and nonerythroid cells. J. Cell Biol. **100**: 1548-1557.

Mechanisms of Altered Hormone and Neurotransmitter Action during Aging: The Role of Impaired Calcium Mobilization

GEORGE S. ROTH

Molecular Physiology and Genetics Section
Laboratory of Cellular and Molecular Biology
Gerontology Research Center
National Institute on Aging
Francis Scott Key Medical Center
Baltimore, Maryland 21224

INTRODUCTION

Regulation of physiological functions by hormones and neurotransmitters represents a key mechanism by which homeostatic balance is maintained.[1,2] Senescence is characterized by a general inability to preserve such balance, and this dysfunction is due largely to impaired physiological adaptation.[3,4] It has, thus, become essential to elucidate those mechanisms by which hormone and neurotransmitter action become altered during aging.

Many recent reviews have addressed the problem of age changes in hormone/neurotransmitter responsiveness.[5-8] In general, they have categorized and analyzed a multitude of studies which have examined the problem over a spectrum of levels ranging from the physiological and behavioral to the cellular and molecular. Due to space limitations, such analyses are well beyond the scope of the present report. Instead, it seems most fruitful to assess general areas of progress in the field, problems in conceptualization as well as practice, and promising prospects for future research.

Initially, most gerontological studies of hormone/neurotransmitter action attempted to determine whether receptor changes might be related to alterations in responsiveness.[5] Although this proved to be true in a number of cases, it soon became apparent that age changes in cellular components and events distal to the receptor were equally if not more important. Clearly, no single causal mechanism for altered hormone/neurotransmitter action during aging has emerged. Indeed, almost every step in various signal transduction sequences is a viable candidate or established case for age-related modification. Nevertheless, certain broad categories of age-associated changes can now be recognized in the action of many hormones, neurotransmitters and related agents.

RECEPTOR CHANGES

As previously reviewed,[5,9] the most consistent and best agreed upon receptor change during aging is the loss of D_2 dopamine receptors from the corpus striatum of mice, rats, rabbits and humans. Loss of beta adrenergic receptors from several brain regions is also fairly well established (for a review see REFERENCE 5).

In the case of steroid receptors, strong concensus for loss of estrogen receptors from aged rodent uterus and selected brain regions as well as for androgen receptor loss in senescent rat prostate has been reached (for a review see REFERENCE 5). However, some recent discrepancies concerning glucocorticoid receptor changes have arisen.[8] Possible explanations for these differing results have been discussed elsewhere.[5,8] Nevertheless, it is interesting to note that age-related reductions in glucocorticoid receptor levels in liver,[10-13] certain brain regions,[14-19] skeletal muscle,[18,20,21] lymphoid cells and tissues,[11,22,23] and cultured lung fibroblasts[24-27] from various species including humans have been reported by at least three independent laboratories. In contrast independent agreement on stable glucocorticoid receptor concentrations during aging exists for rodent liver[18,28,29] and several brain regions.[14,15,30]

Ultimately, the value of such investigations will probably be determined by generalized relevance to human aging. Thus, it becomes important to focus on areas of basic agreement. Consequently, if results of experimental animal studies mimic findings in specific human hormone/neurotransmitter response systems or serve simply as models of general mechanisms of age changes they would seem to be worthwhile.

Age-related changes in receptors have been closely linked to altered responsiveness in a number of cases (for a review see REFERENCE 5). Probably the greatest agreement exists for loss of striatal dopaminergic receptors and motor responsiveness, cerebellar cortex beta adrenergic receptors and stimulated adenylate cyclase activity, and uterine estrogen receptors and estrogenic regulation of enzymes governing energy metabolism and cell proliferation. Most of these studies were performed in rodents, but several other unconfirmed correlations between receptor and responsiveness loss have been reported for various species including humans (for a review see REFERENCE 5). Despite some disagreements between laboratories and specific model systems, therefore, it seems reasonable to conclude that receptor change constitutes one important class of alterations resulting in impaired hormone/neurotransmitter action during aging.

POST-RECEPTOR CHANGES

In many situations in which receptor changes do not occur, or appear to be functionally unimportant during aging, post-receptor mechanisms have been examined. These also have been reviewed extensively elsewhere.[1,5-8] However, several new trends in this area appear to be emerging.

Various steroid hormone-receptor complexes exhibit an impaired ability to bind to nuclear acceptor sites with high affinity during aging, even in cases where total cellular receptor concentrations may be unaltered. Such reductions have been reported for estrogens in rodent uterus,[31-37] liver[38] and brain,[34,39] for glucocorticoids in rat liver[40,41] and cultured human fibroblasts,[25] and for androgens in rat prostate.[42] At least two studies[33,37] have concluded that age-related reductions in the ability of steroid hormone-receptor complexes to bind to nuclei with high affinity are the consequence of alterations at both the receptor and nuclear levels.

Stimulation of cyclic AMP production by various hormones and neurotransmitters also appears to be altered during aging in a number of systems (for reviews see REFERENCES 43 and 44). In some cases this may be due to impaired coupling of receptors to adenylate cyclase due to inability to form high-affinity complexes with ligands.[45-47] However, a variety of possible explanations can be offered for other reports of age-related reductions in stimultion of adenylate cyclase. These include loss of the enzyme catalytic or regulatory subunits, increased levels of inhibitory components, changes in membrane fluidity, and/or other chemical alterations which might render the cyclase system less functional.

IMPAIRED CALCIUM MOBILIZATION

Probably the most exciting class of post-receptor changes to be identified recently includes those calcium-dependent, hormone/neurotransmitter responses that decline during aging. In general, such dysfunctions appear to be due to impaired stimulation of calcium mobilization, even in the absence of receptor changes. In fact, many of these impaired responses can be at least partially restored if sufficient calcium can be moved to the proper intracellular locations in aged cells. These include beta-adrenergic-stimulated myocardial contraction,[48] alpha-adrenergic-stimulated parotid cell glucose consumption[49] and electrolyte secretion,[50] alpha-adrenergic- and serotonergic-stimulated aortic contraction,[51] cholinergic regulation[52-56] of cognitive[57] and motor function,[52] compound 48-80-stimulated histamine release from mast cells,[58] lectin-stimulated thymic lymphocyte mitogenesis,[59,60] luteinizing-hormone-releasing-hormone-stimulated gonodotropin release from pituitary cells,[61] and release of beta-glucuronidase and elastin like protease from polymorphonuclear leukocytes.[62] While not tested directly, impaired cholinergic stimulation of cardiac inotropic responsiveness may also be reversible by appropriate calcium stimulation, since studies with nifedipine blockade suggest a defect proximal to activation of calcium channels.[63]

Although at first glance it would appear that stimulation of calcium movement, from both extra- and intracellular sites, becomes impaired during aging, elucidation of the precise mechanisms involved is clearly much more difficult. For example, calcium movement may occur through a number of processes involving various cellular components in different cell types.[64] While in some cases stimulation of calcium mobilization from these sites is clearly reduced with age,[65-69] in other systems calcium movement seems unaffected[70] and actual increases in intracellular calcium content[71,72] or uptake components[73,74] may occur during aging. Moreover, in at least two cases it has been reported that even when directly exposed to relatively high calcium concentrations, aged fibroblasts[75] and cortical synaptosomes[53] exhibit reduced responsiveness.

Some of the apparent inconsistencies in these studies may come from differences in cell types or the categories of calcium mobilization being examined. Timing of calcium movement mechanisms is also critical and the actual relationship between the calcium flux(es) in question and the final biological response must be ascertained. Since responsiveness is usually dependent on free rather than total calcium it is conceivable that high total intracellular calcium concentrations in some aged cells[53,75] may actually impede normal fluxes of free calcium, thus resulting in impaired responsiveness. Obviously such systems need to be examined on a case-by-case basis for precise elucidation of the molecular mechanisms responsible for age-associated decrements in calcium-dependent functions.

One calcium-dependent systems which has been subjected to extremely close scrutiny during aging is the alpha-adrenergic-stimulated rat parotid cell aggregate. Both stimulated potassium release[50,76] and glucose oxidation[49,77] are reduced with increasing age, although the temporal pattern of change differs somewhat. Nevertheless, both processes are dependent on stimulated mobilization of calcium from both intracellular and extracellular locations, and age-associated decrements are completely reversible in the presence of the calcium ionophore, A23187[49,50] Both responses are also dependent on the binding of adrenergic agents to the $alpha_1$ adrenergic receptor subtype,[78,79] and this interaction is unaltered during aging.[50] Subsequent to receptor binding, the enzyme, phospholipase C, is activated to cleave phosphatidylinositol[4,5] bisphosphate to inositol trisphosphate and diacylglycerol. Preliminary results suggest that generation of the former, believed to be a second messenger in many calcium mobilizing processes, is not significantly affected by age.[80] However, the ability of inositol trisphosphate to stimulate release of calcium from intracellular stores is reduced by approximately 50%. This reduction is consistent with the overall age-related reductions in both $alpha_1$-adrenergic-stimulated calcium efflux,[77,80] glucose oxidation[49,77] and potassium release.[50,76] In addition, a post-receptor impairment in the ability to mobilize calcium is consistent with the ability of A23187 to reverse age changes in glucose oxidation[49] and potassium release[50] by allowing sufficient calcium flux to appropriate cellular sites.

Future studies in this system must examine the quantity of calcium available for mobilization as well as the inositol trisphosphate receptor which may mediate such calcium fluxes. Clearly, in other systems which move calcium in different ways, various cellular components and events are candidates for a causal role in impaired responsiveness. Nevertheless, the similar phenomenology associated with age-related dysfunctions in calcium-dependent processes suggests that at least some common mechanistic alterations may exist.

SUMMARY AND CONCLUSIONS

Age-related changes in hormone and neurotransmitter regulation of physiological functions result from various mechanistic alterations. In many cases changes in the receptors for these agents appear to be closely linked to altered responsiveness. In other instances, receptors are unaffected by aging, and various post-receptor changes result in functional deterioration. Examples of the latter situation include stimulation of cyclic AMP production and high-affinity association of steroid receptor-hormone complexes with nuclear acceptor sites in various cell and tissue types.

One of the most noteworthy post-receptor changes appears to be an impaired ability to stimulate calcium mobilization in many aged systems resulting in reductions in various biological responses. Although the processes which govern regulation of calcium fluxes vary with cell type, many such dysfunctions can be at least partially reversed if sufficient calcium can be transported to appropriate cellular sites. Thus, elucidation of the molecular mechanisms involved in impaired calcium mobilization may provide the basis for new therapeutic strategies.

ACKNOWLEDGMENTS

Thanks are due to my many colleagues, past and present, who contributed to the evolution of the concepts presented here and to Mrs. Rita Wolferman for the typing of the manuscript.

REFERENCES

1. ROTH, G. S. 1985. Changes in hormone/neurotransmitter action during aging. *In* Homeostatic Functions and Aging. B. B. Davis & W. G. Wood, Eds. 41-58. Raven Press. New York, NY.
2. WILLIAMS, R. H., Ed. 1981. Textbook of Endocrinology. Saunders. Philadelphia, PA.
3. SHOCK, N. W. 1962. Sci. Am. **29:** 100-113.
4. ADELMAN, R. C. 1971. Exp. Gerontol. **6:** 75-87.
5. ROTH, G. S. & G. D. HESS. 1982. Mech. Ageing Dev. **20:** 175-194.
6. PRADHAN, S. N. 1980. Life Sci. **26:** 1643-1656.
7. BURCHINSKY, S. G. 1984. Exp. Gerontol. **19:** 227-239.
8. KALIMI, M. 1984. Mech. Ageing Dev. **24:** 129-138.
9. ROTH, G. S., J. M. HENRY & J. A. JOSEPH. 1987. Prog. Brain Res. **70:** 473-484.
10. BOLLA, R. 1980. Mech. Ageing Dev. **12:** 119-122.
11. PETROVIC, J. S. & R. Z. MARKOVIC. 1975. Dev. Biol. **45:** 176-182.
12. PARCHMAN, G. L., M. H. CAKE & G. L. LITWACK. 1978. Mech. Ageing Dev. **7:** 227-240.
13. SINGER, S., H. ITO & G. L. LITWACK. 1973. Int. J. Biochem. **4:** 569-573.
14. DEFIORE, C. H. & B. B. TURNER. 1981. Abstr. Soc. Neurosci. **7:** 947.
15. CARMICKLE, L. J., M. KALIMI & R. D. TERRY. 1979. Fed. Proc. **30:** 482.
16. SAPOLSKY, R. M., L. C. KREY & B. S. MCEWEN. 1983. Brain Res. **289:** 235-240.
17. SAPOLSKY, R. M., L. C. KREY, B. S. MCEWEN & T. C. RAINBOW. 1984. J. Neurosci. **4:** 1479-1485.
18. ROTH, G. S. 1974. Endocrinology **94:** 82-90.
19. ROTH, G. S. 1976. Brain Res. **107:** 345-354.
20. MAYER, M., R. AMIN & E. SHAFRIR. 1981. Mech. Ageing Dev. **17:** 1-10.
21. SHARMA, R. & P. S. TIMIRAS. Mech. Ageing Dev. In press.
22. ROTH, G. S. 1975. Biochim. Biophys. Acta **399:** 145-156.
23. JANCOURT, F., Y. WANG, F. KRISTENSEN & A. L. DEWECK. 1985. Gerontology **31:** 293-300.
24. ROSNER, B. A. & V. J. CRISTOFALO. 1981. Endocrinology **108:** 1965-1971.
25. FORCIEA, M. A. & V. J. CRISTOFALO. 1981. Gerontologist **21:** 179.
26. KONDO, H., H. KASUGA & T. NOUMORA. 1978. Abstracts of the XII International Congress of Gerontology. 26-27.
27. KALIMI, M. & S. SEIFTER, 1979. Biochim. Biophys. Acta **583:** 352-361.
28. LATHAM, K. R. & C. E. FINCH. 1976. Endocrinology **98:** 1480-1489.
29. KALIMI, M., S. GUPTA, J. HUBBARD & K. GREENE. 1983. Endocrinology **112:** 341-347.
30. NELSON, J. F., C. F. HOLINKA, K. R. LATHAM, J. K. ALLEN & C. E. FINCH. 1976. Brain Res. **115:** 345-351.
31. CHUKNYISKA, R. S., M. HAJI, R. H. FOOTE & G. S. ROTH. 1985. Endocrinology **116:** 547-551.
32. CHUKNYISKA, R. S. & G. S. ROTH. 1985. J. Biol. Chem. **260:** 8661-8663.
33. CHUKNYISKA, R. S., C. JUSTINIANO & G. S. ROTH. 1986. Exp. Gerontol. **21:** 255-265.
34. JIANG, M. J. & M. T. PENG. 1981. Gerontology **27:** 51-57.
35. BELISLE, S., C. BEAUDRY & J. G. LEHOUX. 1983. Exp. Gerontol. **17:** 417-423.
36. BELISLE, S., D. BELLABARBA & J. G. LEHOUX. 1985. Endocrinology **116:** 148-153.

37. BELISLE, S., D. BELLABARBA, J.-G. LEHOUX, P. ROBEL & E. E. BAULIEU. 1986. Endocrinology **118:** 750-758.
38. KONOPLYA, E. F., G. L. LUKSKA, S. K. SAVATEEV & A. D. NAUMOV. 1986. Mech. Ageing Dev. **35:** 95-107.
39. WISE, P. M., B. S. MCEWEN, B. PARSONS & T. C. RAINBOW. 1984. Brain Res. **321:** 119-126.
40. BOLLA, R. 1980. Mech. Ageing Dev. **12:** 119-122.
41. PARCHMAN, G. L., M. H. CAKE & G. L. LITWACK. 1978. Mech. Ageing Dev. **7:** 227-240.
42. SHAIN, S. A. & R. W. BOESEL. 1977. Mech. Ageing Dev. **6:** 219-232.
43. ROTH, G. S. 1979. Mech. Ageing Dev. **9:** 497-514.
44. DAX, E. M. 1985. Receptors and associated membrane events in aging. *In* Review of Biological Research in Aging. M. Rothstein, Ed. Vol. 2: 315-336. Academic Press. New York, NY.
45. SCARPACE, P. J. & J. B. ABRASS. 1983. J. Gerontol. **38:** 143-147.
46. NARAYANAN, N. & J. DERBY. 1982. Mech. Ageing Dev. **19:** 127-139.
47. FELDMAN, R. D., L. E. LIMBIRD, J. NADEAU, D. ROBERTSON & A. J. J. WOOD. 1984. N. Engl. J. Med. **310:** 815-819.
48. GUARNIERI, T., C. R. FILBURN, G. ZITNIK, G. S. ROTH & E. G. LAKATTA. 1980. Am. J. Physiol. **239:** H501-H508.
49. GEE, M. V., Y. ISHIKAWA, B. J. BAUM & G. S. ROTH. 1986. J. Gerontol. **41:** 331-335.
50. ITO, H., B. J. BAUM, T. UCHIDA, M. T. HOOPES, L. BODNER & G. S. ROTH. 1982. J. Biol. Chem. **246:** 9532-9538.
51. COHEN, M. L. & B. A. BERKOWITZ. 1976. Blood Vessels **67:** 139-149.
52. PETERSON, C. & G. E. GIBSON. 1983. Neurobiol. Aging **4:** 25-30.
53. MEYER, E. M., F. T. CREWS, D. H. OTERO & K. LARSON. 1986. J. Neurochem. **47:** 1244-1246.
54. CREWS, F. T., E. M. MEYER, R. A. GONZALES, C. THEISS, D. H. OTERO, K. LARSEN, R. KARULLI & G. CALDERINI. 1986. Presynaptic and postsynaptic approaches to enhancing central cholinergic neurotransmission. *In* Treatment Development Strategies for Alzheimer's Disease. T. Crook, R. Bartus, S. Ferris & S. Gershon, Eds. 385-419. Mark Powley Associates. Madison, CT.
55. PETERSON, C. & G. E. GIBSON. 1984. J. Biol. Chem. **258:** 11482-11486.
56. PETERSON, C., D. G. NICHOLLS & G. E. GIBSON. 1985. Neurobiol. Aging **6:** 297-304.
57. DAVIS, H. P., A. IDOWA & G. E. GIBSON. 1983. Exp. Aging Res. **9:** 211-214.
58. ORIDA, N. & J. D. FELDMAN. 1982. Fed. Proc. **41:** 822.
59. WU, W., M. PAHLAVANI, A. RICHARDSON & H. T. CHEUNG. 1985. J. Leuk. Biol. **38:** 531-540.
60. MILLER, R. A. 1986. J. Immunol. **137:** 805-808.
61. CHUKNYISKA, R. S., M. R. BLACKMAN & G. S. ROTH. 1987. Am. J. Physiol. **253:** E233-E237.
62. FULOP, T., G. FORIS, I. WOUN, G. PARAGH & A. LEOVEY. 1985. Mech. Aging Dev. **29:** 1-8.
63. ELFELLAH, M. S., A. JOHNS & A. M. M. SHEPHERD. 1986. J. Cardiovas. Pharmacol. **8:** 873-877.
64. SHAMOO, A. E. & I. S. AMBUDKAR. 1984. Can. J. Physiol. Pharmacol. **62:** 9-22.
65. SEGAL, J. 1986. Mech. Ageing Dev. **33:** 295-303.
66. MICHAELIS, M. L., K. JOBE & T. E. KITOS. 1984. Mech. Ageing Dev. **25:** 215-225.
67. VITORICA, J. & J. SATCUSTEGUI. 1986. Biochim. Biophys. Acta **851:** 209-216.
68. GAFNI, A. & K. YUH. 1985. Gerontologist **25:** 215-216.
69. HANSFORD, R. G. & F. CASTRO. 1982. Mech. Ageing Dev. **19:** 5-13.
70. WILLIAMS, P. B. 1984. Biochem. Pharmacol. **33:** 3097-3099.
71. PETERSON, C. & J. E. GOLDMAN. 1986. Proc. Natl. Acad. Sci. USA **83:** 2758-2762.
72. LANDFIELD, P. W. & T. A. PITLER. 1984. Science **276:** 1089-1091.
73. GOVONI, S., A. RUIS, F. BATTAINI, A. BIANCHI & M. TRABUCCHI. 1985. Brain Res. **333:** 374-377.
74. BATTAINI, F., S. GOVONI, R. A. RIUS & M. TRABUCCHI. 1985. Neurosci. Lett. **61:** 67-71.

75. PRAEGER, F. C. & V. J. CRISTOFALO. 1984. Gerontologist **24:** 226-227.
76. BODNER, L., M. T. HOOPES, M. GEE, H. ITO, G. S. ROTH & B. J. BAUM. 1983. J. Biol. Chem. **258:** 2774-2777.
77. GEE, M. V., Y. ISHIKAWA, B. J. BAUM & G. S. ROTH. 1986. J. Gerontol. **41:** 331-335.
78. UCHIDA, T., H. ITOH, B. J. BAUM, G. S. ROTH, C. R. FILBURN & B. SACKTOR. 1982. Mol. Pharmacol. **21:** 128-132.
79. GEE, M. V., B. J. BAUM & G. S. ROTH. 1983. Biochem. Pharmacol. **32:** 3351-3354.
80. ISHIKAWA, Y., M. V. GEE, I. S. AMBUDKAR, L. BODNER, B. J. BAUM & G. S. ROTH. Biochim. Biophys. Acta. In press.

Immune Senescence Contributes to the Slow Growth of Tumors in Elderly Subjects[a]

MARC E. WEKSLER,[b] TADAAKI TSUDA, WILLIAM
ERSHLER,[c] YOUNG T. KIM, GREGORY W. SISKIND,
DIANE ESPOSITO,[d] GIANFRANCO FASSINA,[d]
AND MARCELLO SINISCALCO[d]

Cornell University Medical College
New York, New York 10021
[c]*University of Wisconsin*
Medical Sciences Center
Madison, Wisconsin 53706
[d]*The Sloan Kettering Institute*
New York, New York 10021

Cancer occurs more frequently in old than in young humans. Epidemiological studies reveal that the prevalence of cancer increases with age—from youth until 85 years of age. In fact, increasing age is the greatest single risk factor with respect to the development of cancer.[1]

The explanation for this direct correlation between age and the risk of cancer is not clear. In part, the explanation may be related to the fact that biological existence of an untransformed cell is finite while that of a cancer cell is infinite. Thus, as normal cells begin to reach the end of their biological life span the random chance of observing an immortal cell increases on purely statistical grounds as untransformed cells disappear.

However, there is also experimental evidence that cells from old animals are more susceptible to the intracellular processes that lead to neoplastic transformation than are cells from young animals. Thus, with increasing age the chance of a cell undergoing neoplastic transformation increases. One of the clearest demonstrations of this thesis is the experiment reported by Ebbesen.[2] In these studies, skin from young and old mice were transplanted to young, syngeneic animals in order to eliminate an effect of age of the host. This permitted a direct comparison of the susceptibility of old and young skin cells to neoplastic transformation. The transplanted skin was then exposed to a carcinogen and the numbers of papillomas and carcinomas in transplanted young and old skin was compared. Benign and malignant tumors arose significantly more frequently in the skin from the old as compared to the young donors.

The biological basis for the increased susceptibility of cells from old animals to

[a]Supported in part by United States Public Health Service Grants AG 00239 and AG 00541.
[b]To whom correspondence should be addressed.

177

neoplastic transformation is not certain. However, as virtually all tumor cells can be shown to have chromosomal abnormalities[3] a change in chromosomal stability with age might contribute to the increased susceptibility of cells from old subjects to neoplastic transformation. For this reason, we investigated whether chromosomes in lymphocytes from older individuals are more fragile than are chromosomes in these cells from younger donors. The susceptibility of chromosomes to radiation-induced damage was studied in lymphocytes from young and old humans. Very low doses of tritiated thymidine induced significantly more chromosomal aberrations in lymphocytes from old as compared to young humans.[4]

More recently, we have extended these findings using a gene co-transfer technique to compare the stability of the human X chromosome in lymphocytes from young and old humans. The results are consistent with the hypothesis that the human X chromosome from lymphocytes of old men is more fragile than is this chromosome from lymphocytes of young men. This conclusion is based on the decreased co-transfer of two genes carried on the human X chromosome in lymphocytes from old as compared to young men. In this technique, human lymphocytes from young or old men are fused with mutagenized chinese hamster ovary (CHO) cells which lack HGPRT enzyme activity. Hybrids are cultured in HAT medium in order to select for hybrids that have retained the human HGPRT gene which is located on the human X chromosome. The hybrids are then screened for the presence of a human cell surface antigen, 12E7, coded for by another gene on the human X chromosome. Seventy percent of cells derived from a single hybrid cell resulting from a fusion with a lymphocyte from a young man with the mutagenized CHO cell co-transferred 12E7 with the HGPRT gene. In contrast, only 40 percent of cells derived from a single hybrid product of the fusion of a lymphocyte from an old man and the mutagenized CHO cell co-transferred 12E7 and the HGPRT gene.

Although the risk of neoplastic transformation increases with age, tumors in older patients appear to grow more slowly than do comparable tumors in younger patients. Clinical studies have suggested that the rate of local growth and distant spread, metastasis, are inversely related to age. For example, breast cancer in young women is frequently a very rapidly progressing disease while breast cancer in elderly women may be indolent with many older patients dying with and not from their breast cancer. Clinical studies suggest that carcinoma of the lung, colon, kidney and prostate also grow more rapidly in young as compared to old patients (reviewed in REFERENCE 5).

Metastasis, another index of tumor growth, is more common in young as compared to old patients with cancer. Thus, in a study of 10,000 patients dying of cancer, more than 80% of patients between 20 and 30 years of age had metastases while less than 50% of patients over 70 years of age had metastases.[6] The influence of age on metastatic potential has also been carefully studied by Ershler and his colleagues.[7] These investigators reviewed the charts of 700 patients with lung cancer. Eighty percent of the young patients (less than 50 years of age) had metastatic disease while less than 40% of older patients (over the age of 70) had metastatic disease. As it is possible that older patients die earlier in the course of neoplastic disease, before metastases develop, a group of patients of different ages but with comparable survival were also studied.[7] In this group, in which survival was comparable, the rate of metastatic disease was also found to be lower in old as compared to young patients.

Fewer investigators have looked into the mechanism for the slower growth of tumors in older patients. Clearly, the rate of tumor growth depends upon both the biology of tumors that occur at different ages and the effect of age upon the host environment. Certain tumors, for example, Wilm's tumors, neuroblastoma and acute lymphobastic leukemia, occur predominantly in children. In contrast, other tumors, chronic lymphocytic leukemia, colon cancer and multiple myeloma are far more common in elderly patients. Even when the same tumor develops both in mid-life and late in life, the biology of the tumor may be different. Thus, carcinomas of the breast that develop in young women usually express a higher degree of aneuploidy, mitotic activity and have a lower frequency of estrogen-receptor proteins. These characteristics are correlated with a shorter disease-free interval and with a shorter survival.[8]

For these reasons, the factors that lead to the more rapid growth of tumors in young organisms could only be studied in experimental animals where it is possible to measure the growth of the same tumor cell in animals of different ages. The tumor chosen for study should have arisen spontaneously in order to assure the closest relationship to the clinical situation. We have studied the effect of the age of C57B1/6 mice and their immune competence on the rate of growth of the B16 melanoma, a spontaneous tumor of the C57B1/6 strain of mouse. Ershler and his colleagues had shown that this tumor grew more rapidly in young as compared to old mice following subcutaneous inoculation.[9] Our working hypothesis has been that the more rapid growth of the tumor in young mice was related to the integrity of the immune system in young animals and the slower growth of the tumor in old mice related to immune senescence.

It has been known for some time that the immune response of old humans and experimental animals to foreign antigens is lower than that of younger hosts. In contrast, the frequency and level of auto-antibodies are increased in old as compared to young subjects. These fundamental changes in immune function appear to be related to changes in the thymus gland with age. The universal involution of the thymus gland, the decline serum thymic hormone activity, and the impaired capacity of the thymus gland to differentiate T-lymphocyte precursors beginning at sexual maturity are hallmarks of immune senescence. For these reasons, T-dependent immunity is more markedly compromised with age than is T-independent immunity. As changes in T-dependent immunity is the central determinant of immune senescence and as the proliferative capacity of T lymphocytes is the most basic attribute of this cell, we have studied the proliferative response of T-lymphocytes from old and young donors.

Initially, we used plant lectins to stimulate T lymphocytes to divide. We found that thymidine incorporation by T cells from healthy persons over 65 years of age cultured with PHA was very much lower than that by T cells from young subjects.[10] This was not due to changes in the relative or absolute number of T lymphocytes in the blood of elderly people. Despite there being as many T cells in the blood of old and young humans, the number of T cells from old persons that could be activated by mitogen was only 20 to 50% the number found in blood from young persons.[11] Furthermore, the mitogen-responsive blood T cells were not capable of dividing as many time in culture when activated by plant lectins. Thus the number of T cells dividing for a second or third time in lymphocyte cultures established from the blood of old donors was only 50 or 25%, respectively, that seen in cultures from young donors.[12] The biochemical basis for the two defects in the proliferative response of T cells from elderly persons—I. the reduced number of T lymphocytes responsive to mitogens and II. the impaired capacity of the responsive T cells to divide repeatedly in culture—is not entirely clear. With respect to the first defect, it appears that the nuclei of T lymphocytes from elderly persons, whose T cells do not respond mitogens, do not respond to cytoplasmic signals that drive DNA replication and thus cannot enter the proliferative cycle.[13] The impaired capacity of T cells that do enter the proliferative cycle to divide repeatedly in culture appears to be due to the decreased production of the T cell growth factor, IL-2.[14]

Inasmuch as production of growth factors by T cells from old animals and elderly humans is decreased, we investigated the contribution of peripheral T cells on the rate of growth of the B16 tumor in C57B1/6 mice of different ages.[15] We have found that the thymus gland and T lymphocytes contribute to the rapid growth of the B16 tumor in young animals. Thus, tumor growth is significantly slowed in young animals whose T cell function is compromised by adult thymectomy. Growth of the B16 tumor was even slower in thymectomized mice which were also treated with anti-theta anti-serum, and the rate of growth of the B16 tumor was almost as slow as the rate observed in old animals. The importance of the T cell population in regulating tumor growth was confirmed by the fact that the characteristic rate of growth of the B16 tumor in young or old animals could be transferred to lethally-irradiated, syngeneic young recipients by spleen cells from young or old donors.

Recently, we have found that only T cells in the spleen cell preparation from young or old mice can transfer the rapid or slow rate of B16 tumor growth, respectively, to young, lethally irradiated syngeneic animals reconstituted with non-T cells from young mice. This clearly demonstrates that T cells are capable of influencing the rate of tumor growth. The capacity to transfer the age-associated growth rate of the B16 tumor has allowed us to investigate whether the growth of the B16 tumor was inhibited in old mice or the growth of the B16 tumor was stimulated in young mice. When animals were reconstituted with a mixture of old and young T cells and inoculated with B16 tumor cells, the rate of tumor growth was rapid and comparable to that observed in mice reconstituted with young T cells.

These findings are not consistent with the production of cytotoxic anti-tumor factors, antibodies or cells by old animals. Rather, it appears that young T cells lead to the increased production of tumor growth factors, enhancing antibody, or circulating blocking factors. The production of specific antibody to B16 tumor cells are unlikely as host immunity to the B16 tumor is uncommon and when induced slows tumor growth. We have been more attracted to the concept that T cells from young animals produce growth factors that might facilitate tumor growth. The first T cell growth factor we tested was IL-2. There are no IL-2 receptors on the B16 melanoma cells and the addition of Il-2 did not facilitate but inhibited the growth of B16 tumor cells in vitro and in vivo.

Recently our attention has been drawn to the fact that there is a difference in blood vessels supplying the B16 tumors of the same size in young and old animals. The more rapidly growing tumors in young mice have a greater blood supply. This suggested that the difference in the vascular supply of tumors in young and old mice might be due to the increased production of an angiogenic factor by T cells in young animals. Angiogenesis factor activity has been reported to be produced by proliferating T lymphocytes.[16] It is our current working hypothesis that the slower growth of neoplasms in older experimental animals results from the compromised function of T cells that leads to a decreased production of angiogenesis factors required for rapid tumor growth.

In any case, the finding that T cells from old animals do not support tumor growth as well as T cells from young animals suggests that immune senescence may confer certain benefits upon the elderly host. For this reason, one should exercise considerable restraint before attempting to augment the immune activity of the older individuals. It is possible that the altered immune reactivity of the elderly host is adaptive at least with respect to the defense of the elderly organism against the formation of auto-antibodies and the rapid growth of tumors.

REFERENCES

1. NEWELL, G. R., W. B. BOUTWELL & D. L. MORRIS. 1982. Epidermiology of cancer. *In* Cancer: Principals and Practice of Oncology. V. T. DeVita, Jr., S. Hellman & S. A. Rosenberg, Eds. 3-32. Lippincott. Philadelphia, PA.
2. EBBESEN, P. 1974. Aging increases susceptibility of mouse skin to DMBA carcinogenesis independent of general immune status. Science 183: 217-218.
3. YUNIS, J. J. 1983. The chromosomal basis of human neoplasia. Science 221: 227.
4. DUTKOWSKI, R. T., R. LESH, L. STAIANO-COICO, H. THALER, G. J. DARLINGTON & M. E. WEKSLER. 1985. Increased chromosomal instability in lymphocytes from elderly humans. Mutation Res. 149: 505-512.
5. ERSHLER, W. B. 1986. Why tumors grow more slowly in old people. J. Natl. Cancer Inst. 77: 837-839.
6. PICKREN, J. W., Y. TSUKADA & W. W. LANE. 1982. Liver metastasis: analysis of autopsy data. *In* Liver Metastases. H. J. Weiss & H. A. Gilbet, Eds. 2-18. GK Hall. Boston, MA.
7. ERSHLER, W. B. 1987. The change in aggressiveness of neoplasms with age. Geriatrics 42(1): 99-103.
8. ROWE, J. W. & E. C. BRADLEY. 1983. The elderly cancer patient: pathophysiological considerations. *In* Perspectives on Prevention and Treatment of Cancer in the Elderly. R. Yancik, P. P. Carbone, K. Skel, W. Patterson & W. D. Terry, Eds. 33-41. Raven Press. New York, NY.
9. ERSHLER, W. B., J. A. STEWART & M. P. HACKER. 1984. B16 murine melanoma and aging: slower growth and longer survival in old mice. J. Natl. Cancer Inst. 72: 161-164.
10. WEKSLER, M. E. & T. H. HUTTEROTH. 1974. Decreased lymphocyte function in aged humans. J. Clin. Invest. 53: 99.
11. INKELES, B., J. B. INNES, M. KUNTZ, A. S. KADISH & M. E. WEKSLER. 1977. Immunological studies of aging. III. Cytokinetic basis for the impaired response of lymphocytes from aged humans to plant lectins. J. Exp. Med. 145: 1176-1187.
12. HEFTON, J. M., C. J. DARLINGTON, B. A. CASAZZA & M. E. WEKSLER. 1980. Immunological studies of aging. V. Impaired proliferation of PHA responsive human lymphocytes in culture. Immunology 125: 1007-1010.
13. GUTOWSKI, J. K., J. B. INNES, M. E. WEKSLER & S. COHEN. 1986. Impaired nuclear responsiveness to cytoplasmic signals in lymphocytes from elderly humans with depressed proliferative responses. J. Clin. Invest. 78: 40.
14. GILLIS, S., R. W. KOZAK, M. DURANTE & M. E. WEKSLER. 1981. Immunological studies of aging: decreased production of and response to T cell growth factor by lymphocytes from aged humans. J. Clin. Invest. 67: 937-942.
15. TSUDA, T., T. T. KIM, G. W. SISKIND, A. DeBLASIO, R. SCHWAB, W. ERSHLER & M. E. WEKSLER. Role of the thymus and T cells in slow growth of B16 melanoma in old mice. Cancer Res. In press.
16. LUTTA, G. A., S. H. LIU & R. A. PRENDERGAST. 1983. Angiogenic lymphokines of activated T-cell origin. Invest. Opthalmol. Vis. Sci. 24: 1595-1601.

Immunoregulation in Aging[a]

GINO DORIA, LUCIANO ADORINI, EDRIS
SABBADINI,[b] CAMILLO MANCINI,
AND DANIELA FRASCA

Laboratory of Pathology
ENEA C.R.E. Casaccia
00100 Rome A.D., Italy C.P. 2400

During senescence the immune system exhibits a decline of immune responsiveness to exogenous antigens and an increased incidence of autoimmune phenomena.

Most of the decline in immune responsiveness to exogenous antigens arises from alterations in regulatory T cell populations rather than in other cell compartments of the immune system. Helper T cells (Th), cytotoxic T cells (Tc) and suppressor T cells (Ts) are mostly affected by aging.[1]

Th Cells

Profound defects have been detected in the Th cell population of old mice. Two types of antigen-specific Th cells have been distinguished, based on different properties such as the surface phenotype and the mode of action. One cell type (Th1) recognizes epitopes of the antigen molecule in association with MHC-encoded class II antigens (Ia) and interacts with B cells through an antigen bridge of physically linked carrier and hapten determinants (cognate B cell activation). The other cell type (Th2) is not MHC-restricted and does not require physical linkage of carrier and hapten determinants for effective T-B cell cooperation (polyclonal B cell activation). Both mechanisms may operate synergistically.

Helper T cell activity declines with advancing age: it is already reduced to 64% in mice at 6 months of age but is not completely lost (30% residual activity) at 24 months of age. The age-related decline in helper T cell activity can be attributed to reduction either in the pool size of Th cell subpopulations or in their ability to interact synergistically in the generation of helper activity. The decrease in helper T cell activity has been attributed to thymus involution[2] and subsequent reduced concentration of thymic factors involved in T cell maturation.[3] The precursor frequency of helper T cells is, indeed, decreased in old mice although the progeny of each precursor cell maintains full capacity to produce lymphokines and to proliferate.[4]

Th cells produce interleukin 2 (IL-2), a growth factor for T and B lymphocytes,

[a] This work was supported by an ENEA-Euratom contract. It is publication No. 2400 of the Euratom Biology Division.

[b] Present address: Department of Immunology, University of Manitoba, Winnipeg, Manitoba, Canada.

in response to mitogens, antigens and other lymphokines. Aging negatively affects IL-2 production which has been found to decline 170-fold in mice from 3 to 22 months of age. Since the decline in helper activity during this life period is only 4-fold, it appears that the dependence of helper activity from IL-2 is not as absolute as other factors, probably less affected by aging, compensates the decreased IL-2 production and contributes to the maintenance of a reduced helper T cell activity in old mice.

Helper activity of Th1 and Th2 cells from old mice can be enhanced to a significant extent by injection of thymosin α_1, a synthetic peptide with thymic hormone-like activity, consisting of 28 amino acid residues. The immunoregulatory activity of thymosin α_1 is restricted to the first 14 amino acids from the N-terminal end of the molecule (N_{14} fragment), whereas the other half of the molecule (C_{14} fragment) is devoid of any discernible effect.

Results from our studies[5] indicate that the thymosin α_1-induced enhancement of helper T cell activity in old mice may be mediated by increased IL-2 production and enhanced expression of IL-2 receptors. Thus, the effect of thymosin α_1 in old mice may result from precursor cell maturation leading, upon T cell activation, to an increased number of IL-2 receptor-bearing cells and to an enhanced production of IL-2 that upregulates the expression of IL-2 receptors.

We have recently investigated whether the injection of old mice with thymosin α_1 can increase the splenic frequency of T cell precursors defined as mitogen responsive cells.[6]

Limiting numbers of spleen cells from 3 month old (young) or 19-20 month old (old) (C57BL/10xDBA/2)F1 (BDF1) mice (20-80 cells/well) were cultured with 2×10^5 irradiated (2500 R) syngeneic spleen cells (feeder), 2 μg/ml Concanavalin A (Con A) and 25 U/ml gibbon IL-2. Test cells at each concentration and feeder cells were cultured in 32 replicate wells. Positive cultures were defined as those in which the mitotic response, measured by ^{3}H-Thymidine incorporation, exceeded by 3 standard deviations the mean from 32 control wells (feeder cells alone). The log fraction of nonresponding cultures was plotted as a function of the number of cells added to culture and a straight line was forced through the origin by the least squares method for graphic inspection of the data. Statistical analysis was performed by the method of maximum likelihood[7] which gives the most likely mitogen responsive T cell precursor frequency in a cell population and an error factor by which the frequency should be multiplied or divided to obtain the variations due to one standard error. Validity of the estimate was assessed by the chi-square criterion to test the goodness of fit of the data to a Poisson distribution.

Old mice were injected intraperitoneally with 0.2 ml saline containing 10 μg synthetic thymosin α_1 3 days before sacrifice. Alternatively, mice received one intraperitoneal injection of 0.2 ml saline containing 5 μg N_{14} or C_{14} synthetic fragment of the molecule. Results demonstrate that injection of thymosin α_1 or its N_{14} fragment, but not of the C_{14} fragment, increases the frequency of responding T lymphocytes to the level displayed in young adult mice (TABLE 1).

The frequency of IL-2-producing cell precursors was also determined. Spleen cells from aging mice, uninjected or injected with thymosin peptides, were cultured under limiting dilution conditions as described above. After 5 days, each microculture was split into two aliquots. One aliquot was assayed for cell proliferation and the other aliquot was extensively washed and then restimulated with Con A and 10 ng/ml Phorbol Myristate Acetate for an additional 24 h to induce IL-2 synthesis in activated cells. Results in TABLE 2 show that aging negatively affects cell precursor frequencies in both assays. Differences between cell frequencies from untreated old and young mice are statistically significant at $p < 0.025$ for proliferation and $p < 0.005$ for IL-

TABLE 1. Precursor Frequency of Proliferating T Cells from Mice of Different Ages Uninjected or Injected with Thymosin Peptides

Exp. No.	Age (Months)	Treatment	Precursors per 10^4 Cells[a]	p
1	3	none	27 (1.35)	
	19	none	9 (1.65)	
	19	α_1 (10 μg)	23 (1.38)	< 0.05
2	3	none	79 (1.21)	
	19	none	24 (1.37)	
	19	N_{14}(5 μg)	95 (1.19)	< 0.005
3	3	none	42 (1.28)	
	20	none	11 (1.57)	
	20	C_{14}(5 μg)	13 (1.51)	> 0.50

[a] Number in parentheses is the error factor by which the frequency should be multiplied or divided to obtain the variations due to one standard error.

2 production in the first experiment, while at $p < 0.05$ for both assays in the second experiment, as shown by the one-tailed Student's t-test. Furthermore, injection of thymosin α_1 or N_{14} fragment was found to significantly increase the frequencies of proliferating and IL-2-producing T cell precursors in old mice, whereas injection of the C_{14} fragment had no significant effect.

Tc Cells

Tc cell activity has been found unchanged or decreased in old mice. This apparent contradiction seems to reflect the requirements for IL-2 and other lymphokines nec-

TABLE 2. Precursor Frequencies of Proliferating and IL-2-producing Cells from Mice of Different Ages Uninjected or Injected with Thymosin Peptides

Exp. No.	Age (Months)	Treatment	Proliferation Precursors/10^4 Cells[a]	p	IL-2 Production Precursors/10^4 Cells[a]	p
1	3	none	94 (1.19)		143 (1.19)	
	20	none	49 (1.26)		54 (1.25)	
	20	α_1(10 μg)	84 (1.20)	< 0.05	105 (1.19)	< 0.02
2	3	none	75 (1.21)		89 (1.20)	
	20	none	46 (1.27)		52 (1.25)	
	20	N_{14}(5 μg)	97 (1.19)	< 0.02	113 (1.18)	< 0.01
	20	C_{14}(5 μg)	52 (1.25)	> 0.50	54 (1.25)	> 0.50

[a] Number in parentheses is the error factor by which the frequency should be multiplied or divided to obtain the variations due to one standard error.

essary for the differentiation of Tc cell precursors as shown under different experimental conditions.[8–10]

In the present study, cultures were set up as follows. Limiting numbers (100-800 cells/well) of responder spleen cells from 3 month old (young) or 10 month old (old) BDF1 mice were cultured with 2×10^5 irradiated (2500 R) allogeneic spleen cells from C3H mice (feeder), in the presence of 2 µg/ml Con A, 25 U/ml gibbon IL-2 and 10 U/ml immune interferon (IFN-γ; gift of Dr. Santo Landolfo). Test cells at each concentration and feeder cells were cultured in 32 replicate wells. At day 4 of culture, wells were resupplemented with fresh medium containing IL-2 and IFN-γ. At day 7, 4×10^7 mitogen-activated spleen cells from C3H mice were labelled with ^{51}Cr and used as target for Tc effector cells. Negative control cultures contained only medium and target cells. Estimates of the responder cell frequency from this limiting dilution assay were determined as already described above for Th cells.[6] The frequency of alloantigen-responsive Tc cell precursors was not affected to a significant extent by 10-fold variations in the number of target cells (data not shown).

Results presented in TABLE 3 show that old mice exhibit about 75% decrease in

TABLE 3. Precursor Frequency of Cytotoxic T Cells from Mice of Different Ages Uninjected or Injected with Thymosin Peptides

Age (Months)	Treatment	Precursors per 10^4 Cells[a]	p
3	none	8 (1.27)	
10	none	2 (1.46)	
10	α_1(10 µg)	5 (1.30)	<0.01
10	N_{14}(5 µg)	6 (1.21)	<0.005
10	C_{14}(5 µg)	2 (1.40)	<0.50

[a] Number in parentheses is the error factor by which the frequency should be multiplied or divided to obtain the variations due to one standard error.

the frequency of alloantigen-responsive Tc cell precursors. However, injection of old mice with thymosin α_1 or its N_{14} fragment, but not the C_{14} fragment, increases the frequency of these Tc cell precursors in the spleen.

Ts Cells

Thymic involution suggests that suppressor T cells (Ts) may be decreased in old mice and, as a result, may account for the expression of autoreactive clones. However, suppressor T cell activity has been found increased,[11–21] unchanged,[22] or decreased[23–29] in aging mice and humans.

The overt contradiction as to age-related changes in immunosuppression reflects the large variety of methods used to assess suppressor cell activity. Suppressor cells of different types have been both induced and tested *in vitro* and *in vivo*, or induced *in vivo* and tested *in vitro*. Besides the different antigens, modes of action, and sensitivities of the test assays used, evaluation of the results is further complicated by alterations in the T lymphocyte recognition repertoire during aging[30] which may hinder suppressor cells from depressing age-mismatched responder cells.[31] Moreover, analysis of antigen-specific immunosuppression has clearly revealed the existence of multiple interactions among suppressor T cells and their soluble products. Thus, different model systems may involve nonidentical parts of the same or different suppressor cell circuits and, therefore, are likely to provide dissimilar results even when the subtle experimental conditions of each assay have been carefully fulfilled.

We have examined age-related alterations of antigen-specific T cell suppression in the NP (4-hydroxy-3-nitrophenyl acetyl) system, a well-defined experimental model characterized by the sequential interaction of several T cell subsets and soluble factors.[32,33] Briefly, antigen presentation by $I\text{-}J^+$, $I\text{-}A^+$ macrophages activates an inducer T cell, Tsi (Ts1; Lyt-1^+,2^-; $I\text{-}J^+$; Id^+), which produces an antigen-specific factor, TsiF (TsF1; $I\text{-}J^+$; Id^+; nonrestricted by MHC and Igh genes; antigen-binding). In the absence of antigen, TsiF presented by $I\text{-}A^+$, $I\text{-}J^+$ macrophages activates transducer T cells, Tst (Ts2; Lyt-1^+,2^+; $I\text{-}J^+$; Id^-), which recognize TsiF by anti-Id receptors and are restricted by I-J and Igh genes. Activated Tst cells produce a factor, TstF (TsF2; $I\text{-}J^+$; anti-Id; restricted by I-J and Igh genes), which, if presented by $I\text{-}A^+$, $I\text{-}J^+$ macrophages, triggers previously primed effector T cells, Tse (Ts3; Lyt-1^-,2^+; $I\text{-}J^+$; Id^+), to produce and release a factor, TseF (TsF3; $I\text{-}J^+$; Id^+; restricted by I-J and Igh genes; antigen-binding). Tse cells are primed by antigen presented on $I\text{-}A^+$, $I\text{-}J^+$ macrophages. TseF suppresses specifically responder target T cells (inhibition of proliferation, lymphokine production) and B cells (inhibition of antibody production) and arms acceptor suppressor T cells, Tsa (Ts4; Lyt-1^-,2^+; $I\text{-}J^+$), and $I\text{-}A^+$, $I\text{-}J^+$ macrophages. Armed acceptor cells are then triggered by antigen associated with I-J products to release factors that are genetically unrestricted and suppress nonspecifically responder target T and B cells.

Tsi cells were activated in BDF1 mice at the age of 3 months (young) or 18 months (old) by intravenous injection of NP-conjugated syngeneic spleen cells (SC). Spleen cells from the NP-SC-injected mice were subcultured in vitro with spleen cells from normal young or old mice to generate Tst cells. Four days later subcultured cells were added to responder cell cultures to trigger Tse cells one day before the plaque-forming cell (PFC) assays. Responder cell cultures, containing NP-conjugated horse red blood cells (HRBC) and spleen cells from HRBC-primed young or old mice, were assayed on day 4 for anti-NP and anti-HRBC PFC. Suppression was found to be antigen-specific and age-restricted. NP-specific suppressor cells are easily induced in subculture if the Tsi and Tst cell populations are both derived from young or old mice. Conversely, if Tsi cells from young or old mice are subcultured with Tst cells from mice of a different age, suppression of the anti-NP PFC response is hardly observed. Age restriction also operates in the interactions between subcultured cells and responder cells indicating that age-matching is required for Tst cells to trigger Tse cells effectively (TABLE 4). These results altogether suggest that aging may affect the idiotypic repertoire expressed in suppressor T cell subsets. Moreover, the finding that suppression is less efficient when exerted on responder spleen cells from old than from young mice provides an explanation for the increased frequency of autoimmune disorders in aging.[21,31]

Conclusions

Age-related modulation of immunoregulatory T cell functions can explain the decline of immune responsiveness to exogenous antigens as well as the increase in autoimmune reactivity. The effects of injecting old mice with thymosin peptides suggest the possibility of repairing T cell activity to the level observed in young mice. The use of thymic hormones is very promising in the treatment of age-related immune dysfunctions but requires accurate protocols to reach antithetic objectives, such as increased immune responsiveness to pathogens and prevention or mitigation of autoimmune reactions.

TABLE 4. Specific Suppression of the Anti-NP Antibody Response

Subcultured Cells from Mice		% Suppression of Responder Cells from Mice[a]			
Tsi	Tst	Young		Old	
young	+ young	49	(1.04)	10	(1.18)
young	+ old	20	(1.06)	0	
old	+ old	39	(1.04)	23	(1.04)
old	+ young	27	(1.06)	0	

[a] Number in parentheses is the error factor by which % suppression should be multiplied or divided to obtain the variations due to one standard error.

REFERENCES

1. DORIA, G., L. ADORINI & D. FRASCA. 1987. Immunoregulation of antibody responses in aging mice. *In* Aging and the Immune Response: Cellular and Humoral Aspects. E. A. Goidl, Ed. 143-176. Marcel Dekker, Inc. New York, NY.

2. HIROKAWA, K. & T. MAKINODAN. 1975. Thymic involution: effect on T cell differentiation. J. Immunol. **114:** 1659-1662.

3. BACH, J. F., M. DARDENNE & J. C. SALOMON. 1973. Studies on thymus products. IV. Absence of serum "thymic activity" in adult NZB and (NZB×NZW)F1 mice. Clin. Exp. Immunol. **14:** 247-258.

4. MILLER, R. A. 1984. Age-associated decline in precursor frequency for different T cell-mediated reactions, with preservation of helper or cytotoxic effect for precursor cell. J. Immunol. **132:** 63-68.

5. FRASCA, D., L. ADORINI, C. MANCINI & G. DORIA. 1986. Reconstitution of T cell functions in aging mice by thymosin α_1. Immunopharmacology **11:** 155-163.

6. FRASCA, D., L. ADORINI & G. DORIA. 1987. Enhanced frequency of mitogen-responsive T cell precursors in old mice injected with thymosin α_1. Eur. J. Immunol. **17:** 727-730.

7. FAZEKAS DE ST. GROTH, S. 1982. The evaluation of limiting dilution assays. J. Immunol. Methods **49:** R11-R23.

8. SHIGEMOTO, S., S. KISHIMOTO & Y. YAMAMURA. 1975. Change of cell-mediated cytotoxicity with aging. J. Immunol. **115:** 307-309.

9. MILLER, R. A. & O. STUTMAN. 1981. Decline, in aging mice, of the anti-2,4,6-trinitrophenyl (TNP) cytotoxic T cell response attributable to loss of Lyt-2⁻, interleukin 2-producing helper cell function. Eur. J. Immunol. **11:** 751-756.

10. THOMAN, M. L. & W. O. WEIGLE. 1982. Cell-mediated immunity in aged mice: an underlying lesion in IL 2 synthesis. J. Immunol. **128:** 2358-2361.

11. GERBASE-DE LIMA, M., P. MEREDITH & R. L. WALFORD. 1975. Age-related changes including synergy and suppression in the mixed lymphocyte reaction in long-lived mice. Fed. Proc. **34:** 159-161.

12. GOIDL, E. A., J. B. INNES & M. E. WEKSLER. 1976. Immunological studies of aging. II. Loss of IgG and high avidity plaque-forming cells and increased suppressor cell activity in aging mice. J. Exp. Med. **144:** 1037-1048.

13. SEGRE, D. & M. SEGRE. 1976. Humoral immunity in aged mice. II. Increased suppressor T cell activity in immunologically deficient old mice. J. Immunol. **116:** 753-738.

14. MAKINODAN, T., J. W. ALBRIGHT, P. I. GOOD, C. P. PETER & L. M. HEIDRICK. 1976. Reduced humoral activity in long-lived old mice: an approach to elucidating its mechanisms. Immunology **31:** 903-912.

15. RODER, J. C., A. K. DUWE, D. A. BELL & S. K. SINGHAL. 1978. Immunological senescence. I. The role of suppressor cells. Immunology **35:** 837-842.

16. DE KRUYFF, R. H., Y. T. KIM, G. W. SISKIND & M. E. WEKSLER. 1980. Age-related changes in the in vitro immune responses: increased suppressor activity in immature and aged mice. J. Immunol. **125:** 142-147.

17. CALLARD, R. E., S. FAZEKAS DE ST. GROTH, A. BASTEN & I. F. C. MCKENZIE. 1980. The immune function in aged mice. V. Role of suppressor cells. J. Immunol. **124:** 52-58.

18. LIU, J. J., M. SEGRE & D. SEGRE. 1982. Changes in suppressor, helper, and B-cell functions in aging mice. Cell. Immunol. **66:** 372-380.

19. AMAGAI, T., K. NAKANO & B. CINADER. 1982. Mechanisms involved in age-dependent decline of immune responsiveness and apparent resistance against tolerance induction in C57BL/6 mice. Scand. J. Immunol. **16:** 217-223.

20. GLOBERSON, A., L. ABEL, M. BARZILAY & I. ZAN-BAR. 1982. Immunoregulatory cells in aging mice. I. Concanavalin A-induced and naturally occurring suppressor cells. Mech. Ageing Dev. **19:** 293.

21. DORIA, G., C. MANCINI & L. ADORINI. 1982. Immunoregulation in senescence: increased inducibility of antigen specific suppressor T cells and loss of cell sensitivity to immunosuppression in aging mice. Proc. Natl. Acad. Sci. USA **79:** 3803-3807.

22. BARTHOID, D. R., S. KYSELA & A. D. STEINBERG. 1974. Decline in suppressor T cell function with age in female NZB mice. J. Immunol. **122:** 9-16.

23. KRAKAUER, R. S., D. A. WALDMANN & W. STROBER. 1976. Loss of suppressor T cells in adult NZB/NZW mice. J. Exp. Med. **144:** 662-680.

24. HALGREN, H. & E. YUNIS. 1977. Suppressor lymphocytes in young and aged humans. J. Immunol. **118:** 2004-2008.

25. THOMAN, M. L. & W. O. WEIGLE. 1983. Deficiency in suppressor T cell activity in aged animals. Reconstitution of this activity by interleukin 2. J. Exp. Med. **157:** 2184-2189.

26. GOTTESMAN, S. R. S., R. L. WALFORD & G. J. THORBECKE. 1984. Proliferative and cytotoxic immune functions in aging mice. II. Decreased generation of specific suppressor cells in alloreactive cultures. J. Immunol. **133:** 1782-1787.

27. GORCZYNSKI, R. M., M. KENNEDY & S. MCRAE. 1983. Alteration in lymphocyte recognition repertoire during aging. II. Changes in the expressed T-cell receptor repertoire in aged mice and the persistence of that change after transplantation to a new differentiative environment. Cell. Immunol. **75:** 226-241.

28. HAUSMAN, P. B., E. A. GOIDL, G. W. SISKIND & M. E. WEKSLER. 1985. Immunological studies of aging. XI. Age-related changes in idiotype repertoire of suppressor T cells stimulated during tolerance induction. J. Immunol. **134:** 3802-3807.

29. DORF, M. E. & B. BENACERRAF. 1984. Suppressor cells and immunoregulation. Annu. Rev. Immunol. **2:** 127-158.

30. ASHERSON, G. L., V. COLIZZI & M. ZEMBALA. 1986. An overview of T suppressor cell circuits. Annu. Rev. Immunol. **4:** 37-68.

31. DORIA, G., C. MANCINI, D. FRASCA & L. ADORINI. 1987. Age restriction in antigen-specific immunosuppression. J. Immunol. **139:** 1419-1425.

The Neuropeptide Network

CANDACE PERT WITH HARRIS DIENSTFREY

Section on Brain Biochemistry
Clinical Neuroscience Branch
National Institute of Mental Health
Bethesda, Maryland 20892

I am going to discuss my laboratory's work on neuropeptides and outline the reasons why we believe that neuropeptides are the biochemical basis of the emotions. Neuropeptides, as we understand them, are not simply one more item in the increasingly more detailed comprehension of the chemistry of the body. We have shown that neuropeptides can suffuse the body, and this is crucial to our understanding of neuropeptides. People sometimes say they are overcome with this or that feeling. Biochemically speaking, we would say that they are overcome with this or that neuropeptide. What we are dealing with in neuropeptides, we believe, is a body-wide system, or, to put it differently, a system that simultaneously includes brain and body. Conventional scientific wisdom tends to see a clear, distinct difference between brain and body. When talking of neuropeptides, the distinction, for all practical purposes, virtually disappears. We are talking about something that can "grip" the whole organism.

This is one reason we contend that this "whole body" system—the system of neuropeptides, the system of emotions—can play a critical part in matters of health and disease. In this connection, I will briefly mention, at the end of the paper, the new understandings of AIDS to which our work on neuropeptides has led us.

The story of neuropeptides, which is evolving so rapidly, is taking us into rather strange new areas for science. My background is largely in the field of brain receptors, particularly their biochemistry. That is to say, the original focus of my attention was on the part of an individual that generally was taken to be his command post, the brain. But it soon became clear that what we were learning about brain receptors had some startling implications about what could command what.

Some years ago, during the early stages of the studies demonstrating the existence of brain receptors, I was asked to talk about the work to lay people and to try and explain, if I could, its practical application. I thought about this for quite a while—or, as some people would now say, I expanded my consciousness as much as I could—and my response came in the last word of a subtitle for a National Institutes of Health lecture that I delivered to lay people in 1981. The title was "Brain Receptors for Opiates and Other Psychoactive Drugs," and the subtitle, "Keys to the Biochemistry of Emotion."

The concept of "emotion" took me out on a limb. Even today, the word is slightly disreputable in many scientific quarters; a half dozen years ago, its use smacked of the scandalous. Emotion, at best, lingered on the periphery of science, and was never a bona fide subject for investigation. People like Sigmund Freud used the word, but whatever people like Freud did, their activity certainly was not science. Walter Pierpaoli said earlier in this workshop that you cannot teach someone something they think they already know. My own work and efforts to investigate emotion suggest a corollary: that it is impossible to teach somebody something that they think is unknowable. Many people think emotions are unknowable in a scientific sense. Our work on neuropeptides strongly suggests otherwise.

What are neuropeptides? What do they do in the life of the brain and body? There used to be heated arguments about what to call these neurosubstances. Were they neurotransmitters or neuromodulators? The general concept first proposed by F. O. Schmitt[1] and independently outlined in our first full-scale effort to explain neuropeptides, "Neuropeptides and their receptors: a psychosomatic network,"[2] is that they are *informational* substances. This is the key thing that neuropeptides do, they are a vehicle for providing information. Where they provide it is equally important. Specifically, they transmit information throughout the brain and body in a *network* of communication, thereby integrating at the level of the whole organism. The concept of network as it applies to the organism is extremely important and deserves a discussion in itself. Here I would just say that a network is nonhierarchical, that it is a system in which there is potentially equal access to all the nodal points.

In the category of informational molecules that constitute part of the neuropeptide informational network, we now include not only the classical neuropeptides but also hormones (including classical peptide hormones like insulin), lymphokines, and growth factors. We have done gel work and are certain that many molecules similar to if not identical with molecules on T-cells and B-cells in the immune system are also found in the brain, in a pattern that we call the typical neuropeptide receptor pattern. We have not yet found a single growth factor that does not have a feedback loop and receptors in the emotion-mediating parts of the brain. The growth factors include insulin-like growth factor I and II, epidermal growth factor, transferring, and the lymphokine, interleuken 1.

What we have, then, are peptides diffusing great distances throughout both the brain (it turns out that most if not all neuropeptides are stored in one part of the brain while the receptors are in another part) and the body, having more of a hormone-like action than a neurotransmitter-like action. In short, the peptides flow. They do not need a neural system to enable them to pass, as in a high-wire act, from one neural platform to another. A word to describe the peptide movement might be neurojuices.

Why is the body not confused by all these oozing chemicals, which flow without the benefit a predetermined road-way system? The answer lies in the exquisite specificity of the receptor recognition molecules. Each type of receptor molecule is different from every other type of receptor molecule, each type has a different molecular weight, and it can be shown that each one recognizes only one class of neuropeptide. Despite the fact that there now are sixty well-documented neuropeptides, and more if one counts all of the growth factor substances, the receptor molecules keep them all straight. There is no confusion because each class of neuropeptide can come to rest, so to speak, in only one kind of receptor molecule.

What has all this to do with emotions? Why do we consider neuropeptides the biochemicals of emotions?

For some years, my laboratory has been working with a receptor-analyzing technique that Dr. Miles Herkenham and I developed in 1979.[3] We call it chemical or molecular neuroanatomy or autoradiography of receptors. Briefly, unfixed frozen sections are incubated in various radio-labeled ligands. The sections are juxtaposed against a film so that we can study the receptor pattern. We then use a computer to transform the pattern into a color gradient according to density. For example, in a section of a rhesus monkey brain which has been incubated with tritiated naloxone, the computer color-translation shows red and yellow areas that represent approximately 40 times the density of opiate receptors that occur in "cooler" areas. Now, brain sections repeatedly show the same receptor pattern. The cool areas, where the receptors are least dense, are in the cortex, and the hot areas, where they are the densest, are in the amygdala and the hypothalamus, which are classically considered to be the core of the so-called limbic system, which in turn is classically considered to be the system that is the neurosubstrate of the emotions. The neuropeptide receptors, in other words, cluster in those areas of the brain that are classically considered to be key juncture points in the production of emotions.

But it turns out that the amygdala and the hypothalamus are not the only areas in the brain that are rich in neuropeptide receptors. This finding, which has arisen in our work, led Dr. Joanna Hill and I to an expanded view of the limbic system. We now think that the appropriate way to characterize the limbic system is not simply in terms of the parts of the brain that show connections to the amygdala and hypothalamus but rather in terms of the nodal points at which information about neuropeptide status converges in the brain.[4]

The amygdala and hypothalamus are two such nodal points, of course. Moreover, they are particularly rich areas, because they contain receptors for essentially every neuropeptide we so far have identified. If our reasoning is correct—that the presence of a heavy density of neuropeptide receptors identifies a part of the limbic system—our research suggests that the usual picture of the limbic system should be extended to include the spinal cord, for a third area enriched with neuropeptide receptors is the dorsal horn of the spinal cord. We have not undertaken a systematic study of the receptors to be found there, but our work, whether on insulin receptors or angiotensin receptors, indicates that it is always the dorsal horn that is enriched.[5]

Now, the dorsal horn has to do with incoming sensory information and not motor outflow, which is associated with another part of the spinal cord, and this central characteristic of the dorsal horn has led to an important theoretical consideration about which Dr. Morton Mishkin and I have speculated in print.[6] We argue that the emotions are very important in determining what an individual pays attention to at any given moment. Put simply, your emotions tell you what to do. At any given moment, you are hearing something, seeing something, feeling something. All of your senses (including what Dr. Edward Blalock calls the sixth sense, which reports on the status of the immune system) are communicating simultaneously, and you need a chemical system to prioritize all of this information. We think it is very interesting that not just the spinal cord with the tactile sense is enriched with neuropeptide receptors. The pathway into the brain of all sensory modality input zones, whether they involve sight, sound, smell, taste, or touch, are marked by neuropeptide receptors.[7]

Above, I spoke of peptides diffusing throughout the body as well as the brain—neurojuices—all connecting at the proper places because of the exquisite sensitivity of the receptor molecules. This picture now needs to be joined to the expanding picture of the emotional network in the body. For it seems to us that the concept of emotions, like the concept of the limbic system, should be defined, in effect, by the presence of neuropeptide receptors.

Angiotensin receptors in the rat provide an example. Angiotensin is a neuropeptide made in the brain and has receptors in the subfornical organ. In a rat, when you inject angiotensin into the subfornical area, within about 30 seconds, the rat, regardless of how water sated he may have been, begins to drink water. Now, the kidney of the rat has the same molecular receptors (the technique of chemical neuroanatomy is also applicable, of course, to the peripheral organs), and when angiotensin occupies those receptors, the kidney works to conserve water. In other words, the chemical angiotensin that makes the rat drink when it is injected into the brain also makes the kidney conserve water. Thus, angiotension leads to water saving and water seeking, two aspects of the same phenomenon. This example seems to us to illustrate a general principle, that the same general mood is integrating to the whole animal level by means of the particular chemical that is diffusing throughout the brain and body.

Where else in the body can neuropeptide receptors be found? Over the past three or four years, Dr. Michael Ruff has accumulated evidence showing that six neuropeptide receptors that have been well documented in brain exist in very similar molecular form on various monocytes.[8] In a study published several years ago, we found that bombesin and other neuropeptides can mediate chemotaxis not just of human monocytes but also of several human tumor cells.[9]

The presence of neuropeptide receptors on monocytes is supported by on-going work on insulin receptors being done by Dr. Joanna Hill and myself. Dr. Hill and I, with Dr. Jesse Roth, have already published a distribution of insulin receptors in rat brains.[10] The distribution follows the standard neuropeptide pattern: the receptors are rich in amygdala, limbic cortex, and other parts of the limbic system. We now are applying our techniques to the spleen, and our early findings suggest that there are similar insulin receptors on monocytes in the spleen.

The presence of neuropeptide receptors on monocytes is the rule not the exception. We now have enough data on enough neuropeptides (not all of it published) to support this proposition.[11]

Looking at this picture of the body-wide, hormone-like distribution of neuropeptides from another angle, we have also begun to explore growth factors. Dr. Hill, an expert in growth factors, had a great interest in transferrin, which has been appreciated as an iron-binding protein and as a major growth factor for a number of cells. Naturally, Dr. Hill wanted to find receptors for transferrin in the brain, and we recently described the limbic-associated pattern of receptors that we found.[12]

Our "mapping" studies, incidentally, are based on a system of carefully graded controls. We validate radioactive ligand-binding distribution patterns by obtaining a rank order of potency of over 20 peptides previously ranked for eliciting a physiological response. We expect the peptides to have the identical rank order in displacing bindings, which is how we know that it is a specific binding. This approach is excellent for peptides, but for larger molecules, for which there is elegant immunological data but not much short peptide work, we need another approach to prove that we have a genuine binding. And in these situations we use what the immunologists have done so beautifully for us—antibodies raised to receptors. The two approaches give us virtually identical patterns. For example, the pattern of transferrin receptors revealed by using classical monoclonal antibodies is the same pattern revealed using a labeled ligand.[12]

In any event, a portion of the receptors are in areas outside the limbic pattern, but many are in areas within the limbic pattern. This suggests that something as unemotional as transferrin and iron has a neuropeptide-like emotional distribution pattern in the brain. And this in turn suggests a feedback loop between brain and body. Again we see an association, a congruence, between peptides and emotions.

Dr. Hill, in collaboration with Dr. Peter Nissley of the National Institutes of Health, has extended this work to other growth factors.[13] With insulin-like growth factor II, for example, both the labeled-ligand and monoclonal-antibody approaches reveal virtually identical patterns of receptors, a large portion of which are, again, in the limbic portions of the brain.

For a final example of the brain/body/neuropeptide network—and one rather closer to the subject of this conference on aging and cancer—I draw on the work of Dr. George Mark of the Cancer Institute. Dr. Mark is an expert on the raf oncogene. He has raised antibodies to synthetic peptides coded by the raf oncogene sequence, and when we use our antibody mapping technique on a slice of brain, we can show that there are receptors for this raf antibody and that they form neuropeptide receptor-like patterns.[14] Indeed, we have not found an oncogene product that is not in the brain, which supports our idea that virtually everything in the immune system, in terms of cell-surface communication molecules, can also be found in brain.

The biochemicals of emotions, because they are so important, are likely to be highly conserved throughout evolution. We believe that this proposition highlights the significance of some findings concerning peptides in unicellular animals. In work done between our laboratory and the laboratory of Dr. Jesse Roth, we demonstrated that the *Tetrahymena* and *E coli.*, simple cellular animals, contain beta-endorphin and other opiate peptides.[15] Dr. Roth had shown previously that they also contained insulin which was immunologically and bioactively indistinguishable from insulin in humans.[16] In more recent work by Dr. Blanche O'Neill, to be published in *Brain Research*, we have shown a single opiate receptor recognition molecule in the *Tetrahymena*. This molecule is generally 110 kD, but it likes to fragment along a weak point to produce a molecule with the molecular weight of 58kD. In the *Tetrahymena*, we have found molecules of these two weights. Protease digests of these bands show that they have the same fragmentation pattern and indistinguishable isoelectric focusing points. These molecules may not be strictly identical. However, they are certainly very similar, and we are awaiting the results of their sequencing in a collaborative venture with Dr. Craig Venter.

It was Freud, of course, who drew our attention to the possibility that the brain has a conscious part and an unconscious or subconscious part. Normally, one thinks of the conscious part on the top and the unconscious part toward the back. But we would go further "back" (or down) and say that the subconscious is in the spinal cord and even "lower." Psychologists talk about deep subconscious processes. Clearly, the network of chemicals that I have attempted to describe suggests that the subconscious extends to one's T-cells, to one's monocytes, and, in a kind of flowing wave, back to one's brain cells.

Freud also made important observations about how emotional status could contribute to disease status. In this context, it seems to us appropriate to consider that with all the circulating neurojuices—and all the neuropeptides can be found in different proportions in different organs throughout the brain, the glands, and the immune system cells—we are seeing a constant aqueous solution that makes a continuum of the brain and the body.

Such a formulation obviously raises the issue of the blood-brain barrier. This barrier exists for only a limited number of substances. We must stay open to the possibility that cells themselves may cross the barrier, just like the microglial cells that start life as macrophages/monocytes in the bone marrow and then actually travel into the brain where they become glial cells. It is possible that there is more cellular trafficking between these two compartments than is currently appreciated. We have no experimental evidence to support this proposition—perhaps at the moment it should be labeled a "wild theory"—but we consider it one worthy of serious investigation.

A brief word, finally, on the significance of neuropeptides to health and disease, specifically with regard to AIDS. Our work on neuropeptides has led us to appreciate the AIDS virus in a neurochemical and neuropeptide context.[17] We have shown that the AIDS virus wreaks its havoc through its envelope, gp 120, which blocks vasoactive intestinal peptide binding throughout the brain and the body.[18] We believe that the capacity of gp 120 to negate the important positive effects of vasoactive intestinal peptide provides the solution to the dilemma of why an organism can be so severely damaged by AIDS even though only a small percentage of cells are actually infected.

The exogenous peptide blocks the endogenous peptide, preventing it from doing its good work.

REFERENCES

1. SCHMITT, F. D. 1984. Molecular regulation of brain function: a new view. Neuroscience 13: 991.
2. PERT, C. B., M. R. RUFF, R. J. WEBER & M. HERKENHAM. 1985. Neuropeptides and their receptors: a psychosomatic network. J. Immunol. 135: 820s-826s.
3. HERKENHAM, M. & C. B. PERT. 1982. Light microscopic localization of brain opiate receptors: a general autoradiographic method which preserves tissue quality. J. Neurosci. 2: 1129-1149.
4. HILL, J. M. & C. B. PERT. Neurochemical basis of emotional behavior. In Handbook of Neuropsychology. F. Boller & J. Grafman, Eds. Elsevier. Amsterdam. In press.
5. PERT, C. B., M. J. KUHAR & S. H. SNYDER. 1976. Opiate receptor: autoradiographic localization in rat brain. Proc. Natl. Acad. Sci. USA 73: 3729-3733.
6. LEWIS, M. E., M. MISHKIN, E. BRAGIN, R. M. BROWN, C. B. PERT & A. PERT. 1981. Opiate receptor gradients in monkey cerebral cortex: correspondence with sensory processing hierarchies. Science 211: 1166-1169.
7. HERKENHAM, M. & C. B. PERT. 1980. In vitro autoradiography of opiate receptors in rat brain suggests loci of "opiatergic" pathways. Proc. Natl. Acad. Sci. USA 77: 5532-5536.
8. RUFF, M. R. & C. B. PERT. 1986. Neuropeptides are chemoattractants for human monocytes and tumor cells: a basis for mind-body communication. In Enkephalins and Endorphins Stress and the Immune System. N. P. Plotnikoff, R. E. Faith, A. J. Murgo & R. A. Good, Eds. 387-398. Plenum Publishing Corp. New York, NY.
9. RUFF, M., E. SCHIFFMAN, V. TERRANOVA & C. B. PERT. 1985. Neuropeptides are chemoattractants for human tumor cells and monocytes: a possible mechanism for metastasis. Clin. Immunol. Immunopathol. 37: 387-396.
10. HILL, J. M., M. A. LESNIAK, C. B. PERT & J. ROTH. 1986. Autoradiographic localization of insulin receptors in rat brain: prominence in olfactory and limbic areas. Neuroscience 17: 1127-1138.
11. RUFF, M. R., C. B. PERT, R. J. WEBER, L. M. WAHL, S. M. WAHL & S. M. PAUL. 1985. Benzodiazepine receptor-mediated chemotaxis of human monocytes. Science 229: 1281-1283.
12. HILL, J. M., M. R. RUFF, R. J. WEBER & C. B. PERT. 1985. Transferrin receptors in rat brain: neuropeptide-like pattern and relationship to iron distribution. Proc. Natl. Acad. Sci. USA 82: 4553-4557.
13. HILL, J. M., M. A. LESNIAK, W. KIESS & S. P. NISSLEY. Radioimmunohistochemical localization of type II IGF receptors in rat brain. Peptides. In press.
14. HILL, J. M., B. ZIPSER & C. B. PERT. Peptide receptor-rich regions of the brain form nodal points in the circuitry of limbic and associated systems. Brain Res. In press.
15. LEROITH, D., A. S. LIOTTA, J. ROTH, J. SHILOACH, M. E. LEWIS, C. B. PERT & D. T. KRIEGER. 1982. Corticotropin and β-endorphin-like materials are native to unicellular organisms. Proc. Natl. Acad. Sci. USA 79: 2086.
16. LEROITH, D., J. SHILOACH, J. ROTH & M. A. LESNIAK. 1980. Evolutionary origins of vertebrate hormones: substances similar to mammalian insulin are native to unicellular eukaryotes. Proc. Natl. Acad. Sci. USA 77: 6184-6188.
17. PERT, C. B., J. M. HILL, M. R. RUFF, R. M. BERMAN, W. G. ROBEY, L. O. ARTHUR, F. W. RUSCETTI & W. L. FARRAR. 1986. Octapeptides deduced from the neuropeptide receptor-like pattern of antigen T4 in brain potently inhibit human immunodeficiency virus receptor binding and T-cell infectivity. Proc. Natl. Acad. Sci. USA 83: 9254-9258.
18. PERT, C. B., C. SMITH, M. R. RUFF & J. M. HILL. 1988. AIDS and its dementia as a neuropeptide disorder: role of VIP receptor blockade by human immunodeficiency virus (HIV) envelope. Ann. Neurol. January Suppl. In press.

Neurohumoral Mechanisms of the Formation of Antitumoral Activity

V. B. VINNITSKY

Institute for Oncology Problems
Academy of Sciences of Ukrainian SSR
Kiev, USSR

INTRODUCTION

The integrity of the neurohumoral link in the regulation of immunological processes in an organism is a condition of normal functioning of the immunocompetent system.[1,2] However, this concept was not at all taken into account in the investigation of the causes of immunosuppression in cancer and in the development of methods for enhancement of sensitivity of the immunocompetent system of response to tumor antigens. We have hypothesized that one of the main reasons for antitumor inconsistency of the immune system is provided by the morphofunctional disorders in the tumor-carrying organism in different divisions of the nervous system and endocrine organs, as a result of which neurohumoral antitumor immune reactions are not optimal.

The search for means of augmenting activation of antitumor immunity must be directed at (1) the development of methods for the optimization of neurohumoral antitumor immune reactions in the organism and optimal immune response to immunostimuli, and (2) finding methods for increasing the antigenicity and immunogenicity of tumor cells. The practical solution of this problem is made difficult by our lack of knowledge: (a) of the character of neurohumor disorders in cancer and the possibility of their elimination, (b) of the features of neurohumoral rearrangements induced by low- and high-immunogenic antigens of tumoral and nontumoral nature and (c) of the optimum neurohumoral alterations that can provide an effective immune response. No information is available on the character and role of neurohumoral rearrangements in an organism affected by a malignant process, during the antigenic load, or during the administration of immunostimuli.

The present work is dedicated to the elucidation of the aforementioned questions.

Comparative Investigation of the Functional State of the Hypothalamus, Adrenal Cortex and Sympathoadrenal System in Animals after Transplantation of Tumor Cells and Administration of Nontumoral Antigenic Material

In chronic experiments with rabbits comparative investigation of the bioelectrical activity of the middle medial division of the hypothalamus was carried out after subcutaneous transplantation of Brown-Pierce carcinoma and allotransplantation of skin graft.[4] Complete tumor resorption was observed on the 40th-50th day after transplantation, and the skin graft lost its viability after 9-12 days. The amplitude and frequency of the basic rhythm of electroencephalograms (EEG) in rabbits with Brown-Pierce carcinoma revealed maximal increases on the 22th-24th day after transplantation, and in the animals with skin allograft on the 3rd-4th day after transplantation (Fig. 1). The control animals that underwent autotransplantation of skin graft did not show alterations in their EEGs during this period. Inhibition of hypothalamic reaction in tumor-bearing animals may be attributed to the low immunogenicity of tumor cells which provide only a weak stimulus to the neurohumoral systems.

FIGURE 1. Changes in the L-rhythm amplitude of EEG of the hypothalamus in the rabbits: (1) after transplantation of Brown-Pierce carcinoma: (2) after transplantation of Brown-Pierce carcinoma with daily electrical stimulation of the hypothalamus: (3) after allotransplantation of skin graft. Electrodes were implanted into the hypothalamus under sodium-ethaminal narcosis. A stereotaxic atlas was used. The first electrode was oriented in the AP plane l-O.5) and the second one in the AP plane (+5.5). Both electrodes were arranged laterally from the median line at 0.3 mm and introduced into the brain at 15.5 mm. Electrodes were fixed at the skull with the use of protacryl. Amplitude and frequency of the basic EEG rhythm were registered through the chronically implanted electrodes with the use of a 15-channel "Alvar" electroencelograph (France).

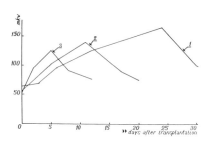

Rabbits with Brown-Pierce carcinoma were subjected to hypothalamic stimulation by the threshold current for 5 minutes daily during the whole period of tumor growth. The stimulation brought about a reversal of tumor growth. Complete resorption of the carcinoma was observed by the 18-25th day after transplantation. It was preceded by the maximal increase in EEG indices, observed on the 12th-13th day after transplantation (Fig. 1). The maximal activation of the sympathoadrenal system (SAS) and adrenal cortex (AC), in the animals with carcinoma subjected to hypothalamic stimulation, was observed on the 5th-7th day after the beginning of electrical stimulation. Normalization of functional state of SAS and AC in these animals occurred by the 15th-17th day after the beginning of electrical stimulation. This short-lived activation of the hypothalamus, SAS and AC was accompanied by an increase in the number of blast-transformed lymphocytes in the phytohemagglutinin (PHA)-test, increased E-rosettes-forming cells (RFC), enhanced interferon reaction of lymphocytes,[5] and positive changes in the ultrastructure of lymphoid cells in regional lymph nodes.[6]

Thus, the experiments with rabbits revealed the possibility of molding, by means of transhypothalamic influences, the neurohumoral rearrangements that contribute to antitumor resistance. The results of comparative studies of hypothalamic bioelectrical activity after transplantation of tumors and skin allografts suggest that analysis, in tumor-bearing animals, of the neurohumoral shifts observed after administration of high-immunogenic antigens, is the most promising approach for increasing antitumor resistance. This statement of the problem required comparative studies of the complex of neurohumoral reactions to antigenic material of different immunogenicity.

Experiments were performed on rats and mice with the use of transplantable tumor strains: Guerin carcinoma, sarcoma 180 and virus-induced Moloney sarcoma. Ram erythrocytes (RE), BCG vaccine, and embryonal tissue were used as the nontumoral antigenic materials.

Biochemical rearrangements in the hypothalamus in animals with Guerin carcinoma included consistent decreases in noradrenalin, which appeared as soon as the 2nd day after inoculation of tumor cells, and elevated levels of serotonin and adrenalin (TABLE 1). The decrease in noradrenalin and increases in adrenalin and serotonin in the hypothalamus were reported to be accompanied by a fall in the level of adrenocorticotropic hormone in the pituitary and a rise in blood concentration of adrenocortical hormone.[7] These data are in good agreement with the results of our investigations that showed consistent increases in 11-oxycorticosteroids (11-OCS) in rat blood plasma, starting from the 7th day of growth of Guerin carcinoma (TABLE 2).

The flux of catecholamines occurred in phased alterations. The first, reactive, phase consisted in a transient (during the first day after tumor inoculation) rise in the excretion of adrenalin and vanillic mandelic acid (VMA). The second phase, which lasted until the formation of tumor foci, did not reveal reliable alterations in catecholamine shifts. The alterations appeared after the 7th day of tumor growth (the third phase), when tumors were observed in all animals. The period of progressive tumor growth indicated both the activation and exhaustion of SAS. Increased noradrenalin and adrenalin contents in the urine and in the adrenal glands were combined with substantial decreases in the level of their precursor dopamine. The fourth phase in the alterations took place at the later stages of tumor growth and involved a sharp fall in dihydroxyphenylalanine (DOPA) and catecholamines in the adrenals and decreased excretion of all of the investigated substances, representing a profound exhaustion of the SAS.[8]

The established biochemical rearrangements in the hypothalamus, alterations in blood level of 11-OCS and in catecholamine shifts reveal the formation of defensive-adaptative reactions in the organism. However, these reactions, developing during the progressive growth of tumor, do not increase the antitumor resistance; moreover, they acquire pathological features characteristic of chronic stress which causes the exhaustion of the functioning of the neurohumoral systems.

Investigation of the hypothalamic content of neuromediators in rats during the development of the primary immune response to administration of RE, in the dose of 5×10^8, revealed phased changes in these indices (TABLE 3).

Alterations in the metabolism of catecholamines after immunization with RE were well balanced. The excretion of noradrenalin and dopamine and their metabolites, VMA and homovanillic acid (HVA), was increased. Elevated excretion of noradrenalin and its main metabolite, VMA, and decreased content of adrenalin in the urine suggest that stimulation of catecholamine methylation and enhanced tonus of SAS can be attributed to the activation of its mediatory role. Normalization of the investigated indices was observed by the 11th day after immunization.[3]

Direct correlation between the immunogenicity of antigens and the character of neurohumoral responses was demonstrated in experiments where Guerin carcinoma

TABLE 1. The Contents of Adrenalin (A), Noradrenalin (NA), Dopamine (DA) and Serotonin (S) in Rat Hypothalamus (mkg per g) after Transplantation of Guerin Carcinoma (M ± m)^a

Time after Tumor Inoculation (days) (n = 6)		Rats with Guerin Carcinoma				Intact Animals			
		A	NA	D	S	A	NA	D	S
1st	M	0.25	1.07	1.18	1.65	0.25	1.61	0.73	1.91
	m	0.01	0.04	0.06	0.04	0.1	0.04	0.02	0.03
	P	>0.1	<0.001	0.001	0.001				
4th	M	0.29	1.17	1.52	1.87	0.26	1.57	0.76	1.42
	m	0.02	0.03	0.03	0.03	0.02	0.07	0.03	0.03
	P	>0.1	<0.001	<0.001	<0.001				
7th	M	0.75	0.84	1.84	2.44	0.21	1.67	0.77	1.64
	m	0.02	0.02	0.03	0.08	0.01	0.06	0.03	0.06
	P	<0.001	<0.001	<0.001	<0.001				
10th	M	0.42	0.91	1.08	1.87	0.22	1.49	0.85	1.39
	m	0.02	0.03	0.04	0.08	0.01	0.05	0.02	0.03
	P	<0.001	<0.001	<0.001	<0.001				
14th	M	0.16	1.08	0.51	1.76	0.24	1.53	0.81	1.45
	m	0.1	0.02	0.02	0.02	0.01	0.03	0.01	0.03
	P	<0.001	<0.001	<0.001	<0.001				
21st	M	0.23	1.48	0.69	1.72	0.26	1.57	0.76	1.42
	m	0.01	0.05	0.04	0.04	0.02	0.07	0.03	0.03
	P	>0.1	>0.1	>0.1	<0.001				

^{a} Hypothalamic contents of dopamine, adrenalin, and noradrenalin were determined by the method in REFERENCE 9, and serotonin concentration by the method in REFERENCE 10 with the use of a Hitachi spectrofluorometer. The experiments were conducted on puberal Wistar male rats.

TABLE 2. Content of 11-OCS (mkg %) in Rat Blood Plasma after Administration of Antigenic Material of a Tumoral and Nontumoral Nature (M ± m)[a]

Groups (n = 20)	Fractions 11-OCS	Time after Administration of Antigenic Material (Days)			
		2	7	15	21
1. Administration of BCG	conjugated	17.7 ± 1.62	23.1 ± 1.54	22.5 ± 1.65	15.9 ± 0.75
	P	> 0.1	> 0.1	< 0.05	< 0.001
	free	13.8 ± 1.50	20.9 ± 2.0	15.9 ± 1.02	9.9 ± 0.63
	P	< 0.001	< 0.001	< 0.001	> 0.1
2. Administration of RE	conjugated	19.65 ± 1.06	21.9 ± 1.59	20.96 ± 2.40	17.73 ± 1.13
	P	> 0.1	> 0.1	> 0.1	< 0.001
	free	12.58 ± 0.84	11.6 ± 0.71	6.72 ± 0.45	6.27 ± 0.53
	P	< 0.001	< 0.001	> 0.1	> 0.1
3. Transplantation of embryonal tissue	conjugated	21.0 ± 0.78	20.7 ± 1.32	18.9 ± 0.96	10.8 ± 0.21
	P	> 0.1	> 0.1	> 0.1	< 0.001
	free	5.5 ± 0.42	9.5 ± 0.80	10.5 ± 0.57	6.9 ± 1.02
	P	> 0.1	< 0.01	< 0.001	> 0.1
4. Transplantation of Guerin carcinoma	conjugated	18.9 ± 0.71	19.1 ± 1.79	25.64 ± 1.59	33.34 ± 1.59
	P	> 0.1	> 0.1	> 0.1	< 0.01
	free	6.68 ± 0.40	8.2 ± 0.63	9.34 ± 0.31	11.08 ± 0.69
	P	> 0.1	> 0.1	> 0.1	< 0.05
5. Control (intact animals)	conjugated	20.7 ± 2.07	22.5 ± 1.2	18.0 ± 1.76	24.8 ± 2.45
	free	6.6 ± 1.14	7.3 ± 0.8	5.73 ± 0.99	7.9 ± 1.36

[a] Concentration of free and conjugated 11-OCS in blood plasma was determined by the method in REFERENCE 11 with the use of a Hitachi spectrofluorometer. BCG vaccine in the dose of 1 mg was introduced subcutaneously; cells of 10-day-old embryos in the dose of 5×10^8, Guerin carcinoma cells in the dose of 5×10^8 and ram erythrocytes in the dose of 5×10^8 were also introduced subcutaneously. The control animals underwent injections of 0.9% NaCl. The experiments were conducted on puberal Wistar male rats.

TABLE 3. Contents of Adrenalin (A), Noradrenalin (NA), Dopamine (DA) and Serotonin (S) (mkg per g) in Rat Hypothalamus after Administration of Ram Erythrocytes in the Dose of $5 \times 10^8 (M \pm m)$[a]

Time after Administration of RE (Days)	Experiment				Control			
	A	NA	D	S	A	NA	D	S
1st	0.36	1.57	0.77	1.75	0.20	1.85	0.71	1.47
	0.02	0.04	0.04	0.06	0.01	0.06	0.03	0.02
P	< 0.001	< 0.01	> 0.1	< 0.01				
4th	0.30	0.60	0.96	1.89	0.21	1.88	0.88	1.46
	0.02	0.07	0.06	0.04	0.01	0.09	0.07	0.04
P	< 0.01	< 0.001	> 0.1	< 0.001				
7th	0.35	1.86	0.83	1.70	0.19	1.62	0.72	1.64
	0.02	0.04	0.05	0.04	0.01	0.03	0.05	0.06
P	< 0.001	< 0.001	> 0.1	> 0.1				
10th	0.53	2.90	0.90	1.36	0.19	1.66	0.92	1.56
	0.06	0.23	0.02	0.05	0.01	0.07	0.03	0.03
P	< 0.001	< 0.001	> 0.1	< 0.01				
21st	0.18	1.43	0.76	0.94	0.23	1.89	0.84	1.37
	0.01	0.03	0.04	0.02	0.01	0.05	0.03	0.02
P	< 0.01	< 0.001	> 0.1	< 0.001				

[a] At each time point, 6 samples, obtained from the animals of each group, were investigated. The experiments were conducted on puberal Wistar male rats.

cells and cells from 10-day old rat embryos were used as low-immunogenic antigenic material, and BCG vaccine and RE were used as high-immunogenic material. Introduction of tumor and embryonic cells was followed by a delayed and durable reaction of SAS and AC, whereas vaccination with BCG and administration of RE induced an active and transient response of AC (TABLE 2).

Comparative investigation of neurohumoral indices in mice after administration of RE, cells of Moloney sarcoma or sarcoma 180, revealed substantial differences in the responses of the hypothalamus and the AC. The animals with sarcoma 180 showed persistently decreased level of noradrenalin and increased serotonin in the hypothalamus; the changes in their concentrations were not phased. A slow but persistent increase in blood 11-OCS content indicated the development of durable stress (TABLE 4). Contrary to this, in response to administration of RE and cells of Moloney sarcoma the phased alterations in neuropeptide content developed in the hypothalamus (similar to those observed in rats after immunization with RE). Rapid but transient increase in 11-OCS content in blood was observed (TABLE 5).

Comparison of our data on the changes in neurohumoral status during growth and resorption of Moloney sarcoma with the data from literature on the immune mechanisms accounting for tumor regression suggests that administration of high-immunogenic virus of Moloney sarcoma[12] induces, in the organism, the neurohumoral rearrangements that provide optimal development of antitumor responses and tumor regression.

Thus, the reaction to the low-immunogenic tumor cells was delayed, phaseless and durable, whereas, in response to administration of high-immunogenic antigens, pronounced but transient alterations in functioning of the neurohumoral systems developed.

Effect of Optimal Neurohumoral Rearrangements on Tumor Survival

Optimal neurohumoral rearrangements in rats was obtained by means of electrical stimulation of the hypothalamus and administration of pharmacological preparations with differing actions, each capable of affecting the functional state of the hypothalamus.

Neurohumoral rearrangements in healthy rats subjected to hypothalamic electrostimulation were similar to those observed in animals after administration of high-immunogenic antigens. This can be attributed to the fact that the hypothalamic region that underwent electric stimulation is involved in the regulation of the neurohumoral stimulation of immune response.[1,14]

The influence of pharmacological preparations on the content of mediators in the hypothalamus was studied in rats and mice. Administration of phenphormin (25 mg/kg via gastric tube) was followed by a reliable reduction in noradrenalin and serotonin and an increase in adrenalin. Subcutaneous injection of L-DOPA (100 mg/kg) decreased the content of noradrenalin and did not affect hypothalamic concentrations of the other neuromediators. Injection of parachlorphenylalanine (PCPA) (300 mg/kg subcutaneously) was accompanied by substantial (2.5-fold) reduction in serotonin and less pronounced reduction in noradrenalin. Administration of L-tryptophane (100 mg/kg subcutaneously) increased hypothalamic serotonin but did not affect the levels of other mediators. Thus, administration of phenphormin and PCPA induced, in the hypothalamus, the biochemical rearrangements similar to those observed during the development of the immune response to RE.

The influence of neurohumoral rearrangements on antitumor resistance was investigated with the use of rats with Guerin carcinoma (TABLE 6). The most pro-

TABLE 4. Contents of Adrenalin (A), Noradrenalin (NA), Dopamine (DA) and Serotonin (S) (mkg per g) in the Hypothalamus of BALB/c Mice after Administration of Ram Erythrocytes, Cells of Sarcoma 180 and Moloney Sarcoma (M ± m)[a]

Days after Introduction of Cells	Physiological Solution (Control)				Ram erythrocytes				Moloney Sarcoma				Sarcoma 180			
	A	NA	DA	S	A	NA	DA	S	A	NA	DA	S	A	NA	DA	S
2nd	0.19 ± 0.01	1.57 ± 0.04	0.68 ± 0.04	1.59 ± 0.06	0.24 ± 0.01	1.37 ± 0.07	0.63 ± 0.03	1.77 ± 0.06	0.25 ± 0.01	1.36 ± 0.03	0.95 ± 0.05	1.59 ± 0.06	0.26 ± 0.01	1.69 ± 0.04	0.58 ± 0.03	1.50 ± 0.06
P					<0.01	<0.05	>0.1	<0.001	<0.001	<0.001	<0.001	>0.1	<0.001		>0.05	>0.1
4th	0.22 ± 0.01	1.63 ± 0.06	0.81 ± 0.05	1.58 ± 0.07	0.26 ± 0.01	1.35 ± 0.06	0.74 ± 0.03	1.92 ± 0.03	0.30 ± 0.01	0.98 ± 0.09	0.79 ± 0.04	1.72 ± 0.04	0.29 ± 0.02	1.86 ± 0.09	0.65 ± 0.06	1.63 ± 0.06
P					<0.02	<0.01	>0.1	<0.01	<0.001	<0.001	<0.1	>0.1	<0.02	>0.05	>0.05	<0.001
7th	0.19 ± 0.01	0.59 ± 0.06	0.67 ± 0.05	1.46 ± 0.05	0.23 ± 0.01	1.00 ± 0.09	0.55 ± 0.04	1.64 ± 0.05	0.24 ± 0.01	2.02 ± 0.07	0.98 ± 0.05	1.77 ± 0.04	0.21 ± 0.01	2.02 ± 0.09	0.60 ± 0.03	1.71 ± 0.08
P					<0.02	<0.001	>0.05	>0.05	<0.01	<0.001	<0.001	<0.001	>0.1	<0.01	>0.1	>0.05
11th	0.21 ± 0.01	1.48 ± 0.05	0.72 ± 0.03	1.63 ± 0.04	0.20 ± 0.01	1.66 ± 0.05	0.67 ± 0.05	1.31 ± 0.06	0.24 ± 0.01	1.25 ± 0.03	0.68 ± 0.03	1.95 ± 0.05	0.25 ± 0.01	1.91 ± 0.1	0.8 ± 0.05	1.76 ± 0.05
P					>0.1	>0.05	>0.1	<0.01	<0.05	<0.01	>0.1	<0.001	<0.02	<0.02	>0.1	>0.05
16th	0.20 ± 0.01	1.52 ± 0.06	0.76 ± 0.02	1.57 ± 0.06	0.20 ± 0.01	1.59 ± 0.06	0.67 ± 0.05	1.42 ± 0.05	0.20 ± 0.01	1.27 ± 0.04	0.58 ± 0.03	1.73 ± 0.04	0.17 ± 0.01	0.76 ± 0.09	0.9 ± 0.04	1.63 ± 0.07
P					>0.1	>0.1	>0.1	>0.05	>0.1	<0.001	<0.001	>0.05	>0.05	>0.05	<0.02	>0.1
20th	0.22 ± 0.01	1.61 ± 0.04	0.73 ± 0.03	1.58 ± 0.04	0.22 ± 0.01	1.3 ± 0.09	0.71 ± 0.03	1.56 ± 0.04	0.20 ± 0.01	1.18 ± 0.04	0.76 ± 0.04	1.66 ± 0.04	0.18 ± 0.01	1.78 ± 0.05	0.84 ± 0.04	1.62 ± 0.08
P					>0.1	<0.02	>0.1	>0.1	>0.1	<0.001	>0.1	>0.1	<0.02	<0.02	>0.05	>0.1

[a] The experiments were performed on puberal BALB/c male mice. Moloney sarcoma was induced by injection of 10% tumor homogenate in the dose of 0.2 ml per mouse into the femur muscle. Cells of sarcoma 180 in the dose of 5×10^8 were introduced subcutaneously.

TABLE 5. Content of 11-OCS (mkg %) in Blood Plasma in BALB/c Mice at Different Time Points after Inoculation of Cells of Sarcoma 180, Moloney Sarcoma and Ram Erythrocytes (M ± m)[a]

Groups of Mice (Influence)(n = 5)	Fractions of 11-OCS	Time after Material Administration (Days)				
		2	4	7	14	20
1. Sarcoma 180	free	1.5 ± 0.11	1.3 ± 0.1	1.6 ± 0.2	4.2 ± 0.4	5.3 ± 0.46
	P	> 0.1	> 0.1	> 0.1	< 0.001	< 0.001
	conjugated	2.7 ± 0.1	2.6 ± 0.2	2.9 ± 0.21	5.0 ± 0.5	6.2 ± 0.4
	P	> 0.1	> 0.1	> 0.1	< 0.001	< 0.001
2. Moloney sarcoma virus	free	1.6 ± 0.2	3.8 ± 0.4	5.7 ± 0.3	5.3 ± 0.2	3.1 ± 0.3
	P	> 0.1	< 0.001	< 0.001	< 0.001	< 0.001
	conjugated	2.6 ± 0.1	4.5 ± 0.5	4.1 ± 0.1	6.8 ± 0.2	5.4 ± 0.3
	P	> 0.1	< 0.01	< 0.001	< 0.001	< 0.001
3. Ram erythrocytes	free	1.3 ± 0.12	7.2 ± 0.61	4.2 ± 0.61	3.0 ± 0.35	2.1 ± 0.23
	P	> 0.1	< 0.001	< 0.01	< 0.01	< 0.05
	conjugated	2.4 ± 0.19	4.3 ± 0.46	4.6 ± 0.31	5.0 ± 0.42	4.6 ± 0.44
	P	> 0.1	< 0.001	< 0.001	< 0.01	< 0.001
4. Physiological Solution (Control)	free	1.4 ± 0.13	1.5 ± 0.1	1.6 ± 0.14	1.5 ± 0.11	1.5 ± 0.13
	conjugated	2.6 ± 0.21	2.9 ± 0.11	3.1 ± 0.1	2.7 ± 0.12	2.9 ± 0.11

[a] Experimental conditions are identical to those described in the note to TABLE 4.

nounced antitumor effects were produced by electrical stimulation of the hypothalamus, administration of phenphormin and PCPA.

These experiments demonstrated that enhancement of antitumor resistance is achieved in the cases when the neurohumoral syndrome is observed after introduction of high-immunogenic antigens. Electrical stimulation of the hypothalamus, which is an optimum method of provoking the rearrangements aftermentioned, is followed by the greatest antitumor effect.

TABLE 6. Effect of Adrenalin, Noradrenalin, L-DOPA, Phenphormin, Parachlorphen-ylalanine, L-Tryptophane and Electrical Stimulation of the Hypothalamus on the Survival of Guerin Carcinoma after Inoculation of 2×10^6 Cells[a]

Preparation (Influence)	Number of Animals in Group	Number of Tumor-bearing Animals	Tumor Survival (%)
Adrenalin	15	13	86. ± 8.8
			P > 0.1
Noradrenalin	15	12	80 ± 10.3
			P < 0.05
L-DOPA	15	14	93.3 ± 6.5
			P > 0.1
Phenphormin	15	6	40 ± 12.6
			P < 0.001
Parachlorphenylalanine	15	7	46.7 ± 12.9
			P < 0.001
L-Tryptophane	15	12	80 ± 10.3
			P < 0.05
Electrical stimulation of the hypothalamus	15	3	20 ± 10.3
			P < 0.001
Control (physiological solution)	15	15	100

[a] The electrodes were implanted into the brain 7-10 days before tumor inoculation. The coordinates of the first electrode—AP = (+2), the second—AP = (+4). Both electrodes were arranged at the distance of 0.3 mm from the median line and introduced into the brain up to 8 mm.[15] Hypothalamic stimulation was administered for 5 minutes daily using square electrical impulses of alternating polarity (1 msec long, 80 impulses per sec) and the threshold current. Adrenalin in the dose of 0.2 mg per kg, noradrenalin in the dose of 0.5 mg per kg, L-DOPA in the dose of 100 mg per kg, parachlorphenylalanine in the dose of 300 mg per kg, L-tryptophane in the dose of 100 mg per kg were inoculated subcutaneously. Phenphormin in the dose of 25 mg per kg was administered through the gastric tube. All the influences commenced at the day of tumor inoculation and were conducted daily for 7 days. Parachlorphenylalanine was administered every three days.

Changes in the Functional State of Hypothalamus, Adrenal Cortex and Sympathoadrenal System During the Development of Chemically Induced Tumors

Experiments conducted on rats and mice showed that the development of 7,12-dimethylbenz(a)-anthracene (DMBA)- and 20-methylcholanthrene (MC)-induced tumors is preceded and accompanied by persistent biochemical rearrangements in the hypothalamus and considerable change in the functioning of the SAS (particularly, of its mediatory link) and AC. These changes are probably the consequence of both (1) functional-adaptive rearrangements in the nervous and endocrine systems as a response to carcinogen administration and tumor formation, and (2) deterioration of the adaptative-defensive capabilities of the organism during the development of morphofunctional disturbances that accompany progressive tumor growth in different parts of the neurohumoral system.[16,17]

These investigations revealed a number of characteristic disturbances in the functioning of neurohumoral systems in carcinogenesis. The most significant alteration in the hypothalamus is a persistent increase in noradrenalin and serotonin starting from the 30th day of carcinogenesis. Taking into account the data available on the ability of various carcinogens to raise the threshold of hypothalamic sensitivity to homeostatic inhibition,[18] we can suppose that the observed biochemical rearrangements account for the altered sensitivity of the hypothalamus to interoceptive signals and thus affect its principal function, homeostatic regulation.

Persistent increase in free noradrenalin excretion and disturbed excretion of catecholamine metabolites during the whole period of carcinogenesis are evidence of disturbances in the methylation of catecholamines. The assumption of suppressed methylation processes is confirmed by the low excretion of adrenalin and dopamine conjugates which are formed by way of O-methylation, catalyzed by catechol-ortho-methyltransferase, with the involvement of S-adenosylmethionine.[16]

The revealed disturbances in catecholamine metabolism are responsible for the absence of SAS activation during the period of carcinogenesis, directly preceding the formation of tumor foci. This is confirmed by the data from the investigation of catecholamine exchange in animals resistant to the carcinogenic action of DMBA, and in rats with developed tumors.

Resistant animals produced a well-balanced reaction of SAS in response to the action of DMBA: elevated excretion of adrenalin, noradrenalin conjugates, VMA. It is worth emphasizing that these animals did not show increased excretion of free noradrenalin during the whole period of investigation. In the period directly preceding the formation of tumor foci, pronounced activation of SAS was observed. This may be one of the important factors providing the timely development of antitumor reactions and enhancement of antitumor resistance.

The data on the absence, in DMBA-sensitive animals, of reaction of the SAS and AC during the latent period of carcinogenesis, the presence of persistent changes in the hypothalamus, and the considerable degree of methylation in catecholamine metabolism enable us to suggest that directed correction of functioning of the neurohumoral systems in the period of carcinogenesis, directly preceding tumor formation, will enhance antitumor resistance.

Influence of Correction of Neurohumoral Status on the Development of Chemically Induced Tumors in Rats and Mice

In the experiments conducted on rats with DMBA-induced carcinogenesis, the effects of electrical stimulation of the hypothalamus on the hypothalamic content of neuromediators; the functional state of the SAS and the AC; and indices of immunological reactivity were studied. Hypothalamic stimulation was started 75 days after

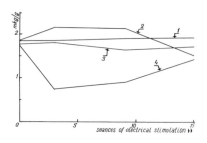

FIGURE 2. Hypothalamic contents of noradrenalin and serotonin in rats with DMBA-induced carcinogenesis subjected to electrical stimulation of the hypothalamus. (**1**) Serotonin content in nonstimulated animals; (**2**) serotonin content in stimulated rats; (**3**) noradrenalin content in nonstimulated rats; and (**4**) noradrenalin content in stimulated rats. Rhabdomyosarcomas were induced in the rats by a single injection of 2 mg of DMBA in 0.2 ml of apricot oil into the femur muscle. The conditions of electrical stimulation are given in TABLE 6.

administration of carcinogen and was carried out daily for 15 days. Electrical stimulation induced phased neurohumoral alterations. Early response of the hypothalamus to electrical stimulation was revealed in an increase in hypothalamic serotonin and a sharp decrease in adrenalin (FIG. 2). Such ratios of the neuromediators were observed until the 9th day. After that, the level of serotonin decreased reliably and noradrenalin was restored to its normal value. Transient increase in blood concentration of 11-OCS and altered urinary excretion of 17-corticosteroids and 17-ketogenic steroids were observed (TABLE 7). It is clear that by the end of electrical stimulation the excretion of androgens increased, and that of glucocorticoids decreased. Data are available that predominance of androgens over glucocorticoids, which stimulate the anabolic processes, contributes to the activation of immunity reactions and enhancement of anti-tumor resistance.[19]

    The activation of catecholamine metabolism by electrical stimulation was shown by a reliable increase in the excretion of DOPA, adrenalin and noradrenalin conjugates, and substantial reduction of free noradrenalin excretion with simultaneous high excretion of the metabolites VMA and HVA. This implies an activation of methylation reactions and a high degree of noradrenalin utilization in the organism (FIG. 3). The aforementioned positive alterations in catecholamines exchange were persistent and were observed until 45 days after the end of electrical stimulation.

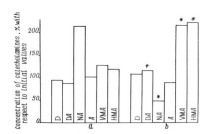

FIGURE 3. Contents of DOPA (**D**), free dopamine (**DA**), free noradrenalin (**NA**), free adrenalin (**A**), vanillic mandelic acid (**VMA**) and homovanillic acid (**HVA**) in the urine of rats on the 90th day after administration of DMBA in nonstimulated rats (**a**) and in rats after 10 electrical stimulations of the hypothalamus (**b**). Simultaneous determination of DOPA, dopamine, noradrenalin and adrenalin in one portion of urine was performed by the method in REFERENCE 21, and determination of VMA and HVA by the method in REFERENCE 22. Fluorescence of catecholamines was measured on a "Hitachi" spectrofluoremeter. * = the differences between the indices in rats with stimulated and nonstimulated hypothalamus are statistically significant.

TABLE 7. Effect of Stimulation of the Hypothalamus on the Content of 11-OCS (mg %) in Blood Plasma and Urinal Excretion of 17-Neutral Ketosteroids (17-KS) and 17-Ketogenic Steroids (17-KGS)—mkg per Day—in Rats with DMBA-induced Carcinogenesis[a]

| Steroids | Seances of Electrical Stimulation | | | | | |
| | Day 3 | | Day 9 | | Day 15 | |
	Experiment	Control	Experiment	Control	Experiment	Control
11-OCS	11.2 ± 0.4	10.6 ± 0.4	10.0 ± 0	10.6 ± 0.8	9.0 ± 0.8	12.4 ± 0.6
P	> 0.1		> 0.1		> 0.1	
11-OCS	7.8 ± 0.2	4.6 ± 0.4	8.9 ± 0.4	5.0 ± 0.4	6.9 ± 0.3	5.8 ± 0.7
P	< 0.001		< 0.001		> 0.1	
17-KS	48.0 ± 6.3	43.0 ± 5.4	54.0 ± 3.9	38.0 ± 4.3	55.0 ± 10.2	43.0 ± 5.7
P	> 0.1		< 0.05		> 0.1	
17-KGS	56.0 ± 8.5	32.0 ± 3.4	49.0 ± 6.6	61.0 ± 10.5	27.0 ± 5.0	60.5 ± 8.5
P	< 0.05		> 0.1		< 0.01	

[a] Experiment (n = 7)—rats subjected to stimulation; control (n = 7)—nonstimulated rats.

FIGURE 4. Indices of immunological reactivity in rats with DMBA-induced carcinogenesis after 10 electrical stimulations of the hypothalamus (1) and in nonstimulated rats (2). (a) AFC in the spleen, (b immune RFC in the regional lymph nodes, (c) E-RFC in the regional lymph nodes. Number of antibody forming cells (AFC) in the spleen was determined by the micromethod of local hemolysis in the chambers with liquid medium in REFERENCE 23, and the number of rosette-forming cells (RFC) in lymph nodes was determined by the method in REFERENCE 24.

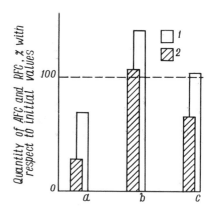

The increased functional activity of neurohumoral systems reestablished the indices of immunological reactivity. The quantity of antibody-forming cells (AFC) in the spleen and of immune RFC in the thymus, spleen and lymph nodes after the 10th and 15th day of electrical stimulation was reliably higher than in nonstimulated animals (FIG. 4). Radioautographic investigations revealed a reliable enhancement of DNA synthesis in lymphoid cells of the thymus, spleen and, particularly, regional lymph nodes.[25]

Correction of the neurohumoral and immune status brought about pronounced enhancement in antitumor resistance, revealed by the decrease of tumor yield (FIG. 5).

In experiments performed on mice, the effect of pharmacological correction of neurohumoral status on the indices of immunological reactivity and development of MC-induced carcinogenesis was studied. We examined the possibility of removing persistent hypothalamic increases in serotonin and noradrenaline in chemical carcinogenesis. Administration of phenphormin, L-DOPA and PCPA reduced hypothalamic noradrenalin. Phenphormin and particularly PCPA, contrary to L-DOPA, also decreased the content of serotonin.

We have mentioned above the possible role of increased noradrenalin and serotonin in the hypothalamus in the mechanism of reducing its sensitivity to homeostatic signals. We have suggested that under decreased content of neuromediators, the sensitivity of the hypothalamus to interoceptive signals (including those involving the test-antigens) would increase. This would contribute, in turn, to the reestablishment of the indices of immunological reactivity in animals with chemical carcinogenesis. Administration of pharmacological preparations to mice before immunization with RE produced a reliable increase in the number of AFC in the spleen when compared with the animals that were not subjected to a correcting influence (FIG. 6). Phenphormin and PCPA

FIGURE 5. Number of tumor-bearing rats, six months after administration of DMBA. (a) DMBA, (b) DMBA + electrical stimulation of the hypothalamus, 3.5 months after administration of carcinogen, (c) DMBA + electrical stimulation of the hypothalamus, 2.5 months after administration of carcinogen.

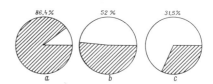

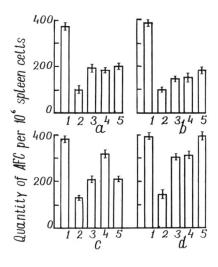

FIGURE 6. Number of AFC in the spleen of BALB/c mice after immunization with ram erythrocytes in the dose of 5 × 10⁸ on the 7th (a), 30th (b), and 60th (c) day after administration of 20-methylcholanthrene (MC) and in healthy animals (d). (1) healthy mice; (2) subjected to MC; (3) subjected to MC and phenphormin; (4) subjected to MC and parachlorphenylalanine; and (5) subjected to MC and L-Dopa. The differences between the indices in the 2nd group and groups 3-5 are statistically significant in all the experiments (p < 0.001). Tumors were induced in mice by a single injection of 1 mg of MC in 0.1 ml of apricot oil into the femur muscle. Phenphormin was administered through a gastric tube in a dose of 25 mg per kg, and parachlorphenylalanine and L-DOPA, intraperitoneally in doses of 300 and 100 mg per kg, respectively. Pharmacological preparations were administered for four days before immunization with RE.

exhibited the most pronounced antiimmunodepressive effects. Preliminary administration of the preparations to healthy animals did not affect the number of AFC in the spleen. It appears reasonable to assume that the correction of hypothalamic functioning would be effective in immunodepression, one of the causes of which is provided by the disturbances in regulatory functions of the hypothalamus.[26]

We investigated the effect of correction therapy on the yield of MC-induced tumors. The preparations were introduced daily (one injection) from the 45th till the 75th day after carcinogen administration. Phenphormin and PCPA showed the most pronounced inhibiting effect on chemical carcinogenesis, shown by a reliable reduction in the number of tumor-bearing animals and an increase in the life term of the animals that underwent treatment (FIG. 7).

Directed correction of the neurohumoral status in the latent period of carcinogenesis provided by electrical stimulation and administration of pharmacological preparations is followed by the activation in the functioning of hypothalamus-hypophysis-

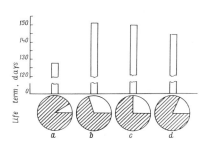

FIGURE 7. Number of tumor-bearing BALB/c mice four months after administration of 20-methycholanthrene (MC) (below) and life term of animals in groups (above). (a) (n = 45) MC, number of tumor-bearing mice, 93.7%; (b) (n = 28) MC + phenphormin, 66.5%; (c) (n = 45) MC + PCPA, 72%; (d) (n = 36) MC + L-DOPA, 75%. Phenphormin, PCPA and L-DOPA were administered for one month, starting from the 45th day after introduction of MC. All the preparations were administered daily, once a day. PCPA was introduced every three days. Method of administration and doses of preparations are given in the legend to FIG. 6.

adrenocortical and sympathoadrenal systems, reestablishment of the indices of immunological reactivity and pronounced enhancement in antitumor resistance.

Effect of Combined Use of Influences That Optimize the Neurohumoral Status and Immunostimuli, on the Development of Experimental Tumors

We have suggested that disturbances in the functioning of the hypothalamus, the AC and the SAS in cancer may account for the defective response of neurohumoral systems to nonspecific immunostimuli, and in this way prevent the activation of antitumor resistance.

TABLE 8. Hypothalamic Contents of Dopamine, Noradrenalin, Adrenalin and Serotonin (mkg per g) in BALB/c Mice with MC-induced Carcinogenesis on the 4th Day after Administration of Zymosan, BCG and Levamysol (M + m)[a]

Groups (Influence)	Dopamine	Noradrenaline	Adrenaline	Serotonin
1. MC	0.79 ± 0.04	1.94 ± 0.01	0.26 ± 0.01	2.14 ± 0.06
2. MC + zymosan	0.57 ± 0.02	1.87 ± 0.05	0.25 ± 0.01	2.18 ± 0.08
P_1	< 0.001	> 0.1	> 0.1	> 0.1
3. MC + BCG	0.73 ± 0.03	2.08 ± 0.08	0.29 ± 0.02	2.03 ± 0.09
P_1	> 0.1	> 0.1	> 0.1	> 0.1
4. MC + levamysol	0.69 ± 0.04	1.14 ± 0.08	0.26 ± 0.01	1.33 ± 0.07
P_1	> 0.1	< 0.001	> 0.1	< 0.001
5. Healthy intact	0.71 ± 0.04	1.72 ± 0.03	0.23 ± 0.01	1.62 ± 0.06
6. Healthy + zymosan	0.68 ± 0.03	1.57 ± 0.06	0.22 ± 0.01	1.37 ± 0.05
P_2	> 0.1	< 0.05	> 0.1	< 0.05
7. Healthy + BCG	0.73 ± 0.03	1.29 ± 0.07	0.26 ± 0.01	1.28 ± 0.05
P_2	> 0.1	< 0.01	< 0.05	< 0.01
8. Healthy + levamysol	0.56 ± 0.05	1.08 ± 0.08	0.28 ± 0.02	1.23 ± 0.07
P_2	< 0.05	< 0.001	< 0.05	< 0.01

[a] P_1—statistical significance of differences between groups 2, 3 and 4 and group 1; P_2—statistical significance of differences between groups 6, 7 and 8 and group 5.

The possibility of enhancement of the antiblastic action of immunostimuli by means of correction of the neurohumoral status was investigated. The preparations that are widely used in oncological practice were taken as immunostimuli: the yeast polysaccharide zymosan, live lyophilized BCG vaccine and levamysol.[28]

A preliminary study was made of the pattern of neurohumoral responses to immunostimuli in rats and mice with chemically induced tumors. Administration of BCG vaccine and zymosan to healthy animals was shown to cause characteristic neurohumoral rearrangements: an increase in the blood plasma level of 11-OCS, decreased noradrenalin and serotonin, and increased adrenalin in the hypothalamus. Administration of immunostimuli during the latent period of carcinogenesis did not produce alterations in 11-OCS in animals; the ratio of neuromediators in the hypothalamus was reversed: noradrenalin content was reliably increased, and that of serotonin slightly decreased (TABLE 8).

Administration of levamysol in animals with MC-induced carcinogenesis brought about a reliable decrease in hypothalamic concentrations of noradrenalin and serotonin, *i.e.*, induced the same change in the concentration of these amines as in healthy mice. This interesting phenomenon can be attributed to the combination of neurotropic and immunostimulating properties of levamysol. Levamysol stimulates the autonomic nervous system by activation of parasympathetic and sympathetic ganglions.[27] Correction of the neurohumoral status of animals with chemical carcinogenesis and simultaneous stimulation of cell immunity[13] are probably enabled by this unique combination of levamysol properties.

The revealed regularities enabled us to start the development of schemes for combined application of the neurotropic influences and immunostimuli.

Inhibition of carcinogenesis by preparations for correction of hypothalamic functioning and immunostimuli (used separately or in combination) was studied in the experiments with BALB/c mice. Live lyophilized BCG vaccine, zymosan and levamysol were administered. The therapy started 45 days after introduction of MC. The course of treatment included 5 injections of phenphormin or L-DOPA, administration of immunostimuli and 7 subsequent injections of the aforementioned neurotropic preparations. PCPA was introduced every three days, twice before and three times after administration of immunostimuli. The treatment was performed in three courses with one-week intervals in between (TABLE 9).

Administration of pharmacological preparations, both separate and in combination with the immunostimuli, increased reliably the life span of tumor-bearing animals. Separate use of BCG and zymosan did not affect life span. Thus, the possibility of increasing the effectiveness of the antitumoral action of immunostimuli by means of preliminary optimization of neurohumoral status was demonstrated.[28]

Conclusion

Our investigations resulted in the development of a new principle for raising the efficiency of action of immunostimuli on antitumor resistance, based on the adequate reactions of the neurohumoral systems to immunostimuli in tumor-bearing animals. This principle makes a basis for directed search for the neurotropic preparations that can provide the best neurohumoral responses to immunostimuli.

The revealed regularities also provide a new approach to the assessment of various effects of neurotropic preparations in oncological practice. While using these preparations one should take into account the effect they exert on the neurohumoral mechanisms that were shown to play an important role in the formation of antitumor reactions.

Complex investigation of the neurohumoral and immune status in animals with experimental tumors made it possible to establish the major neurohumoral mechanisms involved in the formation of antitumor resistance.

Reduced sensitivity of the organism to transplantation of malignant cells was shown to be accounted for by the absence of timely complete reaction of the neurohumoral systems, disorder in the functioning of hypothalamus, AC and SAS which increases progressively with tumor growth, and decrease in the indices of general immunological competence. Artificial modeling of the active complete response of the neurohumoral systems to the transplantation of tumor cells by means of electrophysiological and pharmacological influences, and activation of immune reactions under these conditions were accompanied by substantial enhancement of antitumor resistance. This was revealed in the nonsurvival of tumors in the majority of animals.

Decreased resistance of animals to the blastogenic action of chemical carcinogens results from the development, in the latent period of carcinogenesis, of considerable disturbances in the functioning of hypothalamus, AC and SAS. We suggest that the

TABLE 9. Effect of Phenphormin, Parachlorphenylalanine (PCPA), L-DOPA, Zymosan, BCG and Levamysol on the Development of MC-induced Tumors in BALB/c Mice and the Life Term of Animals with Tumors (M ± m)[a]

Groups of Mice (Influence) (n = 18)	Number of Animals with Tumors (%) at Different Times after Administration of Carcinogen (Months)		Life Term of Animals
	3	4.5	
1. MC + phenphormin	61.1 ± 11.5	88.8 ± 7.4	148.2 ± 6.9
P	>0.1	>0.1	<0.01
2. MC + PCPA	50.0 ± 11.8	83.3 ± 8.8	152.2 ± 7.4
P	>0.1	>0.05	<0.01
3. MC + L − DOPA	72.7 ± 10.6	100.0	139.1 ± 6.4
P	>0.1	>0.1	>0.1
4. MC + phenphormin + BCG	50.0 ± 11.8	72.2 ± 10.6	154.5 ± 7.1
P	>0.1	<0.01	<0.01
5. MC + phenphormin + zymosan	38.8 ± 11.5	66.6 ± 11.1	152.0 ± 6.9
P	<0.05	<0.01	<0.01
6. MC + PCPA + BCG	44.4 ± 11.7	77.7 ± 9.8	156.0 ± 6.6
P	>0.05	<0.05	<0.001
7. MC + phenphormin + levamysol	33.3 ± 9.6	68.0 ± 9.5	147.8 ± 4.6
P	<0.05	<0.01	<0.001
8. MC + PCPA + zymosan	27.7 ± 10.5	61.1 ± 11.5	158.5 ± 8.4
P	<0.01	<0.01	<0.01
9. MC + L − DOPA + BCG	33.3 ± 11.1	88.8 ± 7.4	132.8 ± 6.5
P	<0.02	>0.1	>0.1
10. MC + L − DOPA + zymosan	44.4 ± 11.7	88.8 ± 7.4	136.0 ± 6.6
P	>0.05	>0.1	>0.1
11. MC + BCG	88.3 ± 8.8	100.0	121.1 ± 6.3
P	>00.1	>0.1	>0.1
12. MC + zymosan	77.7 ± 9.8	94.4 ± 5.4	128.1 ± 6.0
P	>0.1	>0.1	>0.1
13. MC + levamysol	50.0 ± 9.1	80.0 ± 7.3	129.7 ± 2.7
P	<0.1	<0.1	<0.1
14. MC + physiological solution (control)	72.7	100.0	123.2 ± 5.7

[a] P—statistical significance of differences between groups 1-13 and group 14.

disturbed ratio of hypothalamic neuromediators (persistent increase in noradrenalin and serotonin) causes a disorder in the regulatory functions of the hypothalamus. Disturbances in hypothalamic control of the actions of AC and SAS account for the absence of their activation in the latent period of carcinogenesis, when the possibility of inhibition of this pathological process by the natural defensive mechanisms still exists. Besides, the function of the SAS is disturbed due to changes in catecholamine metabolism (disturbances in methylation processes, stagnation in the metabolism of catecholamines) and morphohistochemical disturbances in the adrenals. The aforementioned changes also determine the absence of adequate reaction of the neurohumoral systems to test-antigens, which in turn affects the development of immune response. Thus, the neurohumoral disturbances in chemically induced carcinogenesis account for the absence of an adequate defensive reaction in neurohumoral systems in the period directly preceding the formation of tumor foci, the immunodepression, and as a result: reduced resistance of the organism to tumor developments.

The above-stated concepts on the important role of neurohumoral mechanisms in the formation of resistance to chemically induced tumors are confirmed by our experiments on the possibility of enhancement of antitumor resistance by directed correction of neurohumoral disturbances. Correction of the hypothalamic level of neuromediators (reduction in noradrenalin and serotonin), artificial activation of the hypothalamus, AC and SAS in the latent period of carcinogenesis contribute to the increase in the immunological competence of the organism and substantial enhancement of antitumor strength. The latter is revealed by the inhibition of chemical carcinogenesis and prolongation of life span.

The revealed causal-consequential regularities and established general pattern of the neurohumoral rearrangements that account for both reduced and enhanced antitumor resistance confirm our hypothesis that the disturbances in neurohumoral enhancement of immune reactions constitute an important cause of the immunosuppression in cancer. These data provide a stimulus for the further development of a very promising trend: the neurohumoral regulation of antitumor resistance.

REFERENCES

1. KORNEVA, E. A., V. M. KLIMENKO & E. K. SHKHINEK. 1978. Neurohumoral Providing of Immune Homeostasis. Nauka. Leningrad.
2. PIERPAOLI, W., G. I. M. MAESTRONI. 1978. J. Immunol. 120(5): 1600-1603.
3. VINNITSKY, V. B. 1980. Physiologichesky Zhurnal. 26(3): 300-308.
4. VINNITSKY, V. B. & V. F. TSAPENKO. 1977. Oncologiya. Issue 9: 34-38.
5. BALITSKY, K. P., V. B. VINNITSKY, I. G. VEKSLER, O. E. PRIDATKO & V. N. RYABUKHA. 1979. Voprosy Oncologii. 25(5): 38-42.
6. KVATCHEV, V. G. & V. B. VINNITSKY. 1978. Dokl. Acad. Nauk SSSR 238(3): 755-757.
7. ALESHIN, B. V. & A. S. BRESLAVSKY. 1975. Modern State of the Problem of Hypothalamic Regulation of Endocrine Functions. In Mechanism of Hormonal Action. 7-9. Kiev.
8. VINNITSKY, V. B. & Y. P. SCHMALKO. 1980. Exp. Oncol. 2(1): 51-56.
9. KATSNELSON, Z. S. & M. N. STABROVSKY. 1975. Histology and Biochemistry of Chromaffin Tissue of Adrenal Glands. Meditsina. Leningrad.
10. UDENFRIEND, S. 1965. Fluorescent Analysis in Biology and Medicine. Mir. Moscow.
11. DE MOOR, R., O. STEENO & M. RASHIN. 1960. Acta Endocrinol. N33: 297-307.
12. LAMON, E., H. WIGZELL & E. KLEIN. 1973. J. Exp. Med. 137(6): 1472-1493.
13. BALITSKY, K. P., I. G. VEKSLER & V. B. VINNITSKY. 1983. Nervous System and Antitumor Resistance. Naukova Dumka. Kiev.
14. BESEDOVKY, H., E. SORKIN, D. FELIX, H. HAAS. 1977. Eur. J. Immunol. 7(5): 323-325.
15. GROOT, I. 1959. J. Comp. Neurol. 113(3): 383-400.
16. VINNITSKY, V. B., Y. P. SCHAMALKO. 1978. Physiologicheskiy Zh. 24(3): 401-406.
17. VINNITSKY, V. B., O. E. PRIDATKO & Y. P. SCHMALKO. 1983. Exp. Oncol. 5(4): 79.
18. DILMAN, V. M. 1976. Cancrophilic syndrome: tumor cell, risk factors of tumor development and organism. In Organisation of Antitumor Struggle, Prophylaxis of Malignant Tumors. 63-75. Meditsina. Leningrad.

19. MASKAY, W. D., M. H. EDWARDS, R. D. BULBROOK & D. V. WAND. 1971. Lancet 11(7732): 1001-1002.
20. VINNITSKY, V. B., O. E. PRIDATKO & N. S. GUTNIK. 1982. Exp. Oncol. 4(3): 79.
21. MATLINA, E. S., Z. M. KISELYOVA & N. E. SOFIEVA. 1965. Method for determination of adrenaline, noradrenaline, DOPA and dopamine in a single portion of the urine. *In* Methods for Determination of Some Hormones and Mediators. p127. Moscow.
22. DIBOBES, T. K. & T. D. BOLSHAKOVA. 1972. Lab. Delo N4: 221-223.
23. CUNNINGHAM, A. I. & A. SEENBERG. 1968. Immunology 14(4): 599-600.
24. NASKILL, I. S., B. E. ELLIOTT & R. KERBEL. 1972. J. Exp. Med. 135(6): 1410-1415.
25. VINNITSKY, V. B., I. N. SCHEVTCHENKO, E. G. ISAYEVA & N. A. LAPTEVA. 1986. Exp. Oncol. 8(1): 51-54.
26. VINNITSKY, V. B. & V. A. YAKIMENKO. 1981. Vopr. Onkolo. 27(6): 45-50.
27. SYMOENS, I. & M. ROSENTAL. 1974. J. Rethiculoendothel. Soc. 21(3): 33-37.
28. VINNITSKY, V. B. 1980. Exp. Oncol. 2(6): 40-45.

Dysdifferentiation Hypothesis of Aging and Cancer: A Comparison with the Membrane Hypothesis of Aging

IMRE ZS.-NAGY, RICHARD G. CUTLER,[a]
AND IMRE SEMSEI [a]

Verzár International Laboratory for Experimental Gerontology
(VILEG)
Italian Section
Research Department
Italian National Research Centers on Aging (INRCA)
Via Birarelli, 8
I-60121 Ancona, Italy
and
[a]National Institute on Aging
Gerontology Research Center
Francis Scott Key Medical Center
Baltimore, Maryland 21224

INTRODUCTION

Throughout human history, there has always been the great challenge to find an explanation for the phenomena of aging. Since lifespan is genetically determined and species-specific, it is of considerable scientific interest to understand the degree the key features governing aging rate are common and of course the biochemical basis for the wide variations in the lifespans of different species.

In spite of much effort made in this field of biogerontology, considerable controversy still exists among the various workers in the field as to the best experimental approaches to take in studying the problem of aging. Certainly, an important reason for the confusing situation is that gerontology is still lacking a generally accepted theoretical basis. Consequently, most of the data produced in this field are still of phenomenological character, *i.e.,* they remain at a descriptive level, and only rarely do gerontologists attempt to reach generally valid and theoretically coherent conclusions.

Aging was defined by Strehler[1,2] as a process showing the following general phenomena: 1. deleterious (*i.e.,* it reduces functions); 2. progressive (*i.e.,* it occurs gradually and irreversibly); 3. intrinsic (*i.e.,* it is not due to modifiable environmental factors); and 4. universal (*i.e.,* all individuals of a species undergo aging according to the same pattern). The universality of aging also means that all species have a characteristic, genetically-determined aging pattern. The time scale, however, may be extremely variable. In the case of mammalian species, for example, lifespans range from 3 years for mice to 100 years for humans. Lower animals as well as plants display an even wider range in their lifespans. In addition, the onset frequency of cancer appears to be proportional to the aging rate in different mammalian species. Therefore, the large difference in the rate of loss of essentially all physiological processes in different mammalian species is most remarkable, considering their highly conserved biological characteristics.

The common characteristics of aging, as noted above, do not however lead directly to a specific experimental approach without further consideration. It is essential to define first the common properties of all living individuals in chemical, physical, biological and physiological terms. Thus, a considerable descriptive and theoretical study should be completed before we can formulate an acceptable theoretical basis of aging. The obvious application of such an undertaking is that it could lead to the formulation of a reasonable hypothesis of aging that would help guide workers to conduct more meaningful and key experiments.

There have been some recent attempts to solve this task,[3-5] and here only some main points will be reviewed. Two basic questions experimental gerontology should answer are the following: 1. What are the key cellular mechanisms involved in the age-dependent decline of virtually all physiological processes? and 2. What mechanisms govern or control the rate of aging in the different mammalian species? It is obvious that if we are going to search for answers to these two questions with general validity for the living kingdom, only those factors and mechanisms which are present in all living systems (*i.e.,* the most general ones) should be considered seriously. All the factors and cellular mechanisms which are specific only for a given level of evolution (*e.g.,* specific neural or humoral factors, organs, organ systems, etc.) would be omitted automatically from such considerations. This of course does not mean that such specific factors and/or systems do not have possible importance to the aging phenomena. But, in view of the universality of the aging process, it is best to bring into causal relationships with aging only those factors and systems which are common in all organisms that show the aging process.

ON THE NATURE OF THE DAMAGING FACTORS

Although the oxygen-induced free radicals were implicated by Harman[6] some long time ago as possible causative factors to aging, it was only recently more generally accepted that such radicals actually do occur in biological systems[7,8] and are seriously being considered to be involved in cellular aging.[9-14] In the past, biochemists disregarded the role of free radicals in the living processes on the basis that their concentration is too low in the cells and tissues. This concept, however, now seems to be in error, considering the reaction rates these radicals are known to display in various systems. In spite of the fact that most of the recent biochemistry textbooks still do not cover the subject of free radicals, it now seems to be generally accepted that free radicals are involved importantly in many beneficial as well as deleterious biochemical reactions.

The free radical hypothesis of aging has been supported by the generally positive observations obtained in experiments testing the possible role normal as well as artificial antioxidants may have in governing aging rate.[10-14] It has also been supported by the ESR spin-trapping experiments demonstrating the high sensitivity of all amino acids toward the OH· free radicals generated by the Fenton reaction under mild physiological conditions.[15,16]

The types, nature, and mechanisms of formation of oxygen-induced free radicals have been reviewed extensively during recent years. Therefore, it is not necessary to repeat this information here. Nevertheless, it is appropriate to point out some important features which are relevant to the problem of cellular aging.

The major reaction leading to the formation of oxygen-induced free radicals is likely to be the monovalent reduction of molecular oxygen resulting in the formation of superoxide anion radicals. This process takes place as a result of the activity of numerous enzymes like xanthine oxidase, cytochrome P-450, aldehyde oxidase, etc. The evolution of living systems resulted in a potent enzymatic defense against the superoxide anion radicals, which is the enzyme superoxide dismutase (SOD).[7,17,18] It has been shown that SOD activity, if related to the specific metabolic rate of tissues, displays a positive linear correlation with the maximum lifespan potential of mammalian species.[10] The product of SOD is hydrogen peroxide, and there are two enzymes (catalase and glutathione peroxidase) that can eliminate it. In this regard, it is important to stress that the elimination of hydrogen peroxide is never complete; tissues and tissue homogenates display an autoxidation peroxide-producing ability which has proved to be inversely proportional to the longevity of mammalian species.[13] Also, in addition to free radicals, many other types of reactive compounds are produced, such as peroxides and aldehydes. Thus, a general term used for all of these has been active oxygen species.

Hydrogen peroxide flux is present in most tissues, and is freely diffusing throughout the cells. Hydrogen peroxide represents a potential danger to proper cell formation for two reasons: (i) it may cause lipid peroxidation directly,[19,20] and (ii) it may generate OH· free radicals through a heterolysis catalyzed by transition metals like iron(II). It is well established that hydroxyl free radicals are extremely reactive.[21] In fact, the only possible way to protect cell components against the damaging effect of the hydroxyl free radical would be a continuous replacement of the components using the genetic information and protein synthesis mechanisms present in each cell. These damaged components could be eliminated theoretically by the lysosomal system at the same rate they are produced. Therefore, it appears reasonable that the driving force for the continuous turnover of the cellular components observed in all living systems may be related to the continuous free radical-induced damage of these components.

CONSIDERATIONS ABOUT THE POSSIBLE CELLULAR MECHANISMS OF AGING

There is an inherent contradiction concerning the possible important causative role of oxygen-induced free radicals in aging. Namely, the toxic and damaging nature of the free radicals remains unchanged through the whole lifespan, yet younger individuals consume much more oxygen per unit of mass and time than do older individuals. Thus, there must be a more intense free radical formation in the younger ages as compared to the older ones. The problem then is, why young individuals do not age faster than they do as compared to older individuals.[22] An answer to this question may lie in considering the main events of growth and maturation of the organism. On the other hand, any aging hypothesis must be in harmony with the general knowledge regarding the age-dependent alterations of practically all structures and functions.

THE DYSDIFFERENTIATION HYPOTHESIS OF AGING AND CANCER

DHAC goes back to the beginning of this decade.[23-26] It states that aging is largely the result of improper gene regulation that could be caused by active oxygen species interacting with the genetic apparatus of cells. Improper gene regulation would result in a dysdifferentiated cell which has different and less efficient characteristics from its normal differentiated state. Cancer would represent a special case of the general types of dysdifferentiated states that occur. That is, in cancer, amplification occurs in the genetic alteration in terms of greater cell numbers, whereas in all other cases of dysdifferentiation in nondividing cells, each genetic alteration remains with that single cell.

DHAC also involves another general working hypothesis called the "longevity determinant gene hypothesis."[27] This hypothesis states that (i) aging is the result of the side-effects of the normal metabolic processes, (*i.e.,* aging genes do not exist to age an animal for its own good or for the good of the species); and (ii) longevity is determined essentially by the extent the genetic apparatus of cells is stabilized (*i.e.,* longevity of a species is largely determined by quantitative differences in the expression of a common set of longevity determinant genes). One class of these genes could produce elements of the defense mechanisms acting against a common set of damaging processes such as the active oxygen species.[27]

The theoretical basis and the available evidence for DHAC have recently been reviewed.[27,28] Evidence that dysdifferentiation does occur with aging has been the age-dependent increase in expression of specific genes that normally would be expected to be repressed.[23-28] It should be stressed that, although the DHAC may be considered as a theoretically sound approach to the problem of cellular aging, it remains difficult to determine what types of cellular alterations can be considered as good evidence for dysdifferentiation occurring. This point is noted to clarify that the increase in cellular alterations in structure and function may not necessarily involve dysdifferentiation, but rather normal adaptation processes.

Age-dependent alterations in the genome have also been found to support DHAC. For example, the rate of loss of genomic 5-methyldeoxycytidine (5mdC) in two rodent species has recently been found to be proportional to their aging rates.[29] Since 5mdC has been implicated in many of the basic processes of mammalian gene expression, including embryogenesis, differentiation, aging and carcinogenesis,[30-38] it is reasonable to assume that such a systematic alteration of the methylation pattern of the genome could increase the probability of dysdifferentiation occurring.

The possible relation of aging to cancer has been studied by measuring the expression of the c-myc oncogene with age in mice and humans.[39] These preliminary studies used some of the recently developed recombinant cDNA hybridization techniques (Dot blot, Northern blot, etc). The expression as well as the gene dosage of the c-myc gene has been determined in various tissues of C57BL/6J male mice (brain, liver, skin, kidney, spleen, small intestinal mucosa) in five different age groups throughout the lifespan of this species. Typical results observed in brain, liver and skin were the high expression of this gene in the embryonic period, which then decreased considerably in the early postnatal period and eventually reached very low levels by the end of the growth and maturation period. However, after the age of about 10-12 months, there is again an increase of the expression of this gene, which increases as the animal grows older. The spleen behaves differently. Here the c-myc expression decreases instead of increasing continuously throughout the lifespan.

In some of the tissues, an age-dependent change in the gene dosage for c-myc was also found. Spleen, small intestine, and kidney show an increase in gene dosage beyond the young adult age. Other tissues show opposite tendencies. For example, the gene dosage in skin and liver gradually decreases after birth and reaches about 50 % of maximum level by 10 months. Brain tissue is unique in the sense that it displays no change in c-myc gene dosage throughout the lifespan of mice. When considering the relative concentrations of the c-myc mRNA per gene dosage, it is possible to calculate a gene activity ratio. On assigning a value of one for the ratio of c-myc RNA per c-myc gene dosage for newborn, we have the following at the age of 30 months: brain = 0.3; liver = 0.8; skin = 1.2. These data suggest that all the tissues except the skin express the c-myc gene at a relatively lower rate in old animals as compared to the newborn and young ages—but nevertheless are higher than at the young adult age.

The different patterns of c-myc expression and gene dosage levels may be related to tissue-specific regulatory differences. Nevertheless, it is striking that the gene dosage of brain is unchanged and the lowest relative expression value (0.3) was found in this tissue. One can hope that future studies involving agents which are known to suppress c-myc gene expression (retinoids) or enhance them (5-azacytidine) may yield useful new information on the possible role this gene may be playing in normal aging and dysdifferentiation. As previously noted, the link between cancer and aging was discussed recently in the frame of the DHAC.[28] The possibility that cancer and aging may have a common root has far-reaching implications for both theoretical biological research and practical medicine.

THE MEMBRANE HYPOTHESIS OF AGING

The concept of MHA originated during the mid-seventies and was first published in 1978-79.[40,41] since that time, much effort has been made to further elaborate and test this hypothesis. Details have been described in the various publications listed below and extensive reviews are also available.[4,5,22,42] Due to the restriction in length of this paper, only a brief summary can be presented here.

MHA shares a common basis with DHAC since it also attributes an important causative role in aging to active oxygen species-induced alterations in gene expression.[22,42] MHA starts from the fact that all cellular components, including the genome, are randomly exposed to some free radical-induced damage throughout the lifespan. However, when interpreting the effects of this damage, two points need to be taken into consideration. (i) The damages caused by free radicals on the genomic DNA are very efficiently repaired. The failure of efforts to find experimental proofs for the "error-catastrophe" hypothesis indicates excellent maintenance of the structural genes and their expression throughout the lifespan. (ii) The damaging efficiency of the active oxygen species depends on the molecular environment. Diluted systems such as the cytosol are less susceptible than the more compact structures such as the membranes. This is because of the low probability of the formation of intermolecular bonds (cross-links) in the diluted solutions. The probability of cross-links increases exponentially the closer the molecules are to each other. This principle has always been well known in polymer chemistry, but it has been neglected sometimes in biology and biochemistry.

The above considerations resulted from the fact that we were looking for systemic age-dependent alterations of the cellular components determining the physico-chemical composition of the intracellular mass rather than for specific genomic alterations. The density dependency of the free radical reactions is straightforward. The membranes are predicted to be damaged at a much higher rate than anything else in the cells, as indicated by the facts that proteins of considerably shorter half life have been found in the cell membrane than in the cytosol. Since the replacement of the proteins takes a considerably long time, and the proper reassemblage of the membranous structures should also be a time-consuming process, it seemed right to assume that the limiting factor in aging may be the rate of replacement of the damaged membrane components. The accumulating knowledge during the mid-seventies about the lipid peroxidation as the best known mechanism of the free radical-induced membrane damage also strengthened this idea. Furthermore, data regarding the so-called residual heat damage of the cell plasma membrane (see REFERENCE 41 for details) convinced us that an altered permeability of the cell membrane may be the key factor regulating the rate of maturation and aging.

On the basis of the available experimental evidence, MHA can actually be summarized as a circulus vitiosus, in which events and processes are linked to each other according to the following main schedule:

1. Beginning from embryonic life, the cell membrane gradually loses its passive potassium permeability[43–45] as a consequence of the free radical-induced cross-linking and the residual heat-induced damage. This is reflected in physiocochemical changes of the membrane such as found in lipid fluidity,[46,47] lipid asymmetry,[48] lateral diffusion constant of the membrane proteins,[49–53] molecular weight distribution of the protein components,[54] etc. An age-dependent decrease of water permeability is also predicted, although this has not been proved so far.

2. As a consequence of the changes listed under item 1, the intracellular potassium concentration increases considerably (about 30-100 %) if expressed as mEq/kg water.[45, 55–60] This is a beneficial alteration from the point of view of the maintenance of the cell excitability; however, it represents a serious drawback, as listed under item 3.

3. The intracellular colloidal system becomes gradually more and more condensed under the influence of the increasing intracellular ionic strength. This is reflected in a considerable loss of intracellular water content.[45,58,61,62] Aging is known to involve a continuous dehydration of the body, a process which also forms an essential part of the maturation process. The increasing dry mass content of the cells[63] results in a serious limitation for all enzymatic processes sooner or later, in terms of a theoretical molecular enzyme model[64–67] predicting that an increased microviscosity of the enzyme environment exponentially prolongs the lifetime of the enzyme-substrate complexes (i.e., exponentially decreases the enzyme activities). An important point should be stressed here. The inhibition of enzyme activities also involves the enzymatic mechanisms of the free radical defense system (SOD, etc.), which is contributing to an enhanced damage of the system in itself. At the same time, the efficiency of the damaging free radicals is increased also by the increasing density (i.e., a self-destructive cycle is present). It seems to be relevant to mention here that SOD proved to be strongly salt-sensitive in vitro.[68,69]

4. The overall condensation of the intracellular mass manifests itself in a very considerable decrease of the intracellular colloid osmotic pressure.[70,71] The increased physical density of the cells causes a considerable slowing down of the RNA synthesis

rate in the nucleus[4,5,22,42,72] and also the translation processes (see REFERENCES 4,5,82) in the cytoplasm. As a matter of fact, a considerable decrease has been measured in both of these parameters in different cellular models. This also involves a significant reduction of protein turnover.

5. The slowing down of the protein turnover involves the production of lysosomal enzymes eliminating the damaged cell components becoming insufficient also (*i.e.,* damaged waste products such as lipofuscin are accumulated in the cells[20]). The interpretation that lipofuscin accumulation is due to an insufficient "cleaning" activity is fully consistent with important new findings. Namely, it has been shown that the inhibition of certain lysosomal proteinases in the brain of young rats causes a rapid accumulation of lipofuscin-like substances throughout practically the whole brain.[73]

6. As a consequence of the lower protein turnover rate, the cell membrane is forced to work for longer time with the damaged components (*i.e.,* the permeability parameters become even worse, etc.). In this way, the circulus vitiosus becomes closed, and the processes under items 1-6 are repeated until a complete functional incompetence of a given cell is reached. When a certain number of cells in organs of vital importance made of mostly postmitotic cells such as the brain, liver, etc. reach the level of functional disability, the whole organ function becomes compromised, and the individual dies.

MHA as outlined above, is able to interpret all the basic processes taking place during differentiation in general physicochemical terms, and can explain why the young tissues and cells are not showing aging phenomena in spite of the relatively higher rate of the production of damaging oxygen free radicals. MHA assumes that aging is not a specific, separate process but a direct continuation of the maturation of the tissues. On the other hand, such an interpretation is meaningful for all decreases one can observe in gene expression, since a very serious decline (more than 50 %) was observed in the rates of both the total and mRNA synthesis. It is noteworthy that the synthesis and level of mRNA for free radical scavenger enzymes like SOD or catalase decrease with aging.[83]

It should be emphasized, however, that the peroxidation of membranes leads to the production and release of other active oxygen species, peroxides and aldehydes that may directly alter gene expression. Also, changes in ionic strength within the nucleus and/or the nuclear membrane component could alter proper differentiation of cells. Finally, DNA repair after oxidative damage may not be as effective in older animals in remethylation processes. Thus, membranes may be the most critical target for active oxygen species leading to improper gene expression and dysdifferentiation.

The validity of the basic concepts of MHA has been tested in experiments where aging rate was accelerated in rats by a vitamin E deficient diet[74,75] or by intralumbar injection of excessive iron.[76] In both cases one could expect a higher rate of free radical-induced damage and in both interventions a considerable deterioration was found in all the permeability parameters of the cell membrane that MHA predicted as being of basic importance in aging.

One can attribute an even larger significance to the experiments in which a known hydroxyl free radical scavenger drug (centrophenoxine = CPH)[77] was incorporated into the brain cell membranes of aging animals. The result of these experiments was an apparent improvement in practically all membrane physicochemical parameters,[46,54,76] followed by a considerable rehydration[57,58,63] of the intracellular mass, an increased RNA synthesis rate[78] accompanied by an improved synaptic plasticity[79] and a prolongation of the lifespan of the treated animals.[69,78] It is also noteworthy that membrane-active mitogens such as phytohemagglutinin-P, when administered to aging rats in intralumbar injection, improved all cellular parameters including the total and mRNA synthesis rates.[80,81]

GENERAL CONCLUSIONS

Although there are some differences between the concepts of DHAC and MHA, both hypotheses suggest an important cause of aging may be active oxygen species, which could manifest themselves in a gradual deterioration of proper gene expression and/or general cell function. The two hypotheses are therefore largely complementary—where MHA suggests what cellular component may be the most sensitive target of active oxygen species that could lead to the type of improper cell function that has been predicted by DHAC. We therefore believe that further studies, as suggested by both of these hypotheses, may prove helpful in gaining more insight into the biological nature of aging and longevity in mammalian species.

SUMMARY

Our laboratories have been testing the basic concept that the age-dependent deterioration of the molecular components of living systems may be due in part to the biochemical effects of active oxygen species. The dysdifferentiation hypothesis of aging and cancer (DHAC) as well as the membrane hypothesis of aging (MHA) are discussed and compared to each other. These two hypotheses consider cellular mechanisms through which free radical-induced alterations may lead to the aging process.

DHAC emphasizes the importance of the instability of the differentiated state of cells and how active oxygen species may interact with the genetic apparatus of cells, leading to improper gene regulation. The evidence supporting this hypothesis includes an age -dependent increase in the expression of specific genes that normally are expected to be repressed. Such evidence now includes the c-myc oncogene as well as an age-dependent decrease in the average methylation level of the entire genome in liver tissue of mice. The central concept of DHAC is that aging is a result of gene regulatory instability and that lifespan is governed by mechanisms acting to stabilize proper gene regulation.

MHA is based on the concept that all cellular components are exposed to free-radical attacks, and that the damaging efficiency of the radicals is density-dependent. Compact structures like membranes are consequently more susceptible to damage than cytosolic components. In addition, the cell plasma membrane is exposed to another damaging effect called residual heat damage, which is due to the depolarization-induced discharge of the membrane during the action potential. MHA predicts that a key process of normal differentiation as well as aging is a continuous, age-dependent loss of the passive permeability of the cell membrane for potassium and probably also for water. This is due to a constant difference between the rates of damage and replacement of the membrane components and results in a gradual dehydration of the intracellular mass from the embryonic state to the aging state. The increasing intracellular density will eventually become rate-limiting for many different cellular functions, resulting in the cessation of growth and the beginning of aging. MHA also predicts an overall decrease of gene expression and protein turnover rate during aging. Pharmacological interventions on the cell membrane have supported the validity of MHA and have indicated specific mechanisms of how aging and dysdifferentiation may occur.

REFERENCES

1. STREHLER, B. L. 1959. Quart. Rev. Biol. **34:** 117-142.
2. STREHLER, B. L. 1982. *In* Lectures on Gerontology. A. Vidiik, Ed. Vol. 1, Part A: 1-57. Academic Press. London and New York, NY.
3. ESPOSITO, J. L. 1983. Perspect. Biol. Med. **26:** 522-546.
4. ZS.-NAGY, I. 1985. Geriatrika **1(8):** 102-111.
5. ZS.-NAGY, I. 1987. Adv. Biosci. **64:** 393-413.
6. HARMAN, D. 1956. J. Gerontol. **11:** 298-300.
7. FRIDOVICH, I. 1978. Science **201:** 875-880.
8. NOHL, H. & D. HEGNER. 1978. Eur. J. Biochem. **82:** 563-567.
9. TOTTER, J. R. 1980. Proc. Natl. Acad. Sci. USA **77:** 1763-1767.
10. TOLMASOFF, J. M., T. ONO & R. G. CUTLER. 1980. Proc. Natl. Acad. Sci. USA **77:** 2777-2781.
11. HARMAN, D. 1981. Proc. Natl. Acad. Sci. USA **78:** 7128-7132.
12. CUTLER, R. G. 1984. *In* Aging and Cell Function. J. E. Johnson, Ed. 1-147. Plenum Press. New York, NY.
13. CUTLER, R. G. 1985. Proc. Natl. Acad. Sci. USA **82:** 4798-4802.
14. SOHAL, R. S., K. J. FARMER, R. G. ALLEN & S. S. RAGLAND. 1984. Mech. Ageing Dev. **24:** 176-183.
15. FLOYD, R. A. & I. ZS.-NAGY. 1984. Biochim. Biophys. Acta **790:** 94-97.
16. ZS.-NAGY, I. & R. A. FLOYD. 1984. Biochim. Biophys. Acta **790:** 238-250.
17. McCORD, J. M. & I. FRIDOVICH. 1969. J. Biol. Chem. **244:** 6049-6055.
18. McCORD, J. M. & I. FRIDOVICH. 1969. J. Biol. Chem. **244:** 6056-6063.
19. TAPPEL, A. L. 1975. *In* Pathobiology of Cell Membranes. B. F. Trumpf & A. U. Arstilla, Eds. Vol. 1: 145-172. Academic Press. New York, NY.
20. DONATO, H. & R. S. SOHAL. 1981. *In* CRC Handbook of Biochemistry in Aging. J. R. Florini, R. C. Adelman & G. S. Roth, Eds. 221-227. CRC Press. Boca Raton, FL.
21. WALLING, C. 1975. Acc. Chem. Res. **8:** 125-131.
22. ZS.-NAGY, I. 1986. *In* Liver and Aging—1986. Liver and Brain. K. Kittani, Ed. 373-384. Elsevier Biomedical Press. Amsterdam.
23. CUTLER, R. G. 1982. *In* The Aging Brain. E. Giacobini, G. Giacobini, G. Filogamo & A. Vernadakis, Eds. 1-28. Raven Press. New York, NY.
24. CUTLER, R. G. 1982. *In* Testing the Theories of Aging. R. Adelman & G. S. Roth, Eds. 25-114. CRC Press. Boca Raton, FL.
25. CUTLER, R. G. 1984. *In* Aging and Cell Structure. J. E. Johnson, Ed. Vol. 2: 1-147. Plenum Press. New York, NY.
26. CUTLER, R. G. 1984. *In* Free Radicals in Biology. W. A. Pryor. Ed. Vol. 6: 371-428. Academic Press. New York, NY.
27. CUTLER, R. G. 1985. *In* Molecular Biology of Aging. A. D. Woodhead, A. D. Blackett & A. Hollaender, Eds. 15-73. Plenum Press. New York, NY.
28. CUTLER, R. G. 1985. *In* Molecular Biology of Aging: Gene Stability and Gene Expression. R. S. Sohal, L. S. Birnbaum & R. G. Cutler, Eds. 307-340. Raven Press. New York, NY.
29. WILSON, V. L., R. A. SMITH, S. MA & R. G. CUTLER. 1987. J. Biol. Chem. In press.
30. RIGGS, A. D. & P. A. JONES. 1983. Adv. Cancer Res. **40:** 1-30.
31. JAENISCH, R. & D. JEHNER. 1984. Biochim. Biophys. Acta **782:** 1-9.
32. JONES, P. A. 1985. Pharmacol. Ther. **28:** 17-27.
33. HOLLIDAY, R. A. 1979. Br. J. Cancer **40:** 513-522.
34. HOLLIDAY, R. A. 1985. *In* Molecular Biology of Aging. A. D. Woodhead, A. D. Blackett & A. Hollaender, Eds. 269-284. Plenum Press. New York, NY.
35. LEY, T. L., Y. L. CHIANG, D. HAIDARIS, N. P. ANAGNOU, V. L. WILSON & W. F. ANDERSON. 1984. Proc. Natl. Acad. Sci. USA **81:** 6618-6622.
36. KORBA, B. E., V. L. WILSON & G. H. YOAKUM. 1985. Science **228:** 1103-1106.
37. WILSON, V. L. & P. A. JONES. 1983. Science **220:** 1055-1057.
38. FAIRWEATHER, D. S., M. FOX & G. P. MARGISON. 1987. Exp. Cell Res. **168:** 153-159.

39. CUTLER, R. G., S. MA & I. SEMSEI. 1986. Gerontologist **26:** 71A-72A.
40. ZS.-NAGY, I. 1987. J. Theor. Biol. **75:** 189-195.
41. ZS.-NAGY, I. 1979. Mech. Ageing Dev. **9:** 237-246.
42. ZS.-NAGY, I. 1987. *In* CRC Handbook of Biomedicine of Free Radicals. J. Miquel, H. Weber & A. Quintanilha, Eds. *In* CRC Press. Boca Raton, FL.
43. ZS.-NAGY, I., M. GYENES, GY. LUSTYIK, V. ZS.-NAGY & F. JENEY. 1982. *In* Liver and Aging—1982. K. Kitani, Ed. 215-229. Elsevier Biomedical Press. Amsterdam.
44. GYENES, M., GY. LUSTYIK, V. ZS.-NAGY, F. JENEY & I. ZS.-NAGY. 1984. Arch. Gerontol. Geriatr. **3:** 11-31.
45. ZS.-NAGY, I., S. TÓTH & GY. LUSTYIK. 1985. Arch. Gerontol. Geriatr. **4:** 53-66.
46. NAGY, K., V. ZS.-NAGY, C. BERTONI-FREDDARI & I. ZS.-NAGY. 1983. Arch. Gerontol. Geriatr. **2:** 23-39.
47. NAGY, K., P. SIMON & I. ZS.-NAGY. 1983. Biochem. Biophys. Res. Commun. **117:** 688-694.
48. SCHROEDER, F. 1984. Neurobiol. Aging **5:** 323-333.
49. ZS.-NAGY, I., M. OHTA, K. KITANI & K. IMAHORI. 1984. Mikroskopie **41:** 12-25.
50. ZS.-NAGY, I., K. KITANI, M. OHTA, V. ZS.-NAGY & K. IMAHORI. 1986. Arch. Gerontol. Geriatr. **5:** 131-146.
51. ZS.-NAGY, I., K. KITANI, M. OHTA, V. ZS.-NAGY & K. IMAHORI. 1986. Exp. Gerontol. **21:** 555-563.
52. KITANI, K., I. ZS.-NAGY, S. KANAI, Y. SATO & M. OHTA. 1987. Hepatology. In press.
53. ZS.-NAGY, I., Y. OHNO-IWASHITA, M. OHTA, V. ZS.-NAGY, K. KITANI, S. ANDO & K. IMAHORI. 1987. Biochim. Biophys. Acta. In press.
54. NAGY, K. & I. ZS.-NAGY. 1984. Mech. Ageing Dev. **28:** 171-176.
55. ZS.-NAGY, I., C. PIERI, C. GIULI, C. BERTONI-FREDDARI & V. ZS.-NAGY. 1977. J. Ultrastruct. Res. **58:** 22-33.
56. PIERI, C., I. ZS.-NAGY, V. ZS.-NAGY, C. GIULI & C. BERTONI-FREDDARI. 1977. J. Ultrastruct. Res. **59:** 320-331.
57. ZS.-NAGY, I., C. PIERI, C. GIULI & M. DEL MORO. 1979. Gerontology **25:** 94-102.
58. LUSTYIK, GY. & I. ZS.-NAGY. 1985. Scanning Electron Microsc. **1985/I:** 323-337.
59. ZS.-NAGY, I. 1983. Scanning Electron Microsc. **1983/III:** 1255-1268.
60. ZS.-NAGY, I. 1987. Scanning Microsc. In press.
61. ZS.-NAGY, I., GY. LUSTYIK & C. BERTONI-FREDDARI. 1982. Tissue Cell **14:** 47-60.
62. LUSTYIK, GY. & I. ZS.-NAGY. 1987. Scanning Microsc. In press.
63. ZS.-NAGY, I., K. NAGY, V. ZS.-NAGY, A. KALMÁR & É. NAGY. 1981. Exp. Gerontol. **16:** 229-240.
64. DAMJANOVICH, S. & B. SOMOGYI. 1973. J. Theor. Biol. **41:** 567-569.
65. SOMOGYI, B. & S. DAMJANOVICH. 1975. J. Theor. Biol. **51:** 393-401.
66. SOMOGYI, B. & S. DAMJANOVICH. 1986. *In* The Fluctuating Enzyme. R. Welch, Ed. 341-368. J. Wiley. New York, NY.
67. SOMOGYI, B., F. E. KARASZ, L. TRÓN & P. R. COUCHMAN. 1978. J. Theor. Biol. **74:** 209-216.
68. SEMSEI, I. & I. ZS.-NAGY. 1984. Arch. Gerontol. Geriatr. **3:** 287-295.
69. SEMSEI, I. & I. ZS.-NAGY. 1985. J. Free Rad. Biol. Med. **1:** 403-408.
70. TOMITA, M., F. GOTOH, T. SATO, M. YAMAMOTO, T. AMANO, N. TANAHASHI & K. TANAKA. 1979. Exp. Neurol. **65:** 66-77.
71. ZS.-NAGY, I., B. DERECSKEI & GY. LUSTYIK. 1987. Arch. Gerontol. Geriatr. **6:** In press.
72. SEMSEI, I., F. SZESZÁK & I. ZS.-NAGY. 1982. Arch Gerontol. Geriatr. **1:** 29-42.
73. IVY, G. O., F. SCHOTTLER, J. WENZEL, M. BAUDRY & G. LYNCH. 1984. Science **226:** 985-987.
74. BERTONI-FREDDARI, C., C. GIULI, GY. LUSTYIK & I. ZS.-NAGY. 1981. Mech. Ageing Dev. **16:** 169-180.
75. PIERI, C., C. GIULI, C. BERTONI-FREDDARI & A. BERNARDINI. 1986. Arch. Gerontol. Geriatr. **5:** 21-31.
76. NAGY, K., R. A. FLOYD, P. SIMON & I. ZS.-NAGY. 1985. Biochim. Biophys. Acta **820:** 216-222.
77. ZS.-NAGY, I. & R. A. FLOYD. 1984. Arch. Gerontol. Geriatr. **3:** 297-310.
78. ZS.-NAGY, I. & I. SEMSEI. 1984. Exp. Gerontol. **19:** 171-178.

79. BERTONI-FREDDARI, C., C. GIULI & C. PIERI. 1982. Arch. Gerontol. Geriatr. **1:** 365-373.
80. ZS.-NAGY, I., V. ZS.-NAGY, C. PIERI & M. DEL MORO. 1978. Gerontology **24:** 12-26.
81. SEMSEI, I. & I. ZS.-NAGY. 1983. Arch Gerontol. Geriatr. **2:** 307-316.
82. RICHARDSON, A. & I. SEMSEI. 1987. *In* Review of Biological Research in Aging. M. Rothstein, Ed. Vol. 3: 443-459. Alan R. Liss. New York, NY.
83. SEMSEI, I. & A. RICHARDSON. 1986. Fed. Proc. **45:** 217.

Four Models of Medicine: Mechanisms of Aging and Conditions Promoting Cancer Development

V. M. DILMAN

Endocrinology
N. N. Petrov Research Institute of Oncology
Leningrad, USSR

The picture of aging in mammals, including human beings, varies so greatly that the idea of common causes of age- connected changes is usually rejected. Moreover, the physiologic process of aging is thoroughly delimited from age- associated diseases. Since 1958[1,2] the author has been elaborating the conception according to which there are common mechanisms of aging and so- called main noninfectious diseases. The latest version of this conception[6] is as follows: The causes of the main diseases are limited by four groups of factors— ecologic, genetic, accumulative and ontogenetic. The term "accumulative" designates different stochastic endogenic damaging factors, as for example, free radicals; and "ontogenetic" marks the determined mechanisms of deviation of homeostasis, which are necessary for realization of the program of body development. Accordingly, accumulative and ontogenetic factors form the pattern of physiological aging, while ecological and genetic factors control the rate of aging, as a result, the average life span is determined by ecologic and genetic factors, and the maximum life span by accumulative and ontogenetic. The causes inducing malignant tumors are connected with stochastic ecologic and accumulative damaging factors, while ontogenetic factors produce the regular predisposition to tumor development. Consequently, it is not sufficient to remove ecologic carcinogens for prophylaxis of age increase tumor development, but it is necessary to stabilize the hormonal- metabolic homeostasis at optimum level, the latter being reached usually at the age of 20- 25. Besides, the mechanisms of age- associated homeostatic disturbances are considered, in particular, the mechanisms of metabolic immunodepression and hyperadaptosis as well as the means of normalization of homeostasis.

REFERENCES

1. DILMAN, V. M. 1958. Trans. Inst. Physiol. Acad. Sci. USSR, Leningrad, Nauka **7:** 326-336.
2. DILMAN, V. M. 1971. Lancet **1:** 1211-1219.
3. DILMAN, V. M. 1984. Three models of medicine. An integrated theory of aging and age-associated diseases. Med. Hypotheses **15:** 185-208.

4. DILMAN, V. M. 1986. Aging and cancer in the light of the ontogenetic "model of medicine". *In* Age- Related Factors in Carcinogenesis. A. Likhachev, V. Anisimov & R. Montesano, Eds. IARC Scientific Publications No. 58. 21-34. International Agency for Research on Cancer. Lyon, France.

5. DILMAN, V. M. 1986. Ontogenic model of aging and disease formation and mechanisms of natural selection. J. Theor. Biol. **118:** 73-81.

6. DILMAN, V. M. 1987. Four Models of Medicine (in Russian). Meditsina. Moscow, USSR.

7. DILMAN, V. M., S. Y. REVSKOY & A. G. GOLUBEV. 1986. Neuroendocrine- ontogenetic mechanism of aging: toward an integrated theory of aging. Int. Rev. Neurobiol. **28:** 89-156.

8. REVSKOY, S. Y., T. E. POROSHINA, I. G. KOVALEVA, L. M. BERNSTEAN, M. N. OSTROUMOVA & V. M. DILMAN. 1986. Age- dependent metabolic immunodepression and cancer. *In* Age- related Factors in Carcinogenesis. A. Likhachev, V. Anisimov & R. Montesant, Eds. IARC Scientific Publications No. 58. 253- 259. International Agency for Research on Cancer. Lyon, France.

Restoration of *in Vivo* Humoral and Cell-mediated Immune Responses in Neonatally Thymectomized and Aged Rats by Means of Lipid and Protein Fractions from the Calf Thymus[a]

BRANISLAV D. JANKOVIĆ[b] AND DRAGAN MARIĆ

Immunology Research Center
Vojvode Stepe 458
11221 Belgrade, Yugoslavia

INTRODUCTION

The discovery that the thymus plays a crucial role in the development of immune potential[1,2] has introduced completely new notions of the structural and functional correlates of the immune system. This discovery prompted intensive and extensive research activities which *inter alia,* contributed to the comprehension of the humoral function of the thymus, and established a link between the thymus and other glands of the endocrine system. It is now recognized that the thymus is an endocrine organ capable of synthesizing and secreting a variety of hormones different in chemical structures and biological activities.[3] Several extracts partially or completely characterized chemically, prepared from the thymus exhibited biological functions established as characteristic of the thymus.[4]

The importance of the thymus in the development of immune machinery of the body in adolescence and the relationship between the thymus involution and senescence led to the hypothesis that this gland is the "clock for immunologic aging."[5] Thymus involution is associated with a decrease in the number of lymphocytes[6] and atrophic changes in the thymic epithelial cells which are otherwise known to synthesize and secrete thymic hormones.[7] There are also quantitative changes of thymic lymphocytes in aging animals.[8] On the other hand, different hormones exert a considerable influence on the thymus.[9] It is now accepted that several different types of thymic hormones and nonthymic factors are necessary for the generation and functional expression of lymphocytes.[10–12,4,6]

[a]This work was supported by a grant from the Republic of Serbia Research Fund, Belgrade.

[b]Address for correspondence: Branislav D. Janković, Immunology Research Center, Vojvode Stepe 458, 11221 Belgrade, Yugoslavia.

The loss of immune responsiveness in neonatally thymectomized animals can be largely ameliorated by either transplantation of millipore diffusion chambers containing thymic tissue[13] or repeated injections of an extract from the allogenic thymus.[14] In aged animals, declining immune function has been restored by tissue removal, cell grafting, genetic and dietary manipulations and chemical therapy.[6] It should be emphasized, however, that none of the chemically well-defined thymic hormones mimics all the biological actions that have been attributed to the endocrine thymus. These circumstances would imply that preparations containing several thymic hormones may be more effective in the restoration of the immune potential than a single thymic hormone.

Starting from these premises, we assumed that the immune functions which are compromised by early extirpation of the thymus or by thymus involution during aging are amenable to restorative manipulations with multicomponent fractions of the calf thymus, such as a lipid fraction (Thymolip) and protein fraction (Thymex-L). It was deemed prudent to test these thymus fractions in animals before assessing their effects in elderly humans (the next paper in this volume). This report deals, therefore, with the influence of Thymolip (TLP) and Thymex-L (TXL) on humoral and cell-mediated immune responses in 8-week-old thymectomized at birth and aged 22-month-old rats of Wistar and Lewis strains.

MATERIALS AND METHODS

Animals

Experiments were carried out on male 8-week-old neonatally thymectomized[2] Wistar rats (Breeding Center of the Military Medical Academy, Belgrade) and Lewis rats (Microbiological Associates, Bethesda). Lewis rats were used for the production of experimental allergic encephalomyelitis and as skin donors in allograft rejection experiment. Animals had free access to food and tap water. Thymectomized animals showing signs of wasting disease were excluded from the experiment. All thymectomized rats were autopsied and mediastinum inspected for residual thymus. Only animals which had no residual thymus were included in the experiment.

Antigens

Sheep red blood cells, crystalline ovalbumin (Nutritional Biochemical Corp., Cleveland) and fresh guinea pig spinal cord.

Monoclonal Antibodies

Mouse anti-rat W3/25 and MRC OX8 monoclonal antibodies (Serotec, Oxon, England) specific for helper-inducer and suppressor/cytotoxic T cells respectively,

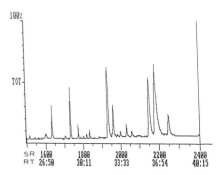

FIGURE 1. Chromatogram of the methyl ester mixture (Thymolip). The mixture consists of unsaturated and saturated, straight chain and branched fatty acids from C_{14} to C_{18}. Among unsaturated acids the most abundant are oleic and linoleic 18:1, 18:2. Among saturated, palmitic and stearic 16:0, 18:0 represent the major fraction. Here are methyl esters as percentage of the total methyl esters: C_{14} saturated (myristic acid) 8.0; C_{14} unsaturated 1.6; C_{15} branched 0.35; C_{15} branched 0.9; C_{16} saturated (palmitic acid) 19.3; C_{16} unsaturated 6.0; C_{17} branched 1.0; C_{17} branched 2.6; C_{17} unsaturated 1.2; C_{18} (stearic acid) 21.0; C_{18} unsaturated (oleic acid) 31.4; and C_{18} unsaturated (linoleic acid) 6.06. **SR**, scan range; **RT**, retention time.

were employed for the immunofluorescence staining of T4 and T8 markers on the rat peripheral blood lymphocyte membrane.

Thymolip

Thymolip (TLP) is a lipid fraction prepared from the calf thymus as described previously.[14] Transesterification of lipids was carried out as follows. Thymic lipids were dissolved in methanol with few drops of concentrated sulfuric acid and left on reflux temperature for 4 h. Methanol was evaporated in a rotary evaporator and the residue dissolved in ether. This lipid solution was washed several times with saturated sodium bicarbonate and then dried over molecular sieve. Ether was removed and infrared and NMR spectra of the residue showed the presence of methyl esters. The mixture of fatty esters was separated and identified in a gas chromatograph with ion trap detector. The capillary column was 0.32 mm I.D. DB WAX 30M, and temperature program from 100 to 250°C. FIG. 1 shows a chromatogram of the methyl ester mixture of TLP. Relative percentage of methyl esters, as determined by ion trap detector, are given in the legend of FIG. 1.

Thymex-L

Thymex-L (TXL) is a commercially available (Thymoorgan Pharmazie, Vienenburg, F.R.G.) preparation of the calf thymus. It contains about 30 proteins of different molecular weights, including small amounts of adenosine desaminase, purine-nucleo-tidephosphorylase, alcaline phosphatase and creatinkinase. One mg of dried TXL contains 0.5-0.6 mg of protein. The therapeutic effect of this protein fraction from the calf thymus was investigated in a variety of diseases.[15]

CNS-lipid

Lipid fraction from the calf central nervous system (CNS) tissue was isolated in an identical manner as that used for the preparation of TLP.[14]

Groups of Animals and Treatment

The following groups of animals were included in the experiment: (a) 8-week-old neonatally thymectomized Wistar and Lewis rats treated with TLP and TXL. The controls for this group consisted of: (1) sham-thymectomized rats treated with saline, (2) thymectomized rats treated with saline, and (3) thymectomized rats treated with CNS-lipid; (b) 22-month-old Wistar and Lewis rats treated with TLP and TXL. Aged rates treated with either saline or CNS-lipid served as controls for this experimental group.

In order to evaluate the prolonged effect of TLP, additional groups of rats were treated with this preparation and immunized, and tested for immune responses on day 1 and day 30 after the last injection of TLP.

A dose of 50 mg of TLP and TXL per kilogram of body weight/injection/day was employed throughout the experiment. Thymus fractions were administered subcutaneously. Different treatment schedules are shown in TABLE 1.

TABLE 1. Different Schedules Used for Treatment of Rats with Thymolip and Thymex-L

	Immunization	
	Before	After
Assay	No. of Days and Injections	
Plaque-forming cells	10	4
Hemagglutinin production	10	4
Delayed skin hypersensitivity	8	14
Experimental allergic encephalomyelitis	10	21
Allograft rejection	10	10
T4$^+$ and T8$^+$ subset detection	16^a (no immunization)	
Leucocyte and lymphocyte counts	16^a (no immunization)	

^{a} Rats were injected every second day; a total of 8 injections. Corresponding 8-week-old normal and neonatally thymectomized controls, and 22-month-old rats were treated with saline and lipid fraction from the central nervous system tissue.

Detection of Plaque-forming Cells (PFC) and Hemagglutinin Titers

Wistar rats were intraperitoneally immunized with 5×10^9 sheep red blood cells (SRBC). Four days later, the spleen was removed, minced, and splenic lymphocytes were isolated on a Isopaque-Ficoll gradient, and then processed for direct PFC assay using normal guinea pig serum as source of complement.

On day of sacrifice, serum samples were taken for the detection of anti-SRBC agglutinin titers. A microhemagglutination reaction was used. Readings were performed microscopically, and agglutination scored from 0 to $+ + + +$, $+$ being taken as the end-point of antibody activity.

Sensitization with Ovalbumin

Wistar rats were immunized for delayed skin hypersensitivity with 0.5 mg of ovalbumin (OA) in complete Freund's adjuvant injected into the left hind foot-pad. All animals were skin tested 14 days later with 30 μg of OA in 0.1 ml of saline injected intradermally in the depilated flank. Delayed skin reactions were read at 24 h, and the diameter and degree of induration (graded from 0 to $+ + + + +$) recorded.

Induction of Experimental Allergic Encephalomyelitis (EAE)

Lewis rats were sensitized with 20 mg of fresh guinea pig spinal cord homogenized in complete Freund's adjuvant injected into the left hind foot-pad. In addition, all animals received in the dorsum of the left leg 1.5×10^{10} pertussis bacilli in 0.5 ml of saline. Rats were daily observed for the onset of clinical signs of disease. At autopsy, cerebrum, cerebellum and spinal cord were dissected free and processed for histological examination. Neurological signs and histological lesions were graded from 0 to $+ + + +$.

Skin Allografting

Circular pieces (6 mm in diameter) of flank skin were removed from Lewis donors and fitted into holes of the same size on the flank of Wistar recipients.[16] Each recipient received two autografts and two allografts. Graft rejection was evaluated grossly and histologically using the criteria described previously.[16] The degree of rejection on day 10 after transplantation was graded from 0 to $+ + + +$.

Mean Score

An arithmetic score reflecting an overall response was calculated for each group of rats, depending on the degree of induration (delayed hypersensitivity reactions; 0

to $+++++$), severity of histological lesions (EAE; 0 to $++++$), and degree of graft rejection (0 to $++++$) defined as follows: $0 = 0$; $+ = 1$; $++ = 2$; $+++ = 3$; $++++ = 4$; and $+++++ = 5$.

White Cell Counts and Detection of T-cell Subsets

An improved Nuebauer-Levy-Hausser chamber was used for the total leucocyte counts, and blood smears were stained with May-Gruenwald and Giemsa for differential counts.

Lymphocytes bearing T4 and T8 markers were detected by means of an indirect immunofluorescence method using mouse anti-rat lymphocyte monoclonal antibodies and sheep anti-mouse Ig conjugated with fluorescein isothiocyanate.

Histology

Thymuses obtained at autopsy were weighed and processed for staining with hematoxylin and eosin, and methyl green and pyronin.

Statistical Analysis

Student's t test was employed. Differences between groups were considered significant if the P values were less than 0.05.

RESULTS

Plaque-forming Cell Response and Hemagglutinin Production

As shown in TABLE 2, there was a striking decrease in the number of splenic hemolysin-releasing cells and level of circulating hemagglutinins in thymectomized animals immunized with SRBC and treated with CNS-lipid. In contrast, these humoral responses were considerably increased in thymusless rats treated with TLP and TXL. All thymectomized animals showed steady weight gain, although TLP- and TXL-treated rats tended to be heavier.

In aged, 22-month-old animals, PFC responses and circulating antibody titers were augmented following treatment with TLP and TXL. In both young thymectomized and aged rats, the immunorestorative effect of TLP was greater than that of TXL.

Delayed Reactions to Ovalbumin

Delayed skin hypersensitivity reactions to ovalbumin (TABLE 3) were sharply reduced in saline-treated and CNS-lipid-treated animals, thymectomized at birth and sensitized at 8 weeks of age. However, thymectomized rats repeatedly injected with TLP and TXL showed an appreciable increase of the delayed response. In aged 22-month-old rats, delayed reactive capacity was significantly enhanced by treatment with TLP and TXL, the lipid fraction being more effective than the protein one.

Experimental Allergic Encephalomyelitis

In neonatally thymectomized Lewis rats that received several injections of saline, there was a striking loss of ability to develop EAE following inoculation of heterologous spinal cord in complete Freund's adjuvant (TABLE 4). On the other hand, a large number of TLP-treated and TXL-treated rats developed clinical and histopathological signs of the disease. Similar increases in incidence and severity of EAE were observed

TABLE 2. The Effect of Thymolip (TLP) and Thymex-L (TXL) on Plaque-forming Cell (PFC) Response and Hemagglutinin Production in TXL Neonatally Thymectomized (Tx) 8-week-old, and 22-month-old Wistar Rats Immunized with Sheep Red Blood Cells

Rats Treated with	n	Humoral Immune Response (Mean ± S.D.)	
		No. of PFC/10^6 Cells	Hemagglutinin Titer (Log_2)
8-week-old Tx rats			
Saline (sham-Tx)	24	2,072 ± 244	7.7 ± 0.5
Saline (Tx)	27	543 ± 361[a]	2.9 ± 0.3[a]
CNS-LP (Tx)	18	609 ± 293	2.8 ± 0.4
TLP (Tx)	32	2,012 ± 301[b,d]	5.8 ± 0.5[b,d]
TXL (Tx)	21	1,720 ± 270[c]	5.2 ± 0.3[c]
22-month-old rats			
Saline	29	1,877 ± 289	6.6 ± 0.4
CNS-LP	30	1,785 ± 246	6.4 ± 0.5
TLP	36	2,620 ± 354[e,g]	7.5 ± 0.4[e,g]
TXL	25	2,048 ± 276[f]	7.0 ± 0.7[f]

Statistically significant differences:
Eight-week-old thymectomized rats
  [a] P <0.001, saline-treated Tx *vs* saline-treated sham-Tx
  [b] P <0.001, TLP-treated Tx *vs* saline-treated Tx
  [c] P <0.001, TXL-treated Tx *vs* saline-treated Tx
  [d] P <0.001, TLP-treated Tx *vs* TXL-treated Tx
Twenty-two-month-old rats
  [e] P <0.001, TLP-treated *vs* saline-treated
  [f] P <0.05, TXL-treated *vs* saline-treated
  [g] P <0.001, TLP-treated *vs* TXL-treated

TABLE 3. The Effect of Thymolip (TLP) and Thymex-L (TXL) on Delayed Skin Hypersensitivity Reactions to Ovalbumin in Neonatally Thymectomized (Tx) 8-week-old, and 22-month-old Wistar Rats Immunized with Ovalbumin in Complete Freund's Adjuvant

Rats Treated with	n	Positive Reactions Diameter (mm) Induration (0 to +++++)						Mean Diameter (mm ± S.D.)	Severity of Reaction (Mean Score)	Positive Reaction (%)
		0 0	7-11 +	12-16 ++	17-22 +++	23-28 ++++	>28 +++++			
8-week-old Tx rats										
Saline (sham-Tx)	24	0	0	7	7	10	0	20.3 ± 4.4	3.1 ± 0.9	100
Saline (Tx)	18	16	2	0	0	0	0	1.8 ± 2.3[a]	0.1 ± 0.3[a]	11.1
CNS-LP (Tx)	20	17	3	0	0	0	0	2.4 ± 2.6	0.1 ± 0.4	15.0
TLP (Tx)	28	4	2	8	13	1	0	15.9 ± 6.3[b,d]	2.2 ± 1.1[b,d]	85.7
TXL (Tx)	21	7	8	4	2	0	0	9.0 ± 5.4[c]	1.0 ± 0.9[c]	66.7
22-month-old rats										
Saline	22	2	3	13	4	0	0	13.8 ± 4.3	1.9 ± 0.8	90.9
CNS-LP	16	1	5	5	5	0	0	13.5 ± 5.1	1.9 ± 1.0	93.8
TLP	31	0	1	3	14	10	3	22.9 ± 4.4[e,g]	3.4 ± 0.9[e,g]	100
TXL	27	0	2	8	15	2	0	17.7 ± 3.8[f]	2.6 ± 0.7[f]	100

Statistically significant differences:

Eight-week-old thymectomized rats
[a] P <0.001, saline-treated Tx vs saline-treated sham-Tx
[b] P <0.001, TLP-treated Tx vs saline-treated Tx
[c] P <0.001, TXL-treated Tx vs saline-treated Tx
[d] P <0.001, TLP-treated Tx vs TXL-treated Tx

Twenty-two-month-old rats
[e] P <0.001, TLP-treated vs saline-treated
[f] P <0.01, TXL-treated vs saline-treated
[g] P <0.001, TLP-treated vs TXL-treated

TABLE 4. The Effect of Thymolip (TLP) and Thymex-L (TXL) on the Development of Experimental Allergic Encephalomyelitis in Neonatally Thymectomized (Tx) 8-week-old, and 22-month-old Lewis Rats

Rats Treated with	n	No. of Rats with Paralysis (0 to ++++)					Mean Score (± S.E.)	% of Rats with Paralysis	No. of Rats with Histological Lesions (0 to ++++)					Mean Score (± S.E.)	% of Rats with Lesions
		0	+	++	+++	++++			0	+	++	+++	++++		
8-week-old Tx rats															
Saline (sham-Tx)	25	7	1	10	7	0	1.7 ± 0.2	72.0	4	3	5	9	4	2.2 ± 0.3	84.0
Saline (Tx)	24	22	1	1	0	0	0.1 ± 0.1[a]	8.3	19	3	2	0	0	0.3 ± 0.1[a]	20.8
TLP (Tx)	28	13	2	4	9	0	1.3 ± 0.3[b,d]	53.6	9	2	8	7	2	1.7 ± 0.3[b,d]	67.9
TXL (Tx)	25	16	3	6	0	0	0.6 ± 0.2[c]	36.0	14	2	7	2	0	0.9 ± 0.2[c]	44.0
22-month-old rats															
Saline	26	9	13	4	0	0	0.8 ± 0.1	65.4	6	8	8	3	1	1.4 ± 0.2	76.9
TLP	30	5	4	6	12	3	2.1 ± 0.2[e,g]	83.3	3	2	8	9	8	2.6 ± 0.2[e,g]	90.0
TXL	24	6	5	10	3	0	1.4 ± 0.2[f]	75.0	3	5	11	3	2	1.8 ± 0.2	87.5

Statistically significant differences:

Eight-week-old thymectomized rats

[a] P <0.001, saline-treated Tx vs saline-treated sham-Tx
[b] P <0.001, TLP-treated Tx vs saline-treated Tx
[c] P <0.05, TXL-treated Tx vs saline-treated Tx
[d] P <0.05, TLP-treated Tx vs TXL-treated Tx

Twenty-two-month-old rats

[e] P <0.001, TLP-treated vs saline-treated
[f] P <0.05, TXL-treated vs saline-treated
[g] P <0.05, TLP-treated vs TXL-treated

in aged animals given TLP and TXL. Again, TLP was more potent than TXL in stimulating the development of EAE in both thymusless and aged rats.

Skin Allograft Rejection

In control sham-thymectomized rats, there was an advanced rejection of allografts at 10 days (TABLE 5). Thymusless rats treated with saline or CNS-lipid showed little or no evidence of rejection. However, thymectomized recipients treated with TLP and TXL developed the ability to reject skin allografts. In the group of 22-month-old animals, allografts were rejected most rapidly in recipients treated with TLP. In general, graft rejection was more advanced in TLP-treated than in TXL-treated rats.

Protracted Effect of Thymolip

In order to ascertain whether TLP exerts a prolonged immunostimulatory action, young thymectomized and aged nonthymectomized rats were challenged for PFC response, hemagglutinin production, and delayed hypersensitivity to ovalbumin (TABLE 6). Immune reactions were evaluated on day 1 and day 30 after treatment with saline and TLP. In saline-treated thymectomized rats, immune responsiveness was very low on day 1 and day 30. In contrast, TLP-treated thymusless rats exhibited a significant increase of PFC response, hemagglutinin formation, and delayed sensitivity reactions on day 1 and 30 after the last injection of TLP. In aged rats, the immunostimulating influence of TLP was evident on day 30. Thus, the enhancement of immune responsiveness induced by TLP appears to be a relatively long-lasting phenomenon.

White Blood Cells and T-lymphocyte Subsets

There was a striking reduction of circulating leucocytes, lymphocytes, and T4-helper/inducer and T8-suppressor/cytotoxic cells in saline-treated thymectomized Wistar rats (TABLE 7). The treatment of thymusless animals with TLP and TXL was accompanied by an increase in the number of these cells. It should be pointed out, however, that the restorative effect of TLP and TXL was much more pronounced on T4 cells. In 22-month-old rats given TLP, the augmented number of leucocytes, lymphocytes and T4 cells was comparable to that observed in 8-week-old, saline-treated, sham-thymectomized rats.

Histology of Spleen and Lymph Nodes of Thymectomized Rats Treated with Thymolip

Histological examination of the spleen and lymph nodes from saline-treated thymectomized 8-week-old rats revealed a striking depletion of lymphocytes in thymus-

TABLE 5. The Effect of Thymolip (TLP) and Thymex-L (TXL) on Skin Allograft Rejection in Neonatally Thymectomized (Tx) 8-week-old, and 22-month-old Wistar Rats

Rats Treated with	n	Degree of Rejection (0 to +++) on Day 10 after Implantation					Mean Score (± S.D.)	Rejected Grafts (%)
		0	+	++	+++	++++		
8-week-old Tx rats								
Saline (sham-Tx)	20	0	0	4	10	6	3.1 ± 0.7	100
Saline (Tx)	24	22	2	0	0	0	0.1 ± 0.3[a]	8.0
CNS-LP (Tx)	24	21	3	0	0	0	0.2 ± 0.3	12.5
TLP (Tx)	26	7	4	9	6	0	1.5 ± 1.1[b,d]	73.1
TXL (Tx)	26	10	11	3	2	0	0.9 ± 0.9[c]	61.5
22-month-old rats								
Saline	19	0	5	8	6	0	2.1 ± 0.8	100
CNS-LP	20	0	6	10	3	1	2.0 ± 0.8	100
TLP	24	0	0	5	10	9	3.2 ± 0.8[e,g]	100
TXL	24	0	1	8	14	1	2.6 ± 0.6[f]	100

Statistically significant differences:
Eight-week-old thymectomized rats
[a] P <0.001, saline-treated Tx vs saline-treated sham-Tx
[b] P <0.001, TLP-treated Tx vs saline-treated Tx
[c] P <0.001, TXL-treated Tx vs saline-treated Tx
[d] P <0.05, TLP-treated Tx vs TXL-treated Tx
Twenty-two-month-old rats
[e] P <0.001, TLP-treated vs saline-treated
[f] P <0.05, TXL-treated vs saline-treated
[g] P <0.01, TLP-treated vs TXL-treated

TABLE 6. Prolonged Effect of Thymolip (TLP) on Plaque-forming Cell (PFC) Response and Hemagglutinin Production, and Delayed Skin Hypersensitivity Reactions in Neonatally Thymectomized (Tx) 8-week-old, and 22-month-old Wistar Rats

Rats Treated with	Day (after Last Injection of TLP)	Antibody Response to Sheep Red Blood Cells (SRBC)		Delayed Sensitivity to Ovalbumin
		No. of PFC/10^6 Cells	Anti-SRBC Titer (Log_2)	Mean Diameter (mm ± S.D.)
8-week-old Tx rats				
Saline (Tx)	1	612 ± 273	2.4 ± 0.4	1.4 ± 2.1
	30	382 ± 325	2.6 ± 0.4	1.6 ± 2.7
TLP (Tx)	1	1,943 ± 311[a]	5.4 ± 0.3[a]	16.8 ± 5.6[a]
	30	1,666 ± 240[b]	4.7 ± 0.4[b]	15.5 ± 4.4[b]
22-month-old rats				
Saline	1	1,819 ± 328	6.1 ± 0.4	15.9 ± 5.2
	30	1,624 ± 303	5.3 ± 0.3	13.1 ± 3.6
TLP	1	2,645 ± 336[c,e]	7.7 ± 0.5[c,e]	23.7 ± 5.3[c,f]
	30	2,308 ± 290[d]	7.1 ± 0.4[d]	19.8 ± 4.8[d]

Twenty-four rats in group.
Statistically significant differences:
Eight-week-old thymectomized rats
[a] P <0.001, TLP-treated Tx (day 1) *vs* saline-treated Tx (day 1)
[b] P <0.001, TLP-treated Tx (day 30) *vs* saline-treated Tx (day 30)
Twenty-two-month-old rats
[c] P <0.001, TLP-treated (day 1) *vs* saline-treated (day 1)
[d] P <0.001, TLP-treated (day 30) *vs* saline-treated (day 30)
[e] P <0.001, TLP-treated (day 1) *vs* TLP-treated (day 30)
[f] P <0.05, TLP-treated (day 1) *vs* TLP-treated (day 30)

TABLE 7. The Effect of Thymolip (TLP) and Thymex-L (TXL) on T4-helper/inducer and T8-suppressor Subpopulations of Lymphocytes in Neonatally Thymectomized (Tx) 8-week-old, and 22-month-old Wistar Rats

Rats Treated with	n	Leucocyte Counts		Lymphocyte Subsets		T4/T8 Ratio
		Le/mm³	Ly (%)	T4 (%)	T8 (%)	
8-week-old Tx rats						
Saline (sham-Tx)	21	9,800 ± 1,450	72 ± 8	58.6 ± 3.8	28.3 ± 3.9	2.1
Saline (Tx)	19	3,200 ± 810[a]	20 ± 13[a]	9.6 ± 4.0[a]	8.2 ± 3.6[a]	1.2
TLP (Tx)	20	7,600 ± 1,380[b,d]	57 ± 10[b,d]	36.3 ± 5.5[b,d]	15.3 ± 4.3[b]	2.4
TXL (Tx)	24	4,700 ± 980[c]	39 ± 7[c]	25.5 ± 4.7[c]	14.6 ± 5.1[c]	1.7
22-month-old rats						
Saline	25	7,100 ± 1,220	48 ± 12	39.5 ± 3.9	29.4 ± 5.8	1.3
TLP	19	9,300 ± 1,070[e,i]	67 ± 10[e,h]	58.2 ± 5.1[e,h]	26.5 ± 5.1	2.2
TXL	22	8,400 ± 1,360[g]	57 ± 7[g]	46.9 ± 4.2[f]	28.7 ± 5.5	1.6

Statistically significant differences:

Eight-week-old thymectomized rats

[a] P <0.001, saline-treated Tx *vs* saline-treated sham-Tx
[b] P <0.001, TLP-treated Tx *vs* saline-treated Tx
[c] P <0.001, TXL-treated Tx *vs* saline-treated Tx
[d] P <0.001, TLP-treated Tx *vs* TXL-treated Tx

Twenty-two-month-old rats

[e] P <0.001, TLP-treated *vs* saline-treated
[f] P <0.001, TXL-treated *vs* saline-treated
[g] P <0.01, TXL-treated *vs* saline-treated
[h] P <0.001, TLP-treated *vs* TXL-treated
[i] P <0.05, TLP-treated *vs* TXL-treated

dependent areas, a finding which is in accordance with an earlier report.[17] In the spleen, there was an almost complete disappearance of small lymphocytes surrounding the while pulp arterioles. In the lymph nodes, lymphocytes of the paracortical area were depleted or absent. These findings are in contrast to the histological features of the spleen and lymph nodes of thymectomized rats treated with TLP: the principal finding was the presence of aggregates of lymphocytes in the white pulp, and small lymphocyte masses surrounding germinal centers in the lymph nodes. These histological features suggest a restorative function of TLP on the thymus-dependent structures in the spleen and lymph nodes.

Histology of Thymus in Aged Animals

In 22-month-old rats at the time of autopsy, *i.e.,* when they were 23 months old, only thymic residues could be detected. Histologically, there were profound changes in the cellular make-up, although cortex and medulla were still recognizable. Aggregates of plasma-cellular elements were present in the medulla, cortico-medullar region and in the vicinity of interlobular septa. On the other hand, in rats treated with TLP, cortical and medullary areas were filled with thymocytes, and pyronin-positive cells were less abundant. Although treatment with TLP and TXL induced an increase in thymus weight, total restoration of the thymus cellular architecture was not complete in any of inspected thymuses from aged rats treated with thymus preparations.

DISCUSSION

The present study demonstrated that Thymolip and Thymex-L, lipid and protein/peptide fraction respectively of the calf thymus, ameliorated immunological impairment in 8-week-old rats thymectomized at birth, and enhanced immune responses in 22-month-old rats. The immune reactions in aged animals treated with TLP were often equivalent to those of young adult normal rats. In contrast, lipid fraction from the central nervous tissue, which served as a control, failed to improve immunodeficiency in thymectomized and senescent rats.

Although chemically different, both TLP and TXL were efficacious in restoring age-dependent immunodeficiencies. These effects of TLP and TXL were similar to immunopotentiating effects produced by chemically defined hormones from the thymus[18–22] or serum.[23,24] Since TXL is a mixture composed of different proteins and peptides from the thymus, the restoration of immune reactivity in thymectomized and aged rats could be ascribed to these bioactive factors. It is, however, difficult to reconsile the beneficial effect of TLP on immune potential with its chemical composition, because this thymic extract contains a large number of saturated and unsaturated fatty acids, such as oleic, stearic, palmitic, myristic and linoleic. Nevertheless, results presented here are in accordance with previous findings[14] that a lipid fraction from the rat thymus increased the number of lymphocytes in the blood and lymphoid tissues, and improved immune responsiveness in rats thymectomized at birth. Similarly, a total lipid extract of the thymus, obtained as a dry residue on evaporation with ethyl ether, was reported to have immunoenhancing activity.[25] Further, it appeared that unsaturated fatty acids from nonthymic sources were capable of affecting the antigenic activation of lymphocytes.[26,27] Linoleic acid was also found to have a marked therapeutic effect on guinea pigs with less severe experimental allergic encephalomyelitis.[28] Although these findings are indicative, it is only the present study that provides direct evidence for the immunorestorative function of thymus lipids.

The immune microenvironment is a complex homeostatic network involving the immune, nervous and endocrine systems.[29,30] Much of the normal, age-related decline in immune capacity of aging animals can be ascribed to the changes in the immune micromilieu,[31,32] and these age-associated changes in the microenvironment may be responsible for immune inadequacy in elderly individuals. This contention is supported by an experiment which showed that parabiosing young mice with old mice caused impairment of T-cell mitogen response and antibody-forming cell response in the young partners without enhancing these two immune responses in the old parabionts.[33] At present, it is difficult to determine whether aging affects more lymphoid cells than nonlymphoid cells of the immune microenvironment, or the cells at remote sites which influence the microenvironment *via* their bioactive products. Since the thymus and lymphoid tissues are directly connected with the central nervous system by parasympathetic and sympathetic fibers,[34,35] the neural component of the immune microenvironment should also be taken into consideration. However, the implication of structural alterations and dysfunctions of the neural components with advancing aging in immune malfunctions related to senescence is still not sufficiently explored.[36,37] Nevertheless, it seems generally accepted that the age-related decline of immune capacity includes both changes of lymphoid cells and their natural microenvironment, and changes in neuroendocrine functions caused by aging.

In this study, monoclonal antibody analysis of T-lymphocyte subsets in neonatally thymectomized and aged rats treated with TLP and TXL revealed a higher increase in the number of T4 cells compared with T8 cells. Immunological dysfunctions associated with aging have been ascribed, *inter alia,* to diminished T-helper/inducer-cell activity,[38] decreased B-cell function,[39,40] enhanced[41] or diminished[42] T-suppressor-cell function, lower production of lymphokines[43] such as interleukin 2,[44] and diminished ability of T cells to respond to environmental signals.[45] The reduction in T-cell precursor frequency[46,47] appears to be due to a defect in antigen presentation by adherent cells.[48] The number of B cells may be normal or increased[49] in old animals but their function impaired.[50] Thus, in senescent rats IgG production was significantly reduced.[51] This may be due to the decreased capacity of these animals to suppress the syngeneic antibody repertoire of primary B cells.[52]

Age-related changes in the pluripotent stem cells, both those which are migrating and those fixed to the tissues, have been described.[53,54] However, it seems that the pluripotent stem cells of the bone marrow of elderly individuals have preserved their functional capacity,[55,56] thus indicating that immunosenescence is not dependent completely on intrinsic changes in immature lymphocytes. Consequently, it is possible that multiple injections of TLP and TXL into thymectomized and aged animals, as performed in this study, may provoke proliferation, differentiation and maturation processes leading to the generation of both T- and B-cell lineages.

In spite of a large body of data on age-associated immune dysfunctions, the mechanisms responsible for the changes of T- and B-cell function are still not understood. Most probably, both extrinsic factors, such as those of the nervous and endocrine systems, and intrinsic factors, such as structural and functional alterations of the epithelial and lymphoid components of the thymus, bone marrow and other lymphoid tissues, may account for the age-related malfunctions of the immune system. The immunopotentiating effects produced by Thymolip and Thymex-L in neonatally thymectomized and senescent rats emphasize, once again, the importance of thymus-associated humoral mechanisms in the maintenance of immune homeostasis.

CONCLUSIONS

Senescence is accompanied by substantial abberations of the immune system function. In order to restore the compromised immune responsiveness, 8-week-old rats thymectomized at birth and 22-month-old Wistar and Lewis rats were repeatedly injected with complex lipid (Thymolip) and protein (Thymex-L) fractions isolated from the calf thymus. Plaque-forming cell response, hemagglutinin production, delayed skin hypersensitivity to ovalbumin, development of experimental allergic encephalomyelitis and skin allograft rejection increased significantly in thymusless and senescent rats treated with Thymolip and Thymex-L. These animals showed an increase in the number of lymphocytes in the peripheral blood as well as in thymus-dependent areas of the spleen and lymph nodes. Such treatment primarily augmented the population of T-helper/inducer cells. It appears that the immunorestorative activity of the lipid fraction is greater than that of protein fraction. It is concluded that thymus lipids and proteins are very effective in inducing prolonged amelioration of immunological impairment in thymusless and elderly rats.

ACKNOWLEDGMENTS

We would like to thank Professor Dragoslav Jeremić and Dr. Vlatka Vajs of the Institute of Chemistry, Faculty of Science,University of Belgrade for chromatographic analysis of Thymolip and valuable suggestions.

REFERENCES

1. MILLER, J. F. A. P. 1961. Immunological function of the thymus. Lancet **2:** 748-749.
2. JANKOVIĆ, B. D., B. H. WAKSMAN & B. G. ARNASON. 1962. Role of the thymus in immune reactions in rats. I. Immunologic response to bovine serum albumin (antibody formation, Arthus reactivity, and delayed hypersensitivity) in rats thymectomized or splenectomized after birth. J. Exp. Med. **116:** 159-175.
3. LUCKEY, T. D., ED. 1973. Thymic Hormones. University Park Press. Baltimore, MD.
4. NATIONAL CANCER INSTITUTE MONOGRAPH 63. 1983. Biological Response Modifiers: Subcommittee Report. Section IV. Thymic Factors and Hormones. 107-137. U.S. Department of Health and Human Services, NIH. Bethesda, MD.
5. KAY, M. 1979. The thymus: clock for immunologic aging? J. Invest. Dermatol. **73:** 29-38.
6. MAKINODAN, T. & M. M. B. KAY. 1980. Age influence on the immune system. Adv. Immunol. **29:** 287-330.
7. GOLDSTEIN, A. L., J. A. HOOPER, R. S. SCHULOF, G. H. COHEN, G. B. THURMAN, M. C. McDANIEL, A. WHITE & M. DARDENNE. 1974. Thymosin and the immunopathology of aging. Fed. Proc. **33:** 2053-2056.

8. SINGH, J. & A. K. SINGH. 1979. Age-related changes in human thymus. Clin. Exp. Immunol. **37:** 507-511.
9. PIERPAOLI, W., N. FABRIS & E. SORKIN. 1970. Developmental hormones and immunological maturation. *In* Hormones and the Immune Response. Ciba Foundation Study Group No. 36. G. E. W. Wolstenholme & J. Knight, Eds. 126-153. Churchill. London.
10. TRAININ, N. 1974. Thymic hormones and the immune response. Physiol. Rev. **54:** 272-315.
11. BACH, J. F. & C. CARNAUD. 1976. Thymic factors. Prog. Allergy **21:** 342-408.
12. TRIVERS, G. E. & A. L. GOLDSTEIN. 1980. The endocrine thymus: A role for thymosin and other thymic factors. *In* The Year in Hematology: 1978. R. Silber, J. LoBue & A. S. Gordon, Eds. 281-319. Marcel Dekker. New York, NY.
13. OSOBA, D. & J. F. A. P. MILLER. 1964. The lymphoid tissues and immune responsiveness of neonatally thymectomized mice bearing thymus tissues in millipore diffusion chambers. J. Exp. Med. **119:** 177-194.
14. JANKOVIĆ, B. D., K. ISAKOVIĆ & J. HORVAT. 1965. Effect of a lipid fraction from rat thymus on delayed hypersensitivity reactions of neonatally thymectomized rats. Nature **208:** 356-357.
15. PEŠIĆ, M. Č. 1984. Immunotherapie mit Thymusextrakt (THX). Haug Verlag. Heidelberg.
16. ARNASON, B. G., B. D. JANKOVIĆ, B. H. WAKSMAN & C. WENNERSTEN. 1962. Role of the thymus in immune reactions in rats. II. Suppressive effect of thymectomy at birth on reactions of delayed (cellular) hypersensitivity and the circulating small lymphocytes. J. Exp. Med. **116:** 177-186.
17. WAKSMAN, B. H., B. G. ARNASON & B. D. JANKOVIĆ. 1962. Role of the thymus in immune reactions in rats III. Changes in the lymphoid organs of thymectomized rats. J. Exp. Med. **116:** 187-206.
18. KLEIN, J. J., A. L. GOLDSTEIN & A. WHITE. 1966. Effects of the thymus lymphopoietic factor. Ann. N.Y. Acad. Sci. **135:** 485-495.
19. DABROWSKI, M. P. & A. L. GOLDSTEIN. 1976. Thymosin-induced changes in cell cycle of lymphocytes from aging neonatally thymectomized rats. Immunol. Commun. **5:** 695-704.
20. GOLDSTEIN, G. 1974. Isolation of bovine thymin: a polypeptide hormone of the thymus. Nature **247:** 11-14.
21. YAKIR, Y., A. I. KOOK & N. TRAININ. 1978. Enrichment of *in vitro* and *in vivo* immunologic activity in purified fractions of calf thymic hormone. J. Exp. Med. **148:** 71-83.
22. MEROBI, P. L., W. BARCELLINI, D. FRASCA, C. SGUOTTI, M. O. BORGHI, G. DE BARTELO, G. DORIA & C. ZANUSSI. 1987. *In vivo* immunopotentiating activity of thymopoetin in aging humans: increase of IL-2 production. Clin. Immunol. Immunopathol. **42:** 151-159.
23. BACH, J. F. & C. CARNAUD. 1976. Thymic factors. Prog. Allergy **21:** 342-408.
24. ASTALDI, A., G. C. B. ASTALDI, P. T. A. SCHELLENKEMS & V. P. EIJSVOOGEL. 1976. Thymic factor in human sera demonstrable by a cyclic AMP assay. Nature **260:** 713-715.
25. POTOP, I. & S. M. MILCU. 1973. Isolation, biologic activity and structure of thymic lipids and thymosterin. *In* Thymic Hormones. T. D. Luckey, Ed. 205-271. University Park Press. Baltimore, MD.
26. MERTIN, J., B. K. SHENTON & E. J. FIELD. 1973. Unsaturated fatty acids in multiple sclerosis. Brit. Med. J.2: 777-778.
27. OFFNER, H. & J. CLAUSEN. 1974. Inhibition of lymphocyte response to stimulants induced by unsaturated fatty acids and prostaglandins. Lancet **2:** 400-401.
28. HUGHES, D., A. B. KEITH, J. MERTIN & E. A. CASPARY. 1980. Linoleic acid therapy in severe experimental allergic encephalomyelitis in the guinea-pig: suppression by continuous treatment. Clin. Exp. Immunol. **41:** 523-531.
29. JANKOVIĆ, B. D. 1973. Structural correlates of immune microenvironment. *In* Microenvironmental Aspects of Immunity. B. D. Janković & K. Isaković, Eds. 1-4. Plenum Press. New York, NY.
30. JANKOVIĆ, B. D. 1979. The immune microenvironment is a multisystem. Immunol. Lett. **1:** 145-146.
31. PRICE, G. B. & T. MAKINODAN. 1972. Immunologic deficiencies in senescence. I. Characterization of intrinsic deficiencies. J. Immunol. **108:** 403-412.

32. PRICE, G. B. & T. MAKINODAN. 1972. Immunologic deficiencies in senescence. II. Characterization of extrinsic deficiencies. J. Immunol. **108**: 413-417.
33. ASTLE, C. M. & D. E. HARRISON. 1984. Effects of marrow donor and recipient age on immune responses. J. Immunol. **132**: 673-677.
34. BULLOCH, K. 1985. Neuroanatomy of lymphoid tissue: a review. In Neural Modulation of Immunity. K. Guillemin, M. Kohn & T. Melnechuk, Eds. 111-141. Raven Press. New York, NY.
35. FELTEN, D. L., S. Y. FELTEN, S. L. CARLSON, J. A. OLSCHOWSKA & S. LIVNAT. 1985. Noradrenergic and peptidergic innervation of lymphoid tissue. J. Immunol. **135**: 755s-765s.
36. LANG, R. W. & D. J. CARLO. 1975. Autoimmunity and aging of the nervous system. In Neurobiology of Aging. J. M. Ordy & K. R. Brizzee, Eds. 233-251. Plenum Press. New York & London.
37. NANDY, K. 1977. Immune reactions in aging brain and senile dementia. In The Aging Brain and Senile Dementia. K. Nandy & I. Sherwin, Eds. 181-196. Plenum Press. New York & London.
38. KROGSRUD, R. L. & E. H. PERKINS. 1977. Age-related changes in T cell function. J. Immunol. **118**: 1607-1611.
39. KISHIMOTO, S., T. TAKAHAMA & H. MIZUMACHI. 1976. In vitro immune response to 2,4,6-trinitrophenyl determinant in aged C57BL/6J mice: changes in the humoral immune response to avidity for the TNP determinant, and responsiveness to LPS effect with aging. J. Immunol. **116**: 294-300.
40. SZEWCZUK, M. R. & R. J. CAMPBELL. 1980. Loss of immune competence with age may be due to auto-anti-idiotypic antibody regulation. Nature **286**: 164-166.
41. RODER, J. C., A. K. DUWE, D. A. BELL & S. K. SINGHAL. 1978. Immunological senescence. I. The role of suppressor cells. Immunology **35**: 837-847.
42. HALLGREN, H. M. & E. J. YUNIS. 1977. Suppressor lymphocytes in young and aged humans. J. Immunol. **118**: 2004-2008.
43. CHANG, M. P., T. MAKINODAN, W. J. PETERSON & B. L. STREHLER. 1982. Role of T cells and adherent cells in age-related decline in murine interleukin 2 production. J. Immunol. **129**: 2426-2430.
44. THOMAN, M. L. & W. O. WEIGLE. 1985. Reconstitution of in vivo cell-mediated lympholysis responses in aged mice with interleukin 2. J. Immunol. **134**: 949-952.
45. GORCZYNSKI, R. M., M. KENNEDY & S. MACRAE. 1984. Altered lymphocyte repertoire during ageing. III. Changes in MHC restriction patterns in parental T lymphocytes and diminution in T suppressor function. Immunology **52**: 611-620.
46. MILLER, R. A. 1984. Age-associated decline in precursor frequency for different T cell-mediated reactions, with preservation of helper or cytotoxic effect per precursor cell. J. Immunol. **132**: 63-68.
47. MILLER, R. A. & D. E. HARRISON. 1985. Delayed reduction in T cell precursor frequencies accompanies diet-induced lifespan extension. J. Immunol. **134**: 1426-1429.
48. EFFROS, R. B. & R. L. WALFORD. 1984. The effect of age on the antigen-presenting mechanism in limiting dilution precursor cell frequency analysis. Cell. Immunol. **88**: 531-539.
49. FARRAR, J. J., B. E. LOUGHMAN & A. A. NORDIN. 1974. Lymphopoietic potential bone marrow cells from aged mice: comparison of the cellular constituents of bone marrow from young and aged mice. J. Immunol. **112**: 1244-1249.
50. CALLARD, R. E., A. BASTEN & R. V. BLANDEN. 1979. Loss of immune competence with age may be due to a qualitative abnormality in lymphocyte membrane. Nature **281**: 218-220.
51. EBERSOLE, J. L., D. J. SMITH & A. TRAUBMAN. 1985. Secretory immune response in ageing rats. I. Immunoglobulin levels. Immunology **56**: 345-350.
52. KLINMAN, N. R. 1981. Antibody-specific immunoregulation and the immunodeficiency of aging. J. Exp. Med. **154**: 547-551.
53. TYAN, M. L. 1977. Age-related decrease in mouse T cell progenitors. J. Immunol. **118**: 846-851.

54. HARRISON, D. E., C. M. ASTLE & J. A. DELAITTRE. 1978. Loss of proliferative capacity in immunohematopoietic stem cells caused by serial transplantation rather than aging. J. Exp. Med. **147:** 1526-1531.
55. GOIDL, E., J. W. CHOY, J. J. GIBBONS, M. E. WEKSLER, G. J. THORBECKE & G. W. SISKIND. 1983. Production of auto-antiidiotypic antibody during the normal immune response. VII. Analysis of the cellular basis for the increased auto-antiidiotypic antibody production in aged mice. J. Exp. Med. **157:** 1635-1645.
56. GORCZYNSKI, R. M., M. CHANG, M. KENNEDY, S. MACRAE, K. BENZING & G. B. PRICE. 1984. Alterations in lymphocyte recognition repertoire during aging. I. Analysis of changes in immune response potential on B lymphocytes from non-immunized aged mice, and the role of accessory cells in the expression of that potential. Immunopharmacology **7:** 179-194.

Immunorestorative Effects in Elderly Humans of Lipid and Protein Fractions from the Calf Thymus: A Double-Blind Study[a]

B. D. JANKOVIĆ,[b,c] P. KOROLIJA,[d] K. ISAKOVIĆ,[c]
LJ. POPESKOVIĆ,[c] M. Č. PEŠIĆ,[e] J. HORVAT,[c]
D. JEREMIĆ,[f] AND V. VAJS[f]

[c]Immunology Research Center
11221 Belgrade, Yugoslavia
[d]Geriatric Clinic
City Hospital
Belgrade, Yugoslavia
[e]Institute of Immunology and Thymus Research
Bad Harzburg, Federal Republic of Germany
[f]Institute of Chemistry
Faculty of Science
Belgrade, Yugoslavia

INTRODUCTION

It is generally believed that the immune system plays a major role in aging,[1-3] and that the elderly human population has an increased susceptibility to infectious and neoplastic diseases due to a decrease in immune potential.[4,5] Regardless of the difficulties in clearly distinguishing the physiological changes of age from physiological alterations which are secondary to diseases that accompany aging,[6] there is a growing body of evidence indicating that abnormalities of the humoral and cell-mediated immune mechanisms[7,8] are inherently involved in the physiology and pathology of senescence.[9]

Decrease in function of the thymus parallels the parenchymal atrophy of the human thymus that occurs with aging.[10] This loss of the thymic function in elderly individuals is caused by both intrinsic defects in lymphoid cells and extrinsic changes in the hormonal environment.[11,12] It has been proposed, *inter alia,* that the decrease of immune responsiveness with increasing age is due to the inability of the thymus to produce

[a]This work was supported by grants from the Republic of Serbia Research Fund, Belgrade.

[b]Address for correspondence: Branislav D. Janković, Immunology Research Center, Vojvode Stepe 458, 11221 Belgrade, Yugoslavia.

247

sufficient amounts of peptide hormones.[13] Therefore, numerous efforts have been made to enhance the immune function in elderly individuals by means of protein and peptide thymic factors.[14] So far, no study has been conducted in humans to assess the effectiveness of thymic lipids in the restoration of immunodeficiencies caused by physiological aging. We report here on the immunorestorative activity in elderly humans of a lipid fraction (Thymolip) and a protein/peptide fraction (Thymex-L) isolated from the calf thymus.

MATERIALS AND METHODS

Thymolip (TLP)

A lipid fraction prepared from the calf thymus[15] containing saturated and unsaturated fatty acids such as myristic, palmitic, stearic, oleic and linoleic.[16]

Thymex-L (TXL)

A commercially available (Thymoorgan Pharmazie, Vienenburg, FRG) extract of the calf thymus which contains proteins and peptides of different molecular weights.[17]

Participants

The elderly subjects were selected according to the criteria suggested for immunogerontologic studies[18] among institutionalized aged individuals. None of them was affected by autoimmune, neoplastic or infectious diseases, nor was any receiving any drugs known to influence the immune capacity. Comprehensive medical histories were obtained from the participants who were subjected to complete physical examination and routine screening laboratory tests. A group of 19 healthy young volunteers was also included in this study. The number, age and sex distribution of participants are shown in TABLE 1. The subjects were tested for immune reactivity before and after treatment with TLP, TXL and placebo.

Treatment

One group of 57 elderly subjects was treated with 100 mg of TLP/injection and another group of 21 aged individuals was given 150 mg of TXL/injection. Twenty aged participants were treated with placebo: a mixture of saline and emulsifiers without TLP and TXL. The treatment consisted of 15 intramuscular injections of TLP, TXL and placebo-mixture given every second day for a period of 30 days. All assays, except those for anti-tetanus toxoid antibody, were performed 2 days before treatment and 7 days after the last injection of TLP, TXL and placebo. The study was conducted in a double-blind fashion.

Evaluation of Delayed Hypersensitivity

Cell-mediated immunity was detected by delayed cutaneous hypersensitivity reactions using Multitest Mériuex (Lyon, France) which measures simultaneously the recall response to seven ubiquitous antigens: tuberculin, tetanus toxoid, diphtheria toxoid, streptococcus, proteus, candida and trichophyton. The puncture application of glycerol served as control. Reactions were inspected at 48 hours by two independent observers who did not have access to the protocol, and diameters (mm) of induration were recorded. Results are expressed as the score derived from the sum of the mean diameters of positive (≤ 2) skin reactions.

TABLE 1. The Subjects Used in the Study

Subjects	Treatment	n	Age		Sex	
			Range	Mean	Males	Females
Aged	Thymolip	57	68–93	78.2	35	22
Aged	Thymex-L	21	66–91	76.5	13	8
Aged	placebo	20	65–88	72.2	12	8
Adults	none	19	25–32	27.4	12	7

Heterohemagglutinin Reaction

Serum agglutinins for sheep, guinea pig and chicken red blood cells were detected by means of a microhemagglutination reaction carried out in 7×45-mm tubes. After 3 h incubation at room temperature, readings were performed microscopically, and the end-point of antibody activity recorded.

Immunization with Tetanus Toxoid

Twelve elderly subjects treated either with TLP, TXL or placebo, and 12 young adult volunteers were immunized with tetanus toxoid: two subcutaneous injections (5 floculation units/inj.) with an interval of four weeks between the injections. Serum anti-tetanus toxoid antibody titers ($\log_2$) were determined 14, 28 and 42 days after booster injection by means of a passive hemagglutination technique.[19]

Determination of T- and B-cell Subsets

Mononuclear cells from heparinized venous blood were isolated by Ficoll-Hypaque density gradient centrifugation. Lymphocyte markers were detected by means of a rosetting-test with sheep red blood cells (E marker), and by indirect immunofluorescence method using OKT3, OKT4, OKT8, OKB7, OKIa and OKM1 monoclonal antibodies (Ortho Pharmaceutical Corp.). Surface immunoglobulins (sIg) were detected by direct immunofluorescent staining using FITC-conjugated F(ab)2 fragments of sheep anti-human Ig serum (Behringwerke AG).

Leucocyte and Lymphocyte Counts

Counts were performed on peripheral blood. Smears used for differential counts were stained with May-Gruenwald and Giemsa.

Statistical Analysis

Statistical evaluation of results was carried out using the Student's *t* test.

RESULTS

Production of Heterohemagglutinins

Titers of "natural" heterohemagglutinins reacting with sheep, guinea pig and chicken erythrocytes in the sera of aged individuals treated with TLP, TXL and placebo are indicated in TABLE 2. Both TLP and TXL induced an increase in antibody formation to heterologous red blood cells. The most pronounced elevation of antibody titers was in aged subjects treated with TLP. Placebo treatment did not produce apparent effects on heterohemagglutinin levels of aged subjects.

Production of Anti-Tetanus Toxoid Antibody

Aged subjects and young adult individuals boostered 4 weeks after primary immunization with tetanus toxoid were tested for specific antibody production at varying time intervals after booster (TABLE 3). The highest mean titer ($\log_2$) was in young adult volunteers (12.7-13.6). The titer was somewhat lower in the group of aged subjects repeatedly injected with TLP (8.8-10.8). Specific antibody formation also

TABLE 2. "Natural" Agglutinin Production for Sheep (SRBC), Guinea Pig (GPRBC) and Chicken (CRBC) Red Blood Cells in Elderly Subjects before and after Treatment with Thymolip, Thymex-L and Placebo

	Mean Titer ($\log_2 \pm$ S.D.) of Heterohemagglutinins before and after Treatment					
	TLP-treated (n = 57)		TXL-treated (n = 21)		Placebo-treated (n = 20)	
Antibody	Before	After	Before	After	Before	After
Anti-SRBC	1.90 ± 1.13	2.74 ± 1.50	1.62 ± 1.43	2.33 ± 1.76	1.86 ± 1.16	2.02 ± 1.34
Anti-GPRBC	0.74 ± 0.92	2.31 ± 1.39^a	1.83 ± 1.04	2.99 ± 1.42^b	1.96 ± 1.18	1.85 ± 1.22
Anti-CRBC	2.06 ± 1.35	3.22 ± 1.95^a	0.70 ± 0.81	1.87 ± 0.96^a	0.68 ± 0.84	0.89 ± 0.91

Statistically significant differences: before treatment *vs* after treatment:
[a]P <0.001
[b]P <0.01

increased in TXL-treated individuals (7.2-8.4), but this increase was less significant compared to that in TLP-treated subjects. Aged subjects given placebo attained the lowest titers throughout the investigated period (5.2-5.6), and exhibited a more rapid fall-off of circulating antibody.

DELAYED HYPERSENSITIVITY

Delayed skin hypersensitivity to seven recall antigens (tuberculin, tetanus toxoid, diphtheria toxoid, streptococcus, proteus, candida and trichophyton) is shown in TABLE 4. The incidence and severity of positive delayed reactions were most pronounced in young adults who were not treated with thymus extracts. There was a significant increase both of frequency and intensity of delayed skin response in the

TABLE 3. Production of Anti-tetanus Toxoid Antibodies in Aged Individuals Pretreated with Thymolip, Thymex-L and Placebo

| | | Anti-tetanus Toxoid Antibody Titer (Mean Log$_2$ ± S.D.) | | |
| | | Days after Second Injection of Tetanus Toxoid | | |
Group[a]	Treatment	14	28	42
Aged	placebo	5.8 ± 0.5	6.2 ± 0.5	5.6 ± 0.6
Aged	Thymolip	8.8 ± 0.7[c,e]	10.3 ± 0.4[c,e]	10.8 ± 0.5[c,e]
Aged	Thymex-L	7.2 ± 0.4[d]	8.3 ± 0.3[d]	8.4 ± 0.9[d]
Adults[b]	none	12.7 ± 0.9	13.6 ± 1.1	13.2 ± 0.7

[a] Twelve subjects per group
[b] Untreated subjects
Statistically significant differences:
[c] P < 0.001, Thymolip-treated group vs placebo-treated group
[d] P < 0.001, Thymex-L-treated group vs placebo-treated group
[e] P < 0.001, Thymolip-treated group vs Thymex-L-treated group

aged population treated with TLP. Notably, 10 out of 14 nonresponders (anergic subjects) in this group reacted to ubiquitous antigens after treatment with TLP. The percentage and severity of positive reactions in TXL-treated aged individuals also increased to some extent. In placebo group, however, the number of responders remained at the same level before and after treatment with a mixture lacking thymus components.

T- and B-cell Subsets

In aged individuals treated with TLP and TXL, there was a significant elevation in the total number of lymphocytes, and T3$^+$, T4$^+$, B7$^+$, Ia$^+$ and sIg$^+$ cells (TABLE 5). TLP-treated subjects also exhibited an increase of E$^+$ cells. However, neither TLP

TABLE 4. Delayed Skin Hypersensitivity Reactions to Recall Microbial Antigens

Group	n^a	Treatment	Before Treatment Positive (%)	Before Treatment Mean ± S.D. Diameter (mm)	After Treatment Positive (%)	After Treatment Mean ± S.D. Diameter (mm)	No. of Anergic Subjects (Nonresponders) Before Treatment	No. of Anergic Subjects (Nonresponders) After Treatment
Aged	20 (15)	placebo	75.0	1.9 ± 1.1	75.0	2.2 ± 1.0	5	5
Aged	57 (44)	Thymolip	77.2	1.8 ± 1.3	91.2	4.4 ± 1.4 [b,c,e]	13	5
Aged	21 (16)	Thymex-L	76.2	1.7 ± 0.9	80.9	3.5 ± 1.5 [b,d]	5	4
Adults	19 (19)	none	94.7	5.5 ± 1.2				

[a] In parentheses, no. of responders to microbial antigens (Multitest Mérieux)

Statistically significant differences:

[b] P < 0.001, before treatment *vs* after treatment with Thymolip or Thymex-L.P.

[c] P < 0.001, Thymolip-treated group *vs* placebo-treated group

[d] P < 0.01, Thymex-L-treated group *vs* placebo-treated group

[e] P < 0.05, Thymolip-treated group *vs* Thymex-L-treated group

TABLE 5. Proportions of T- and B-cell Subsets in Aged Subjects Treated with Thymolip (TLP), Thymex-L (TXL) and Placebo

Mean (± S.D.) Number (× 10^9/l) of Cells before and after Treatment

Cells	TLP-Treated (n = 57)		TXL-treated (n = 21)		Placebo-treated (n = 20)	
	Before	After	Before	After	Before	After
Leucocyte	6.01 ± 1.76	6.48 ± 1.13	5.83 ± 2.11	6.20 ± 1.67	5.88 ± 1.84	6.17 ± 2.33
Lymphocyte	1.59 ± 0.22	2.99 ± 0.41[a]	1.74 ± 0.37	2.06 ± 0.31[b]	1.66 ± 0.36	1.80 ± 0.41
E+	1.20 ± 0.36	1.35 ± 0.35[c]	1.16 ± 0.40	1.23 ± 0.32	0.87 ± 0.34	1.03 ± 0.37
T3+	1.05 ± 0.24	1.22 ± 0.39[b]	1.19 ± 0.26	1.37 ± 0.25[c]	0.95 ± 0.32	1.10 ± 0.28
T4+	0.78 ± 0.19	1.97 ± 0.26[a]	0.82 ± 0.17	1.35 ± 0.20[b]	0.73 ± 0.18	0.79 ± 0.16
T8+	0.31 ± 0.12	0.33 ± 0.09	0.38 ± 0.15	0.41 ± 0.18	0.38 ± 0.20	0.45 ± 0.22
T4/T8 ratio	2.62 ± 0.74	6.04 ± 1.25[a]	2.16 ± 0.60	3.83 ± 0.95[b]	2.07 ± 0.63	1.86 ± 0.85
B7+	0.17 ± 0.06	0.51 ± 0.20[a]	0.25 ± 0.21	0.47 ± 0.28[b]	0.20 ± 0.14	0.23 ± 0.15
sIg+	0.33 ± 0.11	0.86 ± 0.21[a]	0.32 ± 0.13	0.51 ± 0.19[a]	0.30 ± 0.15	0.34 ± 0.18
Ia+	0.32 ± 0.08	0.77 ± 0.12[a]	0.31 ± 0.10	0.44 ± 0.08	0.28 ± 0.09	0.32 ± 0.06
M1+	0.34 ± 0.23	0.39 ± 0.27	0.31 ± 0.11	0.42 ± 0.23	0.40 ± 0.18	0.38 ± 0.21

Statistically significant differences: before treatment vs after treatment:
[a] P < 0.001
[b] P < 0.01
[c] P < 0.05

nor TXL influenced the populations of T8$^+$ and M1$^+$ cells. In placebo-treated, aged individuals, the number of cells bearing E, T3, T4, T8, B7, Ia and M1 markers, and surface immunoglobulins remained constant during the entire study period.

DISCUSSION

The results of this study demonstrate that elderly subjects treated with complex lipid (Thymolip) and protein/peptide (Thymex-L) fractions of the calf thymus exhibited an increased ability to form antibodies against particular and soluble antigens, develop delayed hypersensitivity reactions, and produce lymphocytes bearing T3, T4, B7 and Ia antigens, E marker and surface immunoglobulins. The immunorestorative activity of Thymolip was more pronounced than that of Thymex-L. Delayed sensitivity responses to microbial antigens and increase in subpopulations of T and B cells following treatment with thymus lipid fraction illustrate this difference between TLP and TXL.

In humans, different levels of immunoglobulins were described in the elderly.[20-22] Impaired formation of IgM, IgG and IgA in cultures of pokeweed mitogen-stimulated peripheral blood lymphocytes was found in 77-99-year-old individuals.[23] The mean titers of total and IgG anti-tetanus toxoid antibodies were significantly lower in aged subjects than in young adults.[19] Bach *et al.*[24] described a relationship between decrease in serum heteroantibody level and decline in serum thymic factor. In the present study, a lower formation of both anti-tetanus toxoid antibody and "natural" heterohemagglutinins was found in the aged population treated with placebo. On the other hand, these impaired humoral immune responses were markedly improved by treatment with TLP and TXL.

In spite of a generally held view that aging is associated with a decline in cellular immunity, there are conflicting data in the literature concerning delayed skin hypersensitivity to common microbial antigens.[25-28] In discussing these conflicting reports, Makinodan and Kay[2] stated that decreases in delayed skin sensitivity in the elderly reflect aging of the skin rather than aging of the immune system. The increased incidence and severity of positive skin-sensitivity reactions to common antigens induced by treatment of aged subjects with TLP and TXL do not support the view that diminished delayed response is solely due to the age-associated changes of the skin. It is of interest to mention that the major determinant of decreased cellular immunity in elderly individuals appears to be age itself and not age-related diseases.[29]

Regarding the number of blood T lymphocytes in aged humans, both a significant reduction in the absolute number of lymphocytes[30] and no changes in the circulating pool of T lymphocytes[31] have been described. Discrepant results have also been reported for E-positive lymphocytes; Kishimoto *et al.*[30] reported that the proportion of these lymphocytes was higher in 60-89-year-old subjects. In contrast, Brohee *et al.*[32] found that E-positive lymphocytes in healthy individuals over 75 years of age were unaffected. With respect to T cells, the populations of T3 and T4 cells were reported lower and that of T8 cells higher in elderly when compared to young adults.[33] However, Nagel and co-workers[34] observed that the total number of T cells did not change with age, although the number of helper cells increased and that of suppressor cells decreased. Moreover, the mitogen-induced T cell proliferative response declined significantly in the elderly.[35-37] As for B lymphocytes in aged humans, it appears that there are small variations in the number of these cells.[36]

The present study does not compare the difference in T- and B-cell divisions between young adults and aged subjects. It rather deals with changes in the number of T and B lymphocytes in elderly humans induced by lipid and protein fractions of the calf thymus. Both preparations significantly increased T3[+], T4[+], B7[+], Ia[+] and sIg[+] subpopulations of peripheral blood lymphocytes. A characteristic finding was that TLP and TXL did not affect the T8[+] subpopulation. These data are in accordance with the observed potentiation of humoral and cell-mediated immune responses in aged subjects treated with TLP and TXL. The increased delayed hypersensitivity reactions may be due to a higher number of T lymphocytes, and T3 and T4 in particular. It is now known that T3 protein, which is closely related to T-cell receptor,[38] plays a role in transduction of signals from T-cell receptor to the cytoplasmic components.[39,40] Such an activation of helper lymphocytes may result in a higher production of interleukin 2 (IL-2) which has a central role in T-cell cycle progression from G1 to S phase.[41] In elderly humans, the defective T-cell activity seems to be associated with both decreased secretion of IL-2 and reduced responsiveness to IL-2.[42] It has been shown that thymopentin, a synthetic polypeptide, is able to improve the cutaneous delayed hypersensitivity and proliferative response to PHA and ConA in immunocompromised aged subjects by stimulating the production of IL-2.[43] In aged mice, the diminished cell-mediated cytotoxicity can be markedly enhanced by injections of IL-2.[44] On this basis, since B lymphocytes contain receptors for IL-2,[45] one may assume that the enhanced antibody response in TLP- and TXL-treated aged subjects may be due to the increased number of T helper cells and their activity, and subsequent higher secretion of IL-2. TLP-induced and TXL-induced potentiation of humoral immunity in aged humans may also be associated with the increased amount of Ia on B lymphocytes. Ia is known to play a role in the presentation of antigen to T helper cells and activation of these cells.[46]

The above-mentioned experimental and clinical observations concerning the function of T and B lymphocytes may account, at least in part, for the enhanced cell-mediated and humoral immune responses in aged humans who were treated with Thymolip and Thymex-L. However, whether these thymic preparations can be used in the treatment of primary immunodeficiency diseases in children and other malfunctions of the immune system associated with thymic hypoplasia and dysplasia, or as adjunct therapy in treatment of cancer and in prevention of infections, remains to be elucidated.

CONCLUSIONS

This double-blind study was performed on 98 healthy old-age people (64-93 years; 60 men and 38 women) and 19 young adults (25-32 years; 12 men and 7 women). Aged subjects were given a total of 15 subcutaneous injections of lipid fraction (Thymolip) and protein/peptide fraction (Thymex-L) isolated from the calf thymus every second day, for a period of 30 days. A single dose contained 100 mg of Thymolip and 150 mg of Thymex-L. Control elderly individuals were treated with placebo in an identical manner. Immune reactions were evaluated before and after treatment with thymic preparations and placebo. Thymolip and Thymex-L, but not placebo, significantly increased production of anti-tetanus toxoid antibody, formation of "natural" agglutinins for sheep, guinea pig and chicken erythrocytes, and delayed skin hypersensitivity reactions to recall antigens (tuberculin, tetanus toxoid, diphtheria toxoid, streptococcus, proteus, candida and trichophyton). Characterization of peripheral blood cell markers, by means of monoclonal antibodies of the OKT series, revealed a significant increase of $T3^+$, $T4^+$, $B7^+$ and Ia^+ lymphocyte subpopulations in elderly subjects following treatment with Thymolip and Thymex-L. In these individuals, the number of sIg^+ cells also increased, as well as the absolute number of lymphocytes. Neither Thymolip nor Thymex-L affected the number of $T8^+$ lymphocytes and $M1^+$ cells. The data favour the possibility of using Thymolip and Thymex-L in the treatment of age-associated immunodeficiencies.

REFERENCES

1. WALFORD, R. L. 1969. The Immunologic Theory of Aging. Munksgaard. Copenhagan.
2. MAKINODAN, T. & M. M. B. KAY. 1980. Age influence on the immune system. Adv. Immunol. **29:** 287-330.
3. FABRIS, N. 1981. Body homeostatic mechanisms and aging of the immune system. *In* Handbook of Immunology and Aging. M. Kay & T. Makinodan, Eds.: 61-78. CRC Press. Boca Raton, FL.
4. PHAIR, J. P. 1979. Aging and infection: a review. J. Chron. Dis. **32:** 535-540.
5. MAKINODAN, T. & K. KIROKAWA. 1985. Normal aging of the immune system. *In* Relations between Normal Aging and Disease. H. A. Johnson, Ed. 117-132. Raven Press. New York, NY.
6. KIMMEL, D. C. 1974. Adulthood and Aging. John Wiley & Sons. New York, NY.
7. NORDIN, A. A. & T. MAKINODAN. 1974. Humoral immunity in aging. Fed. Proc. **33:** 2033-2035.
8. STUTMAN, O. 1974. Cell-mediated immunity and aging. Fed. Proc. **33:** 2028-2032.
9. WALFORD, R. L. 1974. Immunologic theory of aging: current status. Fed. Proc. **33:** 2020-2027.
10. SINGH, J. & A. K. SINGH. 1979. Age-related changes in human thymus. Clin. Exp. Immunol. **37:** 507-511.
11. KAY, M. 1984. Immunologic aspects of aging: Early changes in thymic activity. Mech. Ageing Dev. **28:** 193-218.
12. PRICE, G. B. & T. MAKINODAN. 1972. Immunologic deficiencies in senescence. II. Characterization of extrinsic deficiencies. J. Immunol. **108:** 413-417.
13. GOLDSTEIN, A. L., G. B. THURMAN, T. L. K. LOW, G. E. TRIVERS & J. L. ROSSIO. 1979. Thymosin: the endocrine thymus and its role in the aging process. *In* Aging, Physiology and Cell Biology of Aging. A. Cherkin, N. Kharasch, F.L. Scott, C. E. Finch, T. Makinodan & B. Strehler, Eds. Vol. **8:** 51-60. Raven Press. New York, NY.
14. NATIONAL CANCER INSTITUTE MONOGRAPH NO. 63 1983. Biological Response Modifiers: Subcommittee Report. Section IV. Thymic Factors and Hormones. 107-137. U. S. Department of Health and Human Services. NIH. Bethesda, MD.
15. JANKOVIĆ, B. D., K. ISAKOVIĆ & J. HORVAT. 1965. Effect of a lipid fraction from rat thymus on delayed hypersensitivity reactions on neonatally thymectomized rats. Nature **208:** 356-357.
16. JANKOVIĆ, B. D. & D. MARIĆ. 1988. Restoration of *in-vivo* humoral and cell-mediated immune responses in neonatally thymectomized and aged rats by means of lipid and protein fractions from the calf thymus. Ann. N.Y. Acad. Sci. This volume.
17. PEŠIĆ, M. Č. 1984. Immunotherapie mit Thymusextrakt (THX). Haug Verlag. Heidelberg.
18. LIGHART, G. J., C. CORBERAND, P. FOURNIER, W. GALANAUD, B. KENNES, H. K. MÜLLER-HERMELINK & G. G. STEINMANN. 1984. Admission criteria for immunogerontological studies in man: the senior protocol. Mech. Ageing Dev. **28:** 47-56.
19. KISHIMOTO, S., S. TOMINO, H. MITSUYA, H. FUJIWARA & H. TSUDA. 1980. Age related decline in the *in vitro* and *in vivo* synthesis of anti-tetanus toxoid antibody in humans. J. Immunol. **125:** 2347-2352.

20. ALFORD, R. H. 1968. Effects of chronic bronchopulmonary diseases and aging on human nasal secretion of IgA concentrations. J. Immunol. 101: 984-988.
21. BUCKLEY, C. G., E. G. BUCKLEY & F. C. DORSEY. 1974. Longitudinal changes in serum immunoglobulin levels in older humans. Fed. Proc. 33: 2036-2039.
22. RADL, J., J. M. SEPARS, F. SKVARIL, A. MORELL & W. HIJMANS. 1975. Immunoglobulin patterns in humans over 95 years of age. Clin. Exp. Immunol. 22: 84-90.
23. TAURIS, P., P. ANDERSEN & S. E. CHRISTIANSEN. 1985. Plaque-forming cell capability in the senescent. Immunol. Lett. 9: 3-8.
24. BACH, J.-F. M. DARDENNE & F. C. SALOMON. 1973. Studies on thymus products. Clin. Exp. Immunol. 14: 247-256.
25. NIELSEN, H. E. 1974. The effect of age on the response of rat lymphocytes in mixed leucocyte culture to PHA, and in the graft-vs-host reaction. J. Immunol. 112: 1194-1200.
26. GOODMAN, S. A. & T. MAKINODAN. 1975. Effect of age on cell-mediated immunity in long-lived mice. Clin. Exp. Immunol. 19: 533-542.
27. STUTMAN, O. 1975. Tumor development after polyoma infection in athymic nude mice. J. Immunol. 114: 1213-1217.
28. WALTERS, C. S. & H. N. CLAMAN. 1975. Age-related changes in cell-mediated immunity in BALB/c mice. J. Immunol. 115: 1438-1443.
29. GOODWIN, J. S., R. P. SEARLES & K. S. TUNG. 1982. Immunological responses of healthy elderly population. Clin. Exp. Immunol. 48: 403-410.
30. KISHIMOTO, S., S. TOMINO, K. INOMATA, S. KOTEGAWA, T. SAITO, K. KUROKI, H. MITSUYA & S. HISAMITSU. 1978. Age-related changes in the subsets and functions of human T lymphocytes. J. Immunol. 121: 1773-1780.
31. HALLGREN, H. M., J. M. KERSEY, D. P. DUBEY & E. J. YUNIS. 1978. Lymphocyte subsets and integrated immune function in aging humans. Clin. Immunol. Immunopathol. 10: 65-78.
32. BROHEE, D., B. KENNES, C. HUBERT & P. NEVE. 1980. Human lymphocyte affinity for sheep erythrocytes in young and aged healthy subjects. Clin. Exp. Immunol. 42: 399-401.
33. MASCART-LEMONE, F., G. DELEOESSE, G. SERVAIS & M. KUNSTLER. 1982. Characterization of immunoregulatory T lymphocytes during ageing by monoclonal antibodies. Clin. Exp. Immunol. 48: 148-154.
34. NAGEL, J. A., F.J. CHREST & W. H. ADLER. 1981. Enumeration of T lymphocyte subsets by monoclonal antibodies in young and aged humans. J. Immunol. 127: 2086-2088.
35. HALLGREN, H. M., E. C. BUCKLEY III, V. A. GILBERTSEN & E. J. YUNIS. 1973. Lymphocyte phytohemagglutinin responsiveness, immunoglobulins and autoantibodies in aging humans. J. Immunol. 111: 1101-1107.
36. BECKER, M. J., R. FARKAS, M. SCHNEIDER, I. DRUCKER & A. KLAJMAN. 1979. Cell-mediated cytotoxicity in humans: age-related decline as measured by xenogeneic assay. Clin. Immunol. Immunopathol. 14: 204-210.
37. STAIANO-COICO, L., Z. DARZYNKIEWICZ, M. R. MELAMED & M. E. WEKSLER. 1984. Immunological studies of aging. IX. Impaired proliferation of T lymphocytes detected in elderly humans by flow cytometry. J. Immunol. 132: 1788-1792.
38. ACUTO, O., S. C. MEURER, J. C. HODGDON, S. F. SCHLOSSMAN & E. L. REINHERZ. 1983. Peptide variability exists within alpha and beta subunits of T cell receptor for antigen. J. Exp. Med. 158: 1368-1373.
39. IMBODEN, J. B. & J. D. STOBO. 1985. Transmembrane signaling by the T cell antigen receptor. Perturbation of the T3-antigen receptor complex generates inositol phosphates and releases calcium ions from intracellular stores. J. Exp. Med. 161: 446-456.
40. OETTGEN, H. C., C. TERHORST, L. C. CANLEY & P. M. ROSOFF. 1985. Stimulation of the T3-T cell receptor complex induces a membrane-potential-sensitive calcium influx. Cell 40: 583-590.
41. KLAUS, G. G. B. & C. M. HAWRYLOWICZ. 1984. Cell-cycle control in lymphocyte stimulation. Immunol. Today 5: 15-19.
42. FRASCA, D., M. GARAVINI & G. DORIA. 1982. Recovery of T-cell functions in aged mice injected with synthetic thymosin-$\alpha 1$. Cell. Immunol. 72: 384-391.
43. MERONI, P. L., W. BARCELLINI, D. FRASCA, C. SGUOTTI, M. O. BORGHI, G. DEBARTOLO,

G. DORIA & C. ZANUSSI. 1987. *In vivo* immunopotentiating activity of thymopentin in aging humans: increase of IL-2 production. Clin. Immunol. Immunopathol. **42:** 151-159.

44. THOMAN, M. L. & W. O. WEIGLE. 1985. Reconstitution of *in vivo* cell-mediated lympholysis responses in aged mice with interleukin 2. J. Immunol. **143:** 949-952.

45. MURAGUCHI, A., J. H. KEHRL, D. L. LONGO, D. J. VOLKMAN, K. A. SMITH & A. S. FAUCI. 1985. Interleukin 2 receptors on human cells. Implications for the role of interleukin 2 in human B cell function. J. Exp. Med. **161:** 181-197.

46. GREENSTEIN, J. L., M. V. SITKOVSKY & S. J. BURAKOFF. 1987. Distinct roles for L3T4 in T cell activation. Fed. Proc. **46:** 313-316.

Hormonal Intervention: "Buffer Hormones" or "State Dependency"

The Role of Dehydroepiandrosterone (DHEA), Thyroid Hormone, Estrogen and Hypophysectomy in Aging

WILLIAM REGELSON, ROGER LORIA, AND
MOHAMMED KALIMI

Departments of Medicine, Microbiology, and Physiology
Medical College of Virginia
Richmond, Virginia 23298

Multiple effects from hormones or agents which effect aging relate to concepts of state-dependent changes in physiology. This was discussed recently by Lydic[1] who described how serotogenic neurons provide a link between the central generation of behavioral states and the regulation of sleep cycles, heat generation and cardiovascular responses. This provides a unifying strategy, *i.e.,* modulate serotonin and you can effect all these responses which regulate the above fundamental aspects of behavior or survival.

In regard to the state dependent regulatory concepts important to aging, another way to describe what is occurring are the action of "buffer" or modulating hormones that work in conjunction with targeted hormones of more specific responses. "Buffer hormones" demonstrate their presence during physiologic changes in response to stress or injury. They act by facilitating, inhibiting or delaying broad physiologic responses as distinct from classical hormonal action narrowly targeted for specific cells or tissues.

Dehydroepiandrosterone (DHEA), thyroid and estrogen are hormones with "buffer" action possession a wide range of physiologic effects, some of which are important to age intervention.

Hypophysectomy, with corticosteroid and thyroid replacement, is a rejuvenating operative manipulation that alters the aging process in rodents, probably by altering hormone relationships that program the aging process. This paper is a summary of hormonal effects and relationships that may play a role in aging.

DEHYDROEPIANDROSTERONE (DHEA)

For many years DHEA has been thought of as an intermediate in the synthesis of the sex steroids as it is the most abundant steroid produced in man. Renewed interest has accrued to its role in aging because levels of DHEA decline with progressive age so that an individual in his eighties may produce only 10-20% of what he made in his second decade, making DHEA a major biomarker for chronologic age.[2,3]

DHEA has anti-obesity[4-10] and weight-losing effects[11] as well as anti-stress effects to corticosteroid action,[12,13] and it has striking anti-diabetogenic action.[14-16] Coleman *et al.*[14-16] have observed that DHEA feeding prevents diabetes in the db/db mouse and protects mice from streptozotocin-induced diabetes via an insulin-sparing and/or -enhancing action.

In addition, DHEA feeding prevents the development of renal failure and hemolytic anemia associated with autoimmune disease in the NZB mouse[7,8] and can enhance immune responsiveness[9] in association with weight loss. This suggests that the anti-diabetic action of DHEA could result from modulating dietary or caloric factors, or from effects on corticosteroid action.

We have shown that DHEA given subcutaneously can protect mice from mortality induced by the coxsackie B_4 enterovirus and herpes intracranial type II virus infection. The effect against the coxsackie B_4 enterovirus infection is associated with stimulation of immune response in virus-infected animals.[17]

Schwartz, 1985[18] has reviewed the broad effects of DHEA on cancer prevention, autoimmune disease and obesity which highlight the important place of this native steroid in a broad series of age-related pathophysiologic events.

The anti-obesity and weight-losing action of DHEA may be dosage-, rodent-strain- or species-related and can constitute separate but time-related events in DHEA-treated animals. However, the anti-diabetic[14-16] and anti-carcinogenic or anti-tumor activity[8,18-20] reported for DHEA is not necessarily associated with anorexia or significant weight loss, as weight loss is a strain-related effect. Weindruch *et al.*[9] feel that anorexia alone does not account for the initial degree of weight loss on DHEA feeding in mice, which they think is due to a decline in food efficiency. In our clinical experience, DHEA administered to 17 cancer patients P.O. at tolerated doses up to 50 mg/kg/day resulted in no significant weight loss for periods as long as 2½ years.

In regard to DHEA effects on lipid metabolism, mature rats on low cholesterol diets fed DHEA 0.5% for 14 days had a significant decrease in liver triglycerides and cholesterol. In a rodent study by Kritshevsky's group,[21] on DHEA feeding, although serum cholesterol levels were increased, GI absorption of cholesterol was decreased and cholesterol and fatty acid synthesis was increased from acetate but not mevalonate. DHEA has also been shown to inhibit cholesterol biosynthesis in the lactating mammary gland.[22] Aldercreutz *et al.*[23] have found changes in steroid hormone levels and blood lipids in association with DHEA levels, and DHEA values are decreased clinically in individuals on high animal fat diets[24] or with obesity[125] where DHEA may be held in fat stores.

Ben-David *et al.*[26] have found DHEA to have anti-hypercholesterolemic effects in propylthiouracil-treated rats which has been confirmed by Furman *et al.*,[27] who have reported a thyromimetic action for DHEA. The effect of DHEA on lowering cholesterol levels are pertinent to Barrett-Conner *et al.*,[28] who have found that clinically elevated DHEA-S values correlate with survival in aged males in contrast to the low values in cardiac disease.

The possible importance of DHEA in thyroid-mediated responses is seen in a paper by Foldes *et al.*,[29] who have shown that DHEA levels are altered by thyroid disease. There is a fall in DHEA levels with hypothyroidism with a distinct change in the ratios of DHEA to DHEA-S dependent on thyroid status which again stresses the broad modulating actions of thyroid or DHEA hormones and their importance to aging.

In view of the increasing interest in declining DHEA values as a clinical biomarker for age or for risk assessment in coronary-prone patients and its effects on fat stores in obese mice and rats continued studies of DHEA effects on lipid metabolism are warranted. In this regard, Coleman et al.[15] have confirmed the oral place for DHEA in fat metabolism, where they have shown that increased insulin production and improved glucose tolerance could be achieved in feeding DHEA to 2-year-old obese mice with DHEA. The latter is important to the pattern of obesity and diabetes that characterize aging in man. We have seen insulin-related hypoglycemia with DHEA dosage of 80 mg/kg/day in an insulin-dependent diabetic with adenocarcinoma of the lung.

In regard to the above, quantitative changes in urinary steroid profiles in diabetes show a decreased DHEA production, and increases in plasma corticosterone concentration have been found in db diabetic mice. The rise in cortisol production in diabetes, with a decline in DHEA, as discussed previously, may be pertinent to Riley's observations[12] that DHEA aborts stress or corticosterone-induced thymic involution in young mice.

Coleman et al.[16] have found that the natural metabolite of DHEA, DHEA-S is more effective in preventing diabetes than DHEA. More importantly, they have observed that estrogen and alpha and beta hydroxyetiocholanolone, alone or in combination, prevent the development of diabetes in the db/db mouse, particularly when combined with the action of sub-optimal estradiol given parenterally. At sub-optimal dosage estradiol with etiocholanolone in the diet had a distinctly potentiating action in preventing diabetes and increasing insulin blood levels and preserving islet integrity.

The late Vernon Riley[12] showed that rotational stress in mice produced consistent thymic involution and T cell lymphopenia with significant effects on tumor induction and growth. This was related to stress-stimulated corticosterone production. Riley showed that DHEA given subcutaneously (1 mgm/mouse) 30' before 45 rpm rotational stress blocked stress-related thymic involution and could also decrease corticosterone-induced thymic involution by 50% when given 1 hour prior to corticosterone. Evaluation of thymic weights was made 48 hours post rotational stress. The effect was age related as there was a 2-fold decline in protection in 20-28-week mice as compared to 4-10-week-old mice.

Most recently, Marrero et al.[30] found that DHEA feeding (0.45%) increased mouse liver weight associated with more numerous and smaller liver mitochondria accompanied by a specific pattern of liver protein induction. It will be of interest to see if DHEA, like dietary restriction, can restore RNA and protein synthesis in aging mice.

Apart from DHEA's age-related decline, retrospective studies have found that women with either advanced or primary operable breast cancer have low plasma levels of DHEA and DHEA-S[31,32] as well as low urinary excretory rates of androsterone and etiocholanolone, the primary metabolites of DHEA. Bulbrook et al.[33] initiated a prospective study on the island of Guernsey in 5,000 apparently healthy women aged 30 to 59 years. The excretion of 17-hydroxycorticosteroids and the DHEA metabolites androsterone and etiocholanolone showed subnormal excretion up to nine years before breast cancer diagnosis, and that the highest cancer risk was associated with the lowest values.

The above is of interest as glucose-6-PO$_4$ dehydrogenase (G-6PD) plays a role in DNA synthesis, cell proliferation and carcinogen activation. DHEA[34] is a potent inhibitor of mammalian glucose-6-phosphate dehydrogenase (G-6-PDH), which is the rate-controlling enzyme in the pentose phosphate shunt and a major source of extra mitochondrial NADPH, a necessary co-factor for a variety of reductive biosyntheses, including the synthesis of fatty acids and ribo and deoxyribonucleotides.

Based on the above observations, Schwartz' group [8,18-20,35,36] reported that DHEA treatment was associated with tumor inhibition, including complete inhibition of spontaneous breast cancer formation in female C3H A^{vy}/a mice and lung tumors in A/J mice.[8,18-20] Pashko *et al.* [11,37,38] showed that a single i.p injection of DHEA into C3H or ICR mice inhibits the rate of ^{3}H thymidine incorporation into epidermal TC. *In vitro*, both DHEA and the Br-Epi DHEA derivative (more effective as a G-6-PD inhibitor) were instrumental in inhibiting Epstein Barr virus-induced morphologic transformation following stimulation of DNA synthesis in human lymphocytes.[38] The synthetic DHEA-sulfatide was also more active in reducing the rate of ^{3}H thymidine incorporation into mouse breast epithelium and epidermis.

The above has been reviewed by Schwartz *et al.* [18] and Nyce *et al.* [36] who have shown DHEA to inhibit dimethyl hydrazine bowel cancer in mice. Dworkin *et al.* [39] have found DHEA to block growth of HeLa and WI-38 cells *in vitro* which can be modulated by nucleotides. We have shown mitotic inhibiting effects for DHEA *in vitro* using hepatocarcinoma cells as compared to normal hepatocytes.[40]

G-6-PD hepatic levels increase with age by 20% in 6-month versus 20-month-old C57B1/6J female mice.[30] This is of interest to the neuroendocrine control of aging as DHEA declines with age[2,3] and could conceivably reverse the pentose shunt effects modulating G-6PD values.[41,42]

Lopez has postulated that DHEA played a metabolic role in modulating lipid metabolism and the youthful state,[41] and the implications of DHEA's role in atherosclerosis was first discussed by Kask as early as 1959, an idea which is now establishing its validity.[7,18,28,34,41,43-49]

In regard to the inhibition of G-6-PD by DHEA,[39,42,47-49] it is of interest that genetically determined deficiencies of G-6-PD in erythrocytes are associated with a decreased solid tumor incidence in Sephardic Jews, Sicilians[50,51] and American Negroes which have a high incidence of G-6-PD deficiency as a mutational adaptation to regional malaria incidence.

In another area, Merriman *et al.* [52] have studied the effect of DHEA on *in-vitro* malignant transformation. They studied the effect of DHEA on 12-0-tetradecanoyl phorbol-13-acetate (TPA) promotion of malignant transformation in C3H10T1/2 cells and showed that cancer initiation by 3-methylcholanthrene (MCA) promoted by TPA was inhibited by DHEA. This was related to inhibition of ornithine decarboxylase, the polyamine synthesizing enzyme which was induced 100-fold by TPA. DHEA inhibited polyamine synthesis to the same extent as retinyl acetate. In addition, G-6-PD activity in C3H10T1/2 cells was significantly inhibited.

As mentioned previously, we have treated 17 advanced solid tumor cancer patients for periods of up to 2½ years with DHEA at doses of 10-80 mgm/kg/day. The tolerated dose is 40 or 50 mgm/kg/day with nausea and vomiting the major limiting toxicity. Increased insulin sensitivity was seen in one diabetic patient at the highest doses given. Significant transient regression of mastosarcomas in dogs and cats were seen at 10 and 20 mgm/kg/day, but no significant anti-tumor activity was observed in man.

With an alternative interest in DHEA, Roberts[53] has suggested that acetylcholine (Ach) neurotransmitter activity manifests its physiologic action through inhibition of K$^+$ channels in the cell membrane which serves to maintain neuroexcitatory activity. Based on this, Roberts postulated that the progressive debilitation of aging, as is seen in Alzheimer's disease, could be due to gradual decrease in "the capability for genetic transcription of major K$^+$ channel components so that the ability of cells to adjust to changing conditions would be lost." He felt that the progressive decline in the hormonal DHEA, DHEA-S levels with advancing age may be a key factor producing the debility of aging leading to Alzheimer's disease through the loss of K^+ channel inhibition.

The postulate that DHEA would inhibit K^+ channels was based on DHEA's broad physiologic action: modulation of diabetes, tumor induction, and effects on autoimmune response which Roberts[53] felt were key factors in preventing age-related events. Regardless of the validity of his concept, he has found that DHEA and its sulfate in tissue culture enhanced neuron and glial survival and induced differentiation, i.e., neurite outgrowth from disassociated 14-day-old mouse embryo cultures.[54] In addition, they showed memory enhancement on direct intracerebral inoculation of DHEA in an avoidance T maze memory paradigm in mice.

Robert's concept may be further supported by the high concentration of DHEA-S found in the brain,[55] which suggests that DHEA may have modulating effects on cell membranes which alter response to neurotransmitters. In this regard, the concentration of DHEA-S in the rat brain is equivalent to what is found in the adrenal cortex, which could make DHEA a significant steroidal constituent of neural CNS function.

Furthermore, DHEA-S has been found to be a digitalis-like factor in the plasma of healthy human adults,[56] in that it inhibits Na,K ATPase in the same fashion as ouabain, which suggests that it is a plasma digoxin-like factor. At the clinical concentrations of DHEA found in plasma the importance of its action to cardiac function, neurite maintenance, natriuretic factor and the fundamental changes seen with advanced age is suggestive.

DHEA-S also has profound effects on collagen metabolism where on intravenous administration it softens cervical collagen in late clinical pregnancy,[57] suggesting that effects of DHEA on the melting point of collagen with age should be investigated.

The potential actions of DHEA are diverse, and DHEA or DHEA-S has had wide clinical trial as an agent alone or with estrogen in the treatment of menopausal symptoms, acne, cirrhosis, coronary disease, gout and psoriasis. Roberts has stimulated a clinical study of its place in Alzheimer's disease which is underway at the Sepulveda, V.A. in Los Angeles and we are studying its action in cancer patients, multiple sclerosis, and amyotrophic lateral sclerosis and will extend our program to patients with the post-polio syndrome as well as those with Alzheimer's disease and the AIDS syndrome.

As an agent for trial in advanced cancer, it was well tolerated in a Phase I, II clinical study. However, in contrast to transient mastosarcoma regression seen in veterinary practice, no tumor regression was seen clinically, but we wish to examine its clinical action in conjunction with chemotherapy because of DHEA effects on inhibiting the pentose shunt with possible synergistic effects on the DNA control of cell proliferation when combined with anti-metabolites to DNA synthesis.

Because of DHEA's metabolism to the sex steroids, we were concerned in clinical study with possible effects on the normal prostate. However, on prolonged clinical administration no prostate enlargement was seen and because of DHEA's anti-carcinogenesis action, we wish to evaluate its effects on prostatic carcinoma, as it is reported to block prostatic tumor growth in the Copenhagen rat.[58] Of importance to this, the timing of DHEA's age-related clinical decline is associated with prostatic hypertrophy.

DHEA and DHEA-S have wide clinical potential, and the role of DHEA as a biomarker and its benign clinical experience suggest that it and/or its analogs be looked at both in animal models and clinically for potential broad-based anti-aging action. The important clinical epidemiologic study of Barrett-Conner et al.,[59] which showed age and disease related decline in DHEA, solidly suggests that DHEA may play a profound role in preventing atherosclerosis, which combined with its potential anti-carcinogenic action and immunomodulating effects suggests it needs clinical trial in controlled studies for anti-aging or cancer prevention in man.

DHEA is an excellent example of a eustatic or "buffer hormone" that may modulate aging. The fact that it declines with age and effects so many systems and patterns of pathology associated with aging suggests that it is perhaps our best hormone to study as an agent for intervention or modulation of age-related disease.

THYROID

The clinical decline in thyroid function with age and its significance to physiologic decline has been discussed in detail in our review "The Evidence for Pituitary and Thyroid Control of Aging".[60] The role of the thyroid hormones in aging is supported by the action of thyroid combined with growth hormone for post-weaning 30-day periods in Snell-Begg progeric dwarf mice, which resulted in a doubling or tripling of life span.[61] Most recently, Fabris *et al.*[61] have shown that thyroid function clinically modulates thymic endocrine activity through effects on thymulin, a zinc-dependent thymic hormone. This is not surprising in view of the classical work of Lurie,[63] who reported in 1964 that resistance in rabbits to tuberculosis was governed by thyroid hormone activity related to its stimulation and maintenance of immune and phagocytic function.

Thyroidectomy increases rat hepatic ferritin iron by fivefold, suggesting a role for thyroid in iron metabolism and its related pro-oxidant action.[63] Ca^{2+} ATPase activity in reticulocyte membranes is stimulated by thyroid hormone modulated by testosterone or estrogen action,[64] and this latter expression of thyroid action demonstrates the modulating or "buffer" hormone action that might explain how hypophysectomy restores an age-related thyroid action on oxygen consumption by removing or changing a hormonal influence. Thyroxine can also act as an antioxidant to prevent lipid peroxidation of rat liver mitochondrial inner membrane.[65]

Again, an additional involvement in thyrotrophic influences is its catecholaminergic effect,[66] which is present in adult, as well as foetal or neonatal brains. In this regard, the influence of thyroid on a wide range of physiological events serves to emphasize an age-related control of thyroid on cardiac function as well as effects on renal weight, systemic blood pressure, adult cerebral and immune effects that are not generally thought of in relation to aging.

HORMONAL ESTROGEN INTERACTION

Finch *et al.*,[67] have reviewed the role of the neuroendocrine clock as it effects sexual cycling in female rodents. He quotes Ascheim as suggesting in 1965 that hypothalamic aging was the key to the loss of estrous cycles in female rats. These studies suggest that, in females, endocrine impairments relate to ovarian steroids and/ or the trophic loss of follicles which trigger a pituitary aging clock. In this regard, in younger animals, estrogen, given exogenously, or produced during pregnancy, accelerates pituitary aging while early ovariectomy attentuates hypothalamic pituitary age changes permitting ovarian recycling in young ovaries grafted into older mice. If mice are ovariectomized when young, removing ovaries maintains a "youthful" pituitary state through modulation of a feedback mechanism. Clinical intervention to control this pattern of neuroendocrine feedback may now be possible, as a gonadotropin-releasing (GnRH) antagonist is now available as a synthetic peptide which can inhibit ovulation at will.[68]

The GnRH antagonist is now available for study as a potential birth control peptide, whose first pre-clinical exploration has been in the area of controlled ovulation for clinical in-vitro fertilization. The GnRH antagonist now provides an opportunity in similar fashion to clomiphene, to see if its judicious use, at a dose which will not severely compromise estrogen production, could extend the youthful survival of pituitary function, by modulating ovarian cyclicity and follicular atresia. The clinical value of extending the time of reproductive capacity, relates to the fundamental question as to whether maintaining the hormonal balance of reproductive life truly improves survival or the quality of life.

While the menopause has been thought to be due to ovarian "exhaustion," we may now have the means to physiologically arrest ovarian atresia or "exhaustion" which can delay menopause to produce its own risk versus benefit. This will require primate models and will raise serious questions before clinical trial.

In relation to the clinical needs for estrogen, the reader is referred to the paper by Purdy and Goldheizer,[69] "Toward a safer estrogen in aging," in our text on Intervention in Aging. In summary, there are more than 33 million women in the U.S. over the age of 50 with menopausal symptoms which contribute to over 200,000 hip fractures each year. In addition, a decline in estrogen contributes to an increase in diabetes, hypertension, cardiovascular disease, postural changes and neuropsychiatric disorders. Although not an isolated factor, female sexuality, the quality of skin, form, figure and reciprocal sexual drive governing male sexual perceptions relate in large measure to female estrogen levels.

Clinical use of estrogen for post-menopausal replacement is governed by the attitude of physicians, many of whom are afraid of its carcinogenic properties because of enhanced endometrial or breast cancer or its action in increasing thrombosis or gall stone formation. Of interest, there is less concern among gynecologists who widely prescribe estrogen replacement versus the internists who are more cautious, and there is increased intermittent use of progesterone with estrogen to avoid the risks of endometrial cancer.

Purdy and Goldheizer[69] discuss the mutagenic or carcinogenic action of estrogens currently available in this country whose metabolism generates free radicals of mutagenic potential related to estrogen catechol formation. In contrast, in France, moxestrol is available as an effective clinical estrogen replacement without catechol carcinogenic intermediates. It is most unfortunate that moxestrol will most likely never reach the U.S. because of FDA regulatory concerns governing the cost of establishing the safety and efficacy of this estrogen used successfully for many years in France.

HYPOPHYSECTOMY

Hypophysectomy with hormonal supportive maintenance in aged mice and rats has resulted in a significant reversal of age-related pathology. As stated in my review,[60] to my knowledge, this is the only demonstration of a confirmed, broadly based physiologic rejuvenation currently accessible to further research, exploration and eventual clinical intervention. Caloric restriction which retards aging does not appear to lead to significant rejuvenation in older animals, but hypophysectomy does!

Pituitary removal in aged mice or rats with thyroid and corticosteroid maintenance restores: immunologic responsiveness, thymic weight, fur growth, phagocytic activity, vascular response to beta adrenergic stimulation, hepatic RNA synthesis, and oxygen consumption. In addition, hypophysectomy restores glomerular size, basement membrane anatomy and collagen structure to a more youthful pattern. Beneficial effects on absolute survival, motor activity, hepatic enzyme induction, tumor incidence, cardiac weight and aortic elasticity have also been described.[60] Unfortunately, these studies are limited in number, but the data regarding the reversal of age-related immunologic, renal and collagen changes has been confirmed for mice and rats in separate laboratories and by independent investigators.[60,70,71]

Most recently, Everitt and Burgess[71] showed that hypophysectomy in young, 70-day male Wistar rats, like food restriction, retards collagen aging in tail tendon, and inhibits age-associated proteinuria and renal histopathology. Additional localized brain lesions in hypophysectomized rats that result in obesity did not alter the hypophysectomy delay in collagen aging, proteinuria, or life expectancy, but age-related glomerular abnormalities were observed in rats made obese by CNS lesions. Evritt and Burgess were among the first to review the role of the hypothalamus in age control.[71]

It was Denckla's hypothesis that aging is in large measure the result of neuroendocrine action of an unidentified but physiologically defined Decreased Oxygen Consumption Hormone (DECO), produced by the hypophysis which programs aging.[72] Denckla felt that this DECO hormone blocked the metabolic regulating action of thyroid hormone, and that this block to thyroid action programs the aging syndrome. Removal of the pituitary removes this DECO hormone which restores thyroid response and "youthful" function.[60]

Unfortunately, this hypophyseal DECO hormone has not been identified, although like hypophysectomy as reported in our review,[60] caloric restriction restores minimal oxygen consumption in aging rats.[72] It was Denckla's assertion that this is the prime benefit of caloric restriction. The action of caloric restriction on restoring minimal oxygen consumption was recently confirmed by Masoro's group.[73]

Apart from surgical hypophysectomy, pituitary function can be influenced by pharmacologic intervention. The pharmacologic modulation of pituitary function has been reviewed by Lindfoot[74] in his discussion of the treatment of acromegaly and in the text of Cox *et al.*[75] Although growth hormone decline is a factor in aging, its administration at high levels produces vascular changes similar to those seen in aging or diabetes.[60] In this regard, the L-dopa decrease of growth hormone production in acromegaly reported by Luzizzi *et al.*[76] could have a bearing on the significant increase in survival and motor function seen in long-term L-dopa administration to mice,[77] and, as discussed, under tryptophane dietary restriction should be looked at as an alternative approach to neuroendocrine-mediated age control.

As an approach to eliminating DECO, specific immunologic destruction of the adenohypophysis is possible.[78,79] This would permit selective destruction of specific growth hormone, and prolactin pituitary producing areas, which could result in a more localized approach to dissecting hypophyseal function without surgery. Pierpaoli and his colleagues reviewed the relationship between thymus, immunology and the hypophysis as early as 1967.[78-81]

It is our feeling that while Denckla's concept of the DECO aging hormone deserves extensive research, an alternative to the concept of a hypophyseal pro-aging hormone is that with age we lose a compensatory hormonal balance, *i.e.,* the age-related decline of dehydroepiandrosterone (DHEA). Similarly with age we may lose a hormone or hormones that balance the eventual damaging action of prolactin or growth hormone produced by the pituitary. The appropriate balance between hormones is in effect the "youthful state," and this has been discussed by Dilman[82] and others.[83]

It is tragic that Denckla's hypothesis,[72] supported by the pioneering work of Everitt[71] and confirmed in several key independent experiments,[60] has not been taken up by his peers. The problem relates to the simplicity of the concept, the difficulties in working with hypophysectomized animals and measuring minimal metabolic oxygen consumption as the primary biologic assay. The rejuvenating action of hypophysectomy supports the concept that there is a neuroendocrine aging clock, and the evidence supports our capacity to manipulate it.

DISCUSSION

DHEA has profound effects on a wide variety of physiologic or pathophysiologic events. DHEA is a source of the sex steroids and modulates diabetes, obesity, carcinogenesis, neurite outgrowth, tumor growth, virus infection, stress, pregnancy and immune responses.

Does the above work via its inhibition of G-6-PD, ornithine decarboxylase, and K channel blockade or its action on Na,K ATPase and lipid metabolism? Does DHEA and/or its metabolites work via interaction with insulin or specific receptors? As DHEA is perhaps our most significant endocrine biomarker that declines with age, we must ask if DHEA decrease is pertinent to the pathologies or functional changes seen in aging, and this is supported by good epidemiologic data.[59]

Thyroid hormone is classically a broad modulating hormone as its influence on neural, catechol, muscle, renal, vascular and immune function may be distinct from its well-known effect on metabolic rate. As another example, Thyrotropin Releasing Hormone (TRH), apart from its targeted thyroid relationships demonstrates its protective presence in shock and as an endorphin-reversing agent, only when specific or extreme physiologic changes call for this action. Thyroid hormone effects are modulating and in that regard, similar to those of DHEA in that DHEA is a "buffer hormone" as it is both a source of sex steroids and, as discussed, a widely active agent in preventing a variety of pathologies.

The more we think about state-dependent regulation, modulating or "buffer hormones" in man, the more we will find. Melatonin is a prime example. It declines with age and governs diurnal and seasonal cyclicity, opiate sensitivity, sleep, sexual maturity, estrogen receptors, and immunologic responses.[83] Thymic-related hormones probably function in a similar manner.

In regard to the clinical utilization of estrogen, we must find mechanisms to permit foreign clinical data to support the entry of non-carcinogenic estrogens with an adequate overseas track record to clinical practice in this country in a manner that is economically practical for drug development.[69]

We have reviewed the influence of hypophysectomy on aging and the results are reproducible and cry out for understanding mechanism.[60] As the hypophysis is under neural or hormonal control, we can expect to effect its role in aging via hormonal or pharmacologic manipulation. As an example, prolactin production is inhibited by dopaminergics and these agents prevent striatal pathology and improve the length and quality of life in rodent models and are available clinically.[77,84] Could their judicious use or the immunologic anti-acidophilic cell antibody approaches described by Pierpaoli *et al.*[78,79] enable us to effect survival without recourse to removing the hypophysis physically? The evidence of Papavasiliou *et al.*[77] and others[84] for dopaminergic effects on survival and function is suggestive in this regard.

A new observation has been reported relevant to the action of dietary restriction extending survival in mice.[85] The National Center for Toxicologic Research has reported that with dietary restriction, there is a significant decline in body temperature with sleep. This suggests that sleep-related "mini hibernation" would be related to life extension and that lowered body temperature effects would be a factor in endocrine modulation of aging.

Endocrine intervention has great potential in relation to control of the intrinsic clock. DHEA and related steroid structures represent both bioquantitative markers and clinical intervention opportunities of great potential, as does the broad action of thyroid and estrogen-related hormones and the manipulation of hypophyseal function.

ADDENDUM

Most recently, Nestler *et al.*[86] have given oral DHEA to five male, normal weight, mature volunteers as a study to evaluate DHEA effects on insulin sensitivity. DHEA, 1600 mg/day was given for 28 days as 400 mg capsules QID in a double blind randomized study. Normal diet and activity was unchanged. In the DHEA group, mean percent body fat decreased in 4 of 5 men by 31% with the greatest change in the most obese, but with no change in total body weight suggesting that fat mass decrease was associated with an increase in muscle mass. Although DHEA-S levels increased 2.5–3.5-fold, there was no increase in insulin sensitivity. However, there was a fall of 7.5% in serum low density lipoprotein levels. Androgen and estrogen levels did not change in the Nestler 28-day study. The absence of weight change supports our own clinical experience in 37 cancer and multiple sclerosis patients, but recently we have seen increased libido and hirsuitism in multiple sclerosis women at the higher dose of 40 mg/kg/day treated daily for periods of several months.

DHEA effects on aging in man will probably not be similar to those seen on caloric restriction in rodents, but resemble, to some extent, those seen clinically on mild androgen administration. The effect on decreasing LDL may be of clinical interest to atherosclerosis studies, and it is most important to continue to test DHEA in both insulin dependent and in adult onset diabetes where obesity can be a factor.

REFERENCES

1. LYDIC, R. 1987. State-dependent aspects of regulatory physiology. FRSEB J. **1**: 6-15.
2. MIGEON, C. J., A. R. KELLER, B. LAWRENCE, *et al.* 1957. Dehydroepiandrosterone and androsterone levels in human plasma. Effect of age and sex; day-to-day and diurnal variations. J. Clin. Endocrinol. Metab. **17**: 1051-1062.
3. ORENTREICH, N., J. L. BRIND, R. L. RIZER, *et al.* 1984. Age changes and sex differences in serum dehydroepiandrosterone sulfate concentrations throughout adulthood. J. Clin. Endcrinol. Metab. **59**: 551-555.

4. YEN, T. T., J. A. ALLAN, D. V. PEARSON, et al. 1977. Prevention of obesity in A-VY/a mice by dehydroepiandrosterone. Lipids 12: 409-413.
5. CLEARY, M. P., R. SEIDENSATT, R. H. TANNEN, et al. 1982. The effect of dehydroepiandrosterone on adipose tissue cellularity in mice. Proc. Soc. Exp. Biol. Med. 171: 276-284.
6. CLEARY, M. P., A. SHEPHERD & B. JENKS. 1984. Effect of dehydroepiandrosterone on growth of lean and obese Zucker rats. J. Nutr. 114: 1242-1251.
7. TANNEN, R. H. & A. C. SCHWARTZ. 1982. Reduced weight gain and delay of coombs positive hemolytic anemia in NZB mice. Fed. Proc. 41: 463.
8. SCHWARTZ, A. G., L. L. PASHKO & R. H. TANNEN. 1983. Dehydroepiandrosterone: an anti-cancer and possible anti-aging substance. In Intervention in the Aging Process. Part A: Quantitation, Epidemiology and Clinical Research. W. Regelson & F. M. Sinex, Eds. 267-278. Alan R. Liss. New York, NY.
9. WEINDRUCH, R., G. MCFEETERS & R. L. WALFORD. 1984. Food intake and immune function in mice fed dehydroepiandrosterone. Exp. Gerontol. 19: 297-304.
10. CLEARY, M. P., R. SEIDENSTAT, R. H. TANNEN, et al. 1982. The effect of dehydroepiandrosterone on adipose tissue cellularity in mice. Proc. Soc. Exp. Biol. Med. 171: 276-284.
11. PASHKO, L. I. & A. G. SCHWARTZ. 1983. Effect of food restriction, 3 dehydroepiandrosterone, or obesity on the binding of H-7, 12 dimethyl-benz(A) anthracene to mouse skin DNA, J. Gerontol. 38: 8-12.
12. RILEY, V. 1982. Basic and applied studies on the physiology and pathology of stress: the anti-stress action of dehydroepiandrosterone. Report to the M. J. Murdoch Foundation of the late Vernon T. Riley Pacific Northwest Research Foundation.
13. SULMAN, F. G. 1980. The effect of air ionization electric fields, atmospherics and other electric phenomena on man and animal. American Lecture Series. Thomas. Springfield, IL.
14. COLEMAN, D. L., E. A. LEITER & R. W. SCHWIZER. 1982. Therapeutic effects on dehydroepiandroterone (DHEA) in diabetic mice. Diabetes 31: 830-833.
15. COLEMAN, D. L., R. W. SCHWIZER & E. H. LEITER. 1984. Effect of genetic background on the therapeutic effects of dehydroepiandrosterone (DHEA) in diabetes-obesity mutants and in aged normal mice. Diabetes 33: 26-32.
16. COLEMAN, D. L., E. H. LEITER & N. APPLEZWEIG. 1984. Therapeutic effects of dehydroepiandrosterone metabolites in diabetes mutant mice (57BL/KS-db/db). Endocrinology 115: 238-243.
17. LORIA, R. M., T. H. INGE & W. REGELSON. 1987. Up modulation of anti-viral immune response by dehydroepiandrosterone. Submittted.
18. SCHWARTZ, A. 1985. The effects of dehydroepiandrosterone on the rate of development of cancer and autoimmune processes in laboratory rodents. Basic Life Sci. 35. In Molecular Biology of Aging. A. D. Woodhead, Ed. 181-191. Plenum Pub. Co. New York, NY.
19. SCHWARTZ, A. G. 1979. Inhibition of spontaneous breast cancer formation in female (C3H-A'y /A) mice by long term treatment with dehydroepiandrosterone. Cancer Res. 39: 1129-1132.
20. SCHWARTZ, A., G. HARD, L. PASHKO, et al. 1981. Dehydroepiandrosterone: an anti-obesity and anti-carcinogenic agent. Nutr. Cancer 3: 46-53.
21. KRITCHEVSKY, D., S. A. TEPPER, D. M. KLURFIELD, et al. 1983. Influence of dehydroepiandrosterone (DHEA) on cholesterol metabolism in rats. Pharmacol. Res. Commun. 15: 797-802.
22. GIANELLY, A. A. & C. TERNER. 1968. Inhibition of cholesterol biosynthesis by DHEA in lactating mammary gland. Endocrinology 83: 1311-1315.
23. ADLECREUTZ, H., J. KERSTELL, JR., K. O. SCHAUMANN, et al. 1972. Plasma lipids and steroid hormone in patients with hypercholesterolemia or hyperlipemia during dehydroepiandrosterone sulfate administration. Eur. J. Clin. Invest. 2: 91-95.
24. WYNDER, E. L., F. MACCORMAK, P. HILL, et al. 1976. Nutrition and the etiology and prevention of breast cancer. Cancer Detect. Prev. 1: 293-310.
25. LOPEZ, S. A., C. WINGO, J. A. HERBERT, et al. 1976. Total serum cholesterol and urinary DHEA in humans. Atherosclerosis 24: 471-481.

26. BEN-DAVID, B., S. DIKSTEIN, G. BISMUTH, *et al.* 1967. Anti-hypercholesterolemic effect of DHEA in rats. Proc. Soc. Exp. Med. Biol. **125:** 1136-1140.
27. FURMAN, R. H. & R. P. HOWARD. 1962. Effects of androsterone and triodothyronine on serum lipids and lipoproteins, nitrogen balance and related metabolic phenomena in subjects with normal and decreased thyroid function with hyperglyceridemia and/or hypercholesterolemia. Metabolism **11:** 76-93.
28. BARRET-CONNER, E., K.-T. KHAE & S. S. C. YEN. 1986. A prospective study of dehydroepiandrosterone sulfate, mortality, and cardiovascular disease. N. Engl. J. Med. **315:** 1519-1524.
29. FOLDES, J., T. FEHER, K. G. FEHER, *et al.* 1983. Dehydroepiandrosterone sulphate (DS), dehydroepiandrosterone (D) and "free" dehydroepiandrosterone (FD) in the plasma of patients with thyroid diseases. Horm. Metab. Res. **15:** 623-624.
30. MARRERO, M., S. M. SNYDER, R. A. PROUGH, *et al.* 1987. Influence of orally administered dehydroisoandrosterone (DHA) on mouse liver protein synthesis and liver mitochondrial morphology. Fed. Proc. ABS. 748.
31. WANG, D. Y., R. D. BULBROOK, M. HERIAN, *et al.* 1974. Studies on the sulphate esters of DHEA and androsterone in the blood of women with breast cancer. Eur. J. Cancer **10:** 477-482.
32. ZUMOFF, B., J. LEVIN, R. S. ROSENFELD, *et al.* 1981. Abnormal 24 hour mean plasma concentrations of dehydroepiandrosterone and dehydroepiandrosterone sulfate in women with primary operable breast cancer. Cancer Res. **41:** 3360-3363.
33. BULBROOK, R. D., J. L. HAYWARD & C. C. F. SPICER. 1971. Urinary androgen and corticoid excretion and subsequent breast cancer. Lancet **2:** 395-398.
34. MARKS, P. A. & J. A. BANKS. 1960. Inhibition of mammalian glucose-6 phosphate dehydrogenase by steroids. Proc. Natl. Acad. Sci. USA **46:** 447-452.
35. SCHWARTZ, A. G. & R. A. TANNEN. 1981. Inhibition of 7,12-dimethyl benz (A) anthracene and urethane induced lung tumor formation in A/J mice by long term treatment with dehydroepiandrosterone. Carcinogenesis **2:** 1335-1337.
36. NYCE, J. W., P. N. MAGEE & A. G. SCHWARTZ. 1982. Inhibition of 1, dimethylhydrazine induced colon cancer in balb/c mice by dehydroepiandrosterone. Proc. Am. Assoc. Cancer Res. **23:** 91.
37. PASHKO, L. L., A. G. SCHWARTZ, M. ABOU-GHARBIA, *et al.* 1981. Inhibition of DNA synthesis in mouse epidermis and breast epithelium by dehydroepiandrosterone and related steroids. Carcinogenesis **2:** 717-721.
38. HENDERSON, E., A. SCHWARTZ, L. PASHKO, *et al.* 1981. Dehydroepiandrosterone and 16a-bromo-epiandrosterone: inhibitors of Epstein-Barr virus-induced transformation of human lymphocytes. Carcinogenesis **2:** 683-686.
39. DWORKIN, C. R., S. D. GORMAN, L. L. PASHKO *et al.* 1986. Inhibition of growth of HeLa and WI-38 cells by dehydroepiandrosterone and its reversal by ribo and deoxyribonucleosides. Life Sci. **38:** 1451-1457.
40. KALIMI, M. & W. REGELSON. 1985, 1986. DHEA inhibition of [^{3}H] uridine uptake in normal and transformed liver cells. Physiologist **28**(Abs. 64): 18. Characterization of dehydroepiandrosterone (DHEA) binding protein in rat liver. Physiologist **29**(Abs. 30): 9.
41. LOPEZ, S. A., C. WINDO, J. A. HERBERT, *et al.* 1976. Total serum cholesterol and urinary DHEA in humans. Atherosclerosis **24:** 471-478.
42. LOPEZ, S. A. & W. A. KREAL. 1967. In vivo effect of dehydroepiandrosterone in red blood cells on glucose-6-phosphate dehydrogenase. Proc. Soc. Exp. Biol. Med. **126:** 776-778.
43. SONKA, J., J. HILGERTOVA, O. KRATOCHVIL, *et al.* 1974. Inhibitory effect of DHEA on utilization of oxygen. Possibility of using DHEA in treatment of local hypoxia. Unitrini Lek. **24:** 655-666.
44. LOPEZ, S. A. & A. RENE. 1978. Effects of 17 keto steroids on G-6-PD and on G-6-PD isoenzymes. Proc. Soc. Exp. Biol. Med. **142:** 258-261.
45. LOPEZ, S. A. 1984. Metabolic and endocrine factors in aging. *In* Risk Factors for Senility. H. Rothschild & C. F. Chapman, Eds. 205-219. Oxford University Press. New York, NY.

46. LOPEZ, S. A. & B. YATES. 1978. Relationship between serum lipids and DHEA in humans. Circulation Pt. II **58**: Abs. 108.
47. OERTEL, G. W. & P. BENES. 1972. The effects of steroids on glucose-6 phosphate dehydrogenase. J. Steroid Biochem. **3**: 493.
48. OERTEL, G. W., P. BENES, M. SHIRAZI, et al. 1974. Interaction between dehydroepiandrosterone, cyclic adenosine-3, 5, monophosphate and glucose-6-phosphate dehydrogenase in normal and diseased subjects. Experientia **30**: 872-873.
49. TSUTUSUI, E. A., P. A. MARKS & P. REICH. 1962. Dehydroepiandrosterone on glucose 6-phosphate dehydrogenase activity and reduced triphosphopyridine nucleotide formation in adrenal tissue. J. Biol. Chem. **237**: 3009-3013.
50. BEACONSFIELD, P., R. RAINSBURY & G. KALTON. 1965. Glucose-6 phosphate dehydrogenase deficiency and the incidence of cancer. Oncologia **1**: 11-19.
51. SULIS, E. & G. SPANO. 1968. Osservazioni preliminari sull, incidenza neoplastica, sul comportamento enzimatico proliferative pel tessuto tumorale negli individui caronti di gloicosio-6 fosfato deidrogenasi (G-6-PD). Boll. Sci. Ital. Biol. Sper. **44**: 1246-1249.
52. MERRIMEN, R. L., L. R. TANZER, N. B. STAMM, et al. 1981. Chemoprevention of malignant transformation by dehydroepiandrosterone (DHE) in C3HlOT1/2 cells. 13th Int. Cancer Cong. Seattle, WA.
53. ROBERTS, E. 1986. Guides through the labyrinth of AD: dehydroepiandrosterone, potassium channels and the C4 component of complement. In Treatment Development Strategies for Alzheimer's Disease. 173-219. T. Crook, R. T. Bartus, S. Ferris, S. Gershon, Eds. Mark Powley and Associates.
54. ROBERTS, E., L. BOLOGA, J. F. FLOOD, et al. 1987. Effects of dehydroepiandrosterone and its sulfate on brain tissue in culture and memory in mice. Brain Res. **406**: 357-362.
55. CORPECHOT, C., P. ROBEL, M. AXELSON, et al. 1983. Characterization and measurement of dehydroepiandrosterone sulfate in rat brain. Brain Res. **270**: 119-125.
56. VASDEV, L., LONGERICH, E. JOHNSON, et al. 1985. Dehydroepiandrosterone sulfate as a digitalis-like factor in plasma of healthy human adults. Res. Commun. Chem. Pathol. Pharmacol. **49**: 387-397.
57. MOCHIZUKI, M. & T. MARVO. 1985. Effect of dehydroepiandrosterone sulfate on uterine cervical ripening in late pregnancy. Acta Physiol. Hungarica **65**: 267-274.
58. ORENTREICH, N. 1987. Work in Progress. Report to the Orentreich Foundation.
59. BARRET-CONNER, E., K. T. THAW & S. S. C. YEN. 1986. A prospective study of dehydroepiandrosterone sulfate mortality and cardiovascular disease. N. Engl. J. Med. **315**: 1519-1524.
60. REGELSON, W. 1983. The evidence for pituitary and thyroid control of aging: is age reversal a myth or reality?! The search for a "death hormone." In Intervention in the Aging Process. Pt. B. W. Regelson & F. M. Sinex, Eds. 3-52. Alan R. Liss. New York, NY.
61. FABRIS, N., W. PIERPAOLI & E. SORKIN. 1972. Lymphocytes, hormones and aging. Nature **240**: 557-559.
62. FABRIS, N., P. MOCCHEGIANI, S. MARIOTTI, et al. 1986. Thyroid function modulates thymic endocrine activity. J. Clin. Endocrinol. **62**: 474-478.
63. LURIE, M. B. 1964. Resistance to tuberculosis. In Experimental Studies in Active and Acquired Defensive Mechanisms. 265-301. Harvard University Press. Cambridge, MA.
64. WINKELMANN, J. C., C. N. MARIASH, H. C. TOWLE, et al. 1981. Thyroidectomy increases rat hepatic ferritin iron. Science **213**: 569-571.
65. LAWRENCE, W. D., P. J. DAVIS, S. D. BLAS, et al. 1984. Interaction of thyroid hormone and sex steroids at the rabbit reticulocyte membrane in vitro: control by 17B--estradiol and testosterone of thyroid hormone responsive Ca activity. Arch. Biochem. Biphys. **235**: 78-85.
66. PUYMIRAT, J. 1985. Effects of dysthyroidism on central catecholaminergic neurones. Neurochem. Int. **7**: 969-977.
67. FINCH, C. E., L. S. FELIGO, C. V. MOBBS, et al. 1984. Ovarian and steroidal influences on neuroendocrine aging process in female rodents. Endocrine Rev. **5**: 466-497.
68. KENIGSBERG, D. & G. D. HODGEN. 1986. Ovulation inhibition by administration of weekly gonadotropin releasing hormone antagonist. J. Clin. Endocrinol. Metab. **62**: 734-738.
69. PURDY, R. H. & J. W. GOLDZIEHER. 1983. Toward a safer estrogen in aging. In Intervention

in the Aging Process. Part A. ed. W. Regelson & M. Sinex, Eds. 247-266. Alan R. Liss. New York, NY.

70. MOODY, C. E., J. B. INNES, L. STAINAO-COICO, *et al.* 1981. Lymphocyte transformation induced by autologous cells. XI. The effect of age on the autologous mixed lymphocyte reaction. Immunology **44**: 431-438.
71. EVERITT, A. V. & J. A. BURGESS. 1976. Hypothalamus, Pituitary and Aging. Thomas. Springfield, IL.
72. DENCKLA, W. D. 1974. Role of pituitary and thyroid glands in the decline of minimal 02 consumption with age. J. Clin. Invest. **53**: 572-581.
73. MASORO, E. 1986. Personal communication, re: work of R. McCarter.
74. LINDFOOT, J. A. 1981. Acromegaly and giantism. *In* Endocrine Control of Growth. W. H. Daughaday, Ed. 207-267. Elsevier. New York, NY.
75. COX, B., I. D. MORRIS & A. H. WESTON, EDS. 1977. Pharmacology of the Hypothalamus. University Park Press. Baltimore, MD.
76. LUIZZI, A., P. G. CHIODINI & L. BOTALLA. 1972. Inhibitory effect of L-dopa release in acromegalic patients. J. Clin. Endocrinol. Metab. **35**: 941-943.
77. PAPAVASILIOU, P. S., S. T. MILLER, L. J. THAL, *et al.* 1981. Age-related motor and catecholamine alterations in mice on levodopa supplemented diet. Life Sci. **28**: 2945-2952.
78. PIERPAOLI, W. & E. SORKIN. 1975. Immunological blockade of the hypophysis. *In* Host Defense in Breast Cancer. B. A. Stoll, Ed. 172-190. New Topics in Breast Cancer. W. Heinemann Med. Books Ltd. London.
79. PIERPAOLI, W. & E. SORKIN. 1972. Immunological blockade of the adenohypophysis and its possible application in prophylaxis and therapy of neoplasia. Experientia **28**: 336-339.
80. PIERPAOLI, W., H. G. KOPP & E. BIANCHI. 1976. Interdependence of thymic and neuroendocrine functions in ontogeny. Clin. Exp. Immunol. **24**: 501-506.
81. PIERPAOLI, W. & E. SORKIN. 1967. Relationship between thymus and hypophysis. Nature **215**: 834-837.
82. DILMAN, V. M. & L. M. BERNSTEIN. 1979. Hypothalamic mechanism of ageing and specific age pathology. IV. Sensitivity threshold of the hypothalamo-pituitary complex to homeostatic inhibition by the thyroid. Exp. Gerontol. **14**: 225-230.
83. REGELSON, W. & W. PIERPAOLI. 1987. Melatonin: a rediscovered antitumor hormone? Its relation to surface receptors, sex steroid metabolism, immunologic response and chronobiologic factors in tumor growth and therapy. Cancer Invest. In press.
84. FELTEN, D. L., S. Y. FELTEN, T. ROMANO, *et al.* 1985. Pergolide slows age-related deterioration of the dopaminergic nigrostriatal system in Fischer 344 rats. ABS Soc. Neurosci. II: Pt 1 2142, pg. 727.
85. HART, R. W. 1987. Personal communication. National Center for Toxicologic Research.
86. NESTLER, J. E., C. O. BARLASCINI, J. N. CLORE *et al.* 1988. Dehydroepiandrosterone reduces serum low density lipoprotein levels and body fat but does not alter insulin sensitivity in normal men. J. Clin. Endocrinol. In press.

The Therapeutic Potential of Lymphokines in Neoplastic Disease[a]

MELANIE S. PULLEY AND D. C. DUMONDE

Department of Immunology
United Medical and Dental Schools
St. Thomas' Hospital
London SE1 7EH, United Kingdom

INTRODUCTION

The long-standing proposition that a tumour-bearing host is unable to reject his tumour by means of his unaided immunological defence mechanisms[1] has provided continued incentive for investigating immunotherapeutic approaches to neoplastic disease. From this standpoint two supplementary views have emerged: (a) that the neoplastic process itself compromises the host's ability to recruit into or activate lymphoid cells within a tumour site to initiate or maintain tumour-cell destruction; and (b) that the accepted modalities of cancer treatment, comprising major surgery, radiotherapy, chemotherapy and endocrine manipulation, further compromise the host's ability to mobilize inherent mechanisms of defence against tumour spread. Recent knowledge of mechanisms by which activated leucocytes may inhibit tumour-cell growth, and of how the immune system may be impaired in patients with advanced cancer, has revived enthusiasm for integrating cytoreductive with immunotherapeutic approaches to cancer treatment.[2] Here we consider the rationale for administering lymphokines to patients with neoplastic disease against the background of current views concerning the nature and physiological significance of the lymphokine system, and the evident shortcomings of other immunological approaches to cancer therapy. We illustrate growing interest in the therapeutic potential of lymphokines by reference to our own published work and that of others active in the field.

NATURE AND PATHOPHYSIOLOGICAL SIGNIFICANCE OF LYMPHOKINES

This field of study arose from considerations in the 1960's that cellular cooperation in the immunological response might be effected by special mediator molecules in a

[a]Supported by the Trustees of St. Thomas' Hospital, the Cancer Research Campaign, Organon International BV and Interleukin-2, Inc.

fashion analagous to the role of neurotransmitters and endocrine substances in regulating and effecting other complex physiological responses, *e.g.*, of the neuroendocrine system.[3] In 1968 Marcfarlane Burnet had proposed that inherent host defence against neoplasia was effected by means of autopharmacological mediators of immunological surveillance.[4] In 1969 the term 'lymphokine' was introduced to bring together non-antibody lymphocyte factors, such as lymphocyte-mitogenic, migration-inhibitory, skin-inflammatory and cytotoxic factors, which appeared to be involved in the expression of delayed-type hypersensitivity, and which might also be involved in regulation of the immunological response itself.[5] By the end of the 1970's lymphokines (LK's) had become accepted as non-antibody mediators of a wide variety of cellular immune phenomena; more than 100 biological activities ('soluble factors') had been described, apparently arising from lymphoid cell activation, which all appeared relevant to both expression and regulation of lymphoid cell activity.[6] The term 'interleukin' (IL: between leucocytes) was then introduced to emphasize the evident role of some of these factors (IL-1; IL-2) in intrinsic mechanisms of immunoregulation.[7] Since 1980, application of T-cell cloning, monoclonal antibody technology and recombinant DNA methodology is leading to the gene cloning of an increasing number of lymphokines, to the identification of cellular receptors for them, and of the intracellular biochemical pathways triggered by lymphokine: receptor interaction.[8] In extending knowledge of the molecular pharmacology of the cellular immune response[9] it is likely that lymphokines will be classified primarily in molecular terms by reference to specific or preferential ligand-receptor interactions,[10] as are neuroendocrine substances, rather than by reference to their presumed role in immunoregulation, inflammation, stimulation or inhibition of cell growth or motility.[6]

Lymphokines are non-antibody proteins or glycoproteins, generated by cells of the lymphoreticular system as a result of lymphocyte activation. Collectively, these molecules act as intercellular mediators of the effector immunological response and also act as mediators of both intrinsic and extrinsic pathways of immunoregulation. It is likely that controlled generation of lymphokines regulates cellular compartmentation across the microvasculature of both lymphoid and non-lymphoid tissues; and that lymphokines are involved not only in the differentiation and maturation of T cells, B cells and macrophages, but also in signalling to haemopoietic tissue the need for new white-cell elaboration. Growing evidence suggests that lymphokines act as messengers by which the immune system signals its state of activity to other body systems involved with neuroendocrine function, connective tissue metabolism and humoral mechanisms of inflammation and homeostasis. Accordingly the clinical significance of lymphokines arises from their role in mediating intrinsic and extrinsic immunoregulation, allergic and non-allergic inflammation, as well as inherent and adaptive mechanisms of host defence against colonization by unwanted cells such as microbial agents and tumours. A particular challenge to current research is to establish a molecular taxonomy of lymphokines which will also accommodate their 'predominant' biological activities and their presumed role in immunoregulation, inflammation and host defence. This problem is already complicated by increasing evidence of synergistic, cascade and pleiotrophic activities of lymphokines: thus pleiotropism itself is a required feature of any IL-1 candidate molecule which must 'lay claim' to lymphocyte-activating as well as to another biological activity in order to 'qualify' as a member of the IL-1 species.[11] Here we view the existence of lymphokine synergy, cascade interactions and pleiotropism as features which support a physiological approach to investigating the clinical significance of lymphokines.

RATIONALE FOR THE THERAPEUTIC INVESTIGATION OF LYMPHOKINES IN HUMAN CANCER (TABLE 1)

Considerations of the biology of lymphokines, of the behaviour of the immunological system in human cancer, and of other immunological approaches to cancer therapy, all lead to the inference that lymphokines play an important role in the containment of neoplastic disease.[12,13] TABLE 1 assembles a set of general points as a collective rationale for these investigations. Three further considerations are germane to this field: (1) specification of 'intended activity' of lymphokines; (2) indications for lymphokine administration; and (3) whether to study multiple-activity preparations or single-agent (*e.g.,* recombinant) lymphokines.

The first consideration (of specifying 'intended activity') has beset most other immunotherapeutic approaches to human cancer.[14] On the basis of animal experimentation we view the scientific rationale as two-fold:

(a) to assist inherent mechanisms of host defence involved in the elimination of tumour cells and in the containment of tumour spread; and

(b) to combat the occurrence or complications of acquired immunodeficiency arising from disease- or iatrogenically-induced impairment of immunological mechanisms.

The second consideration, of ethical justification for studying the administration of lymphokines to tumour patients, would seem to involve the following:

(a) Where it could be shown that the patient was specifically deficient in the ability to produce a given lymphokine (*e.g.,* IL-2): administration of the specific agent would then be analagous to endocrine replacement therapy;

(b) Where it could be shown that administration *in vivo* or *in vitro* of a given lymphokine could induce local tumour regression or overcome defective white-cell function;

(c) On more circumstantial grounds—as part of the supportive management of patients deemed to have irreversible neoplastic disease (not a truly 'scientific' approach); or

(d) In order to learn more about the physiological and clinical significance of lymphokines in Man (accepting the scientific limitations of working with patients exhibiting abnormalities in immunological and inflammatory cell function).

The third problem, of whether it is 'better' to administer multiple-activity or single-activity lymphokine preparations may be considered as follows:

(a) It seems unlikely that the adverse impact of cancer or cancer treatment on the host will be circumvented by the simple administration of any *single* lymphokine;

(b) At the molecular and cellular level, it is not yet possible to specify the pathophysiology of the whole lymphokine system in the individual patient;

(c The existence of synergistic, cascade and pleiotropic interactions between lymphokines and target tissues supports a therapeutic rationale for giving a 'cocktail' of white-cell-derived lymphokines rather than a single bacterial-derived recombinant agent; and

(d) It seems likely that multiple rather than single defects in lymphokine production or response will characterize the cancer patient.

TABLE 1. Illustrative Rationale[a] for Therapeutic Investigation of Lymphokines in Human Cancer

---

1. Considerations of 'immunological surveillance' predict that there should be a system of autopharmacological mediators of host defence against neoplasia;

2. Lymphokines directly inhibit the growth, migration and metabolism of cultured tumour cells;

3. Lymphokines activate the tumoricidal capacity of rodent macrophages, NK cells and other lymphocytes so as to inhibit tumour-cell viability or growth *in vitro;* and restrict experimental tumour growth or metastasis *in vivo;*

4. Lymphokines augment the metabolic, chemotactic, immunological and tumoricidal activities of human white cells in ways relevant to containment of neoplastic disease and to complications of secondary immunodeficiency;

5. Experimental tumour regression achieved by systemic reactions to bacterial toxins or systemic reactions of delayed hypersensitivity is associated with the appearance of circulating lymphokines;

6. Local or systemic injection of lymphokines can induce experimental tumour regression and augment tumour regression induced by chemotherapy, irradiation or lymphoid-cell transfer;

7. Patients with progressive tumour burden develop cellular immunodeficiency which is a bad prognostic sign;

8. Lymphokines are involved in both intrinsic and extrinsic mechanisms of immunoregulation whose integrity is impaired by conventional cytoreductive treatment modalities of cancer;

9. Cellular immunodeficiency in advanced human cancer is associated with circulating factors blocking production or expression of lymphokine activity;

10. Topical immunotherapy of human tumours by induction of chronic delayed hypersensitivity reactions probably involves the local action of lymphokines;

11. Systemic immunotherapy of human cancer with bacterial toxins and other microbial substances probably induces widespread activation of the lymphokine system;

12. Other systemic immunotherapeutic agents in human cancer (tumour vaccines; transfer factor; lymphoid-cell transfer; thymic hormones; interferons; chemical immunostimulants) affect cell-mediated mechanisms with likely enhancement of local or systemic production of lymphokines.

---

[a] For further details see REFERENCES.

In the last 10 years it has become possible to justify the therapeutic investigation of either mixed-activity or single-agent lymphokines in human subjects at risk of cellular immunodeficiencies, progressive neoplasia and their complications. In the following sections we consider recently published work which illustrates these approaches.

ADMINISTRATION OF MIXED-ACTIVITY LYMPHOKINES

Beginning in 1976 we have studied the local and systemic effects of giving two different types of mixed-activity human lymphokine to patients with advanced cancer. One lymphokine preparation (1788-LK), obtained from Organon International BV, was derived from culture of the human B-lymphoblastoid cell line RPMI 1788; culture supernatants were processed by hollow-fibre filtration and lyophilised. The other lymphokine, developed by our colleague Dr. R. A. Wolstencroft, was a preparation of buffy-coat interleukin (BC-IL) derived by PHA-pulse activation of human peripheral blood mononuclear cells from buffy-coat transfusion residues: culture supernatants were processed by membrane filtration in the liquid state. Quality control of the preparations was done by reference to leucocyte migration inhibitory activity (for 1788-LK) and to TCGF/IL-2 activity (for BC-IL). The two preparations differed in their spectrum of principal lymphokine activities: 1788-LK also contained lymphotoxin (TNF β) and macrophage-activating factor(s) (MAF), but no IL-1, IL-2 or interferon-γ) (IFN-γ); in contrast, BC-IL contained IL-1, IL-2 and IFN-γ activities. The usual sterility, pyrogenicity and safety tests were done on both products and all patients were managed under circumstances of ethical permission, informed consent and compassionate clinical care. Our approach has been to study the intradermal, intratumoural, endolymphatic and intravenous routes of administration, by regimes avoiding short-term or long-term toxicity, and thus to learn about the physiological and clinical significance of lymphokines in Man.[15]

Intradermal Administration

Intradermal injection of either 1788-LK or BC-IL produced dose-related sustained inflammatory responses of erythema and induration resembling in their later phase the classical tuberculin reaction.[16] However, the lymphokine skin reactions had an accelerated development phase, reaching a maximum of 8-24 h, well ahead of the tuberculin reaction. Histological study of excision biopsies of 1788-LK reactions revealed early endothelial margination of polymorphs (evident at 30 min) accompanied by polymorph diapedesis and oedema, and superseded (form 4 h) by mononuclear-cell infiltration with endothelial hypertrophy. With the more intense reactions the injection sites then became progressively indurated but (more commonly) from 18 h the inflammation began to regress clinically. However, at 48 h and 72 h the histological picture of lymphoendothelial inflammation closely resembled that of the tuberculin reaction.[17] The study was of interest in reinforcing the status of lymphokines as physiological mediators of local reactions of delayed-type hypersensitivity in Man, and in revealing that similar inflammatory responses could be induced by two different lymphokine preparations with a different spectrum of lymphokine activities *in vitro*. Accordingly the phenomenon of sustained skin inflammation could not be ascribed solely to the content of IL-1, IL-2 or IFN-γ in the lymphokine preparations; yet 1.0 μg of both types produced substantial reactions of erythema. Control studies showed that the skin reactions could not be attributed to endotoxin.[17] It is likely that both 1788-LK and BC-IL contained interleukin-1 (IL-1)-inducing lymphokines; and that the phenomenon of sustained skin inflammation illustrated synergy, cascade and pleiotropic interactions between lymphokines and cells involved in the inflammatory response.

We then studied clinical correlates of reactivity to lymphokines. Although patients with advanced cancer were often unable to mount a positive tuberculin response, they were able to mount an inflammatory response to lymphokine; however, these reactions became weaker as the clinical condition deteriorated.[15] Additional study revealed that variation between patients in their measurable inflammatory responses to batches of 1788-LK could be reduced by referring the reactions to one such batch designated as a 'standard' preparation.[16] In a group of 22 patients with various malignant tumours of different degrees of disease severity, 24-h skin reactions to a single batch of 1788-LK bore a strongly positive correlation with the extent of recall antigen sensitivity.[16,18]

Patients with less severe disease tended to give both stronger lymphokine reactions and delayed hypersensitivity recall antigen reactions than patients with more severe disease.[18] There was an inverse correlation between lymphokine reactivity and two indices of persistent acute-phase status: C-reactive protein (CRP) levels and circulating neutrophil count.[16] Our findings suggest that impaired delayed hypersensitivity in advanced cancer patients may be due partly to impaired local inflammatory responses associated with systemic indices of inflammation that occur in patients with more severe disease. The role of IL-1 in these phenomena merits investigation;[19] and continued study may lead to pathophysiological criteria relevant to the selection of cancer patients for systemic lymphokine therapy.

Intratumoural Administration

Single or repeated injection of 1788-LK directly into skin metastatic breast carcinoma nodules resulted in clinical regression of tumour and histological evidence of tumour-cell necrosis with a pleomorphic cellular infiltrate consisting mainly of polymorphs and macrophages.[20] Necrosis of tumour cells was frequently confluent but sometimes appeared 'piecemeal' in the neighbourhood of infiltrating leucocytes; yet, electron microscopy failed to show very close contact or cell bridging between leucocytes and tumour cells. Occasionally a ballooning appearance of clumps of tumour cells was observed suggesting the possibility that 1788-LK might have a direct tumoricidal effect, in keeping with its content of lymphotoxin.[20] However, the 1788 cell line is also known to generate a non-interferon macrophage activating factor (MAF)[33] which might have induced resident or blood-borne macrophages to secrete IL-1 and TNFα, thus activating mechanisms of natural cell-mediated cytotoxicity as well as leucocyte-endothelial adhesion leading to diapedesis. An alternative explanation is that the inflammatory cell microenvironment caused by repeated 1788-LK injection was simply 'unfavourable' for tumour-cell survival. The tumour nodules were of scirrhous type, with a dense collagenous stroma which could have protected the tumour cells from the host's inflammatory or immune system; thus microenvironmental activation of the IL-1/TNF family of molecules might have disturbed those tumour-stromal relationships necessary for tumour-cell survival.

As with the intradermal route, detailed study of the intra-tumoural route of lymphokine injection yields information of considerable potential for the understanding of lymphokine action in Man. It seems highly appropriate to study the anti-cancer effects of any 'new' lymphokine or interleukin preparation by intralesional injection in patients with accessible tumour deposits, suitable for excision biopsy, and thus for detailed histological/morphometric examination of the response to lymphokines.

Endolymphatic Administration

Twenty-three melanoma patients received one or more endolymphatic infusions of buffy-coat interleukin (BC-IL): 12 patients had locally recurrent disease, one had lung metastases and the remaining 10 had poor-prognosis primary tumours (*i.e.,* > 1.76 mm deep: Bresselow's classification) which had not recurred following wide excision.[15] Although the original primary tumours had been situated on all major areas of the body, endolymphatic administration of BC-IL was thought to be particularly appropriate in melanoma which spreads by the lymphatic system.[21] Further rationale arose from previous experience of our colleague Dr. J. M. Edwards of the endolymphatic administration of BCG and oil-based isotopes in malignant melanoma,[22] and of our colleagues Dr. R. H. Kelly and Dr. R. A. Wolstencroft who had shown that endolymphatic injection of mixed-activity mitogenic lymphokine in the guinea pig resulted in regional lymph node enlargement (at 1-3 days) accompanied by paracortical distension, germinal centre activation and accelerated differentiation of antibody-forming cells in the regional (preauricular) lymph node.[23-25]

Volumes of BC-IL, which from previous intravenous dose-escalation study the patient was known to tolerate, were infused into one or more regions, and followed directly by contrast lymphoangiography.[15] As judged by TCGF activity, endolymphatic infusions contained 500-4000 units of IL-2. Patients showed clinical enlargement and tenderness of regional nodes at 24 and 48 h and often for longer after infusion. Serial radiography showed that the regional lymph node size was maximal at the follow-ups done 6 or 13 days after a single injection and that enlargement could extend to involve deeper nodes. In 5 patients, block dissection of the regional nodes (inguinal, cervical or axillary) was undertaken between 6 and 13 days post-injection. Lymph node histology revealed marked paracortical distension and follicular hyperplasia; there was extensive plugging of paracortical sinuses with small lymphocytes, a pattern normally associated with an active cellular immunological response. The injections were well tolerated, without adverse toxicity.[15]

The ability of endolymphatic lymphokines to stimulate paracortical (T-zone) activity in human melanoma-draining lymph nodes adds weight to the generalization that lymphokines are physiological mediators of those cellular changes in regional lymphoid tissue that accompany the induction of delayed-type hypersensitivity[23,26] and invites characterization of the molecule(s) responsible for the lymph-node activating (LNAF) effect. In the rabbit, afferent lymph leaving sites of peripheral antigen sensitization contains mitogenic and migration-inhibitory factors whose role may be to prepare the regional node for interactions between antigen-presenting cells and recirculatory lymphocytes.[23] Little is known of the mechanisms whereby lymph nodes limit the survival and proliferation of tumour cells; and in melanoma there is significantly reduced paracortical activity in nodes located near to primary and metastatic tumour.[27] The endolymphatic route of lymphokine administration in Man may well have therapeutic potential in malignant melanoma, as well as offering a means whereby host mechanisms limiting the lymphatic spread of tumour may be investigated.[15,21]

Intravenous Administration

As the two lymphokine preparations contained a different range of activities it was of interest to compare and contrast the effects of lymphoblastoid cell line lymphokine (1788-LK) with buffy-coat interleukin (BC-IL) when given intravenously, by single and repeated injection.[15,28,29] 1788-LK was given to 34 advanced cancer patients of which about half had breast cancer; BC-IL was given to 50 patients of which 32 had malignant melanoma. Following bolus intravenous injection, both lymphokine preparations induced dose-dependent acute-phase symptoms, including pyrexia and rigors. In most cases escalating doses of 1788-LK were given daily or thrice weekly to determine a dose which gave a moderate symptomatic response (without antipyretics) and on which the patient could be maintained for several weeks. Longterm courses of 1788-LK were given to four patients over a 9-25 month period. Likewise, escalating doses of BC-IL were given daily to determine the optimum maintenance dose which was then given intravenously daily or on alternate days (or to determine the dose to be given by endolymphatic infusion). Patients on either lymphokine preparation were followed up and there was no evidence of adverse toxicity attributable to either 1788-LK or BC-IL.[15,28,29]

A single intravenous injection of 1788-LK produced a dose-dependent acute phase reaction characterized by fever, increase in blood neutrophils, decrease in blood lymphocytes and increases in cortisol, ACTH and growth hormone, all maximal between 2-6 hours after injection. Zinc and iron levels started to decrease during this time to reach a trough between 5-12 h; and acute-phase proteins (CRP and α_1-AG) peaked later at 24-48 h.[30] There was insufficient endotoxin in the preparations to account for this reaction and a study using control-processed plasma protein showed that these responses could not be attributed to endotoxin.[31] Patients volunteered feelings of wellbeing during and after the course of 1788-LK; they often remained in a stable clinical condition when previously they had been deteriorating; and an objective response of partial tumour regression was observed in two patients.[32]

A small controlled follow-up study was done in 19 patients with breast cancer, assigned randomly to two groups. Nine of these each received a course of 12 intravenous injections of 1788-LK over a 16-day period in hospital whilst 10 received controlprocessed plasma protein in an identical schedule.[28] Patients receiving control protein showed no symptomatic, haematological or biological changes, in contrast to the group receiving active 1788-LK. Of the 19 patients, 13 entered the study with a mild or moderate tumour burden; of those receiving control protein, mortality at 1 year was 4/7 compared with 1/6 in those receiving active 1788-LK. To our knowledge this is the only controlled follow-up study of lymphokines in human cancer (full details will be published elsewhere).

A single intravenous injection of BC-IL produced similar acute-phase symptoms to that of 1788-LK but with an earlier time-course.[15] Coldness and rigors were first evident at 15 min after injection and the temperature peaked at 2 h; whilst after 1788-LK there was no evidence of a pyrexial response until 30-90 min and the temperature generally peaked at 3 h. Haematological and hormonal responses were also at a maximum earlier: neutrophil and lymphocyte responses peaked at 2-3 h (usually 3-5 h after 1788-LK) and plasma cortisol and ACTH peaked at 60-90 min (3-4 h after 1788-LK). In one patient, levels of β-LPH/β-endorphin were measured after injection and were found to peak with the ACTH response (at 90 min); however, unlike ACTH, the β-endorphin level was still elevated at 6 h. Infusion of hydrocortisone was undertaken to imitate the cortisol levels obtained after BC-IL injection: lymphopenia but not the marked increase in neutrophils as after BC-IL was observed. When BC-IL was given by intravenous infusion over 4-6 h it was less well tolerated than the same dose by bolus injection; patients complained of a 'flu-like feeling' of greater persistence than after bolus injection. In the medium term (2-3 weeks) and on followup there was evidence of changes in immune function. Absolute lymphocyte counts, lymphocyte transformation and delayed hypersensitivity reactions showed an increase in some patients. Most patients had no further increase in tumour load whilst receiving BC-IL and those who subsequently received chemotherapy/irradiation tolerated these treatments well with little evidence of haematological depression. As with 1788-LK, feelings of well-being were volunteered during and after the course of BC-IL; and in some patients there was symptomatic improvement in mobility, appetite, pain and bowel function.[15]

Our studies of the intravenous administration of mixed-activity lymphokines in Man provide evidence that lymphokines are also mediators of systemic reactions of delayed hypersensitivity[26] and draw attention to the therapeutic potential of short-term activation of the acute-phase response. The results also provide evidence in Man that lymphokines activate the neuroendocrine system and may well mediate extrinsic immunoregulatory circuits by feedback mechanisms involving cortisol secretion, metallic cation compartmentation, and acute-phase protein synthesis.[31] It is tempting to ascribe the acute-phase response, induced by both 1788-LK and BC-IL, to the presence of IL-1 or an IL-1 inducer ('MAF') in the preparations. The 1788-LK was known to contain MAF activity[33] but not IL-1, whilst BC-IL contained IL-1 activity: these differences could explain the earlier onset of the acute-phase response to intravenous BC-IL. The associated release of β-LPH/β-endorphin[15] might account for the feelings of well-being induced by the preparations. The lymphopenia may have been cortisol-mediated whilst the neutrophilia could be ascribed to a permissive effect of IL-1 (or IL-1 induction) on granulocyte recruitment from bone marrow. It has been suggested that the changes occurring during the acute-phase response may facilitate immunological defence mechanisms against cancer;[34] and both IL-1- and IL-2-dependent lymphocyte-stimulating activity in vitro are increased by raising the ambient temperature to 39 degrees.[35] Unlike the host response to infection and trauma, cancer appears not to excite acute-phase manifestations in Man until complicated or widespread.[36] We suggest that there is a rationale for inducing recurrent, short-term, self-limiting acute-phase responses with lymphokine preparations that also have additional biological activities relevant to host defence against cancer.

ADMINISTRATION OF INTERLEUKIN-2 AS A 'SINGLE' LYMPHOKINE

Following demonstrations that mitogenic lymphokines could enhance or restore cell-mediated immune responses in vitro or (in mice) in vivo, purified preparations of interleukin-2 were shown to be effective in many of these respects. Particular attention was directed towards purifying human interleukin-2 because of the availability of rapid biological assays based upon T-cell growth, significant advances in protein purification techniques, and the subsequent cloning of the interleukin-2 gene. The rationale for therapeutic investigation of IL-2 as a 'single' lymphokine in human cancer arose from three principal standpoints: (a) the ability of purified IL-2 to expand tumoricidal T lymphocytes to act as antigen-specific (T_c) and non-specific (NK/LAK) killer cells in vitro and to augment chemotherapy-induced suppression of transplantable murine tumours in vivo;[37] (b) demonstrations that purified human IL-2 could stimulate T cells in vitro from patients with congenital and acquired immunodeficiencies;[37] and (c) that whilst infusion of IL-2 into mice stimulated both specifically and non-specifically tumoricidal ('killer') cells in lymphoid tissue, the combined infusion of IL-2 together with IL-2 activated syngeneic lymphocytes was particularly effective in restricting tumour spread.[37,38] Accordingly much interest became focused on the potential of IL-2 'itself' for the therapy of cancer; and this view was reinforced when the pleiotropic activities of the molecule became appreciated.[39] This reasoning is consistent with the above-mentioned rationale (a) to assist anti-tumour host defence mechanisms and (b) to combat associated immunodeficiency states.

Subcutaneous Administration of Low-dose Purified Human IL-2

Human IL-2, generated by phorbol-ester and phytohaemagglutinin treatment of blood lymphocytes co-stimulated with irradiated Daudi cells, was purified by Welte and colleagues to an activity of 10^6 units/mg[40] and administered in 1983-84 to 16 immunodeficient patients in repeated doses over 11 weeks escalating to 20,000 U/m^2: subcutaneous administration was done in order to promote lymphatic drainage.[39] Minor short-term clinical responses occurred in five of the patients, including a clearing of AIDS-related CMV-retinitis; partial regression of a histiocytic lymphoma; appearance of follicles in a lymph node of a patient with Nezelof's syndrome; a decrease in monoclonal immunoglobulin in a second AIDS/Kaposi patient and a decrease in serum alkaline phosphatase in a Hodgkin's patient.[39] Two patients treated for longer than 50 days showed a marked increase in lymphocyte stimulation *in vitro* by a synergistic mixture of OKT3 plus IL-2. In this Phase I study no appreciable toxic effects were observed up to a maximum total dose of around 10^6 units.[39]

Intravenous and Intraperitoneal Administration of Lymphoblastoid and High-dose Recombinant IL-2

Also from 1983-84, human lymphoblastoid cell line IL-2 at 10^6 U/mg, produced at Dupont Laboratories by phytohaemagglutinin/phorbol-ester stimulation of JUR-KAT cells, was administered intravenously to 12 patients with AIDS/Kaposi, melanoma or colonic cancer by Lotze, Rosenberg and colleagues; patients received 4 weekly intravenous bolus doses or 24-h infusions, escalating to a maximum dose of 2 mg (2×10^6 units) of IL-2. At the higher doses patients experienced acute-phase responses of rigors, pyrexia, lymphopenia and raised ACTH and cortisol levels; but no significant changes in clinical or immunological status were observed over the 4-week treatment period.[41,42] It was of interest that intralesional injection of JURKAT IL-2 (in doses of 10^4-10^5 units in 5% albumin) had no anti-tumour activity (M. T. Lotze, pers. comm. 1984).

When bacterial recombinant human IL-2 (rIL-2) became available (from Cetus), Lotze, Rosenberg and colleagues undertook an ascending dose bolus and continuous infusion study of intravenous rIL-2 in some 30 cancer patients, escalating to 30,000 U/kg rIL:hy2 thrice daily (bolus) or 3000 U/kg/h (infusion), usually over 14-21-day study periods.[43] Dose-limiting toxicity involved a generalised 'capillary leak syndrome' with extravascular fluid retention, hypotension and pulmonary, renal and hepatic dysfunction. During rIL-2 administration there was persistent and marked lympho-penia; however, on cessation of rIL-2 or on intermittent treatment, there was often a 'rebound' lymphocytosis of which 25-50% of the cells were Tac (IL-2 receptor) antigen positive. An initial search for evidence of tumour regression proved disappointing; but in a recent report, Lotze and colleagues have reported temporary tumour responses in three patients with disseminated melanoma and one with renal-cell carcinoma.[44] Maximum tolerated doses of rIL-2 given intraperitoneally were also studied (up to 3×10^5 U/kg thrice daily).[45] This regime was associated with the appearance of marked NK-cytotoxicity in peripheral blood, where appreciable serum levels of IL-2 were detected. One of seven advanced cancer patients demonstrated some regression of metastatic tumour; and all experienced major toxicity.[45]

Intravenous Administration of rIL-2 and Lymphokine-activated Killer Cells (LAK Cells)

Based upon synergy between rIL-2- and IL-2-activated syngeneic lymphocytes in inducing regression of murine tumours, Rosenberg and colleagues undertook extensive trials of this approach in advanced cancer patients. In 1985 these investigators reported temporary tumour regression in 11 of 25 patients with disseminated melanoma or renal-cell carcinoma given high-dose thrice daily bolus rIL-2 intravenously with infusions of rIL-2-activated autologous lymphocytes in a protocol designed to maintain killer-cell activity *in vivo.*[46] More recently the same workers reported the occurrence of complete or partial tumour responses of 6-22 months duration in 23 of 108 patients with disseminated tumour (mainly melanoma or renal-cell carcinoma) given a similar regime, which also induced major organ-system toxicity during rIL-2 administration.[47] A confirmatory study was reported by West and colleagues[48] who observed temporary tumour regression in 15 of 40 such patients given rIL-2 by continuous lower-dose intravenous infusion. Tumour responses were associated with good performance status, normal pre-study lymphocyte counts, and marked rIL-2-induced 'rebound' lymphocytosis: a notable feature of the constant-infusion approach was to reduce the total dose of rIL-2 and to reduce the occurrence of major toxicity associated with rIL-2/LAK-cell administration.[47]

Comment: the Pathophysiology of Host Responses to High-dose rIL-2

Whereas temporary regression of highly resistant tumours induced by high-dose rIL-2 or rIL-2/LAK-cell injection is gratifying, it must be conceded that the toxicity ensuing from such regimes has been very substantial, particularly in the more elderly patients or in those in poorer clinical state, in whom quality of remaining life is to be balanced against the uncertain benefits arising from temporary tumour regression. As patients develop raised serum levels of IFN-γ,[47] it is probable that other cytokines are also released into the vascular compartment. Such a patient would be expected to enter a state of persistent acute-phase reactivity and thereby to assume the haematological, endocrine, and metabolic features of response to persistent trauma or infection. Because these responses involve cascade effects on the lymphokine system with widespread activation of humoral, cellular and vascular mechanisms of inflammation, it is unlikely that their analysis will reveal a physiological role for IL-2 alone in host resistance to neoplasia. Accordingly studies of rIL-2 administered systemically as a single-lymphokine anti-cancer agent have demonstrated that if the only 'endpoint' is a 50% regression of measurable tumour, (a) unphysiological quantities of the lymphokine must be given; (b) currently available techniques demand that the IL-2 source is bacterial-recombinant; and (c) the response of patients to toxicological doses of 'foreign' (and hence immunoreactive) rIL-2 may be unrelated to the lymphokine activity of the molecule.

LYMPHOKINES IN CANCER: TACTICS AND STRATEGY
(TABLE 2)

To date, with many recombinant lymphokines eagerly awaiting individual investigation, the single-lymphokine approach to tumour regression, illustrated by experience of systemic rIL-2, clearly leaves much to be desired. There are at least three reasons why the choice of tactics may be inappropriate for the occasion. First, it is unlikely that any single lymphokine regime will cure cancer: for the host response to cancer (and its treatment) involves more than just the immune system, and different patients will be in different states of pathophysiological perturbation. Second, it may be unrealistic to expect that lymphokines will act as if they were cytotoxic drugs: thus a 50% shrinkage in apparent tumor load may be an unrealistic endpoint.[49,50] It would seem more appropriate to devise therapeutic tactics which would optimize the host's metabolic, endocrine, haematological and immunological status and thus promote the ability to tolerate neoplastic disease, to tolerate conventional treatment modalities, and to resist their depressant effects upon host-defence mechanisms.

TABLE 2 illustrates growing evidence of synergistic interactions between lymphokines in effecting and regulating immunological reactions (the phenomena have been itemized as such for descriptive purposes only). Strategic considerations of study design[51,52] will surely take advantage of both synergy and pleiotropism amongst lymphokines. The value of biological response modifiers as a fourth modality[14] in the management of human cancer may lie in helping the host to live with both his disease and his oncologist; and in encouraging assessment of the quality of life as an important criterion of host response.[53] The remarkable diversity of physiological phenomena in which lymphokines have now been implicated places their investigation in the forefront of biomedical research. It may be predicted that further knowledge of the integrative actions of lymphokines[54] will reveal their therapeutic potential in maintaining physiological homeostasis, not only in cancer, but in other disorders which characteristically accompany the aging process.

ACKNOWLEDGMENTS

We thank our many collaborators on publications to which we have referred.

TABLE 2. Physiological Illustrations of Lymphokine Synergism

(Immuno-) Physiological Phenomenon	Predominant Biological Activities of Lymphokines Involved	Illustrative Lymphokines and Synergy
Allergic inflammation Delayed hypersensitivity, granuloma formation, allograft rejection, graft-v-host reactions . . .	'Inflammatory' (complex), chemotactic, cytotoxic, migration-inhibitory, macrophage-aggregating, fibroblast-activating, endothelial cell-activating . . .	SIF, ChF's TNFβ, TNFβ MaggF, FAF IL-1, ECAF, etc. . . .
Protective cellular immunity Restriction of tumour growth and parasite multiplication, destruction of parasitized host cells, activation of host macrophages . . .	Cytotoxic, macrophage-activating, chemotactic, migration-inhibitory, interferon-like, colony-stimulating . . .	IL-1, IL-2, IFN-γ, MIF, LIF, GM-CSF, ChF's, non γ MAF's, TNFα, TNFβ, etc. . . .
'Intrinsic' immunoregulation Control of lymphocyte compartmentation, cellular cooperation during immune induction, physiological suppression of immune responses, non-specific Ig production, maintenance of diversity despite phenotypic restriction . . .	Lymph node activating (complex) lymphocyte-mitogenic (complex) macrophage-activating lymphocyte and macrophage differentiation factors, endothelial-activating factors, helper factors, suppressor factors, colony-stimulating . . .	LNAF (complex); IL-1, IL-2, MAF's, MIF's, TsF's, CSF's, etc. . . .
'Extrinsic' immunoregulation Interactions between immune and neuroendocrine systems; immunological activation of haemopoiesis; interactions between immune system and mesenchymal (connective) tissue; immunological activation of acute-phase and other systemic 'defence' responses . . .	Endogenous pyrogen; leucocyte endogenous mediator; catabolin; colony-stimulating factors; other haemopoietic growth factors; glucocorticoid increasing factor; steroid-modulating factor . . .	IL-1, IL-2, IL-3, GM-CSF, G-CSF, M-CSF, OAF, GIF, etc. . . .

REFERENCES

1. BURNET, F. M. 1970. Immunological Surveillance. Pergamon Press, Ltd. Oxford.
2. MIHICH, E. 1986. Future perspectives for biological response modifiers: a viewpoint. Seminars in Oncology *XIII* (2): 234-254.
3. MORLEY, J., R. A. WOLSTENCROFT & D. C. DUMONDE. 1973. The measurement of lymphokines. *In* Handbook of Experimental Immunology. D. M. Weir, Ed. Second Edition. 28.1-26. Blackwell Scientific Publications. Oxford.
4. BURNET, F. M. 1968. Evolution of the immune response in vertebrates. Nature **218:** 426-428.
5. DUMONDE, D. C., R. A. WOLSTENCROFT, G. S. PANAYI, M. MATTHEW, J. MORLEY & W. T. HOWSON. 1969. 'Lymphokines': non-antibody mediators of cellular immunity generated by lymphocyte activation. Nature **224:** 38-42.
6. COHEN, S., E. PICK & J. J. OPPENHEIM, Eds. 1979. Biology of the Lymphokines. Academic Press. New York.
7. OPPENHEIM, J. J. & GERY, I. 1982. Interleukin-1 is more than an interleukin. Immunol. Today **3:** 113-119.
8. WEBB, D.R., C. PIERCE & S. COHEN, Eds. 1987. Molecular Basis of Lymphokine Action. Humana Press, Inc. New Jersey.
9. DUMONDE, D. C., R. H. KELLY & R. A. WOLSTENCROFT. 1973. Molecular pharmacology of cell-mediated immunity. *In* Microenvironmental Aspects of Immunity. B. D. Jankovic & K. Isakovic, Eds. 705-711. Plenum Press. New York.
10. SMITH, K. A. 1986. Lymphokines as growth factors: interleukin-2 as a prototype lymphocytotrophic hormone. *In* Progress in Immunology VI. B. Cinader & R. G. Miller, Eds. 440-448. Academic Press, Inc. Orlando, FL.
11. POWANDA, M. C., 1985. The role of interleukin-1 in homeostasis. *In* The Physiologic, Metabolic and Immunologic Actions of Interleukin-1. M. J. Kluger, J. J. Oppenheim & M. C. Powanda, Eds 535-546. Alan Liss, Inc. New York.
12. HAMBLIN, A. S., R. A. WOLSTENCROFT, D. C. DUMONDE, F. C. DEN HOLLANDER, A. H. W. SCHUURS, B. M. BACKHOUSE, D. O' CONNELL & F. PARADINAS. 1978. The potential of lymphokines in the treatment of cancer. Dev. Biol. Standard. **39:** 335-345.
13. GOLDSTEIN, A. L. & M. A. CHIRIGOS, Eds. 1981. Lymphokines and thymic hormones: their potential utilization in cancer therapeutics. Raven Press. New York.
14. HERSH, E. M. 1982. Perspectives for immunological and biological therapeutic intervention in human cancer. *In* Immunological Approaches to Cancer Therapeutics. E. Mihich, Ed.: 505-540. John Wiley. New York.
15. PULLEY, MELANIE, S., V. NAGENDRAN, J. M. EDWARDS & D. C. DUMONDE. 1986. Intravenous, intralesional and endolymphatic administration of lymphokines in human cancer. Lymphokine Res. **5** (Suppl. 1): 157-163.
16. PULLEY, MELANIE S., V. NAGENDRAN, D. C. DUMONDE, A. FLECK & B. M. SOUTHCOTT. 1985. Skin reactions induced by two types of lymphokine preparation showing relations to clinical status and the use of a standard preparation. *In* Cellular and Molecular Biology of the Lymphokines. C. Sorg & A.-L. Schimpl, Eds.: 785-790. Academic Press. New York.
17. DUMONDE, D. C., MELANIE S. PULLEY, F. J. PARADINAS, B. M. SOUTHCOTT, D. O'-CONNELL, M. R. G. ROBINSON, F. DEN HOLLANDER & A. H. SCHUURS. 1982. Histological features of skin reactions to lymphoid cell line lymphokine in patients with advanced cancer. J. Pathol. **138:** 289-308.
18. NAGENDRAN, V., B. M. SOUTHCOTT, MELANIE S. PULLEY & D. C. DUMONDE. 1987. Could a single lymphokine skin test replace a battery of delayed hypersensitivity tests in the immunological assessment of cancer patients? Abstr. 5th International Lymphokine Workshop, Clearwater. Lymphokine Res. **6** (1): no. 1510.
19. NAGRENDRAN, V., M. A. MYERS, A. FLECK, MELANIE S. PULLEY & D. C. DUMONDE. 1986. Does protracted IL-1 production cause a depression of cell-mediated immunity? *In* Marker Proteins in Inflammation. J. Bienvenu, J. A. Grimaud & P. Laurent, Eds. Vol. **3:** 55-58. Walter de Gruyter & Co. Berlin.

20. PARADINAS, F. J., B. M. SOUTHCOTT, D. O'CONNELL, F. C. DEN HOLLANDER, A. H. SCHUURS, MELANIE S. PULLEY & D. C. DUMONDE. 1982. Changes induced by local injection of human lymphoid cell line lymphokine into dermal metastases of breast carcinoma: a light and electron microscopical study. J. Pathol. **138**: 309-323.

21. PULLEY, MELANIE S., J. M. EDWARDS, R. A. WOLSTENCROFT & D. C. DUMONDE. 1987. Endolymphatic administration of buffy-coat interleukin in patients with malignant melanoma. Abstr. 5th International Lymphokine Workshop, Clearwater. Lymphokine Res. **6** (1): no. 1509.

22. EDWARDS, J. M. & P. J. PHEILS. 1978. Endolymphatic isotope and BCG in the management of malignant melanoma. Austr. N. Z. J. Surg. **48**: 40-48.

23. KELLY, R. H., R. A. WOLSTENCROFT, D. C. DUMONDE & B. M. BALFOUR. 1972. Role of lymphocyte activation products (LAP) in cell-mediated immunity. II. Effects of lymphocyte activation products on lymph node architecture and evidence for peripheral release of LAP following antigenic stimulation. Clin. Exp. Immunol. **10**: 49-65.

24. KELLY, R. H. & R. A. WOLSTENCROFT. 1974. Germinal centre proliferation in response to mitogenic lymphokines. Clin. Exp. Immunol. **18**: 321-336.

25. KELLY, R. H., V. S. HARVEY, T. E. SADLER & D. C. DUMONDE. 1975. Accelerated cytodifferentiation of antibody-secreting cells in guinea pig lymph nodes stimulated by sheep erthrocytes and lymphokines. Clin. Exp. Immunol. **21**: 141-154.

26. TURK, J. L. 1980. Delayed Hypersensitivity. 3rd edition. North-Holland. Amsterdam.

27. HOON, D. S. B., R. J. BOWKER & A. J. COCHRAN. 1987. Suppressor cell activity in melanoma-draining lymph nodes. Cancer Res. **47**: 1529-1533.

28. DUMONDE, D. C., MELANIE S. PULLEY, V. NAGENDRAN, B. M. SOUTHCOTT, E. VAN VLIET, D. REITSMA & F. DEN HOLLANDER. 1987. A controlled follow-up study of human lymphoblastoid cell line lymphokine in patients with advanced cancer. Abstr. 5th International Lymphokine Workshop, Clearwater. Lymphokine Res. **6** (1): no. 1501.

29. DUMONDE, D. C., MELANIE S. PULLEY, A. S. HAMBLIN, A. K. SINGH, B. M. SOUTHCOTT, D. O'CONNELL, F. PARADINAS, M. R. G. ROBINSON, C. A. RIGBY, F. C. DEN HOLLANDER, A. SCHUURS, H. VERHEUL & E. VAN VLIET. 1981. Short-term and long-term adminstration of lymphoblastoid cell line lymphokine (LCL-LK) to patients with advanced cancer. *In* Lymphokines and Thymic Hormones: Their Potential Utilization in Cancer Therapeutics. A. L. Goldstein & M. A. Chirigos, Eds. 301-318. Raven Press. New York.

30. PULLEY, MELANIE S., D. C. DUMONDE, G. CARTER, B. MULLER, A. FLECK, B. M. SOUTHCOTT & F. DEN HOLLANDER. 1982. Hormonal, haematological and acute-phase protein responses of advanced cancer patients to the intravenous injection of lymphoid cell lymphokine (LCL-LK). *In* Human Lymphokines: the Biological Immune Response Modifiers. A Khan & N. O. Hill, Eds. 651-665. Academic Press. New York.

31. PULLEY, MELANIE S., D. C. DUMONDE, G. CARTER, B. MULLER, B. M. SOUTHCOTT & F. C. DEN HOLLANDER. 1983. Lymphokines as mediators of extrinsic immunoregulatory circuits. *In* Interleukins, Lymphokines and Cytokines. J. J. Oppenheim & S. Cohen, Eds. 723-730. Academic Press. New York.

32. SOUTHCOTT, B. M., D. C. DUMONDE, MELANIE S. PULLEY, E. VAN VLIET, F. C. DEN HOLLANDER & A. SCHUURS. 1982. Systemic lymphokine treatment of selected cancer patients. *In* Human Lymphokines: the Biological Immune Response Modifiers. A. Khan & N. O. Hill, Eds. 641-650. Academic Press. New York.

33. REYNOLDS, R. D., A. KHOJASTEH, B. W. PAPERMASTER & J. E. MCENTIRE. 1986. Phase I clincial trial of MAF-containing preparation of RPMI 1788 B-cell human lymphoblastoid lymphokine in advanced cancer patients. Lymphokine Res. **5** (Suppl. 1): 165-170.

34. GORDON, A. J. & A. KOJ, Eds. 1985. The Acute Phase Response to Injury and Infection. Elsevier. Amsterdam.

35. DUFF, G. W. & S. K. DURUM. 1983. The pyrogenic and mitogenic actions of Interleukin-1 are related. Nature **304**: 449-451.

36. FLECK, A. & M. A. MYERS. 1985. Diagnostic and prognostic signficance of the acute phase proteins. *In* The Acute Phase Response to Injury and Infection. A. H. Gordon & A. Kog, Eds. 249-271. Elsevier. Amsterdam.

37. MERTLESMANN, R. & K. WELTE. 1984. Human Interleukin-2. *In* Immune Suppression and Modulation. M. S. Mitchell & J. L. Fahey, Eds. Clinics in Immunology and Allergy. Vol. 4 (2): 393-413. W. B. Saunders Co. London.
38. GRIMM, E. A. & S. A. ROSENBERG. 1984. The human lymphokine-activated killer cell phenomenon. Lymphokines **9:** 279-312.
39. HERBERMAN, R. B. 1984. Summary: potential of Interleukin-2 for the therapy of cancer. J. Biol. Response Modifiers **3:** 527-532.
40. WELTE, K., C. Y. WANG, R. MERTLESMANN, S. VENUTA, S. P. FELDMAN & M. A. S. MOORE. 1982. Purification of human interleukin-2 to apparent homogeneity and its molecular heterogeneity. J. Exp. Med. **156:** 454-464.
41. LOTZE, M. T., R. J. ROBB, S. O. SHARROW, L. W. FRANA & S. A. ROSENBERG. 1984. Systemic administration of interleukin-2 in humans. J. Biol. Response Modifiers **3:** 475-482.
42. LOTZE, M. T. & S. A. ROSENBERG. 1985. Treatment of tumor patients with purified human interleukin-2. *In* Cellular and Molecular Biology of the Lymphokines. C. Sorg & A.-L. Schimpl, Eds. 711-721. Academic Press. New York.
43. LOTZE, M. T. & S. A. ROSENBERG. 1986. Protocol design for lymphokine testing in studies of human cancer. Lymphokine Res. **5** (Suppl. 1): 177-181.
44. LOTZE, M. T., A. E. CHANG, C. A. SEIPP, C. SIMPSON, J. T. VETTO & S. A. ROSENBERG. 1986. High-dose recombinant interleukin-2 in the treatment of patients with disseminated cancer. J. Am. Med. Assoc. **256:** 3117-3124.
45. LOTZE, M. T., M. C. CUSTER & S. A. ROSENBERG. 1986. Intraperitoneal administration of interleukin-2 in patients with cancer. Arch. Surg. **121:** 1373-1379.
46. ROSENBERG, S. A., M. T. LOTZE, L. M. MUUL, S. LEITMAN, A. E. CHANG, S. E. ETTINGHAUSEN, Y. L. MATORY, J. M. SKIBBER, E. SHILONI, J. T. VETTO, C. A. SEIPP, C. SIMPSON & C. M. REICHERT. 1985. Observations on the systemic administration of autologous lymphokine-activated killer cells and recombinant interleukin-2 to patients with metastatic cancer. N. Engl. J. Med. **313:** 1485-1492.
47. ROSENBERG, S. A., M. T. LOTZE, L. M. MUUL *et al.* 1987. A progress report on the treatment of 157 patients with advanced cancer using lymphokine-activated killer cells and interleukin-2 or high-dose interleukin-2 alone. N. Engl. J. Med. **316:** 889-897.
48. WEST, W. H., K. W. TAUER, J. R. YANNELLI, G. D. MARSHALL, D. W. ORR, G. B. THURMAN & R. K. OLDHAM. 1987. Constant-infusion recombinant interleukin-2 in adoptive immunotherapy of advanced cancer. N. Engl. J. Med. **316:** 898-905.
49. CARTER, S. K. 1980. Biological response modifying agents: what is an appropriate Phase I-II strategy? Cancer Immunol. Immunother. **8:** 207-210.
50. OLDHAM, R. K. 1981. Biological response modifer therapy—an overview. Cancer Bull. **33:** 244-250.
51. DUMONDE, D. C., MELANIE S. PULLEY, B. M. SOUTHCOTT & F. C. DEN HOLLANDER. 1983. Effects of lymphokines in tumour-bearing patients: clinical and laboratory studies. *In* Cancer Management: Proc. 13th Int. Cancer Congress, Seattle. E. A. Mirand, W. B. Hutchinson & E. Mihich, Eds. 83-94. Alan Liss, Inc. New York.
52. DUMONDE, D. C., MELANIE S. PULLEY, A. S. HAMBLIN, B. M. SOUTHCOTT & F. C. DEN HOLLANDER. 1984. The response of tumour-bearing patients to the injection of lymphoid cell line lymphokine. *In* Thymic Hormones and Lymphokines. A. L. Goldstein, Ed. 507-517. Plenum Press. New York.
53. CLARK, A. & L. J. FALLOWFIELD. 1986. Quality of life measurements in patients with malignant disease: a review. J. R. Soc. Med. (London). **79:** 165-169.
54. DUMONDE, D. C., A. S. HAMBLIN, E. KASP, MELANIE S. PULLEY & R. A. WOLSTENCROFT. 1983. Lymphokines and the lymphoendothelial system: an illustration of immunoregulatory integration. *In* Immunoregulation. N. Fabris. E. Garaci, J. Hadden & N. A. Mitchison, Eds. 177-199. Plenum Press. New York.

Relation between Lymphocyte Subpopulations and Pineal Function in Patients with Early or Metastatic Cancer

P. LISSONI, S. BARNI, G. TANCINI, S. CRISPINO,
F. PAOLOROSSI, G. CATTANEO,[a] V. LUCINI,[a]
M. MARIANI,[a] D. ESPOSTI,[b] G. ESPOSTI,[a]
AND F. FRASCHINI [a]

Division of Radiation Oncology
San Gerardo Hospital
Monza, Milan, Italy

[a]*Chair of Chemotherapy*
Faculty of Medicine
University of Milan
Milan, Italy

[b]*Second Institute of Human Physiology*
University of Milan
Milan, Italy

INTRODUCTION

Only a few studies have been carried out to clarify the role played by the pineal gland in the regulation of immunity.

The recent demonstration of the existence of a connection between the neuroendocrine system and immune functions prompted researchers to take into consideration the possible importance of the pineal gland as a regulator of the immune system, on the basis of its well documented role in modulating the psychoneuroendocrine balance, particularly the opioid tone,[1] whose relationship with immune activities is known.[2]

The pineal gland seems to exert a stimulatory action on thymic growth, since the administration of pineal extracts may determine hyperplasia of the thymus gland,[3] while pinealectomy induces thymic atrophy;[4] moreover, blood levels of thymic hormones[5] and melatonin,[6] the most investigated pineal factor, both decrease with the onset of puberty; finally, circulating levels of melatonin[7] and thymosin alpha-1[8] are concomitantly high during the night. In contrast, no data are available about the possible influence of thymus on the pineal function; preliminary results seem to suggest an inhibitory role of thymic hormones on melatonin secretion, and this finding could lead us to the hypothesis that a feed back mechanism may exist between the pineal and the thymus glands.

Pinealectomy reduces some immune reactions in the rat,[9] while the administration of pineal extracts has been seen to enhance antibody production in mice.[10] These data, however, are very contradictory, since other authors[11] did not observe any significant change in immune reactions after pinealectomy.

Melatonin is able to stimulate NK activity in healthy humans,[12] while preliminary results seem to suggest it has no effects *in vitro;* similarly, melatonin does not influence lymphocyte subpopulations *in vitro.* Because of the absence of melatonin effects on lymphocyte functions *in vitro,* it may be hypothesized that the pineal hormone modulates immunity through other mechanisms, particularly the opioid tone; in fact, it has been demonstrated that the stimulatory action of melatonin on immune reactions may be abolished by means of the administration of an opioid antagonist, such as naltrexone.[13] Besides, melatonin seems to be also directly active on granulocytes and monocytes, since it appeared to stimulate granulo-macrophage precursor proliferation[14] *in vitro.* Similarly, melatonin may directly stimulate trombocytopoiesis[15] *in vitro.*

Even if contradictory results exist, at present it is possible to conclude that the pineal gland does not seem to be important in the regulation of immunity in basal conditions, whereas it may play a role in maintaining an effective immune response when the immunological system is stimulated,[13] since in this last case on inhibition of melatonin secretion leads to an immunodepression. The effects of the pineal gland on immunity described by various authors are summarized in TABLE 1.

No relevant data are available up to now about the pineal involvement in influencing immune functions in pathological conditions. We have carried out a study in order to draw some preliminary conclusions on the melatonin-lymphocyte interaction in human neoplastic diseases.

MATERIALS AND METHODS

Two separate studies were carried out.

In a first study, we evaluated 27 patients of both sexes (7 males and 20 females), aged between 38 and 74 years (mean age 49.9 ± 8.7 yrs), with histologically proven neoplastic disease. Six patients were suffering from colorectal cancer, 4 from lung cancer (3 of these with epidermoid and the other with small cell carcinoma), 1 from cancer affecting the pancreas, and the other 16 from breast cancer. All breast-cancer women had been previously treated surgically with radical mastectomy. Lung-cancer patients received chemotherapy, colorectal-cancer patients surgery plus chemotherapy, while only the patient affected by cancer of the pancreas had never been treated. Patients under chemotherapy were studied at least for 20 days after the last administration of cytotoxic drugs. Moreover, 14 patients were without metastases, whereas the other 13 had a metastatic disease. As controls, 46 healthy subjects of both sexes and within the same age range were included in the study. From each subject or patient, venous blood samples were collected during the morning (9:00-11:00 a.m.). Melatonin serum levels were measured by a RIA method after an extraction with diethylether using commercially available kits (EuroDiagnostics, Apeldoorn, Holland). Melatonin serum levels in patients were considered as elevated when higher than 2 SD in comparison to the controls.

TABLE 1. Observations on the Pineal-immunity Relationship in Literature

Authors	Years	
Jankovic et al.[9]	1970	Pinealectomy reduces some immune functions in rat
Milcu and Potop[3]	1973	The administration of pineal extracts determines thymic hyperplasia
Csaba and Barath[4]	1975	Pinealectomy induced thymic atrophy
Belokrylov et al.[10]	1976	Pineal extracts enhance antibody production in mice
Rella and Lapin[11]	1976	Pinealectomy has no significant effects on immunity in rats
Lissoni et al.[12]	1986	Melatonin i.v. infusion enhances NK activity in healthy humans
Maestroni et al.[21]	1986	Melatonin may reverse the immunodepression induced by corticosteroids
Villa et al.[14]	1986	Melatonin stimulates granulo-macrophage precursor cells in vitro
Maestroni et al.[21]	1986	Chemical pinealectomy induces immunodepression
Lissoni et al. (unpublished data)	1987	Melatonin does not influence NK activity and lymphocyte subgroups in vitro

B lymphocytes, total T lymphocytes (T3), T helper/inducer (T4) and T suppressor/cytotoxic (T8) were detected with a flow cytometer using monoclonal antibodies supplied by Ortho (Milan, Italy). Moreover, T helper/suppressor ratios (T4/T8) were also determined.

In a second study, we evaluated the effects of a prolonged administration of melatonin on lymphocyte subpopulations in a group of pretreated metastatic cancer patients. The study included 8 patients (4 males and 4 females) with a mean age of 58.9 ± 9.9 years. Four patients had colorectal cancer, 2 lung cancer, and 2 a cancer of the pancreas. In all patients conventional antineoplastic therapies had failed, and the disease had rapidly progressed. Melatonin was given intramuscularly at a daily dose of 20 mg at 3:00 p.m. for 2 months. Melatonin was supplied by Biosynth (Staad, Switzerland). The clinical protocol was explained in each patient, and an informed consent was obtained. In each patient, venous blood samples were drawn during the morning (9:00-11:00) before and after the 2 months of melatonin treatment in order to determine B lymphocytes, T3, T4, and T8 and T4/T8 ratios. Results were reported as mean ± SD, and the data were analyzed by Student's t test.

RESULTS

Relationship between Serum Levels of Melatonin and Lymphocyte Subpopulations. Individual values of melatonin and lymphocyte sub-set cells observed in the 27 cancer patients are listed in TABLE 2, while TABLE 3 shows mean serum levels of melatonin and the mean percentage of lymphocyte subpopulations found in controls and oncological patients.

Melatonin serum concentrations were high in 10 cancer patients, and within the normal range in the other 17 cases. There were no significant differences in B, T3, T4 and T8 mean percentages, and in T4/T8 mean ratios either between metastatic and nonmetastatic cancer patients, or between patients with normal or high melatonin serum levels. Metastatic cancer patients showed lower T4/T8 mean ratios than patients who had no metastases, without, however, statistically significant differences.

Effects of Melatonin Treatment on Lymphocyte Subpopulations. Individual and mean values of lymphocyte subpopulations observed before and after melatonin therapy in 8 cancer patients are reported in TABLE 4. None of the immunological parameters showed significant differences after melatonin therapy in comparison with the mean values seen before treatment. In one patient only, who was suffering from lung cancer, a decrease of T4/T8 and an increase of T8 percentage higher than 50% were seen after melatonin treatment. No relevant variations in any immune parameter were seen in the other 7 cases. An evident improvement of the performance status and of the quality of life was obtained in 5/8 patients treated with melatonin. Moreover, a weight increase accounting for more than 10% was achieved in 3/8 cancer patients. Nevertheless, despite the clinical improvement found in most cases, no objective tumor regression was observed in any patient. In the only subject in whom T8 lymphocytes enhanced after melatonin treatment, the disease proved to be stabilized, while in the other 7 patients it progressed.

TABLE 2. Individual Values of Serum Melatonin and Lymphocyte Subpopulations in 27 Oncological Patients[a]

Cases	Sex	Age	Tumor	TNM	MLT (pg/ml)	Lymphocytes/mm^3	B	T3 %	T4	T8	T4/T8 Ratio
1	F	39	Breast cancer	T2N1M0	34	1.460	18.4	65.2	46.0	20.3	2.3
2	F	40	Breast cancer	T2N2M0	26	1.524	18.3	68.3	43.0	24.1	1.8
3	F	55	Breast cancer	T2N1M0	32	1.812	12.1	84.5	50.9	36.5	1.4
4	F	56	Breast cancer	T2N1M0	24	2.336	12.8	61.5	32.3	26.1	1.2
5	F	41	Breast cancer	T1N0M0	25	2.178	18.8	72.6	46.6	26.2	1.8
6	F	44	Breast cancer	T2N2M0	38	2.010	12.7	66.4	42.1	28.4	1.5
7	F	46	Breast cancer	T2N1M0	32	2.037	12.6	66.7	43.1	27.1	1.6
8	F	43	Breast cancer	T1N1M0	21	2.056	15.2	71.2	42.1	29.3	1.4
9	F	47	Breast cancer	T1N1M0	31	1.730	13.2	76.1	48.5	33.7	1.4
10	F	49	Breast cancer	T2N1M0	42	1.614	24.6	79.2	47.5	31.3	1.5
11	F	48	Breast cancer	T2N2M0	24	1.776	14.9	68.9	34.9	33.1	1.1
12	F	47	Breast cancer	T×N×M1	16	1.986	16.2	64.6	41.8	24.7	1.7
13	F	45	Breast cancer	T×N×M1	26	1.416	13.2	59.2	33.8	29.3	1.1
14	F	42	Breast cancer	T×N×M1	31	1.848	18.6	69.1	36.9	36.7	1.0
15	F	38	Breast cancer	T×N×M1	14	1.914	27.7	73.0	39.7	37.8	1.1
16	F	46	Breast cancer	T×N×M1	27	1.292	13.4	67.3	27.6	39.8	0.7
17	F	52	Lung cancer	T3N2M1	13	1.479	9.9	77.9	39.5	24.9	1.6
18	M	74	Lung cancer	T2N1M1	31	1.144	14.1	70.9	41.6	25.3	1.6
19	M	58	Lung cancer	T3N2M1	28	1.692	12.5	72.2	38.9	37.3	1.0
20	M	51	Lung cancer	T2N1M1	10	1.530	13.4	72.8	37.2	39.1	0.9
21	M	58	Colorectal cancer	T×N×M1	24	1.575	16.6	73.2	48.7	33.5	1.5
22	M	56	Colorectal cancer	T×N×M0	26	1.344	20.5	66.8	40.2	25.2	1.6
23	M	62	Colorectal cancer	T×N×M1	16	1.671	19.7	72.6	47.3	21.5	2.2
24	M	54	Colorectal cancer	T×N×M0	33	1.675	16.8	75.1	50.9	22.9	2.2
25	F	66	Colorectal cancer	T×N×M1	11	1.860	27.8	65.1	36.7	27.8	1.4
26	F	43	Colorectal cancer	T×N×M1	32	1.140	18.1	74.6	41.4	28.3	1.5
27	F	65	Cancer of the pancreas	T3N1M0	24	1.418	14.2	66.9	47.8	22.4	2.1

[a] MLT: melatonin; B: B lymphocytes; T3: total T lymphocytes; T4: T helper/inducer; T8: T suppressor/cytotoxic.

TABLE 3. Melatonin Serum Levels and Lymphocyte Subpopulations Values ± SD in Healthy Subjects and Cancer Patients[a]

Cases	n	MLT pg/ml	Lymphocytes/ mm^3	B	T3	T4	T8	T4/T8 Ratio
					%			
Healthy subjects	46	16 ± 7	2135 ± 497	15.9 ± 3.6	73.8 ± 7.9	46.7 ± 6.7	25.3 ± 5.1	1.8 ± 0.5
Cancer patients	27	26 ± 8	1686 ± 305	16.6 ± 4.6	70.6 ± 5.6	41.8 ± 5.9	29.2 ± 5.2	1.5 ± 0.4
Patients without metastases	14	29 ± 6	1784 ± 303	16.1 ± 3.6	70.8 ± 6.2	43.9 ± 5.6	27.4 ± 4.7	1.6 ± 0.3
Patients with metastases	13	21 ± 8	1576 ± 280	17.0 ± 5.5	70.2 ± 5.1	39.4 ± 5.3	31.3 ± 6.3	1.3 ± 0.4
Patients with high melatonin	10	34 ± 4	1661 ± 339	16.2 ± 4.0	72.8 ± 6.4	44.9 ± 4.6	28.9 ± 5.6	1.6 ± 0.4
Patients with normal melatonin	17	21 ± 6	1708 ± 305	16.7 ± 5.1	69.2 ± 4.8	39.9 ± 5.8	29.5 ± 6.1	1.4 ± 0.4

[a] MLT: melatonin; B: B lymphocytes; T3: total T lymphocytes; T4: T helper/inducer; T8: T suppressor-cytotoxic.

TABLE 4. Leukocytes and Lymphocyte Subpopulations before and after Melatonin Treatment in 8 Metastatic Cancer Patients[a]

Cases	Tumor		Leukocytes/mm³	% Leukocytes N	E	B	M	L	Total T Lymphocytes (T3)	% Lymphocytes B Lymphocytes	T Helper/Inducer (T4)	T Suppressor/Cytotoxic (T8)	T4/T8 Ratio
1	Colon	B	4.500	55	6	0	4	35	73.2	16.6	48.7	33.5	1.5
		A	6.400	75	3	0	1	21	66.8	20.5	40.2	25.2	1.6
2	Colon	B	4.900	49	9	0	9	33	72.6	19.7	47.3	21.5	2.2
		A	6.700	69	4	0	2	25	75.1	16.9	50.9	22.9	2.2
3	Colon	B	6.000	66	3	0	0	31	65.1	27.8	36.7	27.8	1.3
		A	9.500	65	3	0	0	32	64.2	24.3	37.4	26.4	1.4
4	Colon	B	3.800	65	2	0	3	30	74.6	18.1	41.4	28.3	1.5
		A	9.100	70	0	0	3	27	71.3	17.5	40.2	27.1	1.5
5	Lung	B	10.400	79	2	0	7	11	70.9	14.1	42.6	21.9	1.9
		A	9.400	79	3	0	0	18	72.2	12.5	37.2	39.1	0.9
6	Lung	B	5.100	67	2	0	2	29	77.9	9.9	39.5	24.9	1.6
		A	6.800	77	1	0	0	22	73.2	13.2	38.1	22.4	1.7
7	Pancreas	B	4.800	63	3	0	3	31	66.6	14.6	47.5	22.3	2.1
		A	7.100	72	2	0	2	24	65.7	13.8	38.6	28.4	1.3
8	Pancreas	B	5.300	64	1	0	1	34	66.4	11.5	41.5	23.2	1.8
		A	6.900	73	1	0	0	26	68.3	15.9	42.3	25.1	1.7
$\bar{x} \pm$ SD		B	5.600 ± 2.039	63 ± 9	4 ± 2	0 ± 0	4 ± 3	29 ± 8	70.9 ± 4.5	16.5 ± 5.6	43.1 ± 4.3	24.4 ± 4.2	1.7 ± 0.3
		A	7.737 ± 1.340	73 ± 5	2 ± 1	0 ± 0	1 ± 1	24 ± 4	69.6 ± 3.9	16.8 ± 3.9	40.6 ± 4.5	27.1 ± 5.3	1.6 ± 0.4

[a] B: before; A: after; N: neutrophils; E: eosinophils; B: basophils; M: monocytes; L: lymphocytes.

DISCUSSION

The present study allows us to draw some preliminary conclusions concerning the relationship between the pineal and lumphocyte functions in human neoplasms. The importance of this investigation is justified because both pineal activity[16] and lymphocyte subpopulations[17] have been seen to be altered in patients with cancer.

These preliminary results seem to exclude the existence of an influence of melatonin, the most known pineal hormone, on lymphocyte functions in human neoplasms, since no differences were found between oncological patients with high and normal melatonin blood levels, and moreover, no evident variations in lymphocyte subgroups were achieved after a prolonged administration of the pineal hormone. Nevertheless, it must be remarked that a single determination of melatonin blood concentrations and lymphocyte subpopulations could not be enough to conclude that there is no relationship between the pineal function and T4/T8 ratios, which represent one of the most important immunological parameters for evaluating the status of the immune system in human cancer.[17] Moreover, on the basis of the well documented existence of a circadian variation both in melatonin levels[7] and in lymphocyte subpopulations,[18] an investigation over a 24-hour period would be more appropriate.

Therefore, longitudinal studies, by simultaneously monitoring melatonin levels and lymphocyte variations during the day in relation to the clinical course of the neoplastic disease, will be needed to further clarify, if there is an influence of the pineal hormone on lymphocyte functions in cancer. Moreover, other more sensitive measurements, such as interleukin-2 production in association with a clinical study of the pineal activity, will be required to draw definite conclusions on the pineal-immune interactions in cancer.

As far as the effects of melatonin treatment in advanced untreatable cancer patients are concerned, this study shows that a stable disease was seen in the only patient in whom T8 lymphocytes rose after therapy, while in the all other cases, in whom lymphocyte subpopulations did not change after melatonin administration, a progressive disease was observed. At present, however, it is not possible to establish if T8 increase is due to melatonin treatment or to the clinical course of the neoplastic disease itself; similarly, we cannot establish if T8 rise represents an undesirable effect or a favorable clinical prognostic sign in response to melatonin treatment, since both suppressor and cytotoxic T lymphocytes are included in T8 sub-set cells, the suppressor cells resulting from an inhibitory effect and the cytotoxic ones from a stimulatory action on the host immune response against cancer. Therefore, further studies, by using other monoclonal antibodies in order to be able to distinguish suppressor from cytotoxic T lymphocytes, will be required to clarify which lymphocyte subgroup, if any, if affected by melatonin. Moreover, on the basis of the demonstrated importance of lymphokine-activated killer (LAK) cells, which recently have been reported to be capable of inducing tumor regression in metastatic cancer patients,[19] it would be very interesting to evaluate if melatonin may be able to stimulate this type of cells.

Finally, this study demonstrates that melatonin can play a role in improving the performance status and in counteracting the neoplastic cachexia in advanced oncological patients, despite its apparent lack of effect on tumor growth. Since neoplastic cachexia seems to be due to an hyperproduction of tumor necrosis factor (TNF),[20] this observation leads us to hypothesize that melatonin is effective in decreasing TNF secretion and/or in antagonizing its activity.

SUMMARY

It has been demonstrated that melatonin and other pineal hormones play a role in the neuroendocrine control of immunity.

Anomalies of both pineal and immune functions have been reported in cancer. Pineal and lymphocyte functions, however, have never been simultaneously evaluated in oncologic patients.

This preliminary study was carried out in order to analyze the melatonin-lymphocyte relationship in human neoplasms.

In a first investigation, we evaluated melatonin serum levels and lymphocyte subpopulations on venous blood samples collected during the morning from 46 healthy controls and from 27 cancer patients, 13 of whom had metastases, while the other 14 were without metastases. Moreover, melatonin levels were high in 10 oncological patients and within the normal range in the other 17 cases. B lymphocyte (B), total T lymphocyte (T3), T helper/inducer (T4) and T suppressor/cytotoxic (T8) mean percentages and T4/T8 mean ratios did not significantly differ, either between patients with high and normal melatonin levels, or between metastatic and nonmetastatic cancer patients.

In a second study, we evaluated the effects of a prolonged treatment with melatonin (20 mg/daily intramuscularly at 3:00 p.m. for 2 months) on 8 patients with advanced cancer, in whom conventional antitumor therapies had failed. Mean percentages of B, T3, T4, T8 lymphocytes and T4/T8 mean ratios were not significantly different before or after melatonin treatment. In only one patient did the T4/T8 ratio decrease after therapy; in this case only, a stabilization of the disease was obtained, while in all 7 other patients the neoplastic disease progressed also during melatonin treatment, even if an evident improvement of the performance status was seen as it was in most cases.

These results seem to exclude that melatonin may influence lymphocyte functions in cancer. Longitudinal studies and further data, however, will be needed to clarify this question.

REFERENCES

1. LISSONI, P., D. ESPOSTI, G. ESPOSTI, R. MAURI, M. RESENTINI, F. MORABITO, P. FUMAGALLI, A. SANTAGOSTINO, G. DELITALA & F. FRASCHINI. 1986. A clinical study of the relationship between the pineal gland and the opioid system. J. Neural Transm. **65:** 63-73.
2. MATHEWS, P. M., C. J. FROELICH, W. L. SIBBITT & A. D. BANKHURST. 1983. Enhancement of natural cytotoxicity by B-endorphin. J. Immunol. **130:** 1658-1662.
3. MILCU, S. M. & I. POTOP. 1973. Biologic activity of thymic protein extracts. *In* Thymic Hormones. N. Urban & J. C. Schawarzenberg, Eds. 97-134. Munich.
4. CSABA, G. & P. BARATH. 1975. Morphological changes of thymus and the thyroid gland after postnatal extirpation of pineal body. Endocrinol. Exp. (Bratisl.) **9:** 59-67.
5. IWATA, T., G. S. INCEFY, S. CUNNINGHAM-RUNDLES, C. CUNNINGHAM-RUNDLES, E. SMITHWICK, N. GELLER, R. O'REILLY & R. A. GOOD. 1981. Circulating thymic hormones activity in patients with primary and secondary immunodeficiency diseases. Am. J. Med. **71:** 385-393.
6. SILMAN, R. E., R. M. LEONE, R. F. L. HOOPER, & M. A. PREECE. 1979. Melatonin, the pineal gland and human puberty. Nature **282:** 301-304.

7. ARENDT, J., L. WETTERBERG, T. HEYDEN, P. C. SIZONENKO & L. PAUNIER. 1977. Radioimmunoassay of melatonin: human serum and cerebrospinal fluid. Horm. Res. **8:** 65-75.

8. MCCLURE, J. E., N. LAMERIS, D. W. WARA & A. L. GOLDSTEIN. 1982. Immunochemical studies on thymosin: radioimmunoassay of thymosin α 1. J. Immunol. **128:** 368-373.

9. JANKOVIC, B. D., K. ISAKOVIC & S. PETROVIC. 1970. Effect of pinealectomy on immune reactions in rat. Immunology. **18:** 1-3.

10. BELOKRYLOV, G. A., V. G. MOROZOV, V. K. H. KHAVINSON & B. N. SOFRONOV. 1976. Effect of low-molecular-weight extracts of heterologous thymus and pineal glands and hypothalamus on the immune response in mice. Bull. Exp. Biol. Med. **81:** 218-222.

11. RELLA, W. & V. LAPIN. 1976. Immunocompetence of pinealectomized and simultaneously pinealectomized and thymectomized rats. Oncology **33:** 3-8.

12. LISSONI, P., O. MARELLI, R. MAURI, M. RESENTINI, P. FRANCO, D. ESPOSTI, G. ESPOSTI, F. FRASCHINI, F. HALBERG, R. B. SOTHERN & G. CORNÉLISSEN. 1986. Ultradian chronomodulation by melatonin of a placebo effect upon human killer cell activity. Chronobiologia **13:** 339-343.

13. MAESTRONI, G. J. M., A. CONTI & W. PIERPAOLI. 1987. Role of the pineal gland in immunity: II. Melatonin enhances the antibody response via an opiatergic mechanism. Clin. Exp. Immunol. **68:** 384-391.

14. VILLA, S., P. LISSONI & F. FRASCHINI. 1986. "In vitro" effects of melatonin on CFU-GM proliferation. International Symposium on Normal and Neoplastic Blood Cells: from Genes to Therapy. Rome, June 10-13. Abstracts, p. 93.

15. ROSSI, M. T., L. DI BELLA, L. GUALANO & L. RONCONE. 1986. Melatonin in thrombocytogenesis. J. Neurol. Transm. (Suppl.) **21:** 504.

16. PICO, J. L., G. MATHE, I. M. YOUNG, R. M. LEONE, J. HOOPER & R. E. SILMAN. 1979. Role of hormones in the etiology of human cancer. Pineal indole hormones and cancer. Cancer Treat. Rep. **63:** 1204.

17. DILLMAN, R. O., J. A. KOZIOL, M. I. ZAVANELLI, J. C. BEAUREGARD, B. L. HALLIBURTON, M. C. GLASSY & I. ROYSTON. 1984. Immunoincompetence in cancer patients. Assessment by in vitro stimulation tests and quantification of lymphocyte subpopulations. Cancer **53:** 1484-1489.

18. RITCHIE, A. S. W., I. OSWALD, H. S. MICKLEM, J. E. BOYD, R. A. ELTON, E. JAZWINSKA & K. JAMES. 1983. Circadian variation of lymphocyte subpopulations: a study with monoclonal antibodies. Br. Med. J. **286:** 1773-1775.

19. ROSENBERG, S. A., M. T. LOTZE, L. M. MUUL, S. LEITMAN, A. E. CHANG, S. E. ETTINGHAUSEN, Y. L. MATORY, J. M. SKIBBER, E. SHILONI, J. T. VETTO, C. A. SEIPP, C. SIMPSON & C. M. REICHERT. 1985. Observations on the systemic administration of autologous lymphokine-activated killer cells and recombinant interleukin-2 to patients with metastatic cancer. N. Engl. J. Med. **313:** 1485-1491.

20. BEUTLER, B. & A. CERAMI. 1987. Cachetin: more than a tumor necrosis factor. N. Engl. J. Med. **316:** 379-385.

21. MAESTRONI, G. J. M., A. CONTI & W. PIERPAOLI. 1986. Melatonin regulates immunity via an opiatergic mechanism. Clin. Neuropharmacol. **9**(Suppl. 4): 479-481.

Bone Marrow: A "Morphostatic Brain" for Control of Normal and Neoplastic Growth. Experimental Evidence[a]

WALTER PIERPAOLI,[b] JAYA BALAKRISHNAN,[b]
GEORGES J. M. MAESTRONI,[c] EDGAR SACHE,[d] AND
JEAN CHOAY[d]

[b] Institute for Integrative Biomedical Research
Lohwisstrasse 50
8123 Ebmatingen, Switzerland

[c] Istituto Cantonale di Patologia
6604 Locarno, Switzerland

[d] Institut Choay
46, Avenue Theophile Gautier
75016 Paris, France

EARLY OBSERVATIONS AND AN EMERGING CONCEPT

Hemopoiesis, Bone Marrow Transplantation and the Dogmatic Views

The idea that certain cells and/or their secretory products can monitor and regulate organ volume and size and thus maintain the integrity of the body (homeostasis) is certainly not new.[1-3] This possibility for maintenance of shape and functions by cell replication applies especially to those normal tissues and cells which have preserved in evolution the capacity to divide and proliferate. There is the obvious necessity to repair and substitute cells on surfaces exposed to external and internal environmental agents. These cells, such as those in cutaneous and mucous tissues, which are liable to constant natural erosion or injury; the lymphohemopoietic tissues (thymus, bone marrow, lymph nodes) which deliver cells to lymph and blood and provide a large variety of basic functions (*e.g.,* macrophages, megacaryocytes, leucocytes, mast cells, etc.); connective and other mesenchymal tissues (fibroblasts, microglia and macroglia, bone cells); and to a minor extent the liver, which maintains a moderate capacity for regeneration.

[a] This work was supported in part by the Institut Choay, Paris, and by the Broye-Guisan-Müller Foundation, Zurich.

In earlier work we proposed a possible "trophic" role of lymphocytes in syndromes and diseases which are associated with disturbances or derangements of thymolymphatic functions in early development.[4] These are produced by antigenic loads of toxins, hormones, nociceptive stressors, irradiation, secondary disease (homologous disease, graft-versus-host disease [GVHD]) and a number of naturally occurring syndromes (athymic nude mice, dwarf mice).[4] This concept of the "trophic" function and multifunctionality of lymphocytes is all the more valid when we consider all the recent discoveries on lymphokines, monokines and "classical" peptide hormones which are secreted by lymphoid cells.[5]

The observation, however, which shifted our attention to the bone marrow (BM), has derived from our experimental work on transplantation of BM (BMT) in mice: especially from our observations on the consequences of an incomplete or deranged hemopoietic function when the BM is transplanted into lethally irradiated animals. BMT is a widely used medical procedure for therapy of immunodeficiency diseases and lymphohemopoietic disorders like aplastic anemia, agranulocytosis and leukemias.[6] In most cases, however, even after a careful search for the most suitable, possibly histocompatible donor, a syndrome ensues which leads either to rejection of the grafted marrow or to a reaction of the grafted marrow against the immunodepressed or irradiated host (GVHD). An immense literature exists on the possible causes and cure of a GVHD and on methodologies designed to prevent the syndrome. All such methods are based on the assumption that the immunocompetent T-lymphocytes in the BM inoculum react against the major or minor histocompatibility antigens on the membranes of different categories of the recipient's cells (epithelial, lymphatic, hepatic, etc.). They will initiate an irreversible process which provokes the chronic or acute type of GVHD, thus leading to the demise of the transplanted host. In sum, the immunogenetic diversity between donor and recipient has been and still is, considered to be the primary cause for a GVHD in BMT.[6]

Our observations on the course of experimental BMT in mice led progressively to the concept that the primary cause for a GVHD not only resides in the genetic diversity of the partners, but primarily also in a deficient BM engraftment. We observed that it is possible to avoid the disease when the BM is transplanted *together with its own internal microenvironmental factors.*[7-9] In addition, it was seen that most of the disturbances and alterations secondary to a disturbed or deficient BM engraftment or, in the accepted terminology, during an acute or chronic GVHD, occur in epithelial or hemopoietic tissues and the liver, where the capacity for replication and/or repair is severely affected.[8] Therefore, we reached the conclusion that, although in BMT an immune reaction may certainly *initiate* a secondary disease, in the last analysis a deficient BM engraftment and ill-functioning hemopoiesis (including T-cell functions) lies at the root of the pathological expression of a GVHD on organs and tissues.[8] In fact, a permanent acceptance of a histoincompatible BM in mice was perfectly possible, and this unequivocally demonstrated that, once the BM had been accepted and had populated the host, no GVHD ensued, and the so-called hemopoietic chimera thrived with the foreign, histoincompatible BM.[7-10]

The BM Regulating Factors; Autonomy and Identity of the BM; The Stubborn Chimeras

The existence of long-lived allogeneic chimeras constructed with nonmanipulated, entire BM transplanted from a donor with a genetically different background (H-2 histocompatibility antigens, alloantigens,[11] and even with BM from a different species (rat to mouse, xenogeneic chimeras, see REFERENCES 7,8), clearly demonstrate that the BM, once the engraftment resistance has been overcome, can be firmly established in the "foreign" milieu and will provide its own (endogenous) autoregulation, which apparently is provided by its own cells and factors. In other words, with respect to its host the BM has a primary role in its own control and can be largely autonomous even in a histo-incompatible host.[8-11] We have repeatedly expressed and demonstrated this concept.[7-11] Autoregulation of the BM is possible only if the BM itself produces its own internal self-regulatory factors and itself determines its supremacy with respect to its host. This remarkable feature of the BM for determination and maintenance of immunological identity and for expression of "self" is further reinforced by experimental evidence that we have provided, demonstrating that the long-lived GVHD-free allogeneic chimeras constructed with intact BM containing its regulatory factors[7-9] constituted a real "new" identity which resisted and opposed any change. In fact, the "new" immune character of these "stubborn chimeras" could not be reversed to their original patterns (H-2-type reactivity) even by transfer of massive amounts of immunocompetent, normal lymphocytes of the original recipient H-2 type.[10-14] This astonishing fact shows that the new BM, in spite of the fact that it colonizes a "foreign" environment, reacts vigorously to intrusion from the original, pretransplantation (and now absent) "house master" which has now become foreign to the new chimera.[10-14]

The presence of cell-free extracellular factors in the BM microenvironment which powerfully contributed to allogeneic engraftment[15] suggested that both potent mitogenic and antiproliferative agents must be located in the BM. Such factors could be responsible for the very high rate of cell turnover in the BM. They may also be relevant for replication or nonreplication of *other* cells and tissues with a high mitotic rate (skin, mucosae, tumors).

The Neural Brain and the "Morphostatic Brain"

There exists a necessity for autonomic and automatic control of cell replication with or without intervention of the central nervous system (CNS). The pioneer work of Calvo[16] on innervation of the BM has shown the astonishing complexity of the BM structure and the fine spatial distribution of nerve endings close to single cells or a group of stem cells. Except for its hemopoietic activities, little is known of the BM physiology. The significance of the intricate neural and connectival network in the BM is completely unknown. The BM constitutes an enormous mass of cells distributed in billions of tiny nests, each one of which constitutes a functional niche. This incredibly large and complex beehive must necessarily respond to precise functional demands. If a central organ exists for a fine monitoring of basic functions such as tissue and/or organ homeostasis (growth, regeneration, repair, etc.) then the BM is a suitable candidate. In fact, innervation, changes of blood pressure, temperature and other chemical (*e.g.,* osmolarity and ionic balance) or hormonal variations are certainly detected in the BM, whose spatial distribution in the bones allows a most rapid response to any stimulus. In other words, the BM may be a "morphostatic brain" which serves many relevant functions which do not require purely psychic activity. However, it is feasible that the BM is also affected by psychic and emotional changes.[17]

This automatic "brain," as we have discussed earlier (see above), possesses and maintains the immunological identity (recognition of "self") and is capable of memory (reactivity to "nonself").[10-14] In addition to these basic qualities, the BM, thanks to its intrinsic character of extraordinarily active "cell producer," may be capable of controlling cell proliferation in general, especially of all those tissues with a permanent capacity for regeneration like the epithelia and the liver.[8] Not accidentally, some consequences of an ill-functioning BM (as caused by a deficient engraftment, irradiation, toxic or chemical agents, psychological distress, corticosteroids, etc.) are anemia, leucopenia, liver necrosis and, in particular, epithelial desquamation, especially evident in GVHD in humans and primates.[18] Thus it appears that a central deregulation of the BM leads to a complete alteration of the normal cell proliferation pattern, with degenerative, hyperplastic or hypoplastic changes of epithelia. These changes can regress only when the BM returns to normal functioning. It is possible to devise experiments which will test the working hypothesis that the BM is a "morphostatic brain."

Bone Marrow Factors that Monitor Cell Replication and Tissue Regeneration; Morphostasis

Based on our work on the marrow-regulating factors (MRF) in BMT and the evident presence of regulatory (immunosuppressive?) molecules in the BM environment, the "humoral" approach was chosen in order to demonstrate the presence of pro- or antimitotic agents in the BM *irrespective of the cells of origin of those postulated factors*. This initial step, which was radically divergent from our initial approach,[19] also considered the possibility that a complete integrity of the BM microenvironmental milieu was necessary for the possible identification of the internal regulatory factors. In other words, no further manipulation was necessary on the native cell-free BM supernatant (BM-SN) in view of initiating its analysis.[18]

We observed[18] that besides deeply affecting engraftment of allogeneic BM in lethally irradiated mice, the native BM-SN from freshly prepared BM cell suspensions also profoundly inhibited liver regeneration in partially hepatectomized mice: a stimulatory effect of liver regeneration was obtained when the BM-SN was derived from partially hepatectomized mice. In addition we demonstrated that sublethal irradiation in mice promoted liver regeneration, suggesting a possible constant *inhibitory* activity of the BM on the liver cell mitosis under normal conditions. All these findings indicated the presence of powerful suppressive factors in the BM and the spleen, which could repress tissue regeneration by a negative feedback circuit.[18] Later, additional work demonstrated that, in fact, the bone marrow supernatant (BM-SN) contained, in the course of tissue regeneration as *e.g.*, after laparotomy, factors which first promoted and then strongly inhibited tissue regeneration. This was shown *in vivo* and *in vitro* by experiments of incorporation of DNA precursors by normal cells.[20] We, therefore, came to the conclusion that the BM and other lymphohemopoietic tissues (*e.g.*, the spleen) each contain cell mitosis regulatory factors operating by a constant suppressive, antimitotic activity. This antiproliferative activity was particularly evident in the BM in the course of wound-healing and tissue regeneration in general.[20]

Regulation of Cell Mitosis by Inhibition of Replication

These findings on the production of pro- and more especially of *anti*proliferative agents in the course of regeneration of the liver and of the skin (laparotomy) and during BM regeneration after irradiation[18,20] clearly showed that a basic mechanism for regulation of cell mitosis is located in the BM and under normal conditions *permanently* acts especially when a rapid reconstitution of tissue integrity is required. Completely unexpected, however, was the finding that permanent, powerful and ev-erpresent inhibitory mechanisms of cell mitosis were dominant, while only temporary, short-lived proliferative activity could be seen to appear in the course of tissue re-generation.[20] The conclusion was that the BM and/or other lymphohemopoietic tissues like the spleen seem to possess the capacity to regulate cell mitosis and that, in a broad sense, the BM acts in fact as a "morphostatic brain" through permanent antiproliferative suppression, with short-lived *pro*mitotic activity when regeneration is required.[18,20]

Starting from these concepts, first steps were taken to separate and characterize the BM-derived inhibitory factors. Initial fractionation of the BM-SN led to a fraction called marrow-regulation factors (MRF) (see above, REFERENCE 15). Its application *in vivo* to mice transplanted with the B16 melatonic melanoma provided the first evidence that these inhibitory agents possess the ability to delay and suppress tumor growth *in vivo*.[20]

In this report we present further progress on the characterization and testing of BM-derived tumor-suppressive agents which display remarkable antitumor activity in *in-vivo* assays.

RECENT PROGRESS

Searching for the Antimitotic Agents; The Models

During the last four years we have been investigating the antitumor activity of BM-derived factors. We adhered to the conviction that no anticancer therapy is conceivable A) without a clear-cut and consistently reproducible effect *in vivo* and B) unless the factor(s) exert no noxious side-effects in the course of the treatment. First, all material used was tested for possible contamination with bacterial endotoxin by the *Limulus* test. An acceptable concentration of endotoxin was below 1 ng/mg dry, lyophilized substance.

In-vivo *Models.* Two well studied transplantable tumors were used for *in-vivo* trans-plantation in mice. One was the B16 melanotic melanoma of the H-2^b haplotype in inbred C57BL/6 mice. The second was the CL-26 colon carcinoma of the H-2^d haplotype in inbred BALB/cJ mice. The tumors were maintained *in vivo* by serial transplantation of 4×10^5 cells subcutaneously, in the back, in 0.2 ml isotonic saline. The cell suspensions were prepared by gentle dissociation of the tumor cells, as previously described.[20] The cells were washed twice in TC199 medium (no serum added) and injected subcutaneously under ether anaesthesia in groups of 10 mice. Initially, as described in the previous report, the treatment with the substances was initiated only when the tumor became visible at 5 to 10 days after transplantation. The substances were injected once daily, at 5 p.m. for 4-5 days, and then the mice were sacrificed and the weights of the tumors were recorded.[20] Later we adopted a system where the substances were injected immediately after transplantation of the tumor cells and the treatment was continued for 10 days. This latter method allowed us to evaluate a more prolonged and convincing antitumor activity after a large inoculum of cancer cells.

In-vitro *Models.* For evaluating a possible *in-vitro* activity and a direct cytotoxic or antimitotic activity, the BM factors were tested *in vitro* by using MCF-7 or BR3 human mammary carcinoma, or WiDr human colon carcinoma cells. The established tumor cell lines were cultivated in 0.8 percent methylcellulose in IMDM culture medium supplemented with 2mM L-glutamine and 20 percent fetal calf serum. The proliferation was estimated by counting the tumor colonies after 7 days of incubation at 37°C in 5% CO_2. 10^4 viable tumor cells were plated in 35-mm Petri dishes and samples were prepared and counted in duplicate. Only cell aggregates with one axis exceeding 80 μm were counted as colonies. Concentration of the BM factors was 1, 10, 50, and 100 μg per ml medium.

Fractionation Procedures

Ribs were separated from the carcass of a freshly slaughtered heifer of about one year of age and 700 kg body weight. They were freed of soft tissues and each rib was sawed into four sections. The bones were rinsed repeatedly with sterile ice-cooled isotonic saline and mounted on a bench-vise. The bone marrow was extracted by slow-speed drilling into the spugnosa with a handdrill. The material obtained was immediately suspended in ice-cold sterile isotonic saline and the cells dissociated by prolonged gentle shaking. The whole work was performed under sterile conditions starting from the initial sterile-rinsing of the ribs. The bone marrow cell suspension in isotonic saline represented the starting material for all subsequent purification steps. All manipulations were performed at +4°C. After a first centrifugation at 15,000 × g (30 min) to remove particulate matter such as cells and bone fragments, the supernatant was filtered over sterile gauze to retain any fatty material still present. The precipitate was discarded and the supernatant was immediately frozen. From all the ribs of one heifer about four liters of cell-free bone marrow supernatant (BM-SN) in isotonic saline were obtained, pooled together and frozen in 400-ml aliquots at −30°C. All following steps were performed on the thawed solution, under semisterile conditions.

Bovine BM-SN was again centrifuged (38,000 × g, 30 min) at 4°C to eliminate any residual suspended material. The resulting clear supernatant was gel-filtered on an Ultrogel AcA34 column (IBF Biotechnics, Villeneuve la Garenne, France) under the conditions given in the legend to FIGURE 1. Six fractions were obtained (FIGURE 1). In each fraction the tubes were pooled, dialyzed against freshly distilled water and lyophilized (fraction F, with a very low molecular weight was, in most cases, recovered by dialyzing in calibrated membranes with a defined molecular weight cut-off of 1.000 (Spectrapor, Spectrum, USA). The in-vivo biological activity was found to be associated with fraction C ("peak 3", see below). At this stage 100 ml supernatant usually resulted in a yield of 120 mg lyophilized fraction C material. The protein content of the "peak 3" was estimated to be nearly 100%. Hexose determination revealed a content less than 0.5%.

Tumor-inhibitory Activity in vivo; *The Elusive "Peak 3"*

In the course of four years, we tested the anti-tumor activity *in vivo* of the principal fractions resulting from gel-chromatography of the BM-SN (see previous section). Both B16 melanoma and CL26 colon carcinoma were used. In spite of a number of contradictory and nonreproducible results, finally it was found that a more reliable and reproducible tumor-inhibitory activity was obtained with fraction C, representing the rising slope of fraction D in the gel-filtration by Ultrogel AcA34 (FIGURE 1). This antitumor activity *in vivo* was reproducible with several analogous fractions from different batches.

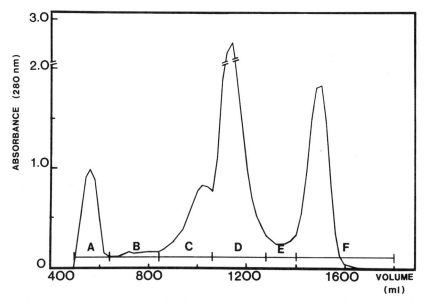

FIGURE 1. Gel filtration on an Ultrogel AcA34 column of bovine bone-marrow supernatant. In a typical run 90-100 ml supernatant are applied to a column (5 × 90 cm) equilibrated and eluted with a 0.9% NaCl solution containing 0.02% NaN$_3$ (w/v); flow rate, 60 ml/hr; volume of fractions, 10 ml; temperature, 4°C; (—), absorbance at 280 nm. Biological activity is associated with fraction C.

The results illustrated on TABLE 1 show that a profound inhibition of CL26 colon carcinoma *in vivo* could be produced in BALB/c mice injected daily for 10 days with a dose of 100 μg of fraction C (peak 3). We could thus conclude that the tumor-inhibitory activity is contained in "peak 3."

The same fractions of "peak 3," when tested *in vitro* in the assay illustrated above, did not show any effect on tumor cell colony formation (negative data not given here). Thus "peak 3" did not display any direct cytotoxic or antimitotic effect on tumor cells *in vitro*.

TABLE 1. Tumor-inhibitory Activity *in vivo* of a Bone Marrow-derived Factor ("Peak 3")

Exp. No.	Fraction (Code No.)	Dose/Day (Micrograms)	Peak 3[a] (No. of Mice)	BSA[a] Controls (No. of Mice)	Percent Inhibition	p Values[c]
1	RB-26114	100	411 ± 174[a] (10)	664 ± 197[a] (10)	38	<0.01
2	RB-26177	100	28 ± 16 (10)	92 ± 38 (10)	70	<0.01
3[b]	RB-26180	100	39 ± 19 (20)	125 ± 65 (20)	69	<0.01
4	RB-27349	100	92 ± 73 (10)	215 ± 78 (10)	57	<0.005

[a] The bone marrow fractions or bovine serum albumin (BSA) were dissolved in phosphate buffer solution (PBS) and injected intraperitoneally daily for 10 days at 5 p.m. in 0.5 ml total volume per mouse.
[b] Two experiments were plotted together.
[c] Analysis of variance (Fisher test).
[a] ± standard deviation.

Histopathology of the Inhibited Tumors

As shown in FIGURE 2, a most remarkable regression or blockade of carcinoma growth was produced by treatment with the antitumor agent contained in "peak 3." The control mice treated with BSA developed much larger tumors (TABLE 1). These tumors showed few necrotic areas and the small amount of connective tissue was composed only of fibroblasts oriented in such a way as to incapsulate the tumor (FIGURES 2A and B). However, the capsule was very thin. Many mitotic figures were clearly visible in the compact tumor mass. The carcinoma was classified as highly malignant and invasive. The tumors of mice treated with "peak 3" showed massive necrotic areas infiltrated by inflammatory tissue (granulocytes, macrophages, lymphocytes) (FIGURES 2C and D). All the tumors examined were completely surrounded by a newly formed granulomatous tissue which had clearly replaced the tumor tissue. In fact, capillaries could be seen which were oriented perpendicularly to the tumor mass, as if the granulomatous tissue had replaced the tumor areas after their necrosis (FIGURE 2D). However, some mitotic figures could still be seen in the remaining tumoral tissue of the mice treated with "peak 3."

Perspectives for Cancer Therapy

A modest number of reports have been published on the tumor-inhibitory activity of BM cells[21] and BM-derived factors[22] *in vivo* and *in vitro*. However, a large literature exists on the presence of hemopoietic, stem cell-inhibitory agents from the BM.[23–26] At the present stage of our investigation, it is not possible to rule out that one of those described BM factors is similar or identical to our tumor-inhibitory, BM-derived, fraction. However, a large number of differences exist between the factor we describe and those described by others. These differences concern mainly the molecular weight range, the kind of *in-vivo* or *in-vitro* testing used, and the target cells chosen to test them. Nevertheless, only a complete chemical and possibly molecular and structural characterization of the anti-tumor agent will allow us to distinguish it from many other so-called "biological response modifiers."

A complete identification of the factor that we have described is our present aim. Its use in experimental and clinical oncology could open a most promising new avenue for *physiological* control of cancer. However, its biological significance may go well beyond just one medical application.

ACKNOWLEDGMENTS

The expert technical skills of M. P. Malazzi, Institut Choay, is gratefully acknowledged. We thank Dr. Chang-Xian Yi for his participation in some of the *in-vivo* experiments. We acknowledge the constant, devoted and most critical collaboration of Ms. Genevieve Babinet, Institut Choay, during the planning of the experimental work and the evaluation of the results.

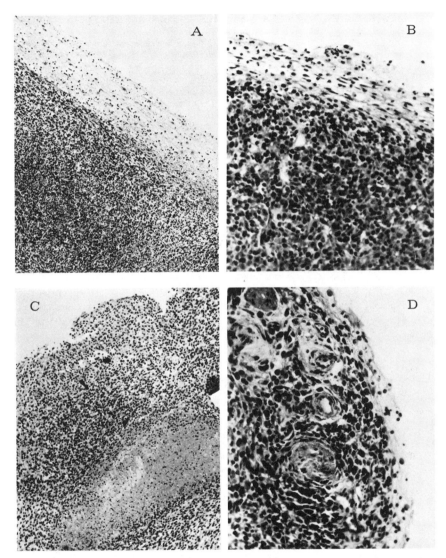

FIGURE 2. CL26 transplantable colon carcinoma in BALB/cJ mice 10 days after transplantation and daily treatment with 100 µg bovine serum albumin (**A** and **B**) or with 100 µg bone marrow-derived "peak 3" (**C** and **D**). Haematoxylin-eosin, ×300 (**A** and **C**) and ×800 (**B** and **D**). For description of the histopathological findings, see the text.

REFERENCES

1. BURWELL, R. G. 1963. The role of lymphoid tissue in morphostasis. Lancet **2:** 69-74.
2. BURCH, P.R.J. 1976. Is normal growth regulated by a central system? *In* The Biology of Cancer, A New Approach. 17-39. MTP Press. Lancaster, PA.
3. LIOZNER, L.D. 1974. Organ Regeneration. A Study of Development Biology in Mammals. Studies in Soviet Science. Consultant Bureau (Division of Plenum Press). New York, NY.
4. PIERPAOLI, W. & E. SORKIN. 1972. Hormones, thymus and lymphocyte functions. Experientia **28:** 1385-1389.
5. COHEN, S., E. PICK & J. J. OPPENHEIM, EDS. 1979. Biology of the Lymphokines. Academic Press. New York, NY.
6. SANTOS, G. W. 1983. History of bone marrow transplantation. Clin. Haematol. **12:** 611-639.
7. MAESTRONI, G.J.M. & W. PIERPAOLI. 1980. Factor(s) elaborated by bone marrow that promote persistent engraftment of xenogeneic and semiallogeneic marrow. J. Clin. Lab. Immunol. **4:** 189-193.
8. PIERPAOLI, W. & G. J. M. MAESTRONI. 1984. Enduring allogeneic and xenogeneic hemopoietic engraftment via marrow-derived regulating factors. *In* Tolerance in Bone Marrow & Organ Transplantation. S. Slavin, Ed. 403-414. Elsevier. Amsterdam.
9. PIERPAOLI, W., R. KELLERHALS, A. BUEHLER & E. SACHE. 1985. Experimental manipulations and marrow-derived factors which affect the outcome of bone marrow transplantation across the H-2 barrier in lethally irradiated mice. J. Clin. Lab. Immunol. **16:** 115-124.
10. PIERPAOLI, W. & G. J. M. MAESTRONI. 1983. Dominance and persistence of donor marrow in long-lived allogeneic radiation chimeras obtained with unmanipulated bone marrow. Immunol. Let. **6:** 197-202.
11. PIERPAOLI, W. & G. J. M. MAESTRONI. 1983. Marrow regulating factors (MRF) and radiation chimeras: a model for bone marrow-directed immunity. *In* Immunoregulation. N. Fabris, E. Garaci, J. Hadden & N. A. Mitchison, Eds. 133-140. Plenum Press. New York, NY.
12. MAESTRONI, G. J. M., W. PIERPAOLI & R. M. ZINKERNAGEL. 1982. Immunoreactivity of long-lived H-2 incompatible irradiation chimeras ($H-2^d \rightarrow H-2^b$). Immunology **46:** 253-260.
13. MAESTRONI, G. J. M., W. PIERPAOLI & R. M. ZINKERNAGEL. 1983. Allogeneic $H-2^d \rightarrow H-2^b$ irradiation bone marrow chimeras: a) failure to transfer chimerism adoptively and b) immune reactivity of immunocompetent lymphocytes adoptively transferred to chimeras. Immunobiology **164:** 417-429.
14. MAESTRONI, G. J. M. & W. PIERPAOLI. 1983. Rejection of P2 skin grafts by long-lived H-2 incompatible graft-versus-host-disease-free bone marrow chimeras ($P1 \rightarrow P2$). Transplantation **36:** 461-463.
15. PIERPAOLI, W. & G. J. M. MAESTRONI. 1981. Enduring allogeneic marrow engraftment via nonspecific bone marrow-derived regulating factors (MRF). Cell. Immunol. **57:** 219-228.
16. CALVO, W. 1968. The innervation of the bone marrow in laboratory animals. Am. J. Anat. **123:** 315-328.
17. PIERPAOLI, W. 1984. The bone marrow, our autonomous morphostatic "brain". *In* Breakdown in Human Adaptation to "Stress". R. E. Ballieux, Ed. Vol. 2: 713-721. Martinus Nijhoff Publishers. The Hague.
18. PIERPAOLI, W. 1985. Immunoregulatory and morphostatic function of bone marrow-derived factors. *In* Neural Modulation of Immunity. R. Guillemin, M. Cohen & T. Melnechuk, Eds. 205-220. Raven Press. New York, NY.
19. ČUK, M., B. RADOSEVIC-STASIC, W. PIERPAOLI & D. RUKAVINA. 1983. Bone marrow-liver-spleen axis in the regulation of morphostasis. Period. Biol. **85:** 23-24.
20. PIERPAOLI, W., J. BALAKRISHNAN, E. SACHE, J. CHOAY & G. J. M. MAESTRONI. 1987. Neuroendocrine and bone marrow factors for control of marrow transplantation and tissue regeneration. Ann. N. Y. Acad. Sci. **496:** 27-38.

21. SCUDERI, P. & C. ROSSE. 1981. The role of bone marrow in the growth of transplanted methylcholanthrene-induced sarcoma (MCA). Transplant. Proc. **13:** 747-751.
22. DITTMER, J. E., S. K. OH, L. CORWIN & M. BENNETT. 1984. Suppression of tumor cell growth in vitro by a bone marrow factor. Cancer Res. **44:** 900-903.
23. LORD, B. I., K. J. MORI, E. G. WRIGHT & L. G. LAJTHA. 1976. An inhibitor of stem cell proliferation in normal bone marrow. Br. J. Haematol. **34:** 441-445.
24. FRINDEL, E. & M. GUIGON. 1977. Inhibition of CFU entry into cycle by a bone marrow extract. Exp. Hematol. **5:** 74-76.
25. WRIGHT, E. G., P. SHERIDAN & M. A. S. MOORE. 1980. An inhibitor of murine stem cell proliferation produced by normal human bone marrow. Leukemia Res. **4:** 309-319.
26. CORK, M., I. ANDERSON, D. B. THOMAS, & A. RICHES. 1981. Regulation of the growth fraction of CFU-S by an inhibitory produced by bone marrow. Leuk. Res. **5:** 101-105.

Opioids: Immunomodulators

A Proposed Role in Cancer and Aging

NICHOLAS P. PLOTNIKOFF

Department of Pharmacology
Oral Roberts University School of Medicine
Tulsa, Oklahoma 74137

INTRODUCTION

Behavioral medicine, in the broadest context, has attempted to include the effects of behavioral changes on states of health.[1] Mood changes have been associated with changes in health status.[2] In more recent decades, an increasing number of studies have suggested that part of these changes in health may be related to changes in immune function. Terms such as psychoneuroimmunology or neuroimmunomodulation attempt to relate alterations in central nervous system function with changes in immune function. Studies have focused on neuroimmunomodulatory effects on antibody formation as well as direct effects on T-cells, B-cells, cytotoxic cells, and macrophages. Connections between the autonomic nervous system, the endocrine system, and the lymphoid organs of the immune system have been established. Finally, the function of specific loci of hypothalamic (limbic system) areas of the brain were altered to evaluate corresponding changes in the immune system.

PATHWAYS OF NEUROLOGIC AND IMMUNE SYSTEM INTERACTION

Autonomic Nervous System

Direct autonomic nervous system connections between the brain and the organs of the lymphoid system (thymus, spleen, bone marrow, and lymph nodes) and gut-associated lymphoid tissue (GALT) have been established. Nerve endings have been identified in the parenchyma of the cortex and medulla of the thymus, spleen, bone marrow, and lymph nodes. In particular, adrenergic neurotransmitters released from nerve endings in the parenchyma have been associated with T-lymphocyte activation. Other factors include cholinergic fibers as well as peptides such as VIP, neuropeptide Y, met-enkephalin, CCK, and neurotensin.[3]

Neuroendocrine System

Earlier studies have demonstrated numerous interactions between the central nervous system and the endocrine system.[4] The principal pathways include the hypothalamus, pituitary gland, and the adrenal glands as well as the gonads.[5] Most of the principal psychoactive agents alter hormone levels and functions of the pituitary gland. Morphine-like agents are known to stimulate release of growth hormone and prolactin, and decrease levels of ACTH as well as gonadonotrophins. Such changes in levels of pituitary hormones can have both direct and indirect effects on components of the immune system. Many of these studies were based on changes in the sizes of thymus, spleen, and lymph nodes. For example, thymic involution has been demonstrated following large doses of ACTH, estrogens, and steroid hormones.[6] Adrenalectomy or gonadectomy results in the increase in the size of the lymphatic organs. Treatment with growth hormone or thyroid hormone increases thymus size. All of the above hormones have direct effects on lymphocytes as well.

Prohormones (Enkephalins-Endorphins) and Psychoneuroimmunology

The source of endogenous enkephalins-endorphins has been discovered to be three large prohormones. The first one to be identified was proopiomelanocortin (POMC). This prohormone was found to be present in the central nervous system, pituitary gland, and human adrenal glands. Processing of this prohormone leads to the release of ACTH, MSH, and beta-endorphin. Thus, the source of ACTH in the pituitary is POMC. However, very recent research has shown that POMC is also found in spleen, bone marrow, and most interestingly, lymphocytes. Extensive studies by Blalock *et al.* (1985) have demonstrated that in the presence of virus, corticotrophin releasing factor (CRF) or arginine vasopressin, lymphocytes release measurable levels of ACTH and beta-endorphin.[7] Thus, the interactions of CRF between the central nervous system and the endocrine and immune systems result in release of ACTH and beta-endorphin. The latter step qualifies both ACTH and beta-endorphin to be considered as "lymphokines." ACTH has been shown to reduce antibody formation in a similar manner to cortisone. More extensive studies on the immune system with beta-endorphin have shown marked effects in activating natural killer (NK) cells and chemotaxis. Beta-endorphin has mixed effects on mitogen-induced proliferation.[8–13]

The second major prohormone found in the central nervous system and the adrenal glands is proenkephalin A. This prohormone is the major source of methionine enkephalin (four copies) and leucine enkephalin (one copy) plus two copies of hepta and octa methionine enkephalin. More recently it has been found that proenkephalin A is found in thymus, spleen, bone marrow and T-helper cells. The specific presence of proenkephalin A in T-helper cells has been documented to release methionine enkephalin into the surrounding media in the presence of the mitogen ConA. Thus methionine enkephalin can be considered to be a "lymphokine."[14,15]

Our group conducted extensive research on the immunological effects of methionine enkephalin both *in vitro* and *in vivo*.[16] Initially methionine enkephalin was shown to stimulate blastogenesis with PHA in mouse spleen cells at extremely low concentrations. Also treatment of mice with methionine enkephalin resulted in enlarged thymus.[17] Methionine enkephalin treatment prolonged survival of mice inoculated with either L1210 (leukemia) or B16 melanoma.[18] In addition, methionine enkephalin enhanced the effect of cis-platinum cyclophosphamide.[19] Additional studies included those demonstrating antagonism of the effects of dexamethasone or prednisolone. Most interesting are the findings that methionine enkephalin can prolong survival of mice inoculated with lethal amounts of Herpes Simplex II or *Listeria monocytogenes.* Morphine, on the other hand, has just the opposite effect and actually shortens survival time.[20] Since morphine binds preferentially to mu receptors and methionine enkephalin to delta receptors, we proposed a Yin-Yang hypothesis of opioid neuroimmunomodulation.[21] That is, mu agonists are down-regulators while delta agonists are up-regulators of the cellular component of the immune system.

Clinical studies of methionine enkephalin in normal volunteers (Phase I studies) in a wide dosage range of 1, 10, 50, 100, 150, 200, and 250 micrograms/kg in a saline 30 minute infusion established safety. No significant changes were seen on blood pressure, heart rate, EKG, respiration, body temperature or neurological reflexes following infusion of methionine enkephalin. There was an increase in serum prolactin and mood elevation in some of the volunteers. However, significant *in-vivo* enhancement of the immune system was discovered. Thus, T-cell subsets, NK cell activity, and blastogenesis (PHA, ConA, pokeweed) were all increased over baseline values, confirming *in-vitro* studies.[22]

Phase II clinical studies were conducted in cancer patients and AIDS patients. These cancers included lung cancer, melanoma, hypernephroma, as well as Kaposi's sarcoma (with AIDS). In all cases, methionine enkephalin treatment, in dose ranges of 10, 20, 50 and 100 micrograms/kg, resulted in significant increases of T-cell subsets and blastogenesis with PHA, ConA and pokeweed. Although there were no significant reductions in the advanced cancers, reports of subjective improvement on the part of the patient were quite uniform. In the case of patients with Kaposi's sarcoma (AIDS), reduction in node size and purplish coloration was seen in all patients.[23,24]

More recently, Wybran *et al.* (1986) reported that methionine enkephalin treatment of ARC patients (Pre-AIDS) markedly reduced lymph node size, fevers, diarrhea, and resulted in significant weight gain and improvement of mood and outlook. All immune system parameters measured including T-cells, NK cells, and blastogenesis showed improvement.[24]

In conclusion, we believe that the prohormones represent a vast potential for investigating the relationships between the central nervous, endocrine, and immune system. All of the fragments of the prohormone, variable in size and number, as determined by the stress(ors) of the individual and environment, result in variable impacts on the three systems. Much remains to be studied in this regard.

Our own studies of methionine enkephalin suggest a major role in the control of immunomodulation. Perhaps methionine enkephalin may be a major fragment of the prohormones responsible for the feedback of processing prohormones. Our clinical studies, to date, suggest that methionine enkephalin may be a useful immunomodulator in the treatment of cancer and AIDS (ARC) patients.

THE YIN-YANG HYPOTHESIS OF OPIOID NEUROIMMUNOMODULATION

In the preceding section a careful distinction was made between the different opioid receptors in the central nervous system and the periphery. It is possible that there are receptor subtypes (mu-1 and mu-2), associated with different functions in the brain and immune systems. Mu receptors are particularly sensitive to the morphine type ligands as well as beta endorphin. In the central nervous system these ligands are particularly effective as analgesics. However, in the periphery, these same mu receptors appear to down-regulate cellular and humoral immunity. Morphine, as the prototype ligand, has been exhaustively reviewed to exert immunosuppressive effects in rodents and man.[25]

Earlier reports on an anecdotal level recorded increased incidence of infections (and cancer) in heroin addicts. Immunological evaluations included measuring mitogen responsivity which was markedly reduced in heroin addicts.[26] Other groups measured and recorded depression of T-cells forming rosettes with sheep red blood cells (SRBC). Finally, Wybran *et al.* (1985) reported that morphine could also depress the number of T-cells forming rosettes (SRBC) *in-vitro* in normal volunteers. This unique finding was confirmed and extended by Donohoe *et al.* (1986).[27–29]

Similar findings of immunodepressant effects of morphine were also found in rodents; suppression of antibody production rosettes, ConA blastogenesis, hemolysis of SRBC, increased infections, suppression of NK cells, decreased helper and suppressor T-cells, and mitogen blastogenesis.[30–34]

Since the three prohormones are processed differently, as determined by various stressors, it is possible to visualize consequent changes in the immune system. The intermediate size fragments from the prohormones bind preferentially to mu and kappa receptors (morphine-type ligands).[25] In contrast, the smaller end products of processing the prohormones, the enkephalins-endorphins, bind preferentially to delta and epsilon receptors (up-regulating receptors). Thus, it is evident that processing of the prohormones into different size fragments determines the state of immunocompetence.

CANCER AND TUMORS

A substantial number of endocrine tumor reports have appeared in the literature indicating that a variety of tumors possess receptors and measurable levels of the various opioids, as well as opioid prohormones.

PHEOCHROMOCYTOMAS

Since POMC and proenkephalin A are found in human adrenals, it is not surprising that significant levels of the endorphins are also found in pheochromocytomas.[35]

NEUROBLASTOMA

Numerous investigators have identified receptor and opioid ligand binding on neuroblastoma cells.[36] All of the morphine (kappa and mu) as well as enkephalin-endorphin (delta and epsilon) receptors have been identified by receptor displacement studies.[37] Most striking are a series of studies conducted by Zagon and McLaughlin (1981) showing that the opioid antagonists, naloxone and naltrexone, can reduce tumor growth and prolong survival time of mice treated with neuroblastoma (S20Y cell line, cloned from A/jax murine C1300 neuroblastoma).[38,39] Of particular interest is the finding that naltrexone has an inhibitory effect on the growth of murine S20Y neuroblastoma in nude mice. This finding would suggest that opioid receptors on tumors may have "direct" modulatory roles in regulating the growth of tumors. In direct contrast to the above, the same group reported that the agonist heroin may also prolong survival time and retard tumor growth if the animals are pretreated before tumor implant.[40] Perhaps there is a secondary feedback loop between mu and delta receptors since the opioid antagonists are more selective for the mu receptor in contrast to the delta receptor.[41] Heterogenous populations of mu and delta receptors have also been characterized in human neuroblastoma (SH-SY5Y)[42] as well as cell lines (1MR-32, NMB and Kelly).

BRAIN TUMORS

Patients with brain tumors have been reported to have impaired cellular immunity.[43] Is it possible that this is psychoneuroimmunology exemplified? Do central mechanisms (autonomic nervous system as well as neuroendocrine systems) alter the immune systems when brain tumors impinge or release "inhibitory factors?" Since all of the opioid prohormones (POMC, proenkephalin A, and prodynorplin) are present in the brain, it can be expected that the prohormones and endorphins would be detected in tumors.[44] One recent study indicates that beta endorphin enhances *in-vitro* lymphokine (leukocyte migration inhibitory factor—LIF) production in patients with squamous carcinoma of the head and neck.[45]

PITUITARY GLAND

The pituitary gland contains POMC and prodynorphin. Patients with pituitary adenoma have measurable beta endorphin (opioid peptides).[46] Ectopic tumors have also been found to contain the prohormones and endorphins.

THYMUS, THYROID, AND PANCREAS

A single tumor cell population was found to produce gastrin, ACTH, beta-endorphin, somastatin, and calcitonin.[47] A patient with Cushing's syndrome was found to have ACTH, MSH, CLIP, beta-endorphin, and met-enkephalin in a thymic tumor.[48] Finally, carcinoma of the thyroid has been found to contain proenkephalin B (dynorphin) as well as ACTH, MSH, beta-endorphin, and somatostatin.[49]

LUNG, RECTUM, BONE MARROW, OVARY, BREAST

Small cell carcinoma line (NC1-H146) was found to contain beta-endorphin, beta-lipotropin, as well as receptors for etorphine.[50] Two cases with endocrine tumors of the colon and rectum were found to contain enkephalin, endorphin, and glucagon cells.[51] Beta-endorphin, methionine-enkephalin, and ACTH were found in the sternal biopsy of leukemic children.[52,53] Ten patients with mucinous cystadenomas of the ovary, were found to contain somastostatin, glucagon, gastrin/CCK, neurotensin, and enkephalin.[54] Methionine enkephalin was also detectable in breast tumors.[55]

MELANOMA

Murgo *et al.* (1986) discovered that methionine enkephalin could reduce the growth rate of B16 melanoma in mice.[16] Dafney *et al.* (1983) reported that morphine had just the opposite effect and actually accelerated rate of mortality of mice with B-16 melanoma.[59]

STRESS, IMMUNITY, AND CANCER

It is tempting to suggest that chronic stress may accelerate rate of tumor growth.[60] Several groups have considered this approach and reported mixed findings.[56,57,61] In light of the preceding sections on the presence of prohormones and endorphins in a large variety of tumors, it is possible to consider environmental conditions as initiators of tumor growth.[58] The studies by Liebeskind *et al.* (1986) would suggest that footshock stress in rats with ascites tumors may be a useful model for considering immunological interactions with tumor growth.[62] Since the effects of stress (enhanced tumor growth) could be reversed by naltrexone, it is possible that intermediate size fragments from the opioid prohormones (from the pituitary and adrenals) may account for the enhanced tumor growth by their effects on the immune system. These peptides, released by stress, have a high affinity for mu and kappa receptors. At the same time, tumors also have receptors for the opioid peptides which may have a direct effect on the growth rate of tumors. Earlier stress studies reviewed by Vernon Riley (1981) would suggest multiple influences on tumor growth including the steroid hormones.[63] Since naloxone has been found to stimulate the release of steroid hormones from the adrenals, tumor growth changes may also be influenced by released steroids.[64]

My working tumor hypothesis, based on the Yin-Yang immune hypothesis, is that mu and kappa receptors and their ligands down-regulate (suppress) the immune system but *up*-regulate (stimulate) tumor growth, since tumors possess opioid receptors. The opposite effect is seen with the enkephalins that up-regulate (stimulate) the delta receptor of the immune system *but* down-regulate (suppress) tumor growth. Receptor subtypes may account for differences in function in the central nervous system versus the immune system. States of mood (depression and bereavement) may contribute to both changes in immunity as well as tumor growth,[65] since NK cells are suppressed in bereavement.[66]

AGING, OPIOIDS, AND IMMUNITY

Simultaneous studies of brain levels and receptor densities (Bmax) for opioids in the brain and the peripheral immune system have not been studied.[67] However, separate studies have shown that brain levels of opioids and receptors diminish with aging.[68,69] For example, Ogawa (1985) showed that methionine-enkephalin and thyrotrophin releasing hormone (TRH) receptor levels in the cerebral cortex of aged rats was markedly lower than that of young adult rats.[70] Petkov et al. (1984) also found that methionine enkephalin receptors decreased with aging (cortex 57% decrease, hypothalamus 84% decrease).[71] Dupont et al. (1981) found almost exclusive decrease of beta-endorphin, and met- and leu-enkephalins in the hypothalamus.[72] Jensen et al. (1980) studied differences between young and old rats on one-trial learning-memory tasks. Aged rats showed impairments. The older rats also had decreased receptor densities (Bmax) for etorphine as well as dihydromorphine in cortex and midbrain.[73] Most interesting, Wilkinson and Dorsa (1986) reported that there are changes in posttranslational processing of peptides during aging (increases in N-terminal acetylation and carboxy-terminal proteolysis of endorphins in the hypothalamus of aged animals).[74] The acetylated endorphins presumably have different agonist functions (neuroleptic-like activity versus opiate analgesic activity). Is it possible that aging results in an imbalance between the mu and delta receptors? Are there more mu receptors than delta receptors? Do the receptor density (Bmax) ratios change? Certainly the inference that aging results in translational changes of the endorphins suggest functional receptor differences. Is there an increase in mu receptor outflow through the autonomic nervous system as well as the neuroendocrine system to the immune system from the brain?

Since there are major opioid receptor changes in the brain, are there similar changes in the immune system? The answer would appear to be yes. However, the evidence is indirect. Since the aged organism has an involuted thymus, are the changes in T-cell numbers and function directly related to the integrity of the thymus?[76]

There is no question that this is true (Pierpaoli's studies, 1981).[77] However, in the remaining T-cells, are there imbalances between mu and delta opioid receptors? Is it possible that endogenous microtumors have imbalances between mu and delta opioid receptors? Certainly the finding by Zurowski et al. (1986) would support the concept that T-helper cells contain proenkephalin A and process methionine enkephalin (in the presence of ConA). Which opioid prohormones are found in the T-suppressor cells?[78]

The search for differential densities (Bmax) between mu and delta receptors in the immune system with aging would be an exciting outcome of this review. The suggestions that came from these studies are the very hard facts that processing of the opioid prohormones varies with stress[25] and now, with aging.[74] In addition receptor densities (Bmax) diminish with aging.[68] Is there an increase of mu agonist fragments from the prohormones resulting in a further down regulation of T-cell functions? Does this combination of down-regulation (involution of the thymus and mu agonists from the opioid prohormones) contribute to aging and malignancy? Can we regain opioid balance by administering delta agonists such as methionine enkephalin? Early clinical studies suggest that methionine enkephalin may have a "replacement hormone" role in therapy of patients with cancer or AIDS (ARC).[79,80] Perhaps similar treatment would also be of benefit in the treatment of aging.[17]

Methionine enkephalin has also been shown to stimulate production of interleukin II (ILII) as well as interleukin I and gamma interferon.[81,82] Since aging includes a decrease in lymphokine production and since lymphokines are used to treat various tumors,[83] it would appear that the clinical use of methionine enkephalin would be appropriate.

I invite you to join me in exploring these issues.

REFERENCES

1. SPECTOR, N. H. 1983. Anatomic and physiologic connections between the central nervous and the immune systems (neuroimmunomodulation). In Immunoregulation. N Fabris, E. Garaci, J. Hadden & N. A. Mitchensen, Eds. Plenum Publishing Corporation. New York, NY.

2. ADER, R. & N. COHEN. 1981. Conditioned immunopharmacologic responses. In Psychoneuroimmunology. R. Ader, Ed. Academic Press. New York, NY.

3. FELTEN, D. L., S. Y. FELTEN, S. L. CARLSON, J. A. OLSCHOWKA & S. LIVNAT. 1985. Noradrenergic and peptidergic innervation of lymphoid tissue. J. Immunol. 135: 755.

4. PLOTNIKOFF, N. P. & A. J. KASTIN. 1977. Neuropharmacological review of hypothalamic releasing factors. In Neuropeptide Influences on the Brain and Behavior. L. H. Miller, C. A. Sandman & A. J. Kastin, Eds. Raven Press. New York, NY.

5. SACHAR, E. J. 1978. Neuroendocrine responses to psychotropic drugs. In Psychopharmacology. M. A. Lipton & A. DiMascio, Eds. Raven Press. New York, NY.

6. DOUGHERTY, T. F. 1952. Effect of hormones on lymphatic tissue. Physiol. Rev. 32: 379.

7. BLALOCK, J. E., K. L. BOST & E. M. SMITH. 1985. Neuroendocrine peptide hormones and their receptors in the immune system. J. Neuroimmunol. 10: 31-40.

8. BERCZI, I. 1986. The influence of pituitary-adrenal axis on the immune system. In Pituitary Function and Immunity. I. Berczi, Ed. CRC Press. Boca Raton, FL.

9. EVANS, C. J., E. ERDELYI & J. D. BARCHAS. 1986. Candidate opioid peptides for interaction with the immune system. In Enkephalins and Endorphins: Stress and the Immune System. N. Plotnikoff et al., Eds. Plenum Press. New York, NY.

10. UNDENFRIEND, S. & D. L. KIRKPATRICK. 1983. Biochemistry of the enkephalins and enkephalin-containing peptides. Biochem. Biophys. 221: 309.

11. BLOOM, F. E. 1983. The endorphins: a growing family of pharmacologically pertinent peptides. Annu. Rev. Pharmacol. Toxicol. 23: 151-170.

12. LEWIS, R. V. & A. J. STERN. 1983. Biosynthesis of the enkephalins and enkephalin-containing polypeptides. Annu. Rev. Pharmacol. Toxicol. 23: 353-372.

13. AKIL, H., S. J. WATSON, E. YOUNG, M. E. LEWIS, H. KHACHATURIAN & J. M. WALKER. 1984. Endogenous opioids: biology and function. Annu. Rev. Neurosci. 7: 223-255.

14. HOLLT, V. 1986. Opioid peptide processing and receptor selectivity. Annu. Rev. Pharmacol. Toxicol. 26: 59-77.

15. PLOTNIKOFF, N. P., G. C. MILLER & J. WYBRAN. 1987. ACTH and endorphins. In Hormones and Immunity. I. Berczi & K. Kovacs, Eds. MTP Press. Norwell, MA.

16. MURGO, A. J., R. E. FAITH & N. P. PLOTNIKOFF. 1986. Enkephalins: mediators of stress-induced immunomodulation. In Enkephalins and Endorphins: Stress and the Immune System. N. P. Plotnikoff et al., Eds. Plenum Press. New York, NY.

17. PLOTNIKOFF, N. P., A. J. MURGO & R. E. FAITH. 1984. Neuroimmunomodulation with enkephalins: effects on thymus and spleen weights in mice. Clin. Immunol. Immunopath. 32: 52.

18. MURGO, A. J. 1985. Inhibition of B-16-BL6 melanoma growth in mice by methionine enkephalin. J. Natl. Cancer Inst. 65: 341.

19. YOUKILIS, E., J. CHAPMAN, E. WOOD & N. P. PLOTNIKOFF. 1985. In vivo immunostimulation and increased in vitro production of interleukin I (IL-1) activity by met-enkephalin. Int. J. Immunopharm. 7: 79.

20. DAFNY, N., J. A. GEORGIADES & C. REYES-VAZQUEZ. 1984. Reduction of Opiate Addiction by Interferon. IUPHAR. London.

21. PLOTNIKOFF, N. P. 1985. The Yin-Yang hypothesis of opioid peptide immunomodulation. Psychopharmacol. Bull. **21:** 489.
22. PLOTNIKOFF, N. P., G. C. MILLER, S. SOLOMON, R. E. FAITH, L. EDWARDS & A. J. MURGO. 1986. Methionine enkephalin: immunomodulator in normal volunteers. *In* Enkephalins and Endorphins: Stress and the Immune System. Plotnikoff *et al.,* Eds. Plenum Press. New York, NY.
23. PLOTNIKOFF, N. P., G. C. MILLER, S. SOLOMON, R. E. FAITH, L. EDWARDS & A. J. MURGO. 1986. Methionine enkephalin: enhancement of T-cells in patients with Kaposi's Sarcoma (AIDS). Psychopharmacol. Bull. **22:** 695-697.
24. WYBRAN, J. & L. SCHANDENE. 1986. Some immunological effects of methionine-enkephalin in man: potential therapeutical use. *In* Leukocytes and Host Defense. J. J. Oppenheim & D. M. Jacobs, Eds. Alan R. Liss. New York, NY.
25. KOYUNCUOGLU, H. & M. GUNGOR. 1986. Effects of morphine opiates on immune function. *In* Enkephalins and Endorphins: Stress and the Immune System. N. Plotnikoff *et al.,* Eds. Plenum Press. New York, NY.
26. SINGH, V. K., A. JAKUBOVIC & D. A. THOMAS. 1980. Suppressive effects of methadone on human blood lymphocytes. Immunol. Lett. **2:** 177.
27. MCDONOUGH, R. J., J. J. MADDEN, A. FALEK, D. A. SHAFER, M. PLINE, D. GORDON, P. BOKOS, J. C. KEUHNLE & J. MENDELSON. 1980. Alterations of T and null lymphocyte frequencies in the peripheral blood of human opiate addicts: *In vivo* evidence of opiate receptor sites on T-lymphocytes. J. Immunol. **125:** 2539.
28. WYBRAN, J. 1985. Enkephalins and endorphins as modifiers of the immune system: present and future. Fed. Proc. **44:** 92-94.
29. DONAHOE, R., J. MADDEN, F. HOLLINGSWORTH, D. SHAFER & A. FALEK. 1986. T-cell E-receptor modulation by opiates, opioids and other behaviorally active substances. *In* Enkephalins and Endorphins: Stress and the Immune System. N. Plotnikoff *et al.,* Eds. Plenum Press. New York, NY.
30. GUNGOR, M., E. GENC, H. SUGDUYU, L. EROGLU & H. KOYUNCUOGLU. 1980. Effect of chronic administration of morphine on primary immune response in mice. Experientia **36:** 1309.
31. LEFKOWITZ, S. S. & D. NEMETH. 1976. Immunosuppression of rosette-forming cells. Adv. Exp. Med. Biol. **733:** 269.
32. LEFKOWITZ, S. S. & C. Y. CHIANG. 1975. Effects of certain abused drugs on hemolysin forming cells. Life Sci. **17:** 1763.
33. SHAVIT, Y., J. W. LEWIS, G. W. TERMAN, R. P. GALL & J. C. LIEBESKIND. 1984. Opioid peptides mediate the suppressive effect of stress on natural killer cell cytotoxicity. Science **223:** 188.
34. MCCAIN, H. W., I. B. LAMSTER & J. BILOTTA. 1986. Immunosuppressive effects of opiopeptins. *In* Enkephalins and Endorphins: Stress and the Immune System. N. Plotnikoff *et al.,* Eds. Plenum Press. New York, NY.
35. CUBEDDU, L. S., S. P. WILSON & O. H. VIVEROS. 1983. Opioid peptides and catecholamine in human pheochromocytoma. Life Sci. **33:** 871-877.
36. ZAGON, I. S. & P. J. MCLAUGHLIN. 1986. Endogenous opioid systems, stress, and cancer. *In* Enkephalins and Endorphins: Stress and the Immune System. N. Plotnikoff *et al.,* Eds. Plenum Press. New York, NY.
37. HAZUM, E., K. J. CHANG & P. CAUTRECASAS. 1980. Cluster formation of opiate (enkephalin) receptors in neuroblastoma cells: differences between agonists and antagonists and possible relationships to biological functions. Proc. Natl. Acad. Sci. USA **77:** 3038-3041.
38. ZAGON, I. S. & P. J. MCLAUGHLIN. 1981. Naloxone prolongs the survival time of mice treated with neuroblastoma. Life Sci. **28:** 1095-1102.
39. ZAGON, I. S. & P. J. MCLAUGHLIN. 1984. Duration of opiate receptor blockade determines tumorigenic response in mice with neuroblastoma: a role for endogenous opioid systems in cancer. Life Sci. **35:** 409-416.
40. ZAGON, I. S. & P. J. MCLAUGHLIN. 1981. Heroin prolongs survival time and retards tumor growth in mice with neuroblastoma. Br. Res. Bull. **7:** 25-32.
41. SIMON, E. J. 1982. History. *In* Endorphins. J. B. Malick & R. M. S. BELL, EDS. MARCEL DEKKER. NEW YORK, NY.

42. KAZMI, S. M. I. & R. K. MISHRA. 1986. Opioid receptors in human neuroblastoma SH-SY5Y cells: evidence for distinct morphine (mu) and enkephalin (delta) binding sites. Biochem. Biophys. Res. Commun. **137:** 813-820.

43. BROOKS, W. M., M. G. NETSKY, D. E. NORMANSELL & D. A. HORWITZ. 1972. Depressed cell-mediated immunity in patients with primary intra-cranial tumors: characterization of a humoral immunosuppressive factor. J. Exp. Med. **136:** 1631-1647.

44. MONSTEIN, H. J., R. FOLKESSON & L. TERENIUS. 1986. Proenkephalin A-like in RNA in human leukemia leukocytes and CNS tissues. Life Sci. **39:** 2237-2241.

45. WOLF, G. T. & K. A. PETERSON. 1986. Beta endorphins enhances *in vitro* lymphokine production in patients with squamous carcinoma of the head and neck. Otolaryn. Head Neck Surg. **94:** 224-229.

46. GILLIES, G., S. RATTER, A. GROSSMAN, R. GAILLARD, P. J. LOWRY, G. M. BESSER & L. H. REES. 1980. ACTH, LPH, and beta-endorphin secretion from perfused isolated human pituitary tumor cells *in vitro.* Horm. Res. **13:** 280-290.

47. ASA, S. L., K. KOVACS, D. W. KILLINGER, N. MARCON & M. PLATTS. 1980. Pancreatic islet cell carcinoma producing gastrin, ACTH, alpha-endorphin, somatostatin, and calcitonin. Am. J. Gastroenterol. **74:** 30-35.

48. BAKER, J., I. M. HOLDAWAY, M. JAGUSCH, A. R. KERR, R. A. DONALD & P. T. PULLAN. 1982. Ectopic secretion of ACTH and met-enkephalin from a thymic carcinoid. J. Endocrinol. Invest. **5:** 33-37.

49. CHARPIN, C., B. ARGEMI, M. CANNONI, C. OLIVER, P. GILLIOZ, J. P. VAGNEUR & M. TOGA. 1984. Detection immunocytochimique de calcitonine, d'ACTH, de beta MSH, de beta-endorphine, et de somatostatine dans les carcinomes medullaires de la thyrode. Ann. Pathol. 1983. **4:** 27-35.

50. ROTH, K. A. & J. D. BARCHAS. 1986. Small cell carcinoma cell lines contain opioid peptides and receptors. Cancer **57:** 769-773.

51. ALUMETS, J., S. FALKMER, L. GRIMELIUS, R. HAKANSON, O. LJUNGBERG, F. SUNDLER & E. WILANDER. 1980. Immunocytochemical demonstration of enkephalin and beta-endorphin in endocrine tumors of the rectum. Acta Pathol. Microbiol. Scand. Sect. A **88:** 103-109.

52. CELIO, M. R. 1979. Distribution of beta-endorphin immunoreactive cells in human fetal and adult pituitaries and in pituitary adenomas. J. Histochem. Cytochem. **27:** 1215-1216.

53. SARDELLI, S., F. PETRAGLIA, F. MASSOLO, A. MESSORI, V. SANTORO, F. FACCHINETTI & A. R. GENAZZANI. 1986. Changes in immunoreactive beta-endorphin, methionine-enkephalin and ACTH in bone marrow cells and fluid from leukemic children. Clin. Immunol. Immunopath. **41:** 247-253.

54. SPORRONG, B., J. ALUMETS, L. CLASE, S. FALKMER, R. HAKANSON, O. LJUNGBERG & F. SUNDLER 1981. Neurohormonal peptide immunoreactive cells in mucinous cystadenomas and cystadenocarcinomas of the ovary. Virchows Arch. (Pathol. Anat.) **392:** 271-280.

55. DI MARTINO, L., A. TARQUINI, I. MITCHELL & N. DESHPANDE. 1982. Effects of opiates and naloxone on certain enzymes of carbohydrate metabolism in human breast carcinomas. Tumori **68:** 397-401.

56. LAUDENSLAGER, M. L., S. M. RYAN, R. C. DRUGAN, R. L. HYSON & S. F. MAIER. 1983. Coping and immunosuppression: inescapable but not escapable shock suppresses lymphocyte proliferation. Science **221:** 568-570.

57. STEIN, M., R. C. SCHIAVI & M. CARMERINO. 1970. Influence of brain and behavior on the immune system. Science **191:** 435.

58. VOGEL, W. H. 1986. Effects of coping and noncoping with stressful events on the immune system. *In* Enkephalins and Endorphins: Stress and the Immune System. N. Plotnikoff *et al.,* Eds. Plenum Press. New York, NY.

59. DAFNEY, N. 1983. Interferon modifies morphine withdrawal phenomena in rodents. Neuropharmacology **22:** 647-651.

60. SOLOMON, G., N. KAY & J. E. MORLEY. 1986. Endorphins: a link between personality stress, emotions, immunity, disease? *In* Enkephalins and Endorphins: Stress and the Immune System. N. Plotnikoff *et al.,* Eds. Plenum Press. New York, NY.

61. MONJAN, A. A. & M. I. COLLECTOR. 1977. Stress-induced modulation of the immune response. Science **196:** 307.

62. LEWIS, J. W., Y. SHAVIT, F. C. MARTIN, G. W. TERMAN, R. P. GALE & J. C. LIEBESKIND. 1986. Effects of stress and morphine on natural killer cell activity and on mammary tumor development. *In* Enkephalins and Endorphins: Stress and the Immune System. N. Plotnikoff *et al.*, Eds. Plenum Press. New York, NY.

63. RILEY, V. 1981. Psychoneuroendocrine influences on immunocompetence and neoplasia. Science **212:** 1100-1109.

64. LYMANGROVER, J. R., L. A. DOKAS, A. KONG, R. MARTIN & M. SAFFRAN. 1981. Naloxone has a direct effect on the adrenal cortex. Endocrinology **109:** 1132-1137.

65. SCHLEIFER, S. J., S. E. KELLER, M. CAMERINO, J. C. THORNTON & M. STEIN. 1983. Suppression of lymphocyte stimulation following bereavement. J. Am. Med. Assoc. **250:** 374-377.

66. IRWIN, M., M. DANIELS, E. T. BLOOM & H. WEINER. 1986. Life events, depression, and natural killer cell activity. Psychopharmacol. Bull. **22:** 1093-1096.

67. MESSING, R. B., B. J. VASQUEZ, V. R. SPIEHLER, J. L. MARTINEZ, JR., R. A. JENSEN, H. RIGTER & J. L. McGAUGH. 1980. 3H-Dihydromorphine binding in brain regions of young and aged rats. Life Sci. **26:** 921-927.

68. MISSALE, C., S. GOVONI, L. CROCE, A. BOSIO, P. F. SPANO & M. TRABUCCHI. 1983. Changes of beta-endorphin and met-enkephalin content in the hypothalamus-pituitary axis induced by aging. J. Neurochem. **40:** 20-24.

69. BARDEN, N., A. DUPONT, F. LABRIE, Y. MERANDI, D. ROULEAU, H. VAUDRY & J. R. BOISSIER. 1981. Age-dependent changes in the beta-endorphin content of discrete rat brain nuclei. Brain Res. **208:** 209-212.

70. OGAWA, N. 1985. Neuropeptides and their receptors in aged-rat brain. Acta Med. Okayama. **39:** 315-319.

71. PETKOV, V. V., V. D. PETKOV, T. GRAHORSKA & E. KOUSTANTINOVA. 1984. Enkephalin receptor changes in rat brain during aging. Gen. Pharmacol. **15:** 491-495.

72. DUPONT, A., P. SAVARD, Y. MERAND, F. LABRIE & J. R. BOISSIER. 1981. Age-related changes in central nervous system enkephalins and substance P. Life Sci. **29:** 2317-2322.

73. JENSEN, R. A., R. B. MESSING, V. R. SPIEHLER, J. L. MARTINEZ, JR., B. J. VASQUEZ & J. L. McGAUGH. 1980. Memory, opiate receptors, and aging. Peptides **1:** 197-201.

74. WILKINSON, C. W. & D. M. DORSA. 1986. The effects of aging on molecular forms of beta and gamma-endorphins in rat hypothalamus. Neuroendocrinology **43:** 124-131.

75. EFFROS, R. B. 1984. Aging and Immunity. *In* Stress, Immunity and Aging. E. L. Cooper, Ed. Marcel Dekker, Inc. New York, NY.

76. KAY, M. M. B. 1978. Effect of age on T-cell differentiation. Fed Proc. **37:** 1241-1244.

77. PIERPAOLI, W. 1981. Integrated phylogenetic and ontogenetic evolution of neuroendocrine and identity-defense, immune functions. *In* Psychoneuroimmunology. R. Ader, Ed. Academic Press. New York, NY.

78. ZURAWSKI, G., M. BENEDIK, B. J. KAMB, J. S. ABRAMS, S. M. ZURAWSKI & F. D. LEE. 1986. Activation of mouse T-helper cells induces abundant preproenkephalin in RNA synthesis. Science **232:** 772.

79. McCAIN, H. W., I. B. LAMSTER & J. BILOTTA. 1986. Modulation of human T-cell suppressor activity by beta endorphin and Glycyl-L- Glutamine. Int. J. Immunopharmacol. **84:** 443-446.

80. WYBRAN, J., D. LATINNE, J. SONNET, H. TAELMAN, J. P. VAN VORREN & N. P. PLOTNIKOFF. 1986. Immunorestorative effect of methionine-enkephalin in ARC and AIDS patients. Int. Conf. Acq. Immunodef. Syndrome. Paris, France.

81. YOUKILIS, E., J. CHAPMAN, E. WOODS & N. P. PLOTNIKOFF. 1985. *In vivo* immunostimulation and increased *in vitro* production of interleukin 1 (IL-1) activity by met-enkephalin. Int. J. Immunopharmacol. **7:** 79.

82. BROWN, S. L. & E. E. VAN EPPS. 1985. Beta endorphin (BE), methionine enkephalin (ME), and corticotrophin (ACTH) modulate the production of gamma interferon (INF) *in vitro.* Fed Proc. **44:** 949.

83. ROSENBERG, S. A. & M. T. LOTZEL. 1986. Cancer immunotherapy using interleukin-2 and interleukin-2-activated lymphocytes. Annu. Rev. Immunol. **4:** 681-711.

Rambunctious Remarks and a Look to the Future

NOVERA HERBERT SPECTOR

Fundamental Neurosciences Program
National Institutes of Health
National Institute of Neurological and Communicative Disorders and
Stroke
Federal Building, Room 916
Bethesda, Maryland 20892

First let's congratulate Walter Pierpaoli for his excellent selection of speakers for this meeting. They have contributed such an amount of rich data and have provided astute discussion and many acute observations, all of which will be of great value in providing clues to the research when each returns to his or her own laboratory. I believe that most of us will agree that this has been one of the best and most fruitful meetings that we have attended in a long time, in the most pleasant ambience that one could imagine. Of course, many questions and problems for future research have been raised by this conference. As with any good meeting, as with any good research, more questions have been raised than have been answered.

I will not attempt to summarize the papers or even the discussion from this meeting—most of it will be available in the same volume in which these concluding remarks will be published. Any summary would be not only redundant but insulting to this audience and to the readers of the book. Instead, I will take upon myself the privilege of making comments on some of the important issues that were raised within the last four days both in the presentations and in the lively discussions. I will presume to correct some historical errors that may have been made by some of the speakers and I will try to point out some questions raised by this meeting, some problems which may or may not have immediate solutions, and some areas for intensive research. When each returns to his or her laboratory, some of the problems and some of the suggestions raised here by the speakers have given us clues for experiments by which we can find some important answers, perhaps in a very short time. Others may require a lifetime or more.

The organization of my remarks seems to lack logic. For its organization and sequence I beg your forgiveness, but I have an excellent excuse. While all of you have had two years in which to carefully prepare your manuscripts and presentations, I have had only a few minutes between the last speaker and the beginning of my talk. I know that despite an occasional indication otherwise, you are all my good friends and you will be very tolerant.

While the term "molecular biology" has become recently a fad and a kind of "catch word," what we have seen here and listened to is some of the *best* of molecular biology: from genetics, biochemistry, neurochemistry, neurophysiology, neuroanatomy, pharmacology; and perhaps the best from the very, very difficult field of behavior.

Occasionally sparks have been seen in the discussion. There has been a lot of heat generated, but the overall effect has been a fruitful interchange. I'm sure that many of you have felt the continuous series of stimuli and waves of excitement at listening to new discoveries, listening to new ideas, new data all put forth in this very small meeting of this most remarkable collection of scientists, from nine countries, who are showing the way to the rest of the world. As at any good scientific gathering we come away with at least a half a dozen new cures for cancer, but what is even more amazing is at least a half a dozen new elixirs of youth. Most of us will rush home and immediately make a cocktail consisting of all of the ingredients shown in TABLE 1, and then we'll all live long enough to have at least ten more—maybe thirty more reunions on this wonderful volcano.

TABLE 1. R$_X$: Stromboli i.v. Cocktail^a

| Volcanic Ash |
| Thymus (whole) |
| Thymus (dessicated, from calf) |
| Thymus (all fractions) |
| Haloperidol |
| Superoxide Dismutase |
| Selected Catalases |
| Activated Charcoal |
| Epsom Salts |
| Butterfly Wings |
| Milk of Magnesia |
| Beta-Carotene |
| Vitamin A |
| Melatonin |
| Arginine |
| Thioproline |
| PCPA |
| Vitamin E |
| Enkephalins |
| Zinc |
| Selenium |
| DHEA |
| Estrogens |
| Prolactin |
| Growth Hormone |
| 3,4-Dimethyl Pyridine |
| Levamysol |

^{a} To be taken with social support, exercise, sex, and electrical stimulation of the hypothalamus.

I made a firm resolution not to bring any slides to this meeting, so we'll have to keep the light on for all of my talk and none of you will have the opportunity to go quietly to sleep.

Without making any pretense of summarizing, I am going to comment on some of the papers that were presented here, *seriatim.*

Professor Baltrusch did Shakespeare one better by further subdividing the stages in the life of man according to physiologic, psychologic, and social factors. He promised us to refine these concepts further and to provide us with good data that will help us not only to classify stages of old age but to understand them better. In discussion of this paper, an excellent question was raised by Candace Pert and raised again in another context by George Solomon. We hear so much about the negative effects of behavior, distress, and so on. Candace wanted to know: what about the protective effects of personality? Dr. Baltrusch has promised to answer this in the future. Prodded by the stimulus of a lay person, the very astute Norman Cousins, various research projects in the United States and perhaps elsewhere are beginning to address such questions. How is the immune system, and health in general, affected by emotions such as happiness and joy and good humor, as opposed to misery, suffering, anxiety, and pain? This is a tricky business, full of semantic and scientific pitfalls, but I believe that current research will contribute some answers: indeed, the preliminary data are very promising.

Bernie Fox gave us an excellent view of epidemiological aspects of psychological and sociological factors in aging and cancer. With regard to his data on distress, a number of issues were raised which need to be answered. One, I question the value of any statistics, and there are a great many such statistics being presented all the time in so-called scientific journals, which differentiate between white and black "races." It has been known for at least fifty years that there are many more genetic and somatic, morphologic and physiologic, differences *among* so-called "blacks" and *among* so-called "whites" than *between* black and white. I think it is high time that we start becoming a little bit more sophisticated and take advantage of at least some of the basic information and concepts that modern anthropology has taught us in approaching sociological problems. (NOTE: After these "Remarks . . ." were submitted, Dr. Fox and I discussed this issue at great length and even with some heat. We are now completely in agreement that (1) "black" and "white" are occasionally useful descriptions, and that (2) the word "race" is totally inappropriate and scientifically inaccurate to describe either "blacks" or "whites".)

Bernie made the point that in a dysphoric mood, stressful events are more often recalled than nonstressful. Of course, I believe he meant *dis*tressful events (see discussion of "stress" below). In this case, we have the usual problem of chicken first or egg first: in either case, I believe, there exists a positive feedback loop. As every good physiologist knows, positive feedbacks are almost always destructive.

Among the many excellent points that Bernie made is that there are usually thirty or more doublings after transformation of cells, before the discovery of cancer clinically. According to at least one theory, everyone may develop these transformations, perhaps even daily. We need to know how these transformations are reversed. Studies need to be made on the rate of reversal, starting with the first doubling and on to full-blown events, *i.e.,* clinical cancer, and disease. There are some epidemiologic studies which are looking at so-called spontaneous remissions. There also are well documented cases, even though anecdotal, of reversal of cancer in advanced stages.

We know also from many experiments including the ones that are reported here by Ghanta, *et al.,* that cancer in mice can develop to a fairly advanced stage, and then can be partially or totally reversed by appropriate prior conditioning. We need more data on this type of phenomenon, and we need to know the mechanisms by which it occurs.

The earliest studies of conditioning of the immune response began about 1924 at the Pasteur Institute in Paris. (This Institute will soon celebrate its 100th anniversary. One of our participants has the honor of being an invited speaker at these celebrations.) From time to time since 1924, a number of people have announced, each in turn, that he or she has discovered a new phenomenon, that is to say, conditioning of immune responses. I think you should all know that there is a sizable literature in this field. I have reviewed this on several occasions and I won't repeat it here; however, I believe that an important new discovery is that natural killer cell activity, and possibly also interferon, can be conditioned either up or down, and that we can demonstrate repeatedly a three to thirty-nine fold increase in natural killer cell activity in the total absence of any antigen or antigenic stimulation with only the stimulus of an immunologically neutral, conditioned stimulus. This is quite exciting and has important clinical implications.

Experiments on conditioning of immunity have been going on for more than half a century. We are reaching a stage now, using modern techniques, where perhaps for the first time we can begin, using all the probes of genetics, membrane physiology, biochemistry, pharmacology, neurochemistry, cellular immunology, to discover the *mechanisms,* to discover *what is going on inside the black box.* This may be music of the future, but I think now that it is music of the near future.

I was very pleased to hear that George Solomon, who has contributed so much to this field over so many years, is now beginning to study healthy people as well as sick people and sick mice.

What does not please me is that George and so many others are still using the word "stress" as if it had some precise meaning. We've had a little discussion on that subject at this meeting. I've raised this question at other meetings, and while I may be just one voice in the wilderness, I think that I heard one or two other voices here and there. Perhaps we can get rid of this word and begin to use terms which can be defined, terms for which we can all agree on a definition, and terms which will be more useful in directing our research. So I bend your tired ears once more for a few words in support of my lonely crusade.

In physics as it should be in physiology, stress has a precise meaning. When you apply *stress* to a material, you can measure the *strain* in the material that has been stressed. In psychology and sociology the word "stress" has been replaced (by some investigators) by "stressor" when they talk about the force that is applied from the outside. This is probably a good step in the right direction, but the word "stress" has been used also to substitute for what the physicists and what good physiologists have called "strain." Any *stimulus,* of any kind, from the exterior or from the interior of an organism, is a *stress.* Stimuli are constantly being received by the organism from the *environment,* in the form of sensory input, in the form of antigenic input, and in other forms; and are constantly being received from the *interior* of the organism in the form of abstract thought, emotions, proprioceptors, and autoimmune reactions. These stimuli (stresses) are constantly producing within the organism a series of responses which are continuous throughout the lifetime of the individual.

Why quibble?

One must make a very careful distinction between one stimulus and another because the number of such stimuli approaches infinity and the number of reactions is equally complex. This confusion of terms will lead to a confusion in our ideas, confusion in our data, and confusion in the design of future experiments. Further confusion is introduced by using the word "stress" to mean either the stimulus (stressor) or the response (strain, etc.).

A simple step in the right direction would be simply to employ the word *"distress."* This could be any type of nociceptive stimulus and this would let us instantly take a leap equal to that which Hans Selye took after many years of talking about "stress responses" (see below).

A very brief look at history would be helpful here. The American physiologist, Walter Cannon, who invented the word "homeostasis," (about whom we have heard already, from one of our discussants, as the author of the book *The Wisdom of the Body*), defined the "fear, fight, and flight reaction" in terms of catecholamines, in other words, the reaction of the adrenal *medulla.* Many years later Hans Selye redefined what he called "stress," or the reactions to a stressor, in terms of the adrenal *cortex* or corticosteroid response.

Today we know that at least a dozen hormones are involved in this type of response, including the catecholamines, the steroids, prolactin, growth hormone, and so on and so forth, as well as a host of neurally active peptides.

After Selye had for many years talked about the harmful effects of stress, Sam Corson from Ohio State University finally convinced him that "stress" in his sense could have beneficial as well as harmful effects, and Selye then began to write books about how to use stress to one's advantage.

Despite all this development many people are still using the word stress when they mean *dis*tress. At a recent gathering of immunologists and behavioral specialists in Arizona I raised this question. After listening for two days to people talking about stress and each one talking about something else, I said, "Hey, fellows, let's define our terms. I don't know what you mean by stress." Whereupon one psychologist jumped up, looking at me with disdain, and said, "Obviously you're unsophisticated. Every good psychologist knows exactly what we mean by stress," and then he gave a definition. Whereupon a psychiatrist at the other end of the table jumped up and said, "Oh no, that's not at all what we mean by stress." Within a few minutes there were five different definitions thrown on the table. I had no need to say anything more. I think my point was validated, but I'm not sure that many people understood this. So I continue my crusade and I hope that at least some of us can begin to clean up this act. (In fairness to George Solomon, after the discussion at the Stromboli meeting, he told me that he agrees fully with my objections.)

With regard to Karen Bulloch's excellent presentation, I will make just two comments. One is that she now has demonstrated again with greatly refined techniques the connection of the thymus to the nucleus retrofacial and the nucleus ambiguous, and distinguished between the neural fibers that innervate the thymus and those that innervate the esophagus, thus protecting her excellent reputation against some recent scurrilous attacks.

The continuing work of Bulloch and of the Feltens and Calvo have given us some insight into the innervation of the organs and tissues of the immune system and with the exception of one nerve-ending described by Karen, we still don't have a clear picture of just what the afferent nerve-ending looks like in terms of its morphology, its histology, or even its functional capabilities. This, I believe, is an important gap in our knowledge, because we want to know more about the "hardwired" loops. It is almost inevitable that we will find such loops between the nervous and immune system just as we have found the many, many loops in which the information is carried by humoral factors. This is an extremely important problem that our neuroanatomists and neurophysiologists should be addressing in the immediate future, although I don't presume to tell them exactly how to do it. To date, the best evidence for *non*humoral influences of the brain upon immune responses remain the experiments of Benetato and Baciu of Romania during the 1940's and 50's, now being continued by Baciu in the '80's (see below)!

With regard to Nicola Fabris' virtuoso experimental performance on the relationship of thymic function to thyroxin, it seems to me that one of the old warriors of neuroimmunomodulation is keeping the faith and giving us some hard new evidence not only about this intriguing relationship but also about the role of amino acids such as arginine in restoring function. Surely these observations will provide a mine of new ideas and will generate new experiments. Not only will this expand our basic concepts of neuroimmunomodulation, but obviously the data will have valuable implications for the clinic.

Not only T-4 but, of course, growth hormone and prolactin have been involved in the interrelationships between the nervous system and the immune system: only in the past few years has this evidence been really nailed down, in part due to the excellent work of Keith Kelley and his colleagues in Illinois.

Keith has run the gamut from behavioral work to genetics with lots of immunochemistry in between. I think it was his observation more than anyone else's that gave us a good foundation for resolving all the controversy about the early work of Blalock and Smith, showing that lymphocytes could produce at least proopiomelanocortin and possibly secrete substances such as ACTH. Keith showed that the genetic precursors were there, which of course made Blalock and Smith very happy. Now he is going further and looking at other peptides and other hormones. His work as well as Fabris' shows us once more that aging may not be an irreversible process.

Piantenelli's work reminds us that a mathematical approach can often save us much time from wasted research or walking down blind alleys. Although in most cases I don't recommend mathematical modeling to biologists, especially when all the data are not in and when there is so much more information to be obtained from *biologic* experiments, I do think it is valuable to have somebody there modeling and somebody there doing the mathematics and somebody who explores the possibilities of this type of approach.

Joseph's and Roth's paper answers several questions and perhaps again, as usual, raises more questions than it answers. Just in passing, Dr. Joseph suggests cerebellar involvement in motor tasks, with the cerebellum possibly being a secondary motor area that can substitute for the striatum. This is not too convincing, since we know that cerebellar ataxia is very different from striatal ataxia such as we see in Parkinson's. On the other hand we know that there are many functions of the cerebellum in motor behavior, and that new ones are still being discovered. In the 19th century, the extirpation of the cerebellum in a pigeon resulted in its inability to maintain its balance. Ever since then we've been discovering bits and pieces, but the cerebellum still remains in many ways a mystery. It would be interesting not only to find the role of the cerebellum as a secondary motor area, which is only suggested by this work, but to see how it is involved in many types of immune responses, which in turn involves thermoregulation, which in turn involves the cerebellum, at least according to one of the pioneers in cerebellar physiology, Snider.

Ed Golub, who cheerfully joins our ranks as a semibeliever and a three-quarter doubter in neuroimmunomodulation, has given us some interesting data on neuropeptides and hemopoietic differentiation. These are some very modern experiments but they remind me of the work of a very much unrecognized pioneer in this field who is still working in it, Ion Baciu of Romania, who, in 1946, gave the best evidence to this date of hardwired connections between the hypothalamus and the hemopoietic system. Baciu used the so-called isolated head preparation, where two dogs side by side had the circulation from one head going to the rest of the body of the other dog. In this when the hypothalamus was mechanically stimulated, Baciu observed changes, not only in hemopoiesis, but also in phagocytosis in the animal whose hypothalamus was stimulated. By means of this preparation he was able to rule out humoral factors. This experiment should be repeated, with careful attention to the vertebral arteries and any other possible source of less-than-total cross-perfusion. Perhaps now, with Dr. Golub's new data, we may be able to postulate the presence of *both* types of information transfer from the central nervous system to the peripheral immune system.

Now, after having retired as Director of the Physiology Institute in Cluj-Napoca, Dr. Baciu is again working full time in research and exploring these interactions by means of brain lesions, brain stimulation and other techniques, both old and new.

I was fascinated by Dr. Levine's presentation and his excellent data on tetrahydrobiopterin (BH_4) teaching at least me another dimension in the complex picture, often oversimplified, of the synthesis of neurotransmitters from amino acids as well as the role of pterins in early and late development of the nervous system. If indeed biopterin is such a scavenger of free radicals and if indeed we are missing pterins in old age, it would be quite interesting to find a method of replacement in the aged, by some fundamental biological procedure or even in a less "physiological" (*i.e.,* pharmacological) procedure. Obviously Levine has his work cut out for him . . . and we need butterfly wings in our "Stromboli Cocktail" (see concluding remarks, below).

No tissue in the history of neuroanatomy and neurophysiology has generated so much misinformation and false leads as the pineal gland. The excellent work of Axelrod, Wurtman and Chu, a few decades ago, on the synthesis of melatonin and the enzymes involved in melatonin synthesis, plus the new work in chronobiology and the relationship of the pineal to the superchiasmatic nucleus of the hypothalamus and the interactions of this system with biorhythmic functions, has given us some new starts which appear to be not only on the right track but this time more promising. Added to these developments, the recent work of Maestroni and his colleagues on the immunoregulatory role of melatonin and the implications of this for so many areas of clinical medicine . . . may be the beginning of a new revolution in our concepts of pineal and melatonin function. Perhaps Pierpaoli, Conti, and Maestroni have discovered the ultimate and most natural tranquilizer or antidistress substance and they've given us cause to revise our favorite old circuit diagrams of neuroimmunomodulation.

Recent claims from several laboratories, still far from being fully verified, ruling out the role of glucocorticoids in neuroimmunomodulation, may have to be revised when we look at the data from Kalimi and the multiple roles played by liver and other tissue glucocorticoid receptors.

Marguerite Kay's paper raised not only the possibility of a senescent cell antigen which may play a role in differentiation and in the aging of many types of cells, but also, in the discussion at this meeting, the old question of the possible limits in the number of cell divisions in any given tissue or in any given species. This may well be a fundamental question in understanding not only aging but many other aspects of growth and development.

This is the other side of the coin, in trying to discover the mechanisms whereby cancer cells and amoeba may be "immortal;" and in this respect I would first like to call your attention to the fact that, although it is accepted dogma that nerve cells do not divide after a rather early age in the development of mammals, this notion is almost surely incorrect. Evidence for this has been accumulating, to my knowledge, for at least thirty years, in a series of papers not too well known, from many countries. In recent years some very good studies have shown that, at least in the amygdala of rodents, and in other cortical areas in birds, there is repeatedly new neuronal cell formation in adults. The fact that one paper, a rather good paper as a matter of fact, from Rakić at Yale, which purports to show there is no new cell division in a primate, does not really settle the question once and for all. It would take at least another hour (and twenty more pages in this book) for me to give you all of my reasons for this personal belief and for the evidence behind this belief. I would just caution you to keep an open mind on the subject, and remember that in the linings of the cerebral ventricles there are neuronal stem cells which probably are there during the entire lifetime of an adult mammal. I would remind you also that in tissue culture, neurons generally do not divide once they have plated out on a substrate, but if they're resuspended into the medium and the neurites are retracted, these cells are quite capable of redivision.

We should bear in mind also that germ cells in so-called higher animals as well as the entire cell of so-called lower animals, such as amoeba, are probably immortal in the sense of the number of potential cell divisions. Here is surely another area for future investigation and a problem for some young investigator to solve (and then to collect a Nobel Prize).

Calcium and the calcium ion has had its ups and downs in physiology for more than half a century. The importance of its role was first recognized in plant cells and then in neurons. Dr. Roth's paper reminds us again of the great complexities of calcium concentration inside and outside of the cell as well as problems of the movement through the membrane. The interaction of calcium with other ions can be extremely complex in a living system and any attempts to simplify it usually lead to disaster. We could express the old Goldman equation or the Hodgkin-Huxley-Keynes-Katz equations, to make room for an unlimited series of ions, each affecting any given membrane potential. In living complex organisms, especially in the brain, these potentials are in turn affected by calcium concentrations in subcellular units as well as in adjacent and even distant cells. To write the general equation for the effects of calcium in the living system will be almost as difficult as writing a general equation in physics that governs the motions of all particles and their interactions.

Weksler promises us that we are "close to resetting the immune thermostat." His own excellent data belies this statement: we are still a long way off, but I like his optimism. Provoked by Weksler's ideas, Dr. Nagy questioned: in general, which is better: immune suppression or immune enhancement? In connection both with the cure of cancer and with the slowing of the aging process, this is an important question, for aside from allergy and autoimmune disease, many of us have simply assumed that it is desirable in general for good health to enhance immune responses.

Often we hear of "*the* immune response," in the singular, as if there were only one! Just as the nervous system functions by a balance between excitation and inhibition, I suspect that we will soon discover that in multidimensional space and time, every "immune response" is a complex of many responses, both "up" and "down."

Dr. Peck's new methods for assaying the tumoricidal function of various lymphocytes raises some important questions of theory as well as of technique. As a neurophysiologist, when I first began to do experiments with immunological reactions, I was appalled. You stimulate a nerve and nine hundred and ninety-nine times out of a thousand, the muscle will twitch, but when you take two mice, even litter-mates of an inbred strain, and you stick them both with the same amount of antigen, one will ave an enormous antibody response and the other may turn out to be a "nonresponder." This is an aspect of biology that still puzzles me, but perhaps immunologists take this variability for granted.

Another type of problem arises, not from biology, but from some "biologists." We may read a paper in an immunology journal which reports that the serum from six animals was pooled and that the assay was repeated twelve times: the investigator now claims that he has statistical significance because the assay comes out the same or close to the same twelve times! I am appalled over and over again at this lack of sophistication in a supposedly advanced science.

In any case all biologists should become aware, if they are not so already, about the problems of *precision* error, aside from biological variability. Precision errors arise from the equipment and/or the techniques of measurement. Every experiment should indicate both precision error and biological variability before any funny statistics are done.

Dr. Peck's techniques (of measuring tumoricidal activity) need to be repeated and verified and compared with other techniques and detailed precision errors worked out. Colorimetric methods are now used to measure such fleeting events as changes in electrical activity during an action potential. Perhaps Peck's simple and rapid methods should be adopted more widely. (NOTE: Unfortunately, a written manuscript from Dr. Peck has not yet been received as this volume goes to press.)

Candace Pert's (with Michael Ruff and John Helm) brilliant presentation was a *tour de force,* exhibiting some fine biological detective work, leading to their finding a potential blocker for the AIDS virus. It was exciting to listen to: it provoked a storm of new ideas, new concepts, and new problems . . . some of which are restatements and refinements of old problems.

With regard to the other half of her report: nine years ago I was writing a review for the *Handbook, Physiology of the Hypothalamus* in which I was trying to deal with aging, drugs and neuroimmunomodulation all at once. In looking at the then existing literature, I noticed a large discrepancy between the anatomical locations of receptors for endogenous opioids and their physiological location, *i.e.*, areas in the brain that seemed to have physiological activity associated with the opioids. So I went to one of my favorite experts, Candace Pert, and discussed this problem with her and she reluctantly admitted how silly the data looked. I was pleased to hear today at least a partial explanation of why these discrepancies exist, as well as a reasonable account of the distribution and function of these receptors. In her linking of neuropeptides' activities with the anatomic and physiologic "limbic system," she has done a fine, logical analysis . . . many parts of which will have to be filled in experimentally before we have a complete picture.

A valuable aspect of the data presented by Pert and her colleagues, as well as in some of the data of others, was the presentation of dose-response curves, in the pharmacological action of neuropeptides. Some of the curves presented at this conference seem to be monophasic. It is my contention (and in the discussion of her paper Dr. Pert agreed with me) that all such responses are *biphasic if not simply in space then certainly in time.* We need to look at such reactions in at least three dimensions and we will always see at least two phases to every curve. Probably *no* physiological response is simply monophasic.

Candace Pert in her discussion of the limbic system frequently placed the hypothalamus at the center of the limbic system. While I agree with her that physiologically this is the case, I must point out that most anatomical descriptions of the limbic system omit the hypothalamus. This is unfortunate and I think that in the future functional anatomy will certainly include the hypothalamus as the very core of the limbic system.

Pert and her colleagues were certainly correct in bravely taking the position that the physiological and anatomical correlates of emotion are *not unknowable.* I believe that in the not too distant future these types of analyses will be considered "hard" science.

In describing the role of the hypothalamus in neuroimmunomodulation, Professor Vinnitsky has carried electrical stimulation of the hypothalamus several steps further. In this case, reporting on some well-conceived experiments showing not only interactions of hypothalamic serotonin, norepinephrine, and corticosteriods in immunomodulation, he also demonstrated their effects on aging, tumor growth and anti-tumor activity. Once again we can see how quickly the gap is being bridged, between basic studies in neuroimmunomodulation and their potential applications in the clinic.

The subject of this extraordinary conference included both aging and cancer: frequently we saw how these two problems were intertwined. With respect to such interaction, I should mention that we all sorely missed Professor Vladimir Dilman, who apparently through no fault of his own, was unable to attend. I would refer the reader of this volume to Dr. Dilman's abstract, which we are including along with a number of references to some of his recent papers. These will help to fill in important parts of his picture. One of Dilman's (and others') "four aging factors" is free radicals. Dr. Nagy also produced some fascinating data and concepts linking free oxygen radicals both to the aging process and to other modulations of functions of normal cells. Based on what we have heard at this meeting we will have to generate a Stromboli Cocktail to improve our health, to prevent cancer, and to live longer. This cocktail will include not only butterfly wings as a source of pterins, but also superoxide dismutase as well as catalase (TABLE 1).

Dr. Janković and his colleagues (as usual) introduced one more dimension into neuroimmunomodulation, in showing the importance of the lipid fractions of thymic extracts in immunomodulation. In the field of neural function it took us more than fifty years to appreciate the work of pioneers in neurochemistry (such as Thudichum), who tried to tell us that fatty substances were essential to brain function. Janković and his co-workers, who only last year reported on brown fat and immunity, have showed us yet another role for lipids in immune functions.

Perhaps at this point it would be a good time to set the record straight with regard to a remark made by one of our participants, in which he gave the credit to Robert Good for being the *first* to show the role of the thymus in immunity. Although Bob Good had made many important contributions to the science of immunology, it has to be stated for the record that this was not one of them. Here we must recognize that Brana Janković was again in the forefront. In 1961, when Janković was a visiting scientist at Harvard University, he and his colleagues, Byron Waxman and Barry Arnason, performed a series of experiments which led to the first report (at Harvard Medical School) demonstrating compromised immune function in neonatally thymectomized rats. In August of 1961 they sent a paper to *Nature* reporting on antibody production, delayed skin hypersensitivity reactions, lymphocyte number and experimental allergic encephalomyelitis in sham-thymectomized compared with thymectomized rats. In September of the same year, a paper by Dr. J. Miller appeared in *Lancet* showing changes in skin allograft reactions in neonatally thymectomized mice. In December of 1961, Waxman, Arnason and Janković inquired of the editors of *Nature* about the fate of their paper submitted in August. They were informed that the manuscripts (all three copies!) had been lost: the authors were asked to submit additional copies. Their paper finally appeared in the April 1962 issue of *Nature*. The same year, three sizable papers from their group appeared in the *Journal of Experimental Medicine* (Vol. 116) dealing with the role of the thymus in immunity. In 1957, Dr. Good had published a paper on the role of the thymus in immunity in *Acta Microbiologica Scandinavica*. He reported on experiments in guinea pigs. Having done thymectomies (which may have been incomplete) on *adult* animals, Dr. Good concluded his study by saying the thymus is not important for immunity. In making these historical corrections, I do not wish to detract at all from the great value of the many contributions of Bob Good,[a] but I do wish to emphasize the seminal role played by Janković in this as well as in so many other areas of immunology, neuroimmunology, and neuroimmunomodulation.

I could make many, many comments on Bill Regelson's many, many contributions. In this discussion, I think that most of his observations stand by themselves, but I think it is important to make a correction to the table that he showed, citing the leading causes of death in the United States. Bill totally omitted two of the major causes of death and disease — the *iatrogenic* and the *nosocomial*. He spoke also of increased longevity in North and South Dakota. Perhaps one of the reasons for this phenomenon might be a reduced concentration of practicing physicians and hospitals

---

[a] Indeed, in 1962, Good and his colleagues published a landmark paper in the *Journal of Experimental Medicine* correctly ascribing an important role to the thymus in immunity.

in the Dakotas. I'm not making these points just to be cute or funny. I think that it is important that we, as basic scientists, pay more attention to the education of physicians in medical schools. We should be teaching them more about the *wisdom of the body* and we should be teaching them more about biochemical and physiological individuality. We should be teaching them the dangers of administering cocktails, mixed pharmacological agents, to elderly, often defenseless, people. We should be teaching them that humane and intelligent approaches to the prevention of disease and to the healing of the sick, take priority over accumulation of wealth and social prestige.

It is refreshing every now and then to have somebody who brings back the fundamentals and to remind us where we're coming from and where we're going. In this respect I was very pleased to hear Professor Dumonde define for us again the multiple role of lymphokines, how they function, and the scientific rationale for the therapeutic use of lymphokines in cancer and aging.

Another area of application of basic neuroscience was illuminated by the fascinating clinical report of Dr. Lissoni and his colleagues on the use of melatonin in the treatment of cancer patients. Thus again another dimension was added to the fundamental studies of Pierpaoli, Maestroni, Conti, and their colleagues.

For several years Pierpaoli and his colleagues have been developing the idea of a "morphostatic brain" in the bone marrow which may control not only normal but neoplastic growth. Hearing the review of Pierpaoli and Balakrishnan helped to put the whole picture together for us and bring us up to date on their latest experimental evidence. Now we are all looking forward to the isolation and characterization of the active fractions (of the "bone marrow factors") and the biochemical analysis of these fascinating substances.

As usual, Nick Plotnikoff gave us more details on his latest work on enkephalins, data on the functioning of endogenous opioids. I will not try to repeat or summarize his important and complex paper, but I think that one observation that he made on cancer patients can be generalized to a great many other studies. He found that elevations of some types of immune responses in leukemia and lymphomas could or could not be observed, depending on the *baseline* that existed prior to an experimental manipulation. Probably every experienced investigator knows, but some of us may forget: failure to demonstrate an increase in some observed function, may be the result of that observed function being already at or near its maximum in an *in vivo* situation.

In conclusion: taken as a whole, this is one of the most stimulating and fruitful meetings that I have attended. I regret we cannot publish all of the discussion because the interaction among the participants was not only intense, but often provocative and mentally stimulating. I think that the best that can be said about a meeting of this sort is the remark, that I heard at least twice, to the effect that "I can't wait to get back to my laboratory to try the experiment that you have just suggested." While not everyone said the same thing in just those words, I know that many new ideas were generated here, that these will result in some wonderful experiments that are going to generate important and useful new data.

Everyday that we were here, Mother Stromboli erupted, spewing flaming rocks into the sky, reminding us of the enormous energy existing beneath this very thin spherical shell that we live on. On a less majestical scale but even more impressive to us, perhaps because we are human, was the constant volcanic activity going on in a small meeting room of the Sirenetta Park Hotel. Perhaps we are beginning now to find the secrets of cancer and aging. Perhaps not. I remember seeing (a year or two ago) a cartoon showing a long-bearded vigorous old man striding up the side of a

STROMBOLI TOAST
(To be loudly sung, following
the ingestion of 1/2 litre wine)

VIVE la VIE!
VIVE le VIN!
VIVE la COMPAGNIE!
VIVE le VIVE, VIVE le VIVE,
VIVE la COMPAGNIE!
VIVE le Walter
VIVE PIERPAOLI!

Key: vie = LIFE (of good quality
                    and long)

       vin = WINE (Sicilian)

compagnie = 35 good people here assembled
                from 9 countries

   Walter = Walter Pierpaoli

Pierpaoli = Walter Pierpaoli

FIGURE 1. Stromboli Toast.

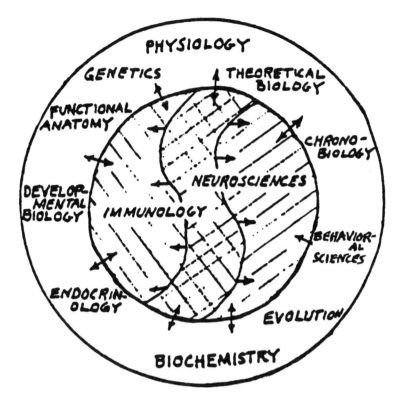

FIGURE 2. Neuroimmunomodulation: an expanding conceptual universe. (Modified and reprinted with permission from Vol. 1, No. 1 of the *NIM Newsletter*, 1969.)

mountain, probably in the Balkans, accompanied by a young eager reporter taking notes on his pad. The old man was saying "We attribute our extreme longevity to a total inability to count."

Over the centuries people have searched diligently for the fountain of youth, for the elixir that will make us young and healthy again. Here at this meeting we have heard many new clues. TABLE 1 shows the Stromboli Cocktail. Perhaps not every reporter can be shown to be correct, but to be on the safe side, each of us will quickly mix this cocktail and we will surely extend our life span and our period of good health for some still unknown period.

At the very minimum, at the end of this meeting we all are certainly a little wiser, as we grow older. Let us hope, finally, that Walter Pierpaoli, having introduced us to this fantastic double volcano, mental and geologic, will succeed in his plan by making this Stromboli Conference a regular event every three years (FIGURE 1).

Index of Contributors

Subject Index